Chronology of
Organized Crime Worldwide,
6000 B.C.E. to 2010

Chronology of Organized Crime Worldwide, 6000 B.C.E. to 2010

MICHAEL NEWTON

McFarland & Company, Inc., Publishers

Jefferson, North Carolina, and London

Contents

Preface

I discovered organized crime at a tender age, when television brought the mob into my living room. It began with NBC's *The Lawless Years*, premiering in April 1959 with actor James Gregory (1911–2002) starring as legendary New York detective Barney Ruditsky (1898–1962), pursuing bootleggers and racketeers during Prohibition. Six months later, ABC aired *The Untouchables*, with Robert Stack (1919–2003) in the career-defining role of Treasury agent Eliot Ness (1903–57). Both shows portrayed real-life gangsters from the 1920s and '30s, while fictionalizing their exploits and downfalls beyond recognition.

The Lawless Years was in its final season, and *The Untouchables* had two years left to run, when I covered the same ground in print, devouring *Meet the Mob* by authors Frank Mullady and William Kofoed. As with the television programs, their accounts of Lucky Luciano, Dutch Schultz, "Mad Dog" Coll, the inimitable "Chicken Head" Gurino and other public enemies of yesteryear bore only a nodding acquaintance to historical fact, but it hardly mattered.

To the everlasting consternation of my parents, I was hooked.

America at large was slow in catching up. FBI Director J. Edgar Hoover denied the existence of organized crime from 1924 until 1962, then blamed all of the underworld's sins on a small clique of Italians. Most reporters have followed his lead, though a few admit that the problem — and threat — may extend across cultural lines. To this day, few acknowledge its antiquity.

While it is true in one sense that the "noble experiment" of Prohibition (1920–33) spawned American organized crime as we know it today, organized criminal gangs are as old as human society. Whenever laws are passed, offenders find a way to circumvent them and corrupt those sworn to punish violators. The so-called *underworld* could not exist without an *upperworld* eager to take advantage of illicit goods and services.

Despite centuries of effort, no universal definition of organized crime exists today. The term *conspiracy* describes any collusion of two or more persons to break any law, great or small, but when does crime become "organized"? Early laws proscribing *criminal syndicalism* applied almost exclusively to political acts of subversion, sabotage and terrorism, extending into Orwellian "thought crimes," without touching on gangsterism. The *racket* label was first applied to criminal activity in 1765, though *racketeer* did not enter the popular lexicon until 1928, and *racketeering* was not legally defined until 1970. Modern terrorists, revolutionaries, and vigilante death squads are highly organized, even subject to military discipline, but do their actions qualify as "organized crime"?

The work in hand defines *organized crime* as any significant criminal activity planned and carried out for profit by a cohesive group of conspirators.

The earliest form of organized crime was piracy at sea, often including raids against coastal communities. Early Vikings set the tone with their attacks on Europe and the British Isles, emulated in due course by pirate fleets from the Far East to the Caribbean. Far from being disorganized bands like America's Wild West desperados and Depression-era bank robbers, pirates — often operating as government-licensed "privateers"—fielded fleets with hundreds of ships and thousands of fighting men aboard. Monarchs and colonial authorities honored some pirates while hunting others, with the line between "heroes" and outcasts in constant flux. Two examples suffice to prove the point: Sir Francis Drake earned a knighthood for his acts of New World piracy against Spain, while pirate Zheng Zhilong retired from buccaneering to become China's supreme "Admiral of the Coastal Seas." Everywhere we turn, collaboration between pirates and authorities prefigured the corruption of modern society. Modern Somalia replicates the pattern, with well-armed pirate fleets operating in complete defiance of— or covert collaboration with — established law enforcement.

While oath-bound criminal societies exist — including, but by no means limited to the Mafia, Triads and Yakuza — many organized criminals operate without benefit of ritual initiations, tattoos, recognition signs and countersigns, or detailed codes of conduct. Violence is a frequent byproduct of organized crime, but some conspiracies thrive without it, particularly in the realm of corporate or "white-collar" crime.

Politicians — and whole governments — may engage in criminal activity for a variety of reasons. Some pursue illegal actions to advance particular agendas, be it "ethnic cleansing" or "containment" of philosophies deemed abhorrent by those in power. Such acts do not qualify as organized crime, within our present definition, but they may place governments in alliance with organized criminals (as when the American Central Intelligence Agency recruited Mafia members to kill Cuban leader Fidel Castro and used profits from drug smuggling to finance guerrilla warfare in Central America). Likewise, while political and religious terrorism generally do not meet our criteria as organized crime, some militant groups support themselves, at least in part, by mercenary acts including robbery, drug trafficking, and kidnapping for ransom.

Likewise, it is not true that all "members" of organized crime live entirely — or even predominantly — on the proceeds of illicit activity. Indeed, most participants in organized crime also have legitimate business investments, and some exist primarily within the upperworld that cultivates and nourishes gangland.

This work includes entries for events that are not "criminal" per se, but which have bearing on the course of underworld history. Such events include births of pertinent characters (both future criminals and crime-fighters), discovery or invention of various drugs and weapons, creation of various law enforcement agencies and legitimate groups or institutions later controlled and corrupted by criminals, and passage of statutes relevant to organized criminal activity. The timeline spans more than eight millennia of human history, encompassing all nations, races, religions and political philosophies.

It is, in effect, a criminal history of the human race itself.

Author's Note

While every effort has been made to ensure precision and accuracy throughout the *Chronology of Organized Crime Worldwide, 6000 B.C.E. to 2010*, exact dates are unavailable for some events, particularly the discovery of certain drugs and the creation of various organizations or institutions in the distant past. Likewise, conspiratorial activity is secretive by nature and necessity, frustrating efforts to pinpoint a date when plots were hatched, alliances were forged or broken, and so on. Where the participants in those events have been willing to speak, timelines may be confused by faulty memory, fear of prosecution, or the habitual compulsion to lie. Deaths and disappearances may be concealed, or simply overlooked. The negligence of journalists — or their reliance on "poetic license" — may obscure the dates and sequence even of notorious events. Therefore, some dates presented here are approximate, the product of scholarly research and educated guesswork. Where conflicting dates for some events appear in print, I have selected the most likely accurate date in historical context.

Abbreviations

AAG   Assistant Attorney General

AB   Aryan Brotherhood

ABA   American Bar Association

AFL   American Federation of Labor

AKA   Also Known As (alias)

AMERIPOL   American Police Community

ATF   Bureau of Alcohol, Tobacco, Firearms and Explosives (U.S.)

BCCI   Bank of Credit and Commerce International

BGF   Black Guerrilla Family

BJA   Bureau of Justice Assistance (U.S.)

BJS   Bureau of Justice Statistics (U.S.)

BNDD   Bureau of Narcotics and Dangerous Drugs (U.S.)

BOPUS   U.S. Federal Bureau of Prisons

CAO   Chief Accounting Officer

CBP   U.S. Customs and Border Protection

CEO   Chief Executive Officer

CFO   Chief Financial Officer

CIA   Central Intelligence Agency (U.S.)

CIO   Congress of Industrial Organizations

DA   District Attorney

DEA   Drug Enforcement Administration (U.S.)

DHS   U.S. Department of Homeland Security

DOJ   Department of Justice (U.S.)

EPA   Environmental Protection Agency (U.S.)

EU   European Union

EUROPOL   European Law Enforcement Organization

FBI   Federal Bureau of Investigation (U.S.)

FBN   Federal Bureau of Narcotics (U.S.)

FDA   Food and Drug Administration

FDR   Franklin Delano Roosevelt

FJP   Federal Judicial Police (Mexico)

FOIA   Freedom of Information Act

FSB   Russian Federal Security Service

FTC   Federal Trade Commission (U.S.)

GAO   General Accountability Office (U.S.)

HUD   Department of Housing and Urban Development (U.S.)

IACP   International Association of Chiefs of Police

IATSE   International Association of Theatrical and Stage Employees

IBT   International Brotherhood of Teamsters

ICC   Interstate Commerce Commission (U.S.)

ICE   U.S. Immigration and Customs Enforcement

ILA   International Longshoremen's Association

ILGWU   International Ladies Garment Workers Union

IMB   International Maritime Board

IMO   International Maritime Organization

INS   Immigration and Naturalization Service (U.S.)

INTERPOL   International Criminal Police Organization

IRS   Internal Revenue Service (U.S.)

JFK   John Fitzgerald Kennedy

KGB   Committee for State Security (USSR)

KKK   Ku Klux Klan

KLA   Kosovo Liberation Army

KMT   Kuomintang (Nationalist Party of China)

LAPD   Los Angeles Police Department

LASO   Los Angeles County Sheriff's Office

LBJ   Lyndon Baines Johnson

LCN   *La Cosa Nostra*

LEIU   Law Enforcement Intelligence Unit (U.S.)

MC   motorcycle club

MCA   Music Corporation of America

NCIC   National Crime Information Center (U.S.)

NIJ   National Institute of Justice (U.S.)

NLRB   National Labor Relations Board (U.S.)

NSA   National Security Agency (U.S.)

NYPD   New York City Police Department

OAS   Organization of American States

ODALE   Office of Drug Abuse Law Enforcement (U.S.)

OGE   Office of Government Ethics (U.S.)

OSS   Office of Strategic Services (U.S.)

RCMP   Royal Canadian Mounted Police

RFK   Robert Francis Kennedy

SEC   Securities and Exchange Commission (U.S.)

SFPD   San Francisco (CA) Police Department

TSA   Transportation Security Administration (U.S.)

UAE   United Arab Emirates

UAW   United Auto Workers

UDN-FARN   Nicaraguan Democratic Union-Nicaraguan Revolutionary Armed Forces

UFW   United Farm Workers

UMW   United Mine Workers

UN   United Nations

U.S.   United States

WCTU   Woman's Christian Temperance Union

WITSEC   Witness Security Program (U.S.)

THE CHRONOLOGY

c. 6000 B.C.E. Cannabis seeds are used as food in China.

c. 6000–4000 B.C.E. Viticulture — the deliberate, selective cultivation of grapes for wine-making — begins in the mountains of present-day Armenia, between the Black and Caspian Seas. Archaeologists later find the oldest known wine residue in jars from Hajji Firuz Tepe, in present-day Iran.

c. 4000 B.C.E. Weavers in China and Turkestan use cannabis (hemp) to make textiles.

c. 3700 B.C.E. Native Americans in the Rio Grande Valley collect peyote buttons, apparently using their mescaline in religious rituals.

c. 3400 B.C.E. Opium poppies are cultivated in Mesopotamia, where Sumerians dub them *hul gil* ("joy plants"). The art of cultivating opium soon spreads to the Assyrians, Babylonians and Egyptians.

c. 3000 B.C.E. South American aboriginal tribes chew coca leaves, revering the plant as a divine gift. Gambling leaves its mark on the Egyptian calendar. A tablet later found at Gizeh, in the pyramid of Cheops, explains that five days were added to the 360-day calendar year after Thoth (the ibis-headed scribe of Egypt's divine pantheon) gambled with the moon and won the extra days.

c. 3000–2000 B.C.E. Production of alcohol flourishes. Mesopotamian brewers record recipes for 20-odd varieties of beer on clay tablets, while wine becomes an increasingly vital component of Mediterranean commerce and society.

2727 B.C.E. Cannabis debuts as a recognized medicine in China.

c. 2350 B.C.E. Urukagina (2380–2360 B.C.E.), ruler of Lagash in Mesopotamia, institutes the first recorded legal code. Known only from secondary sources today, the code imposed penalties for theft, usury, murder and polyandry, while limiting the power the priests and public officials.

c. 2300 B.C.E. China's Emperor Yao (2358–2258 B.C.E.) invents *go*, a board game later known as *igo* in Japan and *baduk* in Korea. Two players manipulate hundreds of pieces, while bystanders bet on the outcome.

2200 B.C.E. A Sumerian cuneiform tablet prescribes beer as a tonic for lactating women.

c. 2060 B.C.E. Ur-Nammu (2112–2095 B.C.E.), the king or Ur (modern Tell el-Mukayyar, Iraq), creates the earliest code of laws known from surviving fragments. Including references to witchcraft and slavery, the laws prescribe capital punishment for murder and robbery, with a prison term and fine (15 shekels of silver) for kidnapping.

c. 1934–1924 B.C.E. Lipit-Ishtar, fifth ruler of the first dynasty of Isin (modern Ishan al-Bahriyat, Iraq), dictates a code of laws including references to slavery, prostitution, and monetary compensation for property damage.

c. 1930 B.C.E. The Laws of Eshunna (modern Tall Ab¨ Harmal, Iraq) are inscribed are recorded on clay tablets, perhaps at the order of Amorite King Bilalama. The text prescribes execution in cases of burglary, murder, and for sexual offenses, while imposing lesser penalties for simple theft, "false distress," bodily injury and property damage.

c. 1800 B.C.E. Brewers in northern Syria produce large quantities of beer.

c. 1760 B.C.E. King Hammurabi of Babylon (1795–1750 B.C.E.) prepares a list of 282 laws delineating capital offenses (murder, child-stealing, "ensnaring," filing false criminal charges, etc.), prescribing mutilation for others, and safeguarding property rights (including the inheritance rights of prostitutes).

c. 1500 B.C.E. Vintners in the Aegean and Mediterranean regions produce large quantities of wine for commercial sale. Farmers in China and Scythia (present-day Kazakhstan, Ukraine, and southern Russia) cultivate cannabis for food and textile fiber. Affluent gamblers in India bet herds of cattle on dice games and chariot races.

c. 1500–1400 B.C.E. The Hittite Empire, based at Hattusa in present-day northern Turkey, develops a system of 200 specific laws governing aggression and assault, marital relationships, obligations and service, assaults on property and theft, contracts and prices, sacral matters, contracts and tariffs, and sexual relationships.

c. 1400 B.C.E. Residents of Thebes begin commercial cultivation of opium poppies. The Egyptian opium trade flourishes from the reign of Pharaoh Thutmose IV (1400–1390 B.C.E.) through that ot King Tutankhamun (1333–1324 B.C.E.). Phoenician and Minoan traders ship opium across the Mediterranean Sea to Greece, Carthage, and Europe.

1400–1300 B.C.E. Pirates from Lukka (modern Anatolia or Asia Minor) raid Mediterranean shipping.

1300 B.C.E. Buccaneers from Thrace (southern Bulgaria, northeastern Greece and European Turkey) dominate piracy on the Aegean and Mediterranean Seas.

1300–1200 B.C.E. Mediterranean pirates from Lukka collaborate with Hittite accomplices.

1220 B.C.E. April: Mediterranean pirates led by Lukki Lukka join Libyan forces to invade Egypt.

1215–1150 B.C.E. Piratical "sea peoples" raid the Mediterranean coastline, including attacks on Cyprus, Hatti (north-central Anatolia), the Levant, and Egypt. Egyptian Pharaoh Merneptay (1213–1203 B.C.E.) describes them in his Great

Karnak Inscription as "the foreign-countries of the sea." Raiding peaks during the reign of Pharaoh Ramesses III (1186–1155 B.C.E.).

c. 1200–800 B.C.E. The Atharvaveda, a Hindu text, describes *bhang* (dried cannabis leaves, stems and seeds) as "sacred grass," one of five Indian plants used both as medicine and as a ritual offering to the god Shiva.

1115–1076 B.C.E. Assyrian King Tiglath-Pileser I enacts a code of laws that leaves punishment of murder to the victim's family and prescribes flogging for a man who strikes a pregnant prostitute and causes her to miscarry. Other offenses rate cropping of ears or noses.

c. 1100 B.C.E. Inhabitants of Cyprus design special knives for harvesting opium. Aboriginal tribes in Mexico and the region of present-day Texas use peyote in religious rituals.

1000–900 B.C.E. Dorian pirates from Crete terrorize their Minoan neighbors.

c. 884–859 B.C.E. King Ashurnasirpal II receives 10,000 skins of wine from Assyrian vintners, delivered to his capital at Nimrud, south of Nineveh on the Tigris River.

c. 800 B.C.E. Brewers produce beer from barley and rice in India.

c. 700–600 B.C.E. The Zend Avesta, a sacred text of Zoroastrianism, described *bhang* (dried cannabis) as the "good narcotic" consumed by Zoroaster. Greek and Phoenician traders suffer constant attacks by Mediterranean pirates.

c. 700–300 B.C.E. Various Scythian tribes place cannabis seeds in royal tombs, as offerings to their gods.

c. 594 B.C.E. Greek statesman Solon (638 B.C.E.–558 B.C.E.) establishes publicly funded brothels in Athens to "democratize" the availability of sexual pleasure. Greek literature describes three classes of prostitutes: slaves (*pornai*), freeborn streetwalkers, and educated prostitute-entertainers (*hetaera*). The first two classes included both males and females, while the third was strictly female.

500–400 B.C.E. Athenian naval forces attack pirate colonies on the Greek islands of Kythnos, Mykonos, and throughout the Sporades archipelago (Alonnisos, Peristera, Skiathos, Skopelos, and Skyros).

c. 500–100 B.C.E. Scythian tradesmen introduce cannabis into northern Europe.

494 B.C.E. Pirate captain Dionysius the Phocaean raids shipping in the Mediterranean Sea.

c. 460 B.C.E. Greek physician Hippocrates (460 B.C.E.–370 B.C.E.) acknowledges the medicinal value of opium as a narcotic and antihemorrhagic for treating internal ailments.

430 B.C.E. Greek historian Herodotus of Halicarnassus (484 B.C.E.–425 B.C.E.) chronicles Scythian use of cannabis in rituals and as a form of recreation.

331 B.C.E. Alexander the Great (356 B.C.E.–323 B.C.E.) orders his admiral to conquer Crete and "clear the pirate fleets."

330 B.C.E. Alexander the Great introduces opium to Persia (now Iran) and India.

315–300 B.C.E. Corsair chief Glaucetas leads pirate raids on the Aegean Sea until the Athenian navy under Thymochares of Sphettos raids his base at Kythnos, capturing Glaucetas and his men.

300–186 B.C.E. The Aetolian League, a confederation of Greek pirates and military forces, dominates the Mediterranean Sea.

300 B.C.E. First use of peyote in the area of present-day Mexico, estimated by Spanish priest Bernardino de Sahagún in his *Florentine Codex*.

246–146 B.C.E. While the Punic Wars with Carthage distract Roman forces, pirate communities flourish in the Mediterranean.

219 B.C.E. Pirate raids ordered by Demetrius of Pharos precipitate the Second Illyrian War with Rome.

168 B.C.E. In a bid to suppress piracy, Rome conquers Illyria (on the modern Balkan Peninsula), establishing four client-republics ruled from Rome.

141–87 B.C.E. After wine is introduced to China along Silk Road trade routes, Emperor Wu of Han establishes a state monopoly on liquor production, which remains in force until 81 B.C.E. During his reign, an unknown Chinese author pens *The Divine Farmer's Herb-Root Classic*, which describes 365 medicines derived from minerals, plants, and animals. The text includes discussion of the psychotropic properties of cannabis.

102–100 B.C.E. Marcus Antonius leads the first Roman campaign against Cilician pirates in the Mediterranean Sea.

74 B.C.E. The second Marcus Antonius, more famous as "Mark Anthony," continues his father's campaign against Mediterranean pirates.

69 B.C.E. Cilician pirate Athenodorus captures and sacks the island of Delos.

67 B.C.E. Pompey the Great (106–48 B.C.E.) assumes command of a naval task force created to suppress Mediterranean piracy. A 40-day campaign clears the Western Sea of buccaneers, restoring communications between Italy, Hispania, and Africa. Pompey then pursues the main pirate force to its stronghold on the coast of Cilicia (now Çukurova, in southern Turkey) and crushes the fleet, inducing surrender by most of the pirates with promises of pardon and resettlement at Soli (near present-day Mersin, Turkey). Piracy is effectively eradicated by early 66 B.C.E.

c. 50 B.C.E. Greek historian Dionysius of Halicarnassus (60 B.C.E.–6 B.C.E.) reports that "the Gauls [French] have no knowledge of wine but use a foul-smelling liquor [beer] made of barley rotted in water."

36 B.C.E. Summer: Pirate captain Apollophanes fights an inconclusive battle with Octavian's Roman fleet off the coast of Sicily.

C.E. 70 Greek physician Pedanius Dioscorides (C.E. 40–90) describes medicinal use of cannabis in Rome.

170 Roman physician Galen of Pergamum (129–200) notes the psychoactive properties of confections made from cannabis seeds.

400 Arab traders introduce Egyptian opium to China.

c. 500 Wine reaches China along the Silk Road from Europe and North Africa.

529–534 Eastern Roman Emperor Justinian I issues the *Corpus Juris Civilis* ("Body of Civil Law"), which includes a ban on gambling in public houses and private homes. Clerics caught gambling are subject to suspension from office.

590 Following his conversion to Christianity, Visigothic King Reccared I of Hispania (the Iberian Peninsula) bans prostitution within his domain. While men who hire prostitutes receive no punishment, women convicted of prostitution receive a virtual death sentence of 300 lashes followed by exile.

768 First specific reference to the use of hops in beer from the Abbey St. Denis in France by King Pepin the Short.

789 Viking raiders stage their first attacks on English coastal towns.

793 June 8: Vikings storm the island of Lindisfarne, off England's northeast coast and "destroy God's church, with plunder and slaughter."

794 Vikings raid Northumbria, England, attacking a monastery at Yarrow.

795 Viking raids begin along the eastern coast of Ireland, from the Irish Sea, striking the islands of Iona, Rathlin and Skye.

797 Vikings assault Lambay Island, off the north coast of County Dublin, Ireland. The *Annála Uladh* (*Annals of Ulster*) record a Viking raid on the Isle of Man. Some modern historians dispute its occurrence.

799 Vikings stage their first raid on continental Europe, attacking the monastery of Saint Philibert of Jumièges on Île de Noirmoutier, off the Atlantic coast of France.

800 King Charlemagne (742–814) organizes French coastal defenses against pirates north of the Seine estuary.

802 Viking pirates attack St. Columba's monastery on the Isle of Iona, in the Inner Hebrides.

805 Vikings return for a second assault on St. Columba's monastery, on Iona.

818 Holy Roman Emperor Louis the Pious (778–840) expands Justinian's gambling ban, mandat-

ing a three-year suspension for clerics caught gambling.

820 Vikings conquer and occupy the Isle of Man, in the Irish Sea. Others raid Flanders, in Belgium, and land at Baie de la Seine in northern France, but native troops kill five and force the rest to retreat.

824–961 Arab pirates operating from Crete raid shipping throughout the Mediterranean.

834 Viking ships approach the mouth of England's River Thames.

836 Viking leaders Björn and Hasting stage the first of many raids against Normandy, in northern France, striking at Avranchin and the Cotentin (or Cherbourg) Peninsula from the English Channel.

839 Viking warlord Turgeis invades Ireland to establish permanent bases.

841 Turgeis and his Vikings conquer Dublin, on the River Liffey.

  May 12: Asgeir's Viking fleet sails up the River Seine, to loot and burn Rouen on May 14. On May 24 the raiders plunder and burn a monastery at Jumiège, then storm another at Fontenell (now St. Wandrille), seizing 68 hostages whom they release on May 28, in exchange for ransom paid by monks from the Abbey of Saint-Denis.

843 Viking raiders from Vestfold, Norway, establish a base of operations on Île de Noirmoutier, using it as a launching pad for raids against Nantes, on the Loire River.

844 Residents of Seville, Spain, repulse a Viking raid.

845 Ragnar Lodbrok leads a Viking fleet of 120 ships against Paris, collecting 7,000 livres from King Charles the Bald of West Francia (823–77) to leave the city in peace; Irish chieftain Máel Sechnaill mac Máele Ruanaid of Clann Cholmáin captures Viking raider Turgeis and drown him in Lough Owel, north of Mullingar, County Westmeath.

846 Muslim pirates based on Sicily sail up the Tiber River and attack Rome, looting the Basilica of St. Peter. Newly-elected Pope Leo IV orders erection of 40-foot "Leonine" walls with 44 watchtowers, surrounding the Vatican, with 44 watchtowers. Construction of the fortress is completed in 852.

851 October 13: Viking chieftain Asgeir leads a fleet up the River Seine and sacks the monastery of Fontenelle.

852 January 9: Asgeir's Vikings return to the monastery of Fontenell, find nothing more to plunder, and burn it to the ground, then march inland toward Beauvais. Blocked by Frankish troops, the Norsemen retreat to winter on Jeufosse island, guarding entry to the Seine, departing on June 5. Before year's end, a new Viking horde under Godfrid and Sigtrygg lands on Jeufosse, where they are besieged by Charles the Bald.

853 Early in the year, Charles the Bald negotiates a truce with Godfrid, who evacuates Jeufosse island. Sigtrygg remains to raid and burn various settlements through March. Another Norse armada led by Olaf the White conquers much of Ireland.

855 July 18: Sigtrygg returns to West Francia, attacking a fortress on the River Seine, below Paris.

August 17: Viking reinforcements arrive on the Seine, led by Björn. The combined forces advance on Chartres, where they are stopped by Frankish troops under Charles the Bald, who forces their retreat with heavy losses.

857 January: Björn and Sigtrygg renew attacks on Paris from their island base on Jeufosse island.

June 12: The Viking army invades Chartres, sacking the town and killing most of its inhabitants.

Summer: The Norse invaders raid Evreux and other Frankish towns from their base on Jeufosse, before retiring in autumn.

858 January 9: Björn, reinforced by Danes under Hasting, raze the abbey of Fontenelle and advance on Paris, demanding ransom to spare Parisian cathedrals. Louis, abbot of Saint Denis (800–67) and his half-brother Joscelin are captured, then released on payment of a large ransom.

859 Viking raiders renew their attacks along the Seine valley, taking advantage of Charles the Bald's conflict with brother Louis the German (806–76), king of Bavaria. Monasteries are sacked and bishops executed at Bayeux, Beauvais, and Laon. During the same year, other Norsemen strike for the first time at Mediterranean targets.

860 Charles the Bald pays Viking chief Veland 3,000 silver livres to cease raiding on the Seine. Rus' Vikings attack Constantinople (now Istanbul, Turkey).

861 A Viking fleet of 200 ships, under Veland, besieges Jeufosse island and stages new raids against Paris, then withdraw, allowing Charles the Bald to erect forts controlling the Seine at Pont-de-l'Arche.

863 Vikings raze the town of Xanten, in the present German state of North Rhine–Westphalia.

865 Viking raiders with a fleet of 50 ships establish a raiding base at Pîtres, on the Seine, in the present-day region of Haute-Normandie. Viking chieftain Ivarr the Boneless leads a "Great Heathen Army" to invade the East Anglian region of England.

866 Viking raiders loot and burn Coutances, in Normandy.

867 Unable to defend Avranchin and the Cotentin Peninsula against Viking attacks, Charles the Bald cedes those portions of Normandy to the Bretons.

873 Ivarr the Boneless dies in England. His brothers and sons continue raiding across the island's northeastern quadrant.

875 Halfdan Ragnarson, brother of Ivarr the Boneless, conquers Northumbria, England, and declares himself king.

876 A fleet of 100 Viking ships invade the Seine, retreating after Charles the Bald pays 5,000 livres in tribute.

877 English warriors expel Halfdan Ragnarson from York. Before year's end, he dies in an attempt to recapture Northumbria.

878 Ubbe Ragnarsson, another brother of Ivarr the Boneless, dies in combat against the West Saxons at the Battle of Cynwit, in Somerset.

885 November 25: Danish warlord Sigfred approaches Paris with a Viking fleet of 700 ships and 30,000 men. Parisians repulse two assaults on the city, on November 26 and 27, resulting in a six-month siege. Frankish king Charles the Fat (839–888), successor to Charles the Bald, pays 700 pounds of silver as tribute in May 886, whereupon the Viking withdraw.

890 Viking raiders sack Saint-Lô, in Normandy.

890–892 Norse warlord Rollo (AKA Rolf) leads multiple raids in the Bessin region of Normandy.

891 French defenders defeat a Viking for at Île de Noirmoutier.

900 Vikings raid various settlements along the Mediterranean coastline.

900–1000 Use of cannabis spreads throughout Arabia, while scholars and clerics debate its effects and value.

902 Muslim pirates led by Leo of Tripoli terrorize island settlements in the Aegean Sea.

904 July: Leo of Tripoli ravages shipping in the Dardanelles with a fleet of 54 galleys and 11,000 pirates.

905 Vikings plunder Vire, in the present-day Basse-Normandie region of France.

907 Viking raids in Brittany effectively destroy Breton sovereignty.

911 Autumn: Frankish king Charles the Simple (879–929) stalls the advance of Viking warlord Rollo's raiders at Chartres, then concludes the Treaty of Saint-Clair-sur-Epte, ceding control of Neustria (between Aquitaine and the English Channel) to Rollo's Norsemen. In return, Rollo submits to Christian baptism, marries Charles's illegitimate daughter Gisele, and agrees to block further invasions by other Vikings.

916 Viking forces based in Bessin and the Cotentin Peninsula launch raids throughout eastern Brittany.

917 Viking raiders seize control of Dublin, Ireland.

923 The Byzantine navy destroys Leo of Tripoli's pirate fleet near Lemnos, in the Aegean Sea.

925 Norsemen from Bessin join forces with native Saxons in raids along the western Seine valley.

941 Rus' Vikings stage new raids on Constantinople.

980 Vikings launch a series of attacks designed to seize control of England.

984 Jomsvikings led by Prince Styrbjörn the Strong suffer a crushing defeat by Styrbjörn's uncle Eric the Victorious (945–95) at the Battle of Fýrisvellir, near present-day Uppsala, Sweden.

991 August 10: Vikings defeat English troops at the Battle of Maldon, in Essex. King Æthelred II (968–1016) subsequently pays the first annual ransom dubbed *Danegeld* ("Danish tax") to prevent further Viking raids against England. The first payment totals 6,600 pounds of silver. Danegeld tribute continues into the 12th century, totaling £23,000 in 1130 alone.

998 Venetian forces crush the Narentan pirates of the Adriatic Sea.

1000 The *Bhavaprakasha*, an Indian medical text, describes use of opium.

1065 Persian scientist Abu Rayhan Biruni publishes his *Kitab al-Saidana fi al-Tibb*, containing the first known reference to the drug khat or *qat*.

1109 Despite ongoing payments of Danegeld, Viking chieftain Olaf Haraldsson (995–1030) attacks London from the Thames, destroying London Bridge.

1020 Persian physician Avicenna (980–1037) describes opium as "the most powerful of stupefacients."

1066 Norman conquerors of England establish the island's first formal courts.

1074–94 Hashish is introduced to Iraq during the reign of Fatimid caliph al-Mustansir.

1090 Hasan ibn al-Sabbah, a missionary of Isma'ilism (second largest branch of Islamic Shi'ism), concludes a two-year siege by capturing the fortress at Alamut, in the Alborz Mountains of northern Persia (now Iran). He establishes a cult of *Hashshashin* ("eaters of hashish"), from which the term "assassin" derives. As the "Old Man of the Mountain," Hasan dispatches killers to spread their religion by eliminating enemies and rivals. The cult evolves into a cadre of slayers for hire to the highest bidder, favored by European nobles for elimination of selected targets. Known or alleged *Hashshashin* victims include: Abu Ali al-Hasan al-Tusi Nizam al-Mulk, a Persian scholar and vizier of the Seljuq Empire, killed on October 14, 1092; al-Malik al-Afdal ibn Badr al-Jamali Shahanshah, a vizier of Egypt's Fatimid caliphs, slain on December 11, 1121; Abu'l-Fal Ibn al-KhashshIb, the *qadi* (judge) of Aleppo, in northern Syria, under Seljuk emir Radwan, assassinated in 1125; Count Raymond II of Tripoli, killed in 1152; Crusader Conrad of Montferrat, who ruled Jerusalem as King Conrad I from November 24, 1190, until his murder on April 28, 1192; and

Prince Edward of England (1239–1307), who survived a wound from a poisoned dagger in 1271 to rule as King Edward I. Mongol warlord Hulagu Khan conquered Alamut on December 15, 1256, and broke the power of the *Hashshashin*, but a Syrian branch of the cult remained active until it was crushed by the Mamluk Sultan Baibars (1223–77) in 1273. *Hashshashin* survivors recaptured Alamut briefly in 1275, and Moroccan scholar Ibn Battuta (1304–69) recorded their persistence as hired killers through the mid–14th century. Their spiritual heirs are the modern NizIrn, officially known as the Shn'a Imami IsmI'nln Tariqah.

1100 Distillation of alcoholic "spirits" documented from the medical school at Salerno, Italy.

1120 Concubines in the harem of Emperor Yelü Yanxi invent the first playing cards, according to the Chinese dictionary *Ching-tsze-tung*, published in 1628.

1155 Sheikh Haidar of Greater Khorasan (including parts of modern-day Afghanistan, Iran, Pakistan, Tajikistan, Turkmenistan and Uzbekistan) enjoys cannabis and encourages its use throughout his domain. In England, a royal charter establishes the Cinque Ports — Dover, Hastings, Hythe, New Romney, and Sandwich — as favored trading settlements exempt from most taxes. That favoritism encourages wholesale smuggling.

1161 While publicly discouraging prostitution, King Heny II of England (1133–89) permits it to continue, mandating that all prostitutes must be unmarried women. Henry also requires weekly inspections of London brothels to ensure that no laws are broken.

c. 1164–71 Syrian mystics introduce cannabis to Egypt under the Muslim Ayyubid dynasty.

1170 Future mercenary pirate Eustace the Monk is born to noble parents in Boulogne-sur-Mer, northern France.

1190 During the Third Crusade (1189–92), King Richard of England (1157–99) and King Philip II Augustus of France (1165–1223) ban gambling for money by any of their subjects below the rank of knight. Kings are allowed to gamble any amount of money they choose, while lesser nobles are restricted to losses of 20 shillings per day.

c. 1200 Three Indian medical texts, the *Dhanvantri Nighantu*, *Sharangdhar Samahita* and *Shodal Gadanigrah* describe opium's value in treating diarrhea and sexual dysfunction.

1204 The Republic of Venice begins conquest of the Greek Ionian Islands with capture of Corfu, striving to suppress local piracy.

1205–12 Eustace the Monk serves King John of England (1166–1216) as a mercenary pirate, raiding French ships and settlements along the English Channel and the Strait of Dover.

1212–17 Eustace the Monk switches sides, to serve King Philip II of France (1165–1223).

1217 August 24: Eustace the Monk's pirate fleet is defeated in combat against British naval forces led by Hubert de Burgh, in the Battle of Sandwich. De Burgh captures Eustace and has him beheaded. As a result, Prince Louis of France (1187–1226) — later King Louis VIII — signs the Treaty of Lambeth on September 20, relinquishing his claim to the English throne and agreeing to eject Eustace's brothers from the Channel Islands.

1223 Summer: Japanese Wokou pirates stage their first recorded raid on the south coast of Goryeo, Korea.

1231 Pope Gregory IX launches the Papal Inquisition to suppress heresy, subsequently expanding to include witchcraft, sorcery — and, by extension, popular use of opium and natural hallucinogens.

c. 1240–45 Spanish physician and herbalist Abu Muhammad Dia'al-Din Abdullah ibn Ahmad ibn Al-Baytar al-Maliqial-Andalusi describes the psychoactive properties of cannabis.

1241 Various European trading states create the Hanseatic League to suppress piracy and monopolize trade along the coast of Northern Europe, from the Baltic to the North Sea and inland.

1271–95 Venetian explorer Marco Polo (1254–1324) tours the Far East, returning to publish second-hand accounts of Hasan ibn al-Sabbah and the *Hashshashin*.

1277 April: Italian pirate Diovanni de lo Cavo captures a Venetian ship in the Mediterranean.

1282 March 30: Residents of Palermo, Sicily, rebel against control of their island by French-born King Charles I of Naples (1226–85), in an insurrection dubbed the "Sicilian Vespers" (because it began at sundown on Easter Monday). Some authors cite this event as the birth of the Sicilian Mafia, claiming that its name derives from the battle cry *Morte alla Francia Italia anela!* ("Death to France, Italy groans!"). However, no contemporary reference to the Mafia exists.

1290 According to Muslim historian Ziauddin Barani (1285–1357), Sultan Jalal-ud-din Firuz Khilji (d. 1296) arrests several members of the Thugee cult in Delhi, procuring information that leads to another 1,000 arrests. Thugs — from the Hindi *thag* ("thief") or the Sanskrit *sthagati* ("he conceals") — are worshipers of Kali, the Hindu goddess of death and destruction. They prey on travelers, strangling, mutilating and robbing lone individuals or whole caravans. Jalal-ud-din Firuz Khilji orders his prisoners transported to Lakhnauti and released. The cult, already well established by this date, persists until suppressed by British colonial authorities in the mid–19th century.

Spring: Danish forces capture and execute Norse pirate Alv Erlingsson off the coast of Scania, Sweden.

c. 1300 England's Cinque Ports establish a league to suppress piracy in the English Channel.

1358 The Great Council of Venice declares prostitution "absolutely indispensable to the world," thus paving the way for state-funded brothels in major Italian cities.

c. 1375–85 Muslim scholar Badruddin Az-Zarkashi (1344–92) writes his *Zahr al-'arish fi tahrim al-hashish*, the oldest known monograph on hashish.

1376–85 Japanese pirates stage 174 raids on Korean coastal towns.

1377 The Florentine senate issues a resolution regulating use of playing cards, while an amendment to the gambling laws of Paris bans them outright. Swiss monk Johannes von Rheinfelden describes the emergence of a new game in Basel, using a deck of 52 cards with four suits.

1378 Emir Soudoun Scheikhouni of the Ottoman Empire issues the first known ban on eating hashish.

1379 Authorities in Regensburg, Bavaria, ban playing cards.

1389 Korean forces attack pirate strongholds on Tsushima, Japan, killing 114 pirates and capturing 21, while rescuing 131 Chinese hostages.

1390 English and French naval forces battle North African pirates in the Mediterranean.

1392 The Dukes of Mecklenberg, Germany, hire a company of privateers called the "Victual Brothers" to raid Danish shipping. Their depredations continue into 1398, when they are expelled from Gotland by the Hanseatic League.

1394 Erich III, Duke of Saxony (1370–1401), plays cards with the Duke of Letzburg to determine ownership of the Ardennes forest.

1399 The provost of Paris, France, adds card-playing to a list of proscribed games, forbidden to the working class on workdays.

1401 October 20: German privateer Klaus Störtebeker dies in battle with forces of the Hanseatic League near Heligoland, in the North Sea.

1402 Agents of the Hanseatic League capture German pirate Gottfried Michaelsen and execute him in Hamburg. Before year's end, the league also captures and executes another German buccaneer, Hennig Wichmann, with 73 of his men.

1416 Jewish resident of Forli, Italy, adopt an ordinance banning gambling parties.

1419 June 9: King Taejon of Korea declares war on Japanese pirates based on Tsushima Island. On June 20 a fleet of 227 ships and 17,285 soldiers attacks Tsushima, burning 109 pirate ships and seizing 20 others. Korean forces kill 200 persons and take 600 prisoners before a Japanese army repels them on July 20. The combatants sign a treaty on September 29.

1430 Amadeus VIII (1383–1451), the Count of Savoy — comprising portions of southeastern France, western Switzerland, and northwest Italy — bans gambling for money, except in the case of women playing cards for "pin-money" (small sums allotted for personal expenses).

1438–1532 The Inca Empire cultivates coca throughout the Andean mountains. *Chasquis*, the empire's professional messengers, chew coca leaves for extra energy on their long-distance runs between relay stations.

1444 The town of Sluis, in Holland, conducts the first documented public lottery.

1445 May 9: L'Ecluse, in the Rhone River valley, conducts a lottery to finance construction of defensive walls around the town. Players purchase 4,304 tickets, for a chance to win 1,737 florins.

1449 Deposed Danish ruler Eric of Pomerania assumes power in the Duchy of Pomerania-Stolp, launching pirate raids "against friend and foe alike" until his death on May 3, 1459.

1453 November: English pirate William Kyd — unrelated to the later William Kidd — seizes a ship owned by the bishop of Saint Andrews, Scotland, and delivers it to Exmouth.

1461 King Eward IV of England (1442–83) bans card and dice games, except during the 12-day Christmas holiday.

1466 February 14: Civic leaders in Bruges, Belgium, sell lottery tickets to raise money for impoverished citizens.

1478 Future Turkish privateer and admiral Hayreddin Barbarossa born on the Mediterranean island of Midilli (present-day Lesbos). He is the youngest of four brothers born in the 1470s, all of whom engage in piracy.

1485 A statute passed in Regensburg, Germany, permits card-playing as long as no money changes hands. Future privateer and Ottoman admiral Turgut Reis born near Bodrum, on the Aegean coast of Turkey.

1496 King Henry VII of England (1457–1509) forbids gambling by the working class, except for card games played during Christmas holidays.

1500 Portuguese mariners and tradesmen on the East China Sea pioneer smoking opium for swift intoxication. Future pirate Jean-François de La Roque de Roberval (AKA "Robert Baal") born in Carcassonne, southern France.

1502 Italian explorer Amerigo Vespucci (1454–1512) returns from the New World to Europe, bearing coca plants among his various discoveries.

1503 Turkish pirate Oruç Reis, brother of Hayreddin Barbarossa, begins operating from Djerba,

an island in the Gulf of Gabbes, off the Tunisian coast. Hayreddin joins him before year's end.

1504 Abu Abdullah Mohammed Hamis, Sultan of Tunisia, grants the Barbarossa brothers permission to operate from the strategic port of La Goulette, in return for one-third of their loot. During the year, the brothers capture two Papal galleys near Elba, and a Sicilian warship — the *Cavalleria* — near Lipari, in transit from Spain to Naples with 60 Spanish knights and 380 soldiers aboard.

1505 The Barbarossa brothers join Turkish privateer Kurto lu Muslihiddin Reis (1487–1535) for raids along the coast of Calabria, southern Italy.

1508 The Barbarossa brothers lead raids against coastal towns in Liguria, northwestern Italy.

1509 Ishak Barbarossa joins brothers Heyreddin and Oruç Reis in pirate raids launched from La Goulette.

1510 The Barbarossa brothers raid Capo Passero, southeastern Sicily, later repulsing Spanish assaults on the Algerian ports of Algiers, Béjaïa, and Oran.

1511 August: The Barbarossas conduct raids around Reggio Calabria, southern Italy.

1512 August: The exiled ruler of Béjaïa commissions the Barbarossa brothers to expel Spanish occupation forces. Their effort fails, and Oruç Reis loses his left arm in combat, replacing it with a silver prosthetic limb.

Autumn: The Barbarossa brothers lead raids along the coast of Andalusia (southern Spain), seize a castle on Minorca (in the Balearic Islands), and capture 23 ships before returning to La Goulette in triumph.

1513 Operating from a new base at Cherchell, 55 miles west of Algiers, the Barbarossa brothers capture four English ships en route to France, seize four more vessels off Valencia, Spain, and capture a Spanish galley near Málaga. They also skirmish with the Spanish fleet on several occasions.

1514 Continuing their private war with Spain, the Barbarossa brothers lead 12 ships and 1,000 Turks to destroy a Spanish fortress at Béjaïa, then raid Ceuta on the Strait of Gibraltar, moving on to wrest Jijel, Algeria, from Genoese control. Next, they capture Mahdiya, Tunisia, followed by lucrative raids on the Balearic Islands, Sardinia, Sicily, and the Spanish mainland. After capturing several ships at Majorca, Oruç Reis pays tribute to Ottoman Sultan Selim I (1465–1520). Selim repays that gesture by furnishing the brothers with two galleys.

1516 Joined once more by Kurto lu Muslihiddin Reis, the Barbarossa brothers lay siege to the Castle of Elba, then strike again at Liguria, capturing 12 ships and sinking or damaging 28 more. Before year's end, they drive Spanish troops from Algiers and Tlemcen, then expel former ruler Abu Hamo Musa III of the Beni Ziyad dynasty, asserting their own authority. Spanish fugitives from Algiers regroup on Peñón de Vélez de la Gomera, off the Moroccan coast, and petition Holy Roman Emperor Charles V for aid, but his forces cannot dislodge the Barbarossa's from Algiers.

April 23: Bavaria's *Reinheitsgebot* ("purity order") bans production of beer from any ingredients other than water, barley and hops.

1517 Oruç Reis declares himself sultan of Algiers, expanding his authority with the capture of Medea, Miliana, and Ténès. Next, the Barbarossa brothers raid Capo Limiti and Calabria's Isola di Capo Rizzuto. Finally, Oruç offers Algiers to the Ottoman Sultan as a new imperial province. The sultan accepts, naming Oruç Governor of Algiers and Chief Sea Governor of the Western Mediterranean, with vows of military support.

1518 May: Emperor Charles V lands at Oran with 10,000 Spanish soldiers, joined by thousands of Bedouins, and marches on Tlemcen. Oruç Reis and brother Ishak defend the city for 20 days, with 1,500 Turks and 5,000 Moors, until both die in battle.

1520 King Francis I of France (1494–1547) signs a bill permitting lotteries in Bordeaux, Lille, Lyons, Paris and Strasbourg. Future Muslim pirate and Ottoman admiral "Uluj Ali" born Giovanni Dionigi, in Italy.

1521 June 15: Spanish colonial authorities ban native use of non-alcoholic intoxicants — hallucinogenic mushrooms and peyote — in New Spain. Catholic priests undertake punishment of offenders.

1521–27 French privateer Jean Fleury raids Spanish shipping in the Caribbean, in the employ of sponsor Jean Ango.

1522 Venetian clothing dealer Geronimo Bambarana inaugurates a lottery with winners paid in cash or decorative carpets.

1523 French pirate Jean Florin captures three Spanish galleons on the Atlantic, returning from the Caribbean with a cargo of gold and precious stones.

1524 Italian explorer Giovanni da Verrazzano (1485–1528) reports the first sighting of wild hemp in North America, during an expedition to the area of present-day Virginia. Most modern historians deny that it was cannabis.

1526 Zāhir ud-Dīn Muhammad bin 'Omar Sheikh (1483–1531), founder of Persia's Mughal Empire, "discovers" hashish.

1527 Swiss physician Paracelsus, né Phillip von Hohenheim (1493–1541), introduces lauda-

num — a mixture of opium, citrus juice and gold, in pill form — as an analgesic. Pirate Jean Florin captured and hanged.

1530 Florence conducts Italy's first public lottery, raising money for public works. Holy Roman Emperor Charles V (1500–58) establishes the Knights of Malta, in part to suppress the Barbary pirates.

July 26: French privateer Jean Ango begins raiding Portuguese shipping in the Atlantic.

1531 August 15: Jean Ango retires from piracy after the king of Portugal pays him 60,000 ducats to desist.

1532 Future pirate and slaver John Hawkins born at Plymouth, England.

1532–33 Francisco Pizzaro González (1471–1541) conquers the Inca Empire in South America. Recipients of Spanish land grants subsequently take possession of Incan coca plantations.

1534 Future Turkish privateer and Ottoman admiral Murat Reis the Elder born at Rhodes.

1537–42 Nobleman-turned-pirate Kristoffer Throndsen raids settlements along the coast of Norway, before receiving a pardon and naval commission from King Christian III of Denmark.

1539 Vicente de Valverde Alvarez (1490–1543), Bishop of Cuzco, claims 10 percent of Peru's coca crop for the Roman Catholic Church.

1540 King Henry VIII of England (1491–1547) bans card games, dice, bowling and tennis, while encouraging his male subjects to practice archery. Future privateer, slaver, and British vice admiral Francis Drake born in Tavistock, Devon.

April — Turgut Reis sacks the island of Gozo, in the Maltese Archipelago, transporting at least 5,000 prisoners for sale as slaves in Libya. He later raids the coasts of Sicily and Spain with a fleet of 25 ships, prompting Charles V to send Genoese admiral Andrea Doria in pursuit, with 81 galleys. Reis escapes, bombarding the southern ports of Corsica, and sacks Capraia in the Tuscan Archipelago.

1544 French Huguenot pirates led by Jean-François Roberval sack Cartagena, in present-day Colombia. Turkish pirates under Barbarossa Hayreddin Pasha capture the island of Ischia, in the Tyrrhenian Sea, seizing 4,000 prisoners. A second raid on Lipari, off the northern coast of Sicily, enslaves another 9,000 captives.

1545 King Philip II of Spain orders *cáñamo* (cannabis) planted throughout his empire, for both medicinal and industrial uses.

1546 July 4: Hayreddin Barbarossa, retired from service as pasha and fleet admiral of the Ottoman navy, dies at his seaside palace in the Büyükdere district of Istanbul.

1547 French theologian John Calvin (1509–64)

issues an edict banning gambling for gold or silver.

1548 February: A large Japanese pirate fleet raids the Chinese coastal counties of Ningbo and Taizhou.

1549 Angolan slaves introduce cannabis to Brazil's sugar plantations. Their Portuguese masters permit them to grow plants between rows of sugar cane and smoke it in their free time, between harvests.

1552 Spring: Hundreds of Chinese pirates led by Wang Zhi raid the coast of Zhejiang, China.

1553 Summer: Wang Zhi's pirates resume attacks on the coast of Zhejiang, with a fleet of several hundred ships.

1554 French pirate François "Peg Leg" Le Clerc captures Santiago de Cuba, occupying the city for a month before he flees with loot valued at 80,000 pesos. In southeastern Italy, pirates sack Vieste and carry off 7,000 slaves.

1555 French pirate Jacques de Sores attacks and burns Havana, Cuba. Turgut Reis sacks Bastia, on Corsica, taking 6,000 prisoners.

1557 China's Ming Dynasty permits establishment of a permanent Portuguese trading base at Macau. Traders soon introduce opium.

1558 July 9: Barbarossa Hayreddin Pasha lays siege to Ciutadella, on Minorca in the Balearic Islands, with 140 ships and 15,000 pirates. The town surrenders on July 17, whereupon 3,452 inhabitants are transported to Constantinople for sale as slaves.

1560 While waiting to ambush a Spanish treasure fleet, François le Clerc ravages settlements along the Caribbean coast of Panama.

May 9–14: Ottoman corsairs Piyale Pasha and Turgut Reis face Spanish and Italian naval forces in battle off the island of Djerba, Tunisia. The pirates win a decisive victory, losing a handful of ships and 1,000 men killed, while their opponents lose 30 galleys, 9,000 dead and 5,000 captured. Spanish survivors evacuate Djerba's garrison on July 29.

1560–73 German pirate Klein Henszlein raids shipping in the North Sea.

1561 Private lotteries are banned in Bruges, Belgium. Cosimo I de' Medici (1519–74) creates the Order of Saint Stephen to combat Muslim pirates on the Mediterranean Sea. The Order subsequently participates in campaigns at Corfu, Dalmatia, and Negroponte.

1562 Sir John Hawkins inaugurates the Atlantic slave trade.

1563 Turgut Reis raids coastal towns in the Spanish province of Granada, seizing 4,000 prisoners at Almuñécar alone. Barbary pirates terrorize the Balearic Islands, depopulating Formentera, while other islands fortify their churches and erect

coastal watchtowers. French pirate Jean Bontemps collaborates with English troops occupying Le Havre, looting French merchant ships.

1565 May 18: A large Ottoman fleet lays siege to Malta, hoping to seize it as a base for raids against European ports. Barbary pirate Turgut Reis suffers critical wounds while leading an attack on June 18. The fortress at Saint Elmo falls on June 23, but resistance continues until a relief expedition arrives from Sicily on September 8, with 60 galleys and 11,000 soldiers. The invaders depart, with more than 6,000 soldiers slain in the fighting.

August 22: Spanish admiral and pirate-hunter Pedro Menéndez de Avilés founds America's oldest port city at St. Augustine, Fla. On August 28 he attacks a French Huguenot settlement at Fort Caroline, on the St. Johns River, slaughtering 200 of the fort's 250 inhabitants. The remainder, mostly women and children, are taken prisoner. Menéndez then erects a Spanish fort on the site, dubbed *Matanzas* ("massacre," in Spanish).

1567 Queen Elizabeth I (1533–1603) conducts England's first public lottery, to finance harbor repairs. A top prize of £5,000 is offered — equivalent to $127,000 in 2009 — but only 33,000 of the original 400,000 tickets are sold by January 1, 1569, when the first drawing is held.

Late April: Pirates led by John Bontemps raid Borburata (now Puerto Cabellos), Venezuela, seizing hostages and robbing them of 1,500 pesos.

1568 April: French nobleman Dominique de Gourgue retaliates for the 1865 massacre of Huguenots at Fort Caroline, Fla., by burning the new Spanish fort and slaughtering its inhabitants.

September — John Hawkins leads a Caribbean slaving expedition, with a crew including young Francis Drake. On September 15, Spanish naval forces surprise the slavers at San Juan de Ulúa, near Veracruz, Mexico, sinking several British ships before the rest escape. Hawkins and Drake thereafter pursue privateering as a means to break Spain's monopoly on Caribbean trade, but lose four of their six ships after a battle at San Juan, Puerto Rico, on September 23.

1568–1648 The Eighty Years' War for control of the Netherlands promotes privateering against Spanish merchant ships.

1569 The Spanish navy surprise Sir John Hawkins and his fleet, including a young Francis Drake, at San Juan de Ulúa, near Veracruz, Mexico. The British privateers narrowly escape.

1570 Jacques de Sore executes 40 Jesuit missionaries at Tazacorte, on La Palma in the Canary Islands, hurling their corpses from a cliff, into the sea. King Philip II of Spain sends Dr. Franciso Hernàndez to study medicinal flora and fauna in Mexico. His subsequent reports include first proper botanical description of peyote.

1570–90 British privateers harass Spanish shipping and colonies throughout the Spanish Main — including Florida, Mexico, Central America, and the northern coast of South America.

1572 German pirate Klein Henzlein and 33 of his men are captured and beheaded.

May 24: Francis Drake leaves Plymouth with two small ships and 73 men, to raid port of Nombre de Dios, in Panama. The July raid is successful, but Drake suffers a serious wound, prompting his men to abandon their loot as they flee. Drake remains in the region for nearly a year, attacking Spanish ships in an effort to recoup the loss.

1573 January: English pirate Martin Frobisher captures a French ship off the Irish coast.

April 29: Francis Drake teams with French buccaneer Guillaume Le Testu to capture a Spanish mule train bearing some 30 tons of gold and silver near Nombre de Dios. Unable to carry the loot, they bury most of it for later retrieval. La Testu is wounded, then captured with his men, all of whom are executed by Spanish troops. One pirate, under torture, directs Spaniards to the buried hoard, but Drake escapes with enough gold to make him wealthy upon his August 9 return to Plymouth.

1575 The coca trade employs an estimated 82 percent of all European settlers in Peru.

September: Moroccan pirates led by Memmi Reis capture Miguel de Cervantes Saavedra, future author of *Don Quixote*. He remains a slave until ransomed, in September 1580.

1576 English pirate Andrew Barker sails for Panama with two ships, to conduct "reprisal" raids against Spanish shipping.

April: Pirate captains John Callice and Simão Fernandes capture a Portuguese ship near the Canary Islands.

May: British authorities jail Portuguese pirate Simão Fernandes, then release him on bail.

December: Dutch pirate Courte Higgenberte is jailed at Cardiff, then released by a friendly judge.

1577 Queen Elizabeth I of England (1533–1603) commissions Francis Drake to plunder Spanish settlements and shipping along the Pacific Coast of North America. Drake leaves Plymouth on November 15, but his ships are damaged by a storm off Cornwall and return to Plymouth for repairs. Drake sails again on December 13, with six ships and 164 men, soon adding a Portuguese merchant ship captured near the Cape Verde Islands. He loses two ships at sea before reaching safe harbor at present-day Puerto San Julián, Argentina.

February: British officers arrest Simão Fernandes for the second time, but a magistrate and fence for pirate loot in Cardiff, Wales, releases him once more.

April: Arrested yet again and packed off to London for trial, Simão Fernandes is freed by intercession of Secretary of State Sir Francis Walsingham.

May: Andrew Barker assaults Veragua, in western Panama, but fails to capture the city. British authorities try pirate John Caliice in London and sentence him to hang. Queen Elizabeth I pardons him November.

June: Andrew Barker's pirates seize a Spanish vessel near Nombre de Dios, Panama.

August: William Coxe leads a mutiny against pirate captain Andrew Barker, marooning Barker and a dozen loyal crewmen on an island off Honduras, where Spanish troops later find and kill them.

October: Captured in Ireland, English pirate Robert Hicks is transported to London, convicted of piracy, and hanged.

December 13: Francis Drake sails from Plymouth on his most famous pirate voyage, with five ships, 160 crewmen, and a dozen "gentleman adventurer" investors.

1578 April: Held in London on a charge of pillaging French ships, Dutch pirate Courte Higgenberte posts £4,000 bail and disappears.

June: William Coxe and 18 fellow pirates stop at the Scilly Isles, off Cornwall, to divide their loot before sneaking into port at Plymouth. Despite their stealth, they are jailed for mutiny and as accessories to Andrew Barker's murder.

June 20: Francis Drake's dwindling fleet enters the Strait of Magellan, reaching the Pacific Ocean in September, with loss of four ships. Despite a wound suffered in battle with Mapuche tribesmen on Mocha Island, off the coast of modern Chile's Arauco Province, Drake moves on to sack Valparaiso on December 5.

July: Paroled pirate John Callice joins Henry Knollys on a voyage to plunder the Spanish Caribbean.

1579 February 5: Francis Drake seizes two Spanish ships near the Peruvian treasure port of Arica, then captures two more en route to Callao, the port of Lima.

March 1: Drake captures the *Nuestra Señora de la Concepción*, a Spanish treasure ship bound from Peru to Manila, in the Philippines, exposing for the first time Spanish shipping to the Far East.

April: Drake's pirates sack Guatulco, Mexico.

June 17: Drake lands somewhere north of Point Loma (near present-day San Diego, Calif.) and claims the land for England.

July: Drake sails eastward across the Pacific, stopping in the Philippines, the Moluccas, at Java, and in Sierra Leone before reaching Plymouth on September 26, 1580.

1581 Moghul conquerors introduce opium to Assam, in northeastern India.

April 4: A French nobleman, Monsieur de Marchaumont, knights Sir Francis Drake. In September, Drake is elected mayor of Plymouth, England.

1582 William Fenner, assigned to hunt pirates in the Atlantic, inexplicably names John Callice as one of his captains.

July: English pirates Stephen Heynes and William Valentine capture a German ship and bring it to Studland, Dorset, England. In search of hidden cash, Heynes tortures the passengers so viciously that some of his own crewmen beg him to stop.

1583 Pirate John Callice loots two Scottish ships and delivers their cargo to Portsmouth.

1584 March 18: Russian Tsar Ivan the Terrible (1530–84), on his deathbed, allegedly bets the national treasury's contents on a chess game with advisor Boris Godunov (1551–1605). Most modern historians deny the story, naming Ivan's final opponent as Russian statesman Bogdan Belsky (d. 1611).

1585 War erupts between England and Spain, continuing intermittently until 1604. Sir Francis Drake sales from Plymouth with 29 ships on September 14, to raid Spanish settlements and shipping.

September: Pirates employed by English privateer Sir George Carrey capture a French-crewed fishing boat from Newfoundland, mistaking it for a Spanish galleon.

September 14: Francis Drake leaves Plymouth with 2,300 seamen and soldiers, for raids in the West Indies.

November 17: Drake's pirates sack and burn Santiago in the Cape Verde Islands.

December 31: Francis Drake's pirates capture and sack the city of Santo Domingo. Burning one-third of the town before they receive a 25,000-ducat ransom.

1586 Frustrated by lax enforcement of European laws penalizing prostitution, Pope Sixtus V (1521–90) mandates execution of convicted harlots.

January 1: Francis Drake's forces capture and loot Santo Domingo on Hispañola (now the Dominican Republic), extorting a ransom of 25,000 ducats.

February 9: Drake occupies Cartagena, looting the city and occupying it until March 26, when he departs with a ransom of 110,000 ducats.

May 28: Drake attacks St. Augustine, Fla., capturing and destroying the town on May 30.

June: Drawings for Britain's second royal lottery span three days, with a suit of armor offered as the main prize.

July 22: Drake returns, triumphant, to Portsmouth, England. The celebration inspired buccaneer Thomas Cavendish to sail at once for the Pacific with three ships and 123 men, including some of Drake's crew.

1587 March: Thomas Cavendish and his pirates reach the Pacific Ocean. Francis Drake receives orders from London to attack the Spanish Armada.

April and May: Sir Francis Drake destroys a large portion of the Spanish fleet in the Bay of Cadiz, lands in the Algarve district of southern Portugal, sacks various coastal forts on the way to Lisbon, and captures a Spanish treasure fleet returning from the Azores. Drake describes the campaign as "singeing the King of Spain's beard."

November 15: Thomas Cavendish captures a Spanish vessel, the *Santa Ana*, hanging its priest and marooning the crew. The haul includes 122,000 pesos and various other prizes. On November 19 Cavendish sails for the Philippines.

1588 July 29: Vice Admiral Sir Francis Drake intercepts and scatters the Spanish Armada in the English Channel, before it can land troops on British soil. On July 30, Drake sinks five Spanish ships in the Battle of Gravelines (a port 15 miles southwest of Dunkirk, France).

September: Pirate Thomas Cavendish returns to England a hero.

October: English pirate George Clifford, Third Earl of Cumberland, captures a Spanish ship off the coast of Brazil.

1589 Britain's Admiralty Court assumes responsibility for regulating prizes seized by privateers and judging whether individual ships were legally captured. Sir Francis Drake and Sir John Norreys receive orders to destroy the remainder of the Spanish Armada; support rebels in Lisbon, Portugal, against King Philip II (1527–98); and capture the Azores. Attacking the Spanish fleet off the coast of A Coruña, in Galicia, the English commanders lose 20 ships and more than 12,000 men.

January 18: King Frederick II of Denmark and Norway executes Faroese privateer Magnus Heinason for piracy. The charges are later withdrawn.

1590 Pope Gregory XIV (1535–91) orders excommunication of any Catholic who bets on the election of a new pontiff.

1591 English privateer James Lancaster sails from Plymouth for the East Indies, robbing every foreign ship he encounters before returning to England in May 1594.

August: Thomas Cavendish mounts a new pirate expedition from England, with five ships.

Storms ravage his fleet in the Strait of Magellan and his surviving crewmen desert Cavendish.

1594 February: English pirate James Langton captures several ships in Jamaican waters.

June 20: Spanish warships overtake the *Destiny*, captained by English pirate Richard Hawkins, off the coast of Ecuador. Hawkins surrenders on June 22, after three days of hard fighting.

1595 March 22: Spanish forces capture English pirate John Crosse near Havana.

September 7: Sir Francis Drake sails from Plymouth with 28 ships, 1,500 seamen and 1,000 soldiers, seeking to capture a Spanish treasure ship with 2 million ducats aboard, awaiting repairs at San Juan, Puerto Rico. Superior defenses prevent him from taking the prize.

November 22–23: Francis Drake's fleet fights inconclusive engagements with Spanish naval forces around Puerto Rico.

December 27–30: After several raids along the Venezuelan coast, Drake spends two days bombarding Nombre de Dios, on the Isthmus of Panama.

1596 January 6: Francis Drake's pirates capture Nombre de Dios, but find no significant treasure.

January 28: Sir Francis Drake dies at sea, offshore from Portobello, Panama. His crew buries him at sea, in a lead casket.

1598 June: Dutch privateers Jacob de Mahu and Simon de Cordes lead Holland's first pirate raids along South America's Pacific coastline.

June 9: English pirate George Clifford, Third Earl of Cumberland, leads eight pirate ships against San Juan, Puerto Rico. The garrison surrenders on June 19, but half of Clifford's 1,200 men are dead or dying from disease within three weeks. The survivors flee in August, with little booty to show for their trouble.

c. 1600 Spaniards in Barbados discover that fermentation of molasses, a by-product of sugar refining, produces rum.

1600 April: Dutch pirates led by Baltazar de Cordes rout Spanish forces on Chiloé Island, off the coast of Chile.

December 31: Queen Elizabeth I grants a royal charter to the East India Company, future overlords of opium trading in Asia.

1601 Merchant ships chartered by Queen Elizabeth I receive instructions to purchase Indian opium and transport it to England.

January: Portuguese authorities imprison Dutch pirate Baltazar de Cordes and his men at Tidore in the Maluku Islands.

February: Portuguese naval forces capture Dutch pirate Baltazar de Cordes and his men, near the Moluccas. English privateer William Parker captures Portobello, Panama, as a base of operations for raiding Peruvian treasure fleets.

May: English pirates Michael Geare and David Middleton capture three ships in the West Indies.

1602 Dutch pirate Jan de Bouff enters Habsburg service to raid shipping during the Dutch Revolt against Spain.

1603 English pirate Nicholas Alvel raids shipping on the Ionian Sea.

January 24: Pirate captains Michael Geare and Christopher Newport attack Santiago, Cuba.

1606 French apothecary and botanist Louis Hébert (1575–1627), the first European to farm in Canada, imports cannabis for cultivation at Port Royal, Nova Scotia. Dutch privateer Simon de Danser ("Simon the Dancer") procures a Dutch Letter of Commission to raid Spanish shipping during the Eighty Years' War. Alarmed by widespread alcoholism, Britain's parliament passes an "Act to Repress the Odious and Loathsome Sin of Drunkenness."

1607 Puritan settlers at Jamestown cultivate hemp, under contract with the Virginia Company. September: The Order of Saint Stephen battles pirates on the Mediterranean, capturing 45 galleys and pillaging the Algerian seaport of Bona, departing with 1,500 prisoners.

1609 Lord Thomas West Delaware (1577–1618), first governor of the Virginia colony, reports that "The countrey is wonderful fertile and very rich, Hempe better than English growing wilde in abundance." Dutch pirate Simon de Danser flees Algiers with three vessels, capturing a Spanish treasure ship before he reaches Marseille. King Henry IV of France (1553–1610) commissions Danser to raid a pirate stronghold in Tunis. Danser vanishes on that mission, his fate still unknown.

1609–1616 England loses 466 merchant ships to Barbary pirates.

1610 British authorities hang pirate Peter Love at Leith, Scotland.

1612 June: Captain William Baughe and his crew surrender at Kinsale, Ireland, under a general amnesty for pirates.

June 29: The Virginia Company, chartered by King James I of England (1566–1625) in April 1606, begins a lottery to generate funds for its Virginia colony in North America. The lottery raises £29,000.

1613 Summer: English pirate Henry Mainwaring launches raids against Spanish settlement at La Mamora (now Mehdya, Morocco).

1614 Sir Thomas Dale (d. 1619) assumes office as governor of Virginia, arriving with orders to establish communal gardens of hemp and flax.

June 4: English pirate Henry Mainwaring attacks a cod-fishing fleet off the coast of Newfoundland, impressing 400 seamen.

1615 June: English pirate Henry Mainwaring

defeats a Spanish squadron sent to capture him in the Mediterranean.

1616 Jamestown's Puritans boast of their hemp crop that there is "none better in England or Holland."

June: King James I of England grants amnesty to Henry Mainwaring's pirates, allowing them to keep their Spanish booty.

1617 Barbary pirates led by Süleyman Reis raid Spanish coastal settlements, sacking Bouzas and Cangas, burning churches at Darbo and Moaña.

1618 March 20: Henry Mainwaring receives a knighthood and commission in the British Royal Navy.

1619 Facing stiff competition from tobacco planters, the Virginia Company orders its colonists to "set 100 [hemp] plants and the governor to set 5,000." Before year's end, the Virginia General Assembly requires colonists to cultivate "both English and Indian hemp"—*Cannabis sativa* and *C. indica*. Gabriel Wisher receives a budget of £100 to import expert hemp-dressers from Poland and Sweden.

1620 French outlaws on Hispañola stage their first attacks on Spanish shipping.

October 10: Barbary pirate Süleyman Reis, born Ivan Dirkie De Veenboer in Holland, suffers fatal wounds in battle with French and English warships, in Amsterdam harbor.

1620–23 Operating from Torbay, Newfoundland, English pirate John Nutt stages raids along the southern coast of Canada and west coast of England.

1621 March 8: King James I issues a proclamation banning further lotteries conducted by the Virginia Company.

June 3: The Dutch West India Company receives a charter from the Republic of the Seven United Netherlands, granting jurisdiction over the African slave trade and other commerce within a vast area spanning the globe from West Africa to the Americas, and the Pacific Ocean extending to eastern New Guinea. Its explicit goal — the elimination of Portuguese and Spanish competition — encourages piracy.

1621–26 Dutch pirate Claes Gerritszoon Compaen serves various commercial sponsors in the Netherlands before retiring with a pardon from Frederick Henry, Prince of Orange.

1622 October: Dutch naval forces capture pirates Juan García and Pedro de la Plesa off the coast of Dunkirk, France.

1623–38 Acting on a "grand design" conceived by the Dutch West India Company, Dutch privateers capture 500 Spanish and Portuguese ships in the Caribbean Sea.

1624 January 26: Privateer Pieter Schouten sails from Holland for the Caribbean, to raid Spanish shipping on behalf of the Dutch West India Company.

May: Dutch pirates led by Piet Heyn and Jacob Willekens capture the port at Bahia, Brazil.

September 13: Pieter Schouten returns to Holland with several chests of stolen Spanish silver, 1,600 chests of sugar, 3,000 animal skins, and other booty.

1625 Future English privateer and admiral Christopher Myngs is born at Norfolk. Dissident Plymouth Puritans, led by Thomas Morton (1576–1647), establish a new colony called Mount Wollaston, whose inhabitants oppose sale of slaves to Virginia and practice a paganized form of Christianity, including maypole dances fueled by alcohol and cannabis. Chinese merchant Zheng Zhilong founds the Shibazhi, a league of 18 notorious pirate captains allied to raid the Ming Dynasty's fleet.

March: A pirate fleet sponsored by the Dutch West India Company sails for Brazil, with orders to reinforce Bahia, conquer Puerto Rico, and harass Spanish treasure fleets. Admiral Boudewijn Hendricksz leads the force of 42 ships.

September 25: The pirate fleet led by Boudewijn Hendricksz shells El Morro fortress in San Juan harbor, killing four soldiers and frightening most inhabitants into flight. Soldiers pillage the abandoned down and desecrate its cathedral. While the looting continues, guns from the fort are turned landward, trapping the pirates inside the harbor until November 2.

1627 Dutch privateer Hendrick Jacobszoon Lucifer suffers fatal wounds while capturing a Honduran treasure ship off the coast of Cuba. His crew nets loot worth 1.2 million guilders.

February: Pirates led by Boudewijn Hendricksz raid Isla Margarita, off the coast of Venezuela, burning a small coastal fort.

March: Dutch pirates led by Piet Heyn attack a Spanish merchant fleet off Bahia, Brazil, capturing or sinking two dozen ships.

July 4–19: Dutch pirate Jan Janszoon van Haarlem (1570–1642), AKA Murat Reis the Younger, raids coastal settlements at Austurland and Vestmannaeyjar, Iceland, kidnapping hundreds of young residents and selling 242 into slavery on the Barbary Coast of North Africa. At Vestmannaeyjar, the pirates force older settlers into a church and burn them alive. The raids become known as "the Turkish Abductions."

1628 The Ming Dynasty's southern fleet surrenders to pirate overlord Zheng Zhilong, who then accepts appointment as a Chinese major general.

May 8: Dutch pirates led by Pieter Adriaanszoon Ita sink a Portuguese ship near Cuba.

Summer: Knights of Malta capture two ships near Crete and two more off the coast of Sicily.

1629 Residents of Salem, Mass., receive their first shipment of hemp seeds. Samuel Cornhill is assigned to cultivate an acre of cannabis, while Pilgrims individually grow hemp for winter clothing.

January: Pirate Piet Heyn returns to Holland bearing loot estimated between 11 and 14 million guilders. Parliament welcomes him as a hero.

March 26: Piet Heyn assumes command of the Dutch navy, ironically assigned to suppress piracy. He dies battling raiders off the coast of Dunkirk on June 18.

1630 French outlaws expelled from Hispañola settle on nearby Tortuga, launching a new era of piracy with raids on shipping in the Windward Channel and beyond, expanding in time to strike coastal towns throughout Spanish America. Plymouth Puritans raid the free-thinkers colony of Mount Wollaston — known by this time as Merry Mount or Mount Dagon — burning the settlement and shipping leader Thomas Morton back to England.

March 22: Boston enacts the first colonial law banning gambling.

June–July: Dutch admiral-pirate Jan Booneter blockades Havana, Cuba, looting various incoming ships. Pieter Ita's pirates raid shipping in the Florida Channel.

1631 Revenue from lotteries funds construction of London's first aqueducts.

June 20: Pirates led by Murat Reis the Younger raid Baltimore, Md., kidnapping 108 settlers for sale as slaves on the Barbary Coast.

1632 Colonists cultivate hemp at Plymouth, in present-day Massachusetts.

June: English ship's captain Dixey Bull turns pirate, capturing three ships along North America's Atlantic seaboard and delivering £500 in loot to Pemaquid, Mass.

1633 July 15: Dutch pirates led by Jan Van Hoorn capture Trujillo, Honduras, exacting a meager 20 pounds of silver as tribute.

October 22: Chinese pirate Zheng Zhilong (1604–61), AKA Cheng Chih-lung' and Nicholas Iquan Gaspard, defeats an armada of the Dutch East India Company.

1633–37 Flemish privateer admiral Jacob Collaert captures 150 Dutch fishing vessels and holds 945 crewmen for ransom.

1634 William Wood's *Description of New England* notes: "This land likewise affords hempe and flax, some naturally, and some planted by the English with rapes if they be well managed."

1635 Future English privateer and admiral Henry Morgan is born in the Welsh county of Monmouthshire.

April: English pirate William Cobb captures an Indian vessel in the Red Sea, torturing its passengers and crew.

1636 William Rous receives a privateering commission and letter of marque from the Providence Island Company to raid Spanish shipping and settlements. He remains active in the Caribbean until 1645.

May: A prisoner exchange between France and Holland liberate Dutch pirate Cornelis Jol.

1636–41 English pirate Samuel Axe raids Spanish shipping for the Providence Island Company.

1637 British traders make their first visit to China, bearing opium. At Hartford, Conn., the colony's General Assembly orders all resident families to plant one teaspoonful of hemp seeds.

May: Pirate William Cobb returns to England with £40,000 in booty. King Charles II and other sponsors of the expedition take £30,000, leaving Cobb to share the rest with his 50 crewmen.

August: Dutch pirate Cornelis Jol stalks Spanish treasure ships off Havana. Flemish privateer Jacob Collaert dies from illness at La Coruña, Spain.

September 6: Cornelis Jol battles Spanish warships off the coast of Cuba.

1638 The Grand Council of Venice opens the Ridotto as Europe's first gambling casino, in the Palazzo Dandolo at San Moisè.

June 20: Thomas Smith is hanged for piracy in Maryland.

August 30: Cornelis Jol's pirates attack a Spanish treasure fleet of 15 ships but are repulsed.

1639 Colonial authorities in Massachusetts follow Connecticut's lead, ordering each family to plant at least one teaspoonful of hemp seeds. Nathaniel Butler, former English governor of Bermuda, raids Spanish shipping in the Caribbean as a privateer.

April: English pirate William Jackson begins raiding along the Nicaragua River, looting several Spanish ships and selling their cargoes in Boston, Mass., in September.

May–September: English privateer James Reiskimmer (or Riskinner) raids Spanish shipping in the Caribbean on behalf of the Providence Island Company.

1639–41 Pirate captain William Jackson raids Spanish shipping and settlements on behalf of the Providence Island Company, established by English Puritans, operating from Guanaja and Roatan in the Honduras Bay Islands.

1640 Connecticut's General Assembly repeats its 1637 order for colonists to plant hemp seeds, "that we might in time have supply of linen cloth among ourselves." Portuguese Jesuit António Vieira (1608–97) documents acts of piracy sponsored by the Dutch West India Company, including capture or destruction of 609 ships between 1623 and 1637. Spanish colonial authorities on Hispañola (present-day Haiti and the

Dominican Republic) launch an abortive campaign to drive pirates from the nearby island of Tortuga, self-identified as "Brethren of the Coast."

May: Sergeant Major Don Antonio Maldonado de Texeda leads a combined Spanish/Portuguese fleet of 13 ships and 700 men against the English colony on Providence Island, in the Bahamas. Maldonado's commander, Captain General of Cartagena Don Melchor de Aguilera, describes Providence Island — occupied by former members of the Massachusetts Bay Colony — as a pirate haven and "den of thieves." Known visitors include British pirate William Jackson, active in the Caribbean since 1639.

July: Cornelis Jol leads another futile campaign to capture Spanish treasure ships in the Caribbean.

1641 William Jackson captures a Spanish slave ship in the port of Trujillo, Honduras, collecting a ransom of 8,000 pounds of indigo as well as 2,000 pieces of eight and two gold chains. He then severs connections with the Providence Island Company, receiving a three-year letter of marque from the Earl of Warwick, sailing with a new pirate fleet including buccaneers Samuel Axe, William Rous and Lewis Morris.

June: The General Court of Massachusetts ordered colonists to grow and harvest "wild hemp" as instructed by local Native American tribes. The court "desired and expected that ... all hands may be employed for the working of hemp and flaxe and other needful things." In China, buccaneer Zheng Zhilong ends his pirate career to accept appointment by Ming Emperor Chongzhen (1611–44) as "Admiral of the Coastal Seas," with a fleet of 800 ships.

October 31: Dutch privateer Cornelis Jol dies from malaria on the island of São Tomé, in the Gulf of Guinea.

1642 An early chronicle of Massachusetts, *New England's First Fruits*, thanks Divine Providence for "prospering hempe and flax so well that it is frequently sowen, spun, and woven into linen cloth (and in short time may serve for cordage)."

March 25: Captain William Jackson leads 500 pirates against the town of St. Jago de la Vega, Jamaica (near present-day Kingston), losing 40 men before he captures the town. Threatened with destruction of the town, locals raise a ransom of 200 cattle, 10,000 pounds of cassava bread, and 7,000 Spanish "pieces of eight" (Spanish dollars).

November: William Jackson's pirates rob pearl fishermen around Isla Margarita, Venezuela.

November 4: Future Chinese pirate and warlord Zheng Jing born in Anhai, Fujian.

December: Pirates led by William Jackson captures Maracaibo, Venezuela.

1643 Britain's parliament imposes an excise tax on distilled spirits, thereby creating a lucrative moonshine trade.

March 25: With 500 pirates, William Jackson attacks Santiago de la Vega, the Spanish capital of Jamaica (now Kingston). After losing 40 men, Jackson collects a ransom of 200 cattle, 10,000 pounds of cassava bread, and 7,000 pieces of eight. He subsequently moves on to capture Trujillo, Honduras.

Winter: William Jackson's pirates stage multiple raids around Cartagena.

1644 Massachusetts colonial governor John Winthrop (1587–1649) writes: "Our supplies from England failing much, men began to look about them, and fell to a manufacture ... of hemp and flax, wherein Rowley, to their great commendation, exceeded all other towns."

Summer: William Jackson's pirates raid small towns along the Gulf of Mexico and Guatemalan coast.

September: Knights of Malta capture a Muslim royal galleon 70 miles from Rhodes, Greece.

1645 Tortuga's acting governor imports 1,650 prostitutes in an effort to suppress disorderly conduct and *matelotage* (homosexuality) among the island's resident buccaneers.

1646 Massachusetts bans gambling in public houses.

1647 January: The Knights of Malta capture Barbary corsair Bekir Reis near Sicily, sentencing him to service as a galley slave.

1649 Author Peter Force, in *A Perfect Description of Virginia*, singles out a Captain Matthews for his production of hemp. Force writes: "He hath a fine house, and all thinges answerable to it; he sowes yearly store of Hempe and Flax, and causes it to be spun ... and in a word, keeps a good house, lives bravely, and a true lover of Virginia; he is worthy of much honour...."

1650 Pirates from Tortuga sack the town of Santiago de los Caballeros, Santo Domingo (the present-day Dominican Republic). British privateer Brown Bushell faces trial for piracy and for his role in the 1642 surrender of Scarborough, North Yorkshire, to Queen Consort Henrietta Maria (1609–69) during England's civil war.

April 1: Captain Thomas Lassells captures Captain Joseph Constant and his 30-man pirate crew off the coast of Yorkshire, England.

1651 August: Future pirate and explorer William Dampier born in East Coker, Somerset, England.

October 21: Future pirate captain Jean Bart born at Dunkirk, France.

1652–54 During the First Anglo-Dutch War, Christopher Myngs captures various Dutch merchant ships, including one complete convoy with two men-of-war.

1653 April 27: The final remnants of Philip O'Reilly's rebel Ulster Army surrender to Cromwellian forces at Cloughoughter, County Cavan. Property owned by the vanquished rebels is disbursed by means of a lottery.

1654 Dutch pirate Gerrit Gerritszoon (c. 1630–71), AKA "Roche Braziliano," makes his first appearance at Port Royal, Jamaica, after operating as a privateer from Bahia, Brazil.

1654–60 The Anglo-Spanish War, spawned by commercial rivalry, encourages privateering in the New World.

1655 Pirate captain Bartolomeo Portugues begins attacks on Spanish shipping from Port Royal, Jamaica, with a small four-gun ship and 30 crewmen.

April: British admiral Robert Blake (1599–1657) receives orders to extract compensation from Barbary pirates for their raids on English shipping. With a fleet of 15 ships, Blake destroys two shore batteries and nine Algerian ships at Porto Farina.

1656 Parisian officials stage a lottery to finance a stone bridge spanning the Seine River.

January: Christopher Myngs arrives in Jamaica as subcommander of an English flotilla, serving until summer 1657.

1657 Despite Puritan influence in the Massachusetts Bay Colony, a rum distillery opens in Boston.

1658 New York City establishes a force of paid night watchmen as the city's first police force.

February: Christopher Myngs returns to Jamaica as commander of English naval forces stationed there. He soon establishes a reputation for brutality, leading swarms of privateers to sack Spanish coastal towns and massacre their occupants, beginning with the ports of Tolú and Santa Maria, in northern Colombia.

1659 Dutch pirate Edward Mansvelt receives a privateering commission from Governor Edward D'Oyley (1617–75) at Port Royal. Another Dutchman, Nicholas van Hoorn (1635–83) turns to piracy against ships of his homeland in the Caribbean. Christopher Myngs plunders Coro, Cumano, and Puerto Caballos on the coast of Venezuela. After sharing half of his £250,000 booty with his buccaneers, against explicit orders from Governor D'Oley, Myngs is charged with embezzlement and sent back to England. An official letter to King Charles II (1630–85) described Myngs as "unhinged and out of tune."

December 13: French pirate Philippe Bequel receives permission to attack Spanish shipping from Governor D'Oyley of Jamaica.

1660 February 25: Retired Dutch pirate Claes Gerritszoon Compaen dies in Oostzaan, Holland.

1661 March 14: Six convicted pirates hang in Massachusetts.

1662 English poet Abraham Cowley (1618–67) publishes "The Legend of Coca," generally regarded as the first mention of coca in English literature. A visitor to Canada, writing in the *Colonial Papers of Virginia*, writes: "Account of the commodities of the Plantation of Quebec: 1. The soil very good to produce hemp. 2. Great store of hemp growing naturally in the Huron's country...." England's Parliament authorizes Virginia Governor William Berkely to offer a bounty of two pounds of tobacco for each pound of cured hemp delivered by colonial planters. French pirate Jean-David Nau (1635–68), AKA "François l'Olonnais," launches attacks on Spanish shipping from Tortuga.

August: Christopher Myngs returns to Jamaica with the *Centurion*, to resume attacks on Spanish shipping. Lord Thomas Windsor, new governor of Jamaica, supports the campaign although England and Spain are no longer at war. Luring pirates with a promises of unrestricted plunder and rapine, Myngs sacks Santiago de Cuba despite its strong defenses.

October 1: English pirate Robert Searle, AKA "John Davis," sails from Port Royal, Jamaica, with 12 ships and 1,300 men to attack Santiago de Cuba. They sack the town on October 27.

1663 Girolamo Cardano's *Liberde Ludo Aleae* (*The Book on Games of Chance*), the first known work on probability in gambling, is published in Italy 87 years after the author's death. Henry Morgan and Dutch pirate Abraham Blauvelt join Christopher Myngs for raids along the Spanish Main.

February: Myngs attacks San Francisco de Campeche, on the Gulf of Mexico, with 14 ships and 1,400 pirates. Myngs is wounded during the attack, forcing his return to England to recuperate.

April: Reports of the atrocities committed at San Francisco de Campeche prompt King Charles II to ban further pirate attacks on coastal settlements. Jamaican governor Sir Thomas Modyford (1620–79) is unable to enforce that order. John Morris and Henry Morgan continue raiding targets in Mexico, Honduras, and Nicaragua through 1664.

April 21: Swedish nobleman-turned-pirate Gustav Adolf Skytte of Duderhoff is executed at Jönköping, Sweden.

1664 The first North American rum distillery opens on Staten Island, N.Y. England's Parliament attempts to ban professional gambling with "An Act against Deceitful, Dishonest, and Excessive Gaming."

1665 North America's first race track opens on Long Island, N.Y. The *Calendar of State Papers* *for Colonial Virginia* reports, "Hemp is so useful that a tariff may well be dispensed with." Dutch officials hold a lottery to raise money for the poor in New Amsterdam (present-day New York).

March 4: The outbreak of the Second Anglo-Dutch War finds Christopher Myngs promoted to "Vice-Admiral of the White" in a squadron commanded by Prince Rupert of the Rhine (1619–82).

May 16: English pirates led by Edward Mansvelt capture a Spanish garrison on Providence Island, off the Honduran coast, seizing 55,000 pesos and 150 black slaves.

June 13: Myngs participates in the Battle of Lowestoft, resulting in a decisive English victory. As a result, Myngs is knighted.

October: Pirates led by John Morris sail up the San Juan River to Lake Nicaragua, sacking the town of Granada.

November: Jamaican Governor Sir Thomas Modyford sends Edward Mansvelt and Henry Morgan to seize Providencia and Santa Catalina in the Archipelago of San Andrés.

December: Governor Modyford's pirates raid Cuba, burning Santo Spirito.

1666 After Spaniards capture and execute Edward Mansvelt, his pirates choose Henry Morgan as their admiral. French authorities commission Nicholas van Hoorn to capture Spanish vessels.

June 11–14: Dutch and English naval forces wage the Four Days Battle, off the coast of North Foreland, England. Christopher Myngs is fatally wounded by musket fire from a Dutch warship, one of some 3,000 combatants lost in the battle.

1667 A rum distillery opens in Boston, Mass. Pirates led by Jean-David Nau sack Gibraltar and Maracaibo, Venezuela, stealing 260,000 pieces of eight, plus large amounts of silver plate, silk, and jewels.

March 15: King Louis XIV creates the Lieutenancy General of Police, which remains in force until its abolition in 1789, during the French Revolution.

1668 Residents of Campeche, Mexico, built a fortified seawall to repel pirates.

January: Sir Thomas Modyford sends Henry Morgan to capture Spaniards in Cuba and secure details of an impending Spanish attack on Jamaica. With 10 ships and 500 men, Morgan captures Santa María del Puerto del Príncipe (now Camaguey), then strikes off with a new commission to ravage Cuban coastal towns. Storms batter his fleet and force its return to Jamaica.

May 2: France and Spain sign the Treaty of Aix-la-Chapelle, ending hostilities between their nations. Dutch pirate Nicholas van Hoorn ignores it and continues his attacks on Spanish shipping, with secret French connivance.

July 11–12: In a savage attack on Portobello, Panama, Morgan's pirates collected some 400,000 pesos in ransom. Spanish investigators document numerous cases of rape and torture. Morgan's fleet returns to Jamaica with its booty on August 17. England's Admiralty Court declared the loot a legal prize in March 1669.

October: Henry Morgan's pirate fleet rendezvous with French buccaneers at Île-à-Vache, off southwestern Hispañola. Governor Modyford donates the *Oxford*, a 34-gun frigate.

1669 Jan. 12: During a drunken party aboard the *Oxford*, reckless gunfire ignites the ship's powder magazine. Henry Morgan survives the blast, while losing some 200 men. The disaster and subsequent desertions scuttle plans to attack Cartagena, forcing Morgan to consider alternate targets.

March: Morgan's pirates sack Maracaibo and Gibraltar, Venezuela, pursuing inhabitants into the jungle, torturing any they capture.

April 27: Spanish warships arrive to confront Morgan's flotilla as Morgan leaves Lake Maracaibo, but he escapes by surrendering a booby-trapped fireship "manned" with dummies dressed to resemble pirates, destroying two Spanish vessels. Morgan salvages 20,000 pesos from the damaged Spanish flagship.

May 27: Morgan returns to Port Royal with several captured ships and 125,000 pesos, using his share to purchase an 836-acre plantation.

June 14: Governor Modyford declares peace with Spain, but Spanish piracy soon prompts him to name Henry Morgan commander-in-chief of all English warships based on the island.

1670 Jean-David Nau captures Puerto de Caballos (now Puerto Cortés) and San Pedro, Honduras. French nobleman Michel de Grammont (1645–86) flees his homeland after killing his sister's suitor in a duel and sails to Hispañola, where he becomes a privateer. He soon captures a Dutch convoy valued at 400,000 livres ($4 million), but hits a reef and sinks his ship on a second outing, then shifts his base of operations to Tortuga. Portuguese pirate Manuel Rivero Pardal stages a false-flag raid on Little Cayman, in the Cayman Islands, burning homes and boats before fleeing with several captives. John Morris and Henry Morgan subsequently meet Rivero off the north coast of Cuba. Despite losing most of his crew in combat, Rivero escapes.

June: The Treaty of Madrid ostensibly ends hostilities between England and Spain, formally granting England control of "all those lands, islands, colonies and places whatsoever situated in the West Indies."

August 1: Despite the recent treaty, Governor Modyford commands Henry Morgan to sink enemy vessels and "to doe and performe all matter of Exployts which may tend to the Preservation and Quiett of Jamayca."

December 15: Henry Morgan seizes Santa Catalina, in the Colombian Archipelago of San Andrés.

December 27: Morgan attacks San Lorenzo, on the Caribbean coast of Panama, emerging victorious from a battle that kills 300 Spaniards and 100 buccaneers.

1671 Maryland grants farmers a bounty of one pound of tobacco for each pound of hemp produced. Manuel Rivero Pardal returns to Cartagena, Colombia, where the governor names him "Admiral of the Corsairs." John Morris meets and kills Rivero before year's end.

January 16: Henry Morgan ascends the Chagress River with 1,500 pirates, to reach Panama City. Over the next four days, skirmishes with Spaniards stall Morgan's advance, while his food and water run out.

January 27: Morgan's starving pirates seize a herd of cattle and eat their flesh raw.

January 28: Morgan's forces assault Panama City, routing its defenders and slaughtering some 400–500 helpless inhabitants. The pirates remain for four weeks, looting the city's charred ruins.

February 24: Morgan's raiders retreat to Chagres and divide their loot — a total of £30,000 leaving only £10–£16 per man. The disappointed pirates accuse Morgan of robbing them. Fearing mutiny, Morgan sails off alone, while the bulk of his force continues raiding along the Central American coastline.

May: Morgan allegedly receives his first notification of the Treaty of Madrid, signed 11 months earlier.

August: Jamaica's new governor, Sir Thomas Lynch, arrests Thomas Modyford for violating the Treaty of Madrid. Modyford spends two years imprisoned in the Tower of London. Lynch offers a pardon to any pirates who desist from raiding, but some notorious captains refuse.

1672 January: John Morris sails from Port Royal toward Havana aboard HMS *Assistance*, under Major William Beeston, hunting privateers. During the six week excursion they capture the *Charity*, under Captain Francis Weatherbourn, and the *Mary*, under Captain Du Mangles, returning to Jamaica with 42 prisoners.

March: Dutch pirate Laurens Cornelis Boudewijn de Graaf (1653–1704) raids Campeche, in southeastern Mexico, and captures a merchant ship bearing silver and cargo worth more than 120,000 pesos.

April: English forces arrest Henry Morgan and transport him to London, but influential friends help him avoid imprisonment.

1673 Spanish pirates seize Captain Edmund Cook's ship near Havana, setting the crew adrift. Cook subsequently obtains a letter of reprisal and begins his own career in piracy.

1674 Henry Morgan is knighted and replaces Sir Thomas Lynch as governor of Jamaica. Thomas Modyford returns to Port Royal as chief justice.

1674–76 French nobleman-turned-pirate Charles François d'Angennes, Marquis de Maintenon, raids Caribbean targets including Isla Margarita and Cumaná, Venezuela.

1676 April: Jamaica's governor sentences English pirate John Deane to die, but authorities in London reprieve him on a legal technicality.

June: William Dampier's pirates raid Alvarado, Mexico, and battle Spanish warships offshore.

1677–80 Algerian pirates capture 160 British merchant ships, while forging alliances with Caribbean buccaneers. Payment of a "license tax" permits pirates from one region to find safe harbor in the other's domain.

1677–82 Pirate John Coxon terrorizes the Spanish Main.

1678 May: Michel de Grammont joins a pirate fleet commanded by Jean II d'Estrées (1624–1707), the Comte d'Estrées, for a raid on the Dutch island of Curaço, aborted when their entire force of 17 ships is wrecked in the Los Roques archipelago, off the Venezuelan coast.

June: Commanding six ships and 700 survivors from the Los Roques catastrophe, Michel de Grammont captures Maracaibo and loots several smaller towns, penetrating inland to Trujillo. For the next six months, he plunders the state of Trujillo.

1679 William Dampier, future explorer and first person to circumnavigate the world three times, serves his apprenticeship as a Caribbean privateer with Captain Bartholomew Sharp. Spanish renegade pirate Juan Guartem loots and burns the coastal town of Chepo, Panama. Reformed pirate Charles François d'Angennes becomes governor of Marie-Galante in the Guadeloupe archipelago, serving until 1686.

Autumn: Laurens de Graaf captures a Spanish frigate of 28 guns and places it in pirate service as the *Tigre*.

1680 British chemist Thomas Sydenham introduces Sydenham's Laudanum, an addictive mixture of opium, sherry, and various herbs. Michel de Grammont stages a daring nocturnal raid on the port of La Guaira, Venezuela, and eludes Spanish naval forces. American pirate Thomas Paine (1632–1715) teams with Dutch raider Jan Willems to raid Riohacha in northern Colombia. Parliament bans British privateers from sailing under foreign flags, a major blow against Caribbean piracy. English pirate Bartholomew Sharp

(1650–90) embarks on a "Pacific adventure," raiding Spanish towns along the west coast of South America. Future pirate Edward "Blackbeard" Teach born in Bristol, England.

February: Bartholomew Sharp and French pirate captain Bournano sack Portobelo, Panama.

April 15: Captain John Coxon and 331 pirates land on the Isthmus of Darien (now Panama) in search of gold reportedly hoarded by local Mosquito Indians.

April 19–20: Coxon's buccaneers capture two Spanish ships in the Bay of Panama.

April 23: Coxon's raiders fight a day-long battle with three Spanish warships, capturing two and forcing the third to withdraw. The pirates lose 19 men, with 30 wounded.

May: Pirates Michel de Grammont, Thomas Paine and William Wright raid Caracas, capturing the seaport of La Guayara.

May 3: Pirates led by John Coxen and Edmund Cook battle Spanish troops outside Panama City. British buccaneer captain Peter Harris is among 20 men killed in the fighting.

May 22: British buccaneer Richard Sawkins dies while attacking Puerta Neva, Panama, with 60 pirates.

June: Michel de Grammont joins Thomas Paine at Isla La Blanquilla, and raid Caracas, Venezuela, with 50 pirates, despite the city's force of 2,000 Spanish defenders. Grammont suffers a sword wound, but survives to command his own eight-ship flotilla.

July: Spanish forces recapture La Guayara.

1681 The British Committee for Trade and Plantations advised the Crown to send hemp and flax seed to the Virginia colony. Rival Thomas Lynch replaces Henry Morgan as governor of Jamaica.

January: Mutinous pirates depose Captain Bartholomew Sharp and appoint John Watling to replace him. Watling raids Arica, Chile, but finds his force outnumbered and dies in the battle. Sharp resumes command and shifts raiding to the Caribbean, capturing 25 Spanish ships and looting numerous coastal towns.

February: Jamaican forces dispatched by Henry Morgan capture Dutch pirate Jacob Everson's ship. Everson escapes, but Morgan hangs 26 crewmen.

March 17: Chinese pirate-warlord Zheng Jing dies of dissipation at Tainan, Taiwan.

May: English pirates plot a raid against the Spanish city of Cartago, Costa Rica, but some miss their rendezvous at San Andrés Island. William Wright leads a depleted force to attack Spanish shipping through August.

May 3: English pirate Peter Harris dies battling a Spanish squadron off the coast of Panama.

September: William Wright joins Dutch pirate Jan Willems to capture Spanish ships off the coast of Colombia, but the Dutch governor of Curaçao refuses to let them sell captured cargo in his jurisdiction.

1682 Virginia's "Act for the Advancement of Manufactures" encourages hemp farming by declaring hemp acceptable as one-fourth payment of any farmer's debts. Maryland re-enacts its bounty granting one pound of tobacco for each pound of hemp produced. The governor of Petit-Goâve, Haiti, commissions Michel de Grammont and Nicholas van Hoorn to raid Spanish shipping in the Caribbean. Henry Morgan sends the frigate *Norwich*, commanded by Peter Haywood, on a futile mission to capture Laurens de Graaf. De Graaf engages a Spanish fleet near Cuba, killing 50 Spaniards against eight pirates slain. He captures the *Princessa*, bearing a 120,000-peso payroll to Spanish forces in Puerto Rico and Santo Domingo. Bartolomeo Sharp and his pirates are arrested on arrival at Port Royal, Jamaica.

May 17: Future pirate Bartholomew Roberts born in Casnewydd Bach, Wales.

June: Pirate Peter Le Pain captures a French merchant ship and delivers it to Jamaica, claiming asylum as a Protestant.

October: Pirate Jean Hamlin captures at 16–18 ships off Jamaica. Governor Lynch sends a frigate to catch him, but Hamlin escapes.

December: Jean Hamlin eludes another British frigate manned by ex-pirates, fleeing his base on Haiti's Île à Vache and finding sanctuary on St. Thomas, under the protection of Governor Adolph Esmit.

December 7: William Penn's Great Law of Pennsylvania includes a ban on gambling throughout the colony.

December 21: Future pirate John "Calico Jack" Rackham born in Bristol, England.

1683 Maryland follows Virginia's lead, declaring hemp legal tender for repaying one-quarter of any farmer's debts. England's parliament passes the Jamaica Act of 1683, banning trade with pirates.

January: French pirate Jean Hamlin captures the British ship *Thomas and William* near the Isle of Ash, off Hispañola, trading the loot at St. Thomas, in the Dutch West Indies.

March: Pirate Thomas Paine, allegedly encouraged by Governor Thomas Lynch of Jamaica, raids coastal villages around St. Augustine, Fla.

April: Pirates under John Cook capture two French ships in the Caribbean and sail for Virginia with their prizes.

May: Jean Hamlin's pirates capture Dutch and English ships off the coast of Sierra Leone, before returning to the Caribbean.

May 17–18: Pirates Laurens de Graaf and Nicholas van Hoorn sack Veracruz, Mexico, then quarrel over the spoils, leaving van Hoorn with a wrist wound that turns gangrenous and claims his life two weeks later.

June 24: Dutch pirate Nicholas van Hoorn dies near Veracruz, Mexico, from a wound received in a duel with Laurens de Graaf.

July 9: Jean Hamlin's pirates exchange fire with a British warship in the harbor at Saint Thomas, in the Virgin Islands.

November: Pirates Laurens de Graaf and Michiel Andrieszoon raid coastal shipping near Cartagena, Colombia.

December: Laurens de Graaf's fleet of seven ships battles three larger Spanish ships off Cartagena, capturing all three. The pirates then establish a blockade offshore.

1684 January: An English convoy reaches Cartagena, bearing Spain's promise of a pardon for Laurens de Graaf. Suspecting betrayal, he rejects the offer and retreats to Haiti. Spanish forces attack New Providence, in the Bahamas, as retaliation for Thomas Paine's raids around St. Augustine in March 1863. Surviving English settlers abandon the Bahamian colony, fleeing to Jamaica and the Carolinas.

March 29: Pirate John Cook meets John Eaton off the coast of Chile, joining forces to raid the Juan Fernández Islands.

July: Laurens de Graff's pirates storm Campeche, Mexico, capturing the town and indulging in a 57-day orgy of looting, burning most of the town and taking 200 prisoners (nine of whom are hanged).

Mid-July: Pirate captain John Cook dies from illness, replaced as commander by Edward Davis.

August: King Louis XIV (1638–1715) sends two officials to French Hispañola, to suppress piracy.

August 15: The Truce of Ratisbon ends the War of the Reunions between France and Spain, temporarily suspending royal contracts with privateers on both sides.

September: William Knight's pirates cross the Isthmus of Panama to capture a Spanish ship off El Salvador and use it in coastal raids against Ecuador.

September 3: Spanish naval forces overtake Laurens de Graaf's pirates as they leave Campeche, capturing and burning two of de Graaf's ships.

October: Adolf Esmit's removal as governor of the Dutch West Indies strips Jean Hamlin of his refuge.

November: Laurens de Graaf rallies pirates on Cuba's Isle of Pines (now Isle of Youth), in preparation for a raid on Campeche. Before the month's end, they capture three more ships, including two Spanish treasure vessels carrying 200,000 pesos.

1685 Captains Edward Davis, John Eaton, and Charles Swan lead 3,000 pirates on an abortive raid against Panama City.

May: Thomas Lynch resumes service as governor of Jamaica. French pirates led by Pierre le Picard cross the Isthmus of Panama and loot Guayaquil.

June 8: The Peruvian navy routs a pirate squadron led by British raider Edward Davis.

July: Robert Clarke loses his post as governor of the Bahamas for illegally issuing letters of marque against Spanish shipping around Florida. Replacement Robert Lilburne is unable to suppress piracy.

July 6: Laurens de Graaf's pirates attack Campeche, oust its Spanish defenders, and occupy the town until September, departing with ransom and prisoners.

July 30: Edward Davis leads eight ships with 640 pirates to raid León and Realejo, Nicaragua.

September 11: Laurens de Graaf fights a daylong battle with superior Spanish forces off the coast of Yucatan, escaping after dumping his cargo and cannons to lighten his flagship for greater speed.

1686 Spanish raiders from St. Augustine advance on Charleston, S.C., to retaliate for piracy, foiled by a "wonderfully horrid and destructive" hurricane.

January: Jamaicans capture English pirate John Coxon, but he subsequently escapes. Pirates led by François Grognier sack Chiriquita, Mexico (now Alanje).

January 24: William Dampier's pirate crew mutinies against him in the Philippines, elects John Read as captain, and sails for Australia.

February: Spanish forces raid Laurens de Graaf's plantation at Saint-Domingue, on Hispañola. De Graaf retaliates with an attack on Tihosuco, Mexico, leaving the town in ashes.

March: Edward Davis's pirates steal £25,000 pesos in jewels and silver from Safia, Peru. A pirate force led by François Grognier and a Captain Townley occupy Granada, Nicaragua.

March 31: Captain Charles Swan, allegedly forced into piracy by his own crew, sails from Cabo Corrientes, Mexico, to raid Spanish shipping from the Philippines.

April: Michel de Grammont is last seen sailing off St. Augustine, Fla. His ship is later reported lost in a storm, with all hands.

May 16: William Dampier's mutinous crew maroons him with seven others on one of the Nicobar Islands, in the Indian Ocean. Dampier later escapes to Sumatra in a native canoe.

August 22: English pirates led by Captain Townley capture two Spanish warships in the Gulf of Panama, but Townley dies from wounds suffered in the battle.

September: Pirate Michel de Grammont embarks on one last pirate mission before accepting a French naval commission in the Caribbean, but vanishes forever with his ship and 180 crewmen.

October 26: French pirates attack the British frigate HMS *Bauden* in the Atlantic.

1687 Laurens de Graaf engages a Spanish frigate and vessels of the Cuban coast guard off southern Cuba, capturing one small ship and sinking several more. Captain Franz Rools leads a crew of 80 pirates against Spanish shipping and coastal settlements of New Spain and Peru, continuing through mid–1689.

January: After two years at large, British pirate Captain Joseph Bannister is hanged aboard HMS *Ruby* at Port Royal, Jamaica.

February: Edward Davis and 80 pirates take £10,000 in loot from Arica, Chile.

April 30: A mixed force of English and French pirates captures Guayaquil, Ecuador, occupying the city until May 27 and torturing residents to discover hidden loot. French pirate captain Le Picard dies in Guayaquil on May 2.

May 19: Edward Davis and his men share £50,000 in booty after defeating a Peruvian squadron sent to liberate Guayaquil.

August 21: Sir Robert Holmes (1622–92) receives a commission from British secretary of state Robert Spencer to suppress piracy in the West Indies. Holmes cedes command of the expedition to Sir John Narborough before it sails, in September.

1688 August 25: Sir Henry Morgan dies in London, with cause of death variously listed as "dropsie," tuberculosis, and liver failure due to alcoholism.

September: Pirate John Coxon surrenders to Jamaican authorities and receives a pardon.

1689 Royal Navy forces capture French pirates Jean Bart (1651–1702) and Claude de Forbin (1656–1733), escorting them to Plymouth for trial. Both escape three days later and flee to Brittany.

January 17: William Coward and Thomas Johnson hang for piracy in Massachusetts.

January 27: Massachusetts authorities hang James Hawkins and six unidentified defendants for piracy.

March: Pirate captain Thomas Pound begins raiding along the coast of New England.

April 13: A large fleet of French buccaneers and regular troops, led by Admiral Jean Baptiste de Casse (1646–1715), lays siege to Cartagena. Bombardment breaches the city's defenses on April 30. Cartagena's governor and troops surrender on May 6.

May: Pirate John Read takes £25,000 from a ship off the west coast of India, then sails for Madagascar, where his worm-eaten vessel sinks on arrival. News of war between England and France reaches the Caribbean, prompting pirate Laurens de Graaf to accept a French naval commission.

June 1–4: Dissatisfied with the loot obtained from Cartagena in May, pirates return to pillage the city again, in a four-day orgy of looting.

July 8: Thomas Pound rallies a small force of pirates on Lovell's Island, in Boston Harbor.

August 16: Pound's buccaneers capture the sloop *Goodspeed* off Race Point, Mass., and converts it to their own use. They sent Captain John Smart ashore, warning that anyone pursuing Pound "should find hot work for they would die every man before they would be taken."

October: Governor de Cussy of Petit Goave leads a pirate expedition against Montego Bay, Jamaica.

December: Laurens de Graaf captures several ships off Jamaica, then blockades the coast for six months before sailing off to further raids among the Cayman Islands. Governor de Cussy leads another raid against Montego Bay. Thomas Pound is captured by the Royal Navy and held for trial in Boston. William Kidd makes his first appearance as a pirate, joining a squadron that raids French shipping in the Caribbean and sacks Marie-Galante in the Guadeloupe archipelago.

1690 William Rittenhouse opens America's first paper mill near Germantown, Pa., utilizing hemp, cotton, and flax. Piracy forces a temporary cessation of trade with North America by England's East India Company. French pirate Pierre le Picard attacks England's Rhode Island colony and is repulsed with heavy casualties.

January 13: Thomas Pound and crewman Thomas Hawkins are convicted of piracy in Boston, but both are later reprieved and return to England, where Pound acquires a new ship and resumes his activities.

January 27: Massachusetts authorities hang pirates William Coward and Thomas Johnson for seizing the ketch *Elenor* in Boston Harbor, the previous year.

February: Mutinous crewmen steal William Kidd's ship while he is ashore on Marie-Galante.

1691 January: Laurens de Graaf battles a large Spanish fleet near Santo Domingo, narrowly escaping with his life.

August: Convicted pirate Christopher Goffe, pardoned in 1687, secures a commission to hunt other buccaneers off the coast of New England.

September: British pirate, explorer, and scientist William Dampier (1651–1715) returns to England after eight years abroad.

1692 January: British pirate James Kelley captures the *Unity* near Bombay, setting her officers adrift while the crewmen join his service.

June 7: An earthquake and tsunami devastate the pirate haven of Port Royal, Jamaica.

December: Rhode Island pirate Thomas Tew launches his first raiding expedition from Rhode Island, with a letter of marque from Bermuda's governor authorizing raids against French holdings in Gambia, West Africa.

1693 The British crown abrogates Virginia's "Act for the Advancement of Manufactures."

June: The governor of the Hudson Bay Company writes to the commander of Fort York, Ontario, saying: "We have sent you some flax and hemp seeds which we will also have sowed upon ground most suitable, and for directions we refer you to the printed book now sent you."

Summer: Laurens de Graaf leads pirate raids along the Jamaican coast.

September 11: Future female privateer Ingela Olofsdotter Gathenhielm, née Hammar, born in Sweden.

Autumn: Thomas Tew captures a large Mughal ship near the Mandab Strait, between present-day Djibouti and Yemen.

December: Thomas Tew captures a treasure ship en route from India to the Ottoman Empire, in the Red Sea, looting the vessel of £100,000 in gold and silver, plus ivory, jewels, silk, and spice.

1694 Britain's Parliament authorizes a state lottery to raise £1 million for war against France. The prize is £1,000, payable in installments spanning 16 years.

April: Thomas Tew arrives at Newport, R.I. He soon establishes a lucrative friendship with Benjamin Fletcher (1640–1703), royal governor of New York.

May 7: First mate Henry Every (or Avery) leads a mutiny aboard the privateer *Charles II*, anchored at La Coruña, Spain. He puts the ship's captain ashore, renames the vessel *Fancy*, and launches his own career as a private captain. His first known raid, in the Cape Verde Islands, nets loot from three English merchantmen.

June 29: French pirate Jean Bart scores his greatest haul, recapturing a huge French grain convoy seized by Dutch privateers earlier in the month.

November: Thomas Tew sails for Madagascar with a letter of marque from Governor Fletcher.

1695 May: English forces attack Port-de-Paix, Haiti, capturing Laurens de Graaf's family but missing their primary target.

June: Pirates led by Henry Every and Joseph Farrell capture two rich prizes in the Red Sea.

August: Thomas Tew reaches the Mandab Strait, joining forces with Captain Henry Every and other pirates.

September: Thomas Tew dies in battle while attacking a Mughal warship, the *Fateh Muhammed*. His demoralized crew surrenders, but is later liberated when Henry Every's pirates capture the *Fateh Muhammed* and a companion, the *Ganj-I-Sawai*. The pirates rape and murder many of those aboard, escaping with cargo valued in excess of 325,000.

December: British pirate John Hoar sails from Boston, Mass., with a privateering commission from New York Governor Benjamin Fletcher.

December 11: William Kidd receives a commission to raid French shipping and hunt various pirates, including Thomas Tew, John Ireland, Thomas Wake, and William Maze.

1696 Henry Every's pirates land in Ireland, where 24 are arrested. Every escapes and vanishes without a trace. Author Charles Johnson's report of Every's death in Devon remains unsubstantiated.

January 26: William Kidd receives a letter of marque from King William III of England (1650–1702), authorizing attacks on French shipping.

May: Captain Kidd sails for New York City from Plymouth, England, aboard the *Adventure Galley.*

June 17: Pirate Jean Bart located a convoy of 112 Dutch merchantmen, escorted by five warships, near Dogger Bank in the North Sea. Outgunned, the Dutch surrender. Bart burns 25 captured ships before a relief force arrives and forces the pirates to flee.

September: Captain Kidd sails from New York City in search of French prizes.

November: Pirates under Dirk Chivers invade Calcutta's harbor, seize four ships, and demand a £10,000 ransom.

1697 February: John Hoar's pirates reach the St. Mary's Islands, off the coast of Malpe, India. Natives rebel against the invaders in July, killing Hoar.

May: British pirate Robert Culliford replaces Ralph Stout as captain of the *Mocha*, after Stout dies in battle.

May 6: French pirates led by Jean Baptiste du Casse join troops under Bernard Desjean, Baron de Pointis (1645–1707), sack Cartagena. Afterward, the commanders have a falling-out and part on bitter terms.

July: English pirate Adam Baldridge, founder of a buccaneer community on Madagascar, flees the island when native tribesmen discover his role in slave trading, destroying his warehouse and killing 30 of his men. Baldridge escapes to North America, then vanishes from the historical record.

October 30: William Kidd fatally bludgeons one of his own crewmen, gunner William Moore, when Moore refuses to fire on a Dutch merchant vessel.

1698 January 30: Captain Kidd captures the 400-ton *Quedagh Merchant*, an Armenian ship carrying gold, silver, fabrics and other loot, off southern India's Malabar coast.

April: Dutch pirate Dirk Chivers captures a British ship, the *Sedgwick*, in the Indian Ocean, then releases it upon receiving a ransom of rum.

April 1: Captain Kidd meets former mutinous crewman Robert Culliford, now captain of the pirate vessel *Mocha*, at Île Sainte-Marie, off eastern Madagascar. Most of Kidd's crew defects to Culliford's command. Only 13 men remain aboard the *Adventure Galley*.

May: Robert Culliford's pirates capture a French ship near Madagascar, stealing £2,000.

September: Robert Culliford joins Dirk Chivers to capture the *Great Mohammed* in the Red Sea, bearing cargo valued at £130,000.

November: London orders all British colonial governors to search for William Kidd.

1699 Parliament bans non-governmental lotteries and other private games of chance in England, along with purchase of foreign lottery tickets.

July 6: Lured to Boston with false promises of clemency, Captain Kidd is arrested for privacy and later transported to England for trial.

1700 Dutch traders ship Indian opium to China and the islands of Southeast Asia, teaching natives to smoke it in tobacco pipes. Virginia lawmakers reinstate the colony's "Act for the Advancement of Manufactures," making hemp, flax, wool, tar and lumber legal tender for payment of debts.

July 18: French pirate Emanuel Wynn, often named as the first buccaneer to fly a "Jolly Roger" flag, engages the HMS *Poole* off the Cape Verde Islands, narrowly escaping capture.

1701 The General Court of Massachusetts subsidizes purchase of hemp from a commercial firm at a farthing per pound, on condition that the company buys all of the colony's "bright, well-cured, water-retted hemp, 4 feet long," for 12 pence per pound.

May: Robert Culliford and several crewmen face trial for piracy in London. Culliford saves himself by agreeing to testify against Samuel Burgess in later proceedings. The crewman all hang.

May 23: Captain Kidd is hanged for piracy at London's Execution Dock. The first rope breaks, necessitating a second attempt. Afterward, Kidd's body is left dangling in an iron gibbet over the Thames, as a warning to would-be pirates.

July 12: English pirate James Gilliam, AKA James Kelley, executed in London.

September: The War of the Spanish Succession begins, spanning the Atlantic. English privateers loot French and Spanish shipping until the war's end in 1714.

November: Créole pirate John Bowen captures several ships off the Malabar coast, before his ship is wrecked at year's end, on St. Thomas's Reef, near Mauritius. Bowen and his briefly stranded crew establish a pirate base at Maratan, on Madagascar.

1702 March 8: Future pirate Anne Bonny born in Kinsale, Ireland.

April 27: Pirate captain Jean Bart dies at Dunkirk, France, from pleurisy.

1703 March: John Bowen captures the *Speedy Return* off Madagascar and converts it to a pirate raider. Pirates led by Thomas Howard capture the *Pembroke* at Johanna Island in the Comoros, killing two crewmen and forcing the ship's captain into piracy.

Spring: John Bowen's pirates capture a 700-ton Muslim merchant ship off Surat, India, seizing £22,000 in gold and additional cargo which they sell at Malabar. Pirate Thomas Howard loots another Muslim merchantman near Surat, netting 84,000 gold chequins.

April 30: William Dampier sails for the Pacific coast of the Americas with two ships and 183 men, to raid French and Spanish shipping. He captures four Spanish ships before reaching South America.

July: Governor Joseph Dudley of Boston commissions Captain Daniel Plowman of the *Charles* with a privateering license to attack French and Spanish ships off the coast of Newfoundland and Arcadia. Before leaving Marblehead, Plowman falls ill and is thrown overboard to drown by mutinous crewmen. The crew elects lieutenant John Quelch as their captain and proceeds to raid Portuguese shipping off the coast of Brazil, capturing gold and other cargo valued at £10,000 (more than £1 million today).

August: John Bowen and Thomas Howard seize two Indian ships in the Red Sea, valued at £70,000.

October: William Dampier's ships separate. The *Cinque Forts* maroons Scotsman Alexander Selkirk (model for the fictional Robinson Crusoe) on the uninhabited Juan Fernández islands, after he complains about the ship's safety.

November: The *Cinque Forts* sinks with most of its crew, confirming Selkirk's qualms about its seaworthiness.

1704 Facing an insatiable demand for hemp imported from its colonies, England's Parliament passes a law mandating bonus payment of £6 per ton, effective through 1754.

April: British pirate George Booth seizes the

Speaker, a 450-ton slave ship with 50 guns, off Majunga, Madagascar.

April 11: Authorities at Leith, Scotland, hang Captain Thomas Green and two of his officers for seizure of the *Speedy Return*, actually committed by John Bowen's buccaneers.

May 24: Laurens de Graaf dies at some uncertain point on the Gulf coast of modern Alabama or Mississippi, after establishing a French colony near present-day Biloxi.

June: John Quelch and his pirates return to Boston, where they are arrested. Quelch and five crewmen hang on June 30. Before the trap is sprung, Quelch delivers a short speech warning spectators, "They should take care how they brought Money into New England to be Hanged for it."

Late August: Irish pirate John Clipperton and 21 men capture a 40-ton ship off the Pacific coast of South America.

September 12: John Clipperton sails for Costa Rica, capturing two ships off Nicaragua and ransoming one for 4,000 pesos.

1705 Queen Anne of Great Britain (1665–1714) endows Greenwich Hospital with £6,472 confiscated from Captain Kidd before his execution.

March: England's High Court of the Admiralty convicts Captain Thomas Green and 14 of his crewmen on piracy charges.

March 10: English, Dutch and Portuguese naval forces crush pirate-turned-admiral Bernard Desjean's combined Spanish-French fleet in the Battle of Marbella, off Gibraltar.

April 4: Thomas Green and three of his crewmen hang at Leith. Eleven other convicted pirates hang in two groups, on April 11 and 18.

October: Colonial authorities in Boston place 788 ounces of gold, formerly held by pirate John Quelch, aboard the HMS *Guernsey* bound for England.

1706 Maryland and Pennsylvania enact legislation permitting use of hemp as legal tender for paying one-quarter of any farmer's debt. Dunkirk closes as a pirate haven, sharply reducing raids on shipping in the English Channel and North Sea. American privateer John Halsey begins raiding in the Indian Ocean. Residents of Charleston, S.C., recruit pirates to join Colonel William Rhett in repulsing Franco-Spanish invaders. Future pirate Mary Read, disguised as a man, joins the Royal Navy.

April: French admiral Pierre Le Moyne d'Iberville leads a force including 1,100 pirates to capture and raze the English colony on Nevis, in the Lesser Antilles. A force of 1,300 buccaneers occupies Martinique, in the Windward Islands, West Indies, using it to launch raids against English and colonial American shipping. Pirates seize control of the Bahamas, ruling it as a "privateer's republic" until 1718.

July 6: Fever claims the life of Pierre Le Moyne d'Iberville, aboard his flagship in Havana harbor.

December: After failing to capture a Dutch merchant ship, pirate captain John Halsey narrowly averts mutiny by his crewmen.

1707 A mixed crew of Irish and Scottish Jacobite pirates sail from France under Thady Doyle, assaulting Fethard, in Ireland's County Tipperary, "full of fire and vengeance." Protestant and Catholic homes are marked, "in order that the former might be plundered and the latter spared." French pirates kidnap a work party building a lighthouse at Eddystone Rocks, southwest of Rame Head, England. They transport the prisoners to France, where King Louis XIV frees the captives and jails their abductors, declaring that "though he was at war with England, he was not at war with mankind."

February: After seizing two merchant ships off the Nicobar Islands, John Halsey sails to the Straits of Malacca, facing continued dissension from his crew.

March: Woodes Rogers (1679–1732) receives a letter of marque to raid Spanish shipping as a privateer.

May 6: Montreal businessmen Guillaume Gaillard and Joseph Riverin enter into partnership with Alexandre Leneuf de Beaubassin, a lieutenant in the French colonial army, to outfit a ship for "privateering ... on and in the neighbourhood of Cape Breton, the island of Newfoundland, the Grand Banks, and surrounding areas." They hire Irish buccaneer Thomas Moore to command the ship, but it sails too late and returns empty-handed in autumn.

May 7: Robert Hunter sails from England to assume office as lieutenant governor of the Virginia colony. French privateers capture him at sea and carry him to France as a prisoner, where he enjoys "a very civilized captivity" before his release in a prisoner exchange.

August: John Halsey engaged a five-ship British squadron in the Red Sea, capturing two of the vessels with cash and cargo valued at £50,000.

1708 Parliament bans Britain's government from accepting loot captured by privateers.

January: A hurricane off Madagascar destroys most of John Halsey's pirate flotilla. Halsey is stricken with fever and dies soon afterward. Dutch botanist German Boerhaave (1668–1738) mentions the coca plant in his paper "Institutions Medicae."

October 18: French privateer Anthony Ferry, with three ships and 300 men, attacks Kiljkoveral in the Galápagos Islands, then sails up the Essequibo River, burning native villages along the way. Ferry anchors off Bartica, where the local garrison's commander pays a ransom valued at 50,000 guilders (2,500 in cash, the remainder in goods and slaves).

1709 February 1: Woodes Rogers and his pirates rescue Alexander Selkirk from Juan Fernández.

April: Pirate captains Woodes Rogers, William Dampier, and Etienne Courtney lead 110 raiders against Guyaquil, on the coast of present-day Ecuador. They loot the town and demand ransom, then leave without collecting it during an outbreak of yellow fever.

December 22: Woodes Rogers captures a Manila galleon, the *Desengaño*, off Cabo San Lucas, Mexico, suffering a wound in the battle.

December 25: Rogers attacks another Manila galleon, the *Begoña*, but his two ships are repulsed with heavy losses.

1710 June: King Charles XII of Sweden (1682–1718) commissions Lars Andersson Gathe (1689–1718) as a privateer to raid Danish and Russian shipping. As a result, Gathe becomes wealthy and is knighted, with his brother Christian, in 1715.

1711 October 14: Woodes Roges returns to England with loot valued at £150,000. Legal wrangling delays distribution of the booty to his sponsors.

1712 November 4: Kanhoji Angre's pirate fleet captures the armed yacht *Algerine*, owned by William Aislabie, British President of Mumbai. Angre's men kill wealthy passenger Thomas Chown and taking his wife hostage, releasing her and the yacht in exchange for a ransom of 30,000 rupees, on February 13, 1713.

1713 April: The Peace of Utrecht ends the War of the Spanish Succession. Privateers employed by various belligerent nations shift to piracy without official support.

1713–14 Winter: English pirate Benjamin Hornigold uses a sloop and sailing canoes to attack merchant vessels off the coast of New Providence, in the Bahamas. His crew includes Edward Teach, AKA "Blackbeard."

1714 British pirates Samuel "Black Sam" Bellamy (1689–1717) and Henry Jennings begin raiding camps that have salvaged sunken Spanish treasure ships in the Caribbean.

1715 March: Pirate captain William Dampier dies in London, without receiving his share of the loot from his last expedition in 1708–09.

Summer: Leading three ships and 300 pirates, Henry Jennings attacks a salvage fleet sent from Cuba to salvage a Spanish treasure fleet lost in a July hurricane off the southeastern Florida coast. Jennings drives off the salvage crews and 60 soldiers, recovering silver worth 350,000 pesos. While sailing for Jamaica with his loot, Jennings

captures another Spanish ship with 60,000 pesos aboard. The incidents provoke Spanish threats, prompting Jamaica's governor to expel Jennings and his buccaneers. Jennings soon resumes operations from New Providence, in the Bahamas.

December 15: Scottish pirate Alexander Dalzeel hangs in London, England.

December 26: Charles Boone replaces William Aislabie as British governor of Mumbai, India, inaugurating a new campaign against pirate captain Kanhoji Angre.

1716 September: John Martel's Caribbean pirates capture the *Berkeley* and the *King Solomon* off Jamaica, seizing cash and cargo valued in excess of £1,000. Later in the month, they loot two sloops off Cuba and capture a third ship, the *John and Martha*, converting it to their own use. Despite those successes, Martel's crewman depose him, replacing him with Irish pirate Walter Kennedy.

September 15: King George I of England (1660–1727) issues a royal decree, the "Act of Grace," pardoning all pirates who surrender to British authorities by September 6, 1718.

October 16: Walter Kennedy loots the ship *Greyhound Galley*, then sails for the Leeward Islands, where he captures several more prize ships by year's end.

December: Caribbean pirates capture the *Kent*.

Winter: Edward Teach assumes authority as second in command of Benjamin Hornigold's pirate flotilla.

1717 January: British warship HMS *Scarborough* shells and wrecks several pirate ships, leaving their crews stranded on St. Croix, in the Virgin Islands.

February: Sam Bellamy's pirates capture the slave ship *Whydah* off the coast of Benin, with a cargo of gold, silver, sugar, and indigo. Bellamy converts the vessel to his own use.

March: Benjamin Hornigold attacks an armed merchant ship sent by South Carolina's governor to hunt pirates around the Bahamas. The ship runs aground on Cat Cay and its crew escapes, the captain reporting that Hornigold now commands five vessels.

Spring: British pirate Stede Bonnet captures several ships off the Eastern Seaboard of North America, between New York and South Carolina.

April: Sam Bellamy seizes a merchant vessel off the coast of South Carolina.

April 27: Captain Sam Bellamy and 143 of his pirates drown when their ship, the *Whyda*, sinks off Cape Cod, Massachusetts. Two *Whyda* crewmen survive, with seven others from a smaller secondary vessel.

Spring: Hornigold and Teach seize three merchantmen in the Caribbean. The first carries 120 barrels of flour bound for Havana; the next is a Bermudan sloop loaded with liquor; the last is a Portuguese vessel sailing from Madeira with a cargo of white whine.

Summer: Barbados resident Stede Bonnet (1688–1718) turns to piracy following the breakup of his marriage. He ranges along the Eastern Seaboard of North America in a ship named *Revenge*, plundering other Barbadian vessels.

May 17: British pirate Samuel Bellamy loses one of his prize ships in fog at Orleans, Mass., then beaches his own ship *Wellfleet*. Bellamy drowns with 143 crewmen, while two survivors are arrested.

July: Stede Bonnet's pirates loot the *Anne*, *Endeavour*, *Turbet*, and the *Young* off the coast of Virginia.

August: Bonnet captures two vessels off South Carolina, looting both and burning one.

October: Bonnet teams with Edward Teach to raid shipping at the mouth of the Delaware Bay.

November: Benjamin Hornigold's pirates vote to override his ban on attacking British-flagged ships. When Hornigold resists, the crewmen replace him with Edward Teach. Teach leaves Hornigold a sloop and token crew for his return to New Providence.

November 15: Six convicted pirates hang in Massachusetts.

November 28: Benjamin Hornigold captures the French slaver *La Concorde* near Martinique.

December: After learning of the British amnesty for pirates, Benjamin Hornigold retires from buccaneering. He gives *La Concorde* to Blackbeard, who renames it *Queen Anne's Revenge.*

1718 Authorities in Williamsburg, Virginia, hang African pirate "Black Caesar."

January 5: Britain's amnesty for pirates who surrender by September 5 is formally announced in Nassau.

January 6: King George I names ex-pirate Woodes Rogers to serve as Captain General and Governor in Chief of the Bahamas.

March: Blackbeard's pirates capture the sloop *Adventure* and the ship *Protestant Caesar* in the Bay of Honduras, then seize pirate Stede Bonnet's *Revenge* and take Bonnet prisoner.

March/April: Charles Vane (1680–1721) and 12 pirates capture a Jamaica sloop in the Bahamas, converting it to their own use.

April: Vane's pirates add another ship to their flotilla, with capture of the sloop *Lark* in the Bahamas. By July 4, Vane's pirates are blamed for looting seven British and French vessels in the same area.

May: Edward Teach blockades Charleston, S.C., with four ships, capturing five vessels and stopping all merchant traffic. Charleston citizens

lift the blockade by paying a ransom of medicine.

June: Blackbeard and Stede Bonnet surrender to are pardoned by Governor Charles Eden of North Carolina under the Act of Grace. Neither lives up to the pardon's provisions. Before the month's end, Blackbeard captures five vessels between North Carolina and Bermuda. Bonnet resumes buccaneering under the pseudonym "Captain Thomas," sailing aboard the *Royal James*. By late July he has captured 13 ships between Delaware Bay and North Carolina. Governor Woodes Rogers of New Providence Island pardons British pirate Phineas Bunce.

Summer through Autumn: Irish pirate Edward Seegar, AKA "Edward England," captures several ships off the coast of Sierra Leone.

July: Pirates capture the slave ship *Cadogan*, whereupon Welsh mate Howell Davis (1690–1720) agrees to join them. Given command of the *Cadogan*, Davis sails for Brazil, but his crew mutinies and diverts the ship to Barbados, where Davis is jailed for piracy. Authorities later release him for lack of evidence, whereupon Davis makes his way to the pirate haven of New Providence.

July 24: Woodes Rogers arrives at Nassau, accompanied by two warships, to assume office as governor. Most resident pirates welcome him and accept the king's pardon, but Charles Vane sails off to continue buccaneering, firing parting shots at Rogers's vessels.

July 27: Vane captures a sloop from Barbados and adds it to his flotilla.

July 29: Vane loots the *John and Elizabeth*, stealing pieces of eight.

August: Liberated by Blackbeard in June, Stede Bonnet anchors in an estuary of the Cape Fear River to effect repairs on the *Royal James*. Governor Robert Johnson of South Carolina sends a naval expedition under Captain William Rhett to clear the river of pirates. In Nassau, Governor Rogers pardons Benjamin Hornigold and commissions him to hunt other pirates. Hornigold spends the next 18 months pursuing Stede Bonnet and Captain John "Calico Jack" Rackham (1682–1720).

August 12: Stede Bonnet captures a shallop on the Cape Fear River.

August 30: Charles Vane loots two ships, the *Emperor* and the *Neptune*, off the Carolinas. Vane's second in command, a Captain Yeats, defects with one of Vane's sloops and surrenders in Charleston, accepting pardon under the Act of Grace.

September: Early in the month, Charles Vane captures five more ships off Charleston, S.C. Pirates led by Englishman Richard Worley score their first prize by capturing a shallop loaded with household goods from a ship on the Delaware River — technically an act of burglary rather than piracy under British maritime law, since the attack did not occur in international waters.

September 27: Stede Bonnet escapes after a protracted battle with Captain Rhett, while most of his crewmen are killed or captured.

Autumn: Howell Davis sails from Nassau aboard the sloop *Buck*, conspiring with six other crewmen to mutiny and seize control off Martinique. The mutineers elect Davis captain and begin raiding from a base on the island of Coxen Hole, off the coast of Honduras. They soon capture two French ships and a Spanish sloop off Hispañola, going on to rob inhabitants of "Isle-atherer" (perhaps Eleuthera, in the Bahamas).

October: En route to the Bahamas, Richard Worley's pirates capture a sloop bound for Philadelphia, thereby gaining four additional crewmen. The HMS *Phoenix* searches for Worley, but he evades capture.

October 8: Searchers find and arrest Stede Bonnet on Sullivan's Island.

October 23: Charles Vane's pirates loot a brigantine and a sloop off Long Island, N.Y., then retire for a week's celebration with Edward Teach and his buccaneers on Ocracoke Island, N.C.

October 24–November 5: Sir Nicholas Trott tries 33 members of Stede Bonnet's crew for piracy in Charleston, S.C. Twenty-nine are convicted and sentenced to hang.

November 8: 20 convicted members of Stede Bonnet's crew hang in South Carolina.

November 10–12: Stede Bonnet is tried on two counts of piracy and sentenced to hang. Governor Johnson rejects his plea for clemency and endorses the verdict.

November 22: Edward Teach dies in battle with British forces off the coast of Virginia. The victors sever his head — valued at £100 under a bounty offered by Virginia's governor.

Late November: Charles Vane's pirates attack a French ship in the Windward Passage, between Cuba and Hispañola, then flee upon discovering that it is a warship. Quartermaster John Rackham favors pressing the attack, paving the way for a later falling-out with Vane.

December: Governor Rogers writes to London's Board of Trade, praising Benjamin Hornigold's efforts to capture Caribbean pirates. Before year's end, Hornigold and all but five of his crewmen die when a hurricane wrecks their ship on an uncharted reef, somewhere between the Bahamas and Mexico. Charles Vane captures a sloop and two periaguas off northwest Jamaica.

December 9–10: Pirate captain John Augur, earlier pardoned by Governor Rogers, stands trial with eight crewmen in Nassau, charged with new acts of piracy. All are convicted and sentenced to hang.

December 10: Stede Bonnet hangs for piracy in South Carolina.

December 16: Charles Vane captures the sloop *Pearl* in the Bay of Honduras.

1719 Dutch farmer Le Page Du Pratz visits New Orleans, writing in his journal: "I ought not to omit to take notice, that hemp grows naturally on the lands adjoining to the lakes on the west of the Mississippi. The stalks are as thick as one's finger, and about six feet long. They are quite like ours in the wood, the leaf and the rind."

February: Charles Vane captures the *Kingston*, giving it to Calico Jack Rackham. Unsatisfied, Rackham leads a mutiny against Vane, deposing him and setting Vane adrift with 15 loyal crewmen. A storm strands Vane on an island in the Bay of Honduras, where he is later rescued and arrested by officers aboard a British warship. Rackham's pirates sail to the Portuguese Island of Princes (whereabouts unclear) and buried their treasure while awaiting the king's pardon. Howell Davis stages unsuccessfully assaults a Portuguese fort on Maio, in the Cape Verde islands.

February 17: Pirate Richard Worley dies in Jamestown, Va. Reports differ as to whether he was hanged for piracy or killed while raiding the port. Colonial records show know executions during 1719.

March: Two British sloops capture Captain Rackham's ship *Kingston*, but Rackham and his men escape to the Cuban interior. Howell Davis plunders Gambia Castle, West Africa, losing one man while capturing gold bars valued at £2,000. Next, Davis teams with French pirate Olivier Levasseur (AKA "The Buzzard") and English pirate Thomas Cocklyn to rout British troops from Bunce Island, off the coast of Sierra Leone.

March 25–June 27: Edward England from the Gambia River to Cape Corso, on Corsica, capturing nine ships along the way, commandeering two and burning four, recruiting 55 prisoners for his crew.

April 1: Thomas Cocklyn, Howell Davis, and Olivier Levasseur capture the slave ship the *Bird Galley* at the mouth of Sierra Leone's Rokel River, remaining on board for a week-long celebration before releasing Captain William Snelgrave and giving him the *Bristol Snow* for his homeward journey, together with the *Bird Galley*'s remaining cargo.

May: Governor Rogers pardons Captain Rackham and his crew at New Providence. After fleeing New Providence and crossing the Atlantic, English pirate Christopher Condent captures several ships off the Cape Verde Islands. One prize is a Dutch warship, which Condent converts to his own use, renamed the *Flying Dragon*.

May 10: Pirate captains Thomas Cocklyn, Howell Davis, and Olivier Levasseur part company. Cocklyn disappears from the public record. Davis sails along the Guinea Coast from Sierra Leone to Anomabu, Ghana, capturing eight ships along the way. One vessel's cargo includes loot worth more than £15,000 and the Dutch governor of Accra, in Ghana.

June: Howell Davis loots a French ship in the harbor of Príncipe, in the Gulf of Guinea, then burns two Portuguese ships at anchor and tries to storm the governor's castle. Davis dies in an ambush during the battle. His crew elects Bartholomew Roberts to succeed him.

July: Christopher Condent arrives on Madagascar, recruiting some of John Halsey's former pirates for his crew.

July: Welsh pirate Bartholomew Roberts begins raiding in the Caribbean and along the Brazilian coast, continuing through May 1720.

Summer: Edward England's pirates capture two ships off Ghana's Cape Coast Castle.

September: Pirates led by Bartholomew Roberts capture a Portuguese ship off Bahía, Brazil, stealing 40,000 gold moidores and many precious stones.

November: Pirate Captains Robert Sample of the *Flying King* and Captain Lane of the *Queen Anne's Revenge* raid shipping off Brazil, until a Portuguese man-of-war drives both vessels ashore, where 38 of the pirates are captured and hanged.

1720 Olivier Levasseur plunders the city of Ouidah, Benin, before a shipwreck strands him on Anjouan, in the Comoros. Edward England raids Malabar coastal shipping, capturing one Dutch vessel and several Indian hulls.

February: Pirate Bartholomew Roberts loots four ships off Barbados.

February 26: Barbadian sailors attack two pirate ships commanded by Bartholomew Roberts and Montigny la Palisse, driving them away with heavy casualties.

March: Two sloops loaded with pirate-hunters from Martinique fail to locate Bartholomew Roberts and his men.

March 22: Charles Vane is convicted of piracy in Jamaica, sentenced to die.

June 21: Bartholomew Roberts invades the harbor of Trepassey, Newfoundland, looting 22 vessels and burning 21 of them.

July: Roberts captures 10 French vessels off Newfoundland's Grand Banks and commandeers a new ship, the 26-gun *Fortune*, using it to loot 10 English ships before he sails back to the Caribbean.

August: Jack Rackham steals John Haman's sloop from Nassau, leading a crew of pirates past the northwest coast of Jamaica, robbing several small boats on the way.

September — Rackham's pirates loot seven or eight fishing boats around Harbour Island, in the Bahamas, then raid French Hispañola for cattle and capture two sloops. Bartholomew Roberts returns to the Caribbean, bombarding Saint Kitts and burning two ships in the harbor. Later in the month, Roberts captures a French ship near Carriacou and commandeers it, renaming it the *Royal Fortune*.

October: Christopher Condent's pirates capture an Arab ship bearing treasure valued at £150,000, off the coast of Bombay, India, then return to Île Sainte-Marie, off Madagascar, to negotiate a French pardon. Condent weds the governor's sister-in-law and departs for France, leaving his crew to settle on the island.

October 19: Jack Rackham's pirates rob a sloop and a schooner off northern Jamaica.

November: A British sloop commanded by Captain Jonathan Barnet captures Jack Rackham and his entire crew.

October/November: Bartholomew Roberts sails for the Cape Verde Islands, but misses his landfall and is forced back to the West Indies by trade winds. Several of his crewmen die of thirst, along the way.

November 16–17: Jack Rackham and his crew stand trial for piracy at St. Jago de la Vega, Jamaica. All are sentenced to hang except female pirates Anne Bonny and Mary Read, who "plead their bellies" and escape death on grounds of pregnancy. Rackham hangs at Gallows Point, in Port Royal, on November 18. His corpse is then tarred and hanged in a gibbet, as a warning to other pirates.

November 20: Edward England and Olivier Levasseur capture the East Indiaman *Cassandra* near Anjouan. England's crew rebels when he refuses to let them kill the *Cassandra*'s sailors. Marooned on Mauritius with two loyal pirates, England builds a raft and sails for Madagascar, where he is reduced to begging and dies around year's end.

1720–22 Connecticut's General Assembly maintains a bounty of four shillings per 100 pounds of retted hemp, while Virginia lawmakers pass several laws mandating hemp cultivation. Olivier Levasseur continues pirate raids from his base on Sainte-Marie, off Madagascar.

1721 Rhode Island pays a bounty of eight pence per pound of hemp and accepts tax payments in hemp at the same rate. Massachusetts and New Hampshire also accept hemp as payment of taxes.

March 29: After an unexplained 12-month delay, Charles Vane hangs for piracy in Jamaica.

April 8: John Taylor and Olivier Levasseur capture the *Nossa Senhora do Cabo* at Réunion Island, in the Indian Ocean, robbing its wealthy passengers of diamonds and other treasures valued at £800,000. Some accounts describe it as the single greatest haul of loot in pirate history.

April 28: Female pirate Mary Read dies in a Jamaican prison.

June: Colonel John Massey and George Lowther seize the British ship on which they serve as crewmen, sailing for the Caribbean as pirates.

July: Pirate Walter Kennedy sails for Ireland but lands on the Scottish coast by mistake. Seventeen of his crewmen are captured, with nine later hanged. Kennedy escapes to London, briefly hiding in a brothel before he is discovered, tried for piracy, and hanged on July 19.

July 19: Walter Kennedy hangs for piracy in London.

August: Bartholomew Roberts captures the *Onslow* at Sestos, off Ghana's Cape Coast Castle, and makes it his flagship.

December: Pirate George Lowther sinks three ships around the Cayman Islands.

1722 Rhode Island grants Newport planter William Borden's petition for a bounty of 20 shillings per bolt of hemp cloth, spanning 10 years. Borden subsequently claims that "if there be so much to spare," he should receive another £500 pound bonus spanning three years. The colonial treasury complies.

January: Pirate George Harris captures a ship in the Bay of Honduras. Bartholomew Roberts raids Ouidah, on the coast of Benin.

February 10: Pirate captain Bartholomew Roberts dies in battle with a British warship, in the Atlantic.

June: Edward Low's pirates attack and loot 13 New England fishing boats anchored at Port Roseway, Shelburne, Nova Scotia.

August: English pirates Thomas Anstis and John Fenn raid shipping around Grand Cayman Island.

December: Pirates Edward Low and Francis Spriggs capture the first of six ships in the Caribbean, continuing raids into January 1723.

1723 January 25: Edward Low's pirates capture a Portuguese ship, the *Nostra Signiora de Victoria*, but lose 11,000 gold moidores (£15,000) when the captain throws them overboard. Furious, Low severs the Portuguese captain's lips, cooks them, and forces his victim to eat them.

March: Pirates Edward Low and Francis Spriggs seize a Spanish ship in the Bay of Honduras.

April: British forces surprise pirates Thomas Anstis and John Fenn at Tobago, capturing Fenn's ship and crew. Anstis escapes, but is killed soon afterward by mutinous crewmen.

June: Edward Low's pirates chase the British warship *Greyhound* off the coast of South Carolina.

June/July: George Lowther's pirates raid shipping in Newfoundland waters.

July 10–12: Rhode Island authorities try 26 of Edward Low's buccaneers stand trial for piracy. All hang at Newport on July 19.

September: Pirate Edward Low begins raiding along the Atlantic coast of Africa with three ships. George Lowther's pirates launch attacks in the Caribbean.

October: A British warship captures 16 of George Lowther's pirates near Venezuela's Blanquilla Island, hanging 11 at Saint Kitts. Some reports claim that Lowther's crewmen found him dead soon afterward, a pistol at his side, with opinions divided as to whether he was murdered or committed suicide. The *Post-Boy* newspaper of May 2, 1724, disputes the report of his death.

December: Pirate Edward Low's ship is wrecked along the coast of South America.

1724 Olivier Levasseur sends a negotiator to Réunion, seeking amnesty from the French colonial governor. He balks at a demand for repayment of loot stolen from French ships and sails instead for the Seychelles.

June 2: John Archer and William White hang for piracy in Massachusetts.

July 4: British pirate Francis Spriggs captures a sloop near St. Kitts and tortures its crew.

1725 January 28: Francis Spriggs captures a Rhode Island slave ship.

April: Francis Spriggs seizes several more ships in the Caribbean.

1726 John Powell of Boston presented a memorial to the General Court of Massachusetts, declaring local hemp well adapted to the manufacture of sailcloth. He proposes to have 20 looms at work within 18 months, receiving a subsidy of 30 shillings per bolt of sailcloth produced.

July 12: English pirate William Fly hangs in Boston.

1727 Maryland authorities authorize another pound-for-pound bounty of tobacco for hemp.

1728 Rhode Island planter William Borden receives an interest-free loan of £3,000 in return for his promise to manufacture 150 bolts of hemp sailcloth yearly. When he fails to meet that quota, the colonial legislature waives his deadline and provides more funds.

October 19: French finance minister Le Pellefier-Desforts announces a lottery to promote Parisian municipal bonds. Purchase of tickets is restricted to bond-holders.

1729 Qing Dynasty Emperor Yongzheng (1678–1735) bans the sale or smoking of opium in

China, except under license for medicinal use. His edict fails to stem the drug trade.

April 29: Retired female pirate Ingela Gathenhielm dies in Sweden.

June 4: Indian pirate and Maratha naval commander Kanhoji Angria dies, succeeded as master of the Arabian Sea by his legitimate sons, Sekhoji and Sambhaji.

1730 June: The French lottery begun in October 1728 concludes. A group of players led by François-Marie Arouet, AKA "Voltaire" (1694–1778), and Charles-Marie de La Condamine (1701–74) dominate the winnings through their knowledge of the laws of probability. Voltaire alone wins more than one million francs.

July 7: Following his capture near Fort Dauphin, Madagascar, Olivier Levasseur is hanged for piracy at Saint-Denis, Réunion.

1732 Pope Clement XII (1652–1740) permits establishment of a Roman lottery.

July 15: Governor Woodes Rogers dies in Nassau, Bahamas, after an extended illness.

1733 South Carolina legislators hire Richard Hall to write a book extolling the virtues of hemp and to promote the industry through 1736. Hall sails to Holland, where he purchases hemp seeds.

1735 Boston bookseller Daniel Henchman prints Lionel Slator's *Instructions for the Cultivating and Raising of Flax and Hemp.*

1737 The Massachusetts public treasury begins accepting hemp in payment of taxes, at a rate of four shillings per pound.

1738 Britain's parliament bans various dice games, including passage and roly-poly.

November 3: Rhode Island authorities hang four convicted pirates.

1739 Parliament bans more games of chance throughout England, ace of hearts, basset, faro, and hazard. Jared Eliot's *Essays Upon Field Husbandry in New England* stresses the value of hemp. He writes: "What I have principally in view is hemp. New England doth not, I suppose, Expend less than several hundred Thousand Pounds worth of Foreign Hemp yearly. If we can raise more than to supply our own Occasions, we may send it Home.... It is not a mere Conjecture that the dreined Lands will produce Hemp. I am informed by my worthy Friend Benjamin Franklin Esq. of Pennsylvania that they raise Hemp upon their dreined Lands."

1741 Female pirate Flora Burn begins raiding on the North America's east coast.

February: Malta's prize court, the Tribunale degli Armamenti, imprisons Maltese corsair Cristofero di Giovanni for illegally seizing a Venetian ship.

1744 Massachusetts conducts a lottery to raise £7,500 for construction of coastal defenses and northern border forts, to ward off French attacks.

1745 Britain's parliament bans the popular "e/o" game, wherein players guess even or odd numbers in play similar to roulette. Another law forbids hosting or playing in a gambling house.

1747 July 16: Benjamin Franklin writes to Jared Eliot: "In your last, you enquir'd about the kind of Land from which our Hemp is rais'd. I am told that it must be very rich land; sometimes they use drain'd swamps and bank'd Meadows; But the greatest part of our Hemp is brought from Canistogo which is a large and very rich tract 70 miles from this city on the banks of the Susquehannah a large fresh water River. It is brought down in Waggons."

1749 Following appointment as London's Chief Magistrate, novelist Henry Fielding joins half-brother John to create the Bow Street Runners, widely regarded as London's first professional police force.

1750 The British East India Company assumes control of India's primary opium-growing districts, Bengal and Bihar. British shipping dominates the opium traffic from Calcutta to China.

1751 New Jersey exports a meager seven tons of hemp to England. Philadelphia establishes its municipal police force.

1753 Carl Linnaeus (1707–78), the "Father of Botany," names the opium poppy *Papaver somniferum* ("sleep-inducing") in a revised edition of his book *Genera Plantarum*. The British Museum is constructed with proceeds from a public lottery.

1754 France inaugurates its *Loterie des Enfants Trouvés* (Orphans Lottery).

February 15: In his *Report on Laws* to the Pennsylvania Assembly Committee, Benjamin Franklin notes a problem with the expanding hemp industry, noting, "That great Frauds are complained of in the Making up of Hemp for Sale in this Province ... and as nothing is more to the Reputation of a People, and the Advantage of Commerce, than Faithfulness in making up their Wares and Merchandize, we think a Law to remedy the above Evils will be very useful."

1755 Overzealous lottery players beat down the doors of English ticket offices on opening day.

1757 The State Council of France approves a new lottery to finance construction of the École Militaire, a French military school, run by Giacomo Casanova and Giovanni Antonio Calasbigi. Drawings are made of five balls from a cage of 90.

1760 August 21: Benjamin Hawkins and Samuel Parks hang for piracy in Rhode Island.

1761 Lottery schemes "run riot" in Philadelphia, Pa. Projects include disposal of 46 acres owned by Alexander Alexander on Petty's Island, paving of the city's streets, and support of various churches. Four opponents of China's Qing Dynasty—Li Amin, Tao Yuan Ti Xi, and Zhu Dingyuan—found the *Tiandihui* (Society of Heaven and Earth) in Fujian Province. Historians recognize it as the first Triad society.

1762 France inaugurates the charitable Loterie de la Pitié. Colonial authorities in Virginia levy fines against farmers who refuse to cultivate hemp.

1763 July 5: In a letter to Alexander Small, Benjamin Franklin mentions a "hemp machine" invented by a Mr. Mures. Franklin writes, "His Proposal is that when the Hemp is thoroughly dry (perhaps laid for some time in an Oven or in a Kiln) it shall be pressed between two Cylinders, a little fluted, so as not only to crush the bun or reed, but also break it in Pieces, so that it may be the more easily separated from the Hemp."

1764 Author M. Mercandier publishes his *Abstract of the Most Useful Parts of a Late Treatise on Hemp*, describing various medical uses of cannabis. Editor Timothy Paine urges New World settlers to cultivate hemp, writing: "Great part of the soils of the North American Colonies, are so well known, to be peculiarly suitable for the growth of hemp, and the mutual interest of Great Britain and those Colonies, to be evidently much dependent upon the increase of this universally useful vegetable, that we persuade ourselves, that every sincere attempt for the encouragement thereof, must be met with the approbation of the public.... Hemp may be said ... to be the most necessary produce of all others, save that of bread corn, in the new settlements of America, where sheep cannot safely be kept, as it may be applied so as to provide for one half of the clothing of the inhabitants.... The principal advantage that Hemp, intended for these uses, will have over wool, grogram yarn, and cotton, is, that it may be used without spinning, or even combing. It will be in no danger from those worms, which commonly eat woolen cloth; and the beauty, as well as the lasting nature and low price of it, will render it preferable to any other material."

1765 May 12–13: Future U.S. president George Washington writes in his diary: "Sowed Hemp at Muddy hole by Swamp. Sowed Ditto above the Meadow at Doeg Run."

May 16: Washington writes, "Sowed Hemp at head of the Meadow at Doeg Run and Southwards Houses with the Barel."

May 18: Washington writes, "Began to Sow the old Dg. next the Orchard at Muddy hole with the Drill and finished 25 Rows then stopd sowing two fast."

July 20: Washington continues hemp cultivation, writing in his diary: "Sowed 14 Rows more ¾ the drill beg. altered with 1 bushel of seed."

August 7: Washington writes, "Began to separate the Male from the Female hemp at Muddy hole ¾ rather too late."

August 9: Washington's diary records: "Abt. 6 Oclock put some Hemp in the Rvr. to Rot."

August 15: Washington writes, "The English Hemp i.e. the Hemp from the English seed was picked at Muddy hole this day 7 was ripe. Began to separate Hemp in the Neck."

August 22: Washington records that he "put some Hemp into the Water about 6 Oclock in the afternoon ¾ note this Hemp had been pulled the 8th Instt. & was well dryed, & took it out again the 26th."

August 29: Washington's diary describes him "pulling up the [male] hemp. Was too late for the blossom hemp by three weeks or a month."

September 20: Washington writes to Robert Cary & Company in London, requesting a price quotation for American hemp: "In order thereto you would do me a singular favour in advising of the general price one might expect for good Hemp in your Port watered and prepared according to Act of Parliament."

September 25: Washington reports that "hempseed seems to be in good order for getting ¾ that is of a proper ripeness ¾ but obliged to desist to pull my fodder."

October 10: Washington writes that he "finished pulling Seed Hemp at River Plantation."

October 12: Washington's diary records that he "finished pulling Do. Do. at Doeg Run. Not much, if any, too late for the seed."

October 31: Washington writes that he has "finished sowing Wheat in Hemp Ground at River Plantation & plowed in a good deal of Shattered Hemp seed—27 bushels in all."

1767 The British East India Company's traffic in opium to China reaches 2,000 chests per year. In China's Zhangzhou Prefecture, Lu Mao directs *Tiandihui* members in a campaign of robberies to finance their anti–Manchu revolutionary activities.

1768 George Washington sponsors a lottery to fund construction of a road across Virginia's Blue Ridge Mountains.

April 30: The first *Tiandihui* uprising begins, when 80 members attack the western gate of

Zhangpu, China. Qing authorities crush the revolt and arrest 365 Triad associates.

1769 Parliament bans lotteries in Britain's North American colonies. The two-story Redoute casino opens in Liège, Belgium.

May 12: Joseph Andrews hangs for piracy in New York.

1770 Benjamin Franklin pens a marginal note to a British pamphlet titled *Another Letter*, describing the trans–Atlantic hemp trade. He writes: "Did ever any North American bring his Hemp to England for this Bounty. We have not yet enough for our own Consumption. We began to make our own Cordage. You want to suppress that Manufacture, and would do it by getting the raw Material from us; You want to be supply'd with hemp for your Manufactures, and Russia demands Money. These were the motives for giving what you are pleased to call a Bounty to us. We thank you for your Bounties. We love you and therefore must be oblig'd to you for being good to yourselves."

1773 Louis Antoine de Gontaut-Biron, duc de Biron (1700–1788), conducts Europe's first organized horse races, on a track located midway near Verviers, Belgium. The British East India Company monopolizes opium production in Bengal, Bihar, and Orissa, India, awarding distribution privileges via contracts awarded by auction.

1774 Virginia planter and politician Robert "Councillor" Carter III (1727–1804) urges mandatory hemp cultivation "as a preparation for war" with England. He writes, "I apprehend that tobacco which may be here, next summer will be in little demand.... [I]n place of tobacco — hemp and flax will be grown." Each Virginia farmer is required to deliver one pound of dressed hemp yearly, "under oath that it was of his own growth."

October: The Articles of Association establishing America's First Continental Congress include a provision declaring that horse-racing, cockfighting, and "all kinds of games" should be discouraged.

November 27: By a vote of 720 to 21, the Great Council of Venice bans gambling, which has impoverished some of the city's leading families.

1775 Kentucky's first cannabis crop is planted.

April: America's rebellion against England inaugurates a new age of privateering.

1776 King Louis XVI of France (1754–93) transforms the Loterie de l'École Royale Militaire into the Loterie Royale de France, with twice-monthly drawings.

January 10: Thomas Paine publishes his revolutionary pamphlet *Common Sense*, including the

observation that "in almost every article of defence we abound. Hemp flourishes even to rankness, so that we need not want cordage."

November 18: Despite its predecessor's opposition to gambling, the Second Continental Congress inaugurates a lottery to finance the war against England.

1780 January 15: Future pirate Hippolyte de Bouchard born in Saint-Tropez, France.

November 29: James Sutton hangs for piracy in Pennsylvania.

1781 Virginia Governor Thomas Jefferson (1743–1826) collects reserves of "the hemp in the back country" to pay for military supplies in the war against England.

May: David Ross, of Richmond, notifies Governor Jefferson that Virginia's delegates receive "no encouragement from Congress ... in money matters. Tobacco will not do there [in Philadelphia] and we have nothing to depend upon but our hemp." In a subsequent letter to the Virginia delegates, Ross says, "I am sorry to be informed by Mr. Nicholson that the present Invasion of Virginia puts it out of his power to Negotiate the Sale of any Tobacco in Philadelphia, that he has no chance of procuring supplys unless he is furnished with Specie or hemp — the former cannot be procured — of the latter I hope to send on 40 tons in the Course of this summer."

June: Virginia's General Assembly asks Governor Jefferson to supply hemp and tobacco for its delegates to sell in Philadelphia.

1782 King George III of England abolishes the office of groom-porter, established in 1660 with duties including "the Inspection of the King's Lodgings, and takes care that they are provided with Tables, Chairs, Firing, &c. As also to provide Cards, Dice, &c. when there is playing at Court: To decide Disputes which arise in Gaming." Since 1702 the groom-porter has received a yearly salary of £680.

April 25: Ex-pirate Anne Bonny dies in South Carolina at age 80, a respected married woman with eight children.

1783–84 Spanish warships bombard Algiers, forcing the Barbary pirates to negotiate a treaty with Spain.

1785 August 13: Fire destroys one wing of the Redoute casino in Liège, Belgium. Wind disperses burning playing cards, igniting the thatched roofs of 50 nearby homes, claiming three lives.

1785–93 Barbary pirates enslave 130 American seamen taken from ships in the Mediterranean and Atlantic.

1786 Yang Gwangxun, leader of a *Tiandihui* spin-off group called the Increase Younger Brothers Society, leads an abortive revolt against Manchu rule on Taiwan.

1787 Author Peter Markoe (1752–92) publishes a satirical novel, *An Algerine Spy in Pennsylvania*, that encourages Congress to finance a U.S. Navy for suppression of Barbary pirates.

January 17: A family feud on Taiwan sparks the Lin Shuangwen rebellion, focusing Qing Dynasty attention on Triad societies. Official records describe Triad initiates sacrificing roosters on an incense altar, swearing blood oaths, and crawling under swords. Later reports claim that initiates must drink a mixture of ash, chicken blood, and wine, sometimes mixed with blood from the recruit's middle finger.

1788 March 3: John White hangs for piracy in Pennsylvania.

July 19: Captured by Qing authorities on Taiwan, *Tiandihui* recruiter Yan Yan breaks his oath of secrecy, explaining that "recognition is ensured by such secret signals as extending three fingers, as well as by saying out loud, 'Five dots twenty-one.'" The numbers are a code for "Hong," as *Tiandihui* also called themselves "Hongmen."

1789 Prominent citizens in Litchfield, Conn., form America's first temperance society, vowing to withhold alcohol from their employees. Angry workmen respond by harassing committee members. New Jersey native Edward Antil (1742–89) publishes his *Observations on the Raising and Dressing of Hemp*, urging "the inhabitants of North America" to cultivate more cannabis as a step toward independence from Europe. He writes: "As it has been thought requisite, by a continental association, to put a stop to the importation of manufactures into America, it is absolutely necessary to fall speedily on some effectual method to furnish, at least, the coarsest articles of our clothing. Our country produces wool, cotton, hemp and flax, materials amply sufficient to answer every demand of necessity and convenience. The quantity may be increased by attention and diligence, and wrought up with a degree of skill easily attainable.... By beginning with coarse manufactures we shall begin at the right end, we shall, every succeeding year, improve upon the past, and, after a fair exertion of the means in our power, we shall look back, with wonder and astonishment, at our present apprehension. We must now exert ourselves in manufactures, or, from an unconquerable indolence, be driven to the basest and most humiliating concessions that others may dispose of our lives, liberties and properties, at their pleasure. When everything valuable to men is thus at stake, the author claims the privilege of a citizen, and entreats the attention to the public, to a subject of so great consequences to this country as that which is now submitted to their consideration. It is no less than a certain and easy method of supplying, internally, the most necessary and considerable parts of our clothing."

May 12: Democratic Party leaders in New York City found the Tammany Society—later Tammany Hall—named for Native American chief Tamanend of the Lenni-Lenape nation. Tammany grows to control city elections by force and fraud from 1829 into the 1960s.

September 10: Rachel Wall faces trial for robbery in Boston, but requests trial for piracy instead. She hangs for that offense on October 8, the last woman hanged in Massachusetts.

September 24: Following congressional passage of the Judiciary Act, President George Washington appoints the first 13 U.S. marshals.

1790 British shipments of opium to China top 4,000 chests annually.

February: U.S. Secretary of the Treasury Alexander Hamilton (1755–1804) receives a report from Assistant Secretary Tench Coxe, advising that "the duty on hemp, wh. is not produced in sufficient quantity for our present demand and which demand will be very much increased by the time the duty will be in operation is menacing circumstance to the makers of those indispensable Articles, Cordage & Sailcloth. If the new invention of the hemp & flax spinning Mill does not prove a deception this duty will be a very unfortunate thing."

March 16: U.S. Secretary of State Thomas Jefferson writes, in his *Farm Journal*: "The culture [of tobacco] is pernicious. This plant greatly exhausts the soil. Of course, it requires much manure, therefore other productions are deprived of manure, yielding no nourishment for cattle, there is no return for the manure expended.... It is impolitic.... The fact well established in the system of agriculture is that the best hemp and the best tobacco grow on the same kind of soil. The former article is of the first necessity to the commerce and marine, in other words to the wealth and protection of the country. The latter, never useful and sometimes pernicious, derives its estimation from caprice, and its best value from the taxes to which it was formerly exposed."

1791 Alexander Hamilton's *Report on Manufactures* includes a reference to cannabis. He writes: "In respect to hemp, something has already been done by the high duty on foreign hemp. If the facilities for domestic production were not unusually great, the policy of the duty, on the foreign raw material, would be highly questionable, as interfering with the growth of manufactures of it.... This is an article of importance enough to warrant the employment of extraordinary means in its favor."

March 3: Congress passes the Whiskey Act, levying an excise tax on whiskey.

June 17: Future pirate Roberto Cofresí y Ramírez de Arellano born in Cabo Rojo, Puerto Rico.

September 24: President George Washington writes to British author and economist Arthur Young, referring to hemp cultivation in Virginia. He says, in part: "Much hemp might be raised in these countries were there the proper encouragement. the foreign hemp gluts the market and there is not sufficient protecting duty to spur the farmer to raise this useful article. Our hemp lands would average a 700 weight to the acre.... Rich fresh bottom lands yield 500 or 600 and highly manured land 6, 8 or 900 pounds to the acre."

October 14: Washington recommends increased hemp production to Alexander Hamilton, as a matter of national security. He writes: "How far, in addition to the several matters mentioned in that letter, would there be propriety do you conceive in suggesting the policy of encouraging the growth of Cotton, and Hemp in such parts of the United States as are adapted to the culture of these articles? The advantages which could result to this Country from the produce of articles, which ought to be manufactured at home is apparent... . The establishment of Arsenals in convenient and proper places is, in my opinion, a measure of high national importance meriting the serious attention of Congress."

December 6: Congress passes a revenue act, imposing an excise tax on distilled spirits, to take effect on June 30, 1792.

1792 Coulter's Brewery is erected at the Five Points intersection of New York City's Lower East Side. Converted into tenement housing in 1837, it becomes the epitome of impoverished, crime-ridden urban life. A French physician living in Switzerland, Dr. Pierre Ordinaire, creates absinthe as a medicinal elixir.

1793 The British East India Company extends its opium monopoly throughout India, forbidding sale of raw opium to competitors. The First French Republic bans France's national lottery.

1794 January 6: President George Washington expands his hemp cultivation to include "India hemp" (*Cannabis indica*), AKA *hashish*. An entry in Washington's diary on this date reads: "I also gave the Gardener a few Seed of East India hemp to raise from, enquire for the seed which has been saved, and make the most of it at the proper season for sowing."

January 19: Washington writes in his diary, "Let the most that can, be made of the pint of Oats which the Gardener raisd last year, and of the Hemp seed."

February 9: Washington writes to his estate manager: "You have never informed me how much St. foin [sainfoin, Eurasian perennial herbs of the legume family] and India Hemp seed he has saved."

February 24: Upon receiving a reply, Washington writes, "I am very glad to hear that the Gardener has saved so much of the St. foin seed, and that of the India Hemp. Make the most of both, by sowing them again in drill.... The Hemp may be sown anywhere."

March 9: Washington offers further advice to his gardener: "The St. foin and India hemp may be sown in the lot which you have mentioned, as more secure perhaps than the other, against Hares; but how they will be annoyed by fowls you can judge better of than I. I wish to have the most that can be made of them."

March 15: Continuing his instructions, Washington writes, "Presuming you saved all you could from the India hemp, let it be carefully sown again, for the purpose of getting into a full stock of seed."

March 30: Still concerned about his cannabis crop, President Washington writes home: "Make the most ... of the Hemp."

May 26: In a letter to Dr. James Anderson of Philadelphia, Washington refers to a soup stock made from hempseed in Silesia, a region of western Poland. He writes: "I thank you as well for the Seeds as for the Pamphlets which you had the goodness to send me. The artificial preparation of Hemp, from Silesia, is really a curiosity; and I shall think myself much favored in the continuance of your correspondence."

July 15: The Whiskey Rebellion begins in Allegheny County, Pennsylvania, when farmers led by William Miller fire on revenue inspector John Neville and a U.S. marshal seeking to serve writs on illegal distillers.

July 16: Thirty armed whiskey rebels approach John Neville's home near Pittsburgh, Pa. An exchange of fire leaves one man dead and several wounded.

July 17: James McFarlane leads 500 whiskey rebels against John Neville's home, now guarded by troops. A gunshot from the house kills McFarlane, after which his men burn Neville's home, barn, and outbuildings.

July 26: Agents acting under orders from U.S. Attorney General David Bradford intercept mail sent by whiskey rebels from Pittsburgh to Philadelphia, Pa.

July 28: David Bradford calls for local militias to rally against whiskey rebels on August 1, at Braddock's Field east of Pittsburgh. An estimated 5,000 to 7,000 militiamen answer the call.

August 7: President George Washington mobilizes 12,950 troops from eastern Pennsylvania, Virginia, Maryland, and New Jersey under General Harry Lee, to suppress whiskey rebels.

August 19: President Washington calls on U.S. Secretary of State Edmund Randolf to answer charges from French minister Joseph Fauchet that Randolf's handling of the Whiskey Rebellion marks him as "a pitiable figure, possessed of some talents and surprisingly little malice, but subject to self-absorbed silliness and lapses of good sense." Randolf subsequently resigns on August 20, 1795.

August 20: A presidential commission meets with Whiskey Rebellion leaders to discuss peace terms and amnesty. The rebels decline to pledge submission.

August 28: Attorney General Bradford recommends war against whiskey rebels.

September 11–12: Residents of western Pennsylvania vote on the question of submission to federal law.

September 19: George Washington leads federal troops from Philadelphia to confront whiskey rebels.

September 24: U.S. commissioners report that force will be required to win compliance with the whiskey excise law.

Late September: Two residents of Carlisle, Pa., die fighting President Washington's troops.

October 2: Whiskey rebels gathered at Parkinson's Ferry (now Monongahela City, Pa.) vote unanimously to obey federal law and accept peace terms offered in August.

October 9–10: Whiskey rebels surrender to President Washington and Secretary of the Treasury Alexander Hamilton at Carlisle, Pa.

October 24: Troops led by General Lee arrive to subdue recalcitrant whiskey rebels in Washington County, Pa.

November 5: Washington writes again to his gardener, saying, "Let particular care be taken of the India Hempseed, and as much good grd. allotted for its reception next year as is competent to Sow."

November 13: Lee's troops capture and confine 150 prisoners during nocturnal raids.

1794–96 While service as America's ambassador to France, future president James Monroe (1758–1831) experiments with hashish, developing a fondness for the drug that endures to the end of his life.

1795 July 10: President Washington issued a proclamation releasing all but five whiskey rebels formally indicted and held over for trial. Jurors later convict two of the five, while the remainder are freed.

1796 Chinese Grand Emperor Qianlong (1711–99) bans opium-smoking in China. Importation by the British East India Company continues, with silver smuggled out of China to pay for drug shipments.

1797 The British East India Company promul-gates "Bengal Regulation IV," permitting appointment of opium agents to purchase crops from native farmers, for processing at the firm's factories in Ghasipur and Patna. The five-member Executive Directory of France reinstates the Loterie Nationale. Samuel Mason establishes a river-pirate enclave at Cave-In-Rock, Ill.

1798 Summer: Napoleon Bonaparte (1769–1821) reports that much of Egypt's lower class habitually smokes hashish. Despite his ban on hashish during French occupation of Egypt, many of Napoleon's soldiers develop a taste for the drug.

November 5: Future pirate Charles Gibbs, né James D. Jeffers, born in Newport, R.I.

1799 February 7: Chinese Emperor Yongyan succeeds his father and initiates prosecution of corrupt grand councilor Heshen. Soon afterward, Yongyan bans opium cultivation and trafficking nationwide, an edict ignored by the British East India Company.

Summer: Kentucky "Exterminators" rout Samuel Mason's river pirates from Cave-In-Rock, Ill. Mason relocates to lead a band of robbers on the Natchez Trace, in Mississippi.

August: A posse kills river pirate and serial murderer Micajah "Big" Harpe in Webster County, Ky.

December 3: George Washington writes to his brother-in-law, Thomas Peter, asking, "Have you succeeded, or are you likely to succeed, in procuring the Hemp seed I required?"

1800 The British Levant Company, chartered in 1580 to promote (and later monopolize) trade with Turkey, purchases half of the opium produced at Smyrna for sale in Europe and the United States.

February 17: French emperor Napoleon I establishes the Prefecture of Police to protect Paris and environs.

April 21–25: Canadian pirate Joseph Baker, AKA Joseph Boulanger, stands trial in Philadelphia, Pa. He hangs on May 9.

1801 January 1: The Acts of Union, passed by lawmakers in Britain and Ireland during July and August 1800, take effect and create the United Kingdom of Great Britain and Ireland. Soon thereafter, state lotteries are banned in Ireland.

March 4: Thomas Jefferson is inaugurated as America's third president. Soon afterward, Yusuf Karamanli, the Pasha of Tripoli, demands tribute in the amount of $225,000 to secure safe passage of U.S. shipping.

May 14: When no tribute is forthcoming, Yusuf Karamanli declares war on the United States, by cutting down the U.S. consulate's flagpole. The Barbary states of Algiers and Tunis soon follow Tripoli's lead. President Jefferson sends frigates to defend American interests in the Mediterranean.

Congress refuses to declare war, but authorizes seizure of Yusuf Karamanli's ships and goods, along with "all such other acts of precaution or hostility as the state of war will justify."

June 29: The USS *Philadelphia* blockades a squadron led by pirate Murat Reis—a Scottish convert to Islam, born Peter Lisle—at Gibraltar.

August 1: The schooner USS *Enterprise* defeats the 14-gun Tripolitan corsair *Tripoli* in a battle at sea.

1802 French authorities establish the Bureau of Public Morals, requiring common prostitutes ("public women") to register and carry at all times an identity card, which must be presented to police upon demand. Other rules inquire health inspections at 15-day intervals, mandate "simple and decent" attire (including bonnets), restrict solicitation to particular neighborhoods, and confine commercial sex to the hours between 7 and 11 P.M. Congress repeals its excise tax on distilled liquors.

March 30: Congress passes a permanent Indian Intercourse Act, replacing the temporary act renewed biannually since July 1790. The new law bans use of liquor for payment in the Indian fur trade.

April: Pirates Samuel Mason and Wiley Harpe attempt to hijack Colonel Joshua Baker on the Mississippi River, between Yazoo and Walnut Hills.

September 4: Chen Lanjisi, a leader of the Increase Brothers Society, leads a Triad uprising in Guangdong, China. Authorities crush the rebellion on October 15, killing Chen and many of his followers. Nine years later, Liangguang Governor-general Ruan Yuan described the rebels as common criminals, writing: "Their intention is only to obtain wealth to use; they are not plotters of illegalities [rebellion], but their intention to incite good people to rob is a local evil."

1803 May 18: An outbreak of hostilities between France and England begins the 13-year Napoleonic Wars. Privateering flourishes once more.

August: Moroccan pirate Ibrahim Lubarez Reis captures an American brig off Malaga, Spain.

October 31: Tripolitan warships capture the USS *Philadelphia* after it runs aground in Tripoli's harbor, holding Captain William Bainbridge and his crew as hostages.

1804 German pharmacist Friedrich Sertürner discovers the active ingredient of opium by dissolving it in acid, then neutralizing it with ammonia. The resultant product—called morphine—is soon dubbed "God's own medicine" by European physicians delighted with its effectiveness as a pain-killer. State legislators in Kentucky ban any game of chance "in which one player is continually opposed to all the others." Chinese

pirate captain Ching Yih forms a confederation including 600 ships and some 150,000 buccaneers.

February 16: Lieutenant Stephen Decatur leads a party of U.S. Marines to burn the captive USS *Philadelphia* in Tripoli harbor.

July 14: Commodore Edward Preble, whose ships have maintained a blockade of Tripoli harbor since 1803, attacks the city itself, but the fireship USS *Intrepid* is destroyed by Tripolitan gunners, killing Captain Richard Somers and his crew.

August 3–September 2: U.S. ships bombard Tripoli on five separate occasions.

September 3: American commanders sent the USS *Intrepid* into Tripoli harbor, loaded with explosives. It detonates prematurely, killing all 16 crewmen aboard.

1805 Charles Cabot, a smuggler from Boston, buys opium from British traders and smuggles it into China with their assistance. The Henriod sisters open an absinthe distillery in Pontarlier, France, under the name Maison Pernod Fils. Frenchman Jean Lafitte (1776–1823) opens a warehouse in New Orleans, La., to store and sell goods smuggled by his brother Pierre (1770–1821).

April 22: Future pirate Benito de Soto Aboal born in Pontevedra, Spain.

April 27–May 13: After an epic desert march from Alexandria, Egypt, former U.S. consul William Eaton and U.S. Marine Corps First Lieutenant Presley O'Bannon storm the Tripolitan city of Derna with eight Marines and 500 native mercenaries. With losses of 11 killed and wounded, the attackers slay more than 800 defenders, wounding more than 1,200. This battle effectively ends the First Barbary War, and is memorialized by the phrase "to the shores of Tripoli" in the Marine Corps Hymn.

May 11: Future U.S. president Andrew Jackson (1767–1845) purchases a racehorse, Truxton, who subsequently wins many races. Its contest with a horse named Greyhound, at Huntsville, Tennessee, nets Jackson a then-record $5,000 purse.

June 6: A peace treaty ends the First Barbary War, with a U.S. payment of $60,000 to ransom hostage crewmen from the USS *Philadelphia*.

June 10: Yusuf Karamanli signs a treaty ending the First Barbary War, but the U.S. Senate delays ratification until 1806.

September: Chinese naval forces raid pirate strongholds on Hangzhou Bay on the East China Sea, capturing 26 ships while many more escape. Frustrated, the commanding general offers a pardon extending through December, which persuades 3,000 pirates to surrender.

Autumn: Captain Joseph Ervin withdraws his

horse Plow Boy from a scheduled $2,000 race against Andrew Jackson's Truxton. Personal insults exchanged in the wake of that forfeiture inspire Jackson to kill one of Ervin's friends, Charles Dickinson, in a Kentucky duel on May 30, 1806.

1806 French Emperor Napoleon I legalizes several gambling rooms.

January: Eight leaders of Philadelphia's Federal Society of Journeymen Cordwainers, a bootmaker's union, are convicted of criminal conspiracy after they strike for higher wages. The trial bankrupts the union and establishes a precedent for "legal" union-busting in America.

1807 A typhoon claims the life of Chinese pirate lord Ching Yih. His widow, His Kai Ching, appropriates his uniform and takes command of his confederation, leading raids by 800 ships in the South China Sea through 1810, when Chinese authorities grant amnesty to end the plague of piracy. Congress forbids further importation of African slaves, thus creating a new bonanza for smugglers of human cargo.

December 22: Congress passes an Embargo Act restricting trade between the United States and foreign nations. Soon afterward, the Lafitte brothers of New Orleans move their contraband warehouse to Grand Terre in Barataria Bay, on the Gulf of Mexico.

1808 July: Pirates led by Chang Pao destroy Chinese naval forces guarding the Pearl River passage between Canton and Macao.

1809 April 18: A horse race at Newmarket, England, boasts a price of 2,000 (42,000 shillings).

July: Chang Pao's pirates destroy Chinese warships on the Pearl River once again.

August: Pirates Chang Pao and Kuo P'o-Tai raid along the Pearl River in China, killing 10,000 victims, taking thousands of women and children as captives.

1810 Future U.S. president John Quincy Adams (1767–1848) publishes a report *On the Culture & Preparing of Hemp in Russia.*

January: Pirate Kuo P'o-tai surrenders to Chinese authorities with 6,000 men, thereby earning a military commission to hunt other pirates. He resigns after a final sweep in May, to finish his life as a scholar, dying before year's end.

April: Pirates Chang Pao and Cheng I Sao negotiate lenient terms before surrendering their Red Fleet of 260 ships, 14,000 crewman, and 1,000 canons to Chinese authorities. In May, Chang leads a new official fleet to hunt and capture other pirates.

September: Thomas Robertson, acting governor of Louisiana, brands the Lafitte brothers "brigands who infest our coast and overrun our country." Few local residents share his antipathy toward the Lafittes, whose smuggled luxury items remain extremely popular with wealthy families.

1811 Lawmakers for the vast Louisiana Territory ban gambling throughout a region equivalent to one-third of the present-day United States.

1812 Criminalist Eugène François Vidocq (1775–1857) founds the Sûreté Nationale (French National Police), serving as its chief until 1827. American trader John Cushing, serving as an agent for the James and Thomas H. Perkins Company of Boston, earns a fortune smuggling Turkish opium into Canton, China. British colonial authorities in India peg the year's death toll from attacks by Thugs at 40,000.

January 4: Anti-Manchu activist Yan Guiqiu organizes a new Triad group, the Sanhehui ("Three Harmonies Society," referring to harmony between Heaven, Earth, and Man), in Guangdong Province.

June 17: U.S. naval forces under Stephen Decatur capture an Algerian warship as the Second Barbary War begins. They seize a second vessel on June 20.

June 18: Congress declares war against England, officially beginning the War of 1812. As during past global conflicts, privateering flourishes.

June 28: Stephen Decatur's force reaches Algiers and accepts the local ruler's surrender, ending the Second Barbary War.

October: Dissatisfied with their income as brokers of pirate loot in New Orleans, the Lafitte brothers buy a schooner and hire a captain to sail it on privateering raids.

November 10: U.S. District Attorney John Grymes charges Jean Lafitte with "violation of the revenue law."

November 16: Soldiers capture the Lafitte brothers and 25 smugglers, confiscating contraband worth several thousand dollars. All but Pierre post bail, then vanish without standing trial.

December 10: Samuel Tully hangs for piracy in Massachusetts.

1813 January: The Lafitte brothers capture their first prize, a Spanish brig with 77 slaves aboard. Sale of the slaves and other cargo nets a profit of $18,000. Converting the ship to their own use, renamed the *Dorada*, the Lafittes soon capture another schooner with cargo valued at $9,000.

March: Jean Lafitte registers himself as captain of *Le Brig Goelette la Diligente*, bound for New York City, but embarks on new privateering raids instead. On March 15, Louisiana Governor William Claiborne denounces Lafitte and his men as "banditti ... who act in contravention of the laws of the United States ... to the evident prejudice of the revenue of the federal government."

October: U.S. revenue agents ambush a party

of Jean Lafitte's smugglers, but the outlaws escape with their contraband after wounding one office.

November: Governor Claiborne of Louisiana offers a $500 reward for Jean Lafitte's capture.

1814 Congress imposes a new tax on whiskey to pay for the War of 1812. The law expires in 1817.

January: Louisiana authorities raid a contraband auction staged by the Lafitte brothers outside New Orleans. One revenue officer dies in the melee, with two others wounded.

September 3: The British warship HMS *Sophie* fires on one of Jean Lafitte's pirate ships, near Lafitte's Grand Terre island. The pirate ship grounds itself in shallow water and hoists a white flag, permitting Lafitte to negotiate with Captain Nicholas Lockyer of the *Sophie* and a captain of the British army. Rowing to the nearby island, the Brits are suddenly surrounded and threatened with lynching by Lafitte's pirates. Lafitte spares them upon receipt of a letter from King George III, requesting Lafitte's aid in the current British war against America. Lafitte requests 15 days to consider the deal, then offers his services to Louisiana's Governor Claiborne. Claiborne signals his agreement with Pierre Lafitte's "escape" from custody.

September 6: Pierre Lafitte visits Philadelphia, carrying an offer of assistance in the war effort to President James Madison.

September 13: With negotiations still in progress for the Lafitte gang's assistance in war against England, U.S. Navy Commodore Daniel Patterson sails to attack the pirates' Grand Terre island in Baratria Bay. Jean Lafitte escapes, but Patterson's force captures 80 prisoners, seven ships, 20 cannon, and goods valued at $500,000, departing the island on September 23. Patterson subsequently files a claim for the confiscated ships and other property.

December 1: General Andrew Jackson arrives in New Orleans and finds the city unprepared for defense against British invaders. Soon afterward, he meets with Jean Lafitte to negotiate a pact for mutual defense.

December 19: Louisiana's state legislature passes a resolution recommending full pardons for all former residents of Grand Terre, whereupon Jean Lafitte's buccaneers join the New Orleans militia. Some serve as sailors, while others for three artillery companies.

December 24: American and British diplomats sign the Treaty of Ghent, formally ending the War of 1812, but hostilities continue in Louisiana, where neither side has knowledge of the treaty.

December 28: British troops shell American forces at New Orleans, but are repulsed by an artillery crew led by two of Jean Lafitte's former lieutenants.

1815 Louisiana's state legislature permits gambling

in New Orleans, under control of municipal authorities.

January 8: The final Battle of New Orleans leaves 278 British soldiers dead, 1,186 wounded, and 484 captured or missing, versus American losses of 13 dead, 39 wounded, and 19 missing. Jean Lafitte's "reformed" pirates play a key role in the American victory.

January 21: General Jackson praises his troops in New Orleans, with a special commendation for "Captains Dominique and Beluche, lately commanding privateers of Barataria with part of their former crews and many brave citizens of New Orleans, were stationed at Nos. 3 and 4." He also praises the Lafitte brothers by name, for having "exhibited the same courage and fidelity."

February 6: The Lafittes and their surviving buccaneers receive a full pardon for all previous crimes from President James Madison.

March 13: Congress authorizes deployment of naval forces against Algiers, to suppress ongoing piracy.

May 20: U.S. Navy Commodore Stephen Decatur Jr. sails for the Mediterranean with a force of 10 warships.

June 17: Decatur's fleet captures the flagship of Algeria's navy off Cape Gatta, Spain, killing 30 Algerian seamen and capturing 406, against American losses of four dead and 10 wounded. The war sputters to an inconclusive resolution, as Barbary pirates continue their raids and enslavement of Christian captives.

September 12: Hippolyte de Bouchard receives a corsair license to raid Spanish shipping in the Western Hemisphere.

1816 America's first multi-millionaire, John Jacob Astor (1763–1848), begins smuggling Turkish opium to China aboard ships owned by his American Fur Company. Hoping to profit from the Mexican War of Independence, brothers Jean and Pierre Lafitte enlist as spies for Spain.

January 10: Hippolyte de Bouchard's pirate fleet bombards Guayaquil, Ecuador.

January 13: Hippolyte de Bouchard captures the *Gobernadora*, followed by four more ships on January 18.

January 21: Hippolyte de Bouchard bombards Guayaquil once more.

June 25: Crewmen on *La Argentina* rebel against Captain Hippolyte de Bouchard, leaving two men dead and four wounded before the uprising is suppressed.

June 27: Hippolyte de Bouchard procures an Argentina letter of marque authorizing attacks on Spanish shipping.

July 9: Hippolyte de Bouchard sails from Argentina on a two-year expedition to plunder Spanish vessels.

August 27: An Anglo-Dutch fleet bombards the harbor at Algiers, destroying 33 ships and losing 818 men killed or wounded. Algerian forces surrender the following day, having exhausted their supply of ammunition.

September: French pirate Louis-Michel Aury accepts a Mexican commission as civil and military governor, raiding the Gulf of Mexico from a base on Galveston Island.

September 24: Britain signs a treaty with Algeria, resulting in release of 1,083 Christian slaves and the British Consul, with a refund of previous ransom payments.

December 23: Algeria's ruler accepts U.S. demand to cease tribute raids against American shipping.

1817 Parliament bans various forms of gambling in its remaining North American colonies. The forbidden games include bowling, cards, checkers, dice, and shuffleboard.

March: Jean Lafitte visits Galveston Island, off the coast of Spanish Texas, a haven for Mexican rebels and French pirate Louis-Michel Aury. Two weeks later, Lafitte seizes control of the island, which lies outside U.S. jurisdiction, and converts it to a new base for piracy.

July: Louis-Michel Aury abandons Galveston Island when its inhabitants fail to heed his calls for revolution.

1818 French physician François Magendie publishes a paper extolling the analgesic properties of morphine. Pirate Benito "Bloody Sword" Bonito raids Spanish shipping on the Pacific coast of the Americas.

January 31: Hippolyte de Bouchard stops and searches an English frigate near Manila.

April: Congress passes a new law banning importation of slaves to the U.S., but permits sale of slaves removed from captures slave ships. Jean Lafitte's pirates take advantage of the loophole, working with smugglers such as Texan Jim Bowie to profit from human trafficking. Before year's end, a hurricane flattens Lafitte's settlement at Campeche, killing hundreds.

July 4: Louis-Michel Aury captures Old Providence Island in the western Caribbean, establishing a community that thrives on proceeds from captures Spanish cargo.

November 24–29: Hippolyte de Bouchard's pirates occupy and loot Monterey, California, burning Spanish military installations.

December 5: Hippolyte de Bouchard's buccaneers attack a Spanish ranch at Santa Barbara, California, slaughtering the livestock.

December 16: Hippolyte de Bouchard loots San Juan Capistrano, California.

1819 January 25: Hippolyte de Bouchard's squadron blockades San Blas, Baja California Sur, remaining into early March.

February 10: Massachusetts authorities hang four convicted pirates.

March 3: Congress passes a law imposing the death penalty on "any person or persons whatsoever shall, on the high seas, commit the crime of piracy."

April 2: Hippolyte de Bouchard attacks El Realejo, Nicaragua, capturing two schooners and burning two more when ransom demands are rejected.

July 12: Chilean authorities arrest Hippolyte de Bouchard in Valparaíso. His trial for piracy begins on July 20 and ends with acquittal on December 9.

August 25: Allan Pinkerton born in Glasgow, Scotland.

November: George Brown hangs for piracy in Texas.

1820 Louisiana lawmakers ban all forms of gambling statewide. British traders deliver 5,000 chests of opium to Chinese ports.

April 13: Israel Denny and John Ferguson hang for piracy in Maryland.

April 21: Louis-Michel Aury leads Colombian forces against the port of Trujillio, on the east coast of present-day Honduras, repulsed by defenders on April 24.

April 25: Commodore Aury attacks the Honduran port of Omoa and is once again defeated, leaving the area on May 6.

April 28: John Hobson hangs for piracy in Georgia.

May 12: South Carolina hangs convicted pirates George Clark and Henry Roberts.

May 15: Congress extends the 1819 Piracy Act for two more years.

May 25: Pirates named only as Desfarges and Johnson hang in Louisiana.

June 15: Three unidentified pirates hang in Massachusetts.

1821 British author Thomas de Quincey (1785–1859) publishes his autobiographical account of drug addiction, *Confessions of an English Opium-Eater*.

May 7: After receiving ultimatums from the captain of the USS *Enterprise*, Jean Lafitte and his pirates burn Campeche and abandon Galveston Island aboard three ships.

May 21: Believing that Jean Lafitte holds a privateering commission, his men help capture a Spanish merchant ship. Lafitte sends the ship to Galveston, hoping that Texas merchant James Long will help smuggle the goods to New Orleans. Frightened by an American patrol boat, Lafitte's men ground the captured ship and bury some of their loot on Galveston Island. Several are arrested and later convicted of piracy, while the rest rejoin Lafitte. On learning that he holds no privateering commission, most of the crew refuse to sail again as pirates. Lafitte permits them to leave aboard his brig, the *General Victoria*, but loyal crewmen board the ship that night, destroying its masts and spars.

July 24: Future Bowery Boys gang member and Know-Nothing political leader William "Bill the Butcher" Poole born in New York City.

August 30: Louis-Michel Aury reportedly dies when thrown from a horse on Old Providence Island, though some accounts claim he lived on in Havana until 1845.

October: While trying to ransom a recent prize, Jean Lafitte is ambushed by U.S. forces and captured.

October 21: While attacking three merchantmen off Cape Antonio, Cuba, pirate Charles Gibbs is surprised by the USS *Enterprise*, which destroys his small fleet. Gibbs and his surviving crewmen flee inland, hiding in the jungle.

1822 February 13: Jean Lafitte escapes from custody, subsequently establishing a new pirate haven on the coast of Cuba, where corrupt local officials accept a share of his loot.

April: An American warship captures Jean Lafitte and delivers him to Cuban authorities, who promptly release him.

June: Seeking a change of scene after Cuban officials crack down on piracy, Jean Lafitte strikes a bargain with Colombian authorities. He receives a privateering commission and a 40-ton schooner, the *General Santander*, with authorization to raid Spanish shipping.

November: Jean Lafitte reaps favorable publicity in the U.S., after escorting an American schooner through pirate-infested Caribbean waters, supplying the ship with food and extra cannon balls.

December 20: U.S., Secretary of the Navy Smith Thompson appoints Captain David Porter "to command the vessels-of-war of the United States on the West India station ... for the suppression of piracy." Financed with an appropriation of $500,000, Porter outfits a "Mosquito Fleet" of small, shallow-draft ships.

1823 Louisiana lawmakers change their minds about gambling, passing a statute that permits New Orleans to license six casinos for a yearly fee of $5,000 each. Parliament votes to abolish England's state lottery. Stephen Austin (1793–1836) recruits the first small band of Texas Rangers.

January 30: Congress makes the death penalty for piracy "perpetual."

February 3: Jean Lafitte attacks two Spanish pirate ships, mistaking them for merchantmen. He suffers a mortal wound in the ensuing battle

and dies on February 5. Crewmen bury him at sea in the Gulf of Honduras.

April: Captain Porter's Mosquito Fleet arrives at Key West, Fla., with a motley collection of vessels and 1,100 men. Porter scores his first victory the same month, with the defeat of Cuban pirate "Diabolito." Porter's fleet kills 30 of Diabolito's 70 crewmen.

April 3: Future Tammany Hall leader William Magear "Boss" Tweed born in New York City.

July: Diabolito meets two of Porter's ships, the USS *Gallinipper* and the USS *Mosquito*, off the coast of Cuba. Although they outnumber the American seamen 80 to 31, the pirates soon abandon ship. The *Gallinipper* and *Mosquito* are "soon in the midst of the swimmers, and, laying about right and left, exterminated dozens of them," including Diabolito.

September 23: Burmese forces attack the British on Shapura, an island close to the Chittagong side, inflicting six casualties.

1824 January: Two Burmese armies invade Cachar, which is under British protection.

March 5: Great Britain declares war on Burma.

May 10: British forces under Commodore Charles Grant and Major-General Sir Archibald Campbell enter the Rangoon River and anchor off the town of Rangoon, which surrenders after brief resistance.

May 17: Burmese troops invade Chittagong and drive a mixed sepoy and police detachment from its position at Ramu.

May 28: Major-General Campbell attacks and captures Burmese posts surrounding Rangoon.

June 10: British forces drive Burmese defenders from the village of Kemmendine.

October: British forces seize control of Burma's Martaban Province.

December 7: A Burmese force of 60,000 assails 5,000 British defenders at Kemmendine, suffering a critical defeat.

December 15: Major-General Campbell pursues retreating Burmese troops and defeats them once more, on the Irrawaddy River.

1825 Underworld figure Rosanna Peers establishes the Center Street Grocery and speakeasy in New York City's Five Points district, on the north side of present-day Foley Square. It remains a center of criminal activity until 1840.

March 5: Pirate Roberto Cofresí hijacks a ship owned by Vicente Antoneti at Salinas, Puerto Rico. Captain John Sloat arrests Confesí and his crew on March 8. A Spanish firing squad executes Confesí and 11 crewmen in San Juan, Puerto Rico, on March 29.

September 17: British and Burmese leaders agree to a one-month armistice in the First Anglo-Burmese War, expiring on November 3.

December 26: Following further military losses, Burmese leaders begin peace negotiations with England. The final Treaty of Yandabo, signed on February 24, 1826, mandates cession of Arakan, together with the provinces of Mergui, Tavoy and Ye, and temporary occupation of large parts of southern Burma until the financial indemnity for the war was paid by the Burmese. The net effect is increased British dominance of the Burmese opium trade.

December 29: Thomas Jefferson writes to associate George Fleming, saying: "Flax is so injurious to our lands and of so scanty produce that I have never attempted it. Hemp, on the other hand, is abundantly productive and will grow forever on the same spot, but the breaking and beating it is so slow, so laborious and so much complained of by our laborers, that I have given it up…. But recently a method of removing the difficulty of preparing hemp occurred to me, so simple and so cheap. I modified a threshing machine to turn a very strong hemp-break, much stronger and heavier than those for the hand. By this the cross arm lifts and lets fall the break twice in every revolution of the wallower. A man feeds the break with the hemp stalks … where it is more perfectly beaten than I have ever seen done by hand…. I expect that a single horse will do the breaking and beating of ten men."

1826 Edward Coleman founds the Forty Thieves, New York City's first noteworthy Irish gang. The gang adopts Rosanna Peers's Center Street Grocery as its unofficial headquarters, while expanding to dominate the Five Points neighborhood.

February 13: Anti-liquor activists in Boston, Mass., found the American Society for the Promotion of Temperance. By 1836 more than 8,000 local chapters claim 1.5 million members who have taken a pledge to abstain from drinking.

July 18: London holds its last sanctioned lottery.

October 18: England concludes its last state lottery.

1827 February 2: Winslow Curtis and Duncan White hang for piracy in Massachusetts. Galician pirate Benito de Soto seizes control of a slave ship in the Atlantic, renames it the *Burla Negra* ("Black Joke"), and converts it to use as a privateer. E. Merck & Company of Darmstadt, Germany, begins commercial manufacturing of morphine. After winning £100,000 at cards, William Crockford (1775–1844) opens a new London casino, Crockford's Gaming Club, on St. James Street. Crockford earns £1,200,000 from the club before retiring in 1840. John Davis opens a New Orleans casino patterned on gaming clubs in London's West End.

1828 February 19: Pirate Benito de Soto meets the trader *Morning Star* en route from Ceylon (now Sri Lanka) to England. After killing some of the crew with cannon fire, de Soto boards the ship, murders the captain and most of his surviving crewmen, then unleashes his pirates to gang-rape several female passengers. Finally, he scuttles the ship with captives locked in the hold, but several escape to report the atrocity.

1829 Parliament creates the Metropolitan Police of London to replace the previously disorganized system of parish constables and watchmen. The new force is headquartered on Great Scotland Yard, a street in Whitehall.

1830 British traders import 22,000 pounds of opium from India and Turkey, as the national addiction rate increases. During the same year, 16,000 chests of opium are shipped to China. U.S. Postmaster General William Barry creates a new Office of Instructions and Mail Depredations, coining the term "special agent" to describe its officers.

January 25: Benito de Soto hangs for piracy on Gibraltar, with his severed head afterward displayed as a warning to others.

June 14: French Admiral Guy-Victor Duperré launches an invasion of Algeria, landing 34,000 soldiers at Sidi Ferruch, 17 miles west of Algiers. The army enters Algiers on July 5, toppling the nation's Muslim regime and ending 313 years of Ottoman rule on July 11.

November 23: Pirates Charles Gibbs and Thomas Wansley lead a mutiny aboard the brig *Vineyard*, killing the captain and first mate, absconding with a cargo of silver. They scuttle the ship at Long Island, N.Y., losing several crewmen and most of the loot. Subsequently arrested for mutiny and murder, Gibbs and Wansley hang Ellis Island, N.Y., on April 22, 1831.

1831 February 12: Future boxer, Dead Rabbits gang boss, and Tammany Hall leader John "Old Smoke" Morrissey born in Templemore, County Tipperary, Ireland.

July 1: Thomas Collinet and Joseph Gadett hang for piracy in Massachusetts.

December 10: America's first weekly horse-racing sheet, the *Spirit of the Times*, begins publication in New York City.

1832 State legislators repeal a statutory limit on the number of casinos allowed in Louisiana, while increasing annual license fees to $7,500. Pirate Benito de Soto is captured at Gibraltar and shipped to Spain for execution.

July: Jardine, Matheson and Company is formed by William Jardine (1784–1843) and James Matheson (1798–1878), following the restructuring of the China firm Magniac & Company. As the British East India Company's monopoly on trade with China expires, Jardine,

Matheson and Company begins importing tea to England and shipping opium to China.

July 9: Congress passes a law banning liquor from Indian reservations.

September 21: Colombian privateer-turned-pirate Pedro Gilbert captures the American brig *Mexican* off the coast of present-day Stuart, Fla., capturing $20,000 in silver bound for Rio de Janeiro. When a crewman asks Gilbert about disposition of prisoners, Gilbert replies, "Dead cats don't mew. You know what to do." His pirates lock the crew belowdecks and set the ship afire, but the captive crewmen manage to escape.

1833 Massachusetts, New York, and Pennsylvania ban state-sanctioned lotteries. Triad member Li Jiangsi informs associate Li Kui that the Increase Brothers Society is now known as the Three Dots Society. Initiates greet one another with the rhyming jingle *"Kaikou buliben, chushou bulisan."* The former "five dot twenty-one" password is replaced by "three, eight, twenty-one."

May 12: A protest against repressive police tactics turns riotous at Coldbath Fields, Clerkenwell, England. Constables suffer heavy casualties, including one officer fatally stabbed. His men lock the *Mexican's* crew below decks and torch the ship, but the prisoners escape and douse the fire, limping back to Salem, Mass., after six weeks at sea.

1834 January 1: New York conducts its final state lottery under prevailing legislation.

The British warship HMS *Curlew* sinks Captain Pedro Gilbert's pirate ship off the coast of West Africa, capturing Gilbert alive for subsequent extradition to the U.S.

June 9: Massachusetts authorities hang five unnamed pirates.

July 7–9: Riotous mobs led by street gangs attack New York City's Bowery Theater and Chatham Street Chapel, along with the homes of prominent abolitionists.

November 1: Poker is first mentioned in print, as a card game played on Mississippi riverboats.

September 12: Francisco Ruiz hangs for piracy in Massachusetts.

December 2: Henry Joseph hangs for piracy in Massachusetts.

1835 Sir William Hooker publishes the first drawing of a coca plant ever seen in England, in an issue of the *Companion to the Botanical Magazine.* Parliament bans all forms of animal fighting in Britain. Louisiana lawmakers once again outlaw casinos. Construction begins on New York City's Halls of Justice, commonly known as "The Tombs." India's colonial government establishes a "Thuggee and Dacoity Department," led by William Sleeman, to pursue homicidal cultists. By 1839 the unit captures 3,000 Thugs,

of whom 466 are hanged, 1,564 transported, and 933 imprisoned for life. While the cult allegedly disbands in the 1850s, the department continues operation until 1904, when it is renamed the Central Criminal Intelligence Department.

April 1: Future financier and robber baron James "Diamond Jim" Fisk Jr. born in Bennington, Vt.

June 11: Pedro Gilbert and three of his crewmen hang in Boston, following their conviction as pirates.

June 21: Two street gangs, the native-born American Guards and the Irish immigrant O'-Connell Guards, fight a pitched battle at the intersection of Crosby and Grand Streets, in New York City. Fighting spreads to the Five Points district, where a local physician, Dr. W.M. Caffrey, is killed while aiding wounded victims.

July 6: After months of unrest, capped by the murder of a local doctor, militia officers hang five gamblers at Vicksburg, Miss.

1836 May 27: Future financier and robber baron Jason "Jay" Gould born in Roxbury, N.Y.

June 17: The French Chamber of Deputies abolishes the national lottery and announce that all casinos nationwide will close by December 31, 1837.

1837 Condemned for its dilapidation, Coulter's Brewery in New York City is converted to squalid tenement housing. Most of its new residents are Irish or African American, living in constant tension.

September 24: Future U.S. political kingmaker Marcus Alonzo "Mark" Hanna born in New Lisbon (now Lisbon), Ohio.

December 31: Casino gambling becomes illegal in France.

1838 As opium smuggling reaches 200,000 chests (1,400 tons) per year, Chinese Emperor Mínníng imposes a death penalty for drug smuggling.

January 1: South Australia's first official horse track opens in Adelaide.

May: Ilanun pirates attack a combined fleet of Malayan, Chinese and European ships along the eastern Malay Peninsula. A British warship intervenes, sinking one Ilanun vessel and capturing 17 pirates.

May 30: Canadian smuggler and pirate Bill Johnston leads an attack on the passenger steamer *Sir Robert Peel,* docked at Wellesley Island, N.Y., and set it afire.

1839 Kentucky boasts more than 3,500 hemp plantations, producing over 18,000 tons of fiber which sells at prices ranging from $90 to $180 per ton.

January 12: Edward Coleman, a founder of the Forty Thieves, becomes the first man hanged at

New York City's Halls of Justice, for the beating murder of his wife.

February 26: Jockey Jem Mason rides "Lottery" to victory in England's first Grand National Steeplechase.

March 18: Lin Zexu, appointed as imperial commissioner to suppress the opium traffic, orders all foreign traders in China to surrender their opium, thus touching off the First Opium War.

May: Lin Zexu forces Sir Charles Elliott, Chief Superintendent of Trade and British Minister to China, to surrender 20,000 chests of opium. Destruction of the drugs begins on June 3.

July 7: Drunken British and American sailors vandalize a temple in Kowloon, killing a Chinese national named Lin Weixi. British authorities demand the privilege of "extraterritoriality," permitting trial of the rioters before an English judge. Refusing to surrender six accused defendants, British officers "convict" them in Canton (now Guangzhou), but release them upon their return to England.

August: British "adventurer" Sir James Brooke arrives with his pirate crew at Sarawak, on Borneo, to begin local raiding.

August 23: British forces occupy Hong Kong, then a minor trading post.

October: Sir Charles Elliott orders a blockade of the Pearl River, to prevent Chinese attacks on British trading ships.

November 3: A blockade runner, the *Royal Saxon*, draws fire from British warships en route Guangdong. Chinese officials accuse Britain of protecting opium smugglers.

1840 American pharmacies offer medicinal preparations of cannabis, while their counterparts in Persia sell hashish. New England traders import 24,000 pounds of opium, prompting Customs officials to impose a special tax on incoming drugs. Kentucky farmers produce 6,000 tons of hemp (cannabis) fiber, while their slaves enjoy the plant's intoxicating qualities. Behram, a member of the Thugee cult in India, confesses ro 125 murders committed between 1790 and 1830, with another 806 committed by his gang of 25 to 50 stranglers.

January 14: China's Qing Emperor asked all foreigners in China to stop aiding British aggression.

June: A British expeditionary force from Singapore reaches Guandong, China, with 15 barracks ships, 4 steam-powered gunboats and 25 smaller boats with 4000 marines commanded by Sir James Bremer. Bremer demands compensation for losses suffered by interruption of the opium trade, including destruction of confiscated drugs. When Chinese authorities fail to comply, the force

blockades the mouth of the Pearl River and moves on to take Chusan and Xiamen.

1841 January: British forces capture China's Bogue forts, defending the Pearl River, seizing the high ground above Canton, defeating a Chinese army at Ningpo, and capturing the military post at Chinghai.

January 21: Sir Charles Elliott lands at Possession Point, on the island of Hong Kong, declares it a "barren rock," and claims it for England.

May: Construction begins on a new casino in Homburg, Germany.

May 12: The first ladies' temperance union meets in New York City.

1842 August 29: After British forces occupy Shanghai, China's government approves the Treaty of Nanking, ending the First Opium War. Under terms of the treaty, China pays $21 million in compensation to British merchants and the government itself, as reimbursement for the costs of war, while ceding Hong Kong as a British crown colony "in perpetuity."

1843 Le Club des Hachichins — the Hashish Eater's Club — opens in Paris, France.

January 4: A servant murders retired pirate captain Hippolyte de Bouchard at his home, near Palpa, Peru.

July 18: Future lawman-gambler Virgil Earp born in Hartford, Ky.

August 16: The Kursaal casino opens in Homburg, operated by François and Louis Blanc.

November 24: Richard Croker, future boss of New York's Tammany Hall, born in Blackrock, Ireland.

1844 February: British naval forces burn the village headquarters of Malayan pirate captain Tuanku Abbas on northern Borneo.

May 7: New York's state legislature authorized creation of a professional police department for New York City.

May 24: British gambler William Crockford dies in London, leaving a fortune equivalent to $5 million.

May 25: Parliament passes a law permitting police to enter any gaming house upon a request by two or more householders.

September: Pirates under Abdulla Al-hadj loot a British merchant vessel at Murdu, northern Borneo.

1845 New York's state legislature passes a law prohibiting public sale of liquor.

August 8: Britain's new Gaming Act renders gambling debts legally unenforceable. The law remains in effect until September 1, 2007.

1846 May 13: Congress declares war against Mexico. Before the conflict ends on February 2, 1848, future U.S. Presidents Zachary Taylor (1784–1850) and Franklin Pierce (1804–69) serve as military commanders in Mexico, smoking cannabis with their troops. In a letter to his family, Pierce says that marijuana is "about the only good thing" to be found in Mexico.

1847 New York State repeals its ban on public sale of liquor. *Curtis' Botanical Magazine* prints the first image of peyote.

May: A British warship engages Balinini pirates near Brunei, destroying a squadron of their vessels in a day-long battle.

1848 Thomas Chambers opens the El Dorado gambling house in San Francisco, paying $40,000 rent per month from average monthly profits of $200,000. Pirates based at Saribas, on Borneo, kill 300 victims during this year.

Spring: A punitive force from Manila destroys a pirate stronghold on Balanini Island, off Malaya.

March 19: Future lawman, pimp and gambler Wyatt Earp is born in Monmouth, Ill.

1849 Various California towns begin individual licensing of gambling halls.

January: Germany's National Assembly bans all gambling after May 1.

February: Chinese pirate Chui A-poo kills two British officers at Hong Kong, for insulting him.

Spring: Chinese pirate Shap-'ng Tsai sinks four opium ships — three British and one American — in the South China Sea.

August 13: The San Francisco Police Department begins operation with 34 men under Captain Malachi Fallon.

September: A British naval squadron finds 100 captive ships held for ransom by pirate Shap-'ng Tsai at Tien-pai, China, but Shap-'ng Tsai escapes. Another squadron destroys ships belonging to pirate Chui A-poo in Bias Bay, northeast of Hong Kong, killing more than 400 buccaneers and capturing Chui himself. Sentenced to exile for life to Van Diemen's Land (now Tasmania), Chui hangs himself in jail before he can be transported.

October: Three British warships pursue Shap-'ng Tsai's pirates to Haiphong, Vietnam, destroying 58 junks with 1,200 cannon and 3,000 crewmen in a two-day battle at sea. Shap-'ng Tsai escapes once more, with six junks and 400 men, surrendering to the Chinese government and accepting a naval commission.

1850 The Los Angeles County Sheriff's Department is created. Hashish finds its way to Greece, while European surgeons use a tincture made from coca leaves as anesthetic during throat surgery. Philadelphia author Frederick Hollick publishes his *Marriage Guide*, encouraging sexually dysfunctional couples to try hashish. He writes: "The true aphrodisiac, as I compound it, acts upon the brain and nervous system, not as a stimulant, but as a tonic and nutritive agent,

thus sustaining its power and the power of the sexual organs also."

1851 April 22: Susan B. Anthony, Elizabeth Cady Stanton, Lucretia Mott, and other early feminists found the Women's State Temperance Society of New York.

April 24: Future lawman-gambler Morgan Earp born in Pella, Iowa.

August 14: John Henry "Doc" Holliday born in Griffin, Ga.

1852 New Orleans creates a police force with 12 officers and 345 patrolmen under Chief John Youenes.

April 5: Angered by Burma's slow payment of reparations from the First Anglo-Burmese War, British forces ignite a new conflict by occupying Martaban.

April 12: British troops capture Rangoon.

April 14: British forces advance to seize Burma's Shwedagon Pagoda in Yangon.

April 23: Pirates named only as Clements and Reid hang in Virginia.

May 19: British forces seize Bassein, Burma.

June 3: Pegu, Burma, falls to British troops.

October 2: Prince Charles Lucien Bonaparte of Canino ends a week's gambling at the Kursaal casino with a profit of 560,000 francs.

October 9: Rear Admiral Charles Austen, brother of the author Jane Austen, occupies the Burmese city of Prome.

October 23: William Poole and other Bowery Boys beat bartender Charles Owens at Florence's Hotel on Broadway, in Manhattan.

December: James Andrew Broun-Ramsay, 1st Marquess of Dalhousie and British colonial governor of India, informs King Pagan of Burma that Britain will henceforth control tor province of Pegu.

1853 Parliament bans off-track betting on horse races throughout Great Britain, whereupon illegal bookmaking thrives. Scottish physician Alexander Wood (1817–84) invents the hypodermic needle and syringe, experimenting with morphine injections.

January 20: The Second Anglo-Burmese War ends without a treaty, as Britain proclaims annexation of Lower Burma, including the coastal provinces of Ayeyarwady, Bago, and Yangon. British traders immediately begin importing large quantities of Indian opium, selling it through a government-controlled monopoly.

October 12: Dead Rabbits gang leader John Morrissey faces champion James "Yankee Sullivan" Ambrose in a bare-knuckly boxing match, in Boston Corners, Mass. Spectators riot in the 37th round, after Ambrose strikes a kneeling Morrissey, and referees award the bout to Morrissey.

1854 Malay author Abdullah bin Abdul Kadir finds chewing of khat prevalent in Al Hudaydah, Yemen's fourth-largest city.

May: The modern Boston Police Department is founded, after 223 years of experimentation with alternate law enforcement systems. Jonathan Pereira's *Elements of Materia Medica and Therapeutics*, published in Philadelphia, mentions cannabis as a medical agent. American author Bayard Taylor publishes *The Lands of the Saracen; or, Pictures of Palestine, Asia Minor, Sicily and Spain*, including a chapter on "The Vision of Hashish." He describes how the drug "revealed to me deeps of rapture and suffering which my natural faculties never could have sounded." Quaker poet John Greenleaf Whittier (1807–92) uses cannabis as a metaphor for slavery and cotton in "The Haschish."

July 26: Bowery Boys member William Poole faces Dead Rabbits leader John Morrissey in a boxing match at Amos Dock, N.Y. On July 28 the *New York Times* reports Morrissey "terribly beaten and left friendless."

1855 Female temperance activists in Lawrence, Kan., stage the first American saloon raid. Cocaine is extracted from coca leaves for the first time. Before year's end, New York neurologist Leonard Corning (1855–1939) injects a cocaine solution as a spinal anesthetic during surgery.

February: Allan Pinkerton creates the Pinkerton National Detective Agency in Chicago, supported by six major railroads.

February 25: NYPD officer Lewis "Lew" Baker, a friend of John Morrissey and frequent Tammany Hall enforcer, shoots Bowery Boys member William Poole at Stanwix Hall, a bar on Broadway in Manhattan. Poole dies from his wounds on March 8. Baker faces three successive juries on murder charges, all of which deadlock without reaching a verdict.

1856 British colonial authorities tax the cannabis trade in India, while increasing opium production in Lower Burma.

April 26: Prince Florestan I of Monaco grants Albert Aubert and Napoléon Langlois a concession to build and operate a casino and bathing establishment.

October 8: Qing imperial officials board a Chinese ship, the *Arrow*, and arrest 12 Chinese subjects suspected of smuggling and piracy. British officials in Guangzhou demand their release under terms of the Treaty of Nanking, since the *Arrow* is registered in Hong Kong. Although subsequent investigation proves the *Arrow*'s registration has expired, Britain uses the incident to justify the Second Opium War (AKA The *Arrow* War).

October 23–November 13: British forces storm and capture various Chinese positions on the Canton River, including the Barrier Forts, the Blenheim Forts, the Bogue Forts, and the Dutch Folly Forts. They conclude by bombarding Canton and burning its suburbs.

December 14: The Villa Bellevue opens for gambling in Monaco, while Aubert and Langlois finish construction of a more elaborate hotel-casino.

1857 A legal ban on public gambling in France prompts Albert Aubert and Napoléon Langlois to sell their Monaco casino. Pierre Auguste Daval buys the operation. American author-explorer Fitz Hugh Ludlow (1836–70) publishes his memoir *The Hasheesh Eater*, reporting that under the influence of cannabis his "thought ran with such terrific speed that I could no longer write at all."

January: Chinese bakers in Hong Kong join a conspiracy to poison European residents, using bread laced with arsenic, but some botch the recipe, prompting a general alarm.

March 3: Apprised of the January poison plot, Britain's House of Commons narrowly passes a resolution stating, "That this House has heard with concern of the conflicts which have occurred between the British and Chinese authorities on the Canton River; and, without expressing an opinion as to the extent to which the Government of China may have afforded this country cause of complaint respecting the non-fulfilment of the Treaty of 1842, this House considers that the papers which have been laid on the table fail to establish satisfactory grounds for the violent measures resorted to at Canton in the late affair of the Arrow, and that a Select Committee be appointed to inquire into the state of our commercial relations with China." As a result, Prime Minister Henry John Temple, 3rd Viscount Palmerston (1784–1865), dissolves Parliament and schedules a new election on grounds that the House of Commons has voted to "abandon a large community of British subjects at the extreme end of the globe to a set of barbarians — a set of kidnapping, murdering, poisoning barbarians."

March 27–April 24: Britain's general election secures a pro-war Whig majority in the House of Commons. Parliament demands reparations for the *Arrow* incident. France soon joins the British campaign against China, using as its excuse the February 1856 execution of French missionary Auguste Chapdelaine by local authorities in Guanxi Province.

April 18: Future New York mafioso Giuseppe Calicchio born in Sicily.

July: British authorities in Hong Kong try American buccaneer Eli Boggs. While acquitted of murder, he is convicted of piracy.

July 4: Members of the Dead Rabbits gang

attack the Bowery Boys' headquarters in New York City, sparking a two-day street war.

October 28: Dead Rabbits assault a man in New York City's Fourth Ward. Police arrest one gang member, but others attack the officers and secure his release.

November: Future Mafia boss Charles Matranga born in Sicily. Admiral Sir Michael Seymour and James Bruce, 8th Earl of Elgin and 12th Earl of Kincardine, lead a combined Anglo-French force to occupy Guangdong, China.

December 8: Three Dead Rabbits beat and rob victim James Costello on Canal Street, in New York City.

1858 Foreign traders in China import 70,000 chests of opium. In England, the Rev. John Liggins publishes a pamphlet titled *Opium: England's Coercive Policy and Its Disastrous Results in China and India*, condemning the conduct of both Opium Wars.

May: Anglo-French coalition forces capture the Taku Forts near Tianjin, China.

May 28: Russia imposes the Treaty of Aigun on China, expanding Russian territory in China beyond the boundary established in 1689 by the Nerchinsk Treaty.

June 2: China's Xianfeng Emperor ordered Mongolian general Sengge Rinchen to guard the Taku Fort at Tianjin. Sengge soon faces a British naval force of 21 ships and 2,200 troops, commanded by Admiral Sir James Hope.

June 24: British sappers blow up iron obstacles planted by Chinese defenders in the Baihe River, protecting the Taku Fort. After a day-long battle, Chinese artillery repels a British invasion force.

June 26–27: Great Britain, France, Russia, and the United States sign a series of agreements collectively known as the Treaty of Tianjin, ending the first phase of the Second Opium War. The treaties open eleven more Chinese ports to foreign traders, permitted foreign legations in Peking (now Beijing), allow Christian missionary activity, and legalized the import of opium. Despite execution of those treaties, hostilities continue in China.

July 31: NYPD officers try to break up a crowd of "roughs" on Canal and Mott Streets. but are overwhelmed and disarmed, ordered to leave the neighborhood and "mind their own business."

August 1: The Bowery Boys and Dead Rabbits brawl at Centre and Worth Streets in New York City, killing one innocent bystander.

1859 February 13: Dead Rabbits riot on Mulberry Street, in New York. Gang member "Fatty" Welch is killed, with several others wounded.

1860 California lawmakers ban banking games, wherein players bet against the house. Published reports claim that 1,138 legal alcohol distilleries

in the U.S. produce 88 million gallons of untaxed liquor annually.

January: Mafioso Raffaele Agnello arrives in New Orleans from Palermo, Sicily, to join his brother Joseph.

Summer: An Anglo-French force of 173 ships and 17,700 men sails from Hong Kong to seal the Bohai Gulf, capturing the port cities of Dalian and Yantai, China.

July 13: Albert W. Hicks, AKA William Johnson, hangs for piracy in Mew York City. His execution is the last in the U.S. for this offense, although slaver Nathaniel Gordon is hanged on February 21, 1862, under provisions of the Piracy Act of 1820.

August 3: Anglo-French coalition forces land at Bei Tang, two miles from the Taku Fort, while another body of troops captures Tientsin and marches inland toward Peking.

August 21: The Taku Fort falls to foreign troops.

August 30: Future NYPD legend Giuseppe "Joe" Petrosino born in Padula, Italy. His family emigrates to New York City in 1874.

September 12: Spanish gambler Thomas Garcia wins 800,000 francs at the Kursaal casino.

September 18: Anglo-French forces clash with Sengge Rinchen's Mongolian cavalry near Zhangjiawan, before proceeding toward the outskirts of Peking for a decisive battle in Tongzhou District. Negotiations between Britain and China's Xianfeng Emperor break down after British diplomatic envoy Harry Parkes and his entourage are arrested and tortured, with several diplomats executed.

September 21: Western coalition forces annihilate Sengge Rinchen's 10,000 troops at the Battle of Palikao.

October 6: Anglo-French troops invade Peking, liberating Harry Parkes and his surviving companions. Invaders proceed to loot the Summer Palace and Old Summer Palace or artwork and other treasures.

October 18: James Bruce, Lord Elgin, orders Peking's Summer Palace burned, but cancels his original plan to destroy the Forbidden City. Chinese officials belatedly ratify the Treaty of Tianjin, officially ending the Second Opium War with the Convention of Peking.

November 2: Future con artist and gang boss Jefferson Randolph "Soapy" Smith II born in Newnan, Ga.

1861 American author Thomas Bailey Aldrich (1836–1907) writes "Hascheesh," a poem describing his experience with cannabis, which he dubs the "Honey of Paradise, black dew of Hell!"

March 2: In the U.S., Nevada Territory separates from Utah Territory. A new statute soon bans games of chance.

March 27: Parliament proclaims Victor Emmanuel II (1820–78) king of a newly-united Italy. Some historians date the Sicilian Mafia's creation from this period.

April 12: The U.S. Civil War begins with the Confederate bombardment of Fort Sumter in Charleston Harbor, S.C. New Orleans mafioso Joseph Macheca and others soon become wealthy by smuggling contraband past the Union naval blockade. In the North, war profiteers make millions of dollars selling shoddy, overpriced goods to the Union Army.

1862 The Merck pharmaceutical firm in Darmstadt, Germany, begins commercial extraction of cocaine from coca leaves.

January 22: Future mafioso Vito Cascio Ferro born at Bisacquino, in the Sicilian province of Palermo.

February 21: New York authorities hang Nathaniel Gordon, the last defendant executed for piracy in the United States.

July 1: Congress passes the Revenue Act of 1862, including imposition of a $20 license fee on retail liquor dealers, plus a tax of one dollar per barrel on beer and 20 cents per gallon on distilled spirits.

July 23: Future political fixer Timothy Daniel "Big Tim" Sullivan is born in New York City's Five Points district.

1863 Italy inaugurates a national lottery. The term "Mafia" receives its first public use in a Sicilian stage play, *I mafiusi di la Vicaria* ("The mafiosi of Vicaria Prison"). Corsican chemist Angelo Mariani markets Vin Mariani, a beverage mixing wine and cocaine.

March: François Blanc buys the Monaco casino resort concession for 1.5 million francs, with a license valid until April 1, 1913.

July 13–16: Mobs run wild through New York City in riots sparked by conscription for military service in the Civil War. Blacks are particular targets, but organized gangs also clash to settle old scores and engage in extensive looting. Final estimates of casualties range from 120 to 2,000 dead, and 2,000 to 8,000 injured.

1864 Baron Niccolò Turrisi Colonna publishes a study titled *Public Security in Sicily*, including reference to a "sect of thieves" operating throughout Sicily. Scholars now consider this the first published reference to the Mafia, though Colonna never used its name.

1865 New Orleans mafioso Joseph Macheca established a steamship company, involves himself in local Democratic politics, and begins to organize Sicilian immigrant criminals into a gang called the Innocents. Frenchman Pierre Oller creates the first recognized gambling pool, which he calls *parier mutuel* ("mutual stake" or "betting

among ourselves"). In England, the system is called "Paris mutuals," later evolving to its present "pari-mutuel" name.

April 9: The Confederate States of America surrender, ending the U.S. Civil War.

April 14: John Wilkes Booth assassinates President Abraham Lincoln in Washington, D.C.

July 5: The U.S. Department of the Treasury creates a "Secret Service Division" to pursue counterfeiters, led by Chief William Wood.

September: Massachusetts state legislators create the Massachusetts State Police.

1865–70 The first traceable Mafia family operates in Uditore, Sicily, as a religious charity, the "Tertiaries of Saint Francis," led by Antonino Giammona and a priest, Father Rosario, employed as chaplain at Palermo's Vicaria Prison.

1866 Louisiana legislators pass a new law requiring all lottery brokers to register with the state and pay a tax equivalent to 5 percent of their profits. The Jerome Park Racetrack opens in the North-West end of Fordham, Westchester County (now in the Bronx), N.Y.

January 6: Future New York mafioso Nicolo "Nicholas" Morello born in Corleone, Sicily.

March 12: The Gunjah Wallah Company of New York City offers its first batch of imported "Hasheesh Candy" for sale, continuing over the next four decades. Advertisements describe it as "The Arabian Gunje of Enchantment confectionized — A most pleasurable and harmless stimulant — Cures Nervousness, Weakness, Melancholy, &c. Inspires all classes with new life and energy. A complete mental and physical invigorator."

May: Confederate military veterans found the original Ku Klux Klan in Pulaski, Tenn.

October: New York boxer, gambler, and Dead Rabbits associate John "Old Smoke" Morrissey wins election to Congress with support from Tammany Hall. He serves from March 4, 1867, to March 3, 1871, having declined to seek re-election in 1870.

November 12: Future revolutionary leader and high-ranking Triad member Sun Yat-sen born in Cuiheng, China.

1867 Sicilian authorities convict mafioso Rosario Meli of murder. He escapes from custody and surfaces in New Orleans the following year, as a subordinate to Raffaelo Agnello in Agnello's brewing war against rival Joseph Macheca.

April: Leaders of the KKK gather in Nashville, Tennessee, to reorganize their "social club" as a paramilitary terrorist group opposing Congressional Reconstruction in the former Confederacy.

May 2: Future mafioso Giuseppe "The Clutch Hand" Morello is born in Corleone, Sicily.

1868 The Louisiana Lottery Company, a group of illegal gamblers from New York, receives exclusive state authorization to operate a lottery for the next 25 years.

February: Prussian lawmakers pass a statute banning all games of chance after 11:00 P.M. on December 31, 1872.

September 3: Future Chicago "Black Hand" extortionist Samuele Cardinelli, AKA Salvatore Cardinella, born in Italy.

October: Joseph Macheca's Innocents receive their first media attention during the year's presidential campaign, terrorizing black Republican voters in the French Quarter of New Orleans.

October 28: Gunmen ambush and kill Sicilian immigrant Litero Barba following a meeting of the Innocents at the Orleans Ballroom, in New Orleans. Police initially blame African Americans, but later suspect rival gangster Raffaele Agnello.

December: Joseph Agnello, brother of New Orleans mafioso Raffaele Agnello, hosts a party at his Royal Street home to negotiate peace between rival Sicilian factions. The meeting turns violent, with Agnello lieutenant Alphonse Mateo suffering a gunshot to the face, while rival Joseph Banano from Messina is shot in the back. Both victims survive.

1869 Nevada legalizes gambling, with a minimum age of 17 for players and a quarterly licensing fee of $250 payable to county officials. New York's Kew Gardens receives its first shipment of coca seeds. Philadelphia garment workers found America's first major labor union, the Knights of Labor, led by Uriah Smith Stephens (1821–82). Los Angeles creates its first paid police force, with six officers hired to serve under City Marshal William Warren.

February 13: The magazine *Frank Leslie's Chimney Corner* publishes "Perilous Play," an anonymous short story written by Louisa May Alcott (1832–88) which describes misadventures of two young hashish-eaters. They find true love in the end, with the girl telling her paramour, "Heaven bless hashish, if its dreams end like this!"

February 15: Joseph Agnello and other gang members invade the Chartres Street headquarters of their Messinian rivals. Joseph Banano, Giovanni Casabianca, Pedro Allucho and two other targets escape with minor shotgun wound.

April 1: Mafia gunman Joseph Florada kills Raffaele Agnello outside the Macheca produce store in New Orleans.

July 15: Future mafioso Fortunato "Charles" Lo Monte born in Sicily.

July 22: Joseph Agnello avenges his brother's murder, joining Salvador Rosa to execute Messinian rivals Pedro Allucho and Joseph Banano near the French Market in New Orleans.

September 1: Temperance activists found the Prohibition Party in Chicago.

September 24: Efforts by robber barons James Fisk Jr. and Jay Gould to corner the U.S. gold market spark a financial panic on "Black Friday," with the face value of gold Double Eagle coins dropping from 62 percent to 35 percent. Gould loses most of his profit in subsequent litigation.

December 6: A moonshiner in Camden County, Mo., assassinates Deputy U.S. Marshal Theodore Moses as Moses sleeps in a lodging house.

1870 The Stuppagghieri Mafia clan receives its first publicity in Monreale, Sicily.

January 1: Member of New York City's Tenth Avenue Gang beat German immigrant John Merkle to death outside his home. Gangsters Patrick Fitzpatrick and James Strang face trial at the Jefferson Market Street Court on February 25.

January 5: James Logan, a prominent member of New York City's Nineteenth Street Gang, quarrels with ex-gang member Jerry Dunn at a Houston Street saloon, after Dunn insults Logan's girlfriend. They step outside, where Dunn mortally wounds Logan with a pistol. Dunn escapes after police arrive.

February 17: Retired smuggler and pirate Bill Johnston dies in Canada.

April 10: Members of the Nineteenth Street Gang stone two NYPD officers after they arrest Thomas Quinn for drunk and disorderly conduct. One officer suffers a serious head wound before reinforcements arrive.

June 22: President Ulysses Grant (1822–85) signs legislation creating the U.S. Department of Justice, officially beginning operations on July 1.

December 28: Bystanders narrowly avert a pistol duel between Rep. John Morrissey and a stranger who spat on him in a saloon on New York City's 23rd Street.

1871 Congress appropriates $50,000 for the Department of Justice to form a branch for "the detection and prosecution of those guilty of violating federal law." DOJ leaders delegate those duties to the Pinkerton National Detective Agency under contract.

March 14: Authorities in Barton County, Mo., sue Constable Wyatt Earp of Lamar, on charges of misappropriating fees collected for support of local schools.

March 31: James Cromwell of Lamar, Mo., sues Constable Wyatt Earp, alleging that Earp falsified court documents referring to money Earp collected from Cromwell to satisfy a judgment, thereby swindling Cromwell out of $75.

April 1: The prosecutor in Lamar, Mo., charges Constable Wyatt Earp and two codefendants — Edward Kennedy and John Shown — with stealing three horses valued at $100 each from William Keys on March 28. Deputy U.S. Marshal J.G. Owens arrests Earp on April 6. A formal indictment is issued against the three defendants on May 15. Earp subsequently flees Missouri, resulting in dismissal of the criminal charge and two pending civil lawsuits.

July 8: The *New York Times* begins publishing evidence of corruption against William "Boss" Tweed, allegedly after refusing a $5 million bribe to suppress the material. Tweed is arrested in October and held on $8 million bond pending trial. Convicted in 1873, he receives a 12-year prison term (reduced on appeal), and serves one year. He is then rearrested on civil charges and confined to debtor's prison, pending payment of $6 million in debts or submission of a $3 million bond.

October 8–10: The Chicago Fire kills at least 125 persons (based on corpses found), while destroying 17,500 buildings and leaving 90,000 of the city's 300,000 citizens homeless. Looting briefly replaces gambling and prostitution as the Windy City's primary criminal activity.

October 12: India's Criminal Tribes Act, inspired by crimes of the allegedly-extinct Thuggee cult, defines residents of 160 communities in northern India as "born criminals." Subsequent amendments extend the designation to tribes in the Bengal Presidency (1876) and the Madras Presidency (1911).

1872 February 22: The Prohibition Party holds its first national congress in Columbus, Ohio, nominating James Black as its candidate for president of the U.S.

April 20: Joseph Florada, Joseph Maressa, and two other gunmen kill Joseph Agnello at the Picayune Pier in New Orleans.

June 18: Moonshiners ambush two deputy U.S. marshals in Pickens County, S.C., as they escort a prisoner to jail. Deputy Maddison Mitchell dies from his wounds, while his companion survives.

July 26: Future Chicago "Black Hand" leader Vincenzo Cosmano, AKA James "Sunny Jim" Cosmano, born in Brancaleone, Italy.

September 4: The New York *Sun* publishes secret court documents exposing a vast financial scandal surrounding the Crédit Mobilier of America, a firm created in 1862 to build the Union Pacific Railroad. Congress creates a special committee to investigate the scandal on December 2, ultimately revealing the theft of some $21 million, along with "gifts" of stock to Vice President Schuyler Colfax and 30-odd members of Congress representing both major parties. The House of Representatives subsequently censures two members: James Brooks of New York, on February 27, 1873, and Oak Ames of Massachusetts, on February 28. The U.S. Senate voted to expel James Patterson of New Hampshire for his involvement in the scandal, on March 26, 1873, but

no action resulted since Patterson's term had expired on March 3.

October: Prussian authorities close the gambling centers at Ems and Wiesbaden, Germany.

December 31: Homburg's casinos enjoy their last day of action, before shutting down in compliance with anti-gambling legislation.

1873 Englishman Joseph Jaggers wins £80,000 pounds at roulette in Monte Carlo, by exploiting imperfections in the wheel that skews odds in favor of certain numbers.

May 28: Canadian lawmakers establish the North-West Mounted Police, forerunner of the modern RCMP.

December 22: Residents of Fredonia, N.Y., found the Woman's Christian Temperance Union.

1874 Sicily's Mafia gets international attention after leaders Antonino Leone and Giuseppe Esposito kidnap an English banker for ransom, severing his ears and the tip of his nose to accelerate payment. While seeking a nonaddictive alternative to morphine, London chemist C.R. Alder Wright creates an even stronger narcotic, diacetylmorphine, popularly known as heroin. San Francisco authorities ban opium smoking within the city limits, thereby restricting it to Chinatown.

March 17: Future Pittsburgh, Pa., mafioso Gregorio Conti born in Sicily.

April 13: North Carolina moonshiners murder a deputy U.S. marshal named Burns.

August 22: Deputy U.S. Marshal Horace Metcalf is slain while trying to arrest a Missouri bootlegger.

November: Delegates assembled in Cleveland, Ohio, found the National Woman's Christian Temperance Union.

1875 Cultivation of hashish is recognized in Greece. Nevada raises the legal gambling age to 21, increases county license fees to $400, bans three-card monte, and makes cheating a felony. Mafioso Rosario Meli and several associates migrate from New Orleans to San Francisco with several associates. Italian troops pursue Mafia boss Antonino Leone into the Sicilian mountains, suffering major losses before soldiers capture Leone and Giuseppe Esposito. Esposito escapes from custody before trial. Leone receives a life sentence, but soon flees prison to hide in North Africa. Opium smoking is banned in Virginia City, Nev.

April 4: Future New York mafioso Antonio Cecala born in Sicily.

May 10: U.S. Treasury agents stage a nationwide series of "Whiskey Ring" raids, exposing a network of corruption through which mostly–Republican politicians have siphoned millions of dollars from federal taxes on liquor. President

Ulysses Grant (1822–85) appoints ex-senator John Brooks Henderson to serve as special prosecutor. The first trial convenes in St. Louis, Mo., in October 1875. Before the scandal ends, 110 defendants are convicted, with more than $3 million recovered.

August: Dr. Gaspare Galati, owner of the Fondo Riella citrus estate, flees Palermo, Sicily, with his family after refusing Mafia demands for tribute. He informs Italy's Minister of the Interior that mafiosi have killed 23 people in Uditore (a village of 800 inhabitants) during 1874 alone, without any police investigation.

November 1: New York City voters elect John Morrissey to the first of two state senate terms.

December 4: William "Boss" Tweed escapes from Sheriff William C. Conner in New York and flees to Spain in the guise of a common seaman. Spanish police arrest him on arrival and return him to New York City on November 23, 1876.

1876 The first reports of "Black Hand" extortion involving Italian immigrants issue from St. Louis, Mo. NYPD establishes a "Steamboat Squad" to combat gangs and river pirates on the city's waterfront. Future New York City gang leader Paul Kelly is born Paolo Antonio Vaccarelli in Sicily. George Remus, future Ohio attorney and "King of Bootleggers," is born in Germany.

January 16: NYPD officers arrest two members of a burglary ring operating from headquarters on Joiner Street. With two accomplices arrested earlier, they receive eight-year sentences at trial.

March: Alexander Graham Bell (1847–1922) receives a master patent for the electric telephone from the U.S. Trademark Office. Hungarian engineer Tivadar Puskás (1844–93) soon invents the first telephone switchboard.

May 1: Future mayor and political boss Edward Joseph Kelly born in Chicago.

May 10: America's first world's fair, the Centennial International Exhibition, opens in Philadelphia. Before it closes on November 10, many of the fair's 10,164,489 visitors enjoy the Turkish Hashish Exposition.

August 2: Jack McCall murders gambler and occasional lawman James Butler "Wild Bill" Hickok in Deadwood, S.D. Hickok dies holding two pair — aces and eights, henceforth known as the "dead man's hand."

August 8: Future U.S. senator and gambling syndicate ally Patrick Anthony McCarran born in Reno, Nev.

October 1: A dealer in untaxed tobacco murders Deputy U.S. Marshal Felix Torbett in Henry County, Tenn.

December 2: New York's *Illustrated Police News* runs a drawing captioned "Secret Dissipation of

New York Belles: Interior of a Hasheesh Hell on Fifth Avenue," depicting intoxicated young women with hashish water-pipes.

December 18: Future Tammany boss James Joseph "Jimmy" Hines born in New York City.

1877 Propaganda Due (P2) founded as a Masonic lodge in Turin, Italy. Authors Leopold Franchetti and Sydney Sonnino publish their study of the Mafia's "violence industry" in Sicily.

February 11: Future newspaper publisher, race-wire boss, and tax evader Moses Annenberg born in Kalvishken, East Prussia.

March: Ohio-born pirate William Henry "Bully" Hayes suffers a fatal gunshot wound from crewmen Peter "Dutch Pete" Radeck near Jaluit Atoll, in the Marshall Islands.

March 19: Ignazio Lupo, AKA Ignazio "Lupo the Wolf" Saietta, born in Corleone, Sicily.

May 7: Future Ohio mafioso Giuseppe Romano born in Sicily.

May 12: Counterfeiters James and Dee Bailey murder Deputy U.S. Marshal Maston Greene near Comanche, Tex.

June: South Carolina moonshiners murder Deputy U.S. Marshals James Letford and Alfred McCreory in retaliation for a recent liquor raid.

June 21: Ten Irish labor activists identified as members of the "Molly Maguires" hang in Pennsylvania for murder and other acts of coalfield terrorism.

July 14: A general strike paralyzes American railroads, sparking a wave of violence nationwide.

July 24: Future Mafia boss Calogero "Don Calò" Vizzini born in the Sicilian Province of Caltanissetta.

July 26: Federal troops kill 26 union protesters in the "Battle of the Viaduct," at Halsted and 16th Streets in Chicago.

August: Kentucky's Louisville Grays baseball team drop from first place after losing seven games and tying one against the Boston Red Stockings and Hartford Dark Blues, letting Boston win the pennant. Team president Charles Chase receives two anonymous telegrams predicting that the Grays will lose another game on August 21 which they do, with a score of 7–0. League president William Hulbert investigates, securing telegrams from Western Union indicating that indicated that pitcher Jim Devlin, left fielder George Hall, and utility player Al Nichols threw games in return for cash bribes. All three, with team captain Bill Craver, are banned from baseball for life. Craver's expulsion is based on his refusal to cooperate with the investigation, although no hard evidence is found against him.

October: Ex-lawman Wyatt Earp meets dentist-turned-gambler and gunman John Henry "Doc" Holliday at a casino in Fort Griffin, Tex.

December 10: Deputy U.S. Marshal George Ellis suffers fatal gunshot wounds while serving a warrant on an illegal distiller in Casey County, Ky. Before collapsing, Ellis kills his assailant.

December 31: Deputy U.S. Marsha Van Hendrix is shot and killed while arresting a South Carolina moonshiner.

1878 Britain's Parliament passed the All-India Opium Act, limiting recreational opium sales to registered Indian opium-eaters and Chinese opium-smokers, while prohibiting sales to workers from Burma. Pari-mutuel betting is introduced at Churchill Downs, in Kentucky. San Francisco authorities accuse Rosario Meli and several associates with murder, but drop that charge after one suspect confesses to the killing as "a matter of honor." Meli and the rest are convicted of robbery instead, paving the way for Meli's later deportation.

February 16: Vincenzo Colosimo, AKA James "Big Jim" Colosimo, born in Colosimi, Italy.

April 12: William "Boss" Tweed dies from pneumonia at Manhattan's Ludlow Street Jail.

April 19: South Carolina moonshiners shoot and kill Deputy U.S. Marshal Rufus Springs during a liquor raid.

May 1: Ex-gang boss and Tammany Hall leader John Morrissey dies from pneumonia in Troy, N.Y.

September 10: Deputy U.S. Marshal Jack Kimbrew suffers gunshot wounds during a liquor raid in Hancock County, Ga. He dies on September 11.

September 28: Salvatore Marino, boss of a New Orleans Mafia faction known as the Stoppaglieri or Stuppagghieri, dies from yellow fever.

November: Mafioso Giuseppe Esposito flees Sicily via Marseilles, France, bound for New York City.

1879 A New Zealand resident named Ekberg invents the first mechanical totalizer, a hand-operated calculating machine for use in pari-mutuel betting system for horse racing.

Spring: Fugitive mafioso Giuseppe Esposito migrates from New York City to New Orleans, changing his name to "Vincenzo Rebello" and joining Joseph Macheca's crime family.

July 22: John Lynch, a member of the Pitt Street gang, is arrested by NYPD officers for stealing ducks from a merchant on Hester Street. Released for lack of evidence, Lynch is jailed again on July 22 for stealing four pails from the Eldridge Street store of an Abraham Bernstein. This time, Lynch pleads guilty.

October: Despite having a wife and family in Sicily, Giuseppe Esposito marries Sarah Castagno in New Orleans, under his "Vincenzo Rebello" pseudonym.

November 27: Virgil Earp is appointed as a Deputy U.S. Marshal for the Arizona Territory.

December: Wyatt Earp settles in Tombstone, Ariz., with brothers James and Virgil. Over the next nine months, they are joined by brothers Morgan and Warren Earp, as well as Doc Holliday.

1880 Triad societies claim 3,600 members in China, capitalizing on native animosity toward foreigners.

January 4: Future Chicago mobster Michele "Mike" Merlo born in Sambuca Zabut, Sicily.

January 13: Robert Suffrage, a member of New York City's Stable Gang, receives a sentence of two years and three months imprisonment for stealing a gold watch in October 1879. En route to The Tombs, Suffrage attacks his NYPD escort and is returned to the courtroom, indicted of assault within 10 minutes.

February 10: NYPD arrests six members of the Brady Gang — including leaders Edward, Hugh, and John Brady — for operating an illegal distillery. Five of the six are convicted in December, then sentenced to time served and released.

February 29: Members of the Smoky Hollow Gang beat NYPD officer Thomas Stone after he tries to arrest a cohort for loitering on Columbia Street. Bystanders intervene before the thugs can crush Stone's skull with a paving stone, but his injuries prove fatal, claiming his life on April 1.

April 24: A bomb detonates at Monaco's Monte Carlo casino, injuring several persons.

September 1: Rosario Meli arrives in New York City, escorted by an SFPD captain and an Italian detective, pending deportation to Italy for trial on charges of brigandage and murder. Meli denies any criminal activity and subsequently disappears en route to his native country.

April 26: Civilians rescue another NYPD officer, Sergeant Walsh, from assault by the Smoky Hollow Gang, after he arrests member Edward Glynn for loitering. A second gang member, John Mungerford, is held and charged with Officer Stone's murder.

May 5: NYPD officers arrest Dutch Mob member John "Little Andy" Anderson on suspicion of robbing Michell, Myers & Co. on April 29. Stolen jewelry valued in excess of $1,500 is found in Anderson's possession.

July 10: While en route to raid a gathering of 200 gang members in Central Park, NYPD officers disrupt a brawl between the rival Eightieth and Ninetieth Street Gangs, arresting nine combatants.

July 25: Deputy U.S. Marshal Virgil Earp accused Frank McLaury of stealing six army mules from Camp Rucker, near Tombstone, Ariz. McLaury is a member of the "Cowboys" rustling gang led by "Old Man" Newman Haynes Clanton, later deadly rivals of the Earps and Doc

Holliday. Around the same time, Wyatt Earp is appointed deputy sheriff for southern Pima County, surrounding Tombstone.

August 11: NYPD officers charge Portland Street Gang members John Collins and John Murphy with robbing Daniel Reardon, a visitor from Maine.

September 30: Grady Gang leader John "Travelling Mike" Grady dies in his office on Sixth Avenue, in New York City. Relatives claim foul play, but an autopsy attributes his death to cardiac congestion, resulting from a long bout of pneumonia.

October 4: Future journalist and crime writer Alfred Damon Runyan born in Manhattan, Kan.

October 28: Cowboys gang member William "Curly Bill" Brocius fatally shoots town marshal Fred White in Tombstone, Ariz. Wyatt Earp arrests Brocius and transports him to Tucson for trial. Virgil Earp, already a deputy U.S. marshal, succeeds White at Tombstone's town marshal on October 30. A judge rules the shooting accidental and releases Brocius on December 27, 1880.

November 9: Wyatt Earp resigns as a deputy sheriff in Pima County, Ariz., following a vote-fraud scandal in Sheriff Charlie Shibell's campaign to defeat challenger Bob Paul.

December 6: Moonshiners kill Deputy U.S. Marshal John Hardie during a raid in Marshall County, Ala.

1881 Kansas bans manufacture and sale of alcoholic beverages. Missouri state legislators ban gambling. New Zealand's Gaming and Lotteries Act bans casinos, off-track totalizer betting, and most lotteries. Publican George Adams (1839–1904) promotes his first lottery in Sydney, Australia. Members of the Yakuza establish Japan's ultra-nationalist *Genyosha* (Dark Ocean Society). Citizens of New Orleans establish a Vigilance Committee to fight crime and civic corruption.

January: Wyatt Earp becomes part-owner of the gambling concession at the Oriental Saloon in Tombstone, Ariz.

February 1: Arizona's legislature creates Cochise County, a new jurisdiction carved from Pima County, including the town of Tombstone. Wyatt vies for a gubernatorial appointment as sheriff, but Territorial Governor John Fremont chooses John Behan instead. Earp later claims that Behan promised him (Earp) appointment as undersheriff, but Behan denies it. Earp briefly retires from law enforcement, focused on gambling and mining.

February 5: Future Illinois gangster Shachna Itzik Birger, AKA Charles "Charlie" Birger, born in Lithuania.

March 15: Bandits bungle an attempt to rob a stagecoach near Benson, Ariz., killing Wells Fargo guard Bud Philpot and passenger Peter Roerig. Virgil Earp names the gunmen as Cowboy syndicate members. Suspect Luther King quickly escapes from Sheriff John Behan's jail, while alleged accomplices Jim Crane, Harry Head, and Billy Leonard evade arrest but later die in unrelated shootings. Cowboys spread rumors that Doc Holliday led the holdup party.

June 19: Future mayor and mob front man James John Walker born in New York City.

July: Mafia assassin Giutano Ardota murders rival Black Hand leader Anthony Labrusio in New Orleans, reportedly on orders from Giuseppe Esposito. Cowboy gang members "Curly Bill" Brocius and Johnny Ringo murder brothers Isaac and William Haslett at Hauchita, N.M., in retaliation for the death of associates Harry Head and Bill Leonard, shot while robbing the Hasletts' store several weeks earlier. Later in the month, Brocius leads a Cowboy ambush of a Mexican trail herd at San Luis Pass, killing six vaqueros and torturing eight survivors.

July 5: Detective David Hennessy arrests New Orleans mafioso Giuseppe Esposito and delivers him to U.S. Immigration agents for deportation. Brothers Antonio and Charles Matranga assume command of Esposito's crime family.

July 13: At an immigration hearing in New York City, Giuseppe Esposito identifies himself as Vincenzo Rebello and denies any criminal activity. The ruse stalls deportation proceedings.

August 13: Newman "Old Man" Clanton and four Cowboy associates — Jim Crane, Dixie Lee Gray, Billy Lang and Charley Snow — die in an ambush by Mexicans at Guadalupe Canyon, N.M. Gang members Billy Byers and Harry Ernshaw escape unscathed.

September 8: Bandits rob a passenger stagecoach in Cochise County, Ariz. Although masked, two of the gunmen — Cowboy gangsters Pete Spence and Frank Stilwell (a deputy under Sheriff John Behan) — are identified by their voices and the print of Stilwell's custom-made boot heel. County deputies arrest Spence and Stilwell for the robbery, but they post bond.

September 21: With his true identity established, Giuseppe Esposito is deported to face murder charges in Italy. His departure sparks a search for his betrayers among mafiosi in New Orleans and New York. Before year's end, Esposito is convicted in Rome and sentenced to life imprisonment.

October 8: Virgil Earp names Spence and Stilwell as suspects in another stage holdup, near Contention City, Ariz. On October 13 he jails both on that charge, plus a federal charge of interfering with a mail carrier in the September 8 holdup.

October 13: During a bitter competition for the police chief's job in New Orleans, Chief of Detectives Thomas Devereaux engages in a shootout with detective-cousins David and Michael Hennessy. Michael is wounded, while his cousin kills Devereaux.

October 23: NYPD officers arrest four members of the Mulberry Street Gang for assaulting and robbing two men. Defendant John Burke is held for trial, while the other three escape with judicial reprimands.

October 26: Doc Holliday joins brothers Morgan, Virgil and Wyatt Earp for a shootout with members of the Cowboys gang near (but not in) the OK Corral at Tombstone, Ariz. The victorious Earps kill Billy Clanton, Frank McLaury and Tom McLaury, while Holliday and two of the Earps suffer nonfatal wounds. Survivor Ike Clanton files murder charges against Holliday and the Earps on October 30, but Justice of the Peace Wells Spicer declares the shootings justified. A local grand jury declines to reverse Spicer's ruling on December 16.

December 28: Gunmen, presumed to be Cowboy gang members, ambush Virgil Earp on Allen Street in Tombstone, Ariz., leaving him badly wounded by shotgun blasts. A hat alleged to be Ike Clanton's is found lying nearby. Wyatt Earp wires U.S. Marshal Crawley Dake, in charge of Arizona, seeking and receiving appointment as a deputy marshal.

1882 NYPD establishes a detective bureau. Feuding ignites between New Orleans Mafia factions, as Giuseppe Provenzano of Palermo accuses Joseph Macheca and Charles Matranga of failing to support Giuseppe Esposito. Chicago Police Chief William McGarigle forges an alliance with gang boss Michael Cassius McDonald, but loses his mob-backed bid to become Cook County's sheriff.

Mid-January: Wyatt Earp sells his gambling concessions at Tombstone's Oriental Saloon.

January 17: Future gambling czar Arnold "The Brain" Rothstein born in New York City.

February: Future Chicago gang lord Johnny Torrio born Giovanni Torrio, in the village of Irsina, Italy.

February 2: Plagued by public criticism, Virgil and Wyatt Earp tender their resignations as deputy U.S. marshals for Arizona Territory. Presiding marshal Crawley Dake declines to accept them. On the same day, jurors acquit Ike Clanton on a charge of wounding Virgil Earp. Wyatt sends a message to Clanton, seeking reconciliation of their feud.

March 18: Snipers fire on Morgan and Wyatt Earp at a pool hall in Tombstone, Ariz., killing Morgan and wounding a bystander, while narrowly missing Wyatt.

March 20: Wyatt Earp kills Frank Stilwell at the railroad depot in Benson, Ariz., allegedly during a Cowboy ambush of brother Virgil and his wife. Ike Clanton escapes unharmed, calling Stilwell's death a summary execution. On the same day, Wyatt and Warren Earp, with Doc Holliday and various other associates, organize a "posse" and launch a three-week "vendetta ride" against Cowboy rivals, lasting until April 15.

March 21: Authorities in Tucson, Ariz., charge the Earp brothers, Doc Holliday, and two friends with Frank Stilwell's murder. Sheriff John Behan pursues them with a posse in Cochise County.

March 22: Wyatt Earp's "vendetta riders" kill Cowboy gang member Florentino "Indian Charlie" Cruz at South Pass in Arizona's Dragoon Mountains.

March 24: Wyatt Earp and company meet a group of Cowboy gunmen at Iron Springs, in the Whetstone Mountains. The "posse" kills Curly Bill Brocius and sidekick Johnny Barnes, while eight other Cowboys escape.

April: Jurors acquit David and Michael Hennessy of murdering Thomas Devereaux, but Chief Tom Boylan fires both defendants. Hennessy forms a private security agency.

April 2: Pete Spence faces trial on charges of killing Morgan Earp, but prosecutors drop their case after the judge rules incriminating testimony from Spence's wife to be inadmissible.

April 15: The "Earp posse" disbands. Wyatt Earp and Doc Holliday leave Tombstone, Ariz., for Colorado.

May 8: President Chester Arthur (1829–86) signs the Chinese Exclusion Act, banning immigration of "skilled and unskilled laborers and Chinese employed in mining" for a decade. Chinese already living in the U.S. organize the first Tong societies for mutual protection.

July 14: Cowboy gunman Johnny Ringo is found dead, shot through the head, in Turkey Creek Canyon, a day's ride from Tombstone, Ariz. Despite rumors that he was killed by Wyatt Earp and/or Doc Holliday, authorities rule his death a suicide. Subsequent newspaper reports place Holliday in Salida, Colo. — 500 miles from the site of Ringo's slaying — on July 7.

October 19: Opponents of mandatory abstinence from alcohol found the Personal Liberty League of the United States in Milwaukee, Wis.

December 11: Future crime-fighting mayor Fiorello Henry La Guardia born in Greenwich Village, Manhattan.

1883 Vito Cascio Ferro faces his first criminal charge, for assault, in Sicily. Police in Sulphur, Calcasieu Parish, La., uncover a proto–Mafia organization, the Favara Brotherhood, whose members come from Favara, in the Sicilian province of Agrigento. The U.S. Congress increases its tariff on smoking opium from $6 to $10 per pound. Members of the WCTU found the World's Woman's Christian Temperance Union.

March 8: Whyos gang member Mike McGloin hangs at The Tombs, New York City, for the murder of saloonkeeper Louis Hannier.

June: A group of gamblers, pimps and gunmen in Dodge City, Kan., organize the "Dodge City Peace Commission" to intimidate their competition. Members include Wyatt Earp, Bat Masterson, and Luke Short, opposing mayor and saloonowner Alonzo Webster.

September 27: Deputy U.S. Marshals Addison Beck and Lewis Merritt die in a shootout with a bootlegger, in Muskogee County, Indian Territory (now Oklahoma).

October 16: John "Johnny the Mick" Walsh, leader of New York City's Walsh Gang, dies in a shootout with Dutch Mob members John Irving and Billy Porter at Shang Draper's saloon. Irving also dies in the exchange, while Draper and Porter are wounded.

October 19: Joseph Petrosino joins the NYPD.

November: *Harper's Monthly Magazine* publishes an article about a hashish den in New York City, where smokers "indulge their morbid appetites."

1884 New Orleans Police Chief Tom Boylan resigns to form the Boylan Protective Police with partner David Hennessy. The city council commissions Boylan's group "as patrolmen with full police powers." The *New York Times* notes that Boylan's men are "neatly uniformed and are a fine-looking and intelligent body of men, far superior to the regular city force." John Torrio emigrates to New York City with his widowed mother, soon joining Paul Kelly's Five Points Gang. Austrian neurologist Sigmund Freud (1856–1939) treats his personal depression with cocaine, then extolls the drugs virtues of cocaine in his paper "On Coca," writing that cocaine produces "exhilaration and lasting euphoria, which is in no way differs from the normal euphoria of the healthy person…. You perceive an increase in self-control and possess more vitality and capacity for work…. In other words, you are simply more normal, and it is soon hard to believe that you are under the influence of a drug." By year's end, the Merck company extracts 3,179 pounds of cocaine from coca leaves.

March 1: Two Whyos gang members escape from prison on Hart's Island, N.Y., while serving six months for vagrancy. Authorities dismiss two guards on suspicion of aiding the escape.

March 14: Future gang boss Maxwell "Kid Twist" Zwerbach born in New York City.

April 5: NYPD officers find gangster Camillo

Farach's corpse on Staten Island, stabbed in the chest and back. They suspect his business partner, Antonio Flaccomio, of murder, but a coroner's jury rules Farach's death a suicide.

May 24: Deputy Marshal Walter Killion is shot and killed by a saloon owner in Lily, Ky., after citing the proprietor for liquor violations.

June 4: An NYPD officer finds the corpse of George Leonidas Leslie, founder of the Leslie Gang, at Tramps' Rock in Westchester County.

July 1: Allan Pinkerton dies in Chicago, from an infected bite on his tongue.

July 12: A moonshiner murders Deputy U.S. Marshal L.J. McDonald near Mitchellville, Tenn.

July 22: Prosecutors charge New York fence Marm Mandelbaum (1818–94) with multiple counts of grand larceny and receiving stolen goods. She posts bond and flees to Canada with an estimated $1 million, spending the rest of her life in Toronto.

October 20: Future Cleveland, Ohio, mafioso Joseph "Big Joe" Lonardo born in Sicily.

October 21: Jurors convict Whyos gang members John Belfield, James Brown, and James Reilly of assaulting Englishman Henry Stanley in a Pell Street saloon and robbing him of $26.

November 19: Future Los Angeles mafioso Giuseppe Ernesto Ardizzone, AKA Joseph "Iron Man" Ardizzone, born in Piana dei Greci (now Piana degli Albanesi), Sicily.

December 25: Dennis Corcoran, a Poydras Market Gang member and former employee of the New Orleans City Hall Department of Improvements, fatally stabs Deputy Sheriff Daniel Haugherty in a personal quarrel.

1885 California legislators ban gambling. Inspired by the commercial success of Vin Mariani, Georgia druggist John Stith Pemberton (1831–88) begins production of a cocaine beverage called Pemberton's French Wine Coca.

April 6: Future Kansas City mafioso Franco DeMaio, AKA Frank "Chee-Chee" DeMayo, born in Sicily.

June 12: Future mafioso Nicola Gentile born in Siculiana, Sicily.

July 4: New York jurors convict Whyos gangsters John Clinton and John Kelly of assaulting victim Naty Glashiem and stealing his gold watch.

July 6: Unknown gunmen murder Deputy U.S. Marshal William Miller near Goodlettsville, Tenn., as he searches the mountains for illicit whiskey stills.

August 10: NYPD Captain Gunner arrests five members of the 74th Street Gang for killing Bohemian immigrant Nawclaw Kalat in a street brawl, earlier the same day.

October 11: Moonshiners ambush two deputy

U.S. marshals near Jamestown, Tenn., as they escort a prisoner to jail. Deputy Marshal Miller Hurst dies in the attack, while the prisoner escapes.

November 26: NYPD officers arrest Whyos Michael Flannagan and Patrick O'Brien for assaulting and robbing fireman William Clark. O'Brien's brother is jailed later in the day, for stealing a gold watch to finance Patrick's legal defense.

1886 Georgia legislators ban alcoholic beverages statewide, prompting John Pemberton to replace his Pemberton's French Wine Coca with non-alcoholic Coca-Cola. The new "soft" drink contains nine milligrams of cocaine per glass until 1903, when the drug is removed entirely. Britain assumes control of the Shan state in northeastern Burma, attempting to monopolize the local opium trade. The Merck company extracts 158,352 pounds of cocaine from coca leaves. NYPD Chief of Detectives Thomas Byrnes publishes *Professional Criminals of America*. After earning a small fortune — and his famous nickname — from a scheme dubbed "The Prize Package Soap Sell Swindle," Soapy Smith establishes a criminal empire in Denver, Colo. Texas physician John Raleigh Briggs experiments with peyote.

February: Future mobster Frank McErlane born in Chicago, Ill.

March 11: Future Pennsylvania mafioso Stefano LaTorre born in Sicily.

May 3: Pinkerton guards and corporate goons attack striking employees outside the McCormick Harvesting Machine Company plant in Chicago, killing two picketers. On May 4, strikers and sympathizers rally in Haymarket Square. When police attempt to disperse them, someone lobs a pipe bomb, killing Officer Mathias Degan and wounding several others. Police respond with promiscuous gunfire, leaving 12 persons dead (eight police and four strikers) and at least 110 wounded (50 strikers and 60 officers). Eight strike leaders are charged with Officer Degan's murder, convicted at trial in June. Four are hanged on November 11, 1887. Governor John Altgeld pardons the others on June 26, 1893. Meanwhile, the police commander who ordered dispersal of the Haymarket rally has been dismissed for corruption.

May 4: Acting under orders from Governor James Rusk (1830–93), National Guardsmen fire on a crowd of 14,000 strikers at the Milwaukee Iron Company's rolling mill in Bay View, Wis., killing seven protesters.

May 15: Future mafioso Vincenzo "Tiger" Terranova born in Corleone, Sicily.

May 17: Congress passes a law mandating the teaching of temperance in schools throughout Washington, D.C., all U.S. territories, military academies at Annapolis and West Point, on Indian reservations, and at all "colored schools under Federal control." President Grover Cleveland signs the law on May 20.

May 20: Future Chicago mob financier Jacob "Greasy Thumb" Guzik near Kraków, in the Austro-Hungarian Empire (now Poland).

May 28: Future Florida Mafia boss Santo Trafficante Sr. born in Cianciana, Sicily.

July 19: Future New York mobster Alfonso "The Butcher" Sgroia born in Italy.

July 31: Salvatore Maranzano, AKA "Don Turridru," born in Castellammare del Golfo, Sicily.

October 2: Brothers Hugh and Matt O'Brian, leaders of the Live Oak Boys in New Orleans, quarrel at Bill Swan's Fireproof Coffee House saloon on Gallatin Street. Matt wounds Hugh with a gunshot, and is arrested. Hugh flees the city to avoid testifying against his brother, but Matt is still imprisoned on a charge of "assault less than mayhem," effectively crushing the gang.

December 8: Samuel Gompers (1850–1924) founds the American Federation of Labor in Columbus, Ohio, serving as its president until his death (except for one year in 1894–95).

1887 Two Triad groups, the Big Sword Society and White Lotus Society, instigate attacks on Christian missionaries in China. Congress ban importation of opium by Chinese, and forbids anyone from importing weak opium (containing less than 9 percent morphine) to manufacture smoking opium. Parke-Davis and Co., a Michigan-based pharmaceutical firm, furnishes dried peyote buttons to German pharmacologist Dr. Louis Lewin for study.

January 18: Romanian chemist Lazar Edeleano synthesizes amphetamine at Universität Berlin, calling it phenylisopropylamine, but fails to explore its medical properties.

April 14: Mafia gunmen fail in an attempt to kill Manhattan grocer Antonio Flaccomio, suspected of killing mafioso Camillo Farach I in 1884 and aiding police investigation of Sicilian counterfeiting syndicates.

April 25: Future Detroit mobster Gaspari Milazzo born in Castellammare del Golfo, Sicily.

May 26: Race track betting legalized in New York State.

June 1: Detective Jonas Brighton tries to arrest brothers Ike and Phineas Clanton on a charge of cattle-rustling, in Springerville, Ariz. Ike resists and Brighton kills him, whereupon Phineas surrenders.

June 6: Future Detroit mafioso Cesare "Chester" Lemare (often spelled "LaMare") born in Castellammare del Golfo, Sicily.

June 8: Future Texas mafioso Rosario "Papa Rose" Maceo Sr. born in Palermo, Sicily.

November 1: The Knights of Labor strike against sugar plantations in Lafourche, St. Mary, and Terrebonne Parishes, La. Ten thousand mostly-black workers walk off their jobs. On November 23, state militiamen and white vigilantes fire on strikers and their families at Thibodaux. Estimates of the death toll range from 30 to 300.

November 5: Bootlegger John Hogan kills Deputy U.S. Marshal John Carleton while resisting arrest in Denison, Tex.

December 1: Future Manhattan mafioso Bonaventura "Fat Joe" Pinzolo born.

1888 Joseph Shakespeare wins election as mayor of New Orleans, naming David Hennessy to serve as chief of police. Paul Hennings, a botanist at Berlin's Royal Botanical Museum, publishes a description of peyote's properties.

January 12: U.S. Secretary of the Treasury Charles Fairchild writes to Speaker of the House of Representatives John Carlisle, complaining that federal restrictions on opium importation have served "to stimulate smuggling, extensively practiced by systematic organizations on the Pacific coast. Recently completed facilities for transcontinental transportation have enabled the opium smugglers to extend their illicit traffic to our Northern border. Although all possible efforts have been made by this Department to suppress the traffic, it is found practically impossible to do so."

January 23: Whyos co-leader Danny Driscoll is executed for killing prostitute Breezy Garrity during a gunfight with Five Points Gang member Johnny McCarthy.

January 27: Francesco Raffaele Nitto, AKA Frank "The Enforcer" Nitti, born in Salerno, Italy.

March 20: Future Cleveland racketeer Arthur "Mickey" McBride born in Chicago.

March 28: Future New York mafioso Vincenzo Giovanni Mangano, AKA Vincent "The Executioner" Mangano, born in Sicily.

April 23: Future Detroit mafioso Pietro Bosco and future Kansas City mafioso Joseph "Scarface" DiGiovanni born in Sicily.

May 11: Future Detroit mafioso Andrea Licato born in Sicily.

May 13: Zelig Harry Lefkowitz, AKA "Big Jack Zelig," born in New York City.

June 29: Future Melbourne gang leader Joseph Leslie Theodore "Squizzy" Taylor born in Brighton, Victoria, Australia.

July 5: Whyos leader Daniel Lyons kills rival pimp Joseph Quinn in a gunfight over prostitute Kitty McGown. Convicted of murder, Lyons is executed on August 21.

August 21: Deputy U.S. Marshal Sam Huges is shot and killed while arresting two Tennessee bootleggers.

October 14: Sicilian brothers Carlo and Vincenzo Quarteraro stab Antonio Flaccomio to death outside New York City's Cooper Union building. Carlo flees the country, while Vincenzo is arrested and charged with murder on October 22.

December 1: Moonshiners murder Deputy U.S. Marshal Thomas Goodson in Carter County, Tenn. Searchers find his corpse on December 11.

December 25: Future mafioso Nicholas Delmore, AKA "Nicholas Amoruso," born in San Francisco, Calif.

1889 Twelve-year-old Ignazio Lupo flees Sicily for New York City, to avoid prosecution for the murder of Salvatore Morello.

January 5: Future New York judge, missing person, and possible gangland murder victim Joseph Force Crater born in Eaton, Pa.

January 24: New Orleans mafioso Giuseppe Provenzano sends emissary Vincenzo Ottumvo to negotiate peace with rivals Joseph Macheca and Charles Matranga, who hack him to death with an axe. Chief of Police David Hennessey tries calls a peace conference between the warring gangs, but leaves the impression that he favors Provenzano.

February 11: Future Philadelphia mafioso Joseph "Joe Bruno" Dovi born.

March 3: Future Pittsburgh, Pa., mafioso Stefano Monastero born in Sicily.

April: New York jurors acquit Vincenzo Quarteraro of murdering Antonio Flaccomio. A disgruntled NYPD officer tells reporters that Italians are free to "kill each other."

July 15: Future Ohio mafioso Joseph "Big Joe" Porello born in Sicily.

July 20: Future New York mobster Ciro "The Artichoke King" Terranova born in Corleone, Sicily.

August 10: Moonshiners ambush and kill Deputy U.S. Marshal James Hager at his home in Wyoming County, W.Va.

November 21: Mafioso Giuseppe DeLucca murders Edward Cunningham in Dedham, Mass.

1890 Greek and Turkish authorities ban cultivation, importation, or use of hashish. Congress bans delivery of lottery materials via the U.S. mail. Thirty thousand Chinese led by members of the Big Sword and White Lotus Societies attack a Catholic church in Lungshui.

January 1: Jurors convict Giuseppe DeLucca for Edward Cunningham's murder. Mafiosi mark state witness Giacchino Cocchiara for death.

January 6: Future mafioso Nicholas Terranova born in Corleone, Sicily.

January 25: Police in New Haven, Conn., arrest five members of the Oak Street Gang for a series of local burglaries.

April 6: Provenzano family assassins ambush several Macheca-Matranga mobsters in New Orleans, killing two. Police use information from Macheca-Matranga informants to arrest the shooters.

April 13: A liquor violator shoots Deputy U.S. Marshal Robert Cox in Claremore, Okla. Cox dies on April 14.

May 1: Gunmen ambush brothers Antonio and Charles Matranga in New Orleans, wounding Antonio. Police later charge Giuseppe Provenzano with ordering the attack.

May 6: A shootout between longshoremen allied with the rival Matranga and Provenzano crime families leaves three Matranga partisans wounded in New Orleans. Antonio Matranga, shot for the second time in five days, loses one leg.

July: New Orleans jurors convict Provenzano gang members for the murders of April 6, but their judge throws out that verdict and orders a new trial.

July 2: Congress passes the Sherman Antitrust Act, limiting cartels and monopolies.

July 13: While escorting a liquor violator to jail in Ada, Okla., Deputy U.S. Marshal Jim Billy is shot and killed by the prisoner's cousin.

September 27: Future Chicago mafioso Giuseppe "Joe" Aiello born in Bagheria, Sicily.

October 1: Fueled by exposés of the Chinese "Yellow Peril," published in newspapers owned by William Randolph Hearst (1863–1951), Congress passed the McKinley Bill, restricting manufacture of smoking opium in the U.S. to American citizens and imposing a federal tax of $10 per pound. The tariff on imported opium is raised from $10 to $12 per pound.

October 15: Two days before his scheduled testimony in the second trial of Provenzano family killers, shotgunners ambush New Orleans Chief of Police David Hennessy. With his dying breath, Hennessy blames "the dagoes." Police respond by arresting 250 Italians.

October 18: Mayor Joseph Shakespeare appoints a "Committee of Fifty" to investigate Chief Hennessy's murder. That group employs Pinkerton agents, sends threatening letters to the Italian community, and establishes a "system of secret and anonymous denunciation."

November 20: After jail inmate Emmanuelle Polizzi names Joseph Macheca and Charles Matranga as the ringleaders of Hennessy's assassination, prosecutors indict 19 Italian suspects. They

include Macheca, Matranga, and four other mafiosi, plus 13 defendants with no apparent criminal ties.

November 30: Liquor smugglers disarm Deputy U.S. Marshal William Pitts at Lake West, Tex., killing Pitts with his own pistol.

December 8: Future New Jersey mafioso Ruggiero "Richie the Boot" Boiardo born in Naples, Italy.

1891 The Sittman & Pitt Company of Brooklyn, N.Y., markets a precursor to the modern slot machine, containing five drums and 50 card faces based on poker. Clergyman Charles Henry Parkhurst (1842–1933) founds the Society for the Prevention of Crime, challenging corrupt leaders of Tammany Hall and the NYPD.

January 26: Francesco Castiglia, AKA Frank Costello, born in Italy's Cosenza Province.

February 16: Trial begins in New Orleans for nine defendants in Chief Hennessy's murder. The court bars testimony from key witness Emmanuelle Polizzi, after he rambles incoherently on the stand. Two other witnesses refuse to testify. On March 13, Judge Joshua Baker directs a verdict of acquittal for defendants Charles Matranga and Bastian Incardona, based on insufficient evidence. Jurors acquit defendants Joseph Macheca, Antonio Bagnetto, and Antonio Marchesi and Gasperi Marchesi. Matranga and Bastian Incardona, while failing to reach a verdict on Antonio Scaffidi, Emmanuelle Polizzi, Pietro Monasterio. A local newspaper, the Times-Democrat, charges jury-tampering in an editorial that concludes: "Rise, outraged citizens of New Orleans!… Peaceably if you can, forcibly if you must!" On March 14 a lynch mob storms the jail, murdering 11 of the original 19 defendants. After the lynching, Mayor Shakespeare declares, "The Italians had taken the law into their own hands and we had no choice but to do the same." Italian protests to Washington are settled with payment of a $25,000 indemnity.

March 4: Future New York City mafioso Willie "Two-Knife" Altieri born.

April 18: Future Los Angeles mafioso Ignazio "Jack" Dragna born in Corleone, Sicily.

June 24: Future Kansas City mafioso James Balestrere born.

July 7: Future Philadelphia mafioso Salvatore Sabella born in Castellamare del Golfo, Sicily.

August 26: NYPD investigates "Black Hand" threats against cigar store owner Robert Castellano.

October 10: Stefano "The Undertaker" Magaddino, future Mafia boss of Buffalo, N.Y., born in Castellamare del Golfo, Sicily.

November 20: A moonshiner kills Deputy U.S.

Marshal Dan Osborne while resisting arrest in Cleburne County, Ala.

December 18: Future U.S. racketeer Owen "Owney the Killer" Madden born in Leeds, England.

1892 Sir William Robbinson (1836–1912), bans betting on horse races throughout the colony. Canada's criminal code bans all gambling except state-regulated on-track bookmaking. Survivors of the Provenzano Mafia family flee New Orleans, ceding control to the Matranga faction. Agitation from religious groups prompts authorities in New South Wales, Australia, to ban sweepstakes gambling, whereupon millionaire promoter George Adams moves to Tasmania. Anti-gambling and saloon reforms drive Soapy Smith from Denver, to Creede, Colo., where he establishes a new underworld network, operating from the Orleans Club, protected by his brother-in-law and gang member Deputy Sheriff William "Cap" Light. German explorer Carl Lumhotz describes ceremonial peyote use among the Huichol and Tarahumara people of Mexico, sending samples to Harvard University for analysis.

February 14: Charles Parkhurst attacks Tammany Hall in a sermon, saying, "While we fight iniquity, they shield and patronize it; while we try to convert criminals, they manufacture them." In a second sermon, on March 13, Parkhurst produces affidavits and other documentation of civic corruption.

March 4: Tennessee moonshiners shoot and kill Deputy U.S. Marshal Charles Stuart while trying to liberate one of their cohorts from jail.

April 1: Future New York mobster and government informer Alphonse "The Peacemaker" Attardi born.

May 11: Future Detroit mafioso Leonard "Black Leo" Cellura born in Italy.

May 20: Future U.S. drug enforcement leader Harry Jacob Anslinger born in Bern, Switzerland.

July 6: Pinkerton gunmen fire on striking workers at the Carnegie steel mill in Homestead, Pa. The resultant battle claims 11 lives, including seven Pinkertons and 11 strikers or spectators.

July 8: Future Chicago gang leader Charles Dean "Dion" O'Banion born in Maroa, Ill.

July 15: Future New York "White Hand" leader William "Wild Bill" Lovett born in Lixnaw, County Kerry, Ireland.

October 17: Deputy U.S. Marshal John Fields suffers fatal gunshot wounds during a Tennessee liquor raid. Future mobster Thomas Jefferson McGinty born in Cleveland, Ohio.

December 2: Future Detroit mafioso Joseph "Cousin Joe" Bommarito born in Sicily.

December 4: Sicilian mafioso Antonio Morello murders Francesco Meli, a prominent Camorra member in Brooklyn, N.Y. Reports in the *Brooklyn Daily Eagle* of January 19 and 23, 1893, ignore the organized crime connection, describing Morello as a "padrone" and victim "Francisco Mele" as a one-armed organ grinder.

1893 International Association of Chiefs of Police founded in the United States. Unione Siciliana created by Sicilian immigrant businessmen in Chicago, incorporated with the right to sell insurance two years later. Britain establishes the Indian Hemp Drugs Commission to investigate cannabis trafficking in India. British journalist William Thomas Stead (1849–1912) publishes *If Christ Came to Chicago*, exposing corruption in the Windy City.

January 20: Future Atlantic City mobster and political boss Enoch Lewis "Nucky" Johnson born in Galloway Township, N.J.

January 22: Future New York mobster Francesco Ioele, AKA "Frankie Yale," born in Italy.

January 26: Future mafioso Giuseppe Genco Russo born in Mussomeli, Sicily.

February 1: Marquis Emanuele Notarbartolo di san Giovanni, ex-mayor of Palermo and ex-governor of the Bank of Sicily, is stabbed to death by two assailants on the train from Sciara to Palermo. Police name the killers as mafiosi Matteo Filipello and Guiseppa Fontana, acting on orders from Don Raffaele Palizzolo — himself a member of parliament and a director of the Bank of Sicily. Palizzolo allegedly ordered the slaying as revenge for Notarbartolo exposing a bank fraud.

February 12: Future Detroit mafioso Giovanni "Papa John" Priziola born in Partinico, Sicily.

February 14: Deputy U.S. Marshal C.B. Brockus is shot while trying to arrest a North Carolina moonshiner. Brockus kills two assailants, while two others briefly escape. Brockus dies from his wounds on February 16.

February 24: Future Illinois mobster Frank Zito born in Palermo, Sicily.

March 8: The Morello-Terranova family arrives in New York City. Members Giuseppe Morello, Nicolo Morello, Ciro Terranova, and Vincenzo Terranova subsequently join the Mafia family led by Ignazio Lupo.

March 17: Future Kansas City mafioso Giuseppe "Joseph" DeLuca born in Sicily.

April 2: Future mobster Phillip "Dandy Phil" Kastel born on Manhattan's Lower East Side.

May 29: Future bandit and freelance hitman Thomas Camp, AKA Fred "Killer" Burke, born on a farm near Mapleton, Kan.

June 24: Deputy U.S. Marshal Calloway Garner killed during a liquor raid in Hardin

County, Tenn. A second deputy marshal is also wounded.

July 1: Future Buffalo, N.Y., mafioso and elected politician Giovanni "John" Montana born in Montedore, Italy.

July 5: A strike against the Pullman Palace Car Company sparks rioting in Chicago. Strikers set the 1892 World's Columbian Exposition afire in Jackson Park, destroying seven buildings. Mobs continue battling police in the streets, burning and looting railroad cars, until 14,000 federal and state troops arrive to crush the strike on July 10.

August 10: Moonshiners in Cleburne County, Ala., kill Deputy U.S. Marshal J. Perry Griggs while resisting arrest.

August 21: Future Chicago gangster Adelard Cunin, AKA George Clarence "Bugs" Moran, born in St. Paul, Minn.

August 22: Deputy U.S. Marshal Joe Gaines shot and killed by a drunken bystander after a raid on an illegal gambling hall in Pauls Valley, Okla.

August 30: Future political boss and U.S. Senator Huey Pierce Long Jr., AKA "Kingfish," born in Winnfield, La.

November: The On Leong Chinese Merchants Association, or On Leong Tong, begins operation in New York City, with headquarters on Mott Street, in Chinatown.

1894 State senator Clarence Lexow (1852–1910) leads the first public investigation of NYPD corruption, continuing into 1895. The Indian Hemp Drugs Commission issues a seven-volume, 3,281-page report on cannabis, including testimony from nearly 1,200 "doctors, coolies, yogis, fakirs, heads of lunatic asylums, bhang peasants, tax gatherers, smugglers, army officers, hemp dealers, ganja palace operators and the clergy." It concludes, "On the whole, if moderation and excess in the use of drugs are distinguished, which is a thing the witnesses examined have ... found it very hard to do, the weight of evidence is that the moderate use of hemp drugs is not injurious.... The question of the mental effects produced by hemp drugs has been examined by the Commission with great care. The popular impression that hemp drugs are a fruitful source of insanity is very strong, but nothing can be more remarkable than the complete breakdown of the evidence on which it is based. Popular prejudice has over and over again caused cases of insanity to be ascribed to ganja which have no connection whatever with it; and then statistics based on this premise are quoted as confirming or establishing the prejudice itself.... Absolute prohibition is, in the opinion of the

Commission, entirely out of the question.... There is no evidence of any weight regarding mental and moral injuries from the moderate use of these drugs.... Large numbers of practitioners of long experience have seen no evidence of any connection between the moderate use of hemp drugs and disease.... Moderation does not lead to excess in hemp any more than it does in alcohol. Regular, moderate use of ganja or bhang produces the same effects as moderate and regular doses of whiskey. Excess is confined to the idle."

January 1: Future Detroit mafioso Tony Mirabile Rizzo born in Italy.

January 9: Boston resident Pasquale Sacco is slashed to death with razors. Police suspect members of the Camorra or Mafia.

February 15: Future Detroit mobster and Unione Siciliana president Salvatore "Sam Sings in the Night" Catalanotte born in Trapani, Sicily.

March 1: Future Texas mafioso Salvatore "Sam" Maceo, AKA "The Velvet Glove," born in Palermo, Sicily.

March 8: Mafiosi Augusto Ferrari and Dante Regali stand trial in Providence, Rhode Island, for beating and robbing local banker John Caproni.

March 13: Englishman J.L. Johnstone invents the starting gate for horse races.

May 11: Three thousand employees of the Pullman Palace Car Company stage a wildcat strike in Chicago. The American Railway Union, led by Eugene Debs (1855–1926), joins the strike, involving some 250,000 workers in 27 states before President Grover Cleveland (1837–1908) sends U.S. marshals and 12,000 federal troops to Chicago on July 6, crushing the strike within days. The final toll includes 13 strikers were killed and 57 wounded, with $340,000 in property damage ($6.8 million today). Debs receives a six-month prison sentence for violating an anti-strike injunction.

June 4: Arkansas moonshiners ambush and kill Deputy U.S. Marshall Thomas Martin at his home.

June 16: Dave Beck, future president of the International Brotherhood of Teamsters, born in Stockton, Calif.

August 25: Future Detroit mafioso Frank Meli born in Terrasini, Sicily.

September 13: Deputy U.S. Marshal Thomas Grissom shot and killed in Pike County, Ark., while attempting to arrest a moonshiner.

November 24: Triad member Sun Yat-sen founds the revolutionary Revive China Society in Honolulu, Hawaii.

December 13: Future mobster Leo Berkowitz,

AKA Charles "Chuck" Polizzi, born in Cleveland, Ohio.

1895 The French Prefecture of Police creates a canine unit to help combat street gangs in Paris. Heinrich Dreser (1860–1924), a chemist employed by Bayer Laboratories in Elberfeld, Germany, dilutes morphine with acetyls to produce diacetylmorphine, a drug without the common side effects of morphine. Bayer calls the new drug heroin, for its "heroic" pain-relief abilities. Sir Edward Braddon (1829–1904), premier of Tasmania, rallies support for the Suppression of Public Betting and Gaming Act, which creates a state monopoly on betting run by transplanted gambler George Adams. Adams continues sweepstakes promotions until his death in 1904, when four ex-legislators receive five-percent shares of his gambling empire from Adams's will. State lawmakers abolish the Louisiana Lottery Company, which has earned $300 million with only small returns to its players. American mechanic Charles Fey invents a five-cent slot machine with three spinning wheels, called the Liberty Bell, premiering in a San Francisco gambling hall, soon known as the "one-armed bandit." Congress bans interstate transportation of lottery materials.

January 1: Future FBI director John Edgar Hoover born in Washington, D.C.

January 27: Police Chief Dexter Gaster acknowledges continuing Mafia activity in New Orleans.

May 25: Residents of Danville, Ill., lynch two alleged gangsters. Police warn any others still remaining to leave town.

June 21: Fearing that imprisoned mafioso Giuseppe DeLucca is conspiring against him with Antonio Caro Armblissa, Boston barber Gioacchino Cocchiara shoots Armblissa.

June 30: Future Chicago mobster Franklin Rio born in Lovato, Italy.

July 4: Police in Waterbury, Conn., blame mafioso Antonio Spadola for shooting victim Nicolo Errico.

July 20: NYPD Commissioner Theodore Roosevelt (1858–1919) appoints Joe Petrosino to the rank of detective sergeant, commanding the department's homicide division.

August 20: Deputy U.S. Marshal Boyd Arnett shot and killed while attempting to arrest a moonshiner in White Oak, Ky.

September 11: Newspapers report that Patrolman Charles Fiore, expected to testify at Antonio Spadola's murder trial in Waterbury, Conn., has been threatened by members of the local Italian community.

December 12: Future Detroit mobster Santo "Cockeyed Sam" Perrone born in Italy.

December 25: Future racketeer Abraham Landau born in New York City.

1896 January 25: Future gambling magnate John Moores born in Eccles, near Salford, Lancashire, England.

February 10: Deputy U.S. Marshal Edward Thurlo shot and killed while searching a liquor smuggler's wagon in Duncan, Okla.

February 25: Future U.S. Senator and mob investigator John Little McClellan born in Sheridan, Ark.

March 5: Deputy U.S. Marshal John Kirby is shot and killed with his own rifle while arresting two moonshiners near Holly Springs, S.C.

June 17: Future New Orleans mafioso Sylvestro Carolla, AKA "Sam Silver Dollar," born in Palermo, Sicily.

June 18: Mark Hanna's political machine secures the Republican presidential nomination for Ohio Governor William McKinley Jr. (1843–1901). McKinley defeats opponent William Jennings Bryan in the general election, on November 3.

July 6: Future New York mafioso Michele "Big Mike" Miranda born in Naples, Italy.

August 25: Future lawman, bandit, bootlegger, and syndicate hitman Vernon Miller born in Kimball, S.D.

September 21: Violence erupts at Leadville, Colo., during a strike by the Western Federation of Miners. Gunfire and dynamite explosions kill at least four strikers and one fireman, causing $50,000 in property damage. Governor Albert McIntire (1853–1935) sends National Guardsmen to protect strikebreakers, effectively crushing the strike.

December: The *British Medical Journal* publishes two personal reports of peyote's effects on human subjects.

1897 Sweden's government inaugurates a state lottery. Congress lowers the tariff on imported opium to $6 per pound, "experience having at last taught that it could not bear a higher rate without begetting an extensive surreptitious manufacture or serious smuggling operations." Following the tax cut, observers note that "the amount that passed through the customs houses … progressively increased." German pharmacologist Arthur Carl Wilhelm Heffter isolated mescaline from the peyote cactus.

January: Future Detroit mafioso Carmello Castiglione born in Sicily. Leaders of eight Mafia clans in Palermo convene to chart new avenues of commerce after Sicilian police raid their counterfeit currency factory. Quarrels between the clans in Malaspina and Uditore produce a bloody feud continuing through 1900.

January 23: Chinese gangsters Chew Tin Gop

and Le-Lum Jung murder Sum Yop Tong leader Fung Jing Toy in San Francisco, Calif.

February 5: NYPD Captain William Devery is arrested for bribery and extortion. Subsequent conviction on those charges compels his dismissal from the police department.

February 6: Louis "Lepke" Buchalter, future labor racketeer and boss of "Murder, Inc.," born in New York City.

February 10: Future Detroit mafioso Angelo Meli born in Terrasini, Sicily.

February 13: Future Detroit mafioso Vito Guglielmo "Black Bill" Tocco born in Terrasini, Sicily.

February 20: Future Los Angeles Mafia boss Nicolo "Mr. Nick" Licata born in Camporeale, Sicily.

March 4: William McKinley is inaugurated as President of the United States. On March 5 he names Ohio Senator John Sherman to serve as Secretary of State, whereupon Ohio's state legislature picks political boss Mark Hanna to fill Sherman's Senate seat.

April 7: Future journalist and underworld aficionado Walter Winchell (né Winschel) born in New York City.

July: The Klondike gold rush lures Soapy Smith from Colorado to Skagway, Alaska. Smith launches his third criminal empire, protected by Skagway's corrupt deputy U.S. marshal. His scams include a fake telegraph office in which the wires went only as far as the wall.

July 10: John "Legs" Diamond, AKA "Gentleman Jack," born to Irish immigrant parents in Philadelphia, Pa.

July 11: Future U.S. mobster Samuel "Sambo" Tucker born in Lithuania.

August 29: Arkansas moonshiners kill Deputy U.S. Marshals Joe Dodson and B.F. Taylor during a liquor raid in the mountains 35 miles from Russellville.

September 10: A posse led by Luzerne County's sheriff fires on striking coal miners near Lattimer, Pa., killing 19 and wounding 36. The victims, originally imported as strikebreakers, had changed sides to join the local miners' union. Investigators find that most were shot in the back.

September 18: Future mobster Morris Kleinman born in Cleveland, Ohio.

October 2: Future New York mafioso Giuseppe "Joe" Profaci born in Villabate, Sicily.

October 22: Future racketeer Louis Dalitz born in Boston, Mass.

November 14: Future Chicago mob boss Felice DeLucia, AKA Paul "The Waiter" Ricca, born in Naples, Italy.

November 23: Arthur Heffter conducts self-experiments with mescaline isolated from the peyote cactus.

November 24: Salvatore Lucania, AKA Charles "Lucky" Luciano, born in Lecara Friddi, Sicily. An article in the *Kansas City Star* mentions the Mafia for the first time in Missouri.

November 27: Future mafioso Vito Genovese born in Rosiglino, Italy.

December 10: Future Detroit mafioso Giuseppe "Joseph" Zerilli born in Terrasini, Sicily.

December 18: Future mafioso Cesare Manzella born in Cinisi, Sicily.

1898 Authorities in the Congo Free State ban absinthe. Bayer Laboratories markets heroin as an analgesic and a "sedative for coughs."

January 7: Disgraced NYPD Captain William Devery wins an appeal of his felony conviction and is reinstated to the force, with a promotion to inspector. He is promoted again, to deputy chief, on February 14, and to the chief's office on June 30.

January 25: Future gang leader and bootlegger Earl Wojciechowski, AKA "Hymie Weiss," born in Chicago.

March 16: Future mafioso Frank Cammarata born in Sicily.

April 20: Congress declares war on Spain. The "splendid little war" ends on December 10, leaving the U.S. in control of Cuba, Guam, the Philippines, and Puerto Rico.

June 13: Police in Springfield, Mass., charge mafioso Natale Giuliano with the public murder of an in-law, Pietro Fazzio. Intimidated witnesses soon recant their testimony.

July 7: Three members of Soapy Smith's gang steal $2,700 in gold from Klondike miner John Douglas Stewart in Skagway, Alaska. A local "Committee of 101" demands return of the gold, but Smith refuses, insisting that Stewart lost it "fairly" in Smith's casino. Vigilantes confront Smith at the Juneau Company wharf on July 8, killing him in a shootout which also claims the life of posse member Frank Reid.

August: Ermanno Sangiorgi assumes office as chief of police in Palermo, Sicily. Between November 1898 and January 1900 he submits a series of reports on Mafia activities to Palermo public prosecutor Vincenzo Consenza, forwarded to Prime Minister Luigi Pelloux. His December 1898 report states that "regrettably, the mafia's bosses act under safeguard of Senators, MPs, and other influential figures who protect them and defend them and who are, in their turn, protected and defended by the mafiosi."

October 12: In the third month of a miners' strike against the Chicago-Virden Coal Company in Virden, Ill., management imports 180 black strikebreakers and their families. Gunfire erupts, killing seven strikers and five company guards, with 40 strikers, four guards, and the train's engineer wounded.

1899 Gang warfare erupts between the Hip Sing Tong and On Leong Tong, for control of illegal gambling in New York's Chinatown, continuing until a peace treaty is signed in 1909.

January 1: Future gang boss Llewelyn Morris Humphreys, AKA Murray "The Camel" Humphreys, born in Chicago.

January 17: Future gang lord Alphonse Gabriel "Scarface Al" Capone born in Brooklyn, N.Y.

February 6: Future mafioso Joseph Massei, AKA Joe Massey, born in Detroit.

March 14: Deputy U.S. Marshal Joseph Heinrichs shot and mortally wounded by a bootlegger incarcerated overnight at Heinrichs's home in Tahlequah, Okla. Heinrichs dies from his wounds on March 15. The suspect flees, but is recaptured on March 16. A member of Heinrichs's staff is charged after the killer claims the posseman furnished his gun and ammunition for the murder.

April 10: Future Pennsylvania mafioso Giovanni "Johnny" Sciandra born in Montedoro, Sicily.

April 29: Striking members of the Western Federation of Miners dynamite the Bunker Hill Company's mill at Wardner, Ida., causing $250,000 damage. President William McKinley sends black troops from Brownsville, Tex., to arrest thousands and cage them in specially-built "bullpens."

May 5: Future labor racketeer Jacob "Gurrah" Shapiro born in Odessa, Russia.

Summer: WCTU activist Carrie Nation (1846–1911) stages her first saloon raid against Mart Strong's in Medicine Lodge, Kan.

July 27: Abner "Longy" Zwillman, AKA the "Al Capone of New Jersey," born in Newark.

August 18: Future U.S. racketeer Anthony Cornero Stralla, AKA Tony "The Hat" Cornero, born in Lequio Tanaro, Italy.

September 23: Future U.S. Attorney General and Supreme Court Justice Thomas Campbell Clark born in Dallas, Tex.

October 25: Rival mafiosi fail in an attempt to kill Francesca Siino, boss of Palermo's Malaspina family. Police chief Ermanno Sangiorgi persuades Siino to turn informer.

November 2: The Society of Righteous and Harmonious Fists in China, an anti-imperialist and anti–Christian group, begins China's "Boxer Rebellion." While Qing Dynasty forces join foreign troops to crush the rebellion on September 7, 1901, the upheaval and crushing debts from foreign reparations pave the way for dismantling of China's monarchy.

November 11: Trial begins in Milan for two railroad employees charges as accomplices in the February 1893 Mafia murder of Marquis Emanuele

Notarbartolo di san Giovanni. Notarbartolo's son Leopoldo names mafioso Guiseppa Fontana as one of his father's slayers, acting on orders from M.P. Don Raffaele Palizzolo, in testimony given on November 16. Prime Minister Luigi Pelloux calls a vote by Italy's Chamber of Deputies, stripping Palizzolo of immunity from prosecution while suspending telegraphic communications between Sicily and the mainland.

December 1: Future mafioso Gaetano "Tommy" Lucchese, AKA "Three-Finger Brown," born in Palermo, Sicily.

December 3: Chicago police arrest future Outfit mobster James "Fur" Sammons on rape charges. He is sentenced to a state reformatory on February 27, 1900.

December 4: Future New York mobster Morris Rosen born in Russia.

December 24: Future mobster Morris Barney "Moe" Dalitz born in Boston, Mass.

1900 The philanthropic Saint James Society mails free heroin samples to American morphine addicts, in hopes of breaking their addiction. New York saloon bouncer Edward Osterman (1873–1920), AKA Monk Eastman, creates a new 1,100-member gang — the Eastmans — to battle Paul Kelly's Five Points Gang for turf.

February 16: Carrie Nation leads a WCTU raid on O.L. Day's pharmacy in Medicine Lodge, Kan.

March 15: Future U.S. mafioso Alfred "Big Al" Polizzi born in Sicily.

March 18: Future New York mobster and Mafia murder victim Ferdinand "The Shadow" Boccia born.

April: Vincenzo Consenza, public prosecutor for Palermo, Sicily, writes to Italy's new Minister of the Interior, saying, "'During the course of performing my duties I have never noticed the mafia.'"

April 27–28: Overnight raids conducted by police chief Ermanno Sangiorgi jail 33 mafiosi in Palermo, followed by hundreds more in coming days.

May: Prosecutor Vincenzo Consenza frees all but 89 of the Palermo mafiosi recently arrested by Police Chief Sangiorgi, after informer Francesca Siino recants his previous testimony.

June: A court in Palermo convicts 32 mafiosi of forming a criminal association. Prosecutors release most of them on the spot, while Police Chief Sangiorgi complains, "It was never going to turn out any other way, as long as people who denounced the mafia in the evening then went along and defended it the following morning."

June 5: Carrie Nation claims to hear the voice of God in a dream, telling her, "Go to Kiowa. I'll stand by you." She interprets the delusion as a divine order to "take something in your hands, and throw at these [liquor] places in Kiowa and smash them." She departs on June 6 for Kiowa, Kan., and raids several local saloons.

June 28: Future Chicago West Side gambler and suspected hitman Samuele "Sam" Mesi born.

September 25: Sun Yat-sen meets with Taiwan's Japanese governor, receiving a promise that Japan will support an uprising in Guangzhou. Sun orders the rebellion to commence on October 25, but Japanese officers renege and the effort collapses, ending with Sun's deportation from Taiwan to Japan.

November 8: Future ILA president and reputed mob cohort Thomas William "Teddy" Gleason born in New York City.

December 27: Carrie Nation wields her trademark hatchet at the Hotel Carey saloon in Wichita, Kan.

1901 Coca-Cola removes cocaine from its recipe. Prince Edward Island becomes the first Canadian province to enforce prohibition of alcoholic beverages. The U.S. Senate adopts a resolution introduced by Henry Cabot Lodge, banning sale of opium or liquor to "uncivilized elements in America itself and in its territories, such as Indians, Alaskans, the inhabitants of Hawaii, railroad workers, and immigrants at ports of entry." Teamsters National Union (now the IBT) founded in Chicago.

January 16: Future dictator and mob front man Fulgencio Batista y Zaldívar born in Banes, Cuba.

January 23: Carrie Nation raids two more saloons in Wichita. While wrecking a saloon in Enterprise, she is assaulted by the proprietor's wife and several other women.

February 5: Carrie Nation demolishes Topeka's Senate Saloon, a favorite watering hole for Kansas state legislators.

February 9: Inspired by Carrie Nation's speech to the Kansas state legislature on February 7, temperance vigilantes demolish several saloons in Holton, Kan.

February 12: Six hundred Kansans sign WCTU resolutions to close saloons statewide. On February 13 vigilantes raid bars in Arkansas City, Coffeyville, Garden City, Goff, Osage City, Paola, Perry, Smith Center, Solomon, Sterling, Wellington, and Winfield.

February 17: Carrie Nation leads a mob of 55 to demolish seven saloons and a cold-storage facility in Topeka, Kan.

February 18–23: More vigilante attacks close Kansas saloons in Chanute, Eureka, Fort Scott, Garden Plain, Herington, Hutchinson, Junction City, Lawrence, Leavenworth, Millwood, Scott City, Silver Lake, and rural Marshall County.

March 12: Carrie Nation retires from saloon-raiding, announcing that she will continue her fight through a newspaper, *The Smasher's Mail*.

March 15: A new ordinance bans horse racing in San Francisco, with the last legal races run on March 16.

April 18: Future New York mafioso Giovanni "John" Bonventre born in Castellammare del Golfo, in Sicily.

Summer: Monk Eastman survives a Chatham Square ambush by members of the Five Points Gang, knocking three unconscious before another shoots him in the stomach. Eastman walks to Gouverneur Hospital, where he spends several weeks recuperating. A week after his discharge, a Five Points gangster is executed in reprisal.

July 5: Future mobster Charles Birger joins the U.S. Army in St. Louis, Mo., serving with Company G of the newly formed 13th Cavalry Regiment. He receives an honorable discharge on July 4, 1904, at Fort Mead, S.D.

July 20: Deputy U.S. Marshal Thomas Price shot and killed during a liquor raid near Monterey, Tenn. The shootout leaves two local police officers and one moonshiner wounded.

August 8: Future Detroit mafioso Guiseppe Catalonotte born in Trapani, Sicily.

September 5: Anarchist Leon Czolgosz shoots President McKinley at the Pan-American Exposition in Buffalo, N.Y. Surgeons extract one bullet but cannot find the second, refusing to use a new X-ray machine on display at the fair. Gangrene claims McKinley's life on September 14. Czolgosz survives him by six weeks, being convicted of murder and executed in New York State's electric chair on October 29.

September 17: With covert backing from Tammany Hall, 1,500 members of the Five Points Gang swarm polling places and ensure the re-election of district chief Tom Foley.

September 30: Sicilian mafioso Vito Cascio Ferro arrives in New York City aboard *La Champagne* from Havre, France. He joins the Morello crime family to coordinate "Black Hand" extortion rackets.

November 17: Suspected bootleggers and counterfeiters kill two Deputy U.S. Marshals, brothers Hugh and John Montgomery, in Oxford, Miss. Following conviction on murder charges, two defendants are hanged on September 24, 1902.

December 6: New York gang leader Paul Kelly receives a nine-month sentence for assault and robbery.

December 19: Future Pennsylvania mafioso John Sebastian LaRocca born in Villarosa, Sicily.

1902 NYPD mistakenly names Ignazio Lupo as the city's top mafioso, though in fact he is only an enforcer for Giuseppe Morello. Chicago mafioso and Unione Siciliana president Anthony D'Andrea (1872–1921) is indicted for counterfeiting coins, ultimately serving 13 months in federal prison. Belgium bans construction of new casinos, while allowing eight that already exist to continue operating. Physicians debate the efficacy of using heroin to "cure" morphine addicts.

January 2: Future mafioso Gerardo "Jerry" Catena born in South Orange, N.J.

January 11: Deputy U.S. Marshal J.N. Holsonback dies in a shotgun ambush after arresting a moonshiner near Boaz, Ala. His son also suffers wounds in the attack. Jurors convict one defendant of manslaughter on October 28, 1905, resulting in a 10-year sentence.

March 24: Future New York prosecutor, governor, and presidential candidate Thomas Edmund Dewey born in Owosso, Mich.

May: *Popular Science Monthly* runs an article titled "Mescal: A Study of a Divine Plant."

May 11: Future mobster Morris "Mushy" Wexler born in Cleveland, Ohio.

May 25: Future Detroit mafioso Joseph "Misery" Moceri born in Sicily.

June 4: Owney Madden sails from Liverpool, England, with two younger siblings as steerage passengers on board the SS *Teutonic*. They settle in New York's Hell's Kitchen, where Madden soon joins the Gopher Gang.

June 7: Future mafioso Peter Joseph "Horseface" Licavoli born in St Louis, Mo.

June 21: Future LAPD chief William H. Parker born in South Dakota.

July 4: Meyer Sucholjansky (or Suchomlanski), AKA Meyer "The Little Man" Lansky, born in Grodno, Russia (now Belarus).

July 23: Children find the corpse of Brooklyn grocer Joe Catania stuffed in a potato sack, with his throat slashed, on 73rd Street. Police suspect mafiosi Ignazio Lupo and Giuseppe Morello.

July 30: Mafioso Guiseppa Fontana and politician Raffaele Palizzolo are convicted in the 1893 slaying of Marquis Emanuele Notarbartolo di san Giovanni. An appellate court rules that verdict invalid in January 1903, with a new trial beginning on September 5. Both defendants are acquitted on July 23, 1094.

August 4: Future Kansas City mobster Anthony Robert Gizzo born in New York City.

August 6: Future gangster Arthur Flegenheimer, AKA "Dutch Schultz," born in New York City.

August 19: Future "Public Enemy No. 1" Émile "Mimile" Buisson born in Paray-le-Monial, France.

August 24: Future mafioso Carlo Gambino born in Caccamo, Sicily.

September 8: Future Chicago mobster and Unione Siciliana president Philip D'Andrea born.

October 12: Company goons kill 14 striking miners and wound 22 at Pana, Ill.

October 23: Future New Jersey mobster Settimo "Big Sam" Accardi born in Vita, Italy.

September 2: Future mafioso Angelo "Gyp" DeCarlo born in Hoboken, N.J.

September 26: Future mafioso Umberto Anastasio, AKA Albert "The Mad Hatter" Anastasia, born in Tropea, Italy.

November 22: Future mafioso Giuseppe Antonio Doto, AKA Joe Adonis, born in Montemarano, Italy.

December 2: New York District Attorney William Jerome orders a raid on one of gambler-art collector Richard Albert Canfield "resort casinos."

1903 Giuseppe "Joe the Boss" Masseria (1887–1931) flees Sicily to avoid murder charges, arriving in New York City to join the Morello Gang as an enforcer. Another Sicilian immigrant, mafioso Nicola Gentile, settles at 91 Elizabeth Street in New York. William Flynn (1867–1928), chief of the U.S. Secret Service in New York, denounces the "Black Hand" as "the most secret and terrible organization in the world." Luxembourg bans all forms of gambling. Nevada legalizes bookmaking on horse races. President Theodore Roosevelt vows to "clean up" an emerging land-fraud scandal surrounding Edward Harriman's Oregon & California Railroad, granted 3.7 million acres of government land during 1866–69. Federal grand juries indict 1,032 defendants in "the greatest cast of wholesale corruption in U.S. history," but U.S. District Attorney Francis J. Heney narrows the field to 35 before trial begins in 1905.

March 4: Big Tim Sullivan takes his seat in the U.S. House of Representatives, serving until his resignation on July 27, 1906. Sullivan finds Congress tiresome, noting that "in New York we use congressmen for hitchin' posts."

March 17: Future mobster and Al Capone bodyguard Rocco Fischetti born in Chicago.

Spring: Gang warfare flourishes in New York City between the Cherry Hill Gang (supported by Monk Eastman) and the Whyos under Bill "The Brute" Sanger. Hundreds of victims are injured in muggings and gunfights.

April: Benedetto Madonia, a mafioso from Buffalo, N.Y., encroaches on Ignazio Lupo's counterfeiting territory, on Manhattan's Lower East Side. Police find Madonia's mutilated corpse on April 14, stuffed into a barrel filled with sawdust, left at the corner of Avenue D and 11th Street. Lieutenant

Joe Petrosino arrests Lupo, Giuseppe Morello, and nine others for Madonia's murder on April 19, but none are convicted.

April 19: Future lawman Eliot Ness born in Chicago.

April 21: Albert "The Policy King" Adams, AKA "the Meanest Man in New York," receives a sentence of "not less than a year and not more than one year and nine months" in Sing Sing for operating the numbers racket. The state's Board of Parole rejects his bid for early release on April 5, 1904.

May 1: Mobster Joseph Catania arrives in New York City aboard the SS *Trojan Prince*, from Palermo, Sicily.

June 12: Future mobster Louis "Lou Rhody" Rothkopf born in Cleveland, Ohio.

July 26: Future U.S. Senator and mob investigator Carey Estes Kefauver born in Madisonville, Tenn.

August 8: Convening at Niagara Falls, N.Y., the Teamsters National Union and Team Drivers' International Union merge to create the International Brotherhood of Teamsters. Cornelius Shea wins election as the union's first president.

September 16: Members of Monk Eastman's gang rampage through the Lower East Side of Manhattan, killing one man and wounding dozens more in a five-hour rampage of gunfire and stabbings.

September 17: Eastman gangsters fight a pitched battle with members of the Five Points Gang on Rivington Street, in New York, for control of a neighborhood stuss game (a variant of faro). Hundreds of gangsters participate, including members of the Gophers who fire at both Eastmans and Five Pointers.

September 19: Spurred to action by recent violence, NYPD raids the Stanton Street headquarters of the "Paul Kelly Association," arresting several Five Points gangsters. Tammany Hall demands a truce between Kelly and Monk Eastman.

September 22: Future mafioso and federal informant Joseph "Joe Cago" Valachi born in New York City.

September 25: Future Pennsylvania mafioso Russell Bufalino born in Montedoro, Sicily.

Winter: Skirmishing resumes between the Eastman and Five Points Gangs. Tammany leader Tom Foley arranges a boxing match between Eastman and Kelly, which lasts for two hours and ends in a draw with both fighters exhausted. The bout resolves nothing.

1904 The Western Union Company ends transmission of race results to American bookmakers.

January 1: Future gangster Louis Kerzner (or Kushner), AKA "Louis Cohen," born in New York City.

February 2: Monk Eastman and an accomplice beat and rob a man on New York's West Side, unaware that the victim is under police surveillance. Officers charge Eastman and his friend with felonious assault and intent to kill.

February 4: Future mobster Paolo Giovanni "Frankie" Carbo born on New York City's Lower East Side.

February 9: Future mafioso Thomas "Yonnie" Licavoli born in St. Louis, Mo.

February 15: Kingmaker Mark Hanna dies from typhoid fever while planning his campaign to challenge incumbent Theodore Roosevelt for the GOP presidential nomination. In China's Hunan Province, Triad ally Huang Xing founds the *Huaxinghui* (China Revival Society) to overthrow the Manchu dynasty.

February 22: Future New York mafioso Alphonse Frank "Funzi" Tieri born in Naples, Italy.

February 23: William Randolph Hearst's *San Francisco Chronicle* launches a series of articles exposing the "menace" of Japanese laborers, prompting California's state legislature to pass a resolution condemning immigration from Japan.

March 1: Harvey Van Dine, one of Chicago's Car Barn Bandits, hangs in Chicago following a five-month crime spree that claimed eight lives.

March 7: Future Detroit mafioso Benedict Joseph "Scarface Joe" Bommarito born in St. Louis, Mo.

April 14: Monk Eastman receives the maximum 10-year sentence for first-degree assault.

April 22: Peter Niedermeyer, leader of the Car Barn Bandits, hangs with two accomplices in Chicago.

April 30: A spate of drunken brawling among railroad workers prompts residents of West Toronto, Ontario, to ban alcohol. The ban remains in place until 1997.

May 28: Future Outfit mobster James "Fur" Sammons and accomplice John Lynch receive life sentences for the holdup-murder of saloonkeeper Patrick Barrett. Sammons escapes from Joliet penitentiary on June 10, 1917, but is recaptured four months later. His sentence is commuted to 50 years on October 4, 1917. Governor Len Small pardons Sammons on July 28, 1923, and Sammons leaves prison on January 28, 1924.

June 8: A battle between striking miners and units of the Colorado Militia leaves six union members dead and 15 incarcerated at Dunnville. On June 10, authorities deport 79 strikers to Kansas.

June 26: Future mafioso Leonard Calogero "Lips" Moceri born in Detroit.

August 9: The second month of an Amalgamated Meat Cutters strike against Chicago meat packing companies erupts into rioting, with several strikers and strikebreakers beaten and wounded by gunfire.

August 18: Future Missouri and Ohio mafioso Vicentio "James" Licavoli, AKA "Jack White," born in St. Louis, Mo. In Chicago, 4,000 striking meat cutters riot for two hours, leaving dozens injured.

November: A *Huaxinghui* fails in Hunan Province, China. Following a second abortive revolt in early 1905, leader Huang Xing flees to Japan.

November 1: During negotiations for control of the Eastman Gang, a friend of contender Max Zwerbach murders contender Ritchie Fitzpatrick. Zwerbach assumes command of the gang.

November 4: Three gunmen from the On Leong Tong wound rival Hip Sing leader Sai Wing Mock, AKA Mock Duck, on Pell Street, in New York City.

November 20: Future gambler, racketeer and murderer Lester Ben "Benny" Binion born in Grayson County, Tex.

December 4: Future mobster Frank "Buster" Wortman born in East St. Louis, Ill.

1905 Nevada legalizes slot machines, imposing a tax of $80 per year on each machine. Salvatore Sabella murders his boss, an abusive butcher, in Castellamare del Golfo, Sicily.

January: Detective Giuseppe Petrosino assumes command of NYPD's Italian Branch, to combat Black Hand racketeers. Mafia assassin Guiseppa Fontana arrives in New York City from Sicily, joining the family of boss Piddu Morello.

January 9: Two members of the Yayey Yake Gang murder Cherry Hill Gang member "Jimmo" Brennan at Catharine and Madison Streets, in New York City.

January 18: Future mafioso Giuseppe "Joe Bananas" Bonanno born in Castellamare del Golfo, Sicily.

February 21: Future Detroit mafioso Julian Cavataio born in St. Louis Mo.

March 3: Congress bans opium trafficking in the Philippines.

March 27: Five Points Gang leader Paul Vaccarelli legally changes his surname to "Kelly."

April 5: NYPD raids Paul Kelly's New Brighton Hall night club on Great Jones Street. Officers arrest Kelly, but later release him without charges filed.

April 16: Chicago Mayor Edward Dunne receives anonymous bribery charges against IBT President Cornelius Shea (1872–1929) and other leaders of an ongoing strike against Montgomery Ward.

April 29: A Chicago grand jury indicts Cornelius Shea and 11 other IBT leaders on six counts

of conspiracy to restrain trade, commit violence, and prevent citizens from obtaining work.

May 2: Pennsylvania State Police created.

June: Two hundred American socialists, anarchists, and radical trade unionists gather in Chicago to found the Industrial Workers of the World, AKA "Wobblies," led by William "Big Bill" Haywood.

June 2: John Driscoll, secretary of a firm that locked out IBT members in April, tells a Chicago grand jury that union leaders demanded and received $50,000 in bribes to end a recent strike. Cornelius Shea counters with charges that local companies offered the IBT bribes to strike against their competitors. On June 3, Chicago police arrest Cornelius Shea for conspiracy and criminal libel against Montgomery Ward vice president Robert Thorne. Shea is arrested again on June 5, for failure to pay bond on the June 3 charges.

June 12: Chicago newspapers reveal that Cornelius Shea resides in a local brothel, the Kentucky Home, with 19-year-old mistress Alice Walsh.

July 1: Chicago's grand jury issues a new conspiracy indictment against IBT President Cornelius Shea.

July 4: Future U.S. mafioso Filippo Sacco, AKA John "Handsome Johnny" Rosselli, born in Esperia, Italy.

July 5: Future physician and mafioso Michele Navarra born in Corleone, Sicily. Federal jurors in Oregon convict Senator John Hipple Mitchell of accepting bribes from the Oregon & California Railroad. He receives a six-month jail term and a $1,000 fine, but dies on December 8, with his case still on appeal. Thirty-three other defendants convicted in the same scandal include Oregon congressmen Binger Hermann and John Newton Williamson.

July 26: A moonshiner kills Deputy U.S. Marshal Zack Wade near Rocky Mount, Va. The gunman hangs on November 24.

August 5: Five Point Gangsters stage a two hour riot on New York's Lower East Side, beating random victims, looting and burning shops, as a show of strength against the NYPD. Officer Frye arrests one rioter, prompting death threats that force his transfer to another post on August 7.

August 7: Future Buffalo, N.Y., mafioso Sam "The Farmer" Frangiamore born.

August 9: Future New York mafioso Giuseppe Maria Barbara, AKA Joseph "Joe the Barber" Barbara, born in Castellammare del Golfo, Sicily.

August 12: Despite revelations that he lives in a Chicago brothel, Cornelius Shea narrowly wins re-election as president of the IBT.

August 20: Sun Yat-sen, residing in Tokyo, creates a new secret society called *Zhongguo Tongmenghui* ("Chinese United League"), merging his *Xingzhonghui* with ally Huang Xing's *Huaxinghui*.

August 28: Alcoholic laborer Jean Lanfray murders his pregnant wife and two children in the Swiss canton of Vaud. Authorities blame absinthe for the crime, although Lanfray's known alcoholic intake for the afternoon includes seven glasses of wine, six glasses of cognac, one coffee laced with brandy, two crème de menthes, in addition to two glasses of absinthe. Convicted of murder on February 23, 1906, Lanfray receives a 30-year sentence and hangs himself in prison three days later. Meanwhile, a petition bearing 82,000 signatures prompts authorities in Vaud to ban absinthe. The ban goes nationwide in 1908, with a constitutional referendum.

September 29: Future Los Angeles mafioso Frank "Bomp" Bompensiero born in Milwaukee, Wis.

October: NYPD officers arrest future mobster Irving "Waxey Gordon" Wexler for pickpocketing. Upon conviction, he is sentenced to Elmira State Reformatory. Giuseppe DiPrimo, a counterfeiter affiliated with Giuseppe Morello's crime family, leaves prison in New York, vowing revenge for the 1903 "barrel murder" of brother-in-law Benedetto Madonia.

October 3: NYPD officers arrest gangster Benjamin "Dopey Benny" Fein (1889–1962) after administrators at PS 19 complain of his recruiting students for criminal activity.

October 8: "Policy King" Albert Adams announces his retirement from gambling in a letter to the *New York Times*.

October 24: NYPD officers arrest Benny Fein again, for assault and robbery, but later drop the charges. Police in Brownstown, Pa., find Madonia murder suspect Tomaso "Il Bove" Petto slain at his home.

October 31: Future Harlem gangster Ellsworth "Bumpy" Johnson born in Charleston, S.C.

December 24: Future billionaire Howard Robard Hughes Jr. born in Houston, Tex.

1906 Belgium and Brazil ban absinthe. Kentucky legalized pari-mutuel betting at horse tracks.

January 2: NYPD arrests Benny Fein for grand larceny, resulting in a work-detail sentence.

January 6: Future mafioso Nicolo Impastato born in Palermo, Sicily.

January 17: Future Murder, Inc., hitman Albert "Allie" Tannenbaum, AKA "Tick Tock," born in Nanticoke, Pa.

January 20: Suspected Black Hand gunmen kill Antonio Lapaino and wound his brother Savarino at their home on Enterprise Street, Los Angeles.

February 24: Future New York racketeer Anthony "Tough Tony" Anastasio born in Catanzaro, Italy.

February 28: Future mobster Benjamin "Bugsy" Siegel born in Brooklyn, N.Y.

March 7: Kidnap victim John (or Tony) Bozzuffi, son of a New York banker, escapes from his captors and names Ignazio Lupo as the plot's ringleader. Police jail Lupo under $1,000 bond.

April 28: Future mob boss Antonino "Joe Batters" Accardo, AKA "Big Tuna," born on Chicago's Near West Side.

June 11: Emanuel "Mendy" Weiss, future hitman for Murder, Inc., born in New York City.

June 30: Congress passes the Pure Food and Drug Act (effective as of January 1, 1907), creating the U.S. Food and Drug Administration empowered to determine the safety of drugs sold in America and require proper labeling of contents for both drugs and food.

July 29: Fruit peddler George Maisano dies in an ambush on North Main Street, Los Angeles. LAPD suspects Black Hander Joseph Ardizzone.

September 13: Jury selection begins for the Chicago conspiracy trial of former IBT President Cornelius Shea, spanning 66 days. Testimony begins on November 30, with a surprise announcement that IBT official Albert Young has pled guilty and turned state's evidence against Shea. Jurors deadlock on January 19, 1907, resulting in a mistrial.

September 27: Gunmen kill Black Hand leader Giuseppe Cuccio outside his home in Los Angeles. Police suspect mafioso Tony Matranga.

October 1: Ex–"policy king" Albert Adams dies at Manhattan's Ansonia Hotel.

November 14: Unknown gunmen kill Mafia "barrel murder" suspect Girolamo Mondini on East 106th Street, Manhattan.

1907 France legalizes public games of skill, including baccarat and chemin-de-fer. China and England launch a collaborative 10-year campaign against opium, with China reducing domestic cultivation while England tapers off importation of Indian opium. Chicago's leading Italian businessmen form a White Hand Society to combat "Black Hand" extortion. Their group is unrelated to New York City's Irish White Hand gang.

January 20: NYPD detective Joe Petrosino arrests extortionist Giuseppe Palermo under the name "Salvatore Saracena." Judge Finn of Police Court discharges the prisoner.

February 1: Cornelius Shea's second conspiracy trial begins in Chicago. Jurors acquit him of all charges on February 20.

February 21: Future Cleveland mobster Alex "Shondor" Birns born in Lemes, Austria-Hungary (later Czechoslovakia).

February 22: Future mafioso Natale "Joe Diamond" Evola born in Brooklyn, N.Y.

March 29: Ignazio Lupo and Giuseppe Morello,

operating as the Ignatz-Florio Co-operative Association Among Corleonesi, borrow $15,000 from Manhattan's Realty Operating Company, using a property at 137th Street and Home Avenue as security. Realty Operating assigns the bond and mortgage to John A. Philbrick & Brothers on April 26.

April 17: Joe Petrosino arrests Neopolitan camorrista Enrico Alfano and holds him for deportation to Italy as a criminal alien.

June 2: Encouraged by emissaries of Sun Yatsen, members of the revolutionary *Shan He Hui* capture government arms at Huizhou in Guangdong Province. The rebels rout Qing troops at Taiwei on June 5 and defeat another contingent in Bazhiyie, before reinforcements crush the revolt.

July 1: Future mafioso Fred "The Wolf" Randaccio born in Palermo, Sicily.

July 6: Police Commissioner Xu Xilin, a member of the Triad-allied China Recovery League, assassinates Enming, provincial governor of Anhui Province, during graduation ceremonies at the Anhui Police Academy. The murder sparks an uprising, crushed by Qing troops after four hours. A firing squad executes Xu Xilin on July 7, then cuts out his heart.

July 8: Future jeweler, political fixer and underworld associate Harry Rosenzweig born to immigrant Austrian parents in Phoenix, Ariz.

August: As uprisings begin in three counties of Guangdong Qinzhou (now China's Guangxi Zhuang Autonomous Region), Sun Yat-sen sends lieutenant Wang Heshun to aid the rebels. They besiege Qinzhou in September, but are repulsed by Qing forces, whereupon Wang flees to Vietnam.

August 8: Gang lord Michael ("King Mike") McDonald dies in Chicago, leaving his empire to be divided among alderman Jacob "Mont" Tennes, gambler James "Big Jim" O'Leary, and another gambler, J.T. "Bud" White.

August 10: Daniel Tobin replaces Cornelius Shea as IBT president, holding that office until October 14, 1952.

September 1: Future labor leader Walter Philip Reuther born in Wheeling, W.Va.

November 14: Future Detroit mafioso Salvatore Finazzo born in Partinico, Sicily.

November 16: A bootlegger kills Deputy U.S. Marshal George Williams while resisting arrest in Oklahoma.

December: Sun Yat-sen sends lieutenant Huang Mintang to monitor a Qing fort at Zhennanguan, a pass on the Chinese-Vietnamese border. Rebels capture the fort's cannon tower, then retreat as 4,000 reinforcements arrive. Qing agents pursue Sun into Vietnam, but he escapes to Singapore.

December 1: Future Chicago mobster Joseph "Joey Doves" Aiuppa born in Melrose Park, Ill.

December 10: Future Detroit mobster James Bellanca born in Trapani, Sicily.

December 31: Black Hand gunmen kill barber Giovannino Bentivegna in his shop on East 9th Street, Los Angeles.

1908 Lieutenant Pertosino arrests Vito Cascio Ferro for murder in New York. Despite his acquittal, Ferro is deported to Sicily. Johnny Torrio leaves Brooklyn for Chicago, at the request of Windy City vice lord Jim Colosimo. Gang warfare continues between Paul Kelly's Five Points Gang and the former Eastman Gang, now led by Max Zwerbach.

January 11: Future mafioso Santo Sorge born in Sicily.

March 17: Future mafioso Raymond Patriarca born in Worcester, Mass.

March 27: Huang Xing, a lieutenant of Sun Yat-sen, launches raids from Vietnam into Lianzhou and Qinzhou Counties, Guangdong Province. The uprising lasts 40 days, before collapsing due to shortage of ammunition.

April 5: Future pirate John Boysie Singh born in Woodbrook, Port of Spain, Trinidad.

April 25: NYPD arrests Frank Costello for assault and robbery, but later drops the charges.

April 29: Encouraged by Sun Yat-sen, rebel Huang Mintang leads 200 men from Vietnam to stage a revolt in Hekou, Yunnan. The revels soon retreat, as government reinforcements arrive.

May 14: Five Points gangster Louis Pioggi quarrels with Max Zwerbach over mutual girlfriend Carroll Terry, fatally shooting Zwerbach and companion Vach "Cyclone Louie" Lewis at Coney Island's Surf Avenue saloon. Jack Zelig assumes command of the former Eastman Gang. Belatedly arrested in 1908, Pioggi receives an 11-month sentence.

May 16: Future Detroit mafioso Paul Vitale born in Cinisi Palermo, Sicily.

May 19: NYPD arrests Benny Fein for disorderly conduct, resulting in a $3 fine.

May 24: Future mobster Salvatore Giangana, AKA Salvatore "Momo" Giancana, born in Chicago's Little Italy.

June: Chicago police seek to arrest ex–IBT president Cornelius Shea on mail fraud charges, but cannot find him. Boston police jail Shea in July, for deserting his wife and children. Conviction on that charge earns him a six-month jail term, imposed on July 23.

June 29: In defiance of congressional opposition, U.S. Attorney General Charles Bonaparte (1851–1921) creates a detective force within the Department of Justice. He names Chief Examiner Stanley Finch (1872–1951) to command the group on July 26.

June 30: Future Chicago mobster Samuel "Teets" Battaglia born in Kenosha, Wis.

July 2: NYPD officers jail Benny Fein for assault, but he is released without trial. Creditor John A. Philbrick & Brothers seeks to foreclose on the Ignatz-Florio Co-operative Association Among Corleonesi under terms of an outstanding mortgage.

July 17: Future mobster Luigi Tomaso Giuseppi Fratto, AKA Louis "Cock-eyed" Fratto, born in Chicago.

July 20: Canada's Opium Act, banning importation, manufacture or sale of opium "for other than medicinal purposes," receives royal assent.

July 23: Former IBT president Cornelius Shea receives a six-month prison term in Boston, for abandoning his wife and children.

July 30: Another assault arrest finds Benny Fein released without trial in New York.

August 7: Future IBT president Frank Fitzsimmons born in Jeannette, Pa.

September 2: Future racketeer Philip "Little Farvel" Kovolick born in New York City.

October 6: Future mafiosi Philip "Benny Squint" Lombardo born in New York City.

October 7: Future syndicate hitman Harry "Happy" Maione born in Brooklyn, N.Y.

October 16: Future Detroit mafioso Dominic Cavataio born in Palermo, Sicily.

October 29: NYPD charges Benny Fein with burglary. Upon conviction, he receives a 42-month sentence in Sing Sing Prison.

December: NYPD promotes Joe Petrosino to lieutenant and places him in charge of the new Italian Squad, targeting "Black Hand" extortionists and other immigrant felons.

December 1: Ignazio Lupo drops from sight in New York, defaulting on $100,000 in debts from his grocery-importing company on Mott Street.

December 16: Wine merchant Salvatore Manzella files for bankruptcy, charging that Ignazio Lupo has ruined his business. The court orders Lupo to appear before January 14, 1909. When he misses that court date, the judge declares Lupo bankrupt.

1909 An International Opium Commission convenes in Shanghai, China. America's delegates, Dr. Hamilton Wright and Episcopal Bishop Henry Brent, stress the drug's "immorality" and evil effects. Authorities in San Francisco, Calif., ban slot machines. Nevada lawmakers ban slot machines and bookmaking on horse races, along with bridge, craps, fan-tan, faro, poker, and whist. Legislators in the Netherlands outlaw absinthe.

January 12: Future Missouri mobster Charles Binaggio born in Kansas City.

February: Lt. Joe Petrosino assumes command of NYPD's new "secret service" branch, planning mass deportation of convicted Italian felons living in New York.

February 1: NYPD Commissioner Theodore Bingham asks U.S. Secretary of State Robert Bacon to arrange Ignazio Lupo's deportation to Italy.

February 9: Congress passes the Opium Exclusion Act, banning importation of smoking opium to the U.S. after April 1.

February 17: Future Detroit mafioso Joseph "Long Joe" Bommarito (not to be confused with "Scarface Joe") born in Terrasini, Sicily.

February 19: NYPD Commissioner Theodore Bingham publicly discusses Lt. Joe Petrosino's impending visit to Italy, for consultation on "Black Hand" and Mafia felons.

February 21: Joe Petrosino arrives in Rome, spends a week with local police, then moves on to Palermo on February 28.

March: U.S. Attorney General George Wickersham names the DOJ's anonymous detective force the Bureau of Investigation.

March 9: NYPD arrests gangster Nicholas Sylvester on suspicion of bomb throwing. Police Court Judge Herman discharges him.

March 12: An anonymous informant lures Joe Petrosino into a fatal ambush, in Palermo. Authorities detain Vito Cascio Ferro, then release him when friends provide an alibi.

April 12: Some 250,000 mourners attend Joe Petrosino's funeral in Manhattan.

May 21: Former IBT president Cornelius Shea stabs mistress Alice Walsh 27 times in New York City. Jurors convict him of attempted murder on July 23, whereupon Shea receives a sentence of 5 to 25 years in Sing Sing.

June 19: New York authorities parole Monk Eastman from prison.

July 12: Congress passes the Sixteenth Amendment to the U.S. Constitution, authorizing collection of a federal income tax. Alabama is the first state to ratify the new amendment, on August 10. Delaware provides the necessary thirty-sixth ratification on February 3, 1913.

July 17: Future mafioso Frank DeSimone born in Pueblo, Colo.

July 20: Future New York mobster Uinseann Ó Colla, AKA Vincent "Mad Dog" Coll, born in Gaoth Dobhair, County Donegal, Ireland.

July 27: Unknown gunmen ambush and kill Mafia "barrel murder" suspect Giovanni Zarcone outside his home in Danbury, Conn.

July 28: Future syndicate hitman Harry "Pittsburgh Phil" Strauss born.

August 15: In New York City's Chinatown, a

hatchetman murders Bow Kum, a former slave of Low Hee Tong — a high-ranking member of the Four Brothers and Hip Sing Tongs — who escaped to marry an On Leon Tong member. The slaying sparks a year-long gang war, finally ended by intervention of U.S. and Chinese government officials.

August 27: Future Harlem mafioso Charles Urbiaco arrives in New York City from Italy.

September 6: Future mafioso Anthony Joseph Biase born in Omaha, Neb.

September 13: Future Chicago mob enforcer Sam "Mad Sam" DeStefano born in Streator, Ill.

September 23: Chicago jurors convict Police Inspector Edward McCann of accepting bribes to protect vice operations in the Levee district.

October: British evangelist Rodney "Gipsy" Smith (1860–1947) leads protest marches against vice dens in Chicago's South Side Levee District.

October 8: Police arrest Paul Kelly and several associates for voter fraud in Hoboken, N.J.

October 23: Police in Chicago arrest Maurice Van Bever and his wife Julia for operating an interstate "white slave" (forced prostitution) ring.

November 12: Fugitive Ignazio Lupo resurfaces in Manhattan.

November 15: U.S. Secret Service agents arrest Ignazio Lupo, Giuseppe Morello, and 13 other mafiosi for counterfeiting, after a raid on their printing plant in Highland, N.Y., seizing 1,200 counterfeit bills.

November 17: NYPD arrests Ignazio Lupo on extortion charges.

November 23: Dissident Five Points gangsters James "Biff" Ellison, Jimmy Kelly, and "Razor" Reilly botch a murder attempt on Paul Kelly, killing bodyguard William Harrington instead.

December 15: Federal prosecutors in New York charge alleged mob terrorist Nicholas Sylvester with counterfeiting, as part of the Lupo ring.

December 30: Hip Song Tong assassins kill Ah Hoon, a comedian and member of the On Leong Tong, in his New York City home.

1910 Nevada legislators ban all forms of gambling. Herbert Mills produces the Operators Bell slot machine, based on Charles Fey's earlier design, but featuring 20 symbols per reel and a window displaying three rows.

January 1–March 26: Black Hand assassins kills 38 victims in Chicago's Little Italy, with many slayings credited to the still-unidentified "Shotgun Man."

January 26: Trial begins in the federal counterfeiting case of Ignazio Lupo, Giuseppe Morello, and six other mafiosi. Al are convicted on February 19, whereupon Judge George Ray imposes the following sentences: Lupo, 30 years and a $1,000 fine; Morello, 25 years and $1,000;

Giuseppe Calicchio, 17 years and $600; Giuseppe Palermo, 18 years and $1,000; Nicholas Sylvestro, Antonio Cecala, Vincenzo Giglio, and Salvatore Cina 15 years and $1,000 each. Lupo enters the federal prison in Atlanta, Ga., on February 20. His co-defendants arrive on February 21. Leadership of the crime family falls to brothers Ciro, Nicholas, and Vincenzo Terranova.

January 28: Future mafioso Carl "Corky" Civella born in Kansas City, Mo.

February 6: Future New Orleans mafioso Calogero Minacore, AKA Carlos "The Little Man" Marcello, born to Sicilian parents in Tunis, Tunisia.

February 10: Zhao Sheng, a lieutenant of Sun Yat-sen, leads a rebellion in Guangzhou, China. Following his resignation, Ni Yingdian continues the struggle until his death in battle ends the uprising.

February 21: Future mafioso Carmine "Lilo" Galante born in East Harlem, N.Y.

February 24: Federal judge George Ray reports that he received death threats during the Lupo-Morello trial.

March 7: New York defendant Leoluca Vasi pleads guilty to possessing 1,148 counterfeit $2 bills printed by the Lupo gang.

March 10: Future Florida mafioso Albert "Chink" Facchiano born in New York City.

March 15: Private individuals create the Chicago Vice Commission to close brothels and "panel houses" (peep shows) in the Levee District.

March 17: U.S. Secret Service agents in New York arrest Salvatore Matsisi for passing counterfeit currency printed by the Lupo gang.

March 18: Johnny Spanish and two accomplices rob a saloon on Manhattan's Norfolk Street.

April 1: An unknown gunman kills John "Spanish Louie" Lewis, a member of the Humpty Jackson Gang, on New York's East 11th Street.

April 4: New Orleans grocer Pietro Pepitone kills "Black Hand" leader Paulo Marchese, AKA Paul Di Christina, during an extortion attempt at Pepitone shop. Pepitone pleads guilty to manslaughter and receives a 20-year sentence, of which he serves six years. Some researchers link Marchese's slaying to the later unsolved serial murders of the "New Orleans Axeman," whose victims include Pepitone's son Michael, killed in his home on October 27, 1919. None of the Axeman's other targets are linked to Marchese's case.

May 21: Future Philadelphia mafioso Angelo Annaloro, AKA Angelo "The Gentle Don" Bruno, born in Villalba, Sicily.

June 23: Ignazio Lupo loses "good time" credit for trying to bribe a guard at the Atlanta penitentiary.

June 25: Inspired by the Van Bever case in Chicago, Congress passes the White-Slave Traffic Act, AKA the Mann Act, banning forced prostitution and interstate transport of females for "immoral purposes."

July 11: Future syndicate hitman Frank Abbondondola, AKA Frank "The Dasher" Abbandando, born in Brooklyn, N.Y.

July 17: Authorities in Pittsburgh, Pa., arrest Tony Gallucci as a member of the Lupo counterfeiting ring.

July 27: Future mobster Reuben Koloditsky, AKA Ruby Kolod, born in New York City.

September 14: Five Points Gang leader Paul Kelly legally changes his surname back to Vaccarelli.

October 1: An explosion and fire destroy the *Los Angeles Times* building in L.A., killing 20 victims. Newspaper proprietor Harrison Otis blames labor unions, calling it "the crime of the century." Future mafioso Carmine "Mr. Gribbs" Tramunti born in Manhattan.

October 23: Members of a gang led by John Weyler (1891–1919), AKA "Johnny Spanish," clash with patrons of a billiard hall on Eldridge Street, in Manhattan, leaving two dead from gunshot wounds.

November 6: Mafia gunmen in Corleone, Sicily, bungle the attempted murder of socialist leader Bernadino Verro, who has publicized Mafia links to the Catholic Church.

November 10: Sun Yat-sen and other leaders of the *Tongmenhui* meet in Malaya to plot an uprising against the Qing Dynasty in Guangzhou Province.

November 19: Future Detroit mafioso Santo "Sam" Caruso born in Trapani, Sicily.

December 1: Secret Service agents and NYPD officers find 500 counterfeit $2 bills concealed in a home on Chrystie Street. They arrest 13 suspects, subsequently charging mafioso Modesto DiSonna and eight others as member of Ignazio Lupo's gang.

December 10: Federal jurors in Manhattan convict Giuseppe Boscarino of passing counterfeit currency.

December 12: Future Cleveland, Ohio, mafioso John "Peanuts" Tronolone born in Buffalo, N.Y.

December 20: Future Detroit mobster Raffaele Quasarano born in Mauch Chunk, Pa.

December 25: Dynamite blasts destroy part of the Llewellyn Ironworks in Los Angeles, during a bitter strike.

1910–12 Newspaper barons William Randolph Hearst and Robert McCormick wage "circulation wars" for their papers, the *Chicago American* and *Chicago Tribune*. Street gangs such as Ragen's Colts, posing as "athletic clubs," battle for prime territory in a three-year struggle that leaves 27 street vendors beaten, stabbed, or shot. Many future Prohibition gangsters earn their reputations in the circulation wars, which soon spread to Cleveland and other American cities.

1911 California legislators ban slot machines. Nevada lifts its legal ban on bridge and whist.

January: Rumors circulate that Giuseppe Morello has turned state's evidence against fellow mafiosi in New York Secret Service agent William Flynn denies knowledge of any such agreement on January 16.

January 26: Canadian lawmakers introduce eight new anti-drug bills in Parliament, soon merged into an Opium and Narcotic Drug Act that supercedes the 1908 Opium Act.

January 29: Future mafioso Salvatore Pieri born in Buffalo, N.Y.

February 7: NYPD stenographer James Ortelero writes to Atlanta Federal Prison officials, describing Giuseppe Morello's alleged involvement in the 1889 murder of Sicilian police official Giovanni Vella. Ortelero's father was imprisoned for the crime.

February 13: Imprisoned mafioso Ignazio Lupo received three days in solitary confinement on restricted diet and loses 10 days of "good time" for "laughing, talking and making signs" to another inmate. Ortelero sends follow-up correspondence on February 17 and April 17, urging officials to obtain Morello's confession.

February 18: Future Yakuza boss Yoshio Kodama born in Nihonmatsu, Fukushima, Japan.

February 26: Future mobster Michael Matthew Rubino born in Detroit.

March 22: NYPD arrests Johnny Spanish for the murder of Saddie Kaplan, a relative of rival gang leader Nathan "Kid Dropper" Kaplan. At trial, he receives a seven-year sentence.

March 27: Future mobster Rocco Salvatore born in Chicago.

April 11: Detroit police arrest James McNamara, president of the International Association of Bridge and Structural Iron Workers, while Indianapolis officers seize his son John, the union's secretary-treasurer. Both are charged with murder for the *Los Angeles Times* bombing in October 1910; John faces additional charges for bombing the Llewellyn Ironworks on Christmas Day. Both plead not guilty in Los Angeles, on July 12. Jury selection begins on October 11, but a plea bargain ends the proceedings on December 1, as James pleads guilty to murder and John pleads guilty to conspiracy.

April 19: Giuseppe Calicchio writes to the warden of Atlanta's federal prison, claiming that a Mafia chapter exists within the penitentiary.

April 27: Triad-allied rebels led by Huang Xing

and Zhao Sheng storm Governor Zhang Minqi's office on Guangzhou, but are soon defeated with 86 killed by Qing troops.

May 1: Future mafioso Anthony "Fat Tony" Salerno born in East Harlem, N.Y.

May 29: The Sullivan Law, requiring a police permit to own or carry handguns, takes effect in New York.

June 8: Jurors convict Five Points gangster James Ellison for the 1909 murder of Paul Kelly bodyguard William Harrington. Ellison loses his mind at Sing Sing, and later dies in an asylum.

June 13: Future New York mafioso Thomas "Tommy Ryan" Eboli born in Eboli, Italy.

July 11: Future Chicago mobster Marcello Giuseppe Caifano, AKA Marshall Joseph Caifano, born in Sicily.

July 15: Samuel Harris, a member of Johnny Spanish's gang, attempts suicide by slashing his wrists in NYPD custody.

August 11: Future Detroit mobster Nick Ditta born in Italy.

September 9: Future mobster Dominic Blasi, AKA "Joe Bantone," born in Chicago.

October 10: China's Wuchang Uprising, in Hubei Province, sparks the broader Xinhai (or Hsinhai) Revolution, ending with the abdication of Emperor Puyi on February 12, 1912, thereby toppling the Manchu government and ending 4,000 years of monarchy. Triad members play key roles in the revolution and in China's later republican government.

October 29: Mafioso "Chuck" Minaco gains access to the home of Nelly Lenere on Manhattan's East 109th Street, claiming he has information concerning her critically-ill estranged husband. Once inside, Minaco beats Lenere in an effort to obtain the combination of her home safe. Lenere stabs Minaco 25 times, and while police deem the killing self-defense, mafioso Aniello "Zopo" Prisco swears vengeance against Lenere and her stepmother, Pasquarella Spinelli.

November 4: Future mafioso James "Jimmy Nap" Napoli born in New York City.

November 20: Hip Sing Tong member Leing Young shoots Woo Dip, of the On Leong Tong, in Cleveland, Ohio, for failure to pay $2 in protection money. Leing Young eludes police, but jurors later convict two other Hip Sing members.

December 1: Chicago gambling boss James Patrick "Big Tim" O'Leary sells off his interests and "retires" — until Prohibition's advent makes him a millionaire bootlegger.

December 2: Jack Zelig lures Jules Morello — an assassin hired to kill him by dissident lieutenants Jack Sirocco and Chick Tricker, to the Stuyvesant Casino on Manhattan's Second Avenue and kills him there. On the same day, a Chicago

"labor slugger" explains his job in a newspaper interview: "Oh, there ain't nothin' to it. I gets my fifty [dollars], then I goes out and finds the guy they wanna have slugged. I goes up to 'im and I says to 'im, 'My friend, by way of meaning no harm,' and then I gives it to 'im — biff! in the mug. Nothin' to it."

1912 Federal authorities log 5,000 fatalities related to cocaine use in the United States. Congress bans absinthe nationwide. Eugene Cornuché opens a casino in Deauville, France. A new Chinese Tong, the Kim Lan Wui Saw, appears in New York City's Chinatown. Before year's end, its leaders declare war on the Hip Sing and On Leong Tongs.

January 1: Triad member Sun Yat-sen announces the establishment of the Republic of China in Nanking, assuming office as China's first provisional president.

January 8: Future New York mafioso Joseph N. Gallo born in Hartford, Conn. He is not related to 1960s Mafia rebel "Crazy Joe" Gallo.

January 23: Representatives of the U.S., China, France, Germany, Italy, Japan, the Netherlands, Persia, Portugal, Russia, Siam and the United Kingdom sign the International Opium Convention, agreeing that "The contracting Powers shall use their best endeavours to control, or to cause to be controlled, all persons manufacturing, importing, selling, distributing, and exporting morphine, cocaine, and their respective salts, as well as the buildings in which these persons carry such an industry or trade."

March 10: Yuan Shikai, a general from the Qing Dynasty, succeeds Sun Yat-sen as China's second provisional president.

March 19: Future mafioso Giuseppe Nicoli "Nick" Civella born in Kansas City, Mo.

March 20: Aniello Prisco and another gunman shoot Pasquarella Spinelli in her stable, on East 107th Street in Manhattan. Stepdaughter Nelly Lenere witnesses the murder but escapes and later flees the country.

April 12: Future gangster Jack "Spot" Comer born in London, England.

April 16: A shootout between Neapolitan camoristi and Sicilian mafiosi leaves five men dead at Third Avenue and 114th Street, in Manhattan. Victims include Charles Bario, and Calogero Morello (son of imprisoned counterfeiter Giuseppe Morello), and Joseph Pollizzo.

April 30: Alexander Bielaski assumes command of the Bureau of Investigation, holding that post until February 10, 1919.

June 3: Gunman Charles Torti shoots Jack Zelig in the neck, on the steps of Manhattan's Criminal Courts building. Zelig survives the wound.

June 18: NYPD Lieutenant Charles Becker (1870–1915) leads raids on several gang hangouts, arresting 19 men on drug and weapons charges.

July 14: The *New York World* publishes an interview with gambler Herman Rosenthal, accusing Lieutenant Becker of extortion. On July 16, Lennox Avenue Gang members Francesco Cirofici, Harry "Gyp the Blood" Horowitz, Louis Rosenberg, and Jacob Seidenscher kill Rosenthal outside the Metropole Hotel, on Times Square. District Attorney Charles Whitman suspects that Becker ordered the slaying and orders a roundup of Zelig's men to procure evidence.

July 23: Two unidentified gangs wage a gun battle at Avenue A and 12th Street in Manhattan, killing a 15-year-old boy and leaving a 12-year-old girl critically wounded. In a separate incident, Officer Francis Reilly suffers a fractured skull while trying to arrest a member of the Pansy Gang on a charge of picking pockets.

July 29: NYPD officers arrest Lieutenant Charles Becker for the murder of Herman Rosenthal.

August: Triad member Sun Yat-sen and other leaders of the *Tongmenghui* create the new *Kuomingtang* (Nationalist Party).

August 1: Future mafioso John "Big John" Ormento born in New York City.

August 3: Police in upstate New York arrest Zelig gang member Louis "Lefty Louie" Rosenberg for Herman Rosenthal's murder.

August 5: NYPD officers arrest Benny Fein for grand larceny, but the case is dismissed.

August 15: Police in Providence, R.I., arrest Jack Zelig for a $65 robbery. Zelig gives a false name, posts $2,000 bond, and vanishes on August 21.

September: Shortly before his term of office expires, State's Attorney John Wayman officially closes vice dens in Chicago's Levee district.

September 18: Future mafioso John Scalish born in Cleveland, Ohio.

October: Francesco Ioele logs his first arrest as "Frank Yale," for disorderly conduct, in New York City.

October 5: Gunman Philip "Red Phil" Davidson kills Jack Zelig on a trolley car, on 13th Street in Manhattan. A police officer captures Davidson one block from the murder scene. Davidson blames the shooting on a $400 debt, but authorities suspect Zelig was killed to prevent him from testifying against Charles Becker. Davidson receives a 20-year prison term on November 6.

October 7: Charles Becker's murder trial begins in Manhattan. Jurors convict Becker on October 30, whereupon Judge John Goff condemns Becker to die.

October 12: An unknown gunman kills mobster Jack Zelig as he boards a streetcar in New York City, one day before Zelig's scheduled testimony at the murder trial of Charles Becker.

October 16: NYPD officers arrest Frank Costello for assault and robbery, but later drop the charges.

November 7: Future mobster David Yaras, AKA "David Miller," born in Chicago.

December 16: East Harlem mafioso Giosue Gallucci schedules a meeting with Aniello Prisco at Nick DelGaudio's barbershop, to settle Prisco's recent extortion demands. On arrival, Prisco is executed by Gallucci gunman John Russomano, while employee Michael Morelles plays a violin to cover the gunshots.

December 24: Merck & Company files two patent applications describing the synthesis of the psychoactive amphetamine 3,4-Methylenedioxymethamphetamine (MDMA, later called "ecstasy") and its subsequent conversion to methylhydrastinine.

December 28: Future syndicate enforcer William "Willie Potatoes" Daddano Sr., AKA "William Russo," born in Chicago.

1913 Bayer Laboratories halts production of heroin, deletes all mention of the drug from official corporate histories, and focuses on mass production of aspirin. George Alfred Julius (1873–1947), a British engineer living in Australia, invents an electromechanical totalizer which soon becomes a standard pari-mutuel betting device at racetracks worldwide. Nevada legalizes "social games" and slot machines that pay out cash or products worth less than $2. Chicago's White Hand Society disbands in the face of police apathy and vigilantism in Little Italy. Giuseppe Masseria receives a 54-month prison sentence for the botched burglary of a Bowery pawn shop.

February: The Triad-dominated KMT wins a significant victory in elections for China's National Assembly.

February 8: Future mafioso Carmine "The Doctor" Lombardozzi born in New York City.

February 12: Future mafioso Anthony "Tony Ducks" Corallo born in East Harlem, N.Y.

February 14: Future IBT president James Riddle Hoffa born in Brazil, Ind.

February 18: Snipers armed with silencer-equipped rifles wound mafioso John Russomano Tony Capilongo outside and bodyguard outside Russomano's home on East 109th Street, in Manhattan.

February 27: Jack Zelig's widow, Henrietta, wins a $600 settlement for bail money unlawfully retained by New York's court system after Zelig's murder.

March 4: President William Howard Taft

(1857–1930) signs a bill establishing the U.S. Department of Labor, to protect the rights of American workers.

March 20: Assassin Ying Kuicheng wounds KMT president Song Jiaoren at a Shanghai railway station, resulting in his death on March 22. Police catch Ying with a telegram implicating Zhao Binjun, third premier of the Chinese Republic (poisoned by persons unknown in 1914). Many Chinese suspect President Yuan Shikai of ordering Song's murder.

March 22: Future Moe Dalitz employee and mob-allied mogul of the Music Corporation of America Lewis Robert "Lew" Wasserman born in Cleveland, Ohio.

March 26: Future anti-mob journalist Victor Riesel born on New York City's Lower East Side.

March 28: Future Yakuza "Godfather of Godfathers" Kazuo Taoka born in Higashimiyoshi, Tokushima, Japan.

April 9: Unknown gunmen kill mafioso Amadeo Buonomo in a wine cellar at 113th Street and First Avenue, in Manhattan.

April 30: Future mafioso Simone Rizzo "Sam the Plumber" DeCavalcante born in New Jersey.

May 4: Moonshiners in Dickenson County, Va., ambush Deputy U.S. Marshals Marion Ramey and John Sloan as they are smashing an illegal whiskey still. Both officers die in the protracted shootout, with hundreds of rounds fired.

May 22: Leaders of the Hip Sing, Kim Lan Wui Saw, and On Leong Tongs sign a peace treaty in New York City. The Four Brothers Tong refuses to participate.

May 23: Vito Genovese arrives in New York City.

June: Chicago gangster Frank McErlane enters Pontiac Prison, convicted of auto theft charges filed in 1911. Authorities parole him in March 1916.

June 11: New Orleans police shoot three striking employees of the United Fruit Company, killing one.

July: Sun Yat-sen leads a KMT rebellion against Yuan Shikai in seven southern Chinese provinces, dubbed the "Second Revolution." Government forces defeat the KMT in Jiangxi Province on August 1, and capture Nanchang on September 1. Sun Yat-sen and other KMT-Triad leaders flee to Japan, while an intimidated parliament formally elected Yuan Shikai president of the Chinese Republic in October.

July 10: Four assailants fatally shoot and stab gangster Morris "Moshe the Strongarm Man" Reich outside a poolroom on Manhattan's Avenue B. Police arrest suspects Jack Willis and David Wolk near the scene.

July 21: NYPD arrests Benny Fein for interfering with an officer. The case is later suspended.

August 4: Two gunmen wound New York labor racketeer William "Billy" Lustig in a Third Avenue coffee house owned by gangster Humpty Jackson. Surgeons at Bellevue Hospital give Lustig little hope for recovery, discharging him on August 14 with one of two bullets still lodged near his spine. On August 16, Lustig returns to the same coffee shop and is slain by unidentified shooters.

August 29: Residents of Manhattan's Lower East side rally at a synagogue on Rivington Street, to discuss formation of an anti-gang vigilance committee.

August 31: Big Tim Sullivan dies in a Bronx railroad yard, after fleeing a sanitarium. Since his family does not report him missing, burial as a vagrant in Potter's Field is scheduled despite Sullivan's monogrammed clothing. A policeman on the morgue detail identified Sullivan's corpse by chance on September 13.

September: Detroit mafioso Antonio Giannola Jr. suffers severe wounds in an ambush by gunmen from the White Hand Society, but survives.

September 4: Future mobster Meyer Harris "Mickey" Cohen born in Brooklyn, N.Y.

September 19: Arrested by NYPD for felonious assault, Benny Fein posts $2,000 bail.

October 6: Future Chicago mobster and government informant Leonard "Lenny" Patrick born in England.

October 9: Benny Fein faces new assault charges, later dismissed.

October 15: President Woodrow Wilson (1856–1924) commutes the prison sentence of convicted counterfeiter Nicholas Sylvester to five years. Sylvester leaves custody on October 28.

October 16: NYPD officers arrest Benny Fein for violating the Sullivan Law. He posts $5,000 bond.

October 29: Black Handers kill landlady Josephine Bannecorso and one of her boarders in Mountain View, Calif. Police suspect Antonio Pedone.

November 14: Future mafioso and informant Aladena "Jimmy the Weasel" Fratianno born in Cleveland, Ohio.

November 25: Members of the Gianolla gang kill Salvatore and Vito Adamo on Mullet Boulevard, Detroit.

1914 Alabama congressman Richard Hobson proposes national prohibition of alcohol on grounds that "liquor will actually make a brute out of a Negro, causing him to commit unnatural crimes. The effect is the same on the white man, though the white man being further evolved it takes longer time to reduce him to the same level."

January 9: Labor racketeer Jack Sirocco and several members of his gang survive an ambush by Benny Fein's gunmen on St. Marks Place, Manhattan.

February 8: The *New York Times* runs an article entitled "Negro Cocaine 'Fiends' Are New Southern Menace: Murder and Insanity Increasing Among Lower-Class Blacks." The story claims that southern sheriffs are buying larger-caliber pistols to bring down coke-crazed African Americans.

February 14: New York's State Court of Appeals overturns Charles Becker's murder conviction and orders a new trial, accusing trial judge John Goff of "gross misconduct," while citing prosecution witnesses as "dangerous and degenerate." In San Francisco, Calif., Black Hand gangsters murder Calogero Abruzzi.

March 3: Unknown gunmen kill James "Gold Mine Jimmy" Cariggio, founder of the Jimmy Curley Gang, outside a bookstore on Manhattan's East 13th Street.

March 15: Future mafioso Aniello "Mr. Niel" Dellacroce born in New York City's Little Italy.

March 20: Future Detroit mafioso Frank Randazzo born in Terrasini, Sicily.

April 13: Condemned inmates Francesco Cirofici, Harry Horowitz, Louis Rosenberg, and Jacob Seidenscher die in Sing Sing's electric chair for the slaying of Herman Rosenthal.

April 17: Five gunmen die in a battle between gangs led by Joe Baker and Joe Morello, on Manhattan's Third Avenue.

April 20: Company gunmen hired by John D. Rockefeller Jr. and enlisted as special "militia" officers fire on striking miners at Ludlow, Colo., then torch their tent city, killing five men, two women, and 12 children.

April 26: Future mafioso William "Willie Rat" Dominick Cammisano Sr. born in Kansas City, Mo.

April 29: Future mobster Giovanni Ignazio Dioguardi, AKA John "Johnny Dio" Dioguardi, born on Manhattan's Lower East Side.

May: Benny Fein agrees to testify against various New York gangsters and labor leaders, in return for a reduced sentence on assault charges. His testimony results in 33 indictments.

May 5: Convicted Mafia counterfeiter Vincenzo Giglio dies in prison.

May 10: Gunman Benjamin Snyder kills labor racketeer Pinchy Paul on Manhattan's Norfolk Street, presumably acting on orders from rival gang boss Joe Rosenzweig. Snyder subsequently pleads guilty to manslaughter.

May 14: Charles Becker's second murder trial begins, before Judge Samuel Seabury (1873–1958). Jurors convict Becker on May 22, and he is once again condemned. Becker dies in the electric chair at Sing Sing on July 30, 1915, still proclaiming his innocence.

May 23: Mafia hitman Umberto Valenti kills Terranova gang member Fortunato Lo Monte at First Avenue and 116th Street, in Manhattan. Conflicting reports blame the murder on Giuseppe Masseria and Salvatore D'Aquila.

May 31: Future mob enforcer Joseph Gagliano born in Chicago.

June 2: Future mafioso Antonio "Tony G" Giordano born in St. Louis, Mo.

June 9: Ciro Terranova filed a declaration of intent to become a U.S. citizen in New York City. He is formally naturalized on February 11, 1919.

July 7: Future mobster John "Jackie the Lackey" Cerone born in Chicago.

July 16: Chicago Detective Sergeant Stanley Birns suffers fatal gunshot wounds during a vice raid in the Levee District. Police charge Roxie Vanilli, a New York gunman recently imported by Johnny Torrio, with the murder.

July 23: An ex–police chief recently convicted of liquor violations kills Deputy U.S. Marshals Holmes Davidson and William Plank as they attempt to serve a warrant at his home in Tulsa, Okla.

July 28: World War I officially begins in Europe.

August 14: Unknown gunmen ambush Black Hand gangsters Vinzione Forte and Felippo Petrillo on North Main Street, Los Angeles. Petrillo dies from his wounds.

September: Antonio and Joe Pedone murder Black Hander-turned-informer Joseph Mello in Los Angeles. Paul Tribiani retaliates with a bungled attempt on Joe Pedrone's life, then allegedly commits suicide.

October 15: Congress passes the Clayton Antitrust Act, tightening restrictions on monopolies and other anticompetitive practices, while legitimizing nonviolent strikes and boycotts.

November 6: Members of the Hudson Dusters gang shoot rival Gophers boss Owney Madden at the Arbor Dance Hall, on Manhattan's Seventh Avenue. Madden survives five bullet wounds.

November 15: Future mafioso Santo Trafficante Jr. born in Tampa, Fla.

November 19: Future mafioso Domenico Brucceleri, AKA "Dominic Phillip Brooklier," born in California.

November 28: Owney Madden kills Hudson Duster Patsy Doyle at a saloon on Manhattan's Eighth Avenue. At trial in May 1915, Madden is convicted of murder and sentenced to 20 years in Sing Sing Prison.

November 29: Members of Benny Fein's gang clash with rivals from a gang led by Jack Sirocco on Greene Street, in Manhattan. Gangster Max Green suffers fatal gunshot wounds in the battle, which touches off New York's first "labor sluggers' war," lasting into 1917.

December 14: Future mafioso Joseph "Joe" Colombo Sr. born in Brooklyn, N.Y.

December 17: Congress passes the Harrison Narcotics Act, described as "An Act To provide for the registration of, with collectors of internal revenue, and to impose a special tax on all persons who produce, import, manufacture, compound, deal in, dispense, sell, distribute, or give away opium or coca leaves, their salts, derivatives, or preparations, and for other purposes."

1915 Utah lawmakers enact the first state ban on marijuana. France outlaws absinthe. Immigrant mobsters Samuele Cardinelli, Nicholas "The Choir Boy" Viana, and Frank Campione launch a three-year wave of Black Hand terrorism in Chicago, claiming at least 20 lives and leaving hundreds wounded by bombs. Yakuza gangster Harukichi Yamaguchi founds the Yamaguchi-gumi crime syndicate in Kobe, Japan.

January 19: Police in arrest miner and IWW member Joel Emmanuel Hägglund, AKA Joe Hill, for the holdup-murders of John and Arling Morrison in Salt Lake City, Utah. Convicted in a trial where his union membership became a major issue, Hill is executed by a firing squad on November 19. Today, some historians consider his case a classic frame-up.

January 25: The U.S. Supreme Court, in *Coppage v. Kansas*, approves "yellow dog" contracts, which forbid union membership.

February 20: Future mafioso Frank Diecidue born in Florida.

March 12: NYPD arrests Frank Costello for carrying concealed weapons. He receives a one-year jail term and serves 10 months.

March 13: Future Buffalo, N.Y., mafioso Joseph Fino born.

March 21: Future mobster Mario Antonio DeStefano born in Chicago.

March 22: Future IBT president Roy Lee Williams born in Ottumwa, Iowa.

May 14: Moonshiners kill Deputy U.S. Marshal C.P. Phelgar during a raid on their still in Floyd County, Va.

May 17: Unknown gunmen kill Giosue Gallucci, "king" of the East Harlem rackets, and his son Luca at Gallucci's coffeehouse on East 109th Street.

May 27: NYPD and agents of Charles Parkhurst's Society for the Prevention of Crime arrest gamblers Peter Matthews, John Saul and Solomon Goldschmidt for operating a policy network. Held on $10,000 bail, all three later plead guilty and receive short sentences. Matthews dies in custody on July 21, 1916.

June 25: Three convicted killers attack Benjamin Snyder on the day of his scheduled sentencing for manslaughter in the 1914 death of Pinchy Paul. Guards intervene to save his life, reporting that the assailants called Snyder a "rat" and "squealer."

June 26: Future mafioso Paul "Big Paul" Castellano born in Brooklyn, N.Y.

July 1: Monk Eastman receives a two-year sentence for grand larceny. Nevada legalizes pari-mutuel betting at racetracks.

July 6: Prosecutors in New York City charge mafioso Jack Dragna with extortion. He receives a three-year sentence on January 26, 1916, but serves only a fraction of the time.

August 21: Ignazio Lupo receives five days in solitary on restricted diet for "renumbering clothing contrary to prison rules."

October 13: Mafia gunmen kill Thomas Lomonte on First Avenue, in Manhattan. His brother Charles died in similar fashion, in May 1914.

October 27: NYPD arrests three men for running a "white slave" ring on the Lower East Side, allegedly selling women for $10 each.

October 28: Vincenzo Terranova files a petition for naturalization with New York. He files a second petition on May 6, 1920, denied three months later (August 6) with a notation that he "was found to be of not good moral character."

November 3: Mafiosi in Corleone, Sicily, murder activist Bernadino Verro five years after their first attempt on his life.

November 20: Chinese President Yuan Shikai endorses monarchy, subsequently proclaiming himself Emperor of the Chinese Empire on December 12, with his Hongxian Dynasty beginning on January 1, 1916. Yunnan military governor Cai E (or Tsai Ao) rebels against Yuan on December 25, followed by other provinces.

December: Joseph Rosenzweig receives a 10-year sentence for his role in the murder of Pinchy Paul.

December 12: Future singer, actor, and underworld sycophant Francis Albert "Frank" Sinatra born in Hoboken, N.J.

1916 Australia permits the Queensland Patriotic Fund to hold a "Golden Casket" lottery, raising funds for disabled World War veterans and survivors of those killed overseas. The *United States Pharmacopeia* drops whiskey and brandy from its list of medicinal drugs. Chemists at the University of Frankfurt, Germany, synthesize oxycodone from thebaine (paramorphine), an opium alkaloid.

February 12: Future mayor Joseph Lawrence Alioto born in San Francisco, Calif.

March 5: Future "Public Enemy No. 1" Pierre "Crazy Pete" Loutrel born in Château-du-Loir, France.

March 6: Future mob financier Irwin Signey Weiner born in Chicago.

March 22: Yuan Shikai renounces his plan to restore monarchy in China.

April 1: Gus Alex, future protégé of mob financier Jake Guzik, born in Chicago.

Summer: NYPD launches a campaign to purge Manhattan of street gangs, claiming success by year's end.

May 17: President Wilson commutes mafioso Salvatore Cina's prison sentence to 10 years. Authorities schedule his release for November 7.

June 5: President Yuan Shikai dies from uremia in China. Announcement of his death on June 6 begins a 12-year warlord era nationwide, fragmenting China.

June 9: Congress passes the Chamberlain-Ferris Act, reclaiming 2.8 million acres in Oregon from the Southern Pacific Company, successor to the scandal-ridden Oregon & California Railroad.

June 10: Future mobster Peter "Mr. Bread" Lo-Cascio born on Manhattan's Lower East Side.

June 14: Gangsters Lloyd Bopp and Frank McErlane kill Officer Herman Malow Jr. after he interrupts a quarrel with other thugs in Oak Park, Ill. Bopp receives a death sentence at trial and hangs on December 6, 1918. McErlane receives a one-year sentence, with two years added for an attempted escape from Joliet Prison.

June 24: Leaders of New York City's Morello Mafia family meet at Coney Island with officers of two groups allied with the rival Camorra, Pelligrino Morano's Coney Island Gang and Leopoldo Lauritano's Navy Street Gang. Together, they plot the murder of Camorra boss Joseph DeMarco, later accomplished after several false starts.

July 16: Imprisoned numbers racketeer Peter Matthews dies from natural causes on Blackwell's Island, in New York City's East River.

July 20: Gangsters George "Lefty" Esposito, Tom Pagano, and Giuseppe Verizzano murder rivals Joe DeMarco and Charles Lombardi in New York City, escaping with aid from mafiosi Umberto Valenti and Nick Sassi.

July 22: A bomb explodes during a "Preparedness Day" parade in San Francisco, Calif., killing 10 persons and wounding 40. Police frame IWW leaders Thomas Mooney (1882–1942) and Warren Billings (1893–1972), convicting both in separate trials rife with perjury and suppression of evidence. Both are sentenced to hang, with those sentences commuted to life imprisonment in 1918. Governor Culbert Olson pardons both defendants in 1939.

July 25: Unknown gunmen kill gambler and alleged camorista Giuseppe DiMarco. Police speculate that mafiosi shot DiMarco in retaliation for the Lomonte brothers' murders in 1914–15.

August 19: Strikebreakers hired by mill owner Neil Jamison attack striking workers in Everett, Wash., while police stand by and watch, claiming the waterfront site is federal property. Later the same day, local officers arrest workers who defend themselves against another attack, in the same place.

September 1: Congress passes the Keating-Owen Child Labor Act, banning interstate sale of goods manufactured by children.

September 7: Gunmen employed by Pellegrino Morano, American "grand master" of the Neapolitan Camorra, kill mafioso Nicolo Morello and bodyguard Charles Urbiaco at Vollero's Café in Manhattan, as they arrive for a peace conference. Morano receives a life sentence in May 1918, for ordering the murders. NYPD also arrests mafioso Umberto Valenti on September 7, for carrying a concealed pistol, but the charges are later dropped.

October: NYPD officers find the remains of camorista Salvatore DiMarco, brother of murder victim Giuseppe DiMarco, under the Manhattan side of the Queensboro Bridge.

October 30: Vigilantes in Everett, Wash., force speakers at an IWW rally to run a gauntlet of clubs and whips, ending with impalement on a spiked cattle guard.

November 5: Company gunmen fire on an IWW meeting in Everett, Wash., killing seven victims and wounding 50.

November 12: Gunman Mike Marino kills Tony Pariese, a member of the Matranga Mafia family, at Eastlake Avenue and Henry Street, Los Angeles.

November 30: Suspected Black Hand gangsters kill businessman Gaetano Ingrassia on Powell Street, in San Francisco.

1917 Nathan "Kid Dropper" Kaplan and John "Johnny Spanish" Weyler leave prison and join forces to create a new labor-racketeering syndicate in New York City. German physicians begin clinical use of oxycodone, under the brand name Eukodal.

February 6: Future Manhattan mafioso John "Sonny" Franzese born at sea, aboard a ship bearing his parents from Italy to New York City.

February 25: Peter Magaddino, son of Stefano Magaddino, born in Brooklyn, N.Y.

March 16: Members of the Camorra-allied Navy Street Gang murder Joseph "Chuck" Nazzaro in Yonkers, N.Y., leaving his corpse on trolley tracks.

April 6: Congress declares war on Germany. Monk Eastman volunteers for service in the U.S. Army and serves with the 106th Infantry Regiment in France, prompting Governor Al Smith (1873–1944) to reinstate full citizenship privileges suspended after Eastman's felony conviction.

May 24: Future mafioso Anthony "Tony Pro" Provenzano born.

May 25: LAPD officers arrest mafioso Jack Dragna. They deliver him to NYPD escorts on June 15, for trial on pending murder charges, but that case is later dismissed.

June: The American Medical Association passes a resolution endorsing national prohibition of liquor as a means of eradicating syphilis.

July 26: John Edgar Hoover joins the DOJ as a clerk.

July 31: Giuseppe Morello files a petition for executive clemency. President Wilson commutes Morello's sentence to 15 years on January 8, 1918. Prison authorities release Morello on March 18, 1920.

August 1: Vigilantes lynch IWW organizer Frank Little in Butte, Mont.

September 5: Federal agents raid the IWW headquarters in 48 cities.

September 7: Camorra gunmen execute mafiosi Nicolo Morello and Charles Ubriaco in Brooklyn, N.Y.

September 13: Future mafioso Joseph "Piney" Armone born in New York City.

November 5: Boyle Heights gang leader Orsario "Sam" Matranga suffers fatal gunshot wounds in the garage of his home on Darwin Avenue, Los Angeles. LAPD suspects Mike Marino.

November 27: Members of the LaFata gang kill San Francisco fish merchant Mariano Alioto, son-in-law of 1916 murder victim Gaetano Ingrassia and uncle of future mayor Joseph Alioto.

December 17: Congress declares war against German ally Austria-Hungary. In Los Angeles, police find suspected Black Hander Carlo Cono buried in a shallow grave near Florence Avenue.

December 18: Congress passes the 18th Amendment to the U.S. Constitution, banning "the manufacture, sale, or transportation of intoxicating liquors within, the importation thereof into, or the exportation thereof from the United States and all territory subject to the jurisdiction thereof." A gunman kills suspected informer Pietro Matranga on the same Los Angeles street corner where Tony Pariese died in November 1916. Once again, LAPD blames Mike Marino.

December 23: Italian gunmen ambush and murder Officer Guy Norris in Akron, Ohio, after police crack down on brothels and gambling dens.

December 27: An inmate at Atlanta Federal Prison fatally bludgeons Deputy Warden James Brock, while Ignazio Lupo watches from six feet away. Lupo denies knowledge of the crime, but another inmate later says the mafioso positioned himself "to see this thing come off."

1918 New York City's "second labor sluggers war" erupts after a falling out between racketeers Nathan Kaplan and Johnny Spanish, continuing until gunmen kill Spanish in July 1919. The Native American Church incorporates under Oklahoma state law, claiming peyote as a sacrament.

January: NYPD officers detain alleged mafioso Umberto Valenti as a suspect in the murders of Camorra members Joseph DeMarco and Charles Lombardi. He turns state's evidence against another suspect prior to his release without charges in November 1918.

January 10: Mafiosi ambush Officers Edward Costigan and Joseph Hunt on North High Street in Akron, Ohio. Costigan dies instantly, while Hunt survived until January 12.

January 8: Mississippi ratifies the 18th Amendment.

January 11: Virginia ratifies the 18th Amendment.

January 14: Kentucky ratifies the 18th Amendment.

January 24: Former Secret Service agent William Flynn writes to President Wilson, supporting Ignazio Lupo's application for executive clemency. He follows up with a second letter in Lupo's favor on February 5. The effort fails.

January 25: North Dakota ratifies the 18th Amendment.

January 29: South Carolina ratifies the 18th Amendment.

January 31: Future mafioso Phillip "Rusty" Rastelli born in Queens, N.Y.

February 13: Maryland ratifies the 18th Amendment.

February 14: New York wine merchant Allessandro Vollero and eight other camoristi defendants stand trial for the 1917 murders of Nicholas Terranova and Charles Ubriaco. The judge's illness produces a mistrial on February 18. Jurors convicted Vallero and Camorra "grand master" Pellegrino Morano on June 20, 1918, whereupon both were sentenced to death. Both were reprieved, and Vollero's sentence was commuted to life on appeal, in October 1919. Authorities released him on April 28, 1933.

February 19: Montana ratifies the 18th Amendment.

March 4: Texas ratifies the 18th Amendment.

March 12: Another Mafia ambush in Akron, Ohio, claims the life of Patrolman Gothin Richards, shot five times on South Main Street. An anonymous call subsequently implicates Black Hand leader Rosario Borgio and six gang members — Lorenzo Biondo, Pasquale Biondo, Paul Chiavaro, Tony Manfredi, Vito Mezzano, and James Palmeri — in the slaying of four Akron policemen. Manfredi turns state's evidence and receives a 20-year sentence, while his testimony convicts the other at trial. Pasquale Biondo dies in the electric chair on October 4, 1918, followed by Borgio and Mezzano on February 21, 1919, and Chiavaro on July 24, 1919. Lorenzo Biondo and James Palmeri receive life sentences. Governor George White (1872–1953) secretly paroles Biondo on May 25, 1934, whereupon he flees to Italy. Palmeri was still imprisoned as of 1964.

March 17: Matranga gunmen execute Joseph LaPaglia on Central Avenue, Los Angeles.

March 18: Delaware ratifies the 18th Amendment.

March 20: South Dakota ratifies the 18th Amendment.

March 28: Future Mafia associate, CIA contract agent, and alleged JFK assassination conspirator David William Ferrie born in Cleveland, Ohio.

April 2: Massachusetts ratifies the 18th Amendment.

April 17: Future mafioso Eddie Guarella born in Detroit.

May 1: Michigan goes "dry." Liquor smuggling begins the same day.

May 24: Arizona ratifies the 18th Amendment.

May 27: Future mafioso Frank "Mad Bomber" Balistrieri born in Milwaukee, Wis.

June 3: The U.S. Supreme Court, in *Hammer v. Dagenhart*, declares the Keating-Owen Child Labor Act unconstitutional.

June 6: Authorities charge Ciro Terranova and five others with arranging the 1916 contract murders of Charles Lombardi and Joe DiMarco, later dropping the charges on grounds that all prosecution witnesses are co-conspirators. On June 7, defendants James Notaro and Alfonso "Butch" Sgroia plead guilty to first-degree manslaughter, receiving sentence of six to 10 years each.

June 26: Georgia ratifies the 18th Amendment.

August 3: Louisiana ratifies the 18th Amendment.

October 18: Gunmen employed by Detroit mafioso Antonio Giannola execute dissident gang member Pietro Bosco in his garage, at Trumbull and Ash Streets.

November 11: An armistice ends fighting in the First World War, although a state of war technically persists between combatant nations until the Treaty of Versailles is signed on June 28, 1919.

November 27: Florida ratifies the 18th Amendment.

November 30: Matranga gangsters kill rival mafioso Jack Cusimano on Darwin Avenue, Los Angeles.

1919 Japanese chemist Akira Ogata synthesizes crystallized methamphetamine by reducing ephedrine using red phosphorous and iodine. John Thompson (1860–1940) invents the Thompson submachine gun, AKA the "Tommy gun," the "Chicago Piano," the "Chicago Typewriter," and the "Chopper." Chemist Ernst Spath synthesizes mescaline at Austria's University of Vienna.

January 2: Michigan ratifies the 18th Amendment.

January 3: While visiting the home of a friend who was recently murdered, Detroit mafioso Antonio Giannola is shot and killed by his adopted son and personal bodyguard, Tony Alescio. The slaying touches off a bloody power struggle in Detroit.

January 7: Ohio and Oklahoma ratify the 18th Amendment.

January 8: Idaho and Maine ratify the 18th Amendment.

January 9: West Virginia ratifies the 18th Amendment.

January 13: California, Tennessee, and Washington ratify the 18th Amendment.

January 14: Future Italian prime minister and indicted Mafia associate Giulio Andreotti born in Rome. Arkansas and Kansas ratify the 18th Amendment.

January 15: Alabama, Colorado, Iowa and New Hampshire ratify the 18th Amendment.

January 16: Missouri, Nebraska, North Carolina, Utah and Wyoming complete formal ratification of the 18th Amendment, scheduled to take effect at midnight on January 16, 1920.

January 17: Minnesota and Wisconsin ratify the 18th Amendment.

January 19: Future mafioso Anthony "Tony Jacks" Giacalone Sr. born in Detroit.

January 20: New Mexico ratifies the 18th Amendment.

January 21: Nevada ratifies the 18th Amendment.

January 29: New York and Vermont ratify the 18th Amendment.

February 5: National League president John Heydler dismisses charges that Cincinnati Reds first baseman Harold "Prince Hal" Chase bet against his team and bribed pitcher Jimmy Ring to throw a game against the New York Giants, in collusion with gamblers. The Reds trade Chase to the Giants, where he becomes first base coach at the end of the 1919 season. That same year, persons unknown send Heydler a copy of a $500 check ($6,160 today) which Chase received from a gambler for throwing a game in 1918. Heydler ordered Giants owner Charles Stoneham to release Chase, effectively ending his baseball career.

February 10: William Allen briefly serves as director of the Bureau of Investigation, replaced by William Flynn on June 30.

February 24: Congress passes the Child Labor

Tax Law, imposing a 10-percent excise tax on the net profits of a company who employed children "under the age of sixteen in any mine or quarry, and under the age of fourteen in any mill, cannery, workshop, factory, or manufacturing establishment."

February 25: An unknown shotgunner kills mafioso Mike "Rizzo" Marino in Los Angeles. Pennsylvania ratifies the 18th Amendment.

February 26: Gianolla gangsters shoot Vito Renda 21 times in an ambush outside the Wayne County Jail, in Detroit.

March 20: Future mafioso Gennaro "Jerry" Angiulo born in Boston's North End.

April 9: Future mafioso Michael James Genovese born in East Liberty, Pa.

April 21: Future fascist, financier, and Mafia associate Licio Gelli born in Pistoia, Italy.

May 6: Connecticut ratifies the 18th Amendment.

May 27: Ohio goes "dry." Liquor sales and smuggling increase instantly.

July 1: William Flynn assumes command of the U.S. Bureau of Investigation.

July 29: Am unknown gunman, presumably employed by Nathan Kaplan, kills labor racketeer Joseph "Johnny Spanish" Weyler outside a restaurant on Manhattan's Second Avenue.

August 21: Gianolla gunmen execute Joseph Carolla in Detroit.

September 9: Future gambler, sports commentator and Las Vegas bookie Dimetrios Georgios Synodinos, AKA "Jimmy the Greek" Snyder, born in Steubenville, Ohio. On the same day, riots and looting rock Boston, as 1,117 for the right to unionize with the AFL. Governor Calvin Coolidge (1872–1933) deploys militiamen to police the city and becomes an overnight celebrity, securing the Republican vice-presidential nomination for 1920.

October 1: World Series play begins, with the Chicago White Sox facing the Cincinnati Reds. Gambler Arnold Rothstein, acting through lieutenant Abraham "The Little Hebrew" Attell, bribes five White Sox players to throw the series. Players Eddie Cicotte and "Shoeless Joe" Jackson confess their guilt to a Chicago grand jury on September 28, 1920, but later recant, and their confessions mysteriously vanish, resulting in acquittal of the indicted players at trial. Rothstein escapes indictment, while eight White Sox players are banned from Major League Baseball for life. The "Black Sox" scandal prompts team owners to appoint federal judge Kenesaw Mountain Landis (1866–1944) as the first Commissioner of Baseball.

October 2: Vitale gunmen murder rival Sam Gianolla in Detroit.

October 28: Congress passes the National Prohibition Act, AKA the Volstead Act, prescribing criminal penalties for violation of the 18th Amendment's ban on alcoholic beverages. President Woodrow Wilson (1856–1924) vetoes the law, but Congress overrides his veto the same day. During the next six months, more than 15,000 physicians, plus 57,000 druggists and drug manufacturers, apply for licenses to prescribe and sell "medicinal" liquor.

October 29: Congress passes the National Motor Vehicle Theft, AKA the Dyer Act, punishing interstate transportation of stolen cars.

November 11: An Armistice Day parade turns violent in Centralia, Wash., as American Legionnaires storm a local IWW meeting hall. The Wobblies defend themselves, fatally shooting three rioters. Legionnaires beat, castrate, and lynch IWW member Wesley Everest. Police and vigilantes spend the next eight days arresting local union members, while Deputy Sheriff John Haney dies from "friendly fire" by fellow posse members on November 15.

December 14: Suspected bootleggers kill Los Angeles resident William Mead in an apparent case of mistaken identity.

December 27: Detroit police report 20 deaths from lethal homemade liquor since September 1. In Cleveland, Ohio, three drinkers have died, with 21 more hospitalized.

December 29: Police blames bootleggers for the murder of Thomas Leighton on Jefferson Street, Los Angeles.

December 30: Mobster Dean O'Banion hijacks a truckload of whiskey outside Chicago's Bismarck Hotel.

1920 Maryland legalizes pari-mutuel betting at racetracks. Moses Annenberg buys the New York–based *Daily Racing Form*, gaining a virtual monopoly over distribution of racetrack information in the United States. Voters in British Columbia end Prohibition.

January: Christopher Wilson, a member of Lou Blonger's gang in Denver, Colo., pleads guilty to manslaughter in the 1916 slaying of fellow gang member Frank Turner. He receives a one-day jail sentence, on condition that he leave Colorado forever.

January 12: Future gangster and soldier-of-fortune Raymond Couraud, AKA Captain Jack William Raymond Lee, born at Surgères, France.

January 16: America goes "dry" at midnight, under the 18th Amendment and the Volstead Act. Within the hour, masked gunmen steal $100,000 worth of whiskey from two freight cars in Chicago. Police suspect Hershie Miller's gang from the West Side.

February 2: Labor racketeer Maurice "Mossy"

Enright dies in an ambush outside his Chicago home. Prosecutors charge Timothy "Big Tim" Murphy, James Cosmano, Michael "Dago Mike" Carozzo and James Vinci with the slaying. Jurors acquit all but Vinci at trial.

February 22: The first greyhound racetrack employing mechanical rabbits opens in Emeryville, N.Y. Major A.V. Dalrymple, supervisor of Prohibition enforcement for the Midwest, reports that Iron County, Mich., is in revolt against the U.S. liquor ban. U.S. Attorney General Mitchell Palmer countermands Dalrymple's effort to impose martial law on February 27.

February 26: Detroit police arrest bootlegger Louis Dalitz for "uttering and publishing," then drop the nebulous charge.

April 8: Authorities grant parole to convicted mafioso Giuseppe Calicchio. He leaves prison on April 11.

April 13: Roberto Calvi, future banker and Mafia-allied swindler, born in Milan, Italy.

April 15: Gunmen rob and kill a paymaster and guard at the Slater and Morrill Shoe Company in Braintree, Mass., escaping with $15,776. While evidence points to a gang led by Joe Morelli, police arrest Italian-born laborers and anarchists Ferdinando Nicola Sacco and Bartolomeo Vanzetti. Both are convicted of robbery, then of murder in a second trial — both with openly-biased Judge Webster Thayer presiding. Their case becomes a cause célèbre, climaxed with execution of both defendants on August 23, 1927. Fifty years later to the day, Governor Michael Dukakis signs a proclamation reading: "Any stigma and disgrace should be forever removed from the names of Nicola Sacco and Bartolomeo Vanzetti. We are not here to say whether these men are guilty or innocent. We are here to say that the high standards of justice, which we in Massachusetts take such pride in, failed Sacco and Vanzetti."

April 17: Federal authorities release convicted mafioso Antonio Cecala.

May 8: Michele "The Shark" Sindona, future banker with Mafia ties, born in Patti, Italy.

May 9: Detroit police find mafioso Nick Forti with his throat was cut.

May 11: Chicago vice lord Jim Colosimo receives a call from lieutenant Johnny Torrio, alerting him to the arrival of a booze shipment at Colosimo's Café on South Wabash. On arrival, Colosimo is slain by a still-unknown gunman. Torrio assumes command of Colosimo's empire.

May 19: Executives of the Stone Mountain Coal Company join hired gunmen from the Baldwin-Felts Detective Agency to evict striking miners from company-owned homes in Matewan, W.Va. Mayor Cabell Testerman and Police Chief Sid Hatfield oppose the evictions, sparking a shootout that claims the lives of Testerman, two miners, and 15 detectives.

May 20: Police raid the Chicago Cubs' bleachers at Wrigley Field, arresting 24 fans for gambling.

May 28: Future gangster François Marcantoni born in Corsica.

June: Joe Masseria establishes a curbside liquor exchange near NYPD headquarters, with booze openly traded from vehicles on Broome, Elizabeth, Grand and Kenmare Streets.

June 13: Moonshiners murder Prohibition agent William Dorsey while he searches for stills in White County, Ga.

June 15: Future mafioso Ilario "Larry Baione" Zannino born in Roxbury, Mass.

June 17: Mafioso Giuseppe Calicchio, already free on parole, receives a presidential commutation of his sentence, ending official supervision on June 19.

June 18: Future mafioso Matthew "Matty the Horse" Ianniello born in New York City.

June 30: Corrupt U.S. Attorney General Harry Daugherty commutes the remainder of Ignazio Lupo's prison term, in exchange for Lupo's promise to leave America. Lupo leaves prison the same day.

July 18: Future mafioso Louis Tom Dragna born in Los Angeles.

August: Bandits steal $400,000 from U.S. mail train at Chicago's Union Station. Federal prosecutors charge Big Tim Murphy with the crime on February 7, 1921. He posts $30,000 bond on May 27, but is convicted at trial on November 9, 1921, and receives a seven year sentence. Murphy remains free, pending appeal of his conviction.

August 7: President Wilson commutes the remainer of Giuseppe Palermo's prison term. Palermo leaves prison on August 8.

August 10: Drive-by gunmen wound Gianolla gang lieutenant Giuseppi Manzello and Angelo Meli on Larned Avenue, Detroit. Manzello dies on August 13, while Meli recovers to plot revenge against rival John Vitale. Salvatore Catalanotte assumes command of the former Giannola gang.

August 11: Friends of Manzello and Meli in Detroit murder Antonio Badalamenti, John Vitale's nephew and chief lieutenant. Police arrest Manzello loyalists Joe Zerilli, Bill Tocco, Leo Cellura, John Mangone, Vito Paraino, Joseph Delmonico, James Barraco, and Carlo Manzello (Joe's cousin) on suspicion of murder, but later release them.

August 17: Gianolla gangsters kill Joseph Vitale in Detroit.

August 28: Deputy Sheriff Homer Adrean dies in a shootout with moonshiners in Oklahoma County, Okla. The battle leaves one suspect dead, while Prohibition agent Stanton Weiss dies from gunshot wounds on October 28. Vigilantes subsequently lynch a second gunman.

September 5: Wichita gangsters Eddie Adams, Ray Majors and Walter Majors try to rob Harry Trusdell's illegal casino in Kansas City, Mo. The resultant shootout leaves one player dead and the bandits in police custody.

September 13: Rival bootleggers Jack Blandino and Roy Garoldino kill each other in a shootout at Blandino's speakeasy on East Ninth Street, Los Angeles.

September 27: Future carabinieri general and Mafia victim Carlo Alberto Dalla Chiesa born in Saluzzo, Italy.

October 2: Two carloads of gunmen kill John Vitale in Detroit, ending the long Giannola-Vitale war with 18 well-placed bullets.

October 11: Prohibition agents intercept a liquor caravan en route from Milwaukee to Hurley, Wis., sparking a shootout that leaves one man dead and another wounded. Agents seize three cars and $30,000 worth of booze.

October 15: Gunmen slay mafioso Andrea Licato on Clinton Street, Detroit.

October 23: Appointed by Benito Mussolini, Cesare Mori assumes office as prefect of Palermo, Sicily, launching an all-out fascist campaign against the Mafia.

October 25: Prohibition agent J.H. Rose suffers fatal gunshot wounds while raiding a still in Asheville, N.C. Future IBT official and hitman Frank Sheeran born in Philadelphia, Pa.

November 10: Journalists disclose that justices of the peace in New York City sell pistol permits indiscriminately for as little as two dollars each.

November 19: Moonshiners ambush two Prohibition agents while they are inspecting a still in Perry, Okla., wounding both. Agent Kirby Frans dies on November 20, while his partner survives. The gunman eludes pursuers.

December 6: Prohibition agent Richard Griffin suffers fatal gunshot wounds while raiding a still near Gadsden, Ala.

December 7: Ignazio Lupo files an application for executive clemency, seeking a pardon or commutation to end his parole.

December 9: Chicago police announce a new campaign against illegal casinos. Gambling continues unabated.

December 16: Moonshiners murder Prohibition agent Richard Jackson in Taylor County, Ga.

December 23: Detroit police find gambler and murder suspect Dan Cleary shot dead on Mack Road.

December 24: Unknown gunmen slay Prohibition agent James McGuiness in Bayonne, N.J.

December 26: Monk Eastman quarrels with crime partner Jerry Bohan, a corrupt Prohibition agent, at the Bluebird Cafe in Lower Manhattan. Bohan follows Eastman to the entrance of the 14th Street subway station and shoots him dead. Bohan serves three years in prison for the slaying.

December 28: Police in Toledo, Ohio, receive orders to arrest all "suspicious" persons and shoot to kill if resistance is offered.

December 29: Joe Masseria personally executes rival bootlegger Salvatore Mauro on Chrystie Street, Manhattan, apparently ending the long Mafia-Camorra feud. In Cincinnati, Ohio, a whiskey wholesaler pleads guilty, logging the first federal conviction for operating a liquor ring.

1920–1931 The U.S. government hires 17,971 Prohibition agents to enforce the Volstead Act. Of those, 1,604 are fired for bribery, extortion, theft, falsification of records, conspiracy, forgery, and perjury. Another 11,982 are dismissed "without prejudice" or explanation for their termination.

1921 Sangerman's Bombers, an underworld terrorist gang led by John Sangerman, offer demolition services to various Chicago bootlegging gangs. Gang warfare erupts in California among four Chinese Tongs, the Bing Kong, Jung Ying, Suey Don, and Suey Ying. Voters in Manitoba and Saskatchewan, Canada, end Prohibition. The Council of the American Medical Association refuses to confirm the AMA's resolution supporting Prohibition.

January: Salvatore Lucania joins Joe Masseria's Mafia family. Lennington Small (1862–1936) takes office as governor of Illinois, proceeding to pardon 1,000 convicted felons. They include white-slaver Harry Guzik (brother of mob treasurer Jake Guzik) and Chicago bootlegger Edward "Spike" O'Donnell.

January 19: Future mobster William "Billy Batts" Devino born in Brooklyn, N.Y.

January 23: Detroit policeman Harry Sleizinger dies after being shot by a state food and drug officer. Agents say they found "a quantity" of liquor in Sleizinger's car and shot him as he tried to flee arrest.

January 27: Prosecutors in Cook County, Ill., indict "Al Brown"— actually Al Capone — for keeping a "disorderly house" and operating slot machines. "Brown" pleads guilty on April 14, paying a $150 fine and $110 in court costs.

January 28: Prohibition agents seize 400 cases of whiskey en route from New York to Cleveland, Ohio.

February 6: Milwaukee mafioso Vito Guardalabene dies of natural causes, replaced by his son Peter.

February 7: A federal grand jury in Cleveland indicts New York cabaret proprietor Moe Baron and former Deputy Internal Revenue collector Bernard Levy for smuggling liquor into Ohio.

February 24: Peter Marcello Sr., younger brother of Carlos Marcello and owner of the French Quarter's Sho-Bar club, born in New Orleans.

March 1: Bootleggers kill Prohibition agent Jacob Green during a liquor raid near Richton, Miss.

March 2: Prohibition agents confront liquor smugglers in El Paso, Tex., sparking a two-hour firefight that leaves Agent Ernest Walker mortally wounded. He dies at a local hotel on March 5.

March 4: The inauguration of President Warren Harding (1865–1923) brings the corrupt "Ohio Gang" to Washington, D.C. Harry Micajah Daugherty (1860–1941) takes office as Attorney General, transforming the Department of Justice into a "Department of Easy Virtue."

March 8: In separate attacks, Chicago gunmen kill municipal court bailiff Paul Labriola and cigar store proprietor Harry Raimondi, both supporters of 19th Ward alderman John "Johnny de Pow" Powers. Police suspect the Genna gang, employed by rival candidate Anthony D'Andrea.

March 16: Future Cicero, Ill., mob boss Ernest Rocco Infelise (or Infelice) born on in Chicago.

March 21: Prohibition agents raid Neal Shearman's ranch outside El Paso, Tex., seeking 23 cases of liquor. Agents Stafford Beckett and Charles Wood die in the resultant shootout. Jurors fail to reach a verdict at the murder trial of four Shearman family members, in June 1921. Federal judge Duval West dismisses all charges on April 24, 1922, citing lack of authority for the original raid.

April 18: Camorra associate Frank Fevrola receives a death sentence on conviction in the March 1917 murder of Joe "Chuck" Nazzaro. The chief prosecution witness is Fevrola's wife, who recants her testimony on April 14, 1922. An appellate court postpones Fevrola's scheduled execution on June 28, 1923, and later commutes his sentence to life imprisonment.

April 30: Moonshiners kill Prohibition agent Irby Scruggs during a liquor raid in Knox County, Tenn. On the same day, Agents B.W. Holzman and John Watson engage in a shootout with smugglers outside Anthony, N.M. Both suffer wounds, resulting in Watson's death on May 2. Their assailants, though wounded, escape.

May 11: Chicago mobster and political candidate Anthony D'Andrea dies in an ambush outside his apartment. Mike Merlo fills his vacant office as president of the local Unione Siciliana.

May 18: Police in Buffalo, N.Y., find the mutilated corpse of Frank Pizzuto, an informer leaking information from a local liquor ring.

May 20: Chicago police accuse former IBT president Cornelius Shea of conducting a bombing campaign during an engineer's strike, in 1920, but the case is dropped for lack of evidence.

July: Chicago booze hijacker Steve Wisniewski disappears in the company of North Side Gang member Hymie Weiss, who later tells friends, "I took Stevie for a one-way ride." The technique soon becomes a Windy City standard.

July 6: An unknown gunman wounds politician Joseph Sinacola outside his home in Chicago's 19th Ward. He survives to be assassinated seven weeks later.

July 17: Moonshiners ambush and kill Prohibition agent Charles Howell in Limestone County, Ala.

August 1: Retaliating for losses suffered in the previous Matewan shootout, Baldwin-Felts detectives assassinate Police Chief Sid Hatfield and a friend, Ed Chambers, outside the McDowell County courthouse in Welch, W.Va. Gunmen C.E. Lively, George Pence, and William Salters win acquittal at their murder trial, with pleas of self-defense.

August 4: Los Angeles bootleggers Batista and Tony Torizzio murder rival August Martinetto and dump his corpse in Elysian Park Reservoir.

August 6: Ignazio Lupo files a petition with 60-odd signatures, asking Senator William Calder (1869–1945) to help him obtain a presidential pardon. Parole officer Louis Miller writes to President Harding on October 5, requesting a six-month "conditional pardon" that will permit Lupo to visit Italy. Attorney General Daugherty suggests a commutation of sentence instead, on October 10. Harding grants a conditional commutation on October 29, and Lupo leaves New York for Italy in early November.

August 7: Gunmen toss the corpse of gangster Mike Mucich from a speeding car near the Ninth Street bridge in Los Angeles. Prosecutors charge racketeer Phil Stickels and ex–LAPD officer Charles Stevens with the murder in 1930.

August 8: Police find the weighted corpse of Camillo Caizzo in New Jersey's Shark River. On August 12 they arrest Salvatore Rose, proprietor of a Belmar roadhouse. Authorities suspect the murder was ordered by Stefano Magaddino, in retaliation for the slaying of his brother Pietro, in Castellamare del Golfo, Sicily, during 1916. Police arrest Magaddino, with five others, on August 16. Suspect Bartola Fontana describes a total of 16 murders committed by the gang, which he calls "the Good Killers." Magaddino escapes prosecution.

August 14: Chicago gunmen kill Joseph Sinacola in front of his children, marking the 19th Ward's thirteenth political slaying since March 8.

August 21: Future anti–Mafia prosecutor and murder victim Cesare Terranova born in Palermo, Sicily.

August 22: Private detective William Burns (1861–1932) replaces William Flynn as director of the Bureau of Investigation, inaugurating a new era of corruption.

August 26: Moonshiners kill Prohibition agent John Reynolds and Chief James Melvin of the Paintsville Police Department, also wounding a deputy sheriff, as the officers search for stills in Johnson County, Ky.

September 7: Unknown killers shoot bootlegger and hijacker Santo Smiraldo on Avenue A, in Los Angeles.

October 8: Bootleggers kill Sheriff W.S. McPherson in Monarch, Wyo.

October 26: Prohibition agent John Foley accidentally shoots himself, inflicting a fatal wound, during a liquor raid in St. Paul, Minn.

October 30: Attorney General Daugherty reverses his earlier order, granting Ignazio Lupo permission to visit Sicily, then return to the U.S.

November: Camorra member Aniellio Paretti receives a death sentence for the March 1917 murder of Joe "Chuck" Nazzaro in Yonkers, N.Y. The Court of Appeals orders a new trial on January 3, 1923, whereupon prosecutors dismiss the charges. Paretti leaves prison in July 1923.

November 2: Jurors in Youngstown, Ohio, convict the citys safety director of accepting bribes from bootleggers.

November 21: Moonshiners ambush and kill Prohibition agent Jesse Johnson in Saline County, Ark.

December 23: Carlo Gambino arrives in New York City as a stowaway, soon joining the Castellano crime family.

December 24: Future mafioso Anthony Cimini born in Detroit.

1922 Police Chief Michael Gebhardt estimates that 75 percent of St. Paul, Minn.'s residents produce illegal wine or liquor. New Orleans mafioso Carlo Matranga retires, naming Sylvestro Carolla as his successor.

January 4: Drive-by gunmen kill Joe Lunetta on Darwin Avenue, Los Angeles. LAPD suspects Victor Matranga.

January 11: Unknown gunmen execute alleged gangster G.P. Duegani in his car on Mozart Street, Los Angeles.

February 17: While trying to arrest two bootleggers in San Francisco, Calif., Prohibition agent

John O'Toole falls from the running board of their truck and suffers fatal injuries.

March 9: New Jersey belatedly ratifies the 18th Amendment.

April 20: Future mafioso Salvatore La Barbera born in Palermo, Sicily.

April 29: Former Tammany leader Richard Croker Sr. dies in County Dublin, Ireland.

May 6: Unknown gunmen kill Missouri mafioso Pellegrino Scaglia in Colorado, prompting a "general assembly" of Mafia bosses in New York City, to negotiate peace between rivals in Denver and Kansas City. In Chicago, prosecutors charge ex–IBT president Cornelius Shea, "Big Tim" Murphy, Jeremiah "Jerry" Horan and five other labor leaders on charges of murdering a policeman. The charges are withdrawn on May 24, refiled on August 2, and then withdrawn again.

May 8: Unknown gunmen kill Vincenzo Terranova, brother of Harlem mafioso Ciro Terranova, on Manhattan's East 116th Street. On the same day, Umberto Valenti and Silva Tagliagamba ambush Joe Masseria on Grand Street in Manhattan, but Masseria escapes, leaving Tagliagamba mortally wounded. Police charge Masseria with Tagliagamba's slaying, but the case is never tried.

May 10: Unknown gunmen kill Chicago Patrolman Thomas Clark as he investigates a suspicious car parked near the site of a recent labor bombing. Thirty minutes later, in the first minutes of May 11, a second shooting slays Sergeant Terrence Lyons. Prosecutors indict Big Tim Murphy, Cornelius Shea, and six other labor leaders for the Lyons murder on May 16, then drop the charges for lack of evidence on May 24. Grand jurors file a new indictment on August 2, but it is later withdrawn.

May 13: Ignazio Lupo returns from Italy aboard the SS *Dante Alighieri*. Immigration officials detain him as a convicted criminal until May 25.

May 16: Federal jurors in Cincinnati convict bootlegger George Remus of conspiracy to violate the Volstead Act. He receives a two-year prison term and a $10,000 fine.

May 17: Liquor violator Leon Briggs kills Prohibition agent William Floyd during a raid on Briggs's home in Houston, Tex. His five-year prison sentence is later reversed on appeal.

May 26: Congress passes the Narcotic Drug Import and Export Act, AKA the Jones-Miller Act, prescribing fines up to $5,000 and prison terms up to 10 years for any person convicted of illegally importing narcotics.

June 12: U.S. Immigration authorities permit Ignazio Lupo's return from Italy.

June 21–22: In the 12th week of a strike led by the United Mine Workers, a shootout between strikers and company goons claims the lives of two strikers and 19 strikebreakers. Six indicted defendants are acquitted in two separate trials, in November 1922 and in winter 1923.

June 25: Liquor violators kill Prohibition agent Charles Sterner during service of a warrant in St. Louis, Mo. In Pekin, Ill., bootleggers steal 150 cases of whiskey from the American Distillery.

June 29: Fred Kohler Jr., nephew of Cleveland's Mayor Frederick Kohler, receives a 60-day sentence and a $250 fine for smuggling liquor.

July 6: Moonshiners kill Prohibition agent Howell Lynch during a liquor raid near Gainsboro, Tenn.

July 9: Mafioso Joseph Peter DiCarlo dies of natural causes in Buffalo, N.Y., succeeded by Stefano Magaddino as boss of the local crime family.

July 22: A moonshiner murders Prohibition agents Howard Fisher and Gary Freeman during a raid near Titustown, Va. Other officers kill the fugitive suspect several days later.

August 2: Future politician and casino owner Paul Dominique Laxalt born in Reno, Nev.

August 7: Chinese gunmen kill Ko Low, national president of the Hip Sing Tong, on Pell Street in New York City's Chinatown.

August 8: Gunmen sent by Umberto "Rocco" Valenti ambush Joe Masseria outside his home on Second Avenue, in Manhattan. Masseria escapes injury, while two bodyguards are killed and four other persons wounded.

August 11: Masseria gunmen led by Salvatore Lucania ambush Rocco Valenti as he arrives for peace talks at a Twelfth Street restaurant. Lucania kills Valenti, while wild shots wound a street cleaner and an eight-year-old girl.

August 21: Labor racketeer Gurrah Shapiro exchanges gunfire with Nathan Kaplan in New York, subsequently beating an attempted murder charge on grounds of self-defense. The incident sparks Manhattan's third "labor sluggers war," as Kaplan battles Jacob "Little Augie" Orgen for control of the "wet wash" trade.

August 22: Moonshiners wound Prohibition agent Joseph Owen in a shootout near Kosciusko, Miss. Owen dies on September 6.

August 30: Chicago police charge Al Capone with drunk driving after his car strikes a taxi and Capone threatens the cabbie with a gun. The charge is later dismissed.

September 3: Prohibition agents Glenn Price and Grover Todd suffer fatal gunshot wounds while raiding a dance hall in Portland, Ore. Other agents wound and capture their killer.

Autumn: Tommy Pennochio's liquor exchange in Manhattan disbands after multiple shootings.

October 4: Moonshiners in Pasco County, Fla., ambush Prohibition agent John Van Waters and Constable Arthur Crenshaw, killing both officers.

October 21: Three Border Patrol officers challenge liquor smugglers in the Upper Valley of El Paso County, Tex. The resultant shootout leaves Officers Charles Gardiner and Charles Birchfield critically wounded. Gardiner dies on October 21.

October 25: Future Yakuza boss Kazuo Nakanishi born in Japan.

November 6: Future mafioso Dominick Licavoli born in St. Louis, Mo.

November 16: Future bandit and separatist leader Salvatore Giuliano born in Montelepre, Sicily.

November 17: President Harding orders the DOJ to investigate claims that high-ranking bootleggers in Cleveland, Ohio, are hiring substitutes to sever their prison terms.

December 5: Manhattan gangster William Lipshitz murders rival Benjamin Levinski.

December 9: Moonshiners ambush and kill Prohibition agent Robert Duff in Menifee County, Ky. Other lawmen corner the gang on December 15, sparking a shootout that kills the gang's leader and Prohibition agent Guy Cole, before six other suspects surrender.

December 19: Prohibition agent Atha Carter and Officer Peter Dubois engage in a shootout with moonshiners at Palisade, Nev. Carter suffers fatal wounds and dies on December 24.

1923 Mafioso Joseph "Socks" Lanza leads Local 359 of the United Seafood Workers union, dominating Lower Manhattan's Fulton Fish Market. European police officials meet in Austria to form the International Criminal Police Commission, commonly known as INTERPOL. Canada bans marijuana under provisions of the 1911 Opium and Narcotic Drugs Act.

January 3: New York "White Hand" leader William "Wild Bill" Lovett survives two gunshot wounds in a Front Street shanty and refuses to name his attackers.

January 13: Future mafioso Salvatore "Ciaschiteddu" ("Little Bird") Greco born in Palermo, Sicily.

February: In a speech to the Students' Union at Hong Kong University, Sun Yat-sen declares that government corruption drove him to support revolution against the Qing Dynasty.

February 1: Owney Madden leaves Sing Sing Prison after serving eight years for murder.

April: The Chicago Crime Commission publishes a list of 28 gangsters "who are constantly in conflict with the law," including brothers Al and Ralph Capone, Anthony "Mops" Volpe, Frank Rio, "Machine Gun" Jack McGurn, James "Mad Bomber" Belcastro, Rocco Fanelli, "Dago Lawrence" Mangano, Jack Zuta, Jake Guzik, Frank Diamond, George "Bugs" Moran, Joe Aiello, Edward "Spike" O'Donnell, Joe Saltis,

Frank McErlane, William Niemoth, Danny Stanton, Myles O'Donnell, Frank Lake, Terry Druggan, William "Klondike" O'Donnell, George "Red" Barker, William "Three-Fingered Jack" White, Joseph "Peppy" Genero, Leo Mongoven, and James "Fur" Sammons.

April 2: Members of Egan's Rats steal $2.4 million in bonds from a mail truck in St. Louis, Mo. Police recover some of the loot from mobster William "Whitey" Doering's home on April 20.

April 3: Bootleggers murder Prohibition agent Leroy Youmans near Hartsville, S.C.

April 4: A federal grand jury in Minneapolis indicts 20 members of a nationwide ring dealing in stolen bonds.

April 16: Future mafioso Vito "Billy Jack" Giacalone born in Detroit. In Hammond, Ind., Prohibition agent Robert Anderson dies while defending a licensed distillery against armed hijackers.

April 18: Spectators riot in Cleveland, Ohio, after judges award victory in a dubious boxing match to Morris "One-Punch" Kleinman. Mayor Fred Kohler bans prize fights city-wide.

April 22: Third-generation mafioso Giuseppe "La Tigre" Di Cristina born in Caltanissetta, Sicily.

April 24: Future Mexican Mafia leader Henry "Hank" Leyva born in Tucson, Ariz.

May 26: Prohibition agents in Cleveland arrest four suspects—Joseph Shearer, ex-prohibition director for Ohio; ex-prohibition agent Fred Counts; his brother, attorney Frank Counts; and Samuel Hoskins, a prominent politician and church leader—on charges of conspiring to violate the Volstead Act and defraud the U.S. government. A moonshiner kills Deputy U.S. Marshal James Short while resisting arrest near Maulden, Ky.

June: Unknown slayers execute gambler Frank "Fats" Bradley and dump his corpse at Central Station, in Los Angeles.

June 11: A mob on the Detroit River tries to sink a federal patrol boat transporting confiscated liquor. Detroit's top federal prosecutor orders agents to fire on future aggressive crowds.

August 1: Members of Nathan Kaplan's Rough Riders and Jacob Orgen's Little Augies kill two bystanders in a shootout on Essex Street, Manhattan.

August 2: President Warren Harding dies at the San Francisco's Palace Hotel, during a cross-country "Voyage of Understanding." Vice President Calvin Coolidge succeeds Harding.

August 22: Future mafioso Lawrence "Larry Fab" Dentico born in Seaside Park, N.J.

August 28: NYPD officers arrest Nathan Kaplan for carrying a concealed weapon. While leaving his arraignment at the Essex Market Court, Kaplan is shot and killed by Orgen gunman Louis Cohen. At trial, Cohen receives a sentence of 20–25 years in Sing Sing, winning parole in 1937.

September 5: Chicago police arrest Al Capone for carrying a concealed weapon. A judge in municipal court dismisses the charge.

September 7: Chicago mobster Frank McErlane kills Jerry O'Connor, a member of the South Side O'Donnells, in the first documented gangland slaying with a Tommy gun.

September 14: Future mafioso Gaetano Badalamenti born in Cinisi, Sicily.

September 16: Vito Giannola's gang murders a St. Louis wholesale meat distributor who objects to the Mafia's "tax" on his inventory.

September 17: Frank McErlane kills two more South Side O'Donnells, George Bucher and George Meegan.

September 18: Future mafioso Gerlando Alberti born in Palermo, Sicily.

September 21: Prohibition agent Harold Mooring is fatally beaten and shot while investigating an illegal saloon in Washington State.

September 27: A team of 40 gunmen steal $30,000 worth of "medicinal" liquor from a distillery in Philadelphia, Pa.

October 31: A Mafia hit team led by Duit Cuteddi kills White Hand leader William "Wild Bill" Lovett in a Brooklyn speakeasy.

November 11: Prohibition agent George Stewart dies in a shootout with liquor bootleggers, after infiltrating a speakeasy in Buffalo, N.Y.

November 15: Bootlegger Charles Birger kills bartender Cecil Knighton in a shootout at Birger's Halfway resort, between Johnston City and Marion, Ill. Jurors later acquit him on a plea of self-defense.

November 18: Charles Birger kills Egan's Rats member William Doering in another gunfight at the Halfway resort.

December 1: Spike O'Donnell beer runners William Egan and Thomas "Morrie" Keane die in a hijacking ambush. Conflicting reports blame Frank McErlane and the Torrio-Capone gang.

December 2: NYPD spokesmen name Ignazio Lupo as an accomplice in Anthony Forti's extortion racket, targeting New York bakeries.

December 3: New York City prosecutors charge Owney Madden and two codefendants with stealing 200 cases of liquor from a local warehouse.

December 13: Future gangster Francis Davidson "Mad Frankie" Fraser born in London, England.

December 22: Ex-Prohibition agent Glenn Young leads KKK vigilantes in liquor raids throughout southern Illinois.

1924 British gambler John Moores creates the world's first public postal soccer pool with betting on credit permitted. Switzerland legalizes gambling on boules (games played with metal balls). Joseph Amato succeeds Peter Guardalabene as boss of Milwaukee's Mafia. Congress passes the Heroin Act, banning manufacture of the drug in the U.S. Jules Stein and William Goodheart Jr. launch the Music Corporation of America in Chicago, booking talent for syndicate speakeasies.

January 2: Future Detroit mafioso Michael Santo Polizzi born in Cataldo, Sicily.

January 5: Glen Young leads more KKK liquor raids in Williamson County, Ill., continuing on January 7.

February 24: Bootleggers ambush and kill Prohibition agent Willie Saylor while attempting to liberate a prisoner to jail in Pineville, Ky.

March 31: Future mafioso Francesco "Ciccio" Madonia born in Palermo, Sicily.

April 1: Police kill Al Capone's brother Frank during election-day violence in Cicero, Ill.

April 2: Future mobster-politician Vito Ciancimino born in Corleone, Sicily.

April 21: Future Philadelphia mafioso Philip "Chicken Man" Testa born.

May 8: Al Capone fatally shoots bootlegger Joe Howard in a Chicago saloon, following Howard's assault on Outfit bookkeeper Jake Guzik.

May 9: Attorney General Harlan Stone (1872–1946) demands the resignation of William Burns as director of the Bureau of Investigation. J. Edgar Hoover replaces Burns as acting director on May 10, confirmed as permanent director on December 10. Hoover retains the post until his death in 1972.

May 12: Future mafioso Michele "The Pope" Greco born in Ciaculli, Sicily.

May 19: Prohibition agents arrest Johnny Torrio at Chicago's Sieben Brewery, in a sting arranged by rival Dean O'Banion.

May 23: Unknown gunmen, suspected members of the Shelton brothers gang, ambush vigilante leader Glenn Young on the road between Harrisburg and East St. Louis, Ill., wounding Young in the leg and blinding his wife. Klansmen retaliate on May 24 by killing Shelton gangster Jack Skelcher in Herrin, Ill.

May 29: Former On Leong Tong president Yee Hee Kee is shot five times in Cleveland, Ohio.

June 1: Future Detroit mobster Bernard Marchesani born.

June 2: The U.S. Supreme Court rules the 1919 Child Labor Tax Law unconstitutional, in *Bailey v. Drexel Furniture Co.*

June 12: NYPD officers arrest Legs Diamond, brother Eddie, John Montforte and Eddie Doyle for a $100,000 jewel robbery. All are released on June 14.

June 14: Diamond gang member Babe Pioli kills boxer Bill Brennan at a Manhattan speakeasy. Pioli later pleads guilty to manslaughter.

July 3: Future mafioso Angelo La Barbera born in Palermo, Sicily.

Summer: Cleveland jurors convict seven Hip Sing Tong members in a $70,000 extortion scheme.

July 10: Prohibition agent Daniel Cleveland suffers fatal bullet wounds during a moonshine raid near Meridian, Miss.

July 12: A federal judge in Detroit sentences 31 defendants from Hamtramck, Mich., all convicted of conspiring to violate the Volstead Act. Those fined and imprisoned include Mayor Peter Jezewsky, ex–police commissioner Max Wosinski, and ex–police lieutenant John Ferguson.

July 29: Moonshiners ambush Deputy U.S. Marshal Samuel Lilly and Police Officer William George after a liquor raid outside Wilmington, N.C., killing both victims and Officer George's police dog.

September: Members of Egan's Rats murder Mafia bootlegger Sam Palizzola in St. Louis, Mo.

October: Legs Diamond survives a shotgun ambush on Manhattan's Fifth Avenue and drives himself to a hospital.

October 15: A murder in Chinatown brings the yearly death toll to 11 in Manhattan's latest Tong war.

October 16: Prohibition agent James Williams suffers a fatal wound from his partner's pistol while grappling with a narcotics suspect in Chicago.

October 23: A federal grand jury in Cleveland, Ohio, indicts bootlegger Thomas McGinty, his brother Joseph, and nine other participants in a giant liquor wholesale-and-retail conspiracy.

October 30: Deputy U.S. Marshal James Hill suffers fatal gunshot wounds during a liquor raid in Seldovia, Alaska.

November 1: Police ambush bootlegger-bandit John "King of the Everglades" Ashley in Sebastian, Fla., killing Ashley and two gang members, Ray Lynn and Bob Middleton. In Cromwell, Okla., corrupt Prohibition agent Wylie Lynn murders Deputy U.S. Marshal Bill Tilghman.

November 8: Unione Siciliana president Mike Merlo dies from cancer, in Chicago.

November 10: Mafiosi Frankie Yale, Albert Anselmi, and Giovanni "John" Scalise murder North Side gang leader Dean O'Banion in his Chicago flower shop.

November 12: Deputy Sheriff Les Farmer, linked to the Egan's Rats gang in St. Louis, purchases Thompson submachine gun No. 2347 in Marion, Ill. The gun is one of two used in Chicago's 1929 St. Valentine's Day massacre.

November 13: Angelo Genna assumes command of Chicago's Unione Siciliana, with support from Frankie Yale.

November 23: Mobsters Leo Klimas and Eddie Tancl die in a shootout at the Hawthorne Hotel, in Cicero, Ill. Jurors later acquit alleged killers James Doherty and Myles O'Donnell.

December 6: A raid on a saloon in Bend, Ind., leaves two persons dead and five wounded by gunfire.

December 13: Border Patrol agent Frank Clark dies in a shootout with smugglers near Cordova Island, Tex.

December 24: Walter W. Power dies in an ambush on Commonwealth Avenue, Los Angeles. LAPD suspects gangster Matthew "Mattie" Deckert but files no charges.

December 29: Future Detroit mafioso Calogero "Carlo" Licata born in Michigan.

1924–25 Police in Boston, Chicago and New York City blame renewed warfare between the Hip Sing and On Leong Tongs for 80-plus murders.

1925 Benito Mussolini launches a purge of Sicilian mafiosi. Salvatore Maranzano emigrates to Brooklyn, N.Y. "Retired" mafioso Carlo Matranga leaves New Orleans to organize a new crime family in Los Angeles. *Collier's* magazine names San Francisco, Calif., and St. Paul, Minn., as "dry" America's "wettest" cities. A new Chilean law authorizes the University of Concepción to operate a lottery.

January 6: Future mafioso Luciano Leggio born in Corleone, Sicily.

January 7: Police find "King of the Bootleggers" William Keefe, AKA "George Turner," shot to death in Santa Barbara, Calif.

January 8: Gunshots kill racketeer Sam Vassallo in Los Angeles. Police suspect rival Tony Raia.

January 12: North Side gangsters fire on Al Capone's car in Chicago, wounding chauffeur Sylvester Barton. Capone escapes harm and buys an armored limousine.

January 19: Future anti–Mafia magistrate Rocco Chinnici born in Italy.

January 24: North Side gangsters ambush Johnny Torrio in Chicago, leaving Torrio and chauffeur Robert Barton badly wounded. Torrio subsequently "retires," ceding control to Al Capone. In Herrin, Ill., vigilante Glenn Young and Deputy Sheriff Ora Thomas kill each other in a gunfight.

February 6: Alfred "Al Joseph" Uhl suffers fatal gunshots in a confrontation with Milton "Farmer" Page at Bert the Barber's, a blind pig on West 6th Street, Los Angeles.

February 9: Judge Adam Cliffe sentences

Johnny Torrio to nine months in the Lake County Jail, for liquor violations.

February 11: Delegates from various nations sign the Agreement concerning the Manufacture of, Internal Trade in and Use of Prepared Opium in Geneva, Switzerland. The treaty, which takes effect on July 28, 1926, provides that all signatory nations are "fully determined to bring about the gradual and effective suppression of the manufacture of, internal trade in and use of prepared opium." Article I states that, with the exception of retail sale, the importation, sale and distribution of opium be a monopoly of government, which would have the exclusive right to import, sell, or distribute opium. Article II prohibited sale of opium to minors. Article III prohibited minors from entering smoking divans. Article IV required governments to limit the number of opium retail shops and smoking divans as much as possible. Articles V and VI regulated the export and transport of opium and dross. Article VII required governments to discourage the use of opium through instruction in schools, literature, and other methods.

February 13: Detroit Police Superintendent William Rutledge admits the presence of at least 15,000 illegal saloons within his jurisdiction.

February 14: Prohibition agents raid the Flanagan Coal Camp in Premier, W.Va., sparking a shootout with liquor violators that kills Agent Malcolm Day and one of his assailants.

February 16: Moonshiners ambush and kill Prohibition agent James Bowdoin in Caryville, Fla.

February 18: Drive-by gunmen wound mobster Pete Carlino on a public street in Denver, Colo.

March 5: Future Yakuza boss Kenichi Yamamoto born in Chūōku, Kobe, Japan.

March 6: Bootleggers ambush and slay two officers agents, Prohibition agent William Collins and Deputy Sheriff Samuel Duhon, en route to a liquor raid in Calcasieu Parish, La. Jurors later convict two brothers of the murders.

March 19: A federal grand jury in Cincinnati indicts 35 police officers, plus 20 more defendants including politicians, prohibition agents, and narcotics officers on bribery charges. The following day, another indictment names 48 city detectives and patrolmen, with 10 local prohibition agents. Six of those charged plead guilty on April 4, followed by 33 more on April 7. By April 22, 59 guilty pleas have resulted in jail terms and fines.

March 26: Posters displayed in Manhattan's Chinatown announce a truce between the warring Hip Sing and On Leong Tongs.

March 28: Members of the Cornero gang kill Walter Hesketh, bodyguard of Milton Page, in downtown Los Angeles. LAPD suspects Tony Cornero and John Rosselli.

April 10: Charles Scribner's Sons releases F. Scott Fitzgerald's novel *The Great Gatsby*, featuring fictional character "Meyer Wolfsheim," based on Arnold Rothstein. In Chicago, police arrest Al Capone for carrying a concealed weapon, then release him the following day.

April 17: Unknown gunmen kill bootleggers Walter O'Donnell and Harry Hassmiller outside a roadhouse in Evergreen Park, Ill.

April 25: Police find bootlegger Joe Perlini gunned down in his garage on Duane Street, Los Angeles.

May: Assassins kill bootlegger Eddie Hannon in his apartment on South Hope Street, Los Angeles. Police suspect rivals Frank Clark and Jack O'Brien.

May 25: During a strike against the Glendale Gas and Coal Company in Wheeling, W.Va., dynamite blasts destroy two company houses occupied by strikebreakers.

May 26: Unknown shotgunners kill Angelo Genna in a high-speed chase through Chicago. Samuel Samuzzo "Samoots" Amatuna replaces Genna as president of the Unione Siciliana.

June: Members of the Cornero syndicate kill Chicago hijacker George Carrol, dumping his corpse on the outskirts of Los Angeles.

June 10: Jurors in Cleveland, Ohio, convict three defendants on liquor conspiracy charges. They include Ohio's suspended federal Prohibition director, J.E. Russell; chief alcohol permit clerk M.B. Copeland; and lawyer W.E. Barrett. All three receive two-year prison terms and fines on June 20.

June 13: While trolling for his brother's murderers, mafioso Mike Genna clashes with Chicago police, killing Detectives Harold Olson and Charles Walsh, wounding Detective Michael Conway. Genna suffers fatal wounds in the firefight, while officers arrest companions Albert Anselmi and John Scalise. Both are charged with murder, then later acquitted on pleas of self-defense.

June 15: Chicago police detain 500 suspected gangsters.

June 20: Federal and state prohibition agents stage simultaneous raids on the same location, outside Huntington, W.Va. Federal agent William Porter and state officer George Ball die in the chaotic exchange of gunfire.

July 8: Three gunmen execute mafioso Tony Genna on a Chicago street corner.

August: Drive-by gunmen kill mafioso Leo Lanzetti outside a barber shop in Philadelphia, Pa. Police suspect rival mobster Salvatore Sabella.

August 4: A shootout at the St. Regis Hotel in Los Angeles leaves three men dead, including Cornero gangster James Fox and to liquor hijackers, Harry Munson and Harry "Cutter Moran" Schwartz.

August 7: Future mafioso Anthony Frank "Nino Glasses" Gaggi born in Manhattan.

August 16: William Hundley, future head of the Justice Department's Organized Crime and Racketeering Section, born in Brooklyn, N.Y.

September 3: Prohibition agent John Mulcahy dies from gunshot wounds during a liquor raid on a camp near Westford, Mass.

September 14: Members of the Green Ones gang murder John and Catherine Gray in St. Louis, Missouri, for complaining about the price of bootleg liquor.

September 23: On Leong Tong member Yee Chock murdered in Cleveland, Ohio. Three rival Hip Sing Tong members are jailed for the slaying, while Safety Director Edwin Barry orders the arrest of every Chinese male in Cleveland (some 700 in all) and condemns the Chinese settlement on Ontario Street as a "fire hazard." Public protests elicit a belated apology.

September 25: Saltis-McErlane gangsters strafe the Chicago headquarters of Ralph Sheldon's gang with Tommy guns, killing victim Charles Kelly.

October 26: Detroit's "Cleaners and Dyers War" begins, as members of the Purple Gang bomb two laundries whose owners refuse tribute payments.

October 31: Fatally wounded by gunshots at a roadhouse in Baltimore, Md., bootlegger Edwin "Spike" Kenny names his slayer as Richard Reese Whittemore. Whittemore is later convicted and hangs on August 12, 1926.

November 3: A.B. Stroup, deputy administrator of federal Prohibition enforcement for Detroit, resigns after telling reporters, "There is something radically wrong with law enforcement in Detroit." After service in six other states, he calls it "the wettest city I have been assigned to." Superiors term his accusations "greatly exaggerated."

November 13: Unknown gunmen kill Unione Siciliana president Samoots Amatuna outside a Chicago barber shop. Antonio Lombardo fills the presidential vacancy.

November 18: Gunmen kill Edward Zion, exbodyguard of Samoots Amatuna, as he returns home from Amatuna's Chicago funeral.

November 20: Unknown shooters kill another Amatuna bodyguard, Abraham Goldstein, in a Chicago pharmacy.

December: Charles Birger and the Shelton brothers team up to operate slot machines in southern Illinois.

December 9: Purple Gang members kidnap and murder Sam Sigmund, a laundry owner who has rejected demands for "protection" payoffs.

December 22: Chicago police blame Saltis-McErlane gangsters for the slaying of Joseph "Dynamite" Brooks and ex-policeman Edward Harmening in Marquette, Ill.

December 26: A shooting at Brooklyn's Adonis Social Club kills White Hand leader Richard "Peg Leg" Lonergan and two associates, Aaron Harms and Cornelius "Needles" Ferry. Police question Al Capone and other witnesses, but file no charges.

December 28: Mexico bans cultivation of marijuana.

1926 Lebanese lawmakers ban cultivation of hashish. Louisiana legalizes pari-mutuel betting at racetracks. Benito Mussolini's police imprison mafioso Vito Casio Ferro, who remains in custody until his death in 1943 or 1945 (reports differ). Tony Lombardo opens Unione Siciliana membership to non–Sicilian Italians and renames the group the Italo-American National Union, reportedly cutting off dues payments from Chicago to Frank Uale's New York headquarters. San Francisco businessman, Robert Sherman builds the original Cal Neva Lodge at Lake Tahoe, as a guesthouse for friends and real estate clients.

January 1: Italian troops directed by Prefect Cesare Mori sweep through the village of Gangi, Sicily, arresting suspected mafiosi. By week's end, 130 fugitives and 300 accomplices are in custody. The total of arrests reaches 11,000 by 1929, with 5,000 jailed in Palermo alone.

January 19: Unknown gunmen kill attorney Henry Spingola, brother-in-law of Angelo Genna, outside a Chicago restaurant. Police claim Spingola was shot for refusing to support a legal defense fund for Albert Anselmi and John Scalise.

January 23: Gambling czar James Patrick "Big Jim" O'Leary murdered in Chicago.

January 26: Wholesale grocers Agostino and Antonio Morici die in a Chicago ambush, shortly after refusing donations to the Anselmi-Scalise defense fund.

January 29: Policemen John Balke and Ohmer Hockett demand payoffs from the Green Ones in St. Louis, rejecting an offer of $200 and demanding an audience with "the boss." Mafiosi beat them unconscious, then execute and bury them in rural graves on January 30. Investigators find the corpses on February 5.

February 5: New Jersey state legislators restrict sale of machine guns. In Manhattan, a subcommittee of the National Crime Commission drafts legislation banning private ownership of automatic weapons.

February 9: Machine-gunners from the Saltis-McErlane gang shoot up Martin "Buff" Costello's speakeasy, killing John "Mitters" Foley and William Wilson.

February 10: Al Capone orders three Tommy guns from a Chicago sporting goods dealer.

February 15: Unidentified gunmen kill an associate of the Genna brothers, Orazio "The Scourge" Tropea, in Chicago.

February 23: Police find Genna gang member Ecola "The Eagle" Baldelli dead in a ditch outside Chicago.

February 24: Gunmen kill another Genna ally, West Side bootlegger Vito Bascone, in Stickney, Ill.

March 1: Future gangster Haji Mastan Mirza born in Panaikulam, India. On the same day, future "Mumbai Mafia" boss Varadarajan Muniswami Mudaliar is born in Thoothukudi, India.

March 2: Chicago newspapers publish photos of State's Attorney Robert Crowe and other officials at a party thrown by the mafioso Genna brothers.

March 16: Fugitive Antonio Paretti surrenders in Kings County, N.Y., for trial in the 1916 murders of Nicolo Terranova and Charles Ubriaco. Despite sudden amnesia suffered by various witnesses at his June trial, jurors convict him and Paretti receives a death sentence. He dies in Sing Sing's electric chair on February 17, 1927.

March 19: Unknown gunmen kill local Unione Siciliana president Samuzzo "Samoots" Amatuna in a Chicago barber shop.

March 27: Former Major League Baseball player and umpire-turned-casino owner John "Kick" Kelly dies in New York City, at age 69.

April 19: Future mafioso Benjamin "Lefty Two Guns" Ruggiero born in Hell's Kitchen, Manhattan.

April 23: Border Patrol Inspector William McKee suffers fatal gunshot wounds during a high-speed pursuit of liquor smugglers, near Tucson, Ariz. In Chicago, Capone machine-gunners wound rival James "Fur" Sammons at his girlfriend's beauty shop.

April 27: Capone gunmen — some say Al Capone himself — machine-gun three victims outside a speakeasy in Cicero, Ill. The dead include Assistant State's Attorney William McSwiggin and two O'Donnell gang members, James Doherty and Thomas Duffy. Capone is charged with McSwiggin's murder on July 29, but the charge is later dropped without trial.

May 6: Connecticut police arrest Raymond Patriarca for an unspecified offense. Placed on probation, he is jailed again in 1927 for violating its terms, receiving a 30-day suspended sentence and paying a $350 fine.

May 10: Prohibition agent Remus Buckner suffers gunshot wounds while raiding a still near Oneonta, Ala. He dies on May 12.

May 14: LAPD officer James Miller suffers a fatal gunshot wound while raiding a speakeasy owned by the Sciortino brothers on East 25th Street, Los Angeles. The Sciortinos surrendered and confessed on May 19.

May 15: Mobster Tony Raia and Bartolo Panna kill each other in a shootout at Panna's shop, Tenth and Wall Streets, Los Angeles.

May 16: Future mafioso Dominic Bommarito born in St. Louis, Mo.

May 21: The Green Ones kill Mariano Deluca in St. Louis, for rejecting extortion demands.

May 26: Bootleggers ambush and kill Prohibition agent Thomas Lankford in Springfield, Illinois.

June 1: Moonshiners kill Prohibition agent Vaughn Grant during a high-speed chase in Hendersonville, N.C.

June 27: The Green Ones murder St. Louis bootlegger Harvey Dunn for refusing to surrender control of his distillery.

July 2: Chicago prosecutors indict Al Capone for conspiring to swear falsely to qualify voters. The charge is dismissed in December.

July 15: Capone gunmen kill James Russo, an independent bootlegger, in Chicago's Little Italy.

July 25: Border Patrol Inspector Lon Parker dies in a shootout with smugglers, in the Huachucas Mountains of Arizona, killing one assailant before he collapses.

August 3: Chicago police find one of Al Capone's chauffeurs tortured and shot to death, his body dumped in a cistern.

August 6: Future IBT president Jackie Presser, son of labor racketeer William "Bill" Presser, born in Cleveland, Ohio.

August 10: Capone gunmen ambush Hymie Weiss and Vincent "The Schemer" Drucci in Chicago, but both escape unharmed.

August 13: Rhode Island state police arrest Ray Patriarca on charges of escaping from Hopkinton's jail, where he was held on suspicion of hijacking. Conviction earns him a 30-day jail term on February 28, 1927.

August 15: North Side gangsters Weiss and Drucci survive another Chicago ambush.

August 20: Unknown Chicago gunmen execute Joseph "The Cavalier" Nerone, suspected slayer of Tony Genna.

August 21: The Green Ones execute rival gangster Joseph Schamora in St. Louis.

August 22: Unknown gunmen execute mafioso Dominic Rubino in Detroit. Shelton brothers gangsters Everett Smith and Harry Walker suffer fatal gunshots at a roadhouse near Marion, Ill.

August 24: Bootleggers Frank and Sam DiMaria drown after falling into a vat of their illegal liquor distillery in rural Berrien County, Michigan.

September 5: The Green Ones kill Cuckoos Gang member Peter Webbe in St. Louis.

September 20: A convoy of North Side machine-gunners strafe Al Capone's headquarters at the Hawthorne Hotel, in Cicero, wounding several bystanders but missing Capone.

September 22: The Green Ones kill Cuckoos Gang member Joseph Corsiglio in St. Louis.

October 1: A federal grand jury in Chicago indicts Al Capone for conspiring to violate the Volstead Act.

October 4: After a falling out with Charles Birger, members of the Shelton brothers' gang ambush Birger associate Art Newman near Harrisburg, Ill., wounding Newman's wife.

October 8: Detroit mobsters Samuel and Isadore "Sidney" Rubino die in an ambush.

October 11: Capone gunmen ambush North Side gang leader Hymie Weiss outside his lawyer's office in Chicago, killing Weiss and bodyguard Patrick Murray, wounding gang members Benny Jacobs and Sam Pellar. Bugs Moran replaces Weiss as boss of the North Side Gang.

October 15: Cuckoos gangsters kill supposed Green Ones gang Kustandy Ajlouny in St. Louis. Relatives insist that Ajlouny was an innocent door-to-door salesman, shot after visiting a mafioso's apartment on legitimate business.

October 16: Thieves steal several Tommy guns from the Rosiclare Spar Mining Company in Rosiclare, Ill. Police blame the Birger gang.

October 20: Bootlegger Joseph "Polack Joe" Saltis and political henchman John "Dingbat" Oberta convene a peace conference at Chicago's Hotel Sherman, to forge a short-lived truce between Al Capone's gang and Bugs Moran's North Siders.

October 26: Police blame the Shelton brothers' gang for killing to Birger associates — Burnett "High Pockets" McQuay, machine-gunned in a car outside Herrin, Ill.; and Ward "Casey" Jones, pulled from the Saline River near Equality.

October 29: Future mafioso Jack William Tocco born in Detroit.

November 6: Mobsters armed with a tripod-mounted machine gun kill Mayor Jeff Stone and companion John "Apie" Milroy in Colp, Ill. Members of the Birger and Shelton gangs blame each other for the slayings.

November 12: A crop-duster pilot employed by the Shelton gang drops three dynamite charges on Charles Birger's "Shady Rest" stronghold near Marion, Ill. One bomb misses the target, while the other two are duds.

November 24: Prohibition agent George Wentworth dies in a shootout with a bootlegger in Berkeley, California, also killing is man at the scene.

November 28: Unknown kidnappers abduct Theodore "The Greek" Anton, manager of Al Capone's Hawthorne Hotel headquarters, and torture him to death.

November 30: Charles Birger's gang raids a bank in Pocahontas, Ill., stealing $30,000.

December 9: A moonshiner murders Prohibition agents Jacob Brandt and Walter Mobray in Pensacola, Fla.

December 12: Gunmen murder Shelton gang ally Joe Adams, mayor of West City, Ill. Prosecutors charge Charles Birger with the murder on December 28. He is convicted at trial and hangs on April 19, 1928.

December 30: Chicago's cease-fire ends with the murder of Sheldon Gang member Hillary Clements by the Saltis-McErlane Gang.

1927 East Coast bootleggers organize the "Seven Group" to reduce competition and maximize prophets. Ranking members include Johnny Torrio, Lucky Luciano, Meyer Lansky and Benjamin Siegel, Joe Adonis, Abner Zwillman, Waxey Gordon, Nucky Johnson, and Harry "Nig" Rosen. Illinois legalizes pari-mutuel betting at racetracks. Pharmacologist Gordon Alles tests amphetamine on himself and discovers its first known medical use, as an artificial replacement for ephedrine. German author Kurt Beringer publishes *Der Meskalinrausch* (*Mescaline Intoxication*), concluding that the drug induces toxic psychosis.

January: Rival bootleggers kill Chicago saloon owner John Costanaro, a distributor for the Ralph Sheldon Gang.

January 2: Future Detroit mafioso Vincent "Little Vince" Meli born in San Cataldo, Sicily.

January 7: Thieves steal $80 million worth of liquor from a licensed warehouse in New York City.

January 8: Fire razes Charles Birger's Shady Rest roadhouse, leaving three men dead in the wreckage.

January 14: Prohibition agent George Dykeman accidentally kills himself with his own gun during a beer raid in West New York, N.J.

January 19: Illinois Highway Patrolman Lory Price and his wife vanish. Police find Price shot to death outside Dubois, Ill., on February 5. His wife's corpse is retrieved from an abandoned mine on June 13. Authorities later name Price as an accomplice of Charles Birger in a stolen-car ring.

January 31: Brothers Bernie, Carl and Earl Shelton face trial for a 1925 mail robbery in Collinsville, Ill. Jurors convict them on February 5, resulting in 25-year prison terms. Some observers blame the convictions on perjured testimony from Birger gangsters.

February 1: Drive-by shooters kill bootlegger Luther Green at his home on Bonnie Brea Street, Los Angeles. LAPD suspects rival Harry "Mile Away" Thomas.

February 25: Philadelphia, Pa.'s first Tommy-gun slaying claims the life of gangster William Duffy. Police suspect rival Max "Boo Boo" Hoff.

February 27: Prominent bootlegger William Michael Cusick, AKA "Mickey Duffy," survives a Philadelphia ambush by rival mobsters Francis Bailey and Peter Ford.

March 4: Federal agents in Chicago charge James "Fur" Sammons with robbing a bonded liquor warehouse. He pleads guilty on April 12 and receives an 18-month sentence, leaving Leavenworth prison on October 18, 1930.

March 11: Saltis-McErlane gunmen Charles "Big Hayes" Hubacek and Frank "Lefty" Koncil die in an ambush on Chicago's South Side. Police suspect the slayings are retaliation for Koncil's recent acquittal in the 1926 slaying of Sheldon gang member John "Mitters" Foley.

March 16: Future mobster Joseph Anthony "Mr. Clean" Ferriola, AKA "Joe Nagall," born in Chicago.

March 19: Gunfire kills bootlegger and suspected informer Joe Vaccarino at his Macey Street home in Los Angeles. Police suspect Marco Albori, AKA "Albert Marco."

March 28: Milwaukee mafioso Joseph Amato dies of natural causes, succeeded by Joseph Vallone. In Detroit, members of the Purple Gang machine-gun three rival mobsters from St. Louis at the Milaflores Apartments.

March 29: Future mafioso Michael Anthony Rizzitello born in Montreal, Québec.

April 1: Congress creates the Bureau of Prohibition (or Prohibition Unit) within the Bureau of Internal Revenue. In Los Angeles, police find "retired" bootlegger and Matranga relative Antonio Ferraro shot to death in his car on Kohler Street.

April 3: Vincent Drucci ransacks the office of a Chicago alderman allies with Al Capone, prompting the chief of police to issue an arrest-on-sight order for North Side gang members. Officers arrest Drucci and companions on April 4. Drucci scuffles with Detective Dan Healy and suffers fatal gunshot wounds.

April 16: Unknown gunmen kill gangster Ted Werner in New Orleans. Some accounts blame Detroit's Purple Gang.

April 21: Border Patrol Inspector Thaddeus Pippin dies in a shootout with liquor smugglers near El Paso, Tex. The shooters escape, abandoning two burros loaded with whiskey.

April 27: LAPD detectives kill hijacker Harry Thomas during the attempted robbery of a garage on West 38th Street.

May 13: Prohibition agent Charles Bintliff and Deputy State Sheriff Charles Halpin die in a shootout near Redfield, S.D., while trying to arrest a man who wounded another federal agent one week earlier. The suspect kills himself later in the day, while surrounded by a posse of 400 lawmen.

May 23: Mafiosi in Philadelphia, Pennsylvania, kill three members of the rival Zanghi gang in a drive-by shooting at Eighth and Christian Streets. Survivor "Musky" Zanghi blames Salvatore Sabella.

May 27: New York gangster Tony Torchio machine-gunned to death in Chicago, after responding to Joe Aiello's offer of a bounty on Al Capone's life. Rival mobsters kill Luigi "Big Gorilla" Lamendola at his Chatham Street restaurant/headquarters in Pittsburgh, Pa.

May 30: Mafia gunmen execute rebellious family members Vincent Cocozza and Joseph Zanghi in Philadelphia, Pa. Anthony Zanghi fingers boss Salvatore Sabella as his brother's killer.

June 1: Capone gunmen kill Aiello gangster Lawrence LaPresta in Chicago.

June 10: Capone gangster James DeAmato is killed in Manhattan, while spying on Frankie Yale's bootleg operations.

June 12: Prohibition agent Charles Rouse suffers fatal bullet wounds during a liquor raid in Baltimore, Md. His killer escapes to France, then surrenders in July.

June 29–30: Capone assassins kill Aiello gangsters Lorenzo Alagna, Diego Attlomionte, and Numio Jamerrico.

July: Illinois jurors convict Birger gang members Ray Hyland and Arthur Newman of murder. Both receive life sentences.

July 11: Gunmen kill Aiello gangster Giovanni Blandini in Chicago. Prohibition agent William Lewis suffers fatal gunshots while attempting to arrest two moonshiners near Kinston, N.C. Lewis dies on July 15.

July 9: Future gangster Charles Kray born in London, England.

July 17: Capone hitmen slay Aiello gangster Dominic Cinderello in Chicago.

July 20: A bootlegger kills Prohibition agent George Nantz while resisting arrest in London, Ky.

July 21: Drive-by machine-gunners strafe a Purple Gang hangout on Detroit's Oakland Avenue, killing Henry Kaplan and wounding three others.

August 7: Federal agents intercept James "King of the Rumrunners" Alderman with a load of smuggled liquor, offshore from Fort Lauderdale, Fla. Alderman kills Secret Service agent Robert Webster and Coast Guardsman Sidney Sanderlin, fatally wounding Coast Guardsman Victor Lamby (who dies on August 11). A companion turns state's evidence against Alderman, resulting in his murder conviction at trial, in January 1928. Alderman hangs at Fort Lauderdale's Coast Guard station on August 17, 1929.

August 8: Future chief William Parker joins LAPD as a patrolman.

August 10: Chicago Outfit gunmen execute Anthony Russo and Vincent Spicuzza, imported from St. Louis by Joe Aiello to murder Al Capone.

August 16–28: Chicago authorities subject various gangsters to "sanity tests." Reluctant subjects include "Machine Gun" Jack McGurn, Frank and Vincent McErlane, "Polack Joe" Saltis, and John "Dingbat" Oberta.

September: Mafioso Joe Aiello forges an alliance with Chicago's North Side gang, against Al Capone.

September 9: Members of a rival gang ambush Green Ones leader Alphonse Palizzola in St. Louis, killing him and a 10-year-old bystander on Tenth Street.

September 24: Machine-gunners kill Sam Valente, a Cleveland gangster hired by Joe Aiello to kill Al Capone.

October 6: Paroled bootlegger George Remus murders his estranged wife in Cincinnati. At trial, he wins acquittal on a plea of temporary insanity.

October 7: Cleveland mobsters execute would-be extortionists Jack Brownstein and Ernest Yorkell.

October 10: Under the name "John D'Nubile," Ray Patriarca pays a $100 fine in Worcester, Mass., for transporting liquor.

October 13: Leaders of Cleveland's Porello Mafia family invite the rival Lonardo brothers to a peace conference at their barber shop, then murder Joe and John Lonardo. Joe Porello takes control of the local Unione Siciliana.

October 15: New York's fourth labor sluggers' war ends with the murder of racketeer Jacob Orgen on Manhattan's Lower East Side. Orgen gang members Lepke Buchalter and Gurrah Shapiro kill Orgen and wound bodyguard Legs Diamond on Norfolk Street, after Orgen rejects Meyer Lansky's advice to abandon crude strike-breaking tactics in favor of infiltrating and corrupting unions.

October 22: A car bomb intended for bootlegger Tony Domingo kills his wife Mary in Berrien County, Mich. Soon afterward, Tony and brother Sebastiano — better known as Mafia hitman "Buster from Chicago"—fire on suspected bomber Louie Vieglo at the local Fourth Ward Republican Club. Vieglo escapes, while police detain the Domingo brothers overnight, then release them.

October 24: Future mafioso Anthony Joseph Zerilli born in Detroit.

October 27: Melbourne mobster Joseph Taylor and rival John "Snowy" Cutmore fatally wound each other in a shootout on Barkly Street, in suburban Carlton, Australia.

November 9: North Side gangsters Frank and Peter Gusenburg wound Capone mobster "Machine Gun" Jack McGurn at Chicago's McCormick Hotel.

November 10: Capone gunmen kill Frank and Robert Aiello in Springfield, Ill.

November 21: In the fifth week of a strike against the Rocky Mountain Fuel Company, 500 striking coal miners and their families picket the Columbine Mine at Serene, Colo. State police attack the strikers, who respond by hurling stones. Police and company thugs open fire with machine guns, killing six IWW members and wounding 60 more.

November 22: Chicago prosecutors arraign Al Capone on charges of vagrancy and disorderly conduct. A judge dismisses both counts.

November 23: A bomb damages the Chicago headquarters of vice lords Barney Bertsche, Billy Skidmore and Jack Zuta. Chicago police surprise gunmen outside the home of Tony Lombardo, sparking a running gun battle.

November 29: Unknown gunmen kill reputed bootlegger Carmen Ferro, dumping his corpse outside Bensenville, Ill.

December 5: Unknown gunmen murder Anthony Caruso, a witness to the October slayings of Joe and John Lonardo, in Cleveland, Ohio.

December 15: Border Patrol Inspector Franklin Wood drowns during a boat pursuit of human traffickers smuggling illegal aliens across the Detroit River, from Canada into Michigan. Searchers fail to recover his body.

December 17: An explosion at the Haymarket Hotel marks Chicago's 108th bombing of 1927. Al Capone returns to Chicago from Los Angeles, briefly delayed by an arrest in Joliet, Ill.

December 26: Future New England mafioso Louis Failla born.

December 28: Rival mobsters invade the home of Green Ones leader Vito Giannola's mistress, in St. Louis. They find Giannola hiding in a secret upstairs compartment and shoot him 37 times.

1928 Britain bans recreational use of cannabis, while legalizing totalizer betting. Soviet authorities ban private gambling in Russia. Chile legalizes public gambling at the Vina del Mar resort, near Santiago. The Agua Caliente hotel-casino and golf course opens near Tijuana, Mexico.

January: Frankie Yale orders Antonio Lombardo to resign the presidency of Chicago's Unione Siciliana, in favor of Joe Aiello. Lombardo refuses.

January 2: Bootleggers kill Prohibition agent Wesley Fraser in South St. Paul, Minn., as he supervises confiscation of a still and other bootlegging equipment.

January 3: Underworld bombs damage the Newport Hotel in Chicago and the Forest Club, a gambling resort, in Forest Park, Ill.

January 4: Police find Amado Vasquez beaten to death on Date Street, Los Angeles, allegedly by members of a College Park bootlegging gang.

January 5: Capone gunmen fire on the Aiello Brothers Bakery, in Chicago.

January 23: Future mayor of Palermo and Mafia associate Salvatore "Salvo" Lima born in Palermo, Sicily.

January 26: Gangland bombers strike the Chicago homes of Charles Fitzmorris and Dr. William Reid, both members of Mayor William Thompson's cabinet.

January 28: Police find bootlegger and suspected informer William Rosen murdered in his car, in the Palos Verdes Hills, southwest of Los Angeles. LAPD suspects Milton Page.

February 2: NYPD officers raid the Paramount Building on Broadway, arresting brothers Legs and Eddie Diamond with 14 others, seizing stolen furs valued at $20,000.

February 5: New Orleans police arrest Al and Ralph Capone on "suspicion," then release them.

February 12: Members of the North End Gang kill bootlegger Frank De Falco in San Pedro, Calif.

February 21: A bomb damages the Chicago home of Lawrence Cuneo, brother-in-law of State's Attorney Robert Crowe.

February 22: Prohibition agent Walter Tolbert suffers fatal gunshot wounds while raiding a still near Harlem, Ga.

February 27: Jurors in Providence, R.I., convict Ray Patriarca of breaking-and-entering and larceny. He receives a two-year sentence on January 21, 1929, and is paroled on January 25, 1930.

March 18: Unidentified bootlegging suspects kill LAPD Officer James Carter after he stops their car in the city's "brandy center area."

March 20: Unknown gunmen execute rumrunners Morris "Ben" Nadel and Morris Goldman in Cleveland, Ohio.

March 21: Shotgunners kill bootlegger-politician "Diamond Joe" Esposito outside his Chicago home.

March 22: Purple Gang members kidnap and murder Sam Polakoff, a Detroit laundry owner who has marshaled resistance against tribute payments. Judge Charles Bowles issues arrest warrants for nine Purples and labor racketeer Charles Jacoby on March 30. Jurors acquit the defendants of all charges on September 13.

March 26: Bombs explode at the Chicago homes of Senator Charles Deneen and Judge John Swanson.

March 29: Future mafioso Vincent "The Chin" Gigante born in New York City.

March 31: Supporters of Mayor William "Big Bill" Thompson protest federal efforts to track election-season bombers in Chicago. Agents ignore the opposition and begin investigation of two bombings — at the homes of Senator Charles Deneen and Judge John Swanson — on April 3.

April 10: Machine-gunners kill Octavius Granady, a black attorney challenging Capone ally Morris Eller as boss of the 20th Ward.

April 21: Charles Birger hangs in Benton, Ill., for the 1927 murder of West City mayor Joe Adams.

April 22: An unknown assassin kills Ben Newmark, former chief investigator for State's Attorney Robert Crowe, at his Chicago home.

May 9: The Chicago Bar Association files a petition in criminal court, charging supporters of State's Attorney Robert Crowe with murder, kidnapping, bombing and vote theft during the city's "Pineapple Primary."

May 10: A moonshiner kills Prohibition agent James Capen while resisting arrest on a farm near Cumberland, Wyo. Another agent fatally wounds the gunman.

June 7: An opium trafficker fatally shoots Prohibition agent James Brown near Isleton, Calif.

June 10: Gunmen kill saloonkeeper Abe Warshofsky in Cleveland, Ohio. Reporters attribute the murder to "a row over tribute to his silent partners."

June 18: Prohibition agent Warren Frahm dies in a car crash while pursuing rum-runners on the Chateaugay-Brainardsville Highway in Franklin County, N.Y.

June 26: Unknown gunmen kill Big Tim Murphy outside his Chicago home. Prime suspects include Murray Humphreys.

July 1: Drive-by gunmen kill mafioso Frankie Yale in Brooklyn. His death marks the first criminal use of a Tommy gun in New York.

July 7: Members of the College Park Gang shoot teenage saloon hostess Bobbi Lee, cut her throat, and toss her from a speeding car in Downey, Calif.

July 8: Police find College Park bootlegger and suspected police informant William Cassidy mur-

dered in Altadena, Calif. On the same day, gunmen kill wealthy druggist and bootlegger John Glabb outside his home on Ventura Boulevard, Los Angeles. LAPD suspects the College Park Gang in both cases.

July 13: Future mafioso Tommaso Buscetta born in Palermo, Sicily. Prohibition agent Irving Washburn suffers fatal gunshots while raiding a speakeasy in Albany, N.Y.

July 17: Members of the North End Gang kill transplanted Chicago racketeer Leon "Jack" Palmer in a taxi, in San Pedro, Calif.

July 18: North End gangsters kill aspiring rival August Palumbo in his car on Hillcrest Street, Los Angeles.

July 20: Capone gunmen kill Joe Aiello's uncle, Dominic Aiello, outside his Chicago store.

July 25: Capone gunmen slay Aiello gangster Salvatore Canale outside his home, in Chicago. The sheriff of Chelan County, Washington, mistakes federal Prohibition agents for bootleggers during a raid near Leavenworth, killing Agent Ludwig Johnson.

August 23: Future hitman Lucas Francis "Lucky Luke" Cavanaugh born in Chicago, raised by Bugs Moran after his father is jailed for murder in 1929.

August 28: Members of the College Park Gang execute rival Phillip Rubino outside his residence on Holmes Avenue, Los Angeles.

September 4: Mayor H.A. Mackey gives police in Philadelphia, Pa., 24 hours to "clean up" their department, but no change occurs. On September 28 authorities arrest 23 officers in one precinct. On October 1 a former captain and two detectives face indictment on charges of extorting cash from speakeasy owners. By October 31, Mayor Mackey has suspended 21 high-ranking officers and transferred 4,800 patrolmen, while requiring all officers to fill out "wealth questionnaires."

September 7: Aiello gangsters kill Unione Siciliana president Antonio Lombardo in Chicago. Bodyguard Joseph Ferraro (or Moreci) is also wounded, dying on September 9. Pasqualino "Patsy" Lolordo fills the Unione vacancy.

September 28: Prohibition agent James Kerrigan suffers internal injuries from a fall, during a raid on an opium den in Newark, N.J.'s, Chinatown. After weeks of pain, he checks into New York City's Misericordia Hospital, where he dies during surgery on December 27.

October 4: Prohibition agent John Nicola dies in a car crash while pursuing suspected rum-runners outside Baltimore, Md.

October 10: Gunmen employed by Joe Masseria kill rival mafioso Salvatore "Toto" D'Aquila at the corner of Avenue A and 13th Street in Manhattan. Alfred "Al Mineo" Manfredi succeeds D'Aquila as New York's "boss of bosses."

October 15: Unknown gunmen wound Dutch Schultz lieutenant Joe Noe outside the Chateau Madrid, on Manhattan's West 54th Street. Noe survives at Bellevue Hospital until November 21. Schultz blames Legs Diamond for the shooting.

November 3: An unknown gunman fatally wounds Arnold Rothstein at Manhattan's Park Central Hotel. He dies on November 4, at the Stuyvesant Polyclinic Hospital, after telling detectives, "Me mudder did it." Prosecutors indict gamblers Hyman Biller and George McManus on December 8, but drop the case prior to trial.

November 6: Drive-by machine-gunners strafe Eddie Diamond's car in Denver, Colo., but he escapes without injury. Police arrest two former bodyguards of Arnold Rothstein, Eugene Moran and James Piteo, who post $15,000 bond and then flee Colorado.

November 16: Unknown gunmen murder John Clay, secretary of the Laundry and Dyehouse Chauffeurs Union, at his Chicago office. Police link Clay's death to a labor rackets war between Al Capone and rival North Side gangsters.

November 17: NYPD files robbery charges (later dismissed) against Lucky Luciano, George Uffner, and Thomas "Fats" Walsh, also grilling them about the Rothstein murder.

November 23: San Francisco gangster Alfredo Cearisso kills Black Hander leader Gerri Ferri.

November 26: NYPD Commissioner Grover Whalen revives the department's "strong-arm" squad and employs vagrancy laws to harass local gangsters.

November 27: Gambler George "Hump" McManus surrenders to NYPD on suspicion of killing Arnold Rothstein. A grand jury indicts him on December 4, but he is later acquitted at trial.

December 4: A car bomb kills Daniel "Dapper Danny" Hogan in St. Paul, Minn., ending his 19-year career as a saloon proprietor and middleman for mobsters and corrupt police.

December 5: Police interrupt a Mafia confab at the Hotel Statler in Cleveland, Ohio, arresting 21 prominent mobsters. Prohibition agent Patrick Sharp dies in Texas, after inhaling toxic fumes during a raid on an underground still.

December 18: Police find Alfredo Cearisso and a companion murdered on the outskirts of San Francisco, Calif.

December 25: Charles Luciano meets with young associates in Manhattan, to plot the demise of older Mafia "Mustache Petes."

December 31: Gunmen from Chicago's Bubs Quinlan gang kill Hugh "Stubby" McGovern and William "Gunner" McPadden, members of the rival Danny Stanton mob.

1929 New Zealand launches an Art Union lottery pool. U.S. authorities estimate that one gallon of denatured industrial alcohol in every ten gallons manufactured is diverted to produce bootleg liquor, with sometimes fatal results for consumers.

January 1: Future mobster Joseph "Joey the Clown" Lombardo Sr. born in Chicago.

January 3: NYPD's "strong-arm" squad raids 60 underworld hangouts with orders to rough up mobsters. Newspapers report many gangsters fleeing to Chicago, where police vow to return them "in boxes."

January 5: Seeking to halt an influx of fugitive New York gangsters, Detroit Police Commissioner William Rutledge announces a $10 bounty for each criminal killed by his men.

January 6: Federal and state officers seize control of Chicago Heights, arresting the suburb's entire police force on corruption charges.

January 8: Aiello gangsters kill Unione Siciliana president Patsy Lolordo in Chicago. Capone rival Giuseppe Guinta claims the presidency.

January 10: Police find New York rum-runner Harry Vesey shot dead on the waterfront at Hoboken, N.J.

January 12: Cornelius Shea dies in at Chicago's Norwegian-American Hospital, following gall bladder surgery.

January 19: President Calvin Coolidge signs the Porter Act, creating two "narcotic farms" for the confinement and treatment of federal prisoners addicted to drugs.

January 20–21: Chicago police jail 3,944 persons in a record series of liquor and vice raids.

January 21: NYPD Commissioner Grover Whalen publicly names the owners of 996 local "crime nests." On February 3, Whalen optimistically declares that Manhattan's gunmen have been dispersed.

February 10: Future mafioso Rosario Riccobono born in Palermo, Sicily.

February 14: Capone gunmen slaughter six members of the North Side Gang and a "civilian" visitor in a garage at 2122 North Clark Street, Chicago. Victims of the "St. Valentine's Day massacre" include Bugs Moran lieutenant Albert Kachellek, AKA "James Clark"; gang bookkeeper Adam Heyer; brothers Frank and Peter Gusenberg; Albert Weinshank, who managed several cleaning and dyeing operations for Moran (whose resemblance to Moran apparently deceived mob spotters); mechanic John May; and optician Reinhart Schwimmer, identified by author Laurence Bergreen (1996) as a active associate of the North Side Gang. The crime remains officially unsolved, although Capone and Moran both publicly blamed each other. Two Tommy guns used in the massacre were later found in the possession of Fred "Killer" Burke, but he was never charged with the slayings.

February 28: NYPD Commissioner Grover Whalen declares that "strong-arm" tactics will prevent New York City from becoming "another Chicago."

March 4: Herbert Hoover (1874–1965) inaugurated as President of the U.S.

March 7: Former Arnold Rothstein associate Thomas "Fats" Walsh dies in a shooting at Miami's Biltmore Hotel.

March 8: Future Philadelphia mafioso Nicodemo "Little Nicky" Scarfo born in New York City.

March 12: Federal authorities remove Major F.D. Silloway from the Prohibition Bureau's Chicago office, after he says that police may have perpetrated the St. Valentine's Day Massacre.

March 15: West Side O'Donnell gang member George Clifford kills underworld poet William Vercoe at the Pony Inn in Cicero, Ill.

March 20: Gunmen kill bootlegger Max Silverstein in his apartment on Santa Catalina Island, off the coast of southern California. Police suspect rivals Ben Baretti and Dan Kennedy.

March 24: Border Patrol Inspector Earl Roberts suffers fatal gunshot wounds while attempting to arrest liquor smugglers on the St. Clair River in Algona, Mich.

April 2: Gunmen in Cleveland, Ohio, execute police informer Leo Klein.

April 7: Future mafioso Joseph "Crazy Joe" Gallo born in Manhattan.

April 10: Future Mexican Mafia member Joe "Pegleg" Morgan born in San Pedro, Calif.

April 14: Unknown gunmen kill West Side gangsters George Clifford and Michael Reiley in Chicago.

April 15: Detroit police arrest Louis Dalitz as a "disorderly person," then drop the charge.

April 29–May 3: Chicago's grand jury indicts 124 participants in a $10 million slot machine operation. Defendants include six police captains and several public officials.

May: President Herbert Hoover (1874–1964) names former U.S. Attorney General George Wickersham (1858–1936) to chair a National Committee on Law Observation and Enforcement, commonly called the Wickersham Commission. Charged with identifying the causes of criminal activity and making recommendations for appropriate public policy, the panel studies Prohibition enforcement and police "third degree" tactics.

May 7: Al Capone hosts a banquet at the Hawthorne Hotel in Cicero, Ill. During the meal, he bludgeons adversaries Giuseppe Guinta, Alberto Anselmi, and John Scalise to death with a baseball bat. Police find the corpses on May 9, outside Hammond, Ind.

May 9: Meyer Lansky marries Anna Citron in New York City.

May 13–15: Nucky Johnson hosts the first convention of America's national crime syndicate in Atlantic City, N.J. Attendees include John Torrio, Charles Luciano, Frank Costello, Joe Adonis, Vito Genovese, Albert Anastasia, Frank "Cheech" Scalise, Vincent Mangano, Gaetano Lucchese, Meyer Lansky, Benjamin Siegel, Gaetano Gagliano, Carlo Gambino, Lepke Buchalter, Gurrah Shapiro, Dutch Schultz, Owney Madden, and Frank Erickson from New York; Longy Zwillman and Guarino "Willie Moore" Moretti from New Jersey; Al Capone, Frank Nitti, Jake Guzik, Frank Rio, and Frank McErlane from Chicago; Waxey Gordon, Nig Rosen, Max "Boo Boo" Hoff, Irving "Bitzy" Bitz, and Charles Schwartz from Philadelphia; Moe Dalitz, Lou Rothkopf, and Charles Polizzi from Cleveland; Abe and Joseph Bernstein from Detroit; Charles "King" Solomon and Frank "The Cheeseman" Cucchiara from Boston; John Lazia from Kansas City; Frank "Bootsy" Morelli from Providence, R.I.; Santo Trafficante Sr. from Tampa, Fla.; and Sylvestro "Silver Dollar Sam" Carolla of New Orleans.

May 14: Prohibition agent Dano Jackley dies in a car crash while chasing a suspected rum-runner outside Berwyn, Md. Days later, a coroner's jury exonerates the suspect of any wrongdoing.

May 15: Chicago police detective Raymond Martin suffers fatal gunshot wounds while impersonating Moses Blumenthal at a ransom drop for Blumenthal's kidnapped bootlegger-brother Philip.

May 16: College Park gangsters kill Matranga family member Joe Porazzo in Chinatown, Los Angeles. Police in Philadelphia, Pa., arrest Al Capone and bodyguard Frank Rio for carrying concealed weapons. Both plead guilty and receive one-year prison terms, serving 10 months. Historians speculate that leaders of the national crime syndicate ordered Capone to take the "vacation" after rousing public outrage with the St. Valentine's Day massacre.

May 22: Unknown gunmen kill Chicago detective Joseph Sullivan at Red Bolton's speakeasy, while Sullivan investigates the May 15 slaying of Detective Ray Martin.

May 29: Unknown gunmen kill West Side gangster Thomas McElligot in Chicago's Loop district.

June 11: Unknown gunmen murder Mafia boss Salvatore "Black Sam" Todaro in Cleveland, Ohio. Joe Porello takes control of the Cleveland crime family.

June 13: The Detroit *Free Press* reports the creation of "a giant combine of Great Lakes rumrunners" to smuggle liquor from Canada. Legs Diamond and bodyguard Charles Entratta kill three rivals — Peter Cassidy, William Cassidy and Simon Walker — at Diamond's Hotsy Totsy Club on Broadway, in Manhattan. Ten witnesses to the slayings subsequently disappear, while an eleventh — club waiter Walter Wolgast — is found murdered in Bordentown, N.J., on July 19.

June 24: Unknown gunmen execute Frankie Yale ally Gandalfo Civito, AKA "Frankie Marlow," on Queens Avenue in New York City.

June 27: Prohibition agent Lawrence Mommer dies in an auto crash while chasing bootleggers through Fort Wayne, Ind.

July: In Detroit, Purple Gang members Abe Axler, Eddie Fletcher, Irving Milberg and Harry Sutton receive 22-month federal prison terms for conspiracy to violate the Volstead Act.

July 2: Detroit police find cult leader and real estate tycoon Benjamin Evangelista, his wife and four children, beheaded at their home. Some researchers blame organized crime for the "voodoo murders."

July 12: While raiding an illegal distillery in New Orleans, Prohibition agent George Droz falls into a vat of boiling mash and suffers fatal burns.

July 14: Italian businessman and mafioso Antonio "Nino" Salvo born in Salemi, Sicily.

July 20: Border Patrol Inspector Ivan Scotten dies in a shootout with liquor smugglers near Clint, Tex. Officers capture triggerman Ramiro Galvan in 1934, resulting in conviction and a sentence of death, commuted to life imprisonment on February 13, 1936.

July 22: Bootlegger Frank Carnigella dies in a shootout with father-son rivals James and Jesse Pagliasotti, on Solano Street, Los Angeles.

July 24: Bootlegger Frank Sallino dies from multiple stab wounds at his home on Biggy Street, Los Angeles. LAPD suspects Dominick Palestino and Dominic Stea.

July 31: Ex–court bailiff Thomas McNichols and gangland armorer James "Bozo" Sharpe kill each other in a shootout on a Chicago street corner. A moonshiner kills Deputy U.S. Marshal Adrian Metcalf during a liquor raid in Harlan County, Ky.

August 2: While struggling with a liquor smuggler in a boat on the Detroit River, Prohibition agent Richard Sandlands suffers a broken neck and dies at the scene.

August 4: A new East Coast Tong war erupts after assassins kill Yee Sun, a member of the Hip Sing Tong, in Chicago. Another Hip Sing member survives an attack in Boston on the same day.

August 6: Mafia boss Stefano Monastero dies in an ambush outside Allegheny General Hospital, in Pittsburgh, Pa. Giuseppe Siragusa succeeds him as the city's top mafioso.

August 9: Future mobster Albert Caesar Tocco born in Chicago.

August 10: Police in Newark, N.J., find Eugene Morgan — a former bodyguard of Arnold Rothstein — shot and burned in a car at the city dump.

August 29: Rival gangsters kill bootlegger Tony Domingo at a Chicago restaurant owned by Pasquale Spilotro, uncle of future mafioso Tony "The Ant" Spilotro.

September 2: Unidentified gunmen kill mobster Henry "Hoop-a-Daisy" Connors in a Chicago restaurant.

September 4: West Side gangster Frank Cawley dies in a Chicago ambush. Future mafioso Dominic Allevato born in Detroit.

September 25: Bootleggers ambush three Prohibition agents on a rural highway in Atascosa County, Tex., killing Agent Charles Stevens. One assassin suffers fatal wounds in the battle, while six more are later arrested.

October 17: Charles Luciano survives a one-way ride in New York City, with permanent facial scarring. The near-miss earns him his "Lucky" nickname.

October 18: Police name gangsters Fred "Killer" Burke and Gus Winkeler as prime suspects in the $93,000 robbery of a Peru, Ind., bank.

October 24: Wall Street suffers its "Black Thursday" crash, succeeded by catastrophic losses on "Black Monday" (October 28) and "Black Tuesday" (October 29), paving the way for a global Great Depression.

November 8: Los Angeles distiller Frank Baumgarteker disappears after refusing to manufacture booze for local bootleggers, including the Matranga family and the North End Gang.

November 17: Gunmen slay ex–Genna gang bootlegger John "Bilikens" Rito, soon after his formation of a new partnership with North Side gangster Ted Newberry.

December 1: Salesman Edwin Lowe of Atlanta, Ga., invents the game of "beano," subsequently renamed "bingo."

December 2: Future mafioso Louis "Bobby" Manna born in Hoboken, N.J.

December 7: Bandits crash a fundraising dinner for magistrate Albert Vitale at the Roman Gardens, in the Bronx, revealing the attendance of various mobsters, including Ciro Terranova. Telephone calls result in swift return of the loot.

December 10: A bootlegger's wife kills Prohibition agent Otto Butler during a liquor raid in Cushing, Okla. Jurors acquit both husband and wife on grounds that the agents' search warrant was invalid.

December 14: Driving drunk through St. Joseph, Mich., Fred Burke strikes another vehicle, then fatally shoots Patrolman Charles Skelly as he arrives on the scene. Burke escapes, leaving behind loot from a recent Wisconsin bank holdup and an arsenal of weapons, including Tommy guns linked to Frankie Yale's murder and the St. Valentine's Day massacre.

December 29: Chicago police arrest mobster Charles "Babe" Baron for killing bootlegger James Walsh after a prize fight, but the charges are dismissed. Prohibition agent Robert Freeman suffers fatal gunshot wounds while raiding a ranch near Yountville, Calif. He dies on February 8, 1930.

December 30: NYPD officers arrest "Madame" Stephanie St. Clair, the "numbers queen" of Harlem, on gambling charges. She receives an eight-month prison term at trial. Future mobster Jacques "Mad Jacky" Imbert born in Toulouse, France.

1930 Farmers in the Yarkand region of Chinese Turkestan exports 100 tons of hashish into the Northwest Frontier and Punjab regions of India. Ireland's government passes the Public Hospital Act, authorizing lotteries to benefit hospitals. Bolivia bans gambling in mining districts.

January: Nicola "Cola" Schiro, leader of Brooklyns Castellammarese mafioso, disappears after paying $10,000 to rival Joe Masseria. Masseria installs Joe Parrino as head of Schiro's crime family.

January 5: Ciro Terranova publicly denies any improper ties to Magistrate Albert Vitale, calling himself a "man of peace" and pleading for privacy. Unimpressed, the New York State Appellate Court orders Vitale's removal on March 14, citing his ties to notorious mobsters and an unexplained $10,000 deposit to his bank account.

January 14: Prohibition Agent Louis Davies suffers fatal gunshot wounds while trying to arrest a bootlegger in Pamlico County, N.C.

January 18: Minnesota bootlegger Leon Gleckman, "the Al Capone of St. Paul," establishes headquarters at the Hotel St. Paul. Bootleggers in West Palm Beach, Fla., kill Prohibition agents Robert Moncure and Franklin Patterson during a liquor raid, then surrender to other officers.

January 20: A federal grand jury in Buffalo, N.Y., indicts Moe Dalitz, Morris Kleinman, Sam Tucker, and 11 codefendants for conspiracy to defraud the government by selling untaxed liquor. Three boat captains plead guilty, but the rest are never tried. Dalitz later denies any knowledge of the indictment.

February 3: Labor racketeers kill contractor William Healy during a dispute with the Chicago Marble Setters Union.

February 4: Unknown gunmen kill Chicago gangster Julius Rosenheim, soon after he agrees to become a police informant.

February 14: Detroit mafioso Salvatore Catalanotte dies from pneumonia in Grosse Point, Mich., sparking a local power struggle.

February 15: Detroit police blame rising crime rates on transplanted mobsters from Chicago.

February 17: Future mafioso Anthony Thomas "Tony Ripe" Civella born in Kansas City, Mo.

February 20: Mafioso Carlo Piranio dies of natural causes in Dallas, Tex. Brother Joseph Piranio assumes control of the family.

February 26: Vito Genovese, acting on orders from Joe Masseria, murders rival mafioso Gaetano Reina in the Bronx, triggering the American Mafia's "Castellammarese War." Masseria places Joe Pinzolo in charge of Reina's gang.

February 27: Chicago's Association of Commerce announces creation of the "Secret Six"— anonymous merchant-detectives pledged to rid the city of crime within six months.

March 10: Legs Diamond surrenders for trial in the triple-killing at his Hotsy Totsy Club. A judge dismisses the charges on March 21.

March 17: Al Capone leaves prison in Pennsylvania, returning to Chicago.

April 11: Police detain Ray Patriarca as a "suspicious person" in Woonsocket, R.I., then release him without charges.

April 12: Prohibition agent Lamar York dies from gunshot wounds sustained while trying to arrest three suspects in Washington, D.C. Jurors convict two defendants, both of whom are executed on June 29, 1932.

April 13: An unknown shotgunner blasts District Attorney Clinton Price at his home in Milwaukee, Wis. Price dies the following day.

April 19: Gunmen raid the state jail at Howard, R.I., killing guard George McVay and trusty Peleg Champlin in a bungled attempt to liberate inmates James "Pretty" McNeal and John "Whitey" Miller. The case remains unsolved until 1944, when confessed triggerman Walter Sullivan claims that Raymond Patriarca hired him, Johnny McLaughlin, and a man known only as Martin to stage the jailbreak. Authorities subsequently rule Sullivan insane and confine him to a state hospital. Prosecutors indict Patriarca and alleged accomplice Joseph Fisher, but the Rhode Island Supreme Court dismisses those charges on June 25, 1945, on grounds that the statute of limitations has expired.

April 20: A single unknown gunmen kills three Capone soldiers in a Chicago speakeasy.

April 23: The Chicago Crime Commission issues its first list of "public enemies." In order of ranking, the 28 mobsters listed include Al Capone, Anthony "Mops" Volpe, Ralph Capone,

Frank Rio, Jack McGurn, James "Bomber" Belcastro, Rocco Fanelli, Lawrence Mangano, Jack Zuta, Jake Guzik, Frank Diamond, George "Bugs" Moran, Joe Aiello, Edward "Spike" O'Donnell, Joe Saltis, Frank McErlane, Vincent McErlane, William Neimoth, Danny Stanton, Myles O'Donnell, Frank Lake, William "Klondike" O'Donnell, George "Red" Barker, William "Three Finger Jack" White, Joseph "Peppy" Genero, Leo Mongoven, and James "Fur" Sammons.

April 25: A federal judge in Miami enjoins local police from harassing Al Capone with nuisance arrests. Nonetheless, officers jail him, with brother John and two gang members, "for investigation" on May 8. A higher court voids the injunction on May 9. Police then arrest Capone, Nick Circella, and former Chicago alderman Albert Prignano at a prizefight, on May 13. Officers arrest Capone and Prignano at another boxing match on May 19, for vagrancy. A judge dismisses that charge on May 21.

May 6: Matranga gang leader Tony Buccola vanishes after rebuffing merger bids from the North End Gang.

May 7: The Maxim Company announces that it will no longer manufacture firearms silencers.

May 9: Future judge and Mafia associate Corrado Carnevale born in Licata, Sicily.

May 15: NYPD officers find Anna Urbas, lover of murdered gangster Eugene Moran, strangled in the East River.

May 19: Future Detroit mafioso Peter Victor Cavataio born in Grosse Pointe, Mich.

May 31: Ambitious mobster Cesare Lemare schedules a meeting with Eastside Mob leader Angelo Meli at Detroit's Vernor Highway Fish Market. Meli sends negotiators Gaspari "The Peacemaker" Milazzo and Sam "Sasa" Parrino in his place. Assassins armed with shotguns kill both men. Witnesses identify the killers as mafiosi Joe Amico, Joe Locano, and "Benny the Ape." The double slaying sparks reprisals, claiming 14 lives in Detroit by July 23.

June 1: Machine-gunners kill three Capone associates at Manning's a resort on Fox Lake in Lake County, Ill.

June 5: Police find mobster Eugene "Red" McLaughlin's corpse in the Chicago River, weighted with baling wire and 75 pounds of scrap metal.

June 6: Future mafioso Albert "Kid Blast" Gallo Jr. born in New York City.

June 9: An assassin kills *Chicago Tribune* reporter Alfred "Jake" Lingle Jr. at the Illinois Central train station underpass. Initial claims of journalistic martyrdom give way to revelations of Lingle's mob connections and extravagant lifestyle. Prosecutors convict suspect Leo Vincent

Brothers, who receives a 14-year sentence, but some researchers still dispute his guilt. In Modoc County, Calif., liquor violators kill Prohibition agent Albert Brown.

June 13: A bootlegger kills Deputy U.S. Marshal Reuben Hughett while resisting arrest in Knox County, Tenn.

June 14: Congress creates the Federal Bureau of Narcotics, led by Harry Anslinger, consolidating functions of the Federal Narcotics Control Board and the Treasury Department's Narcotic Division. In Miami, Judge Paul Barnes dismisses a state petition to padlock Al Capone's Palm Island estate as a "public nuisance."

June 16: Future mafioso Dominick "Sonny Black" Napolitano born in Brooklyn, N.Y. Chicago city council demand and obtain the resignations of Police Commissioner William Russell and Captain John Stege, announcing an investigation of the whole department following Jake Lingle's murder.

June 17: Liquor smugglers shoot and kill Prohibition agent Rosie Flinchum during a high-speed pursuit in Goldsboro, N.C.

June 24: Chicago's city council names J.H. Alcock as the new police commissioner, dropping calls for a department-wide investigation of corruption.

June 25: Border Patrol Inspector Robert Kelsay dies in a shootout with liquor smugglers on the Rio Grande River, in Texas. Mexican authorities find gunman Juan Espinosa dead on their side of the river, later reporting that Kelsay also killed smuggler Jesus Cantu and wounded two others.

June 30: Police find Chicago Outfit lieutenant Thomas Somneiro strangled on the city's West Side.

July: Fearing betrayal to authorities, fugitive Fred Burke kills Chicago gangster Thomas Bonner at a cottage near Hess Lake, Mich.

July 1: The U.S. Prohibition Bureau transfers from the Treasury Department to the Department of Justice.

July 4: The cabin cruiser *Natchez* explodes and burns at a dock owned by Moe Dalitz in Cleveland, Ohio. Dalitz eludes police, after seeking treatment for burns at a local hospital.

July 5: Gunmen kill mafioso Joe Porello and his bodyguard at a restaurant owned by Frank Milano, in Cleveland, Ohio. Milano succeeds Porello as boss of Cleveland's Mafia family.

July 6: Unknown killers ambush Prohibition agent Dale Kearney near Aguilar, Colo., shooting him 16 times.

July 23: Unidentified mobsters kill crusading radio newscaster Gerald Buckley in the lobby of Detroit's LaSalle Hotel.

July 26: Drive-by gunmen kill mafioso Vincent Porello in Cleveland, Ohio.

July 29: LAPD officers arrest mafioso Jack Dragna on suspicion of robbery, then release him on July 30.

July 31: Chicago bootleggers Thomas McNichols and James "Bozo" Schupe kill each other in a shootout on Madison Street.

August 1: Capone soldiers machine-gun Bugs Moran associate Jack Zuta on the dance floor of a resort in Delafield, Wis. In Miami, Al Capone wins a directed verdict of acquittal on perjury charges.

August 6: Judge Joseph Force Crater leaves a restaurant on Manhattan's 45th Street, en route to a Broadway theater, and vanishes forever. Police receive notice of his disappearance on September 3, after private searches fail. An October grand jury calls 95 witnesses and amasses 975 pages of testimony, concluding that "the evidence is insufficient to warrant any expression of opinion as to whether Crater is alive or dead, or as to whether he has absented himself voluntarily, or is the sufferer from disease in the nature of amnesia, or is the victim of crime." Authorities declare Crater dead on June 6, 1939. On August 19, 2005, police receives posthumous notes from Stella Ferrucci-Good, naming her husband Robert Good and fellow NYPD Detective Charles Burns, with taxi driver Frank Burns, as Crater's killers. The notes claim Crater was buried near West Eighth Street in Coney Island, near the present-day New York Aquarium.

August 15: Castellammerese mafiosi execute Masseria enforcer Giuseppe Morello and bodyguard Giuseppe Pariano at Morello's office East Harlem. Companion Gaspar Pollaro dies later from a single bullet wound. Joe Valachi later names one of the shooters as hitman Sebastiano "Buster from Chicago" Domingo.

August 22: Bootlegger Harry Western vanishes after meeting Legs Diamond at a party in Haines Falls, N.Y. NYPD detains two Diamond gang members after Western's car is found in a Brooklyn garage, but his corpse is never recovered.

August 28: Prohibition Agent Ray Sutton vanishes from his room at the Hotel Seaberg in Raton, N.M. Local gangster Perry Caldwell cashes Sutton's last paycheck in Trinidad, Colo., on September 1. A search of his home reveals jewelry and other items belonging to Sutton. Investigators find Sutton's bloodstained car on October 18, in a canyon 20 miles from Raton. Prosecutors indict Caldwell for forgery on December 8, but Sutton's presumed murder — allegedly committed on orders from New Mexico bootleggers — remains officially unsolved, with his body still missing.

September 5: Retaliating for the murder of Gaetano Reina, mafioso Dominick "The Gap" Petrilli murders Reina successor Joe Pinzolo at a Broadway office rented by Gaetano Lucchese. Reina loyalists join Salvatore Maranzano in his war against Joe Masseria.

September 7: Police in Providence, R.I., arrest Ray Patriarca for playing dice on Sunday. He pays a $5 fine, but the arrest results in revocation of his parole on September 25. Patriarca returns to prison on October 4, and is paroled again on November 6, 1930.

September 9: Allies of Salvatore Maranzano murder John Pinzola, a lieutenant of Joe "The Boss" Masseria in New York City.

September 10: Joseph Neuman, an associate of murdered bootlegger Frank Baumgarteker, vanishes after leaving his office in Ontario, Calif. Police suspect the North End Gang.

September 19: Detroit mafioso Carmello Castiglione dies in a shootout with rival mobsters, killing one of his assailants. Prohibition agent John Finiello suffers fatal gunshot wounds while raiding a brewery in Elizabeth, N.J.

September 20: Prohibition agent Mack Parsons dies in a car crash while chasing bootleggers in Columbia, S.C.

September 22: Legs Diamond arrives in Philadelphia, Pa., after a tour of Europe. Police detain him as a "suspicious" person.

September 27: Enemies of Cesare Lemare kill gang member Joe Marino at his Detroit home.

October 8: NYPD blames Ignazio Lupo for the slaying of baker Roger Consiglio, but no charges result.

October 12: Legs Diamond suffers gunshot wounds in an ambush at Manhattan's Hotel Monticello.

October 23: Machine-gunners kill mafioso Joe Aiello in Chicago. Most historians blame Al Capone for the slaying, but Lucky Luciano later claimed that Joe Masseria ordered the hit. Capone appoints Agostino Loverdo to lead Chicago's Unione Siciliana. In Los Angeles, Calif., U.S. forest ranger Franklin Hooma suffers fatal gunshot wounds during a raid on the ranch of convicted bootlegger William Wilson.

October 28: Unknown gunmen kill mobster Solly "Cutcher-Head-Off" Weissman in Kansas City, Mo.

October 31: Three hours after posting bond on a July 14 assault charge, mobster James Sammons wounds police sergeant James McBride with gunshots in Bellwood, Ill. Arrested the same day, Sammons hears his 1923 pardon on murder charges ruled illegal on November 26. He is returned to finish the remainder of his 50-year term in state prison, but a friendly judge frees him again in July 1932.

November 3: Al Capone reportedly offers to quit racketeering in return for a sanctioned monopoly on beer sales in Chicago. Chief Justice John McGoorty rejects the proposal.

November 4: Joe Masseria convenes a strategy meeting with Lucky Luciano, Vito Genovese, Al Mineo, and Steve Ferrigno at Ferrigno's apartment on Pelham Parkway, in the Bronx. Rival Maranzano gunmen kill Ferrigno and Mineo when they leave the apartment on November 5. Joe Valachi later names the primary shooter as Sebastiano Domingo, AKA "Buster from Chicago."

November 16: Future mafioso Salvatore "Totò" Riina, AKA "The Beast," born in Corleone, Sicily.

November 18: Future mafioso Dominic "Fats" Corrado born in Detroit.

November 26: President Herbert Hoover calls for a nationwide war on gangsters.

December: Future mobster James Vincent "Turk" Torello born in Chicago.

December 15: Chicago bootlegger and white slaver Isaac "Ike" Bloom dies after a long illness.

December 26: Civic leaders in Philadelphia, Pa., declare their city free of "racketeers."

December 30: Federal jurors in Rhode Island convict Ray Patriarca of violating the Mann Act. He receives a one-year prison term, revised to one year and a day on January 3, 1931, to prevent early release. Patriarca remains incarcerated until October 21, 1931.

1931 Massachusetts legalizes bingo games for charitable causes. Florida lawmakers approve pari-mutuel betting at horse and greyhound racetracks. Inventor Ode D. Jennings patents the first electrically powered slot machine, dubbed the "Electrojax." Following his arrest for assault and battery with a motor vehicle in northern New Jersey, Salvatore Sabella retires as boss of Philadelphia's Mafia family, replaced by hand-picked successor John Avena.

January: Japanese troops occupy the Hongkou District of Shanghai, China, establishing the first "comfort station" staffed by alleged volunteer prostitutes. By 1945, an estimated 80,000 to 300,000 "comfort women" are forced into prostitution throughout Asia and the Pacific, in areas occupied by Japan.

January 4: Gunman Frank Phillips kills bootlegger Ted Padgett during a floating craps game in San Bernardino, Calif.

January 7: The Wickersham Commission issues its *Report on the Enforcement of the Prohibition Laws of the United States*, opposing repeal of Prohibition while declaring that "there is yet no adequate observance or enforcement" of the Volstead Act.

January 19: Castellammarese mafiosi murder rival Joe Parrino in New York City.

January 24: Attempting to prevent a turf war, Denver mafioso Joe Roma convenes a meeting of 30 Colorado bootleggers. Police raid the meeting before Roma can negotiate peace terms with rivals Pete and Sam Carlino. In New York City, Dutch Schultz and Waxey Gordon ally Charles "Chink" Sherman suffer gunshots wounds in a duel at the Club Abbey on West 54th Street.

February 3: Maranzano family gunmen wound Joe "The Baker" Catania in New York City, on suspicion of hijacking Castellammarese liquor shipments. Catania dies the following day. Joe Valachi later names the shooters as Sebastiano Domingo (AKA "Buster from Chicago"), Nick Capuzzi and Salvatore Shillitani. Police in Cleveland, Ohio, find ex–city councilman William Potter beaten and shot to death in an apartment on Parkwood Drive. Detectives surmise that he attempted to blackmail local syndicate leaders with incriminating information.

February 7: Unidentified gunmen execute Cesare Lemare at his home in Detroit.

February 12: Police in Pittsburgh, Pa., charge racketeer Hyman Martin with the murder of Cleveland victim William Potter. Jurors convict him on April 3, but a key witness later recants, prompting a new trial. A second jury acquits Martin on June 16, 1932. FBI reports name Moe Dalitz, Morris Kleinman and Lou Rothkopf as the men behind Potter's slaying.

February 17: Miners affiliated with the IWW and UMW strike against the Black Mountain Coal Corporation in Kentucky's "Bloody Harlan" County. Sheriff John Blair hires 170 "special deputies" from Black Mountain payroll, including 27 convicted felons, 11 with prior convictions for murder or manslaughter.

February 18: Drive-by gunmen wound bootlegger Pete Carlino in Denver, Colo.

February 25: Gangster Robert Leslie dies in a shootout with Joseph "Cockeye" Herring on Clinton Street, Los Angeles. Future mafioso Alphonse "Sonny Red" Indelicato born in New York City. Chicago police jail Al Capone for vagrancy.

February 26: NYPD officers find Vivian Gordon, key witness in an ongoing vice investigation, strangled at Van Cortlandt Park in the Bronx. Gordon's teenage daughter, Benita Bischoff, allegedly commits suicide by inhaling gas in Audubon, N.J., on March 3.

March 14: Frank Vito, a friend and neighbor of mobster Dominic DiCiolla, vanishes forever from a dinner party in Los Angeles. Police suspect the rival College District gang. In Chicago, mobster Leo Brothers from St. Louis faces trial for the murder of newsman Jake Lingle. Jurors convict him on April 2, resulting in a 14-year prison term.

March 16: College District gangsters kill Vinciano "Jimmy" Basile in Downey, Calif.

March 18: Shotgunners from the College District gang kill rival mobster Dominic DiCiolla on Van Nuys Boulevard, Los Angeles.

March 19: Future Australian crime boss and drug baron Robert Trimbole born in Calabria, Italy. Nevada Governor Fred Balzar signs Assembly Bill 98, legalizing various forms of gambling at licensed casinos, for players aged 21 and older. The law sets monthly licensing fees at $10 per slot machine, $25 per table for social games, and $50 per table for mercantile games.

March 26: Police capture fugitive Fred Burke on a farm near Green City, Mo. Jurors in St. Joseph, Mich., convict Burke of Officer Charles Skelly's murder, and he receives a life sentence on April 27.

April 15: Lucky Luciano meets Joe Masseria for lunch and cards at Coney Island's Nuova Villa Tammaro restaurant. When Luciano goes to the restroom, gunmen appear and riddle Masseria with bullets, thus ending the Castellammarese War.

April 17: "Special Deputy" Jessie Pace dies in a shootout with striking miners in Evarts, Ky.

April 23: Gunmen Harry Hurwitz and Gus Martin kill Paul Crank in a liquor warehouse on Flower Street, Los Angeles.

April 27: Presumed strikers bomb a coal mine in Harlan County, Ky. Unknown gunmen wound Legs Diamond at the Aratoga Inn, in Acra, N.Y.

April 28: Strikers, "special deputies," and corporate gunmen fight a pitched battle in Harlan County, Ky., firing more than 2,000 shots.

April 30: Arsonists burn 16 company houses in Harlan County, Ky., while gunfire damages several other buildings.

May: Salvatore Maranzano names himself "Boss of Bosses" for the American Mafia, at a Chicago meeting hosted by Al Capone.

May 2: Prohibition agent Holmer Everett dies in a shotgun ambush while en route from Collins to Jackson, Miss., to testify in a liquor trial. His killer receives a death sentence on July 11.

May 5: Striking miners, deputies, and corporate goons fight another battle in Evarts, Ky., leaving four miners and two "special deputies" dead.

May 16: Bootleggers kill Deputy U.S. Marshal Clyde Rivers while resisting arrest near Booneville, Miss.

May 23: North End gangsters kill aspiring mob boss Tony Larraso on Moulton Avenue, Los Angeles.

May 30: Dutch Schultz's gunmen kill Peter Coll, brother of Vincent "Mad Dog" Coll, in New York City, sparking full-scale war between the rival gang leaders.

June 4: Future mafioso Anthony Joseph Tocco born in Detroit.

June 15: Vincent Coll kidnaps George "Big Frenchy" DeMange, partner of Owney Madden in various New York nightclubs. Coll releases DeMange after receiving a ransom variously estimated at $35,000 or $37,000.

June 18: Dutch Schultz and bodyguard Danny Iamascia mistake NYPD detectives for Coll gunmen, sparking a shootout on Manhattan's Fifth Avenue that leaves Iamascia dead and Schultz in custody.

June 23: Denver mafioso Joe Roma posts $5,000 bail for rival Pete Carlino, jailed on charges of conspiracy to commit arson.

June 28: Unknown gunmen kill bootlegger-florist Rosolino Visconti in Cleveland, Ohio.

July 11: Retaliating for an earlier murder attempt and the rape of his girlfriend, future Murder, Inc., hitman Abe "Kid Twist" Reles joins Martin "Bugsy" Goldstein to kill racketeer Irving Shapiro in the Bronx.

July 13: Delegates from various nations, gathered in Geneva, Switzerland, sign the Convention for Limiting the Manufacture and Regulating the Distribution of Narcotic Drugs. Taking effect on July 9, 1933, the treaty establishes two groups of drugs: Group I includes morphine, heroin, cocaine, and dihydrohydrooxycodeinone; Group II includes ecgonine, thebaine and their salts, benzylmorphine and the other ethers of morphine and their salts, except methylmorphine (codeine), ethylmorphine and their salts.

July 16: New York State Police officers raid a farm in Coxsackie, N.Y., bagging eight men and six women associated with Vincent Coll. The raiders seize an arsenal of weapons.

July 21: A racetrack in Reno, Nev., pioneers "daily double" betting, wherein bettors wager on the winners of two races, pre-designated by the track for a particular day. Gunmen in Cleveland execute bootleggers Harry Gertzlin and Al Jaffe.

July 22: Fugitive Charles "Pretty Boy" Floyd kills Prohibition agent Curtis Burke during a liquor raid in Kansas City, Mo. On the same day, Prohibition agents Walter Gilbert and John Wilson die in a shootout with a bootlegger in Fort Wayne, Ind.

July 27: Prohibition agent Raymond Ezzell and a bootlegging suspect die in a gun battle in Fort Worth, Tex.

July 28: While gunning for Dutch Schultz associate Joey Rao in Harlem, N.Y., Coll gunmen wound five children on East 107th Street, killing five-year-old Michael Vengalli.

July 30: Mayor James Walker sanctions NYPD's "shoot-to-kill" orders on gangsters.

July 31: Chicago's Crime Commission adds another 28 names to its list of "public enemies."

August 4: U.S. Attorney General William Mitchell explains that President Hoover's call for a nationwide war on gangsters refers to action by local police, not federal agents.

August 14: The American Legion announces "mobilization" of 30,000 members to combat gangsters.

August 19: During a liquor raid in Washington State, Prohibition agent George Trabing dies from the accidental explosion of another agent's firearm.

August 27: NYPD detectives arrest Ignazio Lupo for homicide. A magistrate releases him on August 31.

August 30: Two woodsmen from Maine volunteer to help NYPD officers stalk racketeers.

September 9: Denver mafioso Pete Carlino drives to Cañon City to visit relatives. Rival mobsters kill him on September 10 or 11, hiding his body beneath a bridge, then return to place it in a more obvious location on September 13.

September 10: Salvatore Maranzano schedules a meeting with Lucky Luciano at Manhattan's Helmsley Building on Park Avenue, intending to have Luciano slain by Irish mobster "Mad Dog" Coll. As Maranzano waits for Coll, four gunmen sent by Meyer Lansky arrive, posing as IRS agents, and execute the "Boss of Bosses." On the same day, assassins kill Maranzano lieutenant James Marino in the Bronx and strangle two more loyalists, Samuel Monaco and Louis Russo, dumping their corpses in Newark Bay. Luciano subsequently reorganizes the New York Mafia into five equal families, with a national commission deciding major policies.

September 13: Gunmen kill Pittsburgh mafioso Giuseppe Sinagusa in his home. John Bazzano assumed control of the local family.

September 16: Members of the Purple Gang kill rivals Joseph Lebold, Hymie Paul, and Joseph Sutker at the Collingwood Apartments in Detroit. Police charge gang leaders Ray Bernstein, Harry Keywell and Irving Milberg with the killings on September 21. Jurors convict them on November 11, resulting in life sentences for each.

September 17: Abe Reles and others continue their assault on the Shapiro brothers in New York, executing Meyer and seizing control of the family's gambling rackets.

September 24: Kidnappers abduct bootlegger Leon Gleckman in St. Paul, Minn., and release him on October 2, upon receipt of ransom.

September 30: Future mafioso Giuseppe "Pippo" Calò born in Palermo, Sicily.

October 2: Vincent Coll allies Frank Giordano and Dominic Odierno murder Dutch Schultz employee Joseph Mullen at a Bronx beer drop.

October 6: Al Capone's trial for income tax evasion opens in Chicago's federal court. Jurors convict him on October 17 and he receives an 11-year prison sentence on October 24.

October 11: Future mafioso Calcedonio Di Pisa born in Palermo, Sicily.

October 15: Mafia boss Joe Ardizonne disappears, presumably murdered, while visiting a cousin's home in Etiwanda, Calif. Jack Dragna assumes command of the local crime family.

October 18: Unidentified shooters kill Matt Kolb, bootlegging partner of Roger Touhy, at Kolb's speakeasy in Morton Grove, Ill. Touhy blames Capone gangsters.

October 19: Coll mobster Edward Popke, AKA "Fats McCarthy," kills NYPD Detective Guido Passagano in a Manhattan shootout.

November 11: NYPD officers raid Manhattan's Hotel Franconia, arresting monsters Lepke Buchalter, Gurrah Shapiro and Bugsy Siegel.

November 14: Police in Riverside, Calif., blame "gangland figures" for the slaying of a local taxi company owner.

November 27: Delegates from various nations sign the Agreement for the Control of Opium Smoking in the Far East in Bangkok, Siam (now Thailand). Taking effect on April 22, 1937, the treaty provides that retail sale and distribution of opium shall be limited to government shops and bars persons below age 21 from purchasing or smoking opium.

November 30: Jurors in New York City convict Coll monsters Frank Giordano and Dominic "Toughy" Odierno of killing Joe Mullen in October. Both are condemned. They die in Sing Sing's electric chair on July 1, 1932.

December 16: Vincent Coll faces trial in Manhattan for Michael Vengalli's murder. Jurors acquit him on December 28.

December 17: Unknown gunmen kill Legs Diamond at a hideout on Dove Street in Albany, N.Y.

December 20: The Chicago Crime Commission reports that its work as "crushed" organized crime citywide.

December 21: LAPD blames bootleggers for the murder of Marvin "Hart" Alperm found shot in a car on Orange Drive.

December 22: Irish mobster Frankie Wallace and lieutenant Bernard "Dodo" Walsh die in a Mafia ambush at the headquarters of Boston's while approaching the site of a supposed Mafia peace conference at Boston's C.K. Importing Company. Mafiosi blame Wallace's gang for recent liquor hijackings.

December 26: Chicago police spokesmen report the killing of 70 "outlaws" since January.

1932 February 1: Moonshiners kill Prohibition

agent Robert Buck in Hancock County, Miss. Unidentified gunmen kill Vincent Coll associates Fiori Basile and Pasquale Del Greco, with female companion Emily Torrizello, at an apartment in the Bronx. Two other victims survive gunshot wounds in the same incident.

February 8: An unidentified machine-gunner kills Vincent Coll in a Manhattan telephone booth, allegedly while Coll is trying to extort cash from Owney Madden.

February 9: A bootlegging suspect kills Prohibition agent Joseph Pearce in Shreveport, La.

February 26: A moonshiner strikes Deputy U.S. Marshal W.F. Deiter with a hammer during a liquor raid in San Juan, Puerto Rico. Deiter dies on March 1.

March 1: Charles Augustus Lindbergh Jr. kidnapped from his parents' home in Hopewell, N.J. Al Capone offers assistance from prison, but is refused. An intermediary delivers $50,000 ransom to an unidentified extortionist on April 2. Truck driver William Allen finds a child's decomposed remains 4.5 miles from the Lindbergh home on May 12, but the family's pediatrician cannot identify the corpse. Immigrant suspect Bruno Richard Hauptmann is arrested and tortured by police in September 1934, convicted of murder at trial, and executed on April 3, 1936. Many researchers still consider the trial a frame-up.

March 2: Future mafioso Nicholas "Nicky" Bianco born in New York City.

March 7: Police fire on striking workers at the Ford Motor Company plant in Dearborn, Mich., killing four and wounding 19.

March 16: Manhattan mobsters Antonio Lonzo and Gerard Vernotico die in a Mafia ambush.

March 24: While pursuing an alien smuggler in Niagara Falls, N.Y., Border Patrol Inspector Frank Vidmar Jr. is struck and killed by a trolley car.

March 25: Frank Loesch, from the Chicago Crime Commission, reports a secret meeting with Al Capone. Capone allegedly offers to police Chicago in return for a monopoly on beer, liquor, gambling and labor unions.

April 9: *Scarface* premieres in U.S. theaters, starring Paul Muni as "Antonio 'Tony' Camonte" in the first film produced to cash in on Al Capone's nickname and reputation.

April 15: Moonshiners ambush Prohibition agent Henry Jackson in Oklahoma, near the Texas border. Jackson dies on April 17.

April 19: Chicago police arrest Lucky Luciano, Meyer Lansky, Rocco Fischetti and Paul Ricca outside the Congress Hotel.

May: Al Capone enters federal prison in Atlanta, Ga. Frank Nitti assumes command of the Chicago Outfit.

June 14: Prohibition agent Jack Kenford dies in the explosion of an outlaw still, during a liquor raid in Prairie du Chien, Wis.

June 16: Unknown machine-gunners kill labor racketeer and Capone associate George "Red" Barker in Chicago.

June 22: Congress passes the Federal Kidnapping Act, AKA the Lindbergh Law, making interstate abduction a federal offense punishable by life imprisonment. A subsequent amendment permits execution in cases where victims are physically injured.

July 1: The DOJ's Bureau of Investigation formally changes its name to the U.S. Bureau of Investigation. J. Edgar Hoover remains in charge.

July 11: State troopers kill Vincent Coll associate Edward "Fats McCarthy" Popke in a battle at his hideout near Albany, N.Y.

July 13: A liquor violator shoots Prohibition agent Eugene Jackson on South Park Way, Chicago, killing him instantly.

July 21: Charles Bozeman, an associate of Farmer Page, dies in a shootout with rivals James O'Keefe and Virgil Roach in Los Angeles.

July 28: Future mafioso and police informant Alphonse "Little Al" D'Arco, AKA "The Professor," born in Brooklyn, N.Y.

July 29: Gunmen slay bootlegging brothers Arthur, James, and John Volpe in a Pittsburgh coffee shop, allegedly on orders from Mafia boss John Bazzano.

August 8: NYPD officers find Pittsburgh mafioso John Bazzano dead in Brooklyn, stabbed, strangled, and sewn into a burlap bag.

September 1: Under pressure from investigators and Governor Franklin Roosevelt (1882–1945), James Walker resigns as mayor of New York City and departs for Europe.

September 20: Future syndicate hitman Joseph "The Animal" Barboza born in New Bedford, Massachusetts.

September 23: A moonshiner kills Prohibition agent James Harney during a liquor raid near Tamarack, Minn. Police in Worcester, Mass., charge Ray Patriarca with bank robbery, but witnesses recant their statements and the charge is dropped.

September 29: Prohibition agents Ballard Turner and Ernest Vlasich suffer fatal gunshot wounds while trying to arrest a bootlegger and the suspect's home in Vancouver, Wash. Vlasich survives until October 14.

October 15: Prohibition agent Frank Mather and Patrolman Blucher Soyars die in a shootout in Russellville, Ky., after Soyars mistakes federal liquor raiders for gangsters.

November 5: Future mafioso Salvatore "Bill" Bonanno born in Brooklyn, N.Y.

November 9: A bomb planted by rival Waxey Gordon's men injures Bugsy Siegel at the Hard Tack Social Club in New York City. Suspected bomber Tony Fabrizzo dies in an ambush on November 20, allegedly shot by Siegel himself, sneaking out of his hospital room to perform the killing.

November 12: A liquor violator kills Prohibition agent Chester Mason during an attempted arrest in Beatrice, Neb.

December 2: Atlantic City, N.J., publishes a list of 60 "public enemies."

December 16: Cleveland mobsters create Buckeye Enterprises as a front for illegal gambling. They rename the firm Buckeye Catering on January 1, 1935.

December 19: Corrupt Chicago detectives, allegedly acting on orders from Mayor Anton Cermak, raid an Outfit office on North LaSalle Street, shooting Frank Nitti while falsely claiming that he "resisted arrest." Nitti survives his wounds to plot revenge.

1932–44 Japanese military forces force an estimated 200,000 to 410,000 women into sexual slavery as "comfort women," serving troops abroad. Victims are taken by force from China, Korea, the Philippines, Thailand, Malaya, French Indochina, the Dutch East Indies, and Taiwan. The first known "comfort station" is established in Shanghai, China.

1933 California, Michigan, New Hampshire, Ohio, and West Virginia legalize pari-mutuel betting at racetracks. German lawmakers approve casino gambling. O.D. Jennings markets the "Little Duke" slot machine, featuring a "fortune teller" and unique sideways mechanism. The American firm Smith, Klein & French market amphetamine inhalers under the brand name "Benzedrine."

January 7: Police charge Ray Patriarca with robbery in Southbridge, Mass., then dismiss the case.

January 17: Mayor Anton Cermak orders Chicago police to cease collaboration with the vigilante "Secret Six."

January 24: Rival gunmen John Burke and James Coyne kill mobster King Solomon at the Cotton Club, in South Boston.

January 31: Future mafioso Bernardo Provenzano born in Corleone, Sicily. Outfit gunmen kill Jimmy O'Brien, an ally of Roger Touhy, outside a Chicago nightclub.

February 3: Federal prosecutors in Cleveland charge Morris Kleinman with tax evasion. He flees into hiding, then surrenders on October 12 and pleads guilty on November 27, receiving a four-year prison term and a $15,000 fine.

February 13: Unknown gunmen murder mafioso Joe "Little Caesar" Roma in Denver, Colo.

February 15: Chicago Mayor Anton Cermak suffers a fatal gunshot wound in Miami, Fla., during a public appearance with president-elect Franklin Roosevelt. Cermak dies on March 6. Police charge supposed anarchist Giuseppe Zangara with the murder, claiming that he meant to shoot FDR, and jurors convict him on March 9, resulting in Zangara's execution on March 20. Multiple crime reporters claim Cermak was actually killed on orders from Frank Nitti.

February 17: Future warlord and "opium king" Chang Chi-fu, AKA Khun Sa, born in Burma (now Myanmar).

February 20: Congress proposes a 21st amendment to the U.S. Constitution, repealing Prohibition.

March 4: Franklin Roosevelt inaugurated as President of the United States, instantly reneging on his promises to mob supporters of his 1932 campaign.

March 7: Philadelphia jurors acquit Salvatore Sabella, John Avena, and Domenico Pollina of killing Vincent Cocozza and Joseph Zanghi in May 1927.

March 29: The Minneapolis city council authorizes sale of 3.2-percent beer.

March 31: Prohibition agent William Grubb suffers fatal injuries in San Francisco, Calif., while trying to stop a liquor smuggler's car. On the same day, Prohibition agent Levi Trexler crashes and dies in a high-speed pursuit of moonshiners in Rockingham County, N.C.

April 8: Mob-connected politician Edward Kelly replaces Anton Cermak as mayor of Chicago. With sponsor Patrick Nash, Chairman of the Cook County Democratic Party, Kelly forms the corrupt "Kelly-Nash Machine."

April 10: Michigan ratifies the 21st Amendment.

April 12: Unknown kidnappers abduct Jerome Factor — teenage son of international swindler and Outfit associate John "Jake the Barber" Factor — in Chicago. In Elizabeth, N.J., gunmen kill Waxey Gordon lieutenants Mandell Hassell and Max "Big Maxey" Greenberg at the Carteret Hotel.

April 16: Moonshiners kill Prohibition agent Leroy Wood in Poinsett County, Ark.

April 22: Jerome Factor reappears in Chicago, allegedly freed by his kidnappers without payment of ransom.

April 25: Wisconsin ratifies the 21st Amendment.

April 26: Police find bootleggers Victor Harmon and Earl "Sprout" Withrow strangled on East 26th Street, Los Angeles. LAPD suspects mafiosi John Bucellato and Frank "Hugo" Cannizzaro.

May: IRS agents arrest Waxey Gordon on tax-evasion charges.

May 8: Rhode Island ratifies the 21st Amendment.

May 21: U.S. marshals arrest Waxey Gordon at a hunting lodge in White Plains, N.Y.

May 25: Wyoming ratifies the 21st Amendment.

May 30: Unknown gunmen invade the Castle Café on Manhattan's East First Street and shoot five card-players, killing two. One of the dead is Mafia hitman Sebastiano Domingo, AKA "Buster from Chicago" (misidentified in newspaper reports of the event as "Charles Dominico").

June 1: New Jersey ratifies the 21st Amendment.

June 10: President Roosevelt merges the U.S. Bureau of Investigation and the Prohibition Bureau into a new Division of Investigation (DOI). On the same day, despite objections from J. Edgar Hoover, U.S. Attorney General Homer Cummings declares that the DOJ will fight racketeering.

June 15: Members of the Barker-Karpis gang, acting with syndicate support, kidnap brewer William Hamm Jr. in St. Paul, Minn.

June 17: A party of gunmen led by ex-sheriff Vernon Miller waylays lawmen escorting fugitive bandit Frank "Jelly" Nash from Kansas City's Union Station to the federal prison at Leavenworth, Kan. A chaotic shootout claims the lives of Nash, DOI Agent Raymond Caffrey, Oklahoma Police Chief Otto Reed, and two Kansas City policemen, W.J. Grooms and Frank Hermanson. A year after the shootings, FBI headquarters names bank robbers Charles "Pretty Boy" Floyd and Adam Richetti as Miller's accomplices. Subsequent investigation reveals that DOI Agent Joseph Lackey accidentally killed Nash, Caffrey, and Hermanson.

June 21: During an attempted holdup in the Bronx, Lottie Coll (widow of Vincent Coll), Alfred Guardino and Joseph Ventre kill loan-shark Izzy Moroh. NYPD officers arrest the trio on June 23. They are indicted for robbery and murder on June 27. On February 26, 1934, all three plead guilty to various charges. Guardino receives a sentence of 20 years to life for second-degree murder; Lottie gets six to 12 years for manslaughter; Ventre receives seven to 15 years for manslaughter.

June 22: A liquor violator kills Prohibition agent Harry Elliot near Creston, Iowa, then commits suicide when surrounded in a cornfield by a posse.

June 24: Delaware ratifies the 21st Amendment.

June 26: Indiana and Massachusetts ratify the 21st Amendment.

June 27: New York ratifies the 21st Amendment.

June 30: NYPD officers find Legs Diamond's widow shot dead at her home in Brooklyn. On the same day, kidnappers allegedly snatch John Factor from a roadhouse outside Chicago, releasing him in LaGrange, Ill., on July 12. Factor claims that $70,000 ransom was paid to secure his freedom. Captain Daniel "Tubbo" Gilbert — chief investigator for the Cook County State's Attorney's office and a hireling of the Chicago Outfit — names Capone rival Roger Touhy as the prime suspect.

July 6: While investigating the Kansas City massacre, local officers and FBI agents arrest Chicago fugitive James "Fur" Sammons at the home of K.C. gangster Frank Malloy. Sought on robbery charges, Sammons posts $20,000 bond on July 18, then skips town.

July 10: Illinois and Iowa ratify the 21st Amendment.

July 11 Connecticut and New Hampshire ratify the 21st Amendment.

July 12: A speakeasy bartender kills Prohibition agent Paul Read while resisting arrest in Missoula, Mont.

July 13: U.S. Attorney General Cummings calls for passage of federal anti-racketeering laws. On July 27, President Roosevelt urges Cummings to creat a "super-police force" to battle interstate crime. J. Edgar Hoover opposes the plan.

July 16: Police in Providence, R.I., jail Ray Patriarca as a suspicious person, then discharge him.

July 19: Following a car crash near Elkhorn, Wis., police arrest Roger Touhy and three companions — Eddie "Chicken" McFadden, "Gloomy Gus" Schaefer, and "Wee Willie" Sharkey — with a small arsenal. FBI agents charge them with the kidnappings of John Factor in Chicago and brewer William Hamm in St. Paul, Minn. A grand jury in St. Paul indicts the four defendants for Hamm's kidnapping on August 12.

July 22: Public Safety Director E.E. Adams orders Cleveland police to purge the city of illegal slot machines. Chief of Police George Matowitz echoes the call on July 25, but no raids occur until October 11.

July 24: California ratifies the 21st Amendment.

July 25: West Virginia ratifies the 21st Amendment.

August 1: Arkansas ratifies the 21st Amendment.

August 7: Oregon ratifies the 21st Amendment.

August 8: Alabama ratifies the 21st Amendment.

August 9: Moonshiners kill Deputy U.S. Marshal Robert Sumter during a liquor raid near Lehigh, Okla.

August 10: The U.S. Bureau of Investigation is renamed the Division of Investigation, incorporating the Bureau of Prohibition. J. Edgar Hoover remains in charge.

August 11: Tennessee ratifies the 21st Amendment.

August 12: Police in Kansas City, Mo., kill mafioso Gas Fascone, shortly after he murders rival mobster Ferris Anthon. Fulgencio Batista leads a military coup — the "Revolt of the Sergeants" — to depose Cuban president Gerardo Machado y Morales. Dr. Ramón Grau San Martín takes office as president on September 10, while Batista rules behind the scenes as Army Chief of Staff.

August 18: Future mafioso Francis "Cadillac Frank" Salemme, AKA "Julian Daniel Selig," born in Boston, Mass.

August 27: Future mafioso Vincent "Fish" Cafaro born in New York City.

August 28: Unknown gunmen execute New York mobsters Frank Keller and Harry Mockley at the Bella Napoli Café, in Los Angeles.

August 29: Missouri ratifies the 21st Amendment.

September 4: Booze hijacker Axel Anderson dies in an ambush on Venice Boulevard, Los Angeles. LAPD suspects gangsters Eddie Edwards and R.C. Johnson.

September 5: Arizona and Nevada ratify the 21st Amendment.

September 6: Acting in collusion with U.S. Ambassador Sumner Welles (1892–1961), Fulgencio Batista leads a "Revolt of the Sergeants" in Cuba, deposing Carlos Manuel de Céspedes y Quesada (1871–1939).

September 8: Reform crusader Charles Parkhurst dies at his home in Ventnor, N.J., after sleepwalking off the roof.

September 17: Future mafioso Peter J. Bellanca born in Detroit.

September 22: Future mafioso Vincenzo "Vinny" Aloi born in New York City.

September 23: Vermont ratifies the 21st Amendment.

September 26: Colorado ratifies the 21st Amendment.

September 27: The DOJ announces that its war on racketeering will include prosecution of lawyers who aid and abet crimes committed by underworld clients.

October 2: Future mafioso Aniello "Neil" Migliore born in New York.

October 3: Washington ratifies the 21st Amendment.

October 4: Federal prosecutors in New York indict Moe Dalitz and three codefendants on charges of smuggling liquor. None are actually prosecuted.

October 6: An unidentified gunman kills Edgar

Lebensberger, manager of Gus Winkeler's Chicago nightclub, at his home on Lake Shore Drive.

October 7: Frank Loesch of the Chicago Crime Commission urges the DOJ to create a national "public enemies" list.

October 9: Unknown gunmen riddle mobster Gus Winkeler at Charles Weber's beer distribution office on Roscoe Street, Chicago.

October 10: Minnesota ratifies the 21st Amendment.

October 11: Police in Cleveland raid five gambling dens identified by a local grand jury, but report no crimes in progress.

October 17: Idaho ratifies the 21st Amendment.

October 18: Maryland ratifies the 21st Amendment.

October 22: Gus Winkeler's widow attempts suicide at her Chicago apartment, but is saved by the wife of Fred "Killer" Burke.

October 24: Future British mobsters Reginald and Ronald Kray born in London, England.

October 25: Virginia ratifies the 21st Amendment.

November 1: Verne Miller, leader of the Kansas City massacre, shoots his way out of an FBI trap in Chicago's Uptown district.

November 2: New Mexico ratifies the 21st Amendment.

November 6: Police capture fugitive "Fur" Sammons at Cedar Lake, Ind. Convicted of bribery on November 31, he receives a life sentence as a habitual criminal.

November 9: Future mobster Daniel Patrick Greene, AKA "The Irishman," born in Cleveland, Ohio. In St. Paul, Roger Touhy and his codefendants face trial for the Hamm kidnapping. Jurors acquit them on November 28.

November 14: Florida ratifies the 21st Amendment.

November 20: Waxey Gordon's tax-evasion trial begins in New York City. Jurors convict him on December 1, resulting in a 10-year prison sentence and an $80,000 fine. Police find mobster Albert Silvers, an associate of Verne Miller, stabbed to death in Somers, Conn.

November 24: Texas ratifies the 21st Amendment.

November 25: Moe Dalitz, Meyer Lansky, Chuck Polizzi and Sam Tucker form Molaska Corporation, chartered in Ohio as a front for continued illegal distilling of liquor after the demise of Prohibition.

November 26: Unknown gunmen execute Purple Gang members Abe Axler and Ed Fletcher outside Pontiac, Mich.

November 27: Kentucky ratifies the 21st Amendment.

November 28: Rum smugglers murder U.S.

Customs Inspector Rollin Nichols in East El Paso, Tex.

November 29: Police find Kansas City massacre ringleader Vernon Miller tortured and shot to death, outside Detroit. In Chicago, girlfriend Vivian Mathias receives a 366-day prison sentence for harboring Miller as a fugitive.

November 30: Roger Touhy codefendant Willie Sharkey hangs himself in jail, in St. Paul, Minn., reportedly unhinged by police torture. Future Yakuza boss Masahisa Takenaka born in Himeji, Hyōgo, Japan.

December 5: Ohio, Pennsylvania, and Utah ratify the 21st Amendment, officially ending Prohibition in the USA.

December 7: Border Patrol officers confront 13 smugglers transporting 150 cases of liquor across the Rio Grande River at El Paso, Tex. The resultant shootout kills Inspector Doyne Melton and two smugglers, while the rest escape into Mexico.

1934 Massachusetts and Rhode Island legalize pari-mutuel betting on horse races. Swedish lawmakers establish a special authority to regulate betting on soccer matches. O.D. Jennings produces the "Dutchess Vendor" slot machine, with a built-in candy dispenser. China bans cannabis cultivation and trafficking in Yarkant (or Yarkand) County (in the present-day Xinjiang Uyghur Autonomous Region).

January 1: Fiorello La Guardia (1882–1947) takes office as mayor of New York City and orders the arrest of Lucky Luciano.

January 5: A moonshiner in Wilmington, N.C., kills Prohibition agent Herman Barbrey while resisting arrest.

January 11: Roger Touhy, Gus Schafer, and new codefendant August Lamarr — AKA Albert "Polly Nose" Kantor — face trial for kidnapping John Factor in Chicago. Jurors deadlock without reaching a verdict on February 2.

January 15: Fulgencio Batista, conspiring with U.S. envoy Sumner Welles, forces Dr. Ramón Grau San Martín to resign as president of Cuba. Carlos Mendieta y Montefur replaces Grau as Batista's front man on January 18.

January 17: Members of the Barker-Karpis gang, collaborating with mobsters and corrupt officials in St. Paul, Minn., kidnap banker Edward Bremer and transport him to Bensenville, Ill. They release him on February 7, after collecting a $200,000 ransom.

February 11: Future dictator and drug trafficker Manuel Antonio Noriega born in Panama City, Panama.

February 13: A second trial convenes in Chicago, for the Factor kidnapping. FBI agents persuade bandits Basil "The Owl" Banghart and Ike Costner — then awaiting trial for mail robbery in North Carolina — to testify for the prosecution. Costner falsely testifies that Touhy hired him to kidnap Factor, while Banghart tells the jury Factor employed him to make the staged abduction look real. Jurors convict the defendants, resulting in 99-year prison terms. Banghart receives the same sentence, as an accomplice to kidnapping.

March 4: Unknown gunmen kill alleged mafioso Ralph Monterastelli outside his home on Norton Avenue, Los Angeles.

March 12: New York City officials propose "official ostracism" of persons with criminal records.

Spring: Lucky Luciano, John Torrio, and Meyer Lansky chair a mob summit conference at New York's Waldorf Astoria Hotel, laying groundwork for a national crime syndicate which incorporates but supercedes the Mafia.

March 14: Police find Touhy gangster and alleged Factor kidnapping accomplice Charles "Ice Wagon" Connors murdered outside Chicago.

March 21: Unknown Chicago gunmen murder Fred Goetz, AKA "Shotgun" George Ziegler, an occasional bank robber and suspect in the 1929 St. Valentine's Day massacre.

April 26: FBI agents arrest Chicago bookmaker William Vidler for passing money from the Bremer ransom. His confession produces a May 4 indictment charging 11 defendants with participation in the Bremer snatch. Those named include Arthur "Dock" Barker and crime partner Alvin "Old Creepy" Karpis; political fixer John "Boss" McLaughlin Sr. and his son; and informer William Vidler.

April 29: Future mafioso Dominic "Crazy Dom" Truscello born in Manhattan's Little Italy.

May/June: Inspired by the Kansas City massacre, Congress passes a series of laws imposing federal penalties for interstate flight to avoid prosecution or confinement, also formally authorizing DOI agents to carry firearms and make arrests — which, in fact, they have done since 1908.

June 18: Congress passes an Anti-Racketeering Act imposing federal penalties on persons using violence or coercion to extract unlawful income from interstate commerce.

July 2: Mafioso Paul Castellano robs a shop in Hartford, Conn., and is arrested upon his return to New York City. Convicted at trial, he receives a one-year sentence and serves three months in prison, released in December.

July 10: Unknown machine-gunners fatally wound Mafia boss John Lazia outside his home in Kansas City, Mo. Lazia dies three hours later, leaving Charles Carrollo in charge of the local crime family.

July 13: Future mobster Michael "Mickey" Spillane born in New York City.

July 19: Future mafioso Anthony "Sonny" Ciccone born in New York City.

July 20: Abe Reles and Martin "Bugsy" Goldstein bury mobster William Shapiro alive at a sandpit in Canarsie, Brooklyn.

July 22: FBI agents kill outlaw John Dillinger at Chicago's Biograph Theater. Decades later, author Jay Robert Nash claims that Dillinger escaped, with mob-owned scapegoat Jimmy Lawrence dying in his place.

July 24: Police in Worcester, Mass., jail Ray Patriarca for lewd cohabitation, then discharge him.

July 25: Immigration agents in Los Angeles issue a "wanted" notice for mafioso Jack Dragna. He avoids deportation with aid from sometime-rival Mickey Cohen and Cohen's sponsor, Moe Dalitz.

August: Eliot Ness arrives in Cleveland, Ohio.

August 4: Future mafioso Vittorio "Little Vic" Orena born in New York City.

August 21: Police find Cleveland gambler Frank Joiner shot to death in a lime pit near Solon, Ohio.

August 22: Al Capone and 52 other prisoners arrive at the new federal prison on Alcatraz Island, in San Francisco Bay. FBI agents in Chicago arrest Oliver "Izzy" Berg for passing Bremer ransom money.

September 19: Acting on orders from Luciano underboss Vito Genovese, Willie Gallo and Ernest "The Hawk" Rupolo kill Ferdinand Boccia and sink his body in the Hudson River.

September 26: FBI agents in Detroit arrest gambler Cassius McDonald for passing Bremer ransom money.

October: Mayor La Guardia orders raids on gambling dens in New York City, destroying 1,000 slot machines owned by Frank Costello.

October 7: U.S. Attorney General Cummings calls for a national conference on crime. It convenes in Washington, D.C., on December 10.

November 2: Future mobster Herbert "Fat Herbie" Blitzstein born in Chicago.

November 27: NYPD Commissioner Lewis Valentine orders his men to "terrorize" known criminals. Mayor La Guardia endorses the plan on January 26, 1935.

November 28: Fugitive Dutch Schultz surrenders to federal authorities in Albany, N.Y., for trial on tax-evasion charges. Jurors at his first trial deadlock without reaching a verdict on April 29, 1935. A second jury acquits Schultz on August 2, 1935.

December 19: Ciro Terranova attorney Martin Littleton Sr. dies at his home on Long Island, N.Y., following a week-long illness.

1935 Mexican American residents of Los Angeles

organize the Hoyo Maravilla gang. Governor Herbert Lehman (1878–1963) appoints Thomas Dewey as special prosecutor in Manhattan. Thailand legalizes gambling enterprises licensed by the state. Florida permits pari-mutuel betting on jai-alai. Arkansas, Delaware, and Maine allow pari-mutuel betting on horse races. O.D. Jennings introduces another slot machine, called "The Chief," tailored to reject worthless slugs. Mexican President Lázaro Cárdenas bans gambling nationwide. Owney Madden leaves New York to open the Hotel Arkansas spa and casino in Hot Springs, Ark. The AMA passes a resolution naming alcoholics as "valid patients." America's first "one-percenter" motorcycle club organizes as the Outlaws MC in McCook, Ill.

January 2: Chicago police arrest mobster "Terrible Tommy" Touhy, brother of Roger Touhy, at his apartment. Subsequent conviction on robbery charges sends him to prison for 23 years.

January 4: Jurors convict defendants Herbert "Deafy" Farmer, Richard Galatas, and Frank "Fritz" Malloy of conspiracy in the 1933 Kansas City massacre.

January 16: Treasury agents raid the largest illegal distillery in U.S. history, owned by Molaska Corporation, in Zanesville, Ohio. Those indicted include Tom McGinty, who receives a six-month sentence. FBI agents arrest Elmer Farmer in Bensenville, Ill. He admits complicity in the Bremer kidnapping. On January 17, agents capture Harold Alderton — owner of the Bensenville farm where Bremer was held — in Marion, Ind. Bremer formally identifies Alderton's farm on January 19.

January 19: Future LSD cook Augustus Owsley Stanley III born in Australia.

January 20: Fugitive Alvin Karpis and companion Harry Campbell shoot their way out of a police trap in Atlantic City, N.J.

January 22: A federal grand jury in St. Paul, Minn., issues new indictments in the Bremer kidnapping, superseding charges filed in May 1934. The latest charges name 25 conspirators in the abduction (four already slain by lawmen or fellow gangsters).

January 26: Treasury agents raid another huge, illegal distiller owned by Molaska Corporation, this one in Elizabeth, N.J.

January 30: Cleveland mafioso Frank Milano flees the U.S. for Mexico, to avoid prosecution. Alfred Polizzi succeeds him as boss of the local crime family.

February 2: Rum-runners murder Deputy U.S. Marshal Herbert Ray in Lexington, Ky. Unknown assailants fatally beat and shoot Joseph Redlick, brother of a prosecution witness in the 1931 William Potter slaying, in Cleveland, Ohio.

February 6–12: NYPD jails hundreds of

persons for associating with known criminals. Most are freed without prosecution.

February 7: Corrupt Sheriff W. F. Cato machine-guns Narcotic Inspector Spencer Stafford outside a veterinary clinic in Post, Tex. Jurors later convict Cato, Deputy Tom Morgan, physician L.W. Kitchen, and veterinarian V.A. Hartman on murder charges. Kitchen and Hartman are also convicted of narcotics trafficking.

February 23: Mobster Frank Rio dies from a heart attack in Chicago. Gambler Harold Smith Sr. opens Harold's Club, Nevada's first modern casino, in Reno.

March: Jurors convict Salvatore Sabella of illegally distilling alcohol in Montgomery County, Pa. He serves three months in prison.

March 2: Molaska Corporation files for bankruptcy in Ohio, officially dissolving on November 15.

March 3: Syndicate hitmen kill mobster John "Spider" Murtha in New York City, sparing a female companion. The woman later identifies Max "The Jerk" Golob as one of the killers. Golob pleads guilty to second-degree assault and received a maximum term of five years.

April: Philadelphia jurors convict Tri-State Gang member Francis Wiley for the 1934 kidnap-murder of racketeer William Weiss.

April 11: Future hitman Richard Leonard "The Iceman" Kuklinski born in Jersey City, N.J.

April 17: William Hamm Jr., kidnapped from St. Paul, Minn., in June 1933, identifies the Bensenville, Ill., home of Postmaster Edmund Bartholmey as the place where he was held captive. FBI agents arrest Bartholmey, who confesses and names his accomplices, finally disproving the false charges filed against Roger Touhy and associates. G-men arrest St. Paul mobster Jack Peiffer as one of the abductors on April 18. A federal grand jury indicts Bartholmey, Peiffer, Dock Barker, Alvin Karpis and three others for the Hamm kidnapping on April 22.

May 1: FBI agents arrest Alvin Karpis and three associates in New Orleans. Chief J. Edgar Hoover falsely claims personal credit for Karpis's capture.

May 3: Police in Worcester, Mass., question Ray Patriarca about a mail robbery in Fall River, then release him. In Pass Christian, Miss., FBI agents arrest political fixer Harry Sawyer and his wife on Bremer kidnapping charges.

May 6: Ray Patriarca pays a $10 fine for an alias in violation of Massachusetts law.

May 7: Alvin Karpis is arraigned in St. Paul for the Bremer and Hamm kidnappings, held on $500,000 bond.

May 11: Trial begins for Lucky Luciano in Manhattan, on charges of compulsory prostitution. Jurors convict him on June 6, and Luciano receives a sentence of 30 to 50 years on June 18. Today, most crime historians agree that his conviction was secured with perjured testimony, obtained under coercion by prosecutor Thomas Dewey.

June 27: Leonard Scarnici, a bank robber and suspect in the death of Vincent "Mad Dog" Coll, dies in Sing Sing's electric chair for the 1933 murder of a policeman in Rensselaer, N.Y.

July: Huey Long announces discovery of a plot to kill him, allegedly hatched at the DeSoto Hotel in New Orleans. He reads a supposed transcript of the meeting on the floor of the U.S. Senate, naming participants that include four congressmen, ex–Louisiana governors John Parker (1863–1939) and Jared Sanders Sr. (1869–1944), and New Orleans Mayor Thomas Walmsley (1889–1942).

July 1: The U.S. Division of Investigation is renamed the Federal Bureau of Investigation. J. Edgar Hoover remains in charge. Thomas Dewey takes office as special rackets prosecutor in New York City.

July 5: President Roosevelt signs the National Labor Relations Act, AKA the Wagner Act, legitimizing labor unions and collective bargaining.

July 16: NYPD detectives arrest Ignazio Lupo and Vincenzo Piazza for extorting money from Italian bakers. A magistrate discharges Lupo on November 12.

July 18: Unknown gunmen kill North Side mobster Leland Verain, AKA Louis "Two Gun" Alterie, at his Chicago apartment.

July 31: Sentences are handed down for the Hamm kidnapping. Alvin Karpis and Charles Fitzgerald receive life terms; Jack Peifer gets 30 years (then commits suicide in jail with poisoned gum); and Edmund Bartholmey receives six years. Karpis enters Alcatraz on August 7.

August: Frank Costello and Dandy Phil Kastel create the Bayou Novelty Company in New Orleans, establishing a new gambling empire with support from "Kingfish" Huey Long.

August 21: Unidentified shooters kill Michael "Jimmy the Needle" LaCapra, a witness from the Kansas City massacre trial, in New Paltz, N.Y.

August 22: Unknown gunmen assassinate Vincent Troia, ex-associate of Salvatore Maranzano, in New York City.

September 1: FBI agents arrest indicted Bremer kidnapper William "Lapland Willie" Weaver and girlfriend Myrtle Eaton in Allandale, Fla.

September 4: Ray Patriarca pays a $100 fine for adultery in Massachusetts.

September 8: Dr. Carl Austin Weiss allegedly shoots Huey Long at the Louisiana Capitol in Baton Rouge, whereupon Long's bodyguards shoot Weiss 61 times. Long dies from his wound on September 10. Some researchers claim Weiss was unarmed and simply punched Long in the face, after which a stray shot from one of Long's bodyguards struck him. Decades later, author Hank Messick claims that Long's physicians had orders from Meyer Lansky to "let him die," in retaliation for demanding more gambling graft. In Philadelphia, Pa., police arrest local "Public Enemy No. 1," mobster Anthony "The Stinger" Cugino. He confesses to eight murders, then hangs himself in his cell.

September 9: Dutch Schultz gunman Abraham "Bo" Weinberg vanishes forever from a club in Midtown Manhattan. Lawyer Dixie Davis later claims that Schultz killed Weinberg on suspicion of collaboration with Lucky Luciano and Lepke Buchalter, dumping his weighted corpse in the East River.

September 19: Police in Pawtucket, R.I., jail Ray Patriarca as a suspicious person, then discharge him.

September 29: Future Mafia associate and FBI informer Wilfred "Willie Boy" Johnson born in Canarsie, Brooklyn.

October 9: Cleveland mobsters found a new Molaska Company, Inc., with John Drew (né Jacob Stein) as president and Moe Dalitz as vice president. Illegal distilleries soon open in Chicago and Buffalo, N.Y.

October 23: NYPD officers find labor racketeer Louis "Pretty" Amberg shot and axed to death in his burning car. At 10:15 P.M., syndicate hitmen Mendy Weiss and Charles "Bug" Workman shoot Dutch Schultz and three gang members — Otto "Abbadabba" Berman, Abraham "Misfit" Landau, and Bernard "Lulu" Rosenkrantz — at the Palace Chophouse in Newark, N.J. Soon afterward, unknown gunmen wound Schultz associate Martin "Little Marty" Krompier in Harlem. Krompier survives his wounds, but the Newark victims expire after reaching a local hospital. Berman dies four hours later, Landau eight hours later, Schultz 22 hours later, and Rosenkrantz 29 hours after the shooting.

October 24: Future mafioso and informer Antonino Calderone born in Catania, Sicily.

October 30: NYPD announces yet another revival of its "strong-arm" squad.

November 5: Future mafioso Frank DeCiccio born in Bath Beach, Brooklyn.

November 9: Leaders of eight American trade (industrial) unions create the Committee for Industrial Organization (renamed the Congress of Industrial Organizations in 1938) under president John Llewellyn Lewis (1880–1969).

November 10: Miami police announce plans to jail "undesirables" on sight.

November 25: Chicago's Crime Commission brands New York City as America's new crime

capital. NYPD Commissioner Valentine denies it on November 26.

December 11: Cuban "puppet president" Carlos Mendieta leaves office, succeeded as front man for Fulgencio Batista by José Agripino Barnet. By this time, Batista has received $500,000 each from Meyer Lansky, Lucky Luciano, Moe Dalitz, Ben Siegel, Chuck Polizzi, and five other high-ranking mobsters to secure gambling franchises in Cuba.

December 12: Mayor Harold Burton (1888–1964) names Eliot Ness as Cleveland's new Public Safety Director.

December 16: Federal wiretappers in St. Louis, Mo., eavesdrop on Lou Rothkopf closing an illegal liquor deal with his partners in Cleveland. Jurors convict Rothkopf and 11 codefendants of conspiracy on May 18, 1937. Rothkopf receives a four-year sentence and a $15,000 fine on May 22, entering prison on June 9, 1937.

December 21: Striking at "artichoke king" Ciro Terranova, Mayor La Guardia temporarily bans sale of artichokes in New York City. He also orders NYPD to arrest Terranova on sight.

December 30: John "Boss" McLaughlin Sr. dies while serving a five-year sentence for the Bremer kidnapping, at Leavenworth federal prison.

1936 Racehorse keno gambling debuts at the Palace Club in Reno, Nev.

January 4: NYPD jails Ciro Terranova for vagrancy.

January 11: Cleveland Public Safety Director Eliot Ness raids an illegal casino, the Harvard Club, in Newburgh Heights, Ohio.

January 15: *Reefer Madness*, an anti-marijuana film produced with aid from Harry Anslinger's FBN, opens in the U.S.

January 24: Jurors in St. Paul convict Cassius McDonald, Harry Sawyer and William Weaver for their roles in the Bremer abduction. Sawyer and Weaver receive life sentences, while McDonald gets 15 years.

January 31: Special Prosecutor Thomas Dewey launches raids against 80 brothels in New York City, holding hundreds of prostitutes and madams for questioning.

February 3: Arsonists torch Peter Schmidt's Beverly Hills Club in Southgate, Ky., after Schmidt rejects offers from the Cleveland Syndicate. A five-year-old girl dies in the fire. The casino reopens as the Beverly Hills Country Club, still resisting mob domination, in April 1937.

February 15: Unknown gunmen execute Vincenzo Antonio Gibaldi, AKA "Machine Gun Jack McGurn," at Chicago's Avenue Recreation Bowling Alley, on North Milwaukee Avenue, leaving a humorous greeting card with his corpse.

March: Thomas Dewey announces the indictment of Lucky Luciano for white slavery. Luciano flees to Hot Springs, Ark., hiding out with Owney Madden, but is arrested on April 1 and extradited for trial.

March 3: Chicago gunmen kill Anthony De-Mora, who vowed to avenge the February murder of his half-brother, "Machine Gun" Jack McGurn.

March 22: Future IBT president Ronald Robert Carey born in Long Island City, N.Y.

March 26: Alvin Karpis eludes FBI agents in Hot Springs, Ark. G-men claim that police helped him escape after Karpis donated $6,500 to the mayor's re-election campaign.

April: Federal agents in Detroit charge four Purple Gang members with operating an illegal distillery. Jurors later convict all four, resulting in eight-year prison terms and $20,000 fines for each.

May 7: New York Governor Herbert Lehman asks President Roosevelt to revoke Ignazio Lupo's conditional commutation of sentence, citing allegations of extortion. Roosevelt declares Lupo in violation on July 10 and orders U.S. marshals to arrest him. Lupo re-enters the Atlanta Federal Prison on July 15, to serve 7,174 days. A prison medical examination, conducted on July 27, deems Lupo "a senile, obese, but well developed white man, 60 years of age, with six missing teeth, systolic murmur, and varicose veins both legs." Lupo's parole is formally revoked on October 12.

May 19: An early-morning bomb explosion in Buffalo, N.Y., kills Mrs. Nicholas Longo, sister and next-door neighbor of mafioso Steven Magaddino.

May 20: William Swartz, manager of Tom McGinty's Mounds Club casino, fatally shoots gambler Harry "Champ" Joyce outside syndicate headquarters at the Hollenden Hotel in Cleveland, Ohio. Jurors convict Swartz of manslaughter on October 27, resulting in a sentence of one to 20 years in prison. Authorities parole Swartz on November 8, 1938. In Cuba, Fulgencio Batista replaces President José Agripino Barnet with successor Miguel Mariano Gómez y Arias.

June 7: New York jurors convict Lucky Luciano and eight co-defendants on 62 counts of compulsory prostitution. Luciano receives a sentence of 30–50 years. Various prosecution witnesses later recant their testimony, prompting some researchers to call the case a frame-up.

June 10: Unidentified gunmen execute mafioso Giuseppe Romano in Cleveland, Ohio. Alfred Polizzi succeeds him as boss of the local crime family.

June 22: Future Yakuza boss Masaru Takumi born in Japan.

June 26: Various nations sign the U.S.-sponsored Convention for the Suppression of the Illicit Traffic in Dangerous Drugs in Geneva, Switzerland, legally effective as of October 26, 1939.

July 22: Eliot Ness raids the Hermitage Hotel in Cleveland, but finds its casino vacated thanks to advance warning from corrupt police.

August 8: Future mafioso Carmine John "The Snake" Persico Jr. born in Brooklyn, N.Y.

August 17: Unidentified gunmen kill John Avena, would-be successor to Salvatore Sabella, in Philadelphia, Pa. Joseph "Joe Bruno" Dovi assumes command of the local Mafia.

August 19: Newspapers claim that Manhattan racketeers are rushing to pay state income taxes, thereby dodging prosecution by Thomas Dewey.

September 12: Benny Binion and a henchman murder rival numbers racketeer Ben Frieden in Dallas, Tex. Although Frieden is unarmed, Binion shoots himself in the shoulder and later wins acquittal with a plea of self-defense.

September 13: Hitmen James Ferraco, Harry Strauss, and Mendy Weiss kill Joseph Rosen, a Brooklyn candy vendor scheduled to testify against Lepke Buchalter and Gurrah Shapiro in a labor racketeering case.

October 4: Jewish gangsters led by Jack "Spot" Comer join other anti–Nazi protesters in London's "Battle of Cable Street" against marching members of the British Union of Fascists. Police arrest 150 persons, while 100 are injured.

December 20: Future mafioso Dominick "Big Trin" Trinchera born in Rockland, N.Y.

December 24: Dissatisfied with Cuban president Miguel Mariano Gómez y Arias, Fulgencio Batista replaces him with Dr. Federico Laredo Brú.

1937 Amphetamine becomes available in tablet form, via prescription, for treatment of narcolepsy and attention deficit hyperactivity disorder. Florida legalizes pari-mutuel betting at racetracks. Future IBT president Dave Beck forms the Western Conference of Teamsters, headquartered in Seattle, Wash.

January 2: Despite a predecessor's claim that Philadelphia, Pa., was free of racketeers in December 1930, Mayor Samuel Wilson announces a new campaign to drive all gangsters out of town.

January 8: The Cuban Cabinet places various gambling operations under the control of future president Fulgencio Batista, allied with Meyer Lansky and other U.S. mobsters.

January 31: "Special deputies" ambush UMW organizer Marshall Musick and his wife in Harlan County, Ky., but the intended victims escape unharmed.

February 8: Company gunmen fire on a carload of UMW organizers in Harlan County, Ky., wounding one.

February 9: Unknown gunmen assassinate Marshall Musick at his Harlan County home.

February 11: General Motors Corporation recognizes the United Auto Workers union, ending a sit-down strike that began on December 29, 1936, at the Rouge River, Mich., plant.

February 22: Unknown gunmen wound mafioso Gaspare D'Amico in Newark, N.J. Upon recovering, D'Amico flees the country, ceding control of the New Jersey crime family to Stefano Bedami.

February 27: Future gangster Aslan Usoyan, AKA "Grandpa Hassan," born in Georgia, USSR.

March 17: Future mobster Francesco "Frankie Breeze" Calabrese Sr. born in Chicago.

April 14: Ray Patriarca pays a $10 fine for a traffic violation in Franklin, Mass.

April 24: A "special" sheriff's deputy shoots and kills UMW organizer Lloyd Clause in Evarts, Ky.

May 7: Police haul the corpse of Ferdinand Boccia from the Hudson River in New York City. Mafioso Vito Genovese soon flees the U.S. for Italy.

May 11: Acting on orders from Lepke Buchalter, hitmen Frank Abbandando, Harry Maione and Harry Strauss kill loan shark George Rudnick in New York City.

May 19: Fire of undetermined origin levels the Cal Neva Lodge at Lake Tahoe, causing $250,000 in damage.

May 21: Molaska Company, Inc., files for bankruptcy in Ohio.

May 26: Ford Motor Company thugs employed by mob-allied "security director" Harry Bennett attack UAW organizers in Dearborn, Mich., sparking the "Battle of the Overpass." Goons also beat reporters and attempt to destroy their photographic plates, but a *Detroit News* photographer preserves images of the riot.

May 30: Chicago police fire on strikers at the Republic Steel mill, killing 10 and wounding 40, beating 100 others with clubs.

May 31: Future mafioso Robert "D.B." DiBernardo born in Hewlett, N.Y.

June: Six bandits rob Pete Schmidt's Beverly Hills Country Club in Southgate, Ky.

June 10: Newspapers credit special prosecutor Thomas Dewey with 61 racketeering convictions in New York City.

June 14: Mafia boss Francesco Lanza dies of natural causes in San Francisco, Calif. Anthony Lima assumes command of the local crime family.

June 19: Police attack another crowd of strikers at Chicago's Republic Steel mill, killing one. The melee leaves six more strikers and four officers injured.

June 21: Future mafioso Vincent DiNapoli born in East Harlem, N.Y.

July 7: Yet another clash between police and CIO strikers at Chicago's Republic Steel mill kills one union member and one "special officer," leaving 28 others wounded. Republic settles the strike on July 11.

July 31: Police retrieve the corpse of New York City racketeer Walter Sage from Swan Lake, in the Catskills. Sage has been stabbed 32 times with an ice pick and weighted with a slot machine.

August 2: FBN Commissioner Harry Anslinger introduces the Marihuana Tax Act before Congress, penalizing sale of cannabis with fines up to $2000 and a maximum five years' imprisonment. Congress passes the bill on October 1.

August 8: Future mafioso Carmine John Persico Jr., AKA "The Snake," born in Brooklyn, N.Y.

October 5: FBN agents arrest mafioso Nicola Gentile in New Orleans, on drug-trafficking charges. Gentile posts $15,000 bond, then absconds to Sicily.

October 25: Mafiosi Frank Bompensiero and Leo Moceri kill George Bruneman at the Roost Café on Temple Street, Los Angeles.

November 15: Gangster Hymie Miller suffers fatal gunshot wounds in his apartment on Yucca Street, Los Angeles. LAPD suspects mafioso Danny Iannone.

November 30: Rhode Island Governor Robert Quinn orders the Registry of Motor Vehicles to revoke drivers' licenses and auto registrations of all known criminals, including mafioso Ray Patriarca.

December 9: Police in Springfield, Mass. detain Ray Patriarca for vagrancy, then deliver him to Cambridge, where officers charge him with auto theft on December 11. That case is soon dismissed.

1938 Bolivian lawmakers ban gambling nationwide. Nazi officials take control of INTERPOL, finally moving its headquarters from Austria to Berlin in 1942. Canada bans production of cannabis under provisions of the 1911 Opium and Narcotic Drugs Act.

January 17: Harukichi Yamaguchi, founder of the Yamaguchi-gumi Yakuza family, dies in Japan.

February 5: A grand jury in Philadelphia, Pa., launches investigation of links between local mobsters and those in Manhattan.

February 12: Federal jurors in New York City convict William J. Graham and James C. McKay —

future underworld kingpins of Reno, Nev.— of using the mails to defraud in a $2,500,000 horse race swindle. On February 17 both defendants receive nine-year prison terms and are fined $11,000 each.

February 17: Police jail Ray Patriarca in Webster, Mass., on charges of breaking and entering at night, carrying a revolver, possession of burglar tools and conspiracy. He posts $25,000 bail. Convicted at trial on August 22, Patriarca receives a three-to-five year sentence on September 28.

February 19: Ciro Terranova suffers a stroke in New York City and dies the following day.

February 28: Mafiosi led by Frank Bompensiero, kidnap, beat, and shoot victim Phil Galuzo, dumping his corpse on East 83rd Street, Los Angeles.

March 24: Police detain Ray Patriarca in Brookline, Mass., on suspicion of armed robbery.

April 14: Fugitive Gurrah Shapiro surrenders to FBI agents, beginning his two-year sentence for labor racketeering.

May 2: Unknown gunmen wound mafioso Joe Tocco in Detroit, resulting in his death on May 6. Various researchers blame successor Joe Zerilli or rival Anthony D'Anna of Wyandotte, Mich., as the instigators.

June 1: Mayor Fiorello La Guardia announces special "rules" for gangsters during New York City's upcoming World's Fair.

June 4: Future mafioso Benedetto "The Hunter" Santapaola born in Catania, Sicily.

June 25: Congress passes the Federal Food, Drug, and Cosmetic Act, replacing the 1906 Pure Food and Drug Act, empowering the U.S. Food and Drug Administration (FDA) to oversee the safety of food, drugs, and cosmetics. On the same day President Roosevelt signs the Fair Labor Standards Act, banning "oppressive" child labor, fixing the maximum work week at 44 hours, and establishing a national minimum wage of 25 cents per hour.

August: A New York grand jury indicts Tammany boss Jimmy Hines for protecting numbers rackets operated by Dutch Schultz. His first trial ends in a mistrial on September 12.

August 14: Rhode Island state police arrest Ray Patriarca at Narragansett Racetrack. He waives extradition to Boston, where he is charged as a suspicious person in a local jewel robbery, subsequently released without prosecution.

August 17–19: Philadelphia's grand jury finds links between gangsters, police, and city officials. It recommends dismissal of 11 police officers, while filing charges against 41 with the city's Civil Service Commission.

August 21: Syndicate hitmen execute former Lepke Buchalter associate Hyman Yuran. Police

later find his corpse in a lime pit near Loch Sheldrake, N.Y.

August 27: *Chicago Tribune* publisher Robert McCormick decries the alliance between gangsters and politicians in northern Indiana.

October 29: A federal jury in Little Rock, Ark., convicts three Hot Springs police officers on charges of harboring fugitive gangster Alvin Karpis. The defendants — Police Chief Joseph Wakelin, Chief of Detectives Hebert Akers, and Lieutenant Cecil Brock — receive two-year prison terms.

October 30: Future mafioso Frank "Curly" Lino born in Brooklyn, N.Y.

November 8: Future Missouri mafioso Matthew "Mike" Trupiano Jr. born in Detroit.

November 16: Swiss chemist Albert Hofmann, employed by Sandoz Pharmaceutical in Basel, synthesizes lysergic acid diethylamide (LSD-25) from ergot alkaloids, while attempting to create a blood stimulant.

November 3: Thomas Dewey condemns criminal activity in Brooklyn, as well as Tammany Hall's ties to notorious racketeers.

December 5: FBN Commissioner Harry Anslinger chairs a Marijuana Conference at the U.S. Bureau of Internal Revenue Building in Washington, D.C.

December 21: Massachusetts Governor Charles Hurley pardons Ray Patriarca in the Brookline and Webster cases. Public outrage prompts impeachment of Daniel Coakley, a member of the Massachusetts Governor's Council, and investigation of the state's pardon system. Coakley loses his impeachment trial and is barred for life from public office, after testimony proves that forged statements from priests were used to procure Patriarca's pardon.

December 28: Police find bookie Weldon Irvin shot dead in his Cadillac on Selma Street, Los Angeles.

1939 Mexican Americans in Los Angeles organize the "Cherries" gang, second generation of the Hoyo Maravilla clique. South African legislators ban lotteries, pinball tables, and slot machines. MCA moves its headquarters from Chicago to Beverly Hills, Calif., creating a movie division and beginning to acquire talent agencies.

January 9: Syndicate hitmen execute Albert "Plug" Shuman in Brooklyn, on orders from Lepke Buchalter.

January 28: Unknown gunmen kill paroled racketeer-turned-informant Louis Cohen in New York City, before his scheduled testimony against Lepke Buchalter. Fellow prosecution witness Isadore "Danny Field" Friedman dies in the same ambush.

January 29: Mobster-informant George Weinberg commits suicide in NYPD custody, using a pistol stolen from one of his guards.

February: New York jurors convict Jimmy Hines on all charges. He receives a sentence of four to eight years on March 23.

February 27: The U.S. Supreme Court bans sit-down strikes, in the case of *National Labor Relations Board v. Fansteel Metallurgical Corporation.*

March 9: Future mobster Louis "Big Louie" DeSorbo born in New York City.

March 27: The U.S. Supreme Court voids New Jersey's Gangster Act of 1934.

March 31: Future mobster and hitman Joseph "Mad Dog" Sullivan born in New York City.

April 23: Future mafioso Stefano Bontade born in Palermo, Sicily.

April 25: Syndicate hitmen execute racketeer and suspected informant Abraham "Whitey" Friedman near his home on East 69th Street, Manhattan.

May: Oxycodone appears on the U.S. market.

May 10: Unknown gunmen murder Lepke associate Samuel "Tootsie" Feinstein in New York City.

May 25: Hitmen execute New York IBT president Morris Diamond, allegedly on orders from Lepke Buchalter.

May 26: Future mafioso Pasquale "Pat the Cat" Spirito born in Trenton, N.J.

Summer: Federal authorities eliminate Jack Dragna's gambling ships off the coast from Los Angeles.

June 12: Authorities in Brighton, Mass., indict Ray Patriarca for a 1937 robbery, on the same day that he pleads not guilty to auto theft charges from August 1937. He posts $10,000 bond in the Brighton case on June 16. Jurors convict him of the auto theft on May 10, 1940, resulting in an 18-month sentence. Patriarca wins parole on September 6, 1941.

July 2: Unknown killers dump the corpse of Philadelphia mobster William Lanzetti in suburban Wynnewood, shrouded in burlap bags. Local residents find the body on July 3. Lanzetti's death ends a three-year war between his family and the local Mafia.

July 14: Labor racketeers kidnap and murder longshoreman and ILA reformer Pete Panto in New York City. Police find his corpse in a lime pit at Lyndhurst, N.J., in January 1941. Hitman Abe Reles later blames Albert Anastasia for the slaying.

August 18: Moses Annenberg, son Walter, and three business associates surrender to U.S. marshals in Philadelphia on charges of evading more than $2 million in taxes and $3 million in penalties and interest. All post bond.

August 24: After 25 months in hiding, Lepke

Buchalter surrenders to J. Edgar Hoover in Manhattan. Despite assurances that he will face trial only on federal antitrust charges, Buchalter is subsequently indicted for murder.

September 3: A federal grand jury in New York City finds racketeering dominated by Meyer Lansky and Bugsy Siegel.

September 4: World War II officially begins in Europe, with Germany's invasion of Poland. Following plans drawn up in advance, Nazi troops begin systematic looting of Poland, stealing at least 516,000 individual art objects. The final documented haul includes 13,800 paintings, 25,000 maps, 75,000 manuscripts, 90,000 books (including more than 20,000 printed before 1800), and various other items of artistic and historical significance, all valued at $20 billion.

September 5: Acting on orders from Lepke Buchalter, Abe Reles, Harry Maione, and Harry Strauss murder gambling racketeer Irving "Puggy" Feinstein at Reles's home in Brooklyn, then torch the corpse in a vacant lot.

September 23: Future Yakuza member Kaneyoshi Kuwata born in Osaka, Japan.

October 1: Unknown gunmen kill mafioso Guiseppe Morello in Ciaculli, Sicily.

October 18: Future alleged presidential assassin Lee Harvey Oswald born in New Orleans, La.

October 20: Charles Carrollo, boss of the Kansas City Mafia, enters Leavenworth federal prison to serve a sentence for tax evasion. Charles Binaggio assumes command of the local crime family.

November: New York voters approve amendment of the state constitution to permit parimutuel gambling on horse races.

November 16: Al Capone leaves federal custody and enters a private hospital for treatment of paresis.

November 22: Bugsy Siegel and brother-in-law Whitey Krakower execute Harry "Big Greenie" Greenberg, AKA Harry Schachter, in Los Angeles, to prevent him from turning state's evidence against fellow mobsters.

1939–45 Various governments issue amphetamine to military personnel during World War II, to combat fatigue and increase alertness.

1940 Waxey Gordon leaves Leavenworth Federal Prison, telling reporters, "Waxey Gordon is dead. From now on it's Irving Wexler salesman." New York state lawmakers legalize pari-mutuel betting at racetracks.

January 2: Future mobster Vyacheslav Kirillovich "Little Japanese" Ivankov born in Georgia, USSR.

January 17: Border Patrol Inspector William Sills dies in a shootout with smugglers of illegal aliens near McAllen, Tex.

February 2: NYPD detectives arrest Abe Reles

for robbery, assault, possession of narcotics, burglary, disorderly conduct, and eight charges of murder. Reles turns state's evidence against Murder, Inc., in exchange for a reduced sentence.

March 17: Future mafioso Nicholas "Little Nick" Corozzo born in Brooklyn, N.Y. The first evidence of "Murder Incorporated" surfaces from Brooklyn D.A. William O'Dwyer.

March 21: Syndicate gambler Morris Rosen pays a $40 fine for illegal bookmaking.

March 23: Future mafioso Tommaso "Thomas" Bilotti — AKA "The Pitbull," "The Zombie," "The Doberman," etc.— born in New York City.

March 27: A New York grand jury indicts Charles Workman for the October 1935 slayings of Dutch Schultz and three confederates. Authorities extradite Workman from New Jersey in April 1941, for trial beginning in June. In mid-trial, Workman changes his plea to "no contest," receiving a life prison term. He serves 23 years, paroled on March 10, 1964.

March 29: Corrupt Deputy Sherriff William Cassele admits syndicate hitman Vito "Socko" Gurino to Queens County's civil prison, where Gurino threatens Joseph "Joe the Baker" Liberto, held as a witness to the 1937 murder of George Rudnick.

April: Moses Annenberg pleads guilty to one count of evading $1,217,296 in federal taxes and agrees to pay almost $9 million in fines and penalties. Prosecutors dismiss all charges against his son Walter. A New York grand jury indicts George Scalise, president of the Building Service and Employee's International Union, for extortion.

May: Camorra hitman Alfonso Sgroia dies in Italy of natural causes. Embattled independent gambler Pete Schmidt finally sells his Beverly Hills Country Club to the Cleveland Syndicate.

May 15: A new Italian law permits totalizator betting on dog and horse races. Brooklyn hitman Abraham "Kid Twist" Reles confesses involvement in six murders. By June 3, D.A. William O'Dwyer claims that his investigation of "Murder, Inc.," has solved 56 homicides.

May 21: Future mafioso Anthony "Gaspipe" Casso born in Brooklyn, N.Y.

May 23: Based on testimony from Abe Reles, jurors convict Frank Abbandando and Harry Maione for the 1937 murder of Brooklyn loan shark George "Whitey" Rudnick. New York's Court of Appeals overturns the verdict in December, but a second jury convicts them on May 23, 1941. Both die in Sing Sing's electric chair on February 19, 1942.

June 21: Despite eyewitness testimony from mobster Abraham "Pretty" Levine, jurors acquit

defendant Jacob "Jack" Drucker of murdering Walter Sage in 1937.

July 10: Fred "Killer" Burke dies from heart disease in a Michigan prison.

September 12: Detectives arrest Vito Gurino at Manhattan's Church of the Guardian Angel, where he is hiding in fear of his life from Murder, Inc., assassins. Gurino confesses to three murders and implicates himself in four others.

September 16: Abe Reles admits participation in five more murders.

September 19: Jurors convict Martin Goldstein and Harry Strauss in the 1939 murder of Puggy Feinstein. The New York Court of Appeals upholds their death sentences on April 24, 1941. Both die in Sing Sing's electric chair on June 12, 1941.

Autumn: German Reichstag President Hermann Göring orders Reichsleiter Alfred Rosenberg's Institute for the Occupied Territories to begin seizing "Jewish" art and other valuables throughout Europe. Subsequently, two other Nazi looting organizations — the Dienststelle Muhlmunn and Sonderkommando Ribbentrop — plunder Scandinavia, Russia and North Africa.

October 9: Roger Touhy, Basil Bangart, and four other inmates escape from Joliet Prison in Illinois. FBI agents enter the case on grounds that the fugitives have violated federal law by changing addresses without notifying their draft board. G-men kill fugitives Clair McInerey and James O'Connor in Chicago on December 28, then capture Touhy, Banghart and Edward Darlak the following day, also in Chicago.

October 10: Fulgencio Batista begins his first four-year term as Cuba's president, replacing front man Dr. Federico Laredo Brú.

October 22: An unidentified shotgunner kills mafioso Ignacio Antinori at the Palm Garden Inn in Tampa, Fla. Police suspect Missouri mobsters James and Nicolo Impastato, retaliating for a $25,000 shipment of bad heroin Antinori sold to the Kansas City family.

October 27: Future mafioso John Joseph Gotti, AKA "The Teflon Don," born in the Bronx.

October 28: Future Nuestra Familia member Robert Joseph "Death Row" Gonzales born in Oxnard, Calif.

November 12: Future mafioso Anthony "T.G." Graziano born in New York City.

December 7: Future Philadelphia mafioso Giovanni "John the Dour Don" Stanfa born in Palermo, Sicily.

December 28: Future mafioso Carlo "Charlie Big Ears" Majuri born in Linden, N.J.

1941 Nevada legalizes race books, initially located in poolrooms. Interruption of hashish supplies from Chinese Turkestan prompts Indian officials to consider cultivation in Kashmir. Actor Ronald Reagan wins election to the Screen Actors Guild board of directors, with support from MCA bosses Jules Stein and Lew Wasserman.

January 8: Future Yakuza boss Yoshinori Watanabe born in Tochigi Prefecture, Japan.

January 16: Future mafioso Daniel "Danny the Lion" Leo born in Rockleigh, N.J.

February: Unknown gunmen kill labor racketeer Emil Nizich on a Manhattan street.

February 6: Hitmen execute New York mobster Benjamin "Benny the Boss" Tannenbaum while he babysits for Bronx real estate agent Max Heitner, silencing Tannenbaum as a potential witness against Lepke Buchalter.

April 3: The El Rancho Vegas hotel/casino opens outside Las Vegas, Nev., launching development of the "Las Vegas Strip" (later Las Vegas Boulevard).

April 14: John Torrio leaves Leavenworth Federal Prison after serving 23 months for tax evasion.

May 23: New York jurors convict hitman Irving "Knadles" Nitzberg in the 1939 murder of Albert Shuman. An appellate court overturns Nitzberg's death sentence on December 10. A second jury convicts him on March 12, 1942, but that verdict is also quashed on appeal.

May 24: A federal grand jury in New York City indicts Willie Bioff and George Browne on racketeering charges, related to mob domination of the IATSE. Both are convicted at trial on October 30. Bioff receives a 10-year sentence, while Browne is sentenced to eight years, each with a $20,000 fine.

June 12: Murder, Inc., hitmen Martin "Buggsy" Goldstein and Harry "Pittsburgh Phil" Strauss die in the electric chair at New York's Sing Sing prison.

June 27: Future mafioso Leonardo Vitale born in Palermo, Sicily.

July 7: Future mobster and gangland patriarch Lewis Moran born in Melbourne, Australia.

July 23: Retired On Leong Tong leader Sai Wing Mock, AKA "Mock Duck," dies of natural causes in Brooklyn, N.Y.

July 24: Future mafioso Joseph "Joe Glitz" Galizia born in New York City.

July 30: Syndicate hitmen murder Whitey Krakower on Delancey Street, Manhattan, to avert his testimony against Bugsy Siegel in the 1939 slaying of Harry Greenberg.

September 5: On the day before Ray Patriarca's scheduled release from a Massachusetts auto theft conviction, Suffolk County authorities indict him on two charges from a 1937 robbery in Brighton and void his original bail in that case, increasing it to $20,000. Unable to pay the bond, Patri-

arca leaves state prison for a local jail on September 6. An acquaintance posts the bail on September 8 and Patriarca returned to Rhode Island, with orders for daily meetings with a probation officer.

September 11: Future politician, Mafia associate, and tax-dodger Marcello Dell'Utri born in Palermo, Sicily. In Germany, I.G. Farben chemists Max Bockmühl and Gustav Ehrhart file a patent application for a synthetic opioid called Hoechst 10820 or polamidon, later known as methadone.

October: Lepke Buchalter, Louis Capone, and Mendy Weiss face trial in New York City for the 1936 murder of Joseph Rosen. Jurors convict all three of first-degree murder on November 30, resulting in automatic condemnation. New York's Court of Appeals upholds the verdicts in October 1942, as does the state supreme court in June 1943. The defendants die in Sing Sing's electric chair on March 4, 1944.

October 2: Future mafioso Steve Raffa born in Florida.

October 22: Massachusetts state police arrest Ray Patriarca on a secret indictment from Worcester, charging possession of firearms and burglar tools during a February 1938 robbery. Patriarca posts $6,000 bail. He pleads guilty in that case on November 13, receiving a sentence of 30 to 36 months in prison. Authorities parole Patriarca on May 11, 1944.

November: While speeding down Broadway in Kansas City, Mo., mafioso Charles Binaggio strikes and kills a 50-year-old pedestrian. Police charge him with manslaughter, but the case is soon dismissed. Thereafter, chauffeur Nick Penna accompanies Binaggio on all outings.

November 12: Hitman-informant Abe Reles dies in a fall from his window at the Half Moon Hotel on Coney Island. Police claim Reles fell during a mock escape, intended as a practical joke on the six detectives assigned to guard him. Lucky Luciano later admits that the syndicate paid $100,000 for the guards to silence Reles. Suspicion focuses on Detective Charles Burns, also allegedly involved in the 1930 disappearance of Judge Joseph Crater.

November 19: Future mafioso Dominick "Skinny Dom" Pizzonia born in Ozone Park, Queens, N.Y.

December: Police in Long Beach, Calif., arrest 38th Street Gang members Henry "Hank" Leyva, Jack Melendez, and Joe Valenzuela on suspicion of armed robbery. Leyva pleads guilty and receives a three-month jail term, while the others are discharged. All later emerge as leaders of the Mexican Mafia.

December 7: Japanese warplanes attack the

U.S. Navy base at Pearl Harbor, Hawaii. Congress declares war against the Axis Powers on December 8.

1942 Congress passes the Opium Poppy Control Act, requiring a federal license to grow or possess the plants. Soldiers worldwide receive amphetamine to keep them alert in combat, while dextro-amphetamine and methamphetamine become commonly available. Waxey Gordon receives a one-year sentence for selling 10,000 pounds of black-market sugar to an illegal whiskey distillery in California.

January 25: Mafioso Gaetano Lucchese becomes a naturalized U.S. citizen. Future Yakuza leader Kenichi Shinoda born in Ōita Prefecture, Japan.

February 3: Future mafioso Leoluca Bagarella born in Corleone, Sicily.

February 9–10: Fire scuttles the troopship USS *Lafayette*, formerly the French luxury liner SS *Normandie*, in New York Harbor. While the fire is accidental, fears of Axis sabotage — coupled with loss of 120 merchant ships to German submarines in the North Atlantic — prompt the U.S. Office of Naval Intelligence to initiate "Operation Underworld." Various New York mobsters insist that the ONI must deal with Lucky Luciano, incarcerated under harsh conditions at the Clinton Correctional Facility in Dannemora, N.Y. Luciano receives a transfer to Great Meadow Correctional Facility in Comstock, on May 12, and begins co-operation with the military.

February 18: Future mafioso and informer Francesco Di Carlo born in Altofonte, Sicily.

February 19: Hitmen Frank Abbandando and Harry "Happy" Maione die in the electric chair at Sing Sing prison.

March: New York hitman Vito Gurino pleads guilty to three murders, receiving a sentence of 80 years to life in April.

March 8: Mexico legalizes "limited" gambling.

April: FBN agents raid several targets in Kansas City, Mo., seizing quantities of heroin and arresting members of the local Mafia family, including lieutenant Joseph DeLuca and Nicolo Impastato. Two of those arrested, Thomas Buffa and Carl Caramusa, turn state's evidence against their cohorts at trial, in 1943.

April 13: Mexico grants fugitive mafioso Frank Milano a permanent immigration visa.

June 10: Future gangster Frank "Dunie" Ryan born in Montreal, Québec.

June 29: Moe Dalitz joins the U.S. Army as a private, at age 42. On December 23 he is commissioned as a second lieutenant, placed in charge of army laundries in New York.

July 18: New Jersey promoters stage the first legal horse race in 50 years, at Garden State Park in Cherry Hill.

July 20: Moses Annenberg dies, soon after his release from federal prison.

July 21: Mickey Cohen and Joe Sica raid independent bookie Russell Brophy's office in Los Angeles, beating Brophy and ripping out phone lines. Prosecutors fine Sica and Cohen $200 and $100, respectively, for the assault.

August 2: 38th Street Gang members rumble with rivals from Downey, in Long Beach, Calif., killing Jose Diaz. Eleven defendants are sentenced to prison for the slaying on January 13, 1943. The U.S. District Court of Appeals overturns those convictions on October 4, 1943.

August 6: Future cocaine smuggler George Jacob "Boston George" Jung born in Boston, Mass.

September 7: Future mafioso-hitman Roy Albert DeMeo born in Brooklyn, N.Y.

October 5: After attempts to deport mafioso Nicholas Delmore, U.S. Commissioner of Immigration Earl Harrison accepts Delmore's claim that he was born in San Francisco, before his immigrant parents returned to their native Italy.

October 14: Noboru Yamaguchi, second godfather of the Yamaguchi-gumi Yakuza gang, dies in Japan.

October 28: Mafioso Carlo Matranga dies of natural causes in Los Angeles.

October 30: R.E. Griffith opens the Hotel Last Frontier as the first themed resort on the Las Vegas Strip, with an Old West motif. Previously known as the Pair-o-Dice (1930–36), the Ambassador Night Club (1936–39), and the 91 Club, the establishment will be renamed the New Frontier on April 4, 1955.

November 2: Russian dictator Josef Stalin creates the Soviet State Extraordinary Commission for Ascertaining and Investigating the Crimes Committed by the German-Fascist Invaders and Their Accomplices, collecting evidence of Nazi war crimes over the next five decades. The final tally for 1941–45 includes 173 museums looted, with missing art objects numbered in the hundreds of thousands.

December: Singer Frank Sinatra terminates his contract with bandleader Tommy Dorsey, via gunpoint intervention by New Jersey mafioso Willie Moretti. Thus liberated, Sinatra opens at New York City's Paramount Theater on December 31.

December 5: FBI agents arrest Pittsburgh mafioso Vincenzo Capizzi for conspiracy to violate the National Bankruptcy Act.

1943 January 9: NYPD detectives witness a hit-and-run attempt on the life of Carlo Tresca, immigrant-anarchist editor of *Il Martello*, whose newspaper has criticized the Mafia. On January 11, a gunman kills Tresca on Fifth Avenue. Police suspect mafioso Carmine Galante, but despite assignment of 1,000 officers to the case, no charges result.

January 22: Sunny him Cosmano dies of natural causes in Rochester, N.Y.

February 2: Chicago firefighters find Estelle Carey — "Queen of the Dice Girls" and girlfriend of mobster Nick Circella — tortured to death in her burning apartment. Investigators speculate that she was slain to prevent testimony in the unfolding Hollywood extortion case.

February 15: Future drug lord Griselda "La Madrina" Blanco born on the northeast coast of Colombia.

March 18: A federal grand jury indicts Chicago Outfit leaders Frank Nitti, Paul Ricca, Louis Campagna, Phil D'Andrea, Frank Diamond, Charles "Cherry Nose" Gioe, and Ralph Pierce, plus associates John Rosselli in Los Angeles and Louis Kaufman of Newark, N.J., on charges of extorting protection payments from Hollywood film studios. Nitti allegedly commits suicide in North Riverside, Ill., on March 19, but gambler-author George Redston later claims he saw Nitti arrested by Chicago detectives shortly before his death. Prosecutors dismiss Pierce's case prior to trial.

April 16: LSD inventor Albert Hofmann accidentally experiences the first known "acid trip," reporting "an uninterrupted stream of fantastic pictures, extraordinary shapes with intense, kaleidoscopelike play of colors" spanning two hours. On April 19, he deliberately ingests 250 micrograms.

April 20: Police find the corpse of mobster Johnny Tudisco discarded on Norfolk Street, Los Angeles.

May 5: Unknown Chicago gunmen kill gambler Danny Stanton and associate Louis Dorman.

May 8: Indiana prison authorities release James "Fur" Sammons on condition that he complete 31 years remaining on a 50-year sentence in Illinois. He remains in custody until December 17, 1952.

May 31: White sailors clash with Latino youths in Los Angeles, sparking a series of "zoot suit riots" characterized by police brutality and bias. Before the outbreak ends on June 3, LAPD arrests more than 500 Hispanics — many of them battered victims — for "rioting" or "vagrancy." The experience prompts organization of defensive neighborhood gangs.

June 15: Future "happy hooker," notorious brothel madam and celebrity author Xaviera de Vries, AKA "Xaviera Hollander," born in Soerabaja, Dutch East Indies (now Indonesia), to a Dutch father and French-German mother.

July 9: Allied forces invade Sicily, with aid from the local Mafia allegedly arranged by Lucky Luciano in New York. Occupation and liberation of the island concludes on August 17. Fugitive mafioso Vito Genovese serves U.S. forces as an interpreter, while running a huge black-market operation with Villalba Mafia boss Calogero Vizzini.

August 11: Future New Jersey mafioso Tino "T" Fiumara born.

September 2: Salvatore Giuliano kills a Sicilian carabiniere at a checkpoint near Quattro Molini, while transporting illegally purchased grain. The slaying drives Giuliano underground as a full-time outlaw.

September 8: Future mobster Marat Balagula, "the Russian Tony Soprano," born in Orenburg, USSR.

October 5: Trial begins in the Chicago Outfit Hollywood extortion case, with prosecution witnesses including film studio bosses Louis B. Mayer, Harry and Albert Warner, Joseph and Nicholas Schenck. Jurors convict all remaining defendants on December 22. Ricca, Campagna, D'Andrea, Diamond, Gioe, and Rosselli receive 10-year terms, while Kaufman is sentenced to seven years. All receive $10,000 fines.

October 6: Patrick A. Nash, mob-connected chairman of the Cook County Democratic Central Committee, dies from natural causes in Chicago.

December 6: Mafia boss Calogero Vizzini attends a secret meeting of the separatist Sicilian Independence Movement in Catania. With other mafiosi including Francesco Bontade, Michele Navarra, and Giuseppe Russo, Vizzini supports the drive for Sicilian secession. He attends another meeting of the group's central committee in Palermo, on December 9.

December 22: A grand jury in Campbell County, Ky., indicts "Maurice Davis" (Moe Dalitz), Sam Tucker, and six other defendants on gambling charges. Two syndicate subordinates plead guilty and pay small fines. The rest are never prosecuted.

1944 January 14: Unknown gunmen murder gambling czar Benjamin "Zookie the Bookie" Zuckerman in Chicago.

January 29: Lee Harvey Oswald moves with his mother from New Orleans to Dallas, Tex.

January 31: Judge John Vest jails Sam Tucker and Police Chief Julius Plummer on contempt charges, after confiscated slot machines vanish from police custody in Campbell County, Ky. Appeals continue until July 4, 1945, when local gambler William Motz claims ownership of the slots, accepting a 30-day jail term and paying a $1,530 fine.

March 4: Lepke Buchalter dies in the electric chair at Sing Sing prison, along with hitmen Louis Capone and Emanuel "Mendy" Weiss.

March 22: Future high-profile private investigator and federal prison inmate Anthony Pellicano born in Chicago.

March 31: Future mafioso Bartholomew "Bobby" Boriello born in South Brooklyn, N.Y.

April 22: Rival mobsters murder racketeer Frank Abatte in Calumet City, Ill.

May 4: New York jurors convict Jacob "Jack" Drucker of second-degree murder in the July 1937 slaying of Walter Sage. Drucker receives a sentence of 25 years to life and dies in Attica prison during January 1962.

May 5: Jurors convict Gurrah Shapiro of extortion and conspiracy in New York, resulting in a 15-year prison term.

June: Narcotics peddler Charles "Big Nose" La-Gaipa vanishes from Oakland, Calif. Police find his car near the Southern Pacific Railroad depot, with blood and brain tissue on the dashboard. Cuban voters reject Fulgencio Batista's hand-picked successor as president, Carlos Saladrigas Zayas, in favor of Dr. Ramón Grau San Martín.

June 21: Jurors at the second Sage murder trial acquit Irving "Big Gangi" Cohen of participating in the crime.

July 10: Mobsters Joe Adonis, Frank Costello and Charles Fischetti visit Long Beach, Calif., to negotiate a truce between Bugsy Siegel and mafioso Jack Dragna.

July17: Spruille Braden, U.S. ambassador to Cuba, tells the U.S. State Department, "It is becoming increasingly apparent that President Batista intends to discomfit the incoming Administration in every way possible, particularly financially. A systematic raid on the Treasury is in full swing with the result that Dr. Grau will probably find empty coffers when he takes office on October 10. It is blatant that President Batista desires that Dr. Grau San Matin should assume obligations which in fairness and equity should be a matter of settlement by the present Administration."

July 25: Mafia boss Corrado Giacona dies in New Orleans. Francesco "Frank" Todaro assumes command of the local crime family.

August 3: Drive-by shooters fatally wound mobster Lawrence Mangano and bodyguard Michael Pontillo on Blue Island Avenue, in Chicago.

August 7: U.S. military police arrest fugitive Vito Genovese in Italy and hold him for extradition to New York City on murder charges.

September 12: Future mafioso Michael Peter "Micky" Spilotro born in Chicago.

September 16: Popular Front leaders Girolamo Li Causi and Michele Pantaleone convene a rally in Villalba, Sicily, to denounce mafioso ex-mayor Calogero Vizzini. Gunmen fire on the rally, wounding both speakers and at least a dozen others (some reports claim 18 wounded). Carabinieri arrest eight suspects and question 60 people, finally charging Vizzini and a bodyguard with attempted manslaughter. While evidence vanishes from police files, the trial drags on until 1958, resulting in acquittal four years after Vizzini's death.

October 10: Dr. Ramón Grau succeeds Fulgencio Batista as president of Cuba. Charges of corruption persist until Grau surrenders the presidency to protégé Carlos Prío Socarrás on October 10, 1948.

October 19: Cleveland mafioso Al Polizzi pleads guilty to evading federal liquor taxes. John Scalish succeeds Polizzi as boss of the local crime family. Upon release from prison in 1945, Polizzi "retires" to Coral Gables, Fla.

November: Unknown gunmen execute Enrique Diart, a narcotics dealer and associate of Bugsy Siegel, in Tijuana, Mexico.

November 28: Throat cancer claims the life of New Orleans Mafia boss Frank Todaro. Sam Carollo succeeds him as head of the family.

December 18: Future gangland matriarch Judy Moran born in Melbourne, Australia.

1945 January 8: Authorities in New York City announce the return of Vito Genovese for trial on murder charges. Gangster Kakuji Inagawa founds the Inagawa-kai Yakuza clan in Yokohama, Japan.

January 15: Mafioso Peter La Tempa, key witness in the murder case against Vito Genovese, dies in custody at the Raymond Street jail after taking medicine for his gallstones. An autopsy reveals enough poison in La Tempa's system "to kill eight horses." Prosecutors try to salvage their case, but finally release Genovese on June 11, 1946. In Atlanta, Ga., thieves steal jewelry valued at $300,000 from Schneider & Son. FBI agents trace the bandits to Moe Dalitz's Ohio Villa casino in Cleveland, then lose their trail.

February 20: Future Nuestra Familia member Robert "Babo" Rios Sosa born.

February 23: Unidentified thieves raid the Cleveland warehouse of "Slots King" Nathan Weisenberg, failing in an attempt to steal his slot machines. Police find Weisenberg shot to death in his car at 1:00 A.M. on February 24.

March 1: Moe Dalitz requests early release from military service. He receives an honorable discharge on May 29.

April 12: President Roosevelt dies from a cerebral hemorrhage in Warm Springs, Ga. Vice President Harry Truman succeeds him.

April 25: Ignazio Lupo completes his federal

sentence and begins to serve another 30 days for failure to pay his original $1,000 fine, discharging that sentence on May 26.

May 15: Gangster Max Shaman suffers fatal gunshot wounds in Mickey Cohen's paint shop, Beverly Boulevard, Los Angeles.

June 21: An unidentified gunman executes mafioso-turned-informant Carl Caramusa outside his home in Chicago.

June 23: A liquor smuggler murders Border Patrol Inspector Earl Fleckiger near Calexico, Calif.

June 27: Tom C. Clark takes office as U.S. Attorney General.

July 20: Future mafioso Salvatore Frank Ruggiero Sr. born in Brooklyn, N.Y.

August 5: Future mafioso George V. "Big Georgie" Remini born in New York City.

August 15: Emperor Hirohito announces Japan's surrender to the Allied Powers. A formal surrender ceremony on September 2 officially ends World War II.

November 24: Future Massachusetts mafioso Adolfo "Big Al" Bruno born in Bracigliano, Sicily.

November 27: Future mafioso Vincenzo Puccio born in Palermo, Sicily.

1946 INTERPOL is re-established as the International Criminal Police Organization, with headquarters in Paris, France. Gamblers spend $500 million on legal betting in the U.S., while British authorities tabulate $1.2 billion in bets on greyhound racing.

January: New York Governor Thomas Dewey announces the commutation of Lucky Luciano's prison term, conditional upon his deportation to Italy. Authorities transport Luciano from Great Meadow Correctional Facility to Ellis Island on February 2. Luciano sails for Italy aboard the SS *Laura Keene* on February 9, after a gala *bon voyage* party thrown by various syndicate bosses.

January 3: Future mafioso Antonio "Nino" Rotolo born in Palermo, Sicily.

January 8: Future Mexican drug lord Miguel Ángel Félix Gallardo born.

January 22: President Harry Truman creates a Central Intelligence Group, renamed the Central Intelligence Agency in 1947.

February 21: Future Canadian mafioso Vito Rizzuto born in Cattolica Eraclea, Sicily.

March: Unknown gunmen execute mafioso-turned-informant Thomas Buffa in Lodi, California.

March 3: Future crime boss Francis "The Belgian" Vanverberghe born in Marseille, France.

May 2: Mickey Cohen gunman Harold "Hooky" Rothman kills Paulie Gibbons at the victim's home on Vista Del Mar, Hollywood, Calif.

June 24: Future Pennsylvania mafioso William "Big Billy" D'Elia born in Trenton, N.J. In Chicago, Outfit gunmen wound racketeer and race-wire owner James M. Ragen in a drive-by shooting. Ragen survives multiple shotgun wounds and signs an affidavit identifying the shooters, then dies from mercury poisoning in the hospital, on August 15. State Attorney William Touhy subsequently "loses" Ragen's statement, precluding prosecution of his would-be killers. Control of Ragen's Nationwide News Service passes to the Chicago Outfit.

June 30: Future mobster-businessman Semion Yudkovich Mogilevich born in Kiev, Ukraine.

July: Police in Atlantic City, N.J., report a gathering of mobsters, described in various accounts as "a small Mafia gathering" and "a conference of the National Crime Syndicate."

July 3: Congress passes the Hobbs Act, penalizing actual or attempted robbery or extortion related to interstate commerce.

July 11: Ignazio Lupo's attorney petitions for his release from federal prison. Atlanta warden Joseph Sanford supports that petition with letters to the parole board, written on July 15 and December 6. Lupo leaves prison on December 21.

August 5: Drive-by gunmen wound Cleveland Syndicate overseer Albert "Red" Masterson in Newport, Ky. Police catch rival gambler Buck Brady near the shooting scene with two guns, but later dismiss a charge of "disturbing the peace."

August 30: Guy McAfee opens the Golden Nugget casino-hotel on Fremont Street, in Las Vegas, Nev.

October: Lucky Luciano flies to Havana, Cuba, for meetings with Meyer Lansky and other syndicate leaders.

October 3: Dominic Farinacci and Hooky Rothman kill rival gangsters Benjamin "Meatball" Gamson and George Levinson in the victims' apartment on Beverly Boulevard, Los Angeles.

October 11: Police in St. Petersburg, Fla., arrest Santo Trafficante Jr. under the name "Samuel Balto." He is detained for investigation, then released.

October 22: Mafioso Joseph Dovi dies of natural causes in a New York City hospital. Joe Ida succeeds him as boss of the Philadelphia crime family.

October 24: Future gangster Richard Blass born in Montreal, Québec.

November: Richard Milhous Nixon defeats incumbent Jerry Voorhis in California's 12th congressional district, with a Red-baiting campaign bankrolled by $50,000 from mobster Mickey Cohen.

December 6: LAPD officers arrest mafioso Jack Dragna on suspicion of robbery, then release him on December 9 without further action.

December 21: Future racketeer James "Jimmy C" Coonan born in Hell's Kitchen, Manhattan.

December 22: Prominent U.S. mobsters gather in Havana for a meeting with Lucky Luciano, at Meyer Lansky's Hotel Nacional. The agenda includes revival of international narcotics traffic interrupted by World War II, settlement of a feud between Luciano and Vito Genovese, and discussion of Bugsy Siegel's overrun on expenses for construction of the Flamingo resort in Las Vegas.

December 26: Bugsy Siegel opens the Flamingo, on the Las Vegas Strip. Bad weather grounds charter flights filled with high-rollers in Los Angeles, and the casino immediately suffers losses. Siegel closes the Flamingo in January 1947, pending completion of its hotel.

1947 Mexico bans all forms of gambling unless authorized by the federal government. Hungary's state bank starts a soccer betting pool. Dr. Werner Stoll, son of Sandoz Pharmaceutical president Arthur Stoll and a colleague of Albert Hofmann, publishes the first article on LSD's mental effects in the *Swiss Archives of Neurology*. Adoption of conflict-of-interest bylaws prompt the president and six board members of the Screen Actors Guild to resign. Ronald Reagan assumes the SAG presidency with MCA support, leading the union through underworld accommodations and anti-communist blacklist campaigns during 1947–52. In later years, Reagan rewrites history to describe himself as a crime-fighter within the SAG.

January 8: Three gunmen ambush New York stevedore and Pier 51 hiring boss Andy Hintz outside his Greenwich Village apartment. On January 11, Hintz names his attackers as John "Cockeye" Dunn, Andrew "Squint" Sheridan, and Danny Gentile. He repeats that statement in a formal dying declaration on January 11. With Dunn and Gentile already in custody, police trace Sheridan to Hollywood, Fla., and arrest him on January 24. Hintz dies on January 29, elevating the charge to murder. Jurors convict all three defendants of first-degree murder on December 31, resulting in automatic death sentences. Governor Dewey commutes Gentile's sentence to life imprisonment on July 6, 1949, declaring that Gentile "has done everything within his power to assist this office in its investigation of waterfront criminal activity." Dunn and Sheridan die in Sing Sing's electric chair on July 7, 1949.

January 13: Ignazio Lupo dies in Brooklyn.

January 25: Al Capone dies at his estate on Palm Island, Fla., following a long bout with syphilis.

February 23: Under pressure from U.S. authorities, Cuban police arrest Lucky Luciano in Havana, deporting him to Italy on March 29.

March: James Ragen Jr. meets Mickey McBride in Florida, selling McBride his Continental Press Service which supplies bookies nationwide with race results.

March 1: Contractor Del Webb finishes construction on Ben Siegel's Flamingo hotel-casino in Las Vegas. The Flamingo reopens on March 4, posting profits of $250,000 by May.

March 11: Smuggler Joseph Trujillo kills Border Patrol Inspector Anthony Oneto in Indio, Calif. Convicted of murder, Trujillo dies in California's gas chamber on October 1, 1948.

March 27: Gangster Tom Buffa dies in an ambush while driving through Lodi, Calif.

April 20–21: The People's Block, a coalition of the Italian Communist Party and Italian Socialist Party, scores a surprise victory in elections for Sicily's Constituent Assembly.

April 30: U.S. Immigration officials deport New Orleans mafioso Sylvestro Carollo to Sicily.

May 1: Hundreds of Sicilian peasants gather for a Labour Day parade in the valley of Portella della Ginestra. Concealed gunmen open fire as the Communist party secretary from Piana degli Albanesi begins to address the crowd, killing 11 persons and wounding 33. Authorities blame bandit and separatist leader Salvatore Giuliano, although he later claims that he ordered his men to fire above the marchers' heads. Modern researchers suggest Mafia infiltration of Giuliano's band.

May 5: The "Black Diamond Meeting" convenes in New Orleans, to choose a successor for deported Mafia boss Sylvestro Carollo. Underboss Carlos Marcello assumes command of the family.

May 7: San Francisco police find mobster Nick DeJohn strangled and stuffed in a car's trunk. Invesitgation suggests that DeJohn left his native Chicago after stealing cash from various Outfit members. Police charge mobster Leonard Calamia with the murder, but jurors later acquit him.

May 10: Gangster Harry Golub shoots and kills Arthur Ruscetta in Los Angeles.

May 24: Future gangster and police informer Kenneth James Noye born in London, England.

June 9: Jacob "Gurrah" Shapiro dies from a heart attack in Sing Sing Prison.

June 18: Future mafioso Steven "Wonderboy" Crea born in New York City.

June 20: An unknown sniper kills Bugsy Siegel

at mistress Virginia Hill's home in Beverly Hills, Calif. Within minutes, mobsters Dave Berman, Gus Greenbaum and Moe Sedway assume control of the Flamingo resort in Las Vegas.

June 22: Gunmen kill Solomon Turkin outside his home on South Cloverdale Road, Los Angeles. LAPD suspects mafiosi Jack Dragna and Rosario Desimone.

June 23: President Truman signs the Labor-Management Relations Act, AKA the Taft-Hartley Act, which bans closed shops, requires 60 days' notice prior to strikes, and permits states to ban union shops under "right-to-work laws."

July 4–6: Members of three outlaw biker clubs — the Boozefighters, Market Street Commandos, and Pissed Off Bastards of Bloomington — run amok at Gypsy Tour motorcycle rally in Hollister, Calif. The riot leaves 60 persons injured and 50 jailed on various charges, while inspiring a 1953 film, *The Wild One*, starring Marlon Brando and Lee Marvin.

August 13: Imprisoned Chicago Outfit members Louis Campagna, Phil D'Andrea, Charles Gioe, Paul Ricca, and John Rosselli receive early parole from federal prison. Declassified FBI files attribute the move to mob bribery of Attorney General Tom Clark.

September 3: Ten bandits armed with machine guns rob the Cleveland Syndicate's Mounds Club in Lake County, Ohio, escaping with at least $250,000 in cash and jewelry taken from patrons. Days later, a gang strikes the Continental Club in Chesapeake, bagging another $60,000. Police make no arrests, but later claim that mob hitmen have been killed all the thieves by March 1948.

September 16: Future mafioso Michael Salvatore "Mad Dog" Taccetta born in Newark, N.J.

September 18: President Truman creates the Central Intelligence Agency.

September 20: Ex-mayor Fiorello La Guardia dies from cancer in the Bronx.

Autumn: The U.S. Navy launches "Project Chatter," including experiments with various drugs for interrogation and recruitment of unwitting agents. The operation continues until mid-1953.

November 12: Anti-communist thugs, employed by Corsican mobsters Antoine and Barthélemy Guerini, attack leftist marchers outside City Hall in Marseille, France, fatally shooting one victim. Local unions initiate a general strike in Marseille the next morning, followed by calls for a national strike on November 14. On November 16, two police officers testify that they saw the Guerinis fire on unarmed demonstrators. Both are charged with murder, but the officers recant their statements on November 20 and the charges are dismissed on December 10. Meanwhile, on

December 9, the Marseille strike collapses in the face of CIA-funded gangland violence. By 1948, the Guerinis and other mobsters in Marseille dominate the U.S. traffic in Turkish heroin, with CIA complicity.

1948 Hisayuki Machii founds the Tōsei-kai Yakuza family in Tokyo, Japan, recruiting Korean gangsters as members.

January 1: Future drug lord Ismael Zambada García born in Sinaloa, Mexico.

January 5: Future anti–Mafia activist Giuseppe "Peppino" Impastato born in Cinisi, Sicily.

January 27: Future gangster Otari "Otarik" Kvantrishvili born in Zestafoni, Georgia, USSR.

February 22: Future 'Ndrangheta captain Giuseppe Bellocco born in Rosarno, Italy.

March 10: Mafioso Luciano Leggio murders trade unionist Placido Rizzotto outside Corleone, Sicily, and hides his corpse in a cave.

March 17: Bored veterans of World War II organize the Hells Angels MC in San Bernardino, Calif. Its founders are ex-members of an earlier club, the Pissed Off Bastards of Bloomington, who participated in the Hollister riot of July 1947.

April: An Italian legislative decree controls betting pools on soccer and horse racing.

April 20: Unidentified gunmen wound UAW leader Walter Reuther at his home in Detroit. President Truman orders an investigation, but J. Edgar Hoover refuses, telling Attorney General Tom Clark that he is "not going to send the FBI in every time some nigger woman gets raped." Hoover's bizarre insubordination goes unpunished.

July 16: Unknown gunmen execute mobster Charles Yarnowsky in Jersey City, N.J.

July 22: Future NYPD detective and Mafia hitman Louis Eppolito born in East Flatbush, Brooklyn.

August 10: Assassins slay John DiBiaso, a lieutenant of murdered gangster Charles Yarnowsky, in Jersey City.

August 18: Hooky Rothman dies in an ambush at Mickey Cohen's haberdashery, in Los Angeles.

September 2: The Thunderbird hotel-casino opens on the Las Vegas Strip.

September 10: Police find Joseph Solloway, owner of two San Pedro nightclubs linked to syndicate gamblers, shot dead in the driveway of his Crestline, Calif., home. Detectives blame the killing on Solloway's expansion to the Inland Valley.

October 12: Cohen gangster David Ogul disappears from Los Angeles while free on bond, pending trial in an assault case. Investigators suspect Jack Dragna's gang.

November 19: Diplomats in New York City sign a Protocol Bringing Under International

Control Drugs Outside the Scope of the Convention of 13 July 1931 for Limiting the Manufacture and Regulating the Distribution of Narcotic Drugs, legally effective as of December 1, 1949.

1949 South Africa's Sports Pool Act bans pool betting on sports activities. Psychiatrist Max Rinkel (1894–1966) begins LSD experiments in Boston, using drugs supplied by the Swiss Sandoz Pharmaceutical firm. Around the same time, Dr. Nick Bercel begins similar tests in Los Angeles, soon drawing support from the CIA. An amendment to the 1938 Fair Labor Standards Act bans child labor in the U.S.

April 10: Mobster Charles "Charlie Blank" Blandini suffers fatal stab wounds at the Los Angeles home of alleged prostitute Barbara Waters.

May: Cleveland Syndicate leaders Moe Dalitz, Morris Kleinman, Sam Tucker and Tom McGinty conclude negotiations with veteran gambler Wilbur Clark to purchase a controlling interest in his Desert Inn hotel-casino, under construction on the Las Vegas Strip.

May 23: Future mobster Martin "The General" Cahill born in Dublin, Ireland.

June 6: Future mafioso William "Billy Fingers" Cutolo born in Brooklyn, N.Y.

July 7: Waterfront racketeers John "Cockeye" Dunn and Andrew "Squint" Sheridan die in Sing Sing's electric chair for the January 1947 murder of New York stevedore Andy Hintz.

July 20: Unknown gunmen ambush Mickey Cohen's dinner party outside Sherry's Restaurant in Los Angeles, killing Edward "Neddie" Herbert, wounding Cohen and companion Harry Cooper.

July 26: Tom Clark resigns as U.S. Attorney General, upon his nomination by President Truman for a seat on the Supreme Court. The Senate confirms his appointment on August 24.

August 2: Future mafioso Joseph "Joey Flowers" Tangorra born in Manhattan's Little Italy.

August 12: Mafioso Frank DeMayo dies of natural causes in Kansas City, Mo.

August 14: Salvatore Giuliano's gang detonates mines under a convoy of police vehicles near the Bellolampo barracks, outside Palermo, killing seven carabinieri and wounding 11.

September 2: Mafiosi Joseph Dippolito, Jimmy Fratianno and Gaspare Matranga murder Frank Niccoli at a ranch owned by Charlie and Joseph Dippolito at Ontario, Calif.

September 16: Alleged murder of Philip "Little Farvel" Kovolick in Valley Stream, Long Island, according to Brooklyn assistant D.A. and author Burton Turkus in his book, *Murder, Inc.,* Conflicting reports claim that Kovolick was slain in Florida, in 1971.

October 24: Future drug lord Francisco Rafael Arellano Félix born in Mexico.

November 18: Unidentified shotgunners wound transplanted Michigan gambler Lincoln Fitzgerald outside his Nevada Club, in Reno. Police suspect ex-members of the Detroit Purple Gang.

December 11: Unknown shotgunners kill Mickey Cohen attorney Samuel Rummel outside his home on Laurel Canyon Drive, in Hollywood.

1950 Voters in Arizona, California, Massachusetts and Montana reject ballot initiatives to legalize casino gambling. New Zealand approves off-track betting on horse races, controlled by the Totalization Agency Board. Endo Pharmaceuticals, Inc., markets Percodan, a mixture of oxycodone and aspirin.

January 17: Armed bandits steal $1,218,211.19 in cash and more than $1.5 million in checks, money orders, and other securities from the Brinks Building in Boston. Participants include Stanley "Gus" Gusciora, Joseph "Big Joe" McGinnis, Joseph "Specs" O'Keefe, and Anthony "Fats" Pino. While the crime is not a syndicate score, the robbers have underworld connections.

February: Invited by Attorney General James McGrath (1903–66), mayors of major cities across the U.S. gather in Washington, D.C., to discuss the problem of organized crime.

February 28: Unknown gunmen kill Abraham Davidian at his mother's home in Fresno, Calif., as he waits to testify in the narcotics case of mafiosi Alfred and Joseph Sica.

March 14: FBI headquarters inaugurates its list of "Ten Most Wanted" fugitives.

April 6: Unknown gunmen execute mafioso Charles Binaggio and driver/bodyguard Charles "Mad Dog" Gargotta at the First Ward Democratic Club near downtown Kansas City, Mo. Anthony Gizzo succeeds Binaggio as boss of the local crime family.

April 24: The Desert Inn hotel-casino opens on the Las Vegas Strip, with Wilbur Clark fronting for members of the Cleveland Syndicate.

April 26: The Havre de Grace Racetrack in Harford County, Md., runs its final horse races. New owners Alfred Gwynne Vanderbilt II (owner of the rival Pimlico Race Course in Baltimore) and Morris Abraham Schapiro (owner of the Laurel Park track in Laurel, Md.) close the facility and transfer the track's racing allotment dates to their own tracks.

May: The first U.S. article on LSD appears in the *American Psychiatric Journal.*

May 3: U.S. Senate Resolution 202 authorizes creation of a Senate Special Committee to Investigate Crime in Interstate Commerce, chaired by Estes Kefauver. Joint Resolution 176 authorizes selection of counsel and staff on May 17.

May 24: Frederick J. Tenuto becomes the first associate of organized crime listed on the FBI's

"Ten Most Wanted" roster. He is deleted from the list on March 9, 1964, based on testimony from Mafia informant Joe Valachi that Tenuto is dead.

May 26–27: The Kefauver Committee holds executive hearings in Miami, Fla., hearing 13 witnesses and issuing subpoenas for the records of local casinos.

June: Pennsylvania police arrest Brinks bandits Gus Gusciora and Specs O'Keefe for burglary. Convicted at trial, Gusciora receives a sentence of five to 20 years, while O'Keefe gets three years. The defendants demand cash from various Boston mobsters to finance their legal defense.

June 5: Unknown shotgunners assassinate mafioso James Lumia in Tampa, Fla. Santo Trafficante Sr. assumes control of the local crime family.

July 5: Salvatore Giuliano suffers fatal gunshot wounds under mysterious circumstances in Castelvetrano, Sicily. Police claim that carabinieri captain Antonio Perenze shot Giuliano while he was resisting arrest, but journalists challenge that story. Giuliano lieutenant Gaspare Pisciotta later claims he was offered a pardon in return for killing Giuliano.

August 9: "Incorruptible" William Parker assumes command of the LAPD.

August 18: The Kefauver Committee publishes its first interim report, describing organized crime in Florida.

September 24: An opium addict kills FBN agent Anker Bangs during a drug raid in St. Paul, Minn.

September 25: Unknown Chicago gunmen kill former police captain William Drury and Marvin Bas, attorney for the Republican nominee for Cook County Sheriff, in separate shootings. Investigators believe both were slain for providing information to the Kefauver Committee. Authorities question Outfit leaders Paul Ricca and Louis Campagna, but file no charges.

September 30: Future drug lord Jorge Luis Ochoa Vásquez born in Medellín, Colombia.

November: State initiatives to legalize gambling appear on ballots in Arizona, California, Massachusetts and Montana. Voters in each state reject them.

November 5: Members of the U.S. Senate's Kefauver Committee visit Las Vegas, sparking an exodus of local mobsters.

December: FBN agents initiate a sting operation against Waxey Gordon, using ex-convict Morris Lipsius to arrange heroin sales.

December 13: New Jersey mafioso Willie Moretti testifies before the Kefauver Committee as its first — and only — cooperative gangland witness. His rambling testimony, coupled with mental deterioration caused by advanced syphilis, seals Moretti's fate.

1950–53 U.S. military personnel receive amphetamine to enhance performance during the Korean War.

1951 E.D. Jennings invents the "Tic-Tac-Toe" slot machine, featuring payoffs on both straight and diagonal lines. Alfred Matthew Hubbard (1901–82), AKA the "Johnny Appleseed of LSD," enjoys his first experience with the drug, subsequently "turning on" more than 6,000 persons including clergymen, diplomats, intelligence agents, and politicians. Sandoz Pharmaceutical of Switzerland contract for delivery of 100 grams of LSD per week to the U.S. government, with a clause banning sales to communist nations.

January 1: Future New York mafioso Cesare "The Tall Guy" Bonventre born in Castellammare del Golfo in Sicily.

January 17–19: Kefauver Committee hearings convene in Cleveland, Ohio, with leaders of the Cleveland Four still evading subpoenas.

February 8: The Kefauver Committee releases its second interim report, declaring that "organized crime does exist" and "connivance of local authorities necessary" for rackets to thrive.

February 16: Mafioso Gaetano "Tommy" Gagliano dies of natural causes in New York City. Gaetano Lucchese succeeds him as boss of the family.

February 28: Moe Dalitz and Sam Tucker testify before the Kefauver Committee in Los Angeles.

March: California congressman Cecil King releases "a secret list of underworld characters" facing IRS investigation for tax evasion. The list includes Moe Dalitz and mafioso Peter Licavoli.

March 5: Future mafioso and informer Francesco Marino Mannoia born in Palermo, Sicily.

March 7: Mobster Anthony "The Duke" Maffetore vanishes from New York City, presumed murdered on the date of his scheduled appearance in Queens County Court to face grand larceny charges related to a nationwide auto theft ring.

March 12–20: Kefauver Committee hearings in New York City air live on television nationwide.

March 26: Longy Zwillman testifies before the Kefauver Committee in New York City, while Morris Kleinman and Louis Rothkopf earn contempt citations for their refusal to speak.

March 28: Future Nuestra Familia member Michael "Mikeo" Castillo born.

April 11: Charles "Trigger Happy" Fischetti, cousin of Al Capone, dies in Chicago.

April 16: Texas mafioso Sam Maceo dies from cancer in a Baltimore, Md., hospital.

April 19: NYPD officers find mafioso Philip Mangano shot to death in Brooklyn. His brother Vincent vanishes the same day, leaving Albert

Anastasia in charge of the former Mangano family.

May 1: The Kefauver Committee issues its third interim report, including discussion of the Mafia, and Estes Kefauver resigns as chairman, citing a desire to spend more time with his family. His name remains attached to the committee in popular usage.

May 27: Future mafioso Michael Franzese born in Brooklyn, N.Y.

May 28: Joe Adonis pleads guilty to gambling violations in New Jersey, receiving a two-year prison sentence. Later the same day, Anthony Brancato and Anthony Trombino, AKA "the Two Tonys," rob the sports book at the Flamingo casino, Las Vegas, escaping with $3,500 cash. The FBI adds Brancato to its Ten Most Wanted list on June 27, as an interstate fugitive. He surrenders in San Francisco on June 29 and posts $10,000 bail. On August 6, police find the Two Tonys shot to death in a car on Hollywood Boulevard, in Los Angeles. Mafioso Jimmy Fratianno later confesses the killing, naming other participants as Charles "Charlie Bats" Battaglia, Nick Licata, Leo "Lips" Moceri, and Angelo Polizzi.

June: Future Australian gangster Keith George Faure born in Norlane, Victoria. Federal jurors in Los Angeles convict Mickey Cohen of tax evasion. He receives a five-year prison sentence, serving four.

July 14: CBS-TV selects a horse race as the first U.S. sporting event broadcast in color.

August 2: FBN agents arrest Waxey Gordon for selling heroin in New York. On December 13, Gordon receives an habitual-offender sentence of 25 years to life. After a brief stay at Sing Sing, he is transferred to Attica prison on March 8, 1952.

August 31: The Kefauver Committee issues its final report, surveying organized crime nationwide.

September: The Silver Slipper casino opens on the Las Vegas Strip.

September 8: A grand jury indicts Meyer Lansky on 21 counts of illegal gambling in Saratoga Springs, N.Y. Lansky pleads guilty to five counts on May 2, 1953, and serves three months in prison, plus a $2,500 fine and three years' probation.

October 4: Four unknown gunmen execute mafioso Willie Moretti at Joe's Elbow Room Restaurant, in Cliffside Park, N.J. When killed, Moretti was awaiting lunch guests Dean Martin and Jerry Lewis, both of whom "forgot" the appointment and later phoned to apologize.

October 20: President Truman signs the Revenue Act of 1951, establishing excise and occupational taxes on bookmaking, and requiring bookmakers to register with the IRS.

October 21: First documented CIA experiment with LSD.

October 26: Congress passes the Durham-Humphrey Amendment to the 1938 U.S. Food, Drug, and Cosmetic Act, requiring prescriptions for any habit-forming or potentially harmful drugs.

November 2: Congress passes the Boggs Amendment to the Harrison Narcotics Act, imposing mandatory prison terms for drug violations: two to five years for a first offense, five to 10 years for a second, 10 to 20 years for a third.

November 20: Governor Thomas Dewey to investigate corruption at the Port of New York, with special emphasis on the mob-dominated International Longshoremen's Association.

December 2: Dragna family lieutenant Frank Borgia vanishes on a business trip to Hanford, Calif.

December 18: A federal grand jury in New York indicts Moe Dalitz and six codefendants on charges of conspiracy to defraud the U.S. government and to register airplanes under fictitious names. The charges relate to an abortive sale of warplanes to Egypt in 1948, earmarked for use against Israel. Authorities dismiss Dalitz's indictment for lack of evidence, on April 7, 1953. Three other defendants pay fines on April 10, followed by three more on May 23.

1952 The Federation of Malaya bans lotteries, with certain exceptions. Norwegian citizens spend $6.9 million on the state lottery. Dr. Charles Savage reports failure in treating 15 patients with LSD for clinical depression. The U.S. Army launches "Project 112" at the Edgewood Arsenal's Bio Medical Laboratory (now the U.S. Army Medical Research Institute of Chemical Defense), northeast of Baltimore, Md., conducting experiments with LSD and other drugs through 1974.

January 18: Future bandit, smuggler and mass-murderer Koose Muniswamy Veerappan born in Gopinatham, India.

February 19: Future gangster Thomas "Tam" McGraw born in Glasgow, Scotland.

March 8: Acting on orders from Albert Anastasia, gunman Frederick Tenuto kills clothing salesman Arnold Schuster in Brooklyn. The murder contract results from Schuster's role in the February 18 arrest of fugitive bank robber Willie Sutton, prompting Anastasia to say, "I can't stand squealers! Hit that guy!" Tenuto, already listed as one of the FBI's Ten Most Wanted fugitives, is subsequently murdered to ensure his silence.

March 10: Fulgencio Batista leads a military coup in Cuba, deposing "Cordial President" Carlos Prío Socarrás.

March 18: "Retired" Milwaukee mafioso Joseph Vallone dies from natural causes.

March 20: Mafioso Joseph DeLuca dies of natural causes in Kansas City, Mo.

March 25: Las Vegas *Sun* publisher Hank Greenspun declares that local gamblers led by Moe Dalitz have launched an advertising boycott of his newspaper, on orders from Senator Patrick McCarran. Greenspun sues for $1 million dollars in damages, then settles out of court in February 1953, days before trial is scheduled to start.

March 29: Future gangster John Gilligan born in the Ballyfermot suburb of Dublin, Ireland.

April 10: A federal grand jury indicts Waxey Gordon for heroin trafficking. Authorities transfer him to San Francisco on May 21. Gordon dies from a heart attack at Alcatraz Prison on June 24, while awaiting trial.

April 15: Future Australian attorney-gangster Mario Condello born in Calabria, Italy.

April 17: Future gangster and war criminal Željko Ražnatović, AKA "Arkan," born in Brežice, Slovenia.

April 27: Authorities observe more than 80 high-ranking mobsters at a party in Providence, R.I., celebrating Raymond Patriarca's promotion to lead New England's Mafia family. Patriarca replaces Philip Buccola (or Bruccola), who fled the country to avoid tax-evasion charges.

May: Authorities note a "small meeting" of mafiosi in the Florida Keys.

June 21: Future Québec Hells Angels leader Maurice "Mom" Boucher born in Montreal's East End.

August 15: Frank Costello receives an 18-month federal prison term for contempt of Congress, based on his testimony before the Kefauver Committee in March 1951. He remains incarcerated until October 29, 1953.

October 1: James Vincenzo Capone, AKA "Richard James Hart"—eldest brother of Al Capone and a renowned lawman, dies from a heart attack in Homer, Neb.

October 7: Milton Prell opens the Sahara hotel-casino on the Las Vegas Strip.

October 14: Dave Beck replaces Daniel Tobin as IBT president, after bribing Tobin to step down.

October 16: Moe Dalitz testifies before New York's State Crime Commission, admitting acquaintance with mafioso Gaetano Lucchese.

November: Milwaukee Mafia boss Sam Ferrara vacates his post, allegedly after a vote by family members. John Alioto succeeds Ferrara as head of the gang.

December: FBN agent George Hunter White, formerly a consultant to the Kefauver Committee, begins administering LSD to unwitting subjects at a CIA safe house in Greenwich Village, N.Y.

December 3: Future drug lord Benjamín Arellano Félix born in Mexico.

December 9: Three unknown gunmen execute mafioso-turned-informer Dominick "The Gap" Petrilli at a tavern in the Bronx.

December 15: Texas gambler Jakie Freedman opens the Sands hotel-casino on the Las Vegas Strip.

December 29: Hitman Lucas Cavanaugh executes Chicago Outfit lieutenant Phil D'Andrea in the restroom of a local saloon.

1953 Dr. Humphry Fortescue Osmond (1917–2004) begins treating alcoholics with LSD in Saskatchewan, Canada. Dr. Ronald Sandison opens England's first LSD clinic. The CIA launches "Operation Bluebird/Artichoke," using hypnosis and sodium pentothal to erase memory, create multiple personalities, and enhance resistance to torture. Experiments continue through 1957.

January 8: Professional tennis player Harold Blauer dies after receiving an injection of a mescaline derivative at the New York State Psychiatric Institute, as treatment for depression. A cover-up ensues, concealing "Project Pelican," a top-secret program of drug experimentation funded by the U.S. Army. Congress repeals the Indian Prohibition Act of 1832, permitting residents of each tribal reservation to vote on legality of liquor sales.

January 20: Dwight Eisenhower (1890–1969) inaugurated as President of the United States, with Vice President Richard Nixon. Future crime boss Alaattin Çakıcı born in Arsin, Turkey.

January 26: Recalled to testify before the New York State Crime Commission, Moe Dalitz admits knowing various mobsters "by sight," while denying any contact with Meyer Lansky, Lucky Luciano, Ben Siegel, Abner Zwillman, Lepke Buchalter or Mickey Cohen. FBI files document his acquaintance with all six, but no perjury charges are filed.

April 1: Kansas City mafioso Anthony Gizzo dies from a heart attack in Dallas, Tex. Nicholas Civella succeeds him as boss of the family.

April 13: CIA Director Allen Dulles (1893–1969) initiates Project MK-ULTRA under Dr. Sidney Gottlieb (1918–99), employing LSD and other drugs in mind-control experiments.

April 16: Mafiosi Frank Bompensiero, Joe Dippolito, and Jimmy Fratianno strangle gambler Louis "Russian Louie" Strauss at Dippolito's ranch in Ontario, Calif., in retaliation for Strauss's attempts to blackmail mobster Benny Binion.

April 27: San Francisco mafioso Anthony Lima enters prison following conviction for grand theft. Michele Abati succeeds Lima as head of the local crime family.

May: British author Aldous Leonard Huxley

(1894–1963) experiments with mescaline for the first time, inspiring his 1954 work *The Doors of Perception.*

June 11: Celinus "Clem" Graver, Republican committeeman for Chicago's 21st Ward, disappears following an altercation with mafioso Sam Giancana.

June 19: Mafioso Joe Valachi murders police informant Stephen Franse in New York City.

June 23: Diplomats gathered in New York City sign a Protocol for Limiting and Regulating the Cultivation of the Poppy Plant, the Production of, International and Wholesale Trade in, and Use of Opium.

July 16: Joe Adonis leaves prison in New Jersey, facing perjury charges for lying under oath about his birthplace. On August 5, Attorney General Herbert Brownell Jr. (1904–96) orders Adonis deported to his native Italy.

August 12: Calling waterfront corruption "a national disgrace," President Eisenhower signs legislation creating the Waterfront Commission of New York Harbor, mandated "to investigate, deter, combat and remedy criminal influence in the Port of New York and New Jersey."

August 23: Future Camorra boss Paolo Di Lauro, AKA "Ciruzzo the Millionaire," born in Naples, Italy.

September 23: AFL-CIO president George Meany announces expulsion of the ILA, calling it "the tool of the New York Waterfront mob." The AFL-CIO creates a new International Brotherhood of Longshoremen to replace the ILA.

November 16: Police in Tampa, Fla., detain Santo Trafficante Jr. for investigation of a vagrancy charge, then release him the same day.

November 28: U.S. Army chemist Frank Olson dies at Fort Detrick in Frederick, Md., after being surreptitiously dosed with LSD as part of the CIA's Project MK-ULTRA.

December 29: Crips founder Stanley "Tookie" Williams III born in New Orleans.

1954 Canada's parliament bans casinos, gambling houses and betting shops, while creating a new drug offense: possession for the purpose of trafficking, punishable by seven years in prison. Czechoslovakia launches a national lottery. Italy's state lottery earns $45 million. Eli Lilly and Company of Indianapolis, Ind., begins synthesizing LSD for the CIA. The CIA begins drug experiments for "Operation MK-PILOT" at the Federal Medical Center in Lexington, Ky. Future Mexican Mafia member Frank "Mosca" Castrejon founds the Black Angels gang in Ontario, Calif. Outlaw bikers found the Highwaymen MC in Detroit, Mich. Japanese authorities combat an amphetamine epidemic, claiming some 2 million users in a population of 88 million.

January 7: U.S. Immigration officials deport Kansas City mafioso Charles Carrollo to Sicily.

January 9: Lee Harvey Oswald returns to New Orleans with his mother and siblings.

February 9: Sicilian bandit Gaspare Pisciotta dies in police custody, after drinking poisoned coffee. He had earlier accused Italian Minister of the Interior Mario Scelba (1901–1991) of complicity in murdering Salvatore Giuliano. On March 18, Pisciotta's mother writes a letter to the press, accusing corrupt government officials of killing her son.

March 25: Federal jurors in Washington, D.C., convict Joe Adonis of perjury.

March 29: Mafioso Rosario Maceo dies from heart disease in Galveston, Tex.

April: Longtime gambler Anthony Cornero seeks a Nevada gambling license for his Stardust resort on the Las Vegas Strip. State authorities object to Cornero's large number of shareholders in May, and he withdraws the application in June.

April 11: Rome's *Avanti!* newspaper exposes a Palermo candy factory, reportedly established by Calogero Vizzini and Lucky Luciano in 1949, as a heroin processing lab. The factory closes that evening, and its chemists vanish.

May 18: Specs O'Keefe and a friend kidnap Vincent Costa, a relative of fellow Brinks bandit Anthony Pinto. FBI spokesmen claim a small ransom is paid, though all concerned deny the incident ever occurred.

May 19: Sheriff's deputies in Tampa, Fla., arrest Santo Trafficante Jr. on a charge of bribery. Jurors acquit Trafficante of that charge on September 14, 1957.

May 20: Sheriff's officers in Tampa file a second bribery charge against Santo Trafficante Jr. He is convicted and receives a five-year prison sentence on September 27, 1954. That verdict is overturned by the state supreme court on January 23, 1957.

June 5: Unknown gunmen miss target Specs O'Keefe in a drive-by assassination attempt, in Dorchester, Mass.

June 14: Brinks bandits Henry Baker and Specs O'Keefe trade gunshots in Dorchester. Both escape unharmed.

June 16: Syndicate hitman Elmer "Trigger" Burke wounds Specs O'Keefe with machine-gun fire in Dorchester, Massachusetts. Police arrest Burke with the weapon on June 17. O'Keefe confesses his involvement in the Brinks robbery to FBI agents on January 6, 1956, resulting in the arrest and conviction of his surviving accomplices.

June 29: Police in St. Petersburg, Fla., arrest

Santo Trafficante Jr. for operating an illegal *bolita* lottery. Jurors acquit him on November 8, 1954.

July: Authorities report a Mafia gathering in a Chicago suburb.

July 10: Mafioso Calogero Vizzini dies in Villalba, Sicily.

August 11: Mafioso Santo Trafficante Sr. dies of natural causes in Tampa, Fla. His son, Santo Jr., assumes command of the family.

September 3: The Showboat hotel-casino opens in downtown Las Vegas, bankrolled by Moe Dalitz and his Cleveland Syndicate partners.

September 28: A heart attack kills Senator Patrick McCarran in Hawthorne, Nev.

October 18: Future Clerkenwell crime syndicate leader Terence George "Terry" Adams born in London, England.

November 11: Future gangster-politician Khozh-Ahmed Tashtamirovich Noukhayev born in the Chechen-Ingush Autonomous Soviet Socialist Republic.

December 2: Future Bonanno Family hitman and drug-trafficker Thomas "Tommy Karate" Pitera born in New York City.

December 13: Police report a Mafia meeting in Mountainside, N.J.

December 20: Minister K.N. Katju introduces the Suppression of Immoral Traffic in Women and Girls Bill before the Lok Sabha (lower house of India's parliament). It becomes law on December 31, 1956, theoretically eradicating prostitution nationwide.

1955 J. Edgar Hoover assigns a team of FBI agents to "determine and document the nonexistence of organized crime." Japan bans private bookmaking. Australian gamblers spend $62 million on lottery tickets, while betting $526 million on horse and dog races. Chicano street gang members incarcerated at the Deuel Vocational Institution in Tracy, Calif., organize the Mexican Mafia. The Parliament of Canada doubles penalties for possession of drugs for the purpose of trafficking, from seven to 14 years' imprisonment. Cuban president Fulgencio Batista announces that his government will grant a gambling license to anyone investing $1 million in a hotel or $200,000 in a new nightclub. The state will also provide matching public funds for construction, a 10-year exemption from taxes, and impose no duties on imports of equipment and furnishings for new hotels.

February 18: Future gangster Yaakov Alperon born in Giv'at Shmuel, Israel.

March 31: An unidentified killer stabs New Jersey mafioso Stefano "Steve" Badami in a Newark restaurant.

April 1: U.S. marshals arrest Santo Trafficante

Jr. in Tampa, Fla., on federal gambling charges. A jury acquits him on December 12, 1959.

April 18: Crime boss Charlie Wall dies in Tampa, Fla., leaving mafiosi in control of the city's rackets.

April 19: The Royal Nevada casino opens on the Las Vegas Strip, advertised as the "Showplace of Showtown, USA."

April 20: Miami investors, including Detroit native Samuel "Sammy Purple" Cohen, open the Riviera hotel-casino on the Las Vegas Strip. Gus Greenbaum assumes management of the resort in July.

May 16: California Mafioso Frank Bompensiero enters prison following conviction on bribery charges. Antonio Mirabile succeed him as boss of the San Diego crime family.

May 23: The Dunes hotel-casino opens on the Las Vegas Strip.

May 30: Chicago mobster Louis Campagna dies from a heart attack while fishing offshore on Florida's Biscayne Bay.

June 16: Ohio state legislators pass a stature imposing sentences of 20–40 years for sale of narcotics.

June 18: Future mafioso and informer Michael "Mikey Scars" DiLeonardo born in Bensonhurst, Brooklyn.

July: Detroit mobster Joe Zerilli and Black Bill Tocco found the 3,900-acre Arrowhead Ranch, north of Phoenix, Ariz., purchased for $2.6 million. Ohio mobster Frank "Screw" Andrews murders black numbers operator Melvin Clark in Newport, Ky., later escaping conviction for murder on a plea of self-defense.

July 27: Lee Harvey Oswald joins the Civil Air Patrol in New Orleans and meets Captain David Ferrie, sometimes employed as a pilot by mafioso Carlos Marcello.

July 31: Tony Cornero dies from an apparent heart attack while shooting craps at the Desert Inn Casino, Las Vegas. Morticians fly his body to Los Angeles for cremation before Las Vegas police are informed of his death. Some authors claim Cornero was poisoned to force sale of his new Stardust hotel-casino to the Cleveland syndicate.

August: Owners of the Desert Inn hotel-casino in Las Vegas launch Wilbur Clark's Casino International in Havana, Cuba. In November the firm leases Meyer Lansky's Hotel Nacional, opening the casino under new management on January 19, 1956.

August 4: A government decree regulates Italian state lotteries.

August 6: Future boxer and mobster Domenic "Mick" Gatto, AKA "The Don," born in Australia.

August 11: Rival gangsters Jack "Spot" Comer and Albert "Italian Al" Dimes engage in a knife fight on Frith Street in Soho, London.

August 20: Future drug baron Carlos Arellano Félix born in Mexico.

August 25: Moe Dalitz and Sam Tucker assume control of Meyer Lansky's Nacional Casino in Havana.

October: U.S. Marine Corps recruiters reject Lee Harvey Oswald.

November 4: A car bomb kills mobster-turned-informant William Morris "Willie" Bioff, AKA "William Nelson," at his home in Phoenix, Ariz. U.S. Senator Barry Goldwater attends his funeral, denying any knowledge of Bioff's true identity, but later changes his story to claim he used Bioff for "research" on labor racketeering. Investigators learn that Goldwater received a $5,000 contribution from Bioff, flew Bioff to parties around the Southwest on his (Goldwater's) private plane, and in 1952 pressured a local newspaper not to publish an exposé on Bioff's criminal background.

December 5: The AFL and CIO merge to form North America's largest labor federation, including 65 unions with more than 10 million members.

December 24: Author Aldous Huxley takes his first LSD "trip," inspiring his 1956 book *Heaven and Hell*.

December 26: Future crime boss and terrorist leader Sheikh Dawood Ibrahim Kaskar born in Ratnagiri, Maharashtra, India.

1956 Great Britain introduces a state-run lottery. Portugal legalizes totalizator gambling at horse tracks.

January 3: U.S. Immigration officials agree to let Joe Adonis leave the country, in lieu of serving his perjury sentence. His departure sparks a power struggle between Frank Costello and Albert Anastasia in New York.

February 14: Ireland's new Gaming and Lotteries Act bans slot machines but permits other forms of gambling "if no stake is hazarded by the players with the promoter or banker other than a charge for the right to take part in the game."

February 21: Jake Guzik dies from a heart attack in Chicago.

February 23: A heart attack kills mafioso Jack Dragna in Los Angeles.

February 28: French authorities execute gangster Émile Buisson for one of his estimated 30 murders.

March 18: Future "D.C. Madam" Deborah Jeane Palfrey born in Charleroi, Pa.

March 26: Rowe Cigarette Service of Pawtucket, R.I., files a civil suit against Ray Patriarca's National Cigarette Service, claiming illegal interference with its operations. The court orders an end to Patriarca's harassment of his competitors on June 5.

April 1: Outlaw bikers found the Gypsy Jokers MC in San Francisco, Calif.

April 3: The owners of Wilbur Clark's Casino International join British gambler George Francis to charter Mohawk Securities in Panama. All stock in WCCI transfers to Mohawk, exempt from IRS reporting since American citizens own only half of the firm.

April 5: Racketeer Abraham Telvi blinds crusading journalist Victor Riesel with sulfuric acid outside Lindy's restaurant in Manhattan, scalding his own face in the process. The attack delays Riesel's testimony before a grand jury investigating labor racketeers. Police trace the crime to Lucchese Family members Dominick Bando, Joseph Carlino, Gondolfo Miranti, and Charles Tuso. Dissatisfied with his initial fee of $1,175, Telvi demands another $50,000, prompting his murder on July 28. FBI agents arrest mafioso John Dioguardi for conspiracy on August 29, whereupon he posts $100,000 bond. Carlino pleads guilty and turns state's evidence on October 22, prompting Bando's guilty plea in turn, while jurors convict Miranti of conspiracy. Carlino and Miranti later recant their statements accusing Dioguardi, resulting in dismissal of his charges in September 1957.

April 11: Elmer Perry, a former associate of Bugsy Siegel and Tony Cornero, suffers fatal gunshots in his car on South Hauser Street, Los Angeles. LAPD suspects Ted Lewin.

April 26: Chicago police arrest mobster Ernest Rocco Infelise and two associates on charges of possessing stolen drugs. The case is subsequently dismissed. Future mafioso Primo Cassarino born in Brooklyn, N.Y.

May: The U.S. Army's chemical warfare laboratory at Edgewood, Md., begins LSD testing on human volunteers.

May 14: Federal jurors in New York City convict Frank Costello of tax evasion, resulting in immediate incarceration.

May 18: NYPD officers observe 35 high-ranking mobsters at a conference in New York City.

June: California hotelier Warren "Doc" Bayley and his wife open the Hacienda Hotel on the Las Vegas Strip. Gaming Commission inquiries into suspected hidden ownership delay opening of the casino until early 1957.

June 18: Enraged by discovery of a romantic affair between his wife and Los Angeles Mafia boss Frank DeSimone, underboss Girolomo "Momo" Adamo shoots his wife, then kills himself in San Diego. His wife survives.

July 17: Cleveland mobster Louis Rothkopf "accidentally" kills himself with carbon monoxide gas in the garage of his Ohio home.

July 18: President Eisenhower signs the Narcotic Control Act, increasing penalties for all drug offenses to two to 10 years, five to 20 years, and 10 to 40 years for succeeding convictions; raising fines in all categories to $20,000; and imposing five to 20 years on first conviction for any smuggling or sale violation, and 10 to 40 years thereafter, with a separate penalty of 10 to 40 years for any sale or distribution by a person over 18 to a minor, and from 10 years to life — or death when recommended by a jury — if the drug is heroin.

August 14: Four rival gangs on Manhattan's Lower East Side agree to a three-week truce, with several leaders leaving town for the duration. Violence resumes at the end of the cease-fire.

October: A federal grand jury indicts John Dioguardi on extortion and conspiracy charges. Trial is scheduled for January 1957, then postponed when key witnesses recant their statements or refuse to testify.

October 3: A 14-year-old member of the Lower East Side Dragons suffers stab wounds at Manhattan's Metropolitan High School.

October 10–12: Anti-communist riots leave 59 persons dead and some 500 injured in Hong Kong, with at least $1 million in property damage. Police blame Triad gangsters for initiating the violence, resulting in crackdowns on underworld activity.

October 11: Future drug baron Eduardo Arellano Félix, AKA "El Doctor," born in Mexico.

October 17–18: FBN agents report a gathering of Mafia leaders in Binghamton, N.Y., reportedly the first of three gatherings held to establish heroin routes between Sicily and the U.S.

October 24: Lee Harvey Oswald joins the U.S. Marine Corps, reporting for duty in San Diego on October 26. On December 21 he earns a "sharpshooter" rating on the rifle range.

October 27: Dallas mafioso Joseph Piranio shoots himself after a brief illness. Joseph Civello succeeds him as boss of the local crime family.

1957 Czechoslovakia permits establishment of two sports betting pools. Betting on horse races in New Zealand totals $130 million. Ireland holds its 91st Hospital Sweepstakes, tied to the Britain's Grand National horse race. British psychiatrist Humphry Fortescue Osmond coins the term "psychedelic" to describe mind-manifesting experiences, such as LSD "trips."

January: Howard Hughes loans $205,000 to Donald Nixon, brother of Vice President Richard Nixon, ostensibly to bankroll a drive-in restaurant in Whittier, Calif. Exposure of the loan in 1960 damages brother Richard's presidential ambitions.

January 8: Future New York mafioso Liborio "Barney" Salvatore Bellomo born in Corleone, Sicily.

January 30: The U.S. Senate establishes a Select Committee on Improper Activities in Labor and Management, chaired by John McClellan. The committee holds its first hearings on February 26.

January 31: The AFL-CIO's Ethical Practices Committee gives IBT leaders 90 days to reform their union or face expulsion.

February 25: Former Chicago mobster George "Bugs" Moran dies from lung cancer at Leavenworth federal prison, while serving time for bank robbery.

March: Hungary's state bank inaugurates a lottery.

March 11: Future hitman Patrick "Patty" Testa born in New York City. Frank Costello wins temporary release from prison on $25,000 bond, while the U.S. Supreme Court considers his appeal. The court denies his appeal and Costello returns to prison on October 21, 1958. He wins parole on June 20, 1961.

March 13: FBI agents arrest IBT official Jimmy Hoffa on charges of trying to bribe a McClellan Committee investigator.

March 18: Lee Harvey Oswald begins radar training at the Naval Air Technical Training Center in Jacksonville, Fla. He transfers to Keesler Air Force Base in Biloxi, with a "Confidential" security clearance, on May 3, then departs for duty in Yokosuka, Japan, on August 22.

March 25: IBT president Dave Beck appears before the McClellan Committee in Washington, D.C. Questioned by counsel Robert Kennedy concerning the disappearance of $322,000 from the union treasury, Beck pleads the Fifth Amendment 117 times.

April 4: Future drug baron Joaquín "Shorty" Guzmán Loera born in Sinaloa, Mexico. The Tropicana Hotel-Casino opens in Las Vegas, Nev., controlled by New York mobsters.

April 16: Johnny Torrio suffers a fatal heart attack in a Brooklyn barber shop.

May: Life magazine publishes Robert Gordon Wasson's account of his experiments with "magic mushrooms."

May 2: Prosecutors indict IBT president Dave Beck for tax evasion. Frank Costello survives an assassination attempt by Vincent Gigante in New York City, suffering a minor scalp wound. Police find a slip of paper in Costello's pocket reading "Gross casino wins, 4–27–57, $651,284," which matches earnings for the Tropicana resort in Las Vegas. Costello refuses to testify against Gigante and begins a 30-day jail term for contempt of court on May 7, serving 15 days. He subsequently retires, ceding control of the former Luciano family to Vito Genovese.

May 14: Under pressure from rebellious subordinates, New Jersey mafioso Philip "Big Phil" Amari leaves the U.S. for Italy. Nicholas Delmore succeeds him as boss of the Elizabeth crime family.

May 16: Eliot Ness dies from a heart attack in Coudersport, Pa.

May 19: Paroled mobster Mickey Cohen grants a televised interview to journalist Mike Wallace, telling the nation, "I killed nobody that didn't deserve killing." He also brands LAPD Chief William Parker "a sadistic degenerate," thus prompting civil litigation.

May 20: Future mafioso Giovanni Brusca born in San Giuseppe Jato, Sicily.

May 21: Future mafioso Michele Vitale born in Partinico, Sicily.

May 25: Dave Beck announces that he will not seek re-election as IBT president in October.

June: A judge in New York City revokes John Dioguardi's bond and empanels a special jury to hear his case. The jurors convict him of extortion and conspiracy on July 25, resulting in a two-year prison sentence. While Dioguardi awaits sentencing, another grand jury indicts him for tax evasion. Convicted on those charges in December, he receives a 15-year sentence and enters Sing Sing Prison on January 10, 1958.

June 16: Mobster and Las Vegas Flamingo boss Dave Berman dies during surgery to remove polyps from his colon.

June 17: Unidentified gunmen kill Anastasia family underboss Francesco "Don Cheech" Scalise at a produce market in the Bronx. Reasons suggested for his murder include unauthorized sale of Mafia memberships and participation in heroin trafficking officially banned by New York's Five Families.

July 19: Jimmy Hoffa announces his candidacy for president of the IBT, winning election on October 4. He takes office on February 1, 1958.

September 7: Mafioso Vincent Squillante, a cousin of Albert Anastasia, murders Joseph Scalise following a party where Scalise threatened to avenge the June murder of his brother Francesco. (Some accounts date the slaying from September 19.)

September 25: After three months of hearings, the AFL-CIO votes to expel the IBT if Teamster leaders do not clean up their union within 30 days. IBT president Dave Beck refuses, prompting

suspension of the union on October 24. Final expulsion follows on December 6.

October 12–16: Mafiosi from the U.S. and Sicily gather at Palermo's Grand Hotel des Palmes for what researchers call an international "heroin summit." Alleged participants include Lucky Luciano, Joseph Bonanno, Giuseppe Genco Russo, Gaetano Badalamenti, and Tommaso Buscetta. The meeting is exposed in testimony before the McClellan Committee, on October 10–16, 1963.

October 25: Unidentified gunmen execute Albert Anastasia in the barber shop of Manhattan's Park Sheraton Hotel (now the Park Central). Vito Genovese remains the primary suspect, though author Hank Messick blames Meyer Lansky in 1973.

November 6: Future police officer-turned-drug lord Wilber Alirio Varela Fajardo born in Colombia.

November 10: Authorities document a Mafia gathering at Livingston, N.J., estate of Genovese family capo Richard Boiardo.

November 14: More than 100 mafiosi from all parts of the U.S. convene at Joseph Barbara's estate in Apalachin, N.Y., presumably to discuss Albert Anastasia's murder and determine a new balance of power. New York State Police officers raid the gathering, arresting 58 participants while 50-odd others escape. Those detained on various charges include Vito Genovese, Santo Trafficante Jr., Carlo Gambino, Gerardo Catena, Paul Castellano, and John Scalish.

November 24: Embarrassed by public proof of the Mafia's existence, J. Edgar Hoover creates the FBI's Top Hoodlum Program, ordering each bureau field office to prepare a list of 10 local gangster — no more, no less — for intensive surveillance.

December 12: A drug-addicted informer kills FBN agent Wilson Shee in San Francisco, California.

December 19: Jurors fail to reach a verdict on Jimmy Hoffa's wiretapping charges, resulting in a mistrial.

1958 Portugal permits construction of casinos at specific authorized locations. The Sicilian Mafia establishes its first governing commission, with members including Michele Cavataio, Salvatore Greco, Antonio Matranga, Mario Di Girolamo, Salvatore Manno, Lorenzo Motisi, Giuseppe Panno, Salvatore La Barbera, Mariano Troia, Calcedonio Di Pisa, Francesco Sorci, Antonio Salamone, and Cesare Manzella. Japanese gangsters form the Minato-kai Yakuza clan, later renamed Sumiyoshi-kai. Other mobsters in Tokyo organize the Kokusui-kai ("Patriotic Society") clan. The U.S. Army begins experiments with the hallucinogen "BZ" (3-Quinuclidinyl benzilate) as an incapacitating agent.

January: Las Vegas newspaper headlines announce that Moe Dalitz and his Cleveland partners will run the new Stardust hotel-casino on behalf of owner Rella Factor, wife of mobster John "Jake the Barber" Factor, who has purchased it for $4.3 million from relatives of founder Anthony Cornero.

January 3: Cuban National Police detain and question Santo Trafficante Jr. in Havana.

January 9: Hitman Elmer "Trigger" Burke dies in Sing Sing's electric chair for the 1955 murder of bartender Edward Walsh. In New York City, mafioso brothers Albert, Joseph and Lawrence Gallo begin unauthorized activities independent of family boss Joseph Profaci.

February 11: Ray Patriarca testified before the McClellan Committee in Washington, D.C., denying any knowledge of strong-arm tactics employed by his National Cigarette Service vending machine company.

February 13: Mexican Mafia members Lorenzo Castro and Reuben Ramos kidnap and shoot rival gangsters Gerald De Lao and George Rodriquez in Los Angeles, killing De Lao.

February 21: Future president and Mafia associate Dr. Salvatore "Totò" Cuffaro born in Sicily.

March 14: Future Norte del Valle Cartel drug lord Luis Hernando Gómez Bustamante born in Colombia.

Spring: The U.S. Department of Justice creates a Special Group on Organized Crime.

April 25: Nevada's Tax Commission orders the Desert Inn's owners to divest themselves of gambling interests in Cuba. Moe Dalitz and company sell the Hotel Nacional to gambler Mike McLaney and two partners on September 30, thus escaping confiscation of their property by Fidel Castro in 1959.

May 13: Mexican Mafia members stab Deputy Sheriff Ned Lovretovich in a Los Angeles courtroom, following his testimony in the robbery-murder trial of East L.A. gangsters Augustin Acosta and Gregory Valenzuela.

May 22: Mafioso Tony Musso dies from natural causes in Rockford, Ill. Jasper Calo briefly serves as acting boss of the family, replaced before year's end by Joseph Zammuto.

June: Luciano Leggio survives an ambush by Michele Navarra's gunmen near Corleone, Sicily.

July 2: Police blame local mafiosi for the murder of gambler Joseph Pelusa Diaz in Tampa, Fla. The Stardust Resort and Casino opens in Las Vegas, Nev., run by Cleveland mobsters who also own the nearby Desert Inn.

August 2: Mafiosi Bernardo Provenzano and Salvatore Riina execute Michele Navarra on orders from Luciano Leggio. Another physician riding in Navarra's car also dies in the ambush. Leggio succeeds Navarra as boss of the Corleonesi Mafia faction.

August 23: Future gangster and Bandidos MC member Jan "Face" Krogh Jensen born in Denmark.

September 7: Unknown gunmen kill mafioso John Robilotto, alleged triggerman in Willie Moretti's 1951 execution, on a Manhattan streetcorner.

September 15: A Jersey Central commuter train derails and plunges from a trestle into Newark Bay with 200 passengers aboard, killing 47 passengers and injuring 48. Newspaper photos of the wreckage, showing the numbers 9-3-2 on the train's side, prompt heavy betting in policy circles and the number wins, leaving syndicate bankers strapped for cash in New Jersey.

October: Three days after the Sicilian newspaper L'Ora publishes a front-page exposé of mafioso Luciano Leggio's activities, a bomb shatters the paper's office.

October 22: Police find bookie Maurice "Goldie" Goldworth dead in the trunk of a car on Ventura Boulevard, Studio City, Calif. LAPD suspects Clifford "Rue" Ruebenstein.

November 11: Future Australian gangster Victor George Peirce born in Port Melbourne, Victoria.

December: Greece inaugurates a state-sponsored betting pool on soccer.

December 3: A maid finds Gus Greenbaum and his wife slain at their Phoenix, Ariz., home, both nearly decapitated. Various authors blame Meyer Lansky, Moe Dalitz, or the Chicago Outfit for the murders, but all agree the contract sprang from Greenbaum's heroin addiction and embezzlement from the Flamingo casino in Las Vegas.

December 18: Owners of the Desert Inn and Stardust hotel-casinos open Sunrise Hospital in Las Vegas, assisted by an IBT contract requiring all local teamsters to use the facility for union-authorized health care.

December 27: Habitual felon Victor Francis Buono and two accomplices kill mafioso Antonio Mirabile during a bungled robbery attempt in San Diego, Calif. Joe Adamo succeeds Mirabile as boss of the local crime family, while the killers receive life prison terms.

1959 New Zealand legalizes betting on bingo. Chilean bettors wager $17 million on horse races. The Josiah Macy Jr. Foundation sponsors the first international "LSD therapy" conference. Outlaw bikers found the Grim Reapers MC in Louisville, Ky., unrelated to a Canadian club of the same name founded in 1967. Other bikers found the Pagans MC in Prince George's County, Md. The Josiah Macy Jr. Foundation convenes a scientific conference on LSD.

January 1: President Fulgencio Batista flees into exile, leaving Cuba and the Mob's casino operations to revolutionary victor Fidel Castro. Future mafioso Giovanni Motisi born in Palermo, Sicily.

January 15: Philadelphia mafioso Joseph Ida flees to Sicily following a narcotics conviction, formally renouncing his U.S. citizenship on April 21, 1960. Angelo Bruno assumes command of the local crime family.

January 21: A secret U.S. Army report recommends that "actual application of LSD be utilized in real situations on an experimental basis."

January 29: Future gangster Nikolai "The Russian" Radev born in Bulgaria.

February 11: The McClellan Committee issues subpoenas to syndicate leaders nationwide. All plead the Fifth Amendment, except for mafioso Ray Patriarca, who complains of police harassment, saying, "I have been a goat around Rhode Island for 20 years."

February 17: Future gangster "Dodgy" Dave Courtney born in London, England.

February 26: Police find Longy Zwillman hanged at his home in Orange, N.J. Authorities rule the death a suicide, despite bruises suggesting that Zwillman's wrists were bound before he died. In 1973 author Hank Messick blames Meyer Lansky for the murder.

March 25: *Al Capone* premieres in U.S. theaters, with Rod Steiger in the title role. Nehemiah Persoff portrays James Colosimo, with Murvyn Vye cast as Bugs Moran.

April 16: *The Lawless Years* premieres on ABC, as television's first series depicting the "Roaring Twenties." Actor James Gregory stars as NYPD detective Barney Ruditsky, pursuing real-life mobsters such as Lepke Buchalter, Mad Dog Coll, Dutch Schultz, etc. The series runs until September 22, 1961, with 47 episodes.

April 17: Federal jurors in New York City convict mafiosi Vito Genovese, Natale Evola, and Vincent Gigante of narcotics violations. Genovese receives a 15-year sentence, while Evola gets 10 years and Gigante gets seven. Today, some researchers claim that Genovese was framed by Meyer Lansky and/or Carlo Gambino.

April 20: CBS airs *The Scarface Mob*, with Robert Stack cast as Eliot Ness, against Al Capone portrayed by Neville Brand (1920–92).

April 29: New York mafioso John Dioguardi receives a four-year prison term and a $5,000 fine for income tax evasion.

June 6: Future mafioso Pietro "The Little Gentleman" Aglieri born in Palermo, Sicily.

June 17: New York mafioso Joseph Barbara dies from a heart attack. Russell Bufalino succeeds Barbara as the Mafia boss of northeastern Pennsylvania.

June 20: Future mafioso Salvatore "Vito" Vitale born in Partinico, Sicily.

June 23: New York's Court of Appeals overturns John Dioguardi's extortion conviction.

August 3: Julio Rosario, age 14, suffers fatal stab wounds during a gangfight in Manhattan. Jurors convict his assailant of second-degree murder on May 21, 1960.

August 8: Future gangster Desmond "Dessie" Noonan born in Manchester, England.

August 16: The CIA attempts to kill Fidel Castro with a box of poisoned cigars. Failure of that effort prompts CIA Deputy Director of Plans Richard Bissell and CIA Chief of Security Sheffield Edwards to consider employing professional mobsters.

September 1: The *New York Times* reports that 150 street gangs with more than 6,500 members operate on Manhattan's Lower East Side.

September 2: CIA Chief of Operational Support James O'Connell reports commencement of efforts to assassinate Castro. Future mafioso Giuseppe Lucchese born in Palermo, Sicily.

September 4: Lee Harvey Oswald applies for a passport. He receives it on September 10 and is discharged from the Marine Corps on September 11. Oswald arrives in New Orleans on September 17, then departs for the USSR via Finland on September 20, arriving in Moscow on October 16. With his visa about to expire, he attempts suicide on October 21 and remains hospitalized until October 28. He applies for Soviet citizenship the same day, and writes to the U.S. embassy on November 3, requesting revocation of his American citizenship.

September 9: Future gangster Stanko "Cane" Subotić born in Kalinovac, Serbia.

September 10: Mafioso Onofrio Sciortino dies from natural causes in San Jose, Calif. Joe Cerrito succeeds him as boss of the local crime family.

September 14: Congress passes the Labor Management Reporting and Disclosure Act, AKA the Landrum-Griffin Act, banning communists and convicted felons from holding union offices, requiring unions to hold secret elections for local union offices on a regular basis and providing for review of alleged improper election activity by the U.S. Department of Labor.

September 24: CIA Operational Support Chief O'Connell meets mafioso John Rosselli and ex-FBI agent Robert Maheu, now a private investigator with CIA ties, at the Plaza Hotel in New York City. They discuss plans to kill Fidel Castro. Rosselli subsequently enlists Sam Giancana.

September 25: Unknown gunmen execute Anthony Carfano and girlfriend Janice Drake in Queens, N.Y.

Early October: CIA Operational Support Chief O'Connell meets with John Rosselli, Sam Giancana, Santo Trafficante Jr., and Robert Maheu at the Fontainebleau Hotel in Miami, Fla., continuing discussions of the Castro plot.

October 15: Encouraged by ratings for *The Scarface Mob*, CBS-TV premieres *The Untouchables*, continuing with Robert Stack as Eliot Ness. The series runs through May 21, 1963, with 118 episodes pitting Ness against Chicago mobsters including Frank Nitti and Bugs Moran. Fictional scripts also send Ness in pursuit of other gangsters nationwide, including Dutch Schultz, Mad Dog Coll, Waxey Gordon, and the Barker-Karpis gang — a deviation from history which enrages FBI Director J. Edgar Hoover.

October 18: J. Edgar Hoover sends a memo to CIA Deputy Director of Plans Richard Bissell, reporting that "during a recent conversation with several friends, [Sam] Giancana stated that Fidel Castro was to be done away with very shortly. When doubt was expressed regarding this statement, Giancana reportedly assured those present that Castro's assassination would occur in November." Giancana claims three meetings with a potential assassin.

October 31: Private detective Arthur Ballentti, hired by Sam Giancana, is caught bugging comedian Dan Rowan's Las Vegas hotel room. FBI agents link the incident to John Rosselli, Robert Maheu, and the CIA's plot against Castro.

November 24: A federal judge frees Roger Touhy, ruling that John Factor was never actually kidnapped.

November 27: CIA Director Allen Dulles and Richard Bissell brief president-elect John Kennedy on a planned invasion of Cuba by exiled commandos.

November 28: The U.S. Fifth Circuit Court of Appeals voids the conspiracy convictions of 20 mafioso who attended the 1957 meeting in Apalachin, N.Y.

November 29: Future gangster Ivo Karamanski born in Dupnica, Bulgaria.

December 2: Mickey Cohen, Sam Locigno and George Piscitelle kill independent bookie Jack O'Hara at Rondelli's Restaurant, in Los Angeles.

December 11: Acting on a proposal from Joseph Caldwell King, chief of the CIA's Western Hemisphere Division, Director Allen Dulles orders that "thorough consideration be given to the elimination of [Fidel] Castro."

December 16: Unidentified shotgunners, presumably Outfit assassins, blast recent parolee Roger Touhy in Chicago. Dying, Touhy tells a bystander, "The bastards never forget."

December 17: Future mafioso Salvatore "Torre" LoCascio, AKA "The X-Rated Mobster," born in Scarsdale, N.Y.

December 18: Twenty mafiosi arrested at the 1957 Apalachin meeting are convicted of conspiracy. At sentencing on January 13, 1960, most receive five-year sentences and $10,000 fines. The U.S. Court of Appeals overturns their convictions on November 28, 1960, freeing all from custody.

December 23: Mexican Mafia member Rudy Cadena begins serving a prison sentence for second-degree murder at the California Institution for Men in Chino.

December 25: Gangster Leonard Brophy allegedly committed suicide in his car after an argument with his girlfriend. The Los Angeles coroner's office rules his death accidental.

December 27: Gangster Tony Mirabile suffers fatal gunshots in his San Diego, Calif., apartment. Police suspect rival Ernest Murray.

1960 Bettors in the U.S. wager $3 billion on horse races nationwide, while New York logs $1 billion in bets on all forms of animal racing. Parimutuel bets on horse races recorded by Canada's Department of Agriculture total $141.4 million. Betting on Belgian horse races reaches $13.6 million. O.D. Jennings introduces the four-reel "Buckaroo" slot machine. Timothy Leary founds the Psychedelic Research Project at Harvard University, including 35 professors, instructors, and graduate students who participate in LSD experiments.

January 5: *The Purple Gang* premieres in U.S. theaters, with Robert Blake cast as fictional Detroit mobster "William Joseph 'Honeyboy' Willard."

January 8: U.S. Army Intelligence receives official orders to coordinate covert LSD testing with the CIA and FBI. Collaboration between the CIA and the U.S. Chemical Corps begins in December 1960.

January 13: CIA Director Dulles inaugurates the "Cuban project," AKA "Operation 40," to carry out "careful planning of covert actions" culminating in the toppling of Fidel Castro's government.

January 15: Chicago police arrest eight fellow officers in the Summerdale district on charges of running a burglary ring, seizing various stolen items worth thousands of dollars. Police Commissioner Tim O'Connor resigns on January 23, replaced by Orlando Wilson on February 22. All eight officers are convicted at trial, with five imprisoned, one sentenced to a term in county jail, and two others paying fines. The case marks Chicago's eighth major police corruption scandal in three decades.

January 18: CIA officer J.D. Esterline leads

"Branch 4 of the Western Hemisphere Division," described in agency memos as "an internal task force created within the CIA in January 1960 to direct the Cuban project."

March 9: Members of a federal task force agree that if U.S. agents cannot "eliminate the leaders [of Cuba] with a single blow," Castro's government "can only be brought down through the use of force." On March 17, President Eisenhower signs a National Security Council directive authorizing the CIA to organize, train, and equip Cuban refugees as a guerrilla force to overthrow Castro.

March 11: Jurors in New York City convict two members of the Forsyth Boys, a street gang, for killing a 15-year-old girl during a "rumble" with rival gangsters.

April: Investigators uncover a burglary ring within the Denver Police Department. Before the scandal runs its course, 53 officers are suspended, 30 plead guilty or are convicted at trial on various charges, and a dozen more resign to avoid prosecution.

April 29: New York jurors convict John Dioguardi of income tax evasion. He receives a four-year prison sentence and a $5,000 fine.

May: Meyer Lansky associates Sam Cohen, Morris Lansburgh and Daniel Lifter seek permission to buy 87.75 percent of the Flamingo resort in Las Vegas. State authorities approve the sale in July, deeming the trio "most cooperative."

May 15: *The Rise and Fall of Legs Diamond* premieres in U.S. theaters, with Ray Danton in the title role and Richard Gardner cast as Vincent Coll.

June: Ghana's first legal opens at the Ambassador Hotel in Accra. Harper & Brothers publishes *The Enemy Within*, by Robert F. Kennedy, detailing evidence of labor racketeering collected by the McClellan Committee. Nevada's Gaming Control Board issues its first list of persons banned from casinos statewide, commonly known as the "Black Book."

June 3: Police find James Delmont beaten to death, dumped beside Mountain Avenue in Ontario, Calif. Officers suspect mafioso Angelo Polizzi.

June 5: Future Hells Angels MC member and convicted murderer Jørn "Jønke" Nielsen born in Gladsaxe, Denmark.

June 17: Owners of the El Rancho hotel-casino in Las Vegas eject Chicago Outfit enforcer Marshall Joseph Caifano, né Marcello Giuseppe Caifano, from the premises, based on his listing in Nevada's "Black Book." Later the same night, arsonists burn the resort to the ground.

June 21: Future mobster Costabile "Gus" Farace Jr. born in Bushwick, Brooklyn.

June 28: Future 'Ndrangheta gunman Giorgio "Angel Face" Basile born in Corigliano Calabro, Italy. *Murder, Inc.*, premieres in U.S. theaters, starring Peter Falk as Abe Reles and David Stewart as Lepke Buchalter.

July 5: Fidel Castro nationalizes all U.S.-owned commercial properties in Cuba, including various mob casinos. Meyer Lansky loses an estimated $17 million and allegedly places a $1 million murder contract on "The Beard."

July 26: Arizona judge Yale McFate rules that the First and Fourteenth Amendments to the U.S. Constitution guarantees Native Americans access to peyote as a religious sacrament. Other states subsequently follow Arizona's lead.

August 6: Ohio mobster Vincent Innocenzi's wife reports him missing. Police find his body outside Akron, a week later.

September 1: Britain's Parliament passes the Betting and Gaming Act, permitting small bets on games of skill (such as bridge) after January 1, 1961, and allowing licensed betting shops to operate after May 1, 1961.

September 7: Fueled by Jimmy Hoffa's hatred of the Kennedy brothers, the IBT's board of directors endorses Richard Nixon for president. Hoffa subsequently delivers a $500,000 campaign contribution from mafioso Carlos Marcello.

September 8: Future mafioso Luigi Putrone born at Porto Empedocle, Sicily.

September 5: Two members of Boston's Winter Hill Gang beat George McLaughlin, of the rival Charlestown Mob, for drunkenly groping Alex "Bobo" Petricone's girlfriends at Salisbury Beach. When Winter Hill leader James "Buddy" McLean refuses to surrender McLaughlin's assailants, McLaughlin's brothers try to plant a bomb in McLean's car. He catches them in the act, and while they escape, the resultant gang war kills numerous Irish mobsters in Boston.

September 23: Mafioso Vincent Squillante, a capo in the Gambino Family, vanishes forever (with his new Chevrolet) from New York City.

November 8: John Kennedy defeats Richard Nixon by two-tenths of one percent in the year's presidential election. Vote fraud in Illinois contributes to JFK's victory and mafioso Sam Giancana boasts of personally placing Kennedy in the White House.

November 24: Future gangster and terrorist Mushtaq Abdul Razak "Tiger" Memon born in Mumbai, India.

1961 Betting on soccer totals $333 million in Britain, $240 million in Australia, and $150 million in Scandinavia. New York authorities report more than $1 billion wagered on all forms of animal racing. Austria collects $1.9 million in casino taxes and $1.3 million from lotteries. West German gamblers lose $425 million. Swedish players bet $38.4 million on soccer matches and spend $55.6 million on the national lottery. Betting on horse races in Japan totals $93.3 million. The Cunard Line places 20 slot machines aboard its *Queen Mary* cruise ship. The Parliament of Canada passes a Narcotic Control Act, imposing a maximum seven-year sentence for cannabis cultivation, with 14 years for importation or exportation. The CIA renames "Project MK-ULTRA" as "MKDELTA," expanding mind-control experiments to universities, hospitals, state and federal institutions.

January 3: The U.S. severs diplomatic relations with Cuba. On January 4, a memo titled "Policy Decisions Required for Conduct of Strike Operations Against Government of Cuba" circulates within top-secret circles in Washington, D.C., describing CIA activities against Cuba over the past year.

January 4: Lee Oswald rejects Russian citizenship.

January 20: John Kennedy inaugurated as 35th president of the United States. Brother Robert Kennedy assumes office as Attorney General.

February: Richard Bissell briefs CIA agent William King Harvey on "Executive Action-ZR/RIFLE," the CIA plot to kill Castro. Soon thereafter, James O'Connell provides poison pills to John Rosselli, for delivery to a Cuban official close to Castro. FBI agents propose charging Moe Dalitz with bribery, labor racketeering and Mann Act violations, but J. Edgar Hoover vetoes the plan.

February 13: Lee Oswald informs the American embassy in Moscow of his desire to leave Russia and return to the U.S. In Langley, Va., the CIA's Technical Services Division delivers a box of Fidel Castro's favorite cigars — treated with poison — to an unidentified agent.

February 27: The Gallo brothers kidnap several of Joe Profaci's lieutenants in New York, touching off an internecine war that will leave at least nine persons dead, three missing, and 15 wounded by August 1963.

March 14: John Rosselli gives the CIA's poison pills to a Cuban contact, in at meeting at Miami's Fontainebleau Hotel.

March 17: A roundup of professional gamblers in New York implicates student athletes at New Jersey's Seton Hall University.

March 30: Various UN member nations sign the Single Convention on Narcotic Drugs, updating the Paris Convention of 1931 to include various synthetic opioids invented in the intervening 30 years and creating a mechanism for more easily including new ones. The treaty becomes effective on December 13, 1964. Today, 180 nations are parties to the agreement.

Early April: John Rosselli and Sam Giancana deliver more CIA poison tablets to Manuel Atonio de Varona, a Cuban ally of Santo Trafficante Jr. in Miami. They promise de Varona $150,000 if he delivers the pills to Castro's personal secretary, Juan Orta.

April 4: Acting on orders from Attorney General Robert Kennedy, federal agents seize mafioso Carlos Marcello and deport him to Guatemala. Marcello returns to the U.S. in June, flown by pilot David Ferrie, and surrenders for an immigration hearing.

April 11: Juan Orta seeks refuge at the Venezuelan embassy in Havana, remaining there until Cuban officials grant him safe passage to Mexico in October 1964. He surfaces in Miami during February 1965. John Rosselli later says that Orta "got cold feet" about poisoning Fidel Castro; Orta claims that he "lost access" to Fidel before receiving the CIA's poison tablets.

April 15: Cuban exiles supported by CIA pilots land at the Bay of Pigs, on Cuba's southern coast. President Kennedy declines to launch a full-scale U.S. invasion of Cuba, whereupon Castro's military crushes the exile assault by April 22. The official death toll includes 114 invaders and 176 Cuban soldiers, with 1,204 insurgents captured. Published reports claim "hundreds" of executions in Cuba, between April and October 1961. A total of 1,179 face trial for treason on March 29, 1962, with all convicted and sentenced to 30-year prison terms on April 7, 1962. On December 21, 1962, Castro agrees to release 1,113 prisoners in exchange for food and medicine valued at $53 million. The prisoners and some 1,000 relatives leave Cuba on December 24. President Kennedy stages a "welcome back" ceremony at Miami's Orange Bowl on December 29, 1962. Various mobsters later claim that Attorney General Robert Kennedy coerced them into donating portions of Castro's ransom.

April 28: The CIA and U.S. Army launch "Operation Third Chance," devoted to overseas "testing" of LSD on unwitting subjects. By July 1962 the drug is deemed ready for operational use in the field.

April 30: Lee Oswald marries Marina Prusakova, whose uncle works for Russia's Ministry of Internal Affairs. On May 25 Oswald tells the American embassy that Marina wishes to join him in traveling to the U.S.

May 3: CIA Chief of Security Sheffield Edwards informs FBI headquarters that Sam Giancana has been recruited "in connection with the CIA's clandestine efforts against the Castro government," adding that "several of the plans are still working and may eventually pay off." Edwards claims that he "had never been furnished with any details of the methods used by Giancana and Maheu because this was 'dirty business' and he could not afford to know the specific actions." He also claims that Richard Bissell had "told the attorney general that some of the [Bay of Pigs] planning included the use of Giancana and the underworld against Castro."

May 4: A grand jury in Kansas City, Mo., reveals evidence that local police have conspired with mafiosi to permit criminal activities spanning a decade.

May 22: J. Edgar Hoover informs Attorney General Kennedy of the Sheffield Edwards memorandum. After receiving assurances that the CIA-Mafia link has been severed, Kennedy tells aide Courtney Evans, "I hope this will be followed up vigorously."

June 6: A memo from Sheffield Edwards to FBI Assistant Director Allen Belmont names Robert Maheu as the CIA's go-between with Sam Giancana.

June 29: Frank Costello leaves prison in New York.

July: J. Edgar Hoover approves installation of covert microphones at the Desert Inn casino in Las Vegas, but hotel security delays planting of bugs until March 22, 1962.

July 8: U.S. Immigration officials deport San Francisco mafioso Michele Abati to Italy, where he dies on September 5, 1962. James Lanza succeeds Abati has boss of the local crime family.

July 21: Mafioso Ray Patriarca sues the *Journal-Bulletin* for libel in Providence, R.I. When that case fails, he buys a advertisement in the paper on September 10, complaining of his alleged harassment by "a newspaper which often has paraded in its obituary columns the peccadilloes of many former decent Rhode Island citizens."

August 6: Future wrestler and mobster Iliya Pavlov Naydenov born in Bulgaria.

August 11: Chicago police find the corpse of mobster and alleged informer William "Action" Jackson in the trunk of his car. Published reports differ as to whether Jackson was killed for "squealing" or for raping an Outfit-connected burglar's girlfriend. FBI bugs recorded a discussion of Jackson's torture-slaying, spanning three days, but author Gus Russo claims that conversation was staged by gangsters aware of the microphone's presence.

August 31: In the wake of sweeping IRS raids, a grand jury in Newport, Ky., indicts 15 local gamblers, including ex-mayor Robert Siddell. Further indictments in early September name 19 more defendants, including the town's current mayor, police chief, and three city councilmen.

September 13: President Kennedy signs the Interstate Transportation in Aid to Racketeering (ITAR), Interstate Transportation of Wagering Information (ITWI) and The Interstate Transportation of Wagering Paraphernalia (ITWP) Acts, facilitating prosecution of nationwide gambling syndicates.

September 24: Cuban officials announce the dismantling of "Operation AM/BLOOD," a plot to murder Castro involving exiles trained by the CIA at Guantanamo Bay.

September 29: Fidel Castro bans casino gambling in Havana.

October 5: Antonio Veciana — founder of the anti–Castro terrorist group Alpha 66, flees Cuba following exposure of his plot to kill Castro in collaboration with CIA agent Maurice Bishop.

October 8: Unknown assailants torture and kill Albert Agueci, "French Connection" heroin smuggler-turned-prosecution informant, dumping his corpse outside Rochester, N.Y. Police find his remains on November 23, noting that 30 pounds of flesh were slashed from Agueci's body before he was killed. The murder prompts brother Vito Agueci to wrongly finger a friend of Albert's, mafioso Joe Valachi, as a "rat."

October 20: Chicago police find John Kilpatrick, International President of the United Industrial Workers of America, shot to death in his car. In December, FBI agents charge Detroit gangster William Triplett and an uncle, Dana Horton Nash, with the slaying. Triplett confesses, naming Nash as the triggerman, then escapes from Cook County's jail with two other inmates in May 1962. G-men recapture Triplett in New York City, three days after his escape.

October 31: Winter Hill gangsters Buddy McLean and Alex Rocco join corrupt policeman Russell Nicholson to murder rival gang boss Bernard McLaughlin before witnesses on Charlestown's public square. All are released when witnesses refuse to testify, but McLaughlin's brothers subsequently murder Nicholson.

November: Syndicate hitmen murder Albert Testa, a counterfeiter and burglar associated with murdered Outfit member William Jackson.

November 1: CIA Deputy Director Edward Lansdale and presidential advisor/speechwriter Richard Goodwin recommend the creation of "Operation Mongoose," an effort to depose Castro's government via coordinated propaganda, psychological warfare, and sabotage, presumably excluding assassination.

November 9: President Kennedy tells *New York Times* reporter Tad Szulc that he is "under terrific pressure from advisors to okay a Castro murder" but is reluctant to agree. Soon afterward, Kennedy tells Richard Goodwin, "If we get into that kind of thing, we'll all be targets."

November 13: CIA headquarters orders agent-assassin David S. Morales to leave Mexico City for Havana.

November 15: Richard Bissell orders William Harvey to implement the ZR/RIFLE murder plan against Castro. Harvey re-establishes contact with John Rosselli.

November 16: President Kennedy delivers a speech at the University of Washington–Seattle, saying, "We cannot as a free nation, compete with our adversaries in tactics of terror, assassination, false promises, counterfeit mobs and crises."

November 30: President Kennedy orders Secretary of State Dean Rusk to "use our available assets to help Cuba overthrow the Communist regime." The CIA creates a new "Special Group Augmented" (SGA) to handle plots against Cuba.

December 25: Soviet officials inform Marina Oswald that she and husband Lee will be granted exit visas to leave Russia.

December 27: A testimonial banquet hosted by Dr. Vito Guardalabene confirms Frank Balistrieri as boss of the Milwaukee Mafia family. Future gangster and Bandidos MC member "Big" Jim Tinndahn born in Copenhagen, Denmark.

1962 The FDA designates LSD an experimental drug and restricts research. Burma bans opium. The U.S. Army adopts "BZ" for its chemical arsenal. American gamblers wager $500 million on legal pari-mutuel greyhound racing. France banks $50 million from its state lottery, while paying out $128 million. Swedish gamblers bet $77 million on horse races and buy 17,980,000 lottery tickets. Finland's government earns $18 million from soccer betting pools. Legal off-track pari-mutuel betting totals $520 million. British gamblers bet $1.5 billion on horse races, $322 million on greyhound races, $239 million on soccer pools, and $84 million on bingo. Italy's state lottery collects $81 million while paying out $37 million. Polish gamblers spend $40 million on the state lottery, while Norway's collects $18 million. Russian-American pharmacologist Alexander "Sasha" Shulgin records the effects of 3,4-Methylenedioxymethamphetamine (MDMA, or "ecstasy") while employed by Dow Chemical Company.

January: Moe Dalitz and associates found the Nevada Resort Hotels Association to address "matters of mutual interest." Attorney and CIA contract agent Paul Helliwell establishes the Merchants Bank of the Americas in Nassau, Bahamas.

January 5: *Portrait of a Mobster* premieres in U.S. theaters, starring Vic Morrow as Dutch Schultz and Joseph Gallison as Vincent Coll. Ray Danton reprises his 1960 role as Legs Diamond.

January 19: After meeting with Attorney General Kennedy, CIA agent George McManus pens

a memo reading: "Conclusion: Overthrow of Castro is Possible … a solution to the Cuban problem today carried top priority in U.S. Government. No time, money, effort — or manpower is to be spared. Yesterday … the president indicated to [RFK] that the final chapter had not been written — it's got to be done and will be done."

January 26: Lucky Luciano dies from a heart attack in Naples, Italy.

January 29: An internal DOJ memo states: "Our primary interest was in Giancana … apparently detective [Robert Maheu] has some connection with Giancana but he claims was because of CIA assignment in connection with Cuba — CIA has objected, may have to drop."

February: The CIA and U.S. Army commence "Operation Derby Hat," testing LSD on military personnel stationed in Hawaii through April 19, 1963.

February 19: Richard Helms succeeds Richard Bissell as CIA Deputy Director of Plans. Helms authorized William Harvey to hire "Principal Agent QJWIN (drug-smuggler and mercenary Jose Mankel) for the services of ZR/RIFLE."

February 20: Edward Lansdale presents a six-phase schedule for Operation Mongoose, scheduled to culminate in October 1962. A CIA meeting on February 26 allegedly curtails Lansdale's plan to simple intelligence-gathering.

March 13: Future mafioso Joseph "Skinny Joey" Merlino born in South Philadelphia, Pa. U.S. Secretary of Defense Robert McNamara receives a plan for "Operation Northwoods" from the Joint Chiefs of Staff, detailing plans for overthrowing Castro's regime in Cuba. On March 16, JFK rejects the plan, telling JCS Chief Lyman Lemnitzer that "there was virtually no possibility of ever using overt force to take Cuba."

March 14: The CIA's SGA approves guidelines for Operation Mongoose, noting that the U.S. will "make maximum use of indigenous resources" to oust Castro, while concluding that "final success will require decisive U.S. military intervention." Cuban natives would be used to "prepare and justify this intervention, and thereafter to facilitate and support it."

March 16: Edward Lansdale suggests killing Castro during an upcoming meeting with JFK and RFK at author Ernest Hemingway's old home in Cuba.

March 22: J. Edgar Hoover lunches with President Kennedy, who accepts his last phone call from mistress Judith Campbell a few hours later. Future gangster and Bandidos MC member Per Michael "Joe" Ljunggren born in Helsingborg, Sweden.

March 26: Chicago bookmaker Harry Polay disappears prior to his scheduled testimony before the Cook County grand jury's inquiry on syndicate gambling.

April: The Isle of Man legalizes gambling casinos. Richard Helms issues "explicit orders" for William Harvey to contact John Rosselli.

April 8: Genovese Family captain Anthony "Tony Bender" Strollo vanishes from New York City. Informant Joe Valachi later claims that Genovese ordered Strollo's murder from federal prison, for dealing narcotics against direct orders.

April 8–9: William Harvey and James O'Connell meet with John Rosselli and Robert Maheu in New York City, to discuss Castro's assassination.

April 11: Italy's Senate approves creation of a government commission to investigate the Mafia. The Chamber of Deputies stalls approval until December 20. The commission is finally formed in February 1963. Its term expires on April 28, without an actual meeting.

April 14: William Harvey receives a new batch of poison tablets from CIA physician Edward Gunn in Washington, D.C. Harvey delivers the pills to John Rosselli in Miami, on April 21. Rosselli passes them to Tony Varona, reporting back that Varona's hit team will also target Raul Castro and Che Guevara.

Late April: William Harvey procures $5,000 worth of firearms, explosives, detonators, boat radar and radios for Tony Varona's assassins. John Rosselli receives a nominal rank of colonel from the CIA.

May: Chicago police find two corpses beaten and stabbed beyond recognition, left in a car's trunk. The double-slaying brings Chicago's total of gangland slayings to 25 since January 1961.

May 7: Attorney General Kennedy meets with CIA Director of Plans Richard Helms, to receive a briefing on plots against Castro. Later the same day, Kennedy meets CIA general counsel Lawrence Houston, who later writes: "Mr. Kennedy stated that upon learning CIA had not cleared its action in hiring Maheu and Giancana with the DOJ he issued orders that the CIA should never again take such steps with first checking with the DOJ."

May 9: Attorney General Kennedy informs J. Edgar Hoover that the CIA has hired gangsters to kill Fidel Castro. Hoover summarizes their conversation in a memo dated May 10.

May 14: Sheffield Edwards sends Attorney General Kennedy a memo stating that CIA-Mafia plots have been terminated. Edwards then writes an internal memo confirming severance of contact with John Rosselli — which, according to William Harvey, "was not true, and Col. Edwards knew it was not true."

May 18: A federal grand jury in Nashville, Tenn., indicts Jimmy Hoffa for receiving $1,000,000 in illegal payments through the Test Fleet Corporation, a trucking company established in his wife's name.

May 22: J. Edgar Hoover sends a memo to RFK, confirming that the CIA has used Sam Giancana in "clandestine efforts" against Castro.

June 6: Mafioso Joe Profaci dies from cancer at Southside Hospital in Bay Shore, Long Island, N.Y. Brother-in-law Joseph Magliocco succeeds Profaci, while the Gallo rebellion against Profaci's family continues.

June 13: U.S. Immigration officials deport Los Angeles mafioso Simone Scozzari. Nicolo Licata succeeds Scozzari as boss of the local crime family. Lee and Marina Oswald arrive in Hoboken, N.J., flying on to Fort Worth, Tex., on June 14.

June 21: John Rosselli informs William Harvey that Tony Varona has landed assassins in Cuba.

June 22: Prisoner Joseph Valachi fatally bludgeons fellow inmate John Saupp at the federal prison in Atlanta, Ga., after mistaking Saupp for a hitman hired by Vito Genovese to kill Valachi. The incident prompts Valachi to become a government witness against the Mafia.

June 26: FBI agents interview Lee Oswald for the first time, in Fort Worth. A second interview follows on August 16.

Summer: John Rosselli fails in two attempts to reach Cuba, losing his boat on the second approach. In July, Rosselli complains to CIA colleagues of ongoing harassment by the DOJ and FBI.

July 1: A car bomb kills William "Billy" Naples, younger brother of gambling kingpin Sandy Naples, at his home in Youngstown, Ohio.

July 3: FBI agents seize more than $2.6 million in cash, plus $13,000 in securities and three guns from the Jersey City garage of imprisoned numbers racketeer Joseph "Newsboy" Moriarty. While refusing to discuss the loot, Moriarty later files a tax return listing it as income derived from various sources. An FBI bug at the Desert Inn casino in Las Vegas catches Moe Dalitz and Sam Tucker discussing incumbent gubernatorial candidate Grant Sawyer. Dalitz says, "We can't let him lose."

July 6: Italy's Antimafia Commission holds its first actual meeting. Thirteen years elapse before completion of its 40-volume report in 1976.

July 7: Future Mexican Mafia member and FBI informer Rene "Boxer" Enriquez born in South Central Los Angeles, Calif.

July 22: Future gangster and presidential crony Roman Igorevich Tsepov born in Kolpino, Leningrad Oblast, USSR.

August: IBT president Jimmy Hoffa meets with Louisiana teamster Ed Partin in Washington,

D.C., to plot the murder of U.S. Attorney General Robert Kennedy.

August 10: Dean Rusk convenes a meeting on Castro, allegedly rejecting CIA plans for widespread sabotage in Cuba. Robert McNamara declares that "the only way to take care of Castro is to kill him. I really mean it." Participants discuss "liquidation" of Castro and other Cuban leaders, but apparently reach no conclusions.

August 14: William Harvey reports on the August 10 meeting to Richard Helms, writing: "The question of assassination, particularly of Castro, was brought up by Secretary McNamara. It was the obvious consensus at that meeting, that this is not a subject which has been made a matter of official record."

August 16: Dandy Phil Kastel commits suicide in New Orleans, after a long bout of poor health.

August 20: SGA chairman Maxwell Taylor informs JFK that the CIA "sees no likelihood that the Castro government can be overthrown without direct U.S. military intervention."

September: Lee and Marina Oswald meet perennial FBI surveillance target George de Mohrenschildt, a Russian immigrant living in Dallas, Tex. John Rosselli tells William Harvey that his "asset" in Cuba still has the CIA's poison tablets. Harvey and Rosselli meet repeatedly over the next four months, achieving nothing. Mafioso Carlos Marcello discusses plans to kill JFK, while "setting up some nut to take the fall for the job, just like they do in Sicily." In Florida, mafioso Santo Trafficante Jr. tells Cuban-exile financier José Alemán that JFK "is going to be hit."

September: Future Serbian gangster and warlord Jusuf "Juka" Prazina born in Sarajevo, Yugoslavia.

September 8: Joe Valachi informs FBI agents that American mafiosi call their organization *La Cosa Nostra*.

September 25: After predicting a 15-round match, boxing champion Floyd Patterson loses his title to Charles "Sonny" Liston in Chicago, with a first-round knockout making this third-fastest knockout in boxing history. Widespread speculation on a "fix" for the benefit of gamblers still persists.

October 4: RFK informs the SGA that JFK desires "massive activity" against Castro under Operation Mongoose.

October 27: A private jet owned by Enrico Mattei, president of Italy's national oil company Ente Nazionale Idrocarburi, crashes in Lombardy while en route from Sicily to Milan, killing Mattei, his pilot, and U.S. journalist William McHale. Giulio Andreotti, Italy's Minister of Defense, orders evidence destroyed at the crash site, including flight instruments dissolved in acid.

Several underworld informers later claim the Mafia accepted a murder contract on Mattei from "some foreigners." Authorities exhume Mattei and his pilot on October 25, 1995, reporting discovery of explosive shrapnel in both skeletons.

October 28: With the Cuban missile crisis just finished, FBI agents report that an informant "believes he could arrange to have Fidel Castro assassinated. Underworld figures still have channels inside Cuba through which the assassination of Castro could be successfully arranged." "He said that in the event the United States Government is interested in having the attempt made, he would raise the necessary money and would want nothing from the Government except the assurance that such an undertaking would in no way adversely affect the national security. He expressed confidence in his ability to accomplish this mission without any additional contact with Governmental representatives and with a minimum of contacts with private individuals." FBI headquarters informs RFK, adding: "The informant was told that his offer is outside our jurisdiction, which he acknowledged. No commitments were made to him. At this time, we do not plan to further pursue the matter. Our relationship with him has been most carefully guarded and we would feel obligated to handle any recontact of him concerning the matter if such is desired."

October 30: JFK orders an immediate halt to Operation Mongoose, but William Harvey orders covert teams into Cuba on his own authority, to support any future U.S. military intervention.

November: Paul Helliwell's Merchants Bank of the America's becomes Mercantile Bank and Trust, still based in Nassau, Bahamas.

November 1: Future drug lord and serial killer Adolfo de Jesus Constanzo born in Miami, Fla.

November 8: One of Harvey's covert teams demolishes a Cuban industrial facility.

November 23: Youngstown, Ohio's 82nd gangland bombing in a decade kills syndicate gambling boss Charles "Cadillac Charley" Cavallaro and his 11-year-old son.

December 26: Sicily's "First Mafia War" begins with the assassination of Calcedonio Di Pisa in Palermo. Police blame brothers Angelo and Salvatore La Barbera, while civilian researchers name Michele Cavataio as the killer.

1963 January 1: The CIA creates a new "Special Group" to pursue anti–Castro activities, chaired by McGeorge Bundy. Futile efforts to kill Fidel Castro continue, allegedly without Mafia assistance.

January 7: Unknown gunmen kidnap jukebox operator Anthony Biernat from the railroad station in Kenosha, Wis. Authorities retrieve his body on January 28, from a lime-filled grave on an abandoned Air Force base 20 miles from Kenosha. On January 23, Governor John Reynolds announces that organized crime has a strong statewide network, centered in Milwaukee, Kenosha and Fond du Lac. Prosecutors in all three cities promptly deny it.

January 17: Mafia boss Salvatore La Barbera disappears in Sicily. Police suspect Tommaso Buscetta of the murder, acting on behalf of two rival mobsters and cousins, both named Salvatore Greco.

January 23: Salvatore "Sally the Sheik" Mussachio, acting boss of the Profaci crime family, dies of natural causes in New York.

January 28: Lee Oswald orders a .38-caliber revolver by mail.

January 31: Future drug lord Zhenli Ye Gon born in Shanghai, China.

February 2: CIA headquarters establishes a new Domestic Operations Division under Tracy Barnes, chief of the agency's psychological and paramilitary staff. Future Watergate burglar E. Howard Hunt becomes Barnes's chief lieutenant.

February 12: A car-bomb destroys the home of mafioso Salvatore "Little Bird" Greco in Ciaculli, Sicily.

February 13: Although demoted and reassigned from Operation Mongoose to the CIA's station in Rome, William Harvey resumed contact with John Rosselli in Miami and Los Angeles. While Mafia assassination plots against Castro are placed "on hold," a $150,000 bounty for Castro's death remains in place.

February 15: Future gangster and war criminal Ramiz Delali born in Priboj, Serbia.

March: Governor John King authorizes a state lottery in New Hampshire, formally established in April.

March 12: Lee Oswald orders a rifle by mail from Chicago, using the name "Alek James Hidell." Both the rifle and revolver ship out on March 20. Oswald collects them in Dallas on March 25.

March 18: Cuban exile terrorists, organized as "Alpha 66" with CIA support, initiate attacks on Cuba and Russian ships in Havana's harbor. JFK publicly condemns the raids on March 21.

March 26: A new exile terrorist group, "Lambda 66," begins raids against Cuba. Russia denounces the attacks as covert CIA activity. JFK convenes a meeting to discuss the issue on March 29, telling advisors: "The question is whether we should take direct action in the U.S. to cut off their supplies or whether we should try to advise them to attack Cuba but not the Russians, with the result that the raids would draw less press attention and arouse less acrimony in Moscow. If we decide that such raids should be conducted,

we should plan them ourselves and see that they are carried out under our control rather than as now occurs."

April 3: McGeorge Bundy terminates official support for exile raids against Cuba. Soon afterward, William Harvey speaks with John Rosselli, whereupon the Mafia begins arming terrorist Cuban exiles.

April 10: Lee Oswald allegedly fires a shot at right-wing extremist leader Edwin Walker in Dallas, hiding his rifle near Walker's home, then retrieving it on April 14.

April 13–21: John Rosselli and William Harvey occupy adjoining rooms at Miami's Fontainebleau Hotel. Phone records document repeated calls from both rooms to Las Vegas and Los Angeles.

April 18: A flier circulates among Cuban exiles in Miami, reading: "Only through one development will you Cuban patriots ever live again in your homeland as freemen, responsible as must be the most capable for the guidelines and welfare of the Cuban people. This blessing would come to pass if an inspired Act of God should place in the White House within weeks a Texan known to be a friend of all Latin Americans."

April 19: A Greco Family hit team kills two fishmongers affiliates with the rival La Barbera Family and wounds two others in Palermo, Sicily. The La Barberas retaliate with a car-bomb that kills the Mafia boss of Cinisi, a Greco ally.

April 24: Lee Oswald leaves Dallas for New Orleans, traveling by bus. On April 25 he moves in with an aunt.

April 26: A car bomb kills mafioso Cesare Manzella in Cinisi, Sicily. Gaetano Badalamenti succeeds him as head of the local Mafia family.

May 6: Unknown assassins kill Irving Vine at a hotel on Chicago's South Side, soon after he agrees to testify against Murray Humphreys in IRS proceedings. Harvard University's board of directors fires LSD guru Timothy Leary on grounds that he "has failed to keep his classroom appointments and has absented himself from Cambridge without permission."

May 19: A front-page story in the *Miami News* that Chicago mobsters are behind recent efforts to form a Cuban government-in-exile.

May 25: Gunmen wound mafioso Angelo La Barbera in Milan. Tommaso Buscetta admits accepting a contract on La Barbera's life, but says unknown gunmen beat him to his intended target.

May 26: From New Orleans, Lee Oswald requests a charter for a local chapter of the left-wing Fair Play for Cuba Committee (FPCC). On May 29 he orders 1,000 FPCC handbills.

May 31: Future gangster Curtis "Cocky" Warren born in Liverpool, England.

June 6: Profaci gunmen kill two Gallo gang members, Emile Colontuono and Alfred Mondello, in separate Manhattan shootings.

June 19: JFK approves a new sabotage campaign against Cuba, designed to nourish a spirit of resistance and disaffection which could lead to significant defections and other by-products of unrest." Around the same time, John Rosselli visits William Harvey in Washington, D.C. Afterward, Harvey tells FBI contacts that he has terminated Mafia participation in anti–Castro efforts.

June 27: Dallas mobster Jack Ruby phones Meyer Lansky front-man Lewis McWillie at McWillie's home in Las Vegas, Nev. McWillie later claims that this and six subsequent calls involve labor problems at Ruby's Texas strip club.

June 30: A Mafia car bomb intended for Salvatore "Little Bird" Greco, of the Sicilian Mafia Commission, detonates in Ciaculli, missing its target but killing seven military and police officers as they attempt to defuse it. The massacre prompts post-war Italy's first serious campaign against the Mafia, thus ending the "First Mafia War." The Commission subsequently meets and votes to dissolve itself, with its members scattering abroad.

July: Gallo loyalists ambush and wound Profaci Family associate Hugh "Apples" MacIntosh in New York City.

July 6: Italy's Antimafia Commission holds its first meeting. Thirteen years elapse before publication of its first report, in 1976.

July 9: U.S. Customs agents arrest armed members of a Cuban exile group in Florida.

July 17: Joe Bonanno flies from New York to Arizona, then tours California with his wife under an assumed name, finally surfacing in Canada with an application for permanent residence during May 1964. Meanwhile, the Mafia's commission meets on August 1, to try Bonanno in absentia for plotting to kill the heads of three other New York families. Accomplice Joe Magliocco admits his complicity and is deposed as acting boss of the former Genovese family.

July 22: Ex-champion Floyd Patterson faces Sonny Liston for a rematch in Las Vegas. Liston wins by another controversial first-round knockout, four seconds slower than their last bout in September 1962.

July 23: Future mafioso Daniele Emanuello born in Gela, Sicily. IBT president Jimmy Hoffa asks mob lawyer Frank Ragano to intercede with Carlos Marcello and Santo Trafficante Jr., urging them to rush the JFK assassination.

July 31: FBI agents raid a Cuban exile training camp on Lake Pontchartrain, La., seizing more than a ton of dynamite, 20 bomb casings, napalm

material, and other explosives on property owned by William McLaney — brother of syndicate gambler Mike McLaney, whose Nacional Casino in Havana was closed by Castro in 1959.

August 5: Lee Oswald paradoxically offers to aid Cuban exile Carlos Bringuier in campaigns against Castro. On August 6 he gives Bringuier a Marine Corps training manual. The two men scuffle on August 9, when Bringuier sees Oswald distributing FPCC fliers in New Orleans. Jailed overnight, Oswald requests and receives a visit from FBI Agent John Quigley. Oswald pleads guilty to disturbing the peace on August 12 and pays a $10 fine.

August 16: The *Chicago Sun-Times* reports Sam Giancana's dealings with the CIA from 1959 to 1961. A follow-up story on August 20 quotes Giancana as asking an FBI agent, "Why don't you fellows leave me alone? I'm one of you."

September 2: Jack Ruby phones Lewis McWillie twice from Dallas, first at home, then at the Thunderbird casino.

September 4: Jack Ruby calls Lewis McWillie again, at the Thunderbird.

September 10: Mafioso Bernado "The Tractor" Provenzano leads an attack on allies of rival Michele "Our Father" Navarra. Police issue a warrant for Provenzano's arrest on murder charges, driving him underground as a fugitive.

September 19: Jack Ruby places another call to McWillie at the Thunderbird.

September 20: Lewis McWillie receives a sixth phone call from Jack Ruby.

September 22: Jack Ruby phones Lewis McWillie once more at the Thunderbird casino.

September 24: Philip "Big Phil" Amari, former Mafia boss Elizabeth, N.J., dies of natural causes in Arcadia, Calif.

September 25: The McClellan Committee opens hearings on "Organized Crime and Illicit Traffic in Narcotics," continuing until August 5, 1964. Mafia defector Joe Valachi appears as the committee's star witness, testifying for the first time on September 27–28.

September 26–October 2: Lee Oswald visits Mexico City, allegedly to speak with officials at the Cuban and Russian embassies. CIA surveillance photos purportedly taken of Oswald outside the Russian embassy depict a man bearing no resemblance to Oswald. Oswald leaves Mexico City by bus on October 2, arriving in Dallas the following day.

September 30: Future mafioso John Edward Alite born in the Bronx, N.Y.

October 7: In Dallas, Jack Ruby receives a 17-minute collect call from Robert "Barney" Baker, described by RFK as Jimmy Hoffa's "traveling ambassador of violence."

October 15: Lee Oswald obtains a job at the Texas School Book Depository in Dallas, beginning work on October 16. In Washington, D.C., on October 15, Col. Walter Stone, superintendent of the Rhode Island State Police, testifies that Ray Patriarca runs a widespread "strong-arm" operation. On October 17, Patriarca issues a press release stating: "I again categorically deny all of his testimony which charges me with criminal involvement or criminal associations.... If I am responsible for all the crime in Rhode Island, why hasn't Colonel Stone presented some evidence against me to a Rhode Island grand jury or, if I have violated federal law, evidence to a federal grand jury?"

October 25: Heavyweight boxing champion Charles "Sonny" Liston angrily confronts Moe Dalitz at the Beverly Rodeo Hotel in Hollywood, Calif. As Liston draws back a fist, Dalitz warns, "If you hit me, nigger, you'd better kill me. Because if you don't, I'll make one phone call and you'll be dead in 24 hours." Liston flees the hotel — and the state, returning to his home in Las Vegas.

October 26: Jack Ruby places a 12-minute phone call to syndicate financier Irwin Weiner in Chicago.

October 29: Anti-Castro activist Rolando Cubela meets CIA agents in Paris, France, requesting a "high-powered, silenced rifle with an effective range of hundreds of thousands of yards" for use in killing Fidel Castro. The agents suggest poison, instead. FBI agent James Hosty attempts to reach Lee Oswald through Oswald's estranged wife. Subsequent visits on November 1 and 5 fail to establish contact. On November 12, Oswald visits the FBI office in Dallas, leaving a note that warns Hosty to stay away from Oswald's family.

October 30: Jack Ruby telephones mafioso Nofio Pecora Sr. in New Orleans. FBI records show that Carlos Marcello called Pecora at the same number on June 24, 1963.

November 8: Jack Ruby places a four-minute phone call from Dallas to IBT official Murray "Dusty" Miller at Miami's Eden Roc Hotel. Later the same day, Ruby phones Barney Baker in Chicago, talking for 14 minutes.

November 9: Police informant William Somersett reports a conversation with underworld associate Joseph Milteer in Miami, including Milteer's prediction that JFK will be shot by a sniper from a tall building, with a "patsy" blamed for the slaying. Secret Service agents cancel JFK's planned motorcade in Miami.

November 10: Future gangster, author and businessman Paul John Ferris born in Glasgow, Scotland.

November 16–18: John Rosselli travels from Los Angeles to Phoenix and Las Vegas. FBI surveillance prompts cancellation of a scheduled flight to Washington, D.C.

November 16–17: Witnesses see Jack Ruby with Lewis McWillie at the Thunderbird casino in Las Vegas. Ruby also cashes a check at Moe Dalitz's Stardust casino, then returns to Dallas on November 19, with sufficient cash to pay his delinquent taxes. McWillie later testifies that he has only a "passing acquaintance" with Ruby.

November 19: The *Dallas Times Herald* publishes a map of JFK's motorcade route for a visit on November 22.

November 20: A CIA officer telephones Rolando Cubela, granting his request for a high-powered rifle, scheduled for delivery on November 22.

November 22: Rifle shots fatally wound JFK in Dallas's Dealey Plaza, at 12:30 P.M. A gunman armed with a .38-caliber revolver kills Officer J.D. Tippit at 1:16 P.M. Police arrest Lee Oswald as a suspect in Tippit's murder at 1:50 P.M., in a local theater. Authorities arraign Oswald for Tippit's slaying at 7:10 P.M., then charge him with JFK's assassination at 11:26 P.M.

November 23: In the midst of marathon interrogations, authorities arraign Lee Oswald for JFK's murder at 1:30 A.M.

November 24: Jack Ruby infiltrates Dallas police headquarters, shooting Lee Oswald at 11:21 A.M., during Oswald's transfer to the county jail for safekeeping. Oswald dies at 1:07 P.M.

November 28: Irwin Weiner refuses to speak with FBI agents concerning his recent contacts with Jack Ruby.

December: The CIA implements techniques from "Operation MKDELTA" as operational tactics in the field, designed to "discredit, implant suggestions, [exercise] mental control, [and] elicit information" from selected targets.

December 28: Joe Magliocco dies from a heart attack at Good Samaritan Hospital in West Islip, N.Y.

1964 Irish inmates at California's San Quentin prison organize the Aryan Brotherhood to counter black-on-white violence, soon expanding into organized criminal activity. Sicily's "first Mafia war" ends. Japanese gangster Yoshio Kodama founds the Kantō-kai Yakuza clan in Honshu's Kantō region. U.S. military "advisors" reportedly experiment with aerial dispersion of BZ gas in Vietnam. The CIA renames "Operation MK DELTA" as "MKSEARCH."

January 19: A car bomb wounds Detroit mafioso Santo Perrone, forcing amputation of his right leg.

January 23: The Lucayan Beach Hotel-Casino,

controlled by Meyer Lansky, opens on Grand Bahama Island.

February 2: Mafioso Nicholas Delmore dies of natural causes in Elizabeth, N.J. Nephew Samuel "Sam the Plumber" DeCavalcante succeeds him as boss of the local crime family.

February 14: Future mafioso John Angelo Gotti III, son of Gambino Family boss John J. Gotti, born in Queens, N.Y.

February 25: Boxing champion Sonny Liston meets rival Cassius Clay (later Muhammad Ali) in Miami Beach, Fla., for his first match since the October 1963 confrontation with Moe Dalitz. Clay defeats him with a technical knockout in the 15th round.

March 10: New Hampshire voters approve the first U.S. state lottery since 1895. Sale of tickets begins on March 12.

March 15: Irish gangster George Mclaughlin murders rival William Sheridan in Roxbury, Mass.

March 18: Mafioso John Montana dies from a heart attack in Buffalo, N.Y.

March 22: In a Palm Sunday sermon, Cardinal Ernesto Ruffini of Palermo issues a pastoral epistle entitled "The True Face of Sicily," accusing the media of exaggerating Mafia crimes and influence.

April 2: Future Albanian drug trafficker Princ Dobroshi born in Peć, Kosovo.

April 5: Selection of Joseph Colombo Sr. as boss of the old Profaci Mafia family formally ends New York's Gallo-Profaci gang war.

May: Police in Corleone, Sicily, capture fugitive mafioso Luciano Leggio at the home of ex-fiancée Placido Rizzotto, whom he was once wrongly accused of murdering.

June 11: Unknown gunmen kill retired IBT official Floyd Hayes in Kansas City, Mo., following his testimony in a perjury case involving union payoffs.

July 4: The Outlaws MC absorbs a smaller club, the Cult MC of Voorheesville, N.Y., in a patch-over ceremony.

July 6: Chicago mobster Rocco Fischetti dies from a heart attack while visiting relatives in Massapequa, N.Y.

July 30: Canadian authorities deport Joe Bonanno to Chicago.

August 31: Future drug lord Ramon Arellano Félix born in Culiacán, Sinaloa, Mexico.

September 19: Sam DeCavalcante meets Joe Bonanno to mediate a dispute with the Mafia's commission, involving Bonanno's plot to kill two rival family bosses. Upon his refusal to appear, the commission expels Bonanno.

October: Paul Helliwell's Mercantile Bank and Trust becomes Castle Bank and Trust. Co-owner Burton Kanter, of Chicago, is a registered agent of Moe Dalitz's La Costa Land Company. Morris

Kleinman contributes $600,000 in startup funds. Other depositors include Dalitz, *Playboy* publisher Hugh Hefner, *Penthouse* rival Bob Guccione, and ex–Vice President Richard Nixon, favored with account No. 1.

October 21: Apparent kidnappers snatch Joe Bonanno from the street outside his apartment building on Park Avenue, Manhattan, on the morning of his scheduled appearance before a federal grand jury. Brother-in-law Frank LaBruzzo assumes command of Bonanno's crime family. Bonanno remains missing until 1966.

November 10: NYPD arrests numerous street gang members after reports of an impending "rumble" at 3rd Street and Avenue D.

1965 Hispanic inmates "Lil John de Valley," Haero Morgan, Freddy Gonzales, "Sammy de New Mexico," and "Chalo de Bakersfield" found the La Familia gang (later Nuestra Familia) at California's Soledad prison. Japan's Sumiyoshi-kai Yakuza family disbands, reorganized in 1969 as a labor union. Police crackdowns on the Tōsei-kai gang prompt leader Hisayuki Machii to form a new syndicate, the Tōa Yūai Jigyō Kumiai ("East Asia Friendship Enterprise Association"). The FDA bans Benzedrine inhalers and limits amphetamine to prescription use.

January: The Kantō-kai Yakuza family disbands after 15 months of operations.

January 15: Federal investigators announce the impending disintegration of the Bonanno Mafia family. On the same day, federal prosecutors in New York grant immunity to mafioso Vincent John Rao, seeking to compel testimony regarding the Lucchese crime family. Based upon his statements, a grand jury indicts Rao for perjury on March 18.

January 22: Future wrestling champion and gangster Vasil Iliev born in Kyustendil, Bulgaria.

February: Owsley "Bear" Stanley synthesizes crystalline LSD in Los Angeles. Distribution begins in March.

March 8: LBJ creates the President's Commission on Law Enforcement and Administration of Justice. On the same day, 3,500 U.S. Marines land at China Beach, South Vietnam, officially launching American entry into the ground war, with its resultant corruption and rapid expansion of heroin smuggling to North America.

March 26: Future Gambino Family *caporegime* Francesco Paolo Augusto Calì born in New York City.

April 22: Based on his recent extortion conviction in Colorado, Nevada's Gaming Control Board adds Desert Inn/Stardust partner Ruby Kolod to its "Black Book" of excluded persons.

April 24: Owney Madden dies in Hot Springs, Ark.

April 26: Detroit mafioso "Scarface" Joe Bommarito dies of natural causes in North Miami, Fla.

May: Italy's Parliament passes Law 575, drafted in September 1963, titled "Dispositions against the Mafia." This represents the first time the term "Mafia" has appeared in legislation.

June 1: Sam Giancana refuses to testify before a federal grand jury in Chicago, despite a grant of immunity. Jailed for contempt until May 31, 1966, he then flees to Mexico, remaining in exile until Mexican authorities expel him on July 19, 1974.

July 15: Congress passes Drug Abuse Control Amendments to the Food, Drug, and Cosmetic Act of 1938, imposing strict federal control over amphetamines, barbiturates, LSD, and any other drug described as having "a potential for abuse because of its depressant or stimulant effect on the central nervous system or its hallucinogenic effect."

July 30: La Familia members Robert Joseph Gonzales, Bobby Joe Barkley, Daniel Alacron and David Alacron murder Jess Ontiveros during a robbery in Oxnard, Calif. Jurors convict Gonzales on November 11 and recommend execution on November 28. Gonzales receives his death sentence on January 11, 1966, and enters San Quentin on January 18.

September 11: Gunmen execute syndicate gambler Manny Skar in Chicago, shortly before his scheduled delivery of evidence to federal investigators.

October 20: Gangster Edward "Punchy" McLaughlin shot and killed at a bus station in West Roxbury, Mass., while en route to attend his brother's murder trial.

October 31: Cornelius and Steve Hughes murder rival mobster James "Buddy" McLean outside a bar in Somerville, Mass.

November 23: Hours after pulling a gun on federal agents and eluding arrest, Murray Humphreys dies from a heart attack in Chicago.

December: A new Bureau of Drug Abuse Control is created within the U.S. Department of Health, Education, and Welfare.

December 7: Future wrestler and Satan's Choice MC member Ion (John) William Croitoru born in Hamilton, Ontario, Canada.

December 8: Police find bookmaker Robert Wrolstad and his wife Susanne murdered in their Burbank, Calif., home, each shot once in the left eye.

December 11: Future Mexican Mafia member Raul Leon born.

December 24: In London, members of the rival Richardson Gang and "The Firm" run by brothers Reginald and Ronald Kray brawl at a Christmas party, after Richardson mobster George Cornell calls Ronnie Kray a "fat poof" (homosexual).

1966 Timothy Leary founds the League of Spiritual Development with LSD as its "sacrament." Don Chambers founds the Bandidos MC in Texas, with the motto "We are the people our parents warned us about." Other bikers found the Sons of Silence MC in Niwot, Colo.

January 6: Police find Kansas City mobster Salvatore Palma, recently indicted for interstate transportation of stolen property, shot to death in Mount Olivet Cemetery, Raytown, Mo.

January 26: Future drug lord Luis Fernando Arellano Félix born in Mexico.

January 28: Salvatore Bonanno escapes unharmed from an ambush by multiple gunmen on Troutman Street, in Brooklyn.

February: U.S. federal authorities transfer the Bureau of Drug Abuse Control to the FDA.

March: Violence erupts between rival Irish gangs led by Mickey Spillane and James Coonan, in Manhattan's Hell's Kitchen district.

March 7: Kray gangster Richard Hart suffers gunshot wounds in a fight with Richardson Gang members at Mr Smith's Club in Rushey Green, south London.

March 9: Mobster Ronald Kray fatally shoots rival George Cornell in London's Blind Beggar's Pub.

March 11: *Time* magazine runs an article on LSD, titles "An Epidemic of 'Acid Heads.'"

March 25: *Life* magazine publishes the cover story "LSD: The Exploding Threat of the Mind Drug That Got Out of Control."

April: Sandoz Pharmaceutical Company recalls LSD it has previously distributed and withdraws its sponsorship of further experimentation.

April 1: Mobster Jackie Coonan murders a bartender in Queens, N.Y., resulting in subsequent conviction and imprisonment at Sing Sing.

April 4: Mobster Eddie Sullivan mistakes two patrons at an East Side bar for hitmen hired by rival Mickey Spillane, transporting them to a vacant lot in Queens where both are shot. One survives his wounds to testify, resulting in a life sentence for Sullivan and a sentence of 5–10 years for an accomplice.

April 12: Federal prosecutors in New York City charge Colombo Family *caporegime* John "Sonny" Franzese with plotting a recent series of bank robberies.

April 26: Future Bosnian gangster Ismet "Ćelo" Bajramović born in Sarajevo.

May 17: Joseph Bonanno surfaces in New York City and surrenders in federal court after 19 months in hiding. Authorities arraign him on a one-count indictment charging obstruction of justice.

May 23: Chicago labor racketeer Benjamin Stein begins an 18-month prison term.

June 12–14: Members of the Young Lords gang join in Chicago's Division Street riots, sparked by a police shooting at the city's downtown Puerto Rican Day Parade.

July 15: Nevada Governor Grant Sawyer orders an investigation of alleged casino-skimming by mobsters. Moe Dalitz and other prominent gamblers deny any wrongdoing, a conclusion echoed by Governor Sawyer.

July 22: Future gangster, rapist, and football team owner Georgi Andreev Iliev born in Kyustendil, Bulgaria.

July 30: British police arrest London gangster Charlie Richardson on charges of torturing various rivals. Upon conviction, he receives an 18-year prison term for fraud, extortion, assault and grievously bodily harm. Brother Eddie Richardson and other members of the gang receive shorter sentences, effectively crushing the gang.

August: Lung cancer claims the life of New York mafioso Frank LaBruzzo.

August 3: Controversial comedian Lenny Bruce dies from an accidental morphine overdose in Hollywood, Calif.

July 13: William "Willie" Marfeo, who has angered Raymond Patriarca by running an unauthorized craps game in Boston, suffers fatal gunshot wounds in a phone booth on Federal Hill.

August 22: Two Hispanic labor unions, the Agricultural Workers Organizing Committee and the National Farm Workers Association, merge to create the United Farm Workers of America led by César Chávez. The group continues a strike against California grape growers, launched at Delano in September 1965. On September 18 the Perelli-Minetti ranch signs a "sweetheart" contract with the IBT, sparking five years of violent Teamster attacks on the UFW.

August 27: Wilbur Clark dies from a heart attack in Las Vegas, Nev.

September 22: Police raid a Mafia gathering at the La Stella Restaurant in Queens, N.Y. Those arrested at the "Little Apalachin" gathering include Carlo Gambino, Joe Colombo Sr., Joey Gallo, Thomas Eboli, Mike Miranda, Aniello Dellacroce, Dominic Alongi, and Anthony Cirillo from New York; Carlos Marcello, Joe Marcello, Anthony Carolla and Frank Gagliano from New Orleans, and Santo Trafficante Jr. from Florida.

October 1: Genovese Family *caporegime* Michael "Trigger Mike" Coppola dies from natural causes at Massachusetts General Hospital in Boston.

October 3: Prosecutors in New York City charged mafioso John Franzese with killing a hit-man who testified against Vito Genovese in a 1946 murder trial.

October 6: California lawmakers ban LSD statewide.

October 13: A federal grand jury in Los Angeles indicts Moe Dalitz and accountant Eli Boyer for conspiring to evade taxes in 1959. Dalitz surrenders on October 14 and posts $1,000 bond. Boyer pleads guilty and exonerates Dalitz of any wrongdoing on February 7, 1968, paying a $1,000 fine. Judge Roger Foley dismisses the charge against Dalitz in March 1968.

October 15: Future gangster Maya Dolas born in Mumbai, India.

November 8: Congress passes the Narcotic Addict Rehabilitation Act, permitting rehabilitative treatment as an alternative to imprisonment.

November 27: Howard Hughes arrives in Las Vegas, occupying the Desert Inn's top two floors with his entourage.

December 12: London gangsters Reginald and Ronald Kray help Frank "The Mad Axeman" Mitchell escape from England's Dartmoor Prison, then kill him and conceal the corpse, which has never been found.

1967 California's Department of Corrections declares that the Mexican Mafia controls the yard at San Quentin prison, with active chapters at Soledad and Folsom. The FBI's computerized National Crime Information Center becomes operational. New York becomes the second U.S. state to sponsor an official lottery. Outlaw bikers found the Devils Disciples MC in Fontana, Calif., and the Grim Reapers MC in Calgary, Alberta, Canada. Masaru Takumi, second-in-command of the Yamaguchi-gumi Yakuza clan, founds the Takumi-gumi gang in the Kansai region of Honshū, Japan. The CIA and U.S. Army launch new collaborative drug experiments under the code name "OFTEN/MK CHICKWIT."

January 2: Paul Laxalt inaugurated as governor of Nevada.

January 10: A car bomb kills transplanted Chicago Outfit associate Gerald Covelli at his home in Encino, Calif.

January 13: Future international arms dealer and "merchant of death" Viktor Anatolyevich Bout born near Dushanbe, Tajik SSR (now Tajikistan).

January 25: Citing excessive publicity, Judge Jacob Mishler declares a mistrial in the federal bank robbery case of mafioso John Franzese and four codefendants, ordering transfer of the case from Brooklyn to Albany, N.Y. Albany jurors convict all five on March 2. On April 14, 1967, Franzese receives an indeterminate prison term with a 50-year maximum, plus a $20,000 fine.

February: Outlaw bikers found the Warlocks MC in Philadelphia, Pa. During the same month, Tom "Grub" Freeland forms a chapter in Orlando, Fla.

February 28: The IBT executive board names Frank Fitzsimmons "acting president" while Jimmy Hoffa serves his federal prison term.

March: Information supplied by imprisoned extortionist Harold Konigsberg leads federal agents to a Mafia burial ground in New Jersey. IBT "ambassador of violence" Frank Chavez travels from Puerto Rico to the U.S., vowing to kill Robert Kennedy if Jimmy Hoffa is imprisoned.

March 1: To avoid impending eviction, Howard Hughes leases the Desert Inn hotel-casino from Moe Dalitz and his partners, leaving Dalitz in charge of the casino.

March 4: Future Australian mafioso Alphonse John Gangitano, AKA "The Black Prince of Lygon Street," born.

March 16: Police find Chicago businessman Alan Rosenburg beaten to death, allegedly for failure to repay a debt owed to mobster Felix Alderisio.

March 22: Howard Hughes leases the Desert Inn hotel-casino from Moe Dalitz and his partners, while leaving Dalitz in charge of the casino. Mafioso John Rosselli receives a $50,000 "finder's fee" from the transaction.

March 23: Federal jurors in Illinois convict Milwaukee mafioso Frank Balistrieri on two counts of income tax evasion.

March 31: Nevada's Gaming Control Board unanimously grants Howard Hughes a license to operate the Desert Inn resort.

May: Police in Montreal, Canada, report that the Bonanno crime family controls narcotics trafficking between their city and Manhattan.

May 9: Federal jurors in Chicago convict acting Outfit boss Sam Battaglia of racketeering. Imposition of a 15-year prison term leaves John Philip Cerone to succeed Battaglia.

May 13: At the tax-evasion trial of Louis "The Fox" Taglianetti, FBI agents reveal that they bugged mafioso Raymond Patriarca's office from March 6, 1962, to July 12, 1965. Unknown gunmen subsequently murder Taglianetti.

May 18: Future drug lord and Gulf Cartel leader Osiel Cárdenas Guillén born in Matamoros, Mexico.

June: Authorities in Westchester County, N.Y., announce that local garbage hauling is monopolized by the Gambino and Genovese Mafia families. San Francisco's "Summer of Love" lures an estimated 100,000 persons to the Haight-Ashbury district, where illegal drugs proliferate. Imprisoned hitman Joseph "The Animal" Barboza turns informer for the FBI.

June 15: Mobster Francis Vanverberghe receives a one-year sentence for assault and battery in Marseille, France.

June 17: Marijuana smugglers disarm, handcuff and execute Border Patrol Inspectors George Azrak and Theodore Newton near Oak Grove, Calif. Police find their bodies on June 19.

June 22: FBI agents and local police arrest Buffalo, N.Y., mafioso Fred "The Wolf" Randaccio and five associates on charges of conspiring to rob banks and armored cars. Though none of the holdups were carried out, jurors convict Randaccio and four codefendants—Pasquale Natarelli, Steven Cino, Charles Caci and Louis Sorgi—on November 25. Randaccio receives a 20-year prison term.

June 23: Two unidentified gunmen execute French-Corsican mob boss Antoine Guerini outside Marseille, France.

June 25: FBI agents charge Ray Patriarca, Enrico "Henry" Tameleo, and Ronald Cassesso (already imprisoned for a Massachusetts robbery) with conspiracy to murder William Marfeo in July 1966. At trial, hitman Joseph "Joe the Animal" Barboza testifies as a prosecution witness, resulting in conviction of all three defendants. Patriarca receives a five-year sentence and a $10,000 fine on March 24, 1968.

June 30: *The St. Valentine's Day Massacre* premieres in U.S. theaters, starring Jason Robards as Al Capone and Ralph Meeker as Bugs Moran.

July: The IBT surrenders its Perelli-Minetti contract in California after the UFW wins a representation election.

July 13: Mafioso Gaetano Lucchese dies from a brain tumor. Carmine Tramunti succeeds him as boss of the family.

July 22: Howard Hughes buys the Sands hotel-casino in Las Vegas for $14.6 million, leaving its old managers in place.

August: An FBI report declares that Meyer Lansky, Moe Dalitz, and other associates control the International Credit Bank of Geneva, Switzerland.

August 1: Manhattan mobster Charles Grandiere receives a ten-year prison term for robbing a fruit stand and attempting to kill its owner.

August 4: Los Angeles mafioso Frank DeSimone dies from natural causes. Nicolo Licata succeeds him as boss of the local crime family.

August 10: Future mafioso Anthony "Superman" Gioia born in New York City's Little Italy.

September 22: Future gangster Jason Matthew Patrick Moran born in Melbourne, Australia.

October: Nevada Governor Paul Laxalt creates a "task force" to investigate charges of skimming in Las Vegas, while declaring that it will not be "an 'anti-skimming' group." The team, consisting of six casino executives, "seeks cooperation of the casinos via an exchange of letters" and conducts no inspections without advance warning.

October 6: San Francisco's Summer of Love officially ends with a mock funeral ceremony mourning "The Death of the Hippie."

October 29: London mobster Reginald Kray fatally stabs Jack "The Hat" McVitie, as punishment for McVitie's failure to complete a £1,500 murder contract.

October 31: Unidentified gunmen execute alleged underworld associate Kenneth A. Lindstrand before 40 witnesses, at a Halloween party in Los Angeles.

November 10: An unidentified machine-gunner kills defecting Bonanno Family members James Di Angelo, Thomas "Smitty" Di Angelo, and Frank "Frankie 500" Telleri at the Cypress Garden restaurant in Queens.

November 14: Justice Albert Bosch declares a mistrial on murder charges filed against mafioso John Franzese and three codefendants in New York City. A new trial begins on December 2, resulting in acquittal of all three defendants on December 15.

November 17: Jurors convict mafioso Vincent Rao of perjury in New York City, resulting in a five-year prison term.

November 24: Mafioso Luigi Tomaso Giuseppi Fratto, AKA Louis Thomas Fratto, dies from cancer in Madison, Wis.

November 30: Future mafioso Richard G. Gotti born in New York City.

December 11: Jurors in Manhattan convict John Dioguardi of bankruptcy fraud, receiving a five-year sentence and a $10,000 fine.

December 19: Drug traffickers murder undercover FBN agent Mansel Burrell in Gary, Ind.

1968 Britain's Parliament passes a Gaming Act, creating the Gaming Board for Great Britain to license casinos. Mafia-backed politician Salvatore Lima elected to Italy's Chamber of Deputies. Outlaw bikers found The Breed MC in Asbury Park, N.J., and the Free Souls MC in Eugene, Ore. Scottish immigrant William George "Jock" Ross founds the Comancheros MC in Sydney, Australia, taking the club's name from a John Wayne film.

January: Richard Nixon attends the grand opening of Meyer Lansky's latest casino on Paradise Island, Bahamas.

January 29: In the case of *Marchetti v. United States*, the U.S. Supreme Court invalidates an occupational tax imposed on gamblers by the 1951 Revenue Act as an unconstitutional form of compulsory self-incrimination.

January 30: A car bomb severs the right leg of Boston lawyer John E. Fitzgerald Jr., representing hitman-turned-informer Joe Barboza. Fitzgerald survives his injuries to become a judge in South Dakota.

January 31: Sirhan Sirhan pens a journal entry reading: "RFK must die."

March: Howard Hughes offers $29 million for the Stardust resort in Las Vegas. Moe Dalitz counters with a demand for $35 million on March 17. Facing opposition from the DOJ's Antitrust Division, Hughes withdraws his offer on August 15.

March 4: Unknown gunmen wound Peter Crociata, underboss of the former Bonanno Mafia family, in New York City.

March 8: Federal jurors convict mafioso Raymond Patriarca of violating the International Traffic in Arms Regulations statute, resulting in a five-year prison sentence.

March 11: Gunman Frank Mari, affiliated with Gaspar DiGregorio faction of the former Bonanno Family, kills Bonanno loyalist Santo "Sam" Perrone in Brooklyn.

April 1: Bonanno Family defector Michael Consolo dies at the hands of his own men in New York, for speaking cordially to Bill Bonanno outside Manhattan's courthouse.

April 4: A sniper kills civil rights leader Martin Luther King Jr. in Memphis, Tenn., during a garbage-handlers strike. Evidence links the slaying to members of Carlos Marcello's New Orleans Mafia family.

April 8: The FNB and Bureau of Drug Abuse Control merge to create a new Bureau of Narcotics and Dangerous Drugs.

April 20: Unidentified shotgunners kill mafiosi Rudolph Marfeo and Anthony Melei in Boston.

May: An inmate at Pennsylvania's Lewisburg Federal Prison tells FBI agents that fellow prisoners Jimmy Hoffa and Carmine Galante have discussed "a contract to kill Bob Kennedy."

May 8: Unknown gunmen murder George B. Piscitelle — a former Mickey Cohen associate linked to Nevada pimp Joe Conforte — at an apartment in Van Nuys, Calif.

May 9: British police arrest mobster Reginald and Ronald Kray on murder charges.

May 16: Sirhan Sirhan pens a diary entry reading: "My determination to eliminate RFK is becoming more of an unshakable obsession."

May 27: Jurors in Madison, Wis., convict mafioso Carlo Caputo of income tax evasion, resulting in a 30-day jail term and 23 months' probation.

May 29: LBJ signs the federal "Truth in Lending Act," banning extortionate credit transactions and granting the FBI jurisdiction over loan-sharking.

June 1: Sirhan Sirhan buys two boxes of .22-caliber hollow-point cartridges.

June 4: RFK suffers fatal gunshot wounds at the Ambassador Hotel in Los Angeles, minutes after winning California's Democratic presidential primary. Members of Kennedy's entourage capture Sirhan Sirhan and relieve him of an eight-shot .22-caliber revolver. Police photographs and other evidence (later destroyed) confirm at least 13 shots fired at the scene. RFK dies from his wounds at 12:15 A.M. on June 5.

June 14: Moe Dalitz ruptures falls from a horse at his DI Ranch in Utah, rupturing a kidney and necessitating emergency surgery to remove it.

June 19: LBJ signs the Omnibus Crime Control and Safe Streets Act, permitting used of court-approved electronic surveillance in certain criminal cases and establishing the Law Enforcement Assistance Administration.

July 3: Snipers fire into the Tucson, Ariz., home of mafioso Sam Giancana's daughter.

July 7: Former Harlem gangster Ellsworth "Bumpy" Johnson dies in New York City.

July 21: A bomb explodes at Pete Licavoli's home in Tucson, Ariz.

July 22: Two bombs detonate at Joe Bonanno's Tucson, Ariz., home.

August 3: Illinois gambling racketeer Frank Wortman dies from complications of larynx cancer surgery.

August 8: Federal jurors convict mafioso Carlos Marcello of assaulting an FBI agent, resulting in a two-year prison term.

August 16: Two bombs rocks the Tucson, Ariz., home of Bonanno Family associate Peter Notaro. Mayor James Corbett Jr. tells reporters he would be "happy if underworld figures chose to live elsewhere."

August 18: Bandits kill mafioso Joe "Misery" Morceri at his warehouse in Detroit.

August 24: Mafia gunmen bungle the first of several attempts to kill rival Richard Blass in Montreal, Québec.

Early September: Members of the Mexican Mafia murder La Familia gangsters Phillip Neri and Sonny Pena at San Quentin prison.

September: Bombers in Tucson, Ariz., strike four more mob-related targets, including a wig shop that employs Charles Battaglia's wife. In Newark, N.J., mafioso Angelo "Gyp" DeCarlo and others beat tardy debtor Louis Saperstein at DeCarlo's office.

September 14: Paul Sciacca, newly confirmed boss of the former Bonanno crime family, stages a reception in New York City to resolve feuds dating from 1964.

September 15: Mexican Mafia leader Robert "Robot" Salas, AKA "Big Hazard," attacks La Familia member Hector Padilla in a dispute over stolen shoes at San Quentin. La Familia retaliates on September 16, with an attack that kills one Mexican Mafia member and wounds 11 more.

September 18: DiGregiorio gunman Frank Mari disappears in New York City, presumably murdered.

September 23: Young Lords founder Jose "Cha-Cha" Jimenez reorganizes the gang on political lines while imprisoned in Illinois, drawing inspiration from Mao Zedong and the Black Panther Party.

October: UAW leaders Victor and Walter Reuther survive the crash of their private plane near Dulles Airport in Washington, D.C. They suspect sabotage of the aircraft.

October 18: Jay Sarno opens the Circus Circus hotel-casino in Las Vegas, Nev., as a "family" resort, built with a $43 million IBT loan. Rumors of mob influence are confirmed when Tony Spilotro takes over the gift shop in 1971.

October 24: Congress passes the Staggers-Dodd Act, amending the Food, Drug, and Cosmetic Act of 1938 to ban LSD and other "depressant or stimulant drugs" nationwide.

November 5: Richard Nixon wins election as President of the U.S.

November 26: FBI agents arrest mafioso Stefano Magaddino and eight subordinates on interstate gambling charges, including operations in Canada. In New Jersey, recent Mafia beating victim Louis Saperstein dies from apparent arsenic poisoning, after mailing the FBI a letter detailing his troubles with mafioso Angelo "Gyp" DeCarlo.

December 20: In Manhattan, U.S. Attorney Robert Morgenthau indicts Tammany Hall leader Carmine DeSapio, mafioso Anthony "Tony Ducks" Corallo and millionaire contractor Henry Fried on charges of bribery and corruption related to government construction contracts. All are subsequently convicted and sentenced to federal prison, effectively breaking the power of Tammany Hall in New York.

December 22: The year-long trial of 114 Mafia defendants in Catanzaro, Italy, ends with conviction of Angelo La Barbera (sentenced to 22 years for a double-kidnap-murder in 1963), Tommaso Buscetta (sentenced to 13 years for kidnapping *in absentia*), and Tommaso Buscetta (sentenced to four years *in absentia* for "organized delinquency").

1969 Teenagers Raymond Washington and Stanley Williams found the Crips street gang in Los Angeles. Amendment of Canada's criminal code allows individual provinces to license and operate lotteries. Outlaw bikers found the Brother Speed MC in Boise, Ida. Clint Jacks founds the Confederates MC in Brisbane, Queensland, Australia (later renamed the Rebels MC). Sicily's Mafia Commission is revived, including members Gaetano Badalamenti, Stefano Bontade and Luciano Leggio.

January: Members of the Young Lords and the Black Panther Party meet in Chicago to discuss cooperation in "a political human rights movement."

January 20: Richard Nixon inaugurated as President of the U.S.

February: Los Angeles DA Evelle Jansen Younger vacations at Mexico's Acapulco Towers, owned by an associate of Moe Dalitz. While there, he receives $50,000 in cash from a friend of mafioso Sam Giancana. Returning to California, Younger quashes various subpoenas issued against owners of the Hollywood Park race track.

February 6: Thomas Zummo, a lieutenant in the DiGregorio-Bonanno Family, dies in a Manhattan shooting, officially the last victim of New York's "Banana War."

February 8: NYPD rounds up members of the Poisoners, a local gang, on charges of committing more than 30 robberies and at least one murder.

February 14: Vito Genovese dies from a heart attack while incarcerated at the Medical Center for Federal Prisoners in Springfield, Mo. Thomas Eboli ascends to leadership of the Genovese crime family.

March: Hitman-turned-informer Joseph Barboza leaves prison after serving one year. Relocated to Santa Clara, Calif., he enrolls in culinary school while allegedly continuing his career as a contract killer.

March 5: While on trial for loan-sharking in Providence, R.I., Ray Patriarca begins serving his five-year sentence for conspiracy to kill William Marfeo. Jurors subsequently acquit him of the latest charge.

March 9: A court in London, England, convicts Reginald Kray of murdering Jack McVitie, while twin brother Ronald Kray is convicted of killing George Cornell. Both receive life prison terms with a mandatory 30 years before parole.

March 12: Future drug lord Michael Christopher "Dudus" Coke born in Kingston, Jamaica.

March 18: NYPD arrests 19 members of a local motorcycle gang on charges of binding a victim and setting him afire in his East Village apartment.

April 17: Jurors in Los Angeles convict Sirhan Sirhan of RFK's assassination, resulting in a death sentence (commuted with others to life imprisonment by the U.S. Supreme Court in 1972).

April 18: Jurors in Minneola, Long Island, acquit imprisoned mafioso John "Sonny" Franzese on charges of robbery, grand larceny, assault and conspiracy related to a $3,000 holdup committed in 1965.

April 23: President Nixon sends a message to Congress proposing a campaign against organized crime in America.

June 17: LAPD suspects mafioso Jimmy Fratianno of killing Julio Anthony Petro, found shot in a car parked at Los Angeles International Airport.

July 3: Brian Jones, guitarist with the Rolling Stones rock band, dies at Cotchford Farm in East Sussex, England, from apparent complications of drug and alcohol abuse.

July 9: A federal judge in Los Angeles convicts mafioso Nicolo Licata of contempt, resulting in imprisonment until September 20, 1970. On the same day, dissident members of the Buffalo, N.Y., Mafia family meet at Frank Valenti's farm near Henrietta. They vote to replace boss Stefano Magaddino with Salvatore Pieri. Journalists credit the rebels with prompting an FBI raid on Magaddino's gambling operations in November 1968, resulting in confiscation of gaming equipment worth $500,000.

July 21: Police in Tucson, Ariz., jail Paul Mills Stevens for a series of bombings that began one year earlier. Suspect William John Dunbar joins him in jail on July 22. While neither man will talk, a girlfriend directs police to "an FBI agent named Dave." Dunbar and Stevens later testify that Agent David Hale coordinated the attacks on local mafiosi and their relatives, with help from Tucson businessman Walter I. Prideaux and college student Frances Angleman — an apparent victim of suicide in Tucson on May 14, 1969. Hale escapes prosecution by resigning from the FBI on August 12, 1969, and fleeing Tucson, leaving his lawyers to claim that U.S. Attorney General John Mitchell "had ordered Hale not to testify about anything he had learned in his official FBI capacity or to disclose anything contained in FBI records." To compensate for the embarrassment, FBI agents raid the Bonanno and Notaro homes in Tucson.

July 26: A Young Lords chapter begins operating in New York City.

August: A federal grand jury in Boston indicts Ray Patriarca, Robert Fairbrothers, Maurice Lerner, John Rossi, and Rudolph Sciarra for conspiracy to murder Rudolph Marfeo and Anthony Melei in 1968. Jurors convict all five defendants on March 27, 1970, with 10-year prison terms imposed on August 31, 1970. Lerner subsequently receives two consecutive life terms for first-degree murder in the same case.

September: Chicago police find the Rev. Bruce Johnson and his wife Eugenia stabbed to death in the parsonage of their People's Church, which serves as headquarters for the Young Lords. Fugitive suspect Julio Roldan subsequently commits suicide under curious circumstances, while in the custody of NYPD.

September 21: U.S. Customs agents launch

"Operation Intercept," a two week campaign to suppress marijuana smuggling across the Mexican border.

September 23: *Look* magazine publishes an article titled "The Web That Links San Francisco's Mayor [Joseph] Alioto and the Mafia." Alioto files a libel suit against *Look*. Jurors at the first trial fail to reach a verdict, but a second panel votes unanimously in Alioto's favor, ruling that the story was substantially false and defamed Alioto.

October 16: Gangster Richard Blass escapes from custody en route to trial in Montreal, Québec. Police recapture him at his wife's apartment.

November 30: Future Serbian mobster Aleksandar "Kristijan" Golubović born in Munich, West Germany.

December 5: New York City's chapter of the Hells Angels, led by Sandy Alexander, receives its charter.

December 6: Hells Angels "security guards" fatally stab an armed man during a Rolling Stones performance at the Altamont Speedway in Altamont, Calif.

December 10: Mafioso Michele "The Cobra" Cavataio and three of his soldiers die in an ambush in Palermo, Sicily. Before collapsing, Cavataio kills assailant Calogero Bagarella and wounds another gunman.

December 11: Future drug lord Francisco Javier Arellano Félix born in Mexico.

December 31: Assassins hired by United Mine Workers president William Anthony "Tony" Boyle kill rival UMW official Joseph Yablonski, his wife and daughter at their home in Clarksville, Pa. Police find the bodies on January 5, 1970, prompting a one-day wildcat strike by 20,000 West Virginia miners. On May 1, 1972, Judge William Bryant invalidates the December 9, 1969, UMW international elections in which Boyle defeated Yablonski. Bryant schedules a new election for December 1972, wherein Arnold Miller unseats Boyle. Prosecutors indict Boyle on three counts of murder in April 1973. His trial begins in September and ends with conviction on all counts in April 1974, resulting in three consecutive life sentences. Pennsylvania's Supreme Court overturns that verdict on January 28, 1977. Jurors convict Boyle a second time in February 1978. He dies in custody on May 31, 1985.

1970 A U.S. government survey estimates that some 2 million Americans have tried LSD. Keith Stroup founds the National Organization for the Reform of Marijuana Laws (NORML) in Washington, D.C., to lobby for decriminalization of cannabis nationwide. The Black Guerrilla Family and Mexican Mafia negotiate a truce. New Jersey authorizes a state lottery, while New York's awards the first $1 million jackpot.

January 15: International bookmaker Gilbert Beckley vanishes from Manhattan while free on bond from a 1967 federal gambling conviction. Published reports allege he was murdered to prevent him from turning informant.

January 17: Mafioso Joseph Francis Civello dies of natural causes in Dallas, Tex.

February: Congress establishes the Narcotics Treatment Administration to consolidate drug rehabilitation programs in Washington, D.C. Dr. Robert DuPont begins using methadone to wean addicts from heroin. Within one year, burglaries in the city decline by 41 percent.

March: The Young Lords open a South Bronx Information Center and printing office for their newspaper, *Pa'lante*. Cleveland mobster Tom McGinty dies in Florida. Federal jurors in New Jersey convict mafioso Angelo "Gyp" DeCarlo of conspiracy to murder Louis Saperstein in 1968, resulting in a 12-year prison term.

March 7: Rival bikers murder Ronald George Hartley, president of the Outcasts MC, in Calgary, Alberta, Canada. Police charge 11 members of the Grim Reapers MC and two club associates with the slaying. Trial jurors later convict 12 defendants.

March 14: Québec launches Canada's first legal provincial lottery, offering a $150,000 prize in return for a $2 bet.

April: Mayor John Lindsay creates a Commission to Investigate Alleged Police Corruption, chaired by future federal judge Whitman Knapp. The commission's final report, published on December 27, 1972, documents extensive graft throughout NYPD.

April 22: Governor Nelson Rockefeller signs a package of revenue legislation for New York City, including legalized off-track betting. The first legal bets are cast on April 8, 1971.

May: New York's branch of the Young Lords, led by Felipe Luciano, formally severs relations with the gang's Chicago headquarters.

May 9: Jurors convict Chicago mafioso John Philip Cerone on interstate gambling charges, resulting in a five-year prison sentence and a $10,000 fine. In Michigan, UAW leader Walter Reuther, his wife, architect Oscar Stonorov, a bodyguard, and two pilots die in the crash of Reuther's Learjet. Brother Victor Reuther tells reporters, "I and other family members are convinced that both the fatal crash and the near fatal one in 1968 were not accidental." The FBI's file on the crash remains classified.

May 21: An unidentified shotgunner kills mafioso Gaspare Magaddino in Brooklyn.

June: The BNDD's *Microgram* newsletter reports the first appearance of "windowpane" LSD, sold as small "flakes" of gelatin.

June 11: Mafioso Gaspare DiGregorio dies from natural causes in New York City.

June 26: "Retired" mafioso Sylvestro Carollo dies in New Orleans from natural causes.

July: Documents submitted to the Bahamian Ministry of Finance reveal that Morris Kleinman owns one-third of Castle Bank and Trust.

July 17: Former drug trafficker and informer Alphonse "The Peacemaker" Attardi dies from natural causes on Manhattan's Lower East Side.

July 27: Meyer Lansky arrives in Israel, announcing his application for citizenship under the Law of the Return. His emigration comes one month after media announcements of a federal investigation into Florida gambling.

August: First published report of recreational MDMA use in the U.S.

August 20: Philadelphia mafioso Ignazio Denaro dies from natural causes in Los Angeles.

August 24: In California, 7,000 lettuce workers led by the UFW strike against growers who have signed sweetheart contracts with the IBT, demanding representational elections.

September 15: Frank Milano, ex-boss of Cleveland's Mafia family, dies in Los Angeles of natural causes.

September 16: Italian journalist Mauro De Mauro vanishes in Sicily while investigating the October 1962 death of Enrico Mattei. Police blame De Mauro's disappearance on the Mafia.

September 18: Musician James Marshall "Jimi" Hendrix dies in London, England, suffocated by his own vomit following an apparent drug overdose.

September 25: Federal jurors in Buffalo, N.Y., convict mafioso Salvatore Pieri on charges of bribery and jury-tampering during an earlier trial. Upon imposition of a five-year sentence, Joseph Fino succeeds Pieri as head of the local crime family.

October 4: Singer Janis Joplin dies in Los Angeles, from an overdose of heroin.

October 13: Future drug dealer and murderer Carl Anthony Williams born in Melbourne, Australia.

October 15: President Nixon signs the Organized Crime Control Act of 1970, including the Racketeering Influenced and Corrupt Organizations (RICO) statute. The same law also creates the federal Witness Security Program (WITSEC). On the same day, he creates a Commission on the Review of the National Policy Toward Gambling, but appoints no members. Carlos Marcello begins serving a six-month jail term for assaulting a federal officer.

October 26: Manhattan gangster Santos Ber-

mudez receives a sentence of 25 years to life for the February 1969 murder of a robbery victim slain for $14.

October 27: Congress passes the Comprehensive Drug Abuse Prevention and Control Act, consolidating previous federal drug laws and reducing penalties for marijuana possession. The new law also includes the Controlled Substances Act, establishing five categories ("schedules") for regulating drugs based on their medicinal value and potential for addiction. It places most of the known hallucinogens (LSD, psilocybin, psilocin, mescaline, peyote, cannabis, and MDA) in Schedule I; cocaine and injectable methamphetamine fall into Schedule II; while other amphetamines and stimulants (including non-injectable methamphetamine) are placed in Schedule III.

October 31: Future Canadian gangster Omid Tahvili born in Tehran, Iran.

November: Boston jurors convict mafioso Ilario Zannino, Joseph Balliro, and Peter Limone, with codefendant Lewis Strauss, for interstate transportation of stolen jewelry. Zannino and Limone receive seven-year terms. The U.S. Supreme Court affirms the convictions on June 7, 1971, and Zannino enters prison on May 9, 1972. Limone is already imprisoned, having been framed by other mobsters and the FBI for a gangland murder in 1965.

November 7: Mafioso Joseph Aiello dies from natural causes in Madison, Wis.

November 21: Future gangster Konstantin "Samokovetsa" Dimitrov born in Samokov, Bulgaria.

November 26: Howard Hughes secretly leaves Las Vegas, placing control of his gambling and real estate empire in the hands of subordinates.

December 30: Former mob lawyer Julius Richard "Dixie" Davis dies from a heart attack at his New York home, after learning that two masked gunmen have bound his wife and grandson, then looted the house of jewels, furs and cash.

1971 Nevada permits legalized prostitution by county option, maintaining a ban in heavily-populated Clark and Washoe Counties (Las Vegas and Reno). Connecticut, Massachusetts, and Pennsylvania authorize state lotteries. Members of the L.A. Brims, a black Los Angeles street gang, reorganize as the Bloods to oppose incursion on their turf by rival Crips. The Bloods adopt red bandanas in contrast to the blue "rags" favored by Crips. Endo Pharmaceuticals patents Percocet, a short-term narcotic pain-reliever containing are oxycodone and acetaminophen, approved for sale by the FDA in 1976.

January: Evelle Younger takes office as California's attorney general, holding the office until January 1979. Questioned about his underworld ties after leaving office, Younger tells a reporter, "I never said I was tough on crime."

January 4: Nevada Governor Paul Laxalt temporarily leaves politics for a career as a casino owner.

January 5: Ex-champion Sonny Liston's wife finds him dead at their home in Las Vegas, Nev. Examiners date Liston's death from December 30, based on the number of milk bottles and newspapers outside his door. Police blame a heroin overdose, but decomposition rules out definitive answers. Speculation of possible murder persists.

January 15: Jurors in New Jersey convict mafioso Sam DeCavalcante on interstate gambling charges, resulting in a five-year sentence and a $10,000 fine.

January 18: The SEC files a lawsuit in Dallas, Tex., alleging stock fraud by former state attorney general Waggoner Carr, former state insurance commissioner John Osorio, Houston financier Frank Sharp, and other defendants, including two of Sharp's companies, the Sharpstown State Bank and National Bankers Life Insurance Corporation. The expanding "Sharpstown Scandal" drives U.S. Assistant Attorney General Will Wilson from office in September, after revelations that he accepted a $30,000 interest-free loan from Sharp. Also in September, a Travis County grand jury indicts Texas Speaker of the House Gus Mutscher and two colleagues ("the Abilene Three") for bribery and conspiracy. Jurors convict that trio on March 15, 1972, and they receive five years' probation on March 16. Sharp subsequently receives a sentence of three years' probation and a $5,000 fine.

January 25: Mafioso Frank Pasqua pleads guilty to income tax evasion in New York City.

February 1: Rival mobsters ambush Jacques "Mad Jacky" Imbert in Marseille, France. Though wounded seven times, he survives because one assailant tells the others, "A swine like him isn't worth le coup de grâce. Let him die like a dog."

February 21: UN delegates in Vienna, Austria, sign the Convention on Psychotropic Substances, containing import and export restrictions and other rules aimed at limiting drug use to scientific and medical purposes. The convention comes into legal force on August 16, 1976. Today, 175 nations worldwide are party to the treaty.

March 6: Hells Angels battle members of The Breed MC at a motorcycle show in Cleveland, Ohio, leaving five persons dead, 21 injured, and 84 in custody. The dead include one Angel and four Breed members (one of whom was castrated). Prosecutors charge 57 bikers with first-degree murder.

March 10: NYPD charges eight Hells Angels with raping a 17-year-old girl at an East Village

leather goods shop. Charges are dropped the following week.

March 16: Jurors in Manhattan convict mafioso Angelo Mele and four associates of conspiring to sell two kilos of heroin. Mele receives a 30-year sentence.

March 22: The National Commission on Marihuana and Drug Abuse, appointed by President Nixon, launches 50-plus research projects, including a study of the effects of cannabis on humans to a field survey of criminal enforcement in six major metropolitan jurisdictions.

March 26: In California, the IBT and UFW sign a three-year collaboration agreement, countersigned by George Meany of the AFL-CIO.

April: New York mobster Joseph "Mad Dog" Sullivan stages the first successful escape from New York's Attica Correctional Facility, remaining at large for several weeks.

April 3: Mafia informer Joe Valachi dies of natural causes at La Tuna Federal Penitentiary, El Paso, Tex.

May: Congressmen Morgan Murphy of Illinois and Robert Steele of Connecticut release an explosive report on epidemic heroin addiction among U.S. soldiers in Vietnam.

May 12: Federal agents arrest Bonanno Family leaders Paul Sciacca and Michael Casale for conspiracy to sell heroin in New York.

May 27: Britain's parliament passes the Misuse of Drugs Act, classifying various drugs and prescribing punishments for their possession, sale, or manufacture. Class A drugs include heroin, cocaine, ecstasy, methamphetamine, LSD and psilocybin mushrooms; Class B includes cannabis, amphetamine, codeine and methylphenidate ("Ritalin"); Class C includes GHB, ketamine, diazepam, flunitrazepam and most other tranquilizers, sleeping tablets and benzodiazepines, as well as anabolic steroids.

June 17: President Nixon declares drug abuse "public enemy number one in the United States," announcing creation of the Special Action Office for Drug Abuse Prevention (SAODAP) under methadone treatment specialist Dr. Jerome Jaffe.

June 28: Black gunman Jerome Johnson shoots mafioso Joe Colombo Sr. on the dais at New York City's second Italian Unity Day rally. Colombo's son and others wrestle Johnson to the ground, whereupon an unknown second gunman kills him, then escapes in the crowd. Colombo remains in a coma, succeeded as family boss by Vincent Aloi, until his eventual death on May 22, 1978. Family members suspect Joey Gallo of ordering the hit.

July 1: Presidential aides Egil Krogh and David Young pen a memo calling for creation of a "White House Plumbers" unit to close leaks like that of the Pentagon Papers, furnished to the *New York Times*. The "plumbers" stage their first known burglary on September 3, rifling the office of a psychiatrist who has treated Pentagon Papers "leaker" Daniel Ellsberg, failing to uncover Ellsberg's file. Elderly mafioso Gaspare Matranga dies of natural causes in Los Angeles.

July 7: New York jurors convict mafioso Joseph "Scotty" Spinuzzi on local gambling charges, resulting in a one-year prison term. In Washington, federal authorities reclassify non-injectable amphetamine and methamphetamine as Schedule II controlled substances.

August 16: White House Counsel John Wesley Dean III writes a memo titled "Dealing with Our Political Enemies," proposing means by which "we can use the available federal machinery to screw our political enemies."

August 21: In California, Black Guerrilla Family founder George Jackson dies in a gun battle at San Quentin Prison, along with three guards and two other inmates. Prison authorities claim that lawyer Stephen Bingham smuggled a pistol to Jackson during a visit, but jurors subsequently acquit him of that charge. The source of Jackson's alleged weapon remains unexplained, while supporters term his death a political assassination.

September: The Pentagon initiates "Operation Golden Flow," requiring urinalysis testing for drugs on all military personnel returning home from Vietnam. In the first round, 4.5 percent test positive for heroin. Israel's Supreme Court rejects fugitive Meyer Lansky's application for citizenship under the Law of the Return.

September 17: NYPD officers find mafioso James Plumer strangled to death, while free on appeal from his March conviction on charges of violating the Welfare and Pension Plans Disclosure Act.

September 25: Chicago mobster Felix Alderisio dies of natural causes at the federal penitentiary in Marion, Ill., while serving a sentence for extortion.

October: Charles Colson, Special Counsel for Public Liaison to President Nixon, asks John Dean to investigate madam Xaviera Hollander's "happy hooker" prostitution ring in New York City, hoping to embarrass clients from the Democratic Party.

October 1: Police Officer Gene Clifton suffers a gunshot wound while aiding BNDD agents on a drug raid in Palo Alto, Calif. He dies on November 19.

October 9: *The French Connection* premieres in the U.S., fictionalizing the exploits of real-life NYPD narcotics detectives Edward "Eddie" Egan and Salvatore "Sonny" Grosso. The film wins five

Academy Awards, including Best Picture, Best Director (William Friedkin), Best Actor (Gene Hackman), Best Film Editing, and Best Writing of a Screenplay Adapted from Another Medium.

October 12: FBI agents arrest mafioso Alexander D'Alessio in a Staten Island gambling raid.

October 23: A federal grand jury indicts Meyer Lansky, Sam Cohen, and Morris Lansburgh for skimming more than $36 million from the Flamingo hotel-casino in Las Vegas. Cohen and Lansburgh later plead guilty, each serving four months of their one-year prison terms. Lansky escapes prosecution with a plea of poor health.

November 9: A federal grand jury indicts six Milwaukee mafiosi — including Frank Balistrieri, already imprisoned on other charges — for concealing the ownership of a restaurant, income tax fraud and other crimes.

November 26: Joe Adonis dies a heart attack at his Italian villa.

December 23: To secure IBT votes for his re-election campaign, President Nixon commutes Jimmy Hoffa's 13-year federal prison term to time served.

December 25: Unknown gunmen execute Manhattan mafioso Bruno Latini in his car.

1972 La Familia supreme commander Robert Rios "Babo" Sosa and first lieutenant Joe Gonzales, both incarcerated at San Quentin Prison (with Gonzales on death row) rename their gang Nuestra Familia. Maryland and Michigan authorize state lotteries.

January: Pakistani financier Agha Hasan Abedi founds the Bank of Credit and Commerce International in Karachi, subsequently operating through some 400 branches in 78 countries, laundering money for the CIA, drug dealers, terrorists, and other criminals before its collapse in 1991.

January 4: French police and agents of the American BNDD seize 110 pounds of heroin at Charles de Gaulle International Airport in Paris. Evidence bagged in that raid leads to the subsequent arrest of Marseilles drug traffickers Jean-Baptiste Croce and Joseph Mari.

January 6: *The Valachi Papers* opens in American theaters, starring Charles Bronson as Mafia informer Joe Valachi.

January 21: Mexican Mafia member Carlos Rodriquez dies in a shotgun ambush in Pomona, Calif.

January 27: At a meeting with Attorney General John Mitchell and other White House aides in Washington, D.C., ex–FBI agent G. Gordon Liddy presents the "GEMSTONE" plan for illegal campaign "dirty tricks." GEMSTONE draws its name from proposed activities including the "DI-AMOND" program (removal and detention of violent demonstration leaders); "CRYSTAL" (electronic surveillance); "SAPPHIRE" (the prostitute program); "OPAL" (covert entry operations); and "RUBY" (agents-in-place). CREEP deputy director Jeb Magruder approve GEM-STONE on April 7.

January 28: President Nixon creates the Office of Drug Abuse Law Enforcement under Director Myles Ambrose, to establish joint federal/local task forces opposing the street-level drug trade.

February: French heroin traffickers offer a U.S. Army sergeant $96,000 to smuggle 240 pounds of heroin home to America. The sergeant informs BNDD agents, resulting in raids on both sides of the Atlantic. On February 29, French authorities seize the shrimp boat *Caprice des Temps* off Marseilles, bound for Miami with 915 pounds of heroin. By year's end, French police make 3,016 narcotics arrests — up from 57 in 1970.

February 3: After several clashes with Mexican Mafia members at California's Chino prison, authorities transfer Nuestra Familia member Fred Charles Castillo to Folsom.

February 7: Morocco issues a 25-centimes postage stamp promoting creation of a national lottery.

February 15: Mexican Mafia hitmen stab George "Poyo" Felix more than 30 times in Los Angeles.

February 17: In Rome, Mafia-linked politician Giulio Andreotti assumes office as Prime Minister of Italy.

February 22: Chicago mafioso Sam DeStefano receives a 42-month sentence for threatening a witness in a murder trial. Authorities release him on bail pending appeal.

March: An interim report from Italy's Antimafia Commission declares, "Generally speaking magistrates, trade unionists, prefects, journalists and the police authorities expressed an affirmative judgement on the existence of more or less intimate links between Mafia and the public authorities ... some trade unionists reached the point of saying that 'the mafioso is a man of politics.'"

March 16: Police in Commerce, Calif., find Mexican Mafia dropout Raymond Ochoa bound to a chair and shot in his apartment, near his hogtied wife and son. Prosecutors charge "Eme" member Gilbert "Shotgun" Sanchez with the slaying. His trial begins on April 3, and jurors acquit him on October 13.

March 18: NYPD officers raid the East Village headquarters of the Hells Angels MC, seizing guns, explosive devices, and illegal knives.

March 22: Mafioso Nicholas Camerota dies of natural causes in Springfield, Mass. On the same day, Chairman Raymond Shafer releases the final report of the National Commission on Marihuana and Drug Abuse, recommending decriminalization of cannabis coupled with "a social control policy seeking to discourage marijuana use, while concentrating primarily on the prevention of heavy and very heavy use." President Nixon ignores the report.

March 24: The film version of Mario Puzo's Mafia novel, *The Godfather*, premiers in the U.S. It subsequently wins three Academy Awards: Best Picture, Best Actor (Marlon Brando), and Best Writing for a Screenplay Based on Material from Another Medium.

March 31: Authorities briefly cripple Gennaro Anguilo's Rhode Island numbers operation by jailing his runners for civil contempt.

April 7: Unidentified gunmen kill Joey Gallo during his 43rd birthday celebration at Umberto's Clam House, in Manhattan's Little Italy. Authorities suspect retaliation for the earlier shooting of Joe Colombo Sr.

April 10: Gunmen execute mafioso Frank Ferriano in his car, near New York City's Holland Tunnel.

April 17: Gambler David Wolosky dies in an ambush outside Manhattan's Beth Israel Hospital, listed by the *New York Times* as the eighth gangland murder victim in three weeks.

April 21: Cementing an alliance with the Mexican Mafia, Aryan Brotherhood members Fred Steve Mendrin and Donald Ray Hale murder Nuestra Familia member Fred Charles Castillo in California's Folsom Prison.

April 26: Federal convict four defendants — St. Louis mafioso Anthony Giordano; Detroit mobsters Michael Polizzi and Anthony Zerilli; and Emprise Corporation, based in Buffalo, N.Y. — on interstate gambling charges. Giordano, Polizzi and Zerilli receive four-year prison terms, while Emprise paid a fine.

May 2: J. Edgar Hoover dies at his home in Washington, D.C. President Nixon names L. Patrick Gray as acting FBI director.

May 14: Hyatt Hotels executive Donald Pritzker meets Moe Dalitz in Honolulu to arrange an IBT loan for purchase of the Four Queens hotel-casino in Las Vegas. The union loans Pritzker $8 million at 4 percent interest, then buys $30 million in Hyatt stock.

May 28: CREEP members burglarize the Democratic National Committee's (DNC) office at Washington's Watergate hotel, photographing files and planting bugs. Detroit mafioso "Black Bill" Tocco dies of cancer in Grosse Pointe, Michigan.

June 5: Unknown gunmen execute mafioso Dominic Chirico, an associate of family boss Frank Valenti in Rochester, N.Y. Valenti vacates his position, succeeded on June 6 by Samuel "Red" Russotti.

June 9: Jeb Magruder orders Gordon Liddy to replace a defective bug at the Watergate DNC office.

June 17: Security guards at the Watergate hotel arrest CREEP burglars Bernard Barker, Vergilio Gonzales, Eugenio Martínez, James McCord and Frank Sturgis during their second break-in at DNC headquarters, launching multiple media and government investigations of White House corruption.

June 29: Turkish authorities impose a nation-wide ban on opium cultivation, debated with U.S. diplomats during 1971.

July 9: A federal grand jury indicts twelve members and associates of the Los Angeles Mafia family on charges of extorting money from bookmakers, loan-sharks and pimps. Defendants include underboss Dominic Brooklier and two *caporegimes*, Peter Milano and Sam Sciortino.

July 12: Federal jurors in New York City acquit mafioso John Dioguardi on charges of fraud.

July 16: Thomas Eboli, acting boss of the former Genovese Family, dies in a machine-gun ambush on a Brooklyn sidewalk. Frank Tiere assumes command of the family.

July 17: The IBT's executive board convenes at Moe Dalitz's La Costa resort in San Diego County, Calif., unanimously endorsing President Nixon's re-election bid.

August 11: An unknown gunman, presumed to be a hitman imported from Sicily, accidentally kills four wholesale meat dealers at the Neapolitan Noodle restaurant in Manhattan. The hitman's actual targets, mafiosi Gennaro Langella, Alphonse Persico, and other Colombo Family members, are present but escape injury.

August 25: A car bomb kills mobster Louis Donald Shoulders in St. Louis, Mo.

August 29: Prison officials release Chicago mobster Samuel "Teets" Battaglia, diagnosed with a terminal illness. He dies at home in Oak Park, Ill., on January 8, 1973.

October 11: Ex-Outfit boss "Felice" DeLucia dies of natural causes in Chicago.

October 12: BNDD Agent Frank Tummillo suffers fatal gunshot wounds during an undercover operation in New York City. Agent Thomas Devine is also wounded, left permanently paralyzed, and dies from his injuries on September 25, 1982. Mafioso Leonard "Black Leo" Cellura dies of natural causes in Detroit.

October 15: President Gerald Ford appoints 15 members to the Commission on the Review

of the National Policy Toward Gambling, created by President Nixon two years earlier. The commission issues its final report on October 15, 1976, declaring that the "pastime indulged in by two-thirds of the American people, and approved of by perhaps 80 percent of the population, contributes more than any other single enterprise to police corruption in their cities and towns and to the well-being of the Nation's criminals."

October 16: Police and FBI agents in New York City and environs serve subpoenas on 677 mafiosi, launching a "massive probe of mob dealings in narcotics, prostitution, and extortion."

October 31: Authorities return Mexican Mafia member Rudy Cadena to California's Chino Institute for men as a parole violator.

November: New Jersey begins a lottery with daily drawings.

November 5: Meyer Lansky leaves Israel, after the Israeli Supreme Court denies extension of his tourist visa and rejects his application for citizenship a second time. Lansky flies on to Switzerland, Africa, and several nations in South and Central America, but his standing offer of $1 million to any country that will grant him sanctuary gets no takers. He surrenders to FBI agents at Miami International Airport on November 7.

November 7: Richard Nixon wins re-election as president.

November 10: Syndicate gambling boss Arthur "Mickey" McBride dies in Cleveland, Ohio.

November 13: A grand jury in New York indicts mobsters Carmine DiBiase, Carmine Persico, Joseph Russo, and Joseph Yacovelli for conspiracy to help Russo avoid murder charges. A mistrial is declared for Persico and Russo on September 25, 1973, due to prejudicial pretrial publicity.

December: President Nixon pardons Angelo "Gyp" DeCarlo, freeing him from prison after 18 months of his 12-year federal sentence, ostensibly due to poor health. Subsequent investigation reveals that DeCarlo used singer Frank Sinatra to deliver a $100,000 campaign contribution to Nixon staffers.

December 7: Manhattan District Attorney Frank Hogan announces 19 indictments against mafioso Vincent Rizzo and 24 other defendants, capping a two-year investigation.

December 12: Nuestra Familia members Santos and Gilbert Arranda suffer stab wounds at California's Chino Institute for Men.

December 18: Retaliating for the attack on the Arranda brothers, Nuestra Familia members murder Eme leader Rudy "Cheyenne" Cadena, stabbing him 70 times before hurling his body from the third tier to the main floor of the maximum security unit. Eme members Gilbert Sandoval and Steven Oropeza are injured in the same attack.

December 28: Irish mobsters Jimmy McBratney and "Crazy Eddie" Maloney kidnap a Gambino Family loan-shark known only as "Junior" from Staten Island, holding him for ransom.

1973 Nepal bans cannabis shops. Afghanistan outlaws cultivation of hashish. President Nixon creates the Commission on the Review of National Policy toward Gambling, to review gambling policies in the U.S. Delaware and Ohio authorize state lotteries. Australian lawyer Frank Nugan and former CIA contract operative Michael Hand create Nugan Hand Ltd. in Sydney, Australia. Subsequently operating as the Nugan Hand Bank, they launder drug money and perform other financial services for organized crime worldwide, until the bank's collapse in 1980.

January 4: Frank Valenti, former Mafia boss of Rochester, N.Y., receives a 20-year prison term after conviction on multiple counts of extortion.

January 30: Howard Hunt and Gordon Liddy receive prison terms for the Watergate burglary.

February 5: Henry Robert Senter pleads guilty to seven counts of an indictment arising out of the alleged kidnapping and murder of Emanuel Gambino, nephew of New York mafioso Carlo Gambino.

February 6: A Manhattan grand jury indicts mafioso Richard J. Todaro on gambling charges and related counts of destroying property to avoid seizure during a March 1972 FBI raid.

February 8: IBT leaders meet in Palm Springs, Calif., then adjourn to Moe Dalitz's La Costa resort near San Diego, joined by Chicago mafiosi Tony Accardo, Tony Spilotro, and Marshall Caifano.

February 12: IBT president Frank Fitzsimmons joins President Nixon aboard Air Force One, promising Nixon "$1 million up front … and more that'll follow to make sure you are never wanting."

February 16: Yoshitaro Nakagawa, founder of the Nakagawa-gumi Yakuza clan, dies from natural causes in Kyoto, Japan.

February 18: Frank Costello dies of natural causes in Manhattan.

February 22: BNDD Agent Richard Heath Jr. suffers a gunshot wound while working undercover in Aruba, Netherlands Antilles. He dies at a hospital in Quito, Ecuador, on April 1.

March 4: NYPD arrests nine members of the Dynamite Brothers in Manhattan's east village, seizing a cache of homemade explosives earmarked for attacks on a rival gang, the Royal Javelins.

March 17: Watergate burglar James McCord writes a letter to Judge John Sirica, stating that he committed perjury on orders from John Dean

and John Mitchell. The letter prompts investigation of White House ties to the break-in and other criminal activities.

March 28: President Nixon signs Reorganization Plan No. 2, merging the BNDD and ODALE into a new Drug Enforcement Administration. The DEA begins operations on July 1, led by Administrator John Bartels Jr.

March 29: Mafia *capodecina* ("captain of ten") Leonardo Vitale surrenders to police and turns informer in Palermo, Sicily, furnishing a full confession of his crimes and a detailed accounting of the syndicate's inner workings. State psychiatrists deem him "mentally semi-infirm" but fit for trial.

March 31: Members of rival gangs led by Francis Venverberghe and Gaetan Zampa battle in Marseille, France, leaving four men dead.

April 14: Mafioso "Mad Sam" DeStefano dies from shotgun blasts in the garage of his Chicago home, while free on bond pending appeal of his 1972 conviction for threatening a witness. Police suspect Tony Spilotro but file no charges.

April 16: A majority of table grape growers in California's Coachella Valley refuse to renew contracts with the UFW, signing with the IBT instead. San Joaquin growers subsequently follow their lead, sparking a renewed UFW strike and grape boycott.

April 23: Mafioso Michael Genovese is jailed for contempt in Pittsburgh, Pa., after refusing to testify before a federal grand jury under a grant of immunity from prosecution.

April 27: Acting FBI Director L. Patrick Gray resigns after revelations that he destroyed evidence taken from Howard Hunt's safe. President Nixon names former EPA director William Ruckelshaus to replace Gray on April 30.

May 17: The U.S. Senate's Watergate Committee begins televised hearings in Washington, D.C.

May 19: Congress appoints special prosecutor Archibald Cox to oversee investigation into possible presidential malfeasance stemming from the Watergate burglary.

May 22: Three mafiosi posing as NYPD officers kill mobster Jimmy McBratney in a Staten Island tavern. Police charge future Gambino Family boss John Gotti with the murder. Gotti later pleads guilty to a reduced charge of attempted manslaughter.

June 1: Confessed extortionist Henry Robert Senter pleads guilty to manslaughter in New York City, receiving a 15-year sentence.

June 3: John Dean tells Watergate investigators that he has discussed the cover-up with Nixon at least 35 times.

July 10: Unidentified kidnappers abduct American oil heir John Paul Getty III in Rome, Italy, demanding $17 million ransom for his safe return. Relatives initially suspect a ploy on the youth's part to swindle his billionaire grandfather. A postal strike in Italy delays a second ransom note, then John Paul Getty II's request for money is refused by his father. In November the kidnappers mail one of their victim's severed ears to a local newspaper, threatening further mutilation of $3.2 million is not paid within 10 days. Procrastination continues, with John Paul Getty Sr. finally negotiating a payment of $2.9 million, obtaining his grandson's release on December 15. Various published reports blame Luciano Leggio's Mafia family or the 'Ndrangheta for Getty's abduction.

June 11: Nuestra Familia member Jess Valenzuela returns to prison as a parole violator.

July 13: Former presidential appointments secretary Alexander Butterfield reveals that all conversations and telephone calls in Nixon's office have been taped since 1971. Nixon orders White House taping systems disconnected on July 18. On July 23 Nixon refuses to turn over presidential tapings to Senate Watergate Committee or the special prosecutor.

July 29: Syndicate hitman Roy DeMeo kills Paul Rothenberg, owner of an illegal film-processing lab in New York City, to prevent Rothenberg from testifying about extortion payments made to the Gambino Family.

August 3: Federal jurors in Cleveland, Ohio, convict mafioso Frank Brancato on gambling charges. Brancato dies of natural causes on December 17, while appealing his conviction.

August 6: Fulgencio Batista dies in Guadalmina, Spain.

August 9: DEA Agent Emir Benitez suffers fatal gunshot wounds during an undercover cocaine investigation in Fort Lauderdale, Fla.

August 11: Future Mexican drug lord Edgar Valdez Villarreal born in Laredo, Tex.

August 15: Kern County sheriff's deputies fatally beat UFW striker Nagi Daifullah at a farm near Arvin, Calif.

August 16: A shootout between Asian gangs in Manhattan's Chinatown leaves two gang members and three bystanders wounded.

August 17: Unidentified drive-by gunmen kill UFW striker Juan de la Cruz on a picket line between Arvin and Weedpatch, Calif. Police accuse Filipino immigrant Bayani Advencula of firing the fatal shots, but jurors acquit him at trial, leaving the crime unsolved.

August 28: Mafioso Natale Evola dies of natural causes in New York City. Philip Rastelli succeeds him as boss of the former Bonanno Family.

September 6: The New York Times reports that nearly all Superfecta harness races run at tracks in Monticello, Roosevelt and Yonkers, between January and March of 1973 were fixed.

September 7: Convicted of extortion in Chicago, Outfit lieutenant Sam "Teets" Battaglia receives a 15-year prison term.

September 9: Mafioso Thomas "Yonnie" Licavoli dies of a heart attack in Ghanna, Ohio.

September 12: A judge in Philadelphia, Pa., jails mafioso Philip Testa, when Testa refuses to testify before a federal grant jury under a grant of immunity. Testa remains in custody until January 10, 1975.

September 26: Future wrestler and gangster Georgi Stoev born in Sofia, Bulgaria.

October 4: A federal jury in Manhattan indicts 43 mafiosi and Mafia associates on drug-dealing charges.

October 10: Spiro Agnew resigns as Vice President of the United States, following exposure of corrupt activities while he was governor of Maryland. Gerald Ford replaces Agnew as Vice President on October 13. Agnew subsequently pleads no contest to tax evasion, thus avoiding trial on charges that he accepted $29,500 in bribes. Agnew pays a $10,000 fine plus taxes and interest due on "unreported income" from 1967, and is sentenced to three years' probation. Former Maryland Attorney General Stephen Sachs calls Agnew's plea-bargain "the greatest deal since the Lord spared Isaac on the mountaintop."

October 19: The film Lucky Luciano, starring Gian Maria Volonté as Luciano and Charles Cioffi as Vito Genovese, premieres in Italy, making its way to the U.S. in November 1974.

October 20: Mafioso Angelo "Gyp" DeCarlo dies in Mountainside, N.J., five days before the deadline for payment of a $20,000 fine imposed in 1970. President Nixon fires special prosecutor Archibald Cox. Attorney General Elliott Richardson and FBI Director William Ruckelshaus resign in protest. Attorney Leonidas "Leon" Jaworski replaces Cox as special prosecutor on November 1.

October 25: Federal jurors in Manhattan convict mafioso Carmine Tramunti of perjury, resulting in a five-year prison sentence.

November 6: A cocaine trafficker kills undercover LAPD Detective Gerald Sawyer during an attempted robbery of a $144,000 flashroll.

November 17: President Nixon stages a televised press conference to tell America, "I am not a crook."

December 20: Unidentified gunmen execute ex-policeman Richard Cain (né Richard Scalzitti) in a Chicago sandwich shop. As a member of the Chicago Police Department in the 1960s, Cain also served both as an enforcer for mafioso Sam Giancana and as an FBI informant. Some conspiracy theorists link Cain to the JFK assassination.

December 22: Jurors in New York City convict mafiosi Vincent Aloi and John Dioguardi on new charges of stock fraud. Aloi receives a nine-year sentence, while Dioguardi (already imprisoned on other charges) gets 10 years.

1974 Illinois, Maine, and Rhode Island authorize state lotteries. New Jersey voters defeat a referendum proposal for government-owned casino gambling. Two cruise lines, Holland America and Home Lines, install slot machines on their cruise ships. Gamex Industries introduces an early electronic slot machine. American gamblers wager $17.3 billion on legal gambling nationwide, including $1.7 billion on bingo and $681 million on state lotteries. The Nugan Hand bank facilitates illegal CIA arms shipments to war-torn Angola. Alexander Shulgin synthesizes the hallucinogen 2,5-dimethoxy-4-bromophenethylamine, AKA "2C-B," while exploring the homologues of another hallucinogen, 2,5-dimethoxy-4-bromoamphetamine, AKA "DOB." Drittewelle, a German pharmaceutical firm, markets 2C-B as an aphrodisiac, under the trade name "Eros." In Palermo, Sicily, the Mafia Commission becomes operative with Gaetano Badalamenti as chairman.

January: John Volpe, U.S. ambassador to Italy, names banker and Mafia money-launderer Michele "The Shark" Sindona "Man of the Year" and "saviour of the lira."

January 23: New York City mafioso Alphonse Persico receives a two-month sentence for contempt, after he refuses to testify before a grand jury despite a grant of immunity.

January 24: Manhattan mafioso Carmine Galante leaves federal prison after serving 12 years for narcotics violations.

January 28: Nixon campaign aide Herbert Porter pleads guilty to perjury.

February 17: The film *Crazy Joe* premieres in New York City, starring Peter Boyle as late mafioso Joey Gallo.

February 25: Herbert Kalmbach, personal counsel to President Nixon, pleads guilty to two charges of illegal campaign activities. Future gangster and assassin Sretko "The Beast" Kalini born in Zadar, Croatia.

March: Police in Rome, Italy, charge mafioso Gerlando Alberti with smuggling 84 kilos of heroin from Italy to New York.

March 1: A federal grand jury indicts John Mitchell, H.R. Haldeman, John Ehrlichman, Charles Colson, Robert C. Mardian, Kenneth W. Parkinson, and Gordon Strachan for conspiracy to hinder the Watergate investigation. The grand jury's report names President Nixon as an unindicted co-conspirator.

March 20: Mafiosi Frank Balistrieri, Nicholas Civella and Carl DeLuna meet with front man Allen Glick in Las Vegas, Nev. Glick agrees to sell part of his Argent Corporation to Balistrieri's sons John and Joseph for the nominal sum of $25,000.

April: The Italian stock market crashes, producing economic ruin for banker Michele "The Shark" Sindona. Profits for his Franklin National Bank of Long Island, N.Y., drop 98 percent, and the bank is declared insolvent on October 8, due to mismanagement and fraud, involving losses in foreign currency speculation and poor loan policies. Mafia informer Francesco Marino Mannoia later describes underworld efforts to save the bank, in order to salvage hidden heroin income.

April 5: Jurors convict Dwight Chapin, Deputy Assistant to President Nixon, of lying to a grand jury.

April 7: A grand jury indicts Ed Reinecke, Republican lieutenant governor of California, on three charges of perjury before the Senate Watergate committee.

May 8: Unknown gunmen execute mafioso John Camilleri in Buffalo, N.Y. Police blame the slaying on rivalry between acting boss Salvatore Pieri and a dissident faction led by Joseph Fino.

May 16: Italian police capture fugitive mafioso Luciano Leggio in Milan. Already convicted *in absentia* for the 1958 murder of Michele Navarra, Leggio begins serving his life prison term.

May 28: The Massachusetts State Lottery offers America's first scratch-off instant-winner game cards.

June 3: Charles Colson pleads guilty to obstructing justice in a burglary staged by White House "Plumbers." On June 21 he receives a sentence of one to three years in prison.

July 12: Jurors convict Watergate defendants John Ehrlichman, Gordon Liddy, Bernard Barker, and Eugenio Martinez of burglary and perjury.

July 18: Mexican authorities deport Sam Giancana, forcing his return to Chicago.

July 19: A heart attack kills mafioso Stefano Magaddino in Buffalo, N.Y. Salvatore "Samuel Johns" Pieri formally succeeds Magaddino as boss of the local crime family.

July 24: The U.S. Supreme Court orders President Nixon to surrender all tapes of Oval Office conversations. During July 27–30 the House Judiciary Committee passes articles of impeachment.

August 9: President Nixon resigns in disgrace, succeeded by Vice President Gerald Ford. On September 8, Ford grants Nixon a "full, free, and absolute pardon" for any criminal acts.

August 22: Frank Zito, boss of the Springfield, Ill., crime family, dies of natural causes.

September 24: Members of a New York City

fornia's Folsom Prison after serving four years on a 1971 guilty plea to second-degree murder. He settles in San Francisco as "Joseph Donati."

October 6: Police in Philadelphia, Pa., arrest bookmaker Joseph Vito Mastronardo Sr. with three sheets of rice paper bearing 1,000 college and professional football bets and "tally work totaling approximately $50,000." Jurors subsequently acquit him on gambling charges.

October 8: Franklin National Bank, based on Long Island, N.Y., collapses under obscure circumstances involving Italian banker Michele "The Shark" Sindona and the Propaganda Due Masonic lodge. The Holy See of Rome loses an estimated $30 million in the crash.

October 9: Richard Nixon makes his first public appearance since resigning as president, at Moe Dalitz's La Costa Resort and Spa in San Diego County, Calif.

October 14: President Ford receives the final report of the Domestic Council Drug Abuse Task Force, recommending that "priority in Federal efforts in both supply and demand reduction be directed toward those drugs which inherently pose a greater risk to the individual and to society." The report ranks marijuana as a "low priority drug" in contrast to amphetamines, heroin, and mixed barbiturates.

November 13: In Los Angeles, Judge Thomas LeSage dismisses the *Penthouse* libel case, ruling that Moe Dalitz and his partners are public figures. LeSage reverses that judgment in part, on April 5, 1976, after a new U.S. Supreme Court decision limits the definition of "public figures." Moe Dalitz and convicted swindler Allard Roen remain excluded from the case, while two other Dalitz partners are permitted to proceed.

November 15: LAPD suspects mafioso Michael Rizzitello in the beating death of Bernard Gusoff, slain for $500,000 life insurance.

November 16: Future drug dealer and suspected mass-murderer Andrew "Benji" Veniamin born in Melbourne, Australia.

November 18: New York gunmen kill Gambino family associate Mario Pannicioli en route to his trial on murder charges.

November 20: FBI agents arrest mafioso and IBT officer John Nardi in Ohio, following his indictment on corruption charges in Florida.

November 22: Colombian police seize 1,320 pounds of cocaine from a private plane at the Alfonso Bonilla Aragón International Airport in Palmira, a suburb of Cali. Over the next 48 hours, enraged drug cartel soldiers retaliate by killing 40 residents of Medellín. The record seizure and ensuing "Medellín Massacre" alert officials to a drastic increase in cocaine trafficking.

November 23: Gunmen execute mafioso Jimmy "The Hammer" Massaro in Rochester, N.Y. Thomas Didio succeeds him as boss of the local crime family. Jurors subsequently convict defendants Eugene Di Francesco, Sam Gingello, Dick Marino, Tom Marotta, Rene Piccaretto, and Red Russotti on murder charges. All receive sentences of 25 years to life on January 1, 1977.

December: Mafioso Francis Consalvo, brother of September murder victim Carmine Consalvo, plummets to his death from the roof of a five-story building in Manhattan's Little Italy. NYPD dubs their case the "Flying Consalvo Murders."

December 19: DEA Agent Larry Wallace dies at the Naval Regional Medical Center in Guam from gunshot wounds received during an undercover drug investigation.

1976 U.S. authorities report the first known cases of drug users smoking "freebase" cocaine. Revenue from sale of lottery tickets in the U.S. hits $975.5 million.

January 23: Police find mafioso Frank Cucchiara and his wife shot to death at their home in Belmont, Mass. Investigators deem the slayings a murder-suicide. The Grand Orient of Italy suspends the P2 lodge, allegedly at the request of master Licio Gelli. A Masonic tribunal convened in 1981 declares that P2 had been illegal since 1974.

February 11: Former hitman-turned-government witness Joe "The Animal" Barboza dies in a shotgun ambush outside an apartment occupied by Boston mobster James Chalmas in San Francisco, Calif.

February 20: A federal appellate court denies Carmine Persico's plea for reduction of his 14-year hijacking sentence.

March 13: Federal authorities return mafioso Ilario Zannino to prison, to complete his seven-year term for fencing stolen diamonds. A friendly judge had released Zannino based on a plea that Zannino was denied parole "because he had been improperly labeled as a member of organized crime."

March 18: Mafioso Giuseppe Genco Russo dies from natural causes in Mussomeli, Sicily.

March 19: A federal grand jury indicts New York mafioso Lawrence Paladino for tax evasion. He already faces charges of bribery and extortion, filed in 1975.

March 31: Federal jurors in Massachusetts convict mafioso Francesco Scibelli and eight associates on illegal gambling charges.

Spring: Police in Washington, D.C., arrest Louisiana congressman Joe Waggonner Jr. after he solicits sex from a female officer posing as a prostitute. No charges are filed, since the U.S.

Constitution forbids arrest of federal legislators on misdemeanor charges while Congress is in session. Louisiana voters overwhelmingly renominate Waggonner for another term on August 14 and he wins that election, then retires in 1978.

April 20: New York mafioso Louis Pucci receives a three-month sentence for criminal contempt after refusing to testify before a grand jury investigating loan-sharking.

April 21: A federal grand jury in New York indicts mafioso Joseph Colombo and 30 others on gambling charges.

April 23: Federal jurors in New York convict mafioso Philip Rastelli of antitrust violations and extortion, arising from his efforts to monopolize the mobile commissary business. On August 27 Rastelli receives three concurrent 10-year terms for extortion and one year on the antitrust count.

May: New York authorities unexpectedly parole hitman Joseph "Mad Dog" Sullivan.

May 1: Gangster Keith George Faure fatally shoots victim Shane Dennis Rowland in Richmond, Victoria, Australia. Faure is later convicted of manslaughter.

May 14: DEA agent Ralph Shaw in a plane crash north of Acapulco, Mexico, during an flight supporting Mexico's opium eradication program.

May 18: Agents of Nevada's Gaming Control Board raid the Stardust casino in Las Vegas, seizing $10,000 in uncounted coins from a hidden "auxiliary bank." Stardust slots manager George Vandermark flees to Mexico and vanishes forever.

May 20: In an unsanctioned slaying, members of the DeMeo murder crew kill New York mafioso Joseph Brocchini.

May 28: A federal grand jury indicts Tampa, Fla., mafioso Frank Diecidue and four associates on RICO charges. All are convicted at trial, on November 16.

June: Police in Salt Lake City, Utah, arrest congressman Allan Howe after he solicits sex from a policewoman posing as a prostitute. Howe claims a "set-up" and refuses to resign, but loses his re-election bid in November.

June 2: A remote-control car bomb wounds investigative reporter Don Bolles in Phoenix, Ariz. Before an ambulance arrives, he gasps, "They got me ... Mafia ... Emprise ... Adamson." Bolles dies on June 13, and Phoenix police arrest dog-racer John Harvey Adamson as a prime suspect. On June 16 detectives question local contractor Max Dunlap, allegedly seen delivering money to Adamson.

June 4: Gangster Keith Faure and two accomplices rob a bank in Clifton Hill, Victoria, Australia, wounding a policeman with gunfire. Faure subsequently receives a four-year sentence for those crimes.

June 12: Roy DeMeo and Gambino Family member Anthony Gaggi shoot Vincent Governara in Brooklyn, in retaliation for a fight between Gaggi and Governara years earlier. Governara dies several days later, at a local hospital.

June 16: Frank Fitzsimmons wins re-election as IBT president.

June 23: Jurors in Rochester, N.Y., convict mafioso Richard Marino of murdering victim Vincenzo Massaro in 1973. A second jury convicts five more defendants, including mafiosi Rene Piccarreto and Salvatore Russotti, of Massaro's slaying on November 10.

July 11: Convicted gambler Ernest Tom Kanakis murders mobsters Nick Ditta, Joseph Siragusa and Frank Randazzo in the basement of Randazzo's Detroit home.

July 13: Miami police find Florida contractor George Zebedie Byrum shot and stabbed to death in his room at the Ocean Shore Motel. The case remains unsolved until 1983, when mob informer Dominick Montiglio names Byrum's slayers as Anthony Gaggi and Roy DeMeo. Montiglio says Byrum was killed for helping robbers target Gaggi's Florida home in 1975.

July 22: Police in Kansas City, Mo., find mafioso David Bonadonna shot to death in the trunk of his car.

August: Following discovery of marijuana at her 13-year-old daughter's birthday party, in a suburb of Atlanta, Ga., Martha "Keith" Schuchard organizes Families for Action, America's first group of parents united to fight drug abuse. In Canada, five provinces form the Interprovincial Lottery Corporation. The new provincial lottery offers $5 scratch-off tickets with a top prize of CDN$1 million. The first drawing occurs on October 31.

August 16: Cleveland mafioso Leo Moceri vanishes from Little Italy, presumed kidnaped and murdered by rival John Nardi, acting in concert with Irish mobster Danny Greene. Police find only his bloodstained car on September 2. Moceri's disappearance sparks a war that decimates the Cleveland Mafia.

August 17: Reputed mobster Casper Vincent Calderazzo beaten and shot to death in the backyard of mafioso Joseph Spencer Ullo's home in Northridge, Calif.

August 20: Recently paroled hit man "Mad Dog" Sullivan kills mobster Edward "Eddie The Butcher" Cummiskey at Manhattan's Sunbrite Saloon. Despite a bartender's identification of

Sullivan, police file no charges and the case remains officially unsolved.

September 5: Former Gallo loyalist John Cutrone, who formed an independent gang after Joey Gallo's murder, dies in a machine-gun ambush at a Brooklyn luncheonette.

September 8: Irish mobster and hitman Lucas "Lucky Luke" Cavanaugh dies from congestive heart failure in Chicago.

September 10: Rival mobsters botch an attempt to kill mafioso John Nardi in Cleveland, Ohio.

October: California authorities arrest 15-year-old parolee Carlos "Casper" Silva on charges of murdering three victims for Nuestra Familia over the past seven weeks.

October 10: Nuestra Familia shot-caller Joe Gonzales orders the slaying of gang member Richard Hernandez for failing to carry out orders. Gang members Rudy Del Real and Rudolfo Quilon execute the contract.

October 15: Mafioso Carlo Gambino dies of natural causes. Son-in-law Paul Castellano succeeds him as boss of New York's dominant crime family.

November 2: New Jersey voters pass a measure authorizing casino gambling in Atlantic City. State legislators formally legalize gambling on November 8.

November 4: Unknown gunmen execute Bonanno Family member Pietro Licata in Brooklyn. Police suspect rival mafioso Salvatore Catalano, but they file no charges.

December: New Jersey inaugurates a "Touchdown" football-themed lottery game.

December 12: Nuestra Familia gangsters fatally stab Mexican Mafia associate Alejandro Moreno at a work camp in Salinas, Calif. On the same day, Delaware cancels its Touchdown II multiple-choice fixed-odds lottery game due to risk of loss.

December 13: An informant fatally shoots DEA Country Attaché Octavio Gonzalez at the agency's office in Bogota, Colombia.

December 15: Mafiosi Joseph Gambino and Carlo Conti assault undercover FBI agent Walter Orrell during a sting operation targeting monopolistic Mafia control of the New York carting industry.

December 31: Police find the corpse of Gloria Rice in California's Salinas Valley, stabbed 94 times by Nuestra Familia soldiers Ernie Castro and Jesse Gomez. Rice had earlier witnessed her husband's murder by gang members at a Salinas tavern.

1977 Vermont legislators authorize a state lottery. Britain classifies MDMA as a Class A drug. In the U.S., physicians report the first emergency case of an MDMA overdose, with only seven more logged by December 1981. The Outlaws MC creates its first Canadian chapter by patching-over Toronto's Satan's Choice MC.

January: A gang of burglars invades mafioso Tony Accardo's home in Chicago, seeking cash and jewels.

January 15: Members of the Mexican Mafia gun down Robert Lewis, special assistant to Senator Alex Garcia, in Los Angeles. On the same day, John Adamson admits planting the bomb that killed Don Bolles and pleads guilty to second-degree murder, accepting a sentence of 20 years and two months in exchange for testimony against other defendants. Phoenix police arrest Max Dunlap and plumber James Robison, accused by Adamson of triggering the remote-control bomb, on charges of first-degree murder.

January 16: Mexican Mafia members Michael Delia and Eddie "The Sailor" Gonzales kill Ysidro Trujillo, a resident of Delia's "Project Get Going" halfway house for parolees in Los Angeles.

February 1: Mexican Mafia members Daniel "Choco" Montellano, Alfred "Alfie" Sosa, and Manuel Torres execute Gilbert Roybal at his home in Fresno, Calif., after Roybal announces plans to leave the gang. Members of the rival Zampa Gang wound Jacques "Mad Jacky" Imbert with gunshots in Marseille, France.

February 2: New York mobsters murder Arthur Milgram, owner of a lottery ticket distribution service.

February 10: Mafioso-turned-informer Frank Bompensiero shot and killed outside his apartment in San Diego, Calif. Police name hitman Thomas Ricciardi as the probable assassin.

February 11: Mexican Mafia members Raymond "Huero Shy" Shyrock and Alfie Sosa stab gang associate Bruno Chavez to death at Glassell Park in Los Angeles.

February 15: Mexican Mafia member Daniel Montellano kills George "Poyo" Felix at his home in Rosemead, Calif.

February 17: Sailor Gonzales and Alfie Sosa fatally shoot Ellen Delia, wife of a Mexican Mafia member, in Sacramento, Calif. Authorities contend that Michael Delia ordered his own wife's murder to prevent exposure of corruption within Project Get Going (financed by a $228,000 state grant).

February 20: Police in Monterey Park, Calif., arrest Mexican Mafia members Robert "Robot" Salas, Alfie Sosa, and Armando Varela on concealed weapons charges. Salas and Sosa post bail, while Varela remains in custody as a cooperating witness in the death of Ellen Delia. His testimony prompts the arrest of Salas for complicity in the Delia and Gilbert Roybal slayings.

March: Kansas City mafioso Fred Bonadonna, brother of 1976 murder victim David Bonadonna, enters the federal Witness Security Program, preparing to testify against Mafia enforcers Joseph and William Cammisano.

March 26: Police in Tijuana, Mexico, arrest fugitive Alfie Sosa, charged with the murders of Ellen Delia and Gilbert Roybal.

March 27: Nuestra Familia soldiers murder gang member Fabio Garza in Calif., for using heroin and stealing money from the gang.

April 1: Police find underworld informant Thomas J. Palermo murdered in New York.

April 14: Mafioso Anthony "Tony Grande" Palmieri pleads guilty to federal extortion charges, admitting that he collected protection payments from contractors in New York and New Jersey, laundering the money through his plumbing company. Palmieri receives a three-year sentence on June 16.

May 2: Unknown gunmen execute mafioso Myron Mancuso in Kansas City, Mo., moments after his meeting with Carl Civella, brother of local mob boss Nicholas Civella. In Los Angeles, mafioso Michael Rizzitello pleads no contest to charges of extortion and filing a false insurance claim. He receives a two- to three-year prison sentence on May 22.

May 4: Police in Kansas City, Mo., find Mafia associate Michael Massy shot to death.

May 5: Acting on behalf of Gambino Family members, Jimmy Coonan's Westies lure New York loan-shark Charles "Ruby" Stein to the 596 Club and murder him there.

May 13: Unknown gunmen kill Westies leader Mickey Spillane outside his apartment in Woodside, Queens, N.Y. Prime suspect Jimmy Coonan succeeds Spillane as boss of the gang.

May 16: Detectives in Kansas City, Mo., blame members of the Civella Family for killing dissident member Mike Spero at a local bar, wounding his brothers Carl and Joe.

May 17: A car bomb kills rebellious mafioso John Nardi in Cleveland, Ohio.

May 30: *Newsweek* magazine publishes a feature article on cocaine, stating, "Among hostesses in the smart sets of Los Angeles and New York, a little cocaine, like Dom Perignon and Beluga caviar, is now de rigueur at dinners. Some party-givers pass it around along with the canapes on silver trays.... [T]he user experiences a feeling of potency, of confidence, of energy." Critics accuse *Newsweek* of glamorizing coke and understating its dangers.

June 2: Nicaraguan authorities arrest drug trafficker Norwin Meneses on charges of murdering the nations top Customs official. General Edmundo Meneses — Norwin's brother and the chief

of Managua's police department, identified as a CIA "asset" — investigates the slaying and "clears" his brother.

June 13: A federal grand jury in Manhattan indicts mafiosi Vincent Napoli and four others for importing and distributing heroin. Jurors convict Napoli on November 14. He receives a 10-year prison term on December 20.

July: Utah police arrest Mexican Mafia member Joe Morgan, a fugitive from California indictments charging narcotics and arms-trafficking violations.

July 6: Trial begins in Phoenix for Bolles murder suspects Dunlap and Robison. An opening statement by Dunlap's lawyer casts suspicion on local attorney Neal Roberts. At trial, John Adamson testified that Bolles was slain to prevent newspaper exposure of unindicted suspect Kemper Marley. Jurors convict both defendants of murder (and of conspiring to kill then–Arizona Attorney General Bruce Babbitt) on November 6. Both receive death sentences on January 10, 1978.

July 15: Anti-drug crusader Donald Mackay vanishes from a hotel parking lot in Sydney, Australia. Police recover his van, containing his car keys, bloodstains, and three spent .22-caliber shells. Police suspect drug lord Robert Trimbole, who blamed Mackay for the loss of a large marijuana cache in 1975, with associates James Frederick Bazley, George Joseph, and Gianfranco Tizzone. Mackay's corpse remains missing, but in 1984 a coroner rules his death the result of "wilfully inflicted gunshot wounds."

July 26: Federal authorities in the U.S. reduce mafioso Nick Civella's gambling sentence to three years. He serves 10 months and is paroled on June 14, 1978.

September 21: During a wild party, Hells Angel "Big Vinny" Girolamo hurls Mary Campbell to her death from the roof of the gang's Manhattan clubhouse. Implicated in the unfolding BCCI scandal, Bert Lance submits his resignation as director of the Office of Management and Budget to President Carter. In January 1978, Lance sells his stock in National Bank of Georgia to Saudi billionaire and BCCI ally Ghaith Pharaon, while on the same day, BCCI founder Agha Hasan Abedi pays off Lance's $3.5 million loan at the First National Bank of Chicago. In February 1978, Lance helps BCCI in its bid for a hostile takeover of Financial General Bankshares of Washington.

September 24: Nuestra Familia officer "Death Row Joe" Gonzales orders the murder of suspected informer Eddie Serna. Gang members Robert Flores and Robert "Brown Bob" Viramontes strangle and hang Serna in his cell at the Salinas County jail.

October 5: Unknown rivals fatally shoot and stab two Hells Angels in Bridgeport, Conn.

October 6: A car bomb kills Irish mobster Danny Greene in Cleveland, Ohio, ending a two-year gang war. Investigation of the slaying leads to indictment of eight defendants on January 6, 1978. They include mafiosi James Licavoli, Angelo Lonardo, John Calandra, Ronald Carabbia, Pasquale Cisternino, Thomas Sinito, Alfred Calabrese, and Jimmy Fratianno (who subsequently turns informer). Two additional defendants, Mafia associates Kenneth Ciarcia and Thomas Lanai, are convicted of aggravated murder on August 25, 1978.

October 11: Police suspect mafiosi Angelo and Salvatore Marino in the gunshot slaying of Peter Catelli in his office, at the California Cheese Company in San Jose, Calif.

October 22: Police find Joseph Bovan shot to death in the parking lot of a Newport Beach, Calif., restaurant. Investigators name reputed mafiosi Jerry Fiori, Anthony Merrone Jr. and Ray Resco as suspects.

October 30: New York mobster and future government informer Frank Lino becomes a "made" member of the Bonanno Family.

November 7: FBI agents arrest Meyer Lansky at Miami International Airport.

November 17: Police in Signal Hill, Calif., find drug dealer Robert Mrazek murdered in his apartment. Jurors later convict Mexican Mafia members Joe Morgan, Ramon Mendoza, Arthur Guzman and Helen Mrazek Pacheco of Mrazek's slaying.

November 19: Detroit mafioso Joseph Zerilli died of natural causes. Jack Tocco succeeds him as head of the local crime family.

December: Nuestra Familia members John Joseph "Mousey" Hernandez and Robert Prado Rocha agree to testify against the gang before a grand jury in Monterey County, Calif.

December 11: Police in Venice, Calif., find Sandra Jones — a potential prosecution witness against drug trafficker Harold Morton — shot dead in her car. Jurors later convict Morton and two codefendants, Thornell McKnight and Gloria Roe, of the murder.

1978 U.S. and Mexican authorities collaborate to reduce production of "Mexican mud," spraying Mexican opium poppy fields with the defoliant Agent Orange. Drug smugglers quickly find an alternate supply from the "Golden Crescent" of Iran, Afghanistan and Pakistan. The FBI launches ABSCAM, a sting operation run from the bureau's office in Hauppauge, Long Island. The operation starts with creation of "Abdul Enter-

prises Ltd.," in Washington, D.C., staffed by agents posing as influence peddlers for a nonexistent Arab sheikh. The operation climaxes in 1981 with criminal convictions of one U.S. senator and five congressmen. New York State launches a successful lotto.

January 20: Police find Bernard Ryan shot to death at Stone Park. Ryan is the first of six suspected burglars murdered for the January 1977 invasion of Tony Accardo's home.

February 2: Chicago police find burglar Steven Garcia in the trunk of a car parked at O'Hare International Airport, with his throat slashed. Garcia is another suspect in the Accardo burglary.

February 4: Accardo burglary suspects Vincent Moretti and Donald Swanson are found stabbed to death in an abandoned car in Stickney Township, Ill.

February 8: A federal grand jury in Los Angeles indicts five leading mafiosi on RICO charges including extortion and obstruction of a criminal investigation. The defendants include Dominic Brooklier, Samuel Sciortino, Louis Tom Dragna, and Jack LoCiero.

February 15: Paroled mafioso Nicholas Virgilio murders lawyer and part-time municipal judge Edwin Helfant in an Atlantic City, N.J., cocktail lounge. The slaying arises from Virgilio's 1972 murder trial, in which the Mafia paid Helfant $12,000 to bribe a Supreme Court judge and secure a lenient sentence. The plan failed, and Virgilio received a term of 12–20 years. In 1988 Virgilio is one of 16 Philadelphia mafiosi convicted on RICO charges, including Helfant's slaying. He receives a 40-year sentence.

February 20: Police find the mutilated corpse of John Mandell, another Accardo burglary suspect, in the trunk of a car on Chicago's South Side.

February 28: A federal grand jury in California indicts mafiosi Dominic Brooklier, Samuel Sciortino, Jack LoCicero, and Louis Tom Dragna on RICO charges including extortion and obstruction of a criminal investigation.

March: Robert Flores, John Hernandez, and Robert Rocha testify before Monterey County's grand jury, describing Nuestra Familia activity in the area.

March 7: Fugitive Salvatore "Ciaschiteddu" Greco, first boss of the Sicilian Mafia Commission, dies in Caracas, Venezuela, from cirrhosis of the liver.

March 21: Unknown gunmen murder IBT official Salvatore Briguglio at the Andrea Doria Social Club, in Manhattan's Little Italy. The murder preempts Briguglio's impending trial, with hitman

Harold Konigsberg, for the 1961 murder of Anthony Castellito.

March 31: Tabulations for the first fiscal year of Lotto Canada reveal ticket sales of CDN$225 million, prize payouts of CDN $74 million, and a CDN$56 million payment on Canada's Olympic debt.

Spring: DEA and FBI agents file independent reports confirming that CIA assets Ernesto and Norwin Meneses are smuggling large quantities of cocaine into the U.S. aboard commercial airliners.

April: Police in Washington, D.C., arrest New York congressman Frederick William Richmond for soliciting sex from a 16-year-old male prostitute. Prosecutors drop the misdemeanor charge when Richmond agrees to psychiatric counseling. Chicago hitmen leave the last Accardo burglary suspect, 43-year-old John McDonald, riddled with bullets in a North Side alley. In Sicily, mafioso-turned-informer Giuseppe Di Cristina warns authorities of an impending war between rival bosses Gaetano Badalamenti and Luciano Leggio.

April 13: The film *F.I.S.T.* premieres in Los Angeles, starring Sylvester Stallone as Johnny Kovak, a mob-allied labor leader patterned on Jimmy Hoffa.

April 23: A car bomb kills mafioso Salvatore "Sammy G" Gingello in Rochester, N.Y.

May 1: Federal jurors convict New England mafioso Joseph Napolitano of conspiring to distribute $3.3 million in counterfeit $100 bills. On September 6 NYPD finds Napolitano and an associate murdered in New York, reportedly due to suspicion that Napolitano had turned informer for the FBI.

May 5: Police in Philadelphia, Pa., arrest bookmaker Joseph Mastronardo Sr. and his brother on gambling charges, then drop the case. Three months later, Joseph marries the daughter of ex–police commissioner and mayor Frank Rizzo.

May 8–9: Mafiosi kidnap anti–Mafia activist Giuseppe Impastato in Cinisi, Sicily, torturing him overnight before wrapping his body in explosives and detonating the charge on nearby railroad tracks. Local voters elect him posthumously as a member of the city's council, on May 11. The Court of Assises convicts mafioso Vito Palazzolo of Impastato's murder on March 5, 2001, imposing a 30-year prison term, but that verdict is overturned on appeal. Mafia boss Gaetano Badalamenti receives a life sentence for the slaying on April 11, 2002.

May 15: Mexican Mafia member Joe Morgan receives a five-year sentence for being a felon in possession of a firearm and transporting a rifle across state lines. Two hours later, a federal judge sentences him to a term of two to 10 years for possession of heroin. Before year's end, state jurors convict Morgan of second-degree murder in the slaying of a fellow Eme member. He receives a life term in that case.

May 16: Members of Roy DeMeo's crew shoot, stab, bludgeon and dismember Lucchese Family associate Michael DiCarlo in New York City.

May 26: Resorts International opens the first legal casino in Atlantic City, N.J.

May 30: Gunmen murder mafioso-turned-informer Giuseppe Di Cristina at a bus stop in Palermo, Sicily. Defendant Antonio Marchese subsequently receives a life sentence for the slaying.

June 12: Authorities revoke the parole of brothers Salvatore Bonanno and Joseph Bonanno Jr., imposing jail terms of 30 and 34 months respectively, for withholding information about unreported income.

June 15: Jurors in Kingston, N.Y., convict hitman Harold "Kayo" Konigsberg and mafioso–IBT official Anthony "Tony Pro" Provenzano in the slaying of IBT rival Anthony Castellito. The defendants receive sentences of 25 years to life on June 21.

June 16: A grand jury in Kansas City, Mo., indicts mafiosi Joseph and William Cammisano for "conspiracy to extort the property of Fred Bonadonna," a local tavern owner who opposed the Mafia's establishment of "adult" entertainment facilities in the River Quay district. The Cammisanos plead guilty on October 23; on November 22 William receives a five-year sentence, while Joseph gets 18 months.

June 17: Cleveland mobster Sam Tucker dies in Florida.

June 28: Mafioso Joe Colombo dies after six years in a coma.

July 7: Aided by Cleveland, Ohio, drug dealer Carmen Zagaria, mobster Hans "the Butcher" Graewe murders Orville Lee Keith aboard a boat on Lake Erie. Graewe fears that Keith may tell police that Graewe swindled him out of $25,000.

August: Death Row Joe Gonzales seeks a new attorney, citing a conflict of interest in sharing an attorney with his murder co-defendants. The move generates rumors of impending defection from Nuestra Familia.

August 5: Mafia underboss Anthony Milano dies of natural causes in Cleveland, Ohio.

September: Québec joins Canada's Interprovincial Lottery Corporation.

August 8: Federal jurors in Pennsylvania convict mafioso Russell Bufalino of extorting $25,000 from a man who owed money to one of the Mafia's fences. Upon receiving a four-year sentence,

Bufalino names Eddie Sciandra as acting boss of the family.

August 25: Jurors in Cleveland, Ohio, convict mobsters Kenneth Ciarcia and Thomas Lanai of aggravated murder charges in the bombing death of Danny Greene.

September: A hit-and-run driver kills the father of anti–Mafia activist Giuseppe Impastato in Cinisi, Sicily. Police rule his death accidental.

September 8: Gunmen kill mafioso Giuseppe "Pippo" Calderone in Palermo, Sicily. Benedetto "Nitto" Santapaola succeeds Calderone as boss of the Mafia in Catania.

September 14: Members of the Poor People's Guerrilla Army wound police chief and drug smuggler Gen. Edmundo Meneses in a machine-gun ambush, in Managua, Nicaragua. Meneses dies on September 29.

September 28: Pope John Paul I dies at the Vatican, 33 days after his selection as pontiff. While authorities blame his death on a heart attack, author David Yallop later claims the pope was murdered by the Mafia and corrupt Vatican insiders.

October: Nuestra Familia "commander" Art Beltran pleads guilty on two counts of second degree murder and one count of conspiracy to commit murder in San Joaquin County, Calif. Authorities grant immunity from further prosecution, as Beltran exposes previously unknown gang units in Oakland, Sacramento, San Francisco, and San Jose. In Los Angeles, Mexican Mafia member Daniel Montellano posts $100,000 in Los Angeles and $150,000 in Fresno, securing release pending trial on homicide charges.

October 14: President Jimmy Carter signs bill H.R. 1337/S.R. 3534, legalizing home brewing of beer for the first time since Prohibition.

October 15: Imprisoned mafioso Carmine "Mr. Gribbs" Tramunti dies of natural causes in New York.

October 25: Congress passes the Interstate Horseracing Act, legalizing transmission of racing odds and results between states where racing is legal. On the same day, Congress passes the Foreign Intelligence Surveillance Act enacted, creating a Foreign Intelligence Surveillance Court and limiting federal government domestic surveillance powers, as recommended by the Church Committee in 1976.

October 30: Mafioso Joseph Zerilli dies in Grosse Pointe, Mich., after a prolonged illness.

November: Canada's Maritime provinces — New Brunswick, Nova Scotia, and Prince Edward Island — join the Interprovincial Lottery Corporation. U.S. Bureau of Prisons authorities grant parole to mafioso John "Sonny" Franzese, on his 50-year bank robbery sentence imposed in 1967.

November 3: Police in Fresno, Calif., launch an investigation of Judge Lenore Schreiber after learning that she has put money on the books for Mexican Mafia members Daniel Montellano and Robert Salas at the county jail. No criminal charges result.

November 8: Chicago police receive a missing-person report on 75-year-old Michael Volpe, longtime housekeeper and bodyguard of mafioso Tony Accardo. Five days before his presumed murder, Volpe appeared before a grand jury investigating the torture-slayings of six burglars suspected of looting Accardo's home in January 1977. FBI agents search Accardo's home, discovering remnants of eyeglasses similar to Volpe's from an incinerator.

November 10: Congress passes the Psychotropic Substances Act, amending the Controlled Substances Act to ensure compliance with the UN's Convention on Psychotropic Substances. Another amendment, passed on the same day, permits confiscation and forfeiture of cash and other assets obtained from illicit drug-trafficking.

November 11: Mexican Mafia members Adolpho "Champ" Reynoso and Pedro Flores stab inmate Thomas Trejo 45 times at the Federal Correctional Institution at Lompoc, Calif. Both are subsequently convicted of murder, receiving terms of life plus 99 years.

November 16: Tony Accardo seeks the return of property seized from his home by officers investigating Michael Volpe's disappearance. Items listed include two .38-caliber revolvers and $275,000 in cash found in a hidden basement vault. The court denies his appeal.

November 20: Mafioso Salvatore Pieri pleads guilty on gambling charges in Buffalo, N.Y.

1979 Medellín drug cartel member Carlos Lehder buys 165 acres on Norman's Cay in the Bahamas, using it as an airstrip for transshipment of cocaine from Colombia to the U.S.

January 12: Imprisoned mafioso Johnny Dioguardi dies of natural causes at a Pennsylvania hospital.

January 15: Cleveland hitman Raymond Ferritto admits to stalking murdered mobster Danny Greene in 1977 and receives a five-year prison term.

January 17: A federal grand jury in New York indicts mafioso Anthony Scotto, son-in-law of Albert Anastasia and president of Brooklyn ILA Local 1814, of taking $200,000 in illegal payoffs.

February 7: Roy DeMeo's New York murder crew kills and dismembers Peter Waring, a cocaine dealer turned informant for NYPD's Narcotics Division.

February 19: The DeMeo crew shoots, stabs, and dismembers mobster Frederick Todaro, leaving his remains at Brooklyn's Fountain Avenue Dump.

February 26: Joseph Vincent "Newsboy" Moriarty, former numbers racket boss of Hudson County, N.J., dies from prostate cancer.

February 27: Crips gang founder Tookie Williams, Alfred "Blackie" Coward, James Garret and Tony Sims rob a convenience store outside Whittier, Calif. They escape with $180 after Williams murders employee Albert Lewis Owens.

March 11: While robbing a motel on South Vermont Avenue in Los Angeles, Tookie Williams murders elderly proprietors Yen-Yi Yang and Tsai-Shai Yang, along with their daughter Yu-Chin Yang Lin. In Chicago, Outfit gunman Gerardo Scarpelli murders George Christofalos, owner of a roadhouse and competitor of mobster John Borsellini. Two months later, police find Borsellini murdered in a field, naming Scarpelli as their prime suspect.

March 17: The DeMeo crew executes out-of-town cocaine dealers Charles Padnick, William Serrano, and two unidentified associates.

March 19: James Padnick arrives in New York City to investigate his father's disappearance. The DeMeo crew immediately murders and dismembers him.

March 20: Gunmen kill journalist Carmine "Mino" Pecorelli in Rome, using a rare brand of pistol ammunition. Identical rounds are later found in the arsenal of a local criminal organization, the Banda della Magliana, concealed in the Health Ministry's basement. Investigation focuses on right-wing terrorists until April 6, 1993, when mafioso-turned-informer Tommaso Buscetta claims Pecorelli was slain by members of Gaetano Badalamenti's Mafia clan, on orders from Prime Minister Giulio Andreotti. A court in Perugia acquits Andreotti on murder charges in 1999, along with codefendants Claudio Vitalone (Italy's former Foreign Trade Minister), Badalamenti, mafioso Giuseppe Calò, and two alleged triggermen: Massimo Carminati and Michelangelo La Barbera. An appellate court convicts Andreotti and Badalamenti on November 17, 2002, sentencing both to 24 years in prison. That verdict, in turn, is reversed on October 30, 2003.

April 14: Detroit mafioso Giovanno "Papa John" Priziola dies of natural causes in Grosse Pointe, Mich.

April 19: Roy DeMeo mistakes 19-year-old college student Dominick Ragucci for a Colombian hitman, pursuing his car and killing Ragucci after a high-speed chase in New York City.

April 26: Police find Anthony "Little Pussy" Russo, ex-chauffeur and bodyguard for mafioso Vito Genovese, shot to death in Long Branch, N.J. The murder terminates FBI investigation of Russo on suspicion of hidden casino ownership and skimming in Las Vegas, Nev.

May 11: Roy DeMeo and Anthony Senter kill Gambino Family associate Harvey "Chris" Rosenberg on orders from mafioso Anthony Gaggi. Gaggi accuses Rosenberg of robbing and killing associates of a Colombian drug dealer linked to the Mafia.

May 30: Police charge Mexican Mafia member Daniel "Choco" Montellano with killing 17-year-old Jerry Granillo outside Montellano's apartment in Visalia, Calif.

June: Former anti–Mafia prosecutor Cesare Terranova seeks reinstatement to the Sicilian judiciary, receiving an appointment as the chief examining magistrate in Palermo. Cocaine traffickers Oscar Danilo Blandón and Norwin Meneses flee Nicaragua, seeking sanctuary in the U.S.

June 17: LAPD officers find sports promoter and suspected mob associate Victor Weiss shot dead in the trunk of his Rolls Royce.

July: Britain's Gaming Board refuses to renew the licenses of three casinos operated by Ladbrokes, Cyril Stein's Middlesex-based international gaming company.

July 1: An international conference on cocaine convenes in Lima, Peru.

July 11: Mafioso Anthony Provenzano receives a 20-year sentence for labor racketeering in Newark, N.J. In Milan, Italy, unidentified gunmen murder Giorgio Ambrosoli, an attorney investigating the 1974 collapse of Michele Sindona's financial empire. Sindona will receive a 25-year sentence in March 1984, for ordering Ambrosoli's assassination. A shootout between rival cocaine-smuggling gangs at Miami's Dadeland Mall leaves two gunmen dead and four bystanders wounded.

July 12: Mafioso Carmine Galante dies with bodyguard Leonard Coppola in a shotgun ambush at Joe & Mary's Italian Restaurant in Bushwick, Brooklyn. The gunmen also kill Giuseppe Turano, Galante's cousin and owner of the restaurant. While the crime remains officially unsolved, published reports name the slayers as Cesare "The Tall Guy" Bonventre, Alphonse "Sonny Red" Indelicato, Anthony "Whack Whack" Indelicato, Dominick "Sonny Black" Napolitano, Dominick "Big Trin" Trinchera.

July 13: Authorities find policeman-turned-drug dealer Felix Garrido and his wife shot to death at their home in Dedeo, Guam. On August 28, convicted heroin dealer Johnny B. Santos tells investigators that Guam Penitentiary inmate Irvin R. Ibanez confessed the murders, saying the hits were ordered by drug trafficker Francisco Palacios. According to Ibanez, Palacios blames Garrido for his arrest on June 22, 1979.

July 17: Nicaragua falls to rebels of the Sandinista National Liberation Front. American pilots airlift deposed dictator Anastasio Somoza and 100 allies to Florida's Homestead Air Force Base.

July 19: Congress opens hearings on cocaine trafficking in Washington, D.C.

July 21: Mafia assassin Leoluca Bagarella murders Chief of Police Giorgio Boris Giuliano at the Lux Bar in Palermo, Sicily. The murder ends Giuliano's investigation of journalist Mauro De Mauro's slaying in September 1970.

August 2: Felon-financier Michele Sindona disappears from New York City in a fake kidnapping staged to avert his federal trial on 65 counts including fraud, perjury, false bank statements and misappropriation of bank funds. Aided by the Mafia, Sindona embarks on an 11-week sojourn to Italy, seeking to extort support from various former allies including Prime Minister Giulio Andreotti. The plot fails, and Sindona reappears in Manhattan on October 16, surrendering to FBI agents. Federal jurors subsequently convict Sindona at trial. He receives a 25-year sentence on March 27, 1980.

August 22: Pennsylvania congressman Michael Joseph "Ozzie" Myers accepts a $50,000 bribe from undercover FBI agents in the ABSCAM sting operation. Following his indictment, the House of Representatives expels him on October 2, 1980. Myers receives a three-year prison term in 1981.

September 25: Mafia gunmen ambush magistrate Cesare Terranova in Palermo, killing Terranova and policeman Lenin Mancuso, who served as Terranova's driver and bodyguard.

October: Playboy Limited of England acquires three casinos and 60 British betting shops for $13 million.

October 1: Roy DeMeo and Anthony Gaggi murder Gambino Family members James Eppolito Sr. and his son, James Jr., in New York City. A witness alerts police, sparking a shootout that leaves Gaggi wounded and in custody, while DeMeo escapes.

October 7: Members of the "Israeli Mafia" murder and dismember victims Esther and Lili Ruven at the Bonaventure Hotel in downtown Los Angeles, afterward dumping their remains in garbage bins around Sherman Oaks and Van Nuys. Police arrest suspect Joseph Zakaria two weeks later. Accomplice Yehuda Avital is captured in Las Vegas, Nev., in March 1980, while Eliahu Komerchero surrenders to police in Van Nuys on April 9, 1981. Komerchero pleads guilty to voluntary manslaughter and turns state's evidence against his codefendants, receiving a four-year sentence. Upon conviction, Avital receives a prison term of life without parole, while Zakaria is sentenced to 21 years. An appellate court affirms Avital's sentence on March 22, 1985, while overturning Zakaria's conviction.

October 8: Brooklyn mobsters Costabile "Gus" Farace Jr., Robert DeLicio, David Spoto and Mark Granato abduct two teenage male prostitutes from Greenwich Village, sexually abusing them before bludgeoning both and leaving them for dead. Victim Steven Charles dies, while Thomas Moore survives, identifying all four assailants at a police lineup. Farace pleads guilty to first-degree manslaughter on December 10, receiving a prison term of seven to 21 years. Authorities release him in June 1985.

October 12: Roy DeMeo's crew murders and dismembers legitimate used-car dealers Khaled Daoud and Ronald Falcaro in New York, after Daoud threaten to inform police of DeMeo's involvement in an international auto-theft ring.

November 3: Police and British Gaming Board inspectors raid four London casinos operated by the Coral Leisure Group.

November 15: A federal grand jury in Detroit indicts mafiosi Raffaele Quasarano and Peter Vitale on charges of racketeering, extortion, mail fraud, and tax fraud, related to the 1972 takeover of a Wisconsin cheese company.

November 21: The local *Review-Journal* hails Moe Dalitz as "an asset to Nevada."

November 27: Michael Hand writes to CIA officer Theodore "Ted" Shackley, concerning a recent meeting in Washington, D.C. His letter reads: "The opportunity of meeting you again on different terms was very enjoyable and I sincerely trust that something worthwhile businesswise may surface and be profitable for both of us."

December: The first reports of "rock" or "crack" cocaine surface in South Central Los Angeles. In London, Metropolitan Police and the British Gaming Board commence proceedings to cancel the gaming license of Victoria Sporting Club for various illegal practices. Three London casinos of the Ladbroke Group are closed during the same month.

December 5: Moe Dalitz protégés Al Sachs and Herb Tobman assume control of the Fremont and Stardust resorts in Las Vegas, after paying Allen Glick $66 million. One week later, the *Wall Street Journal* names Sachs as a target of federal organized crime inquiries.

December 28: Lotto Canada holds its last drawing. Thereafter, the federal government leaves lotteries to the individual provinces.

1980 The World Health Organization classifies khat as a drug of abuse that may produce mild to moderate psychological dependence.

January: Federal jurors in Rochester, N.Y., convict mafioso Francesco Frassetto and six codefendants on racketeering charges, including several bombings.

January 1: Police in Dade County, Fla., blame

a $40,000 drug rip-off for the murder of California resident Kevin Turney. His suspected killer flees the U.S.

January 6: Mafia gunmen in Palermo assassinate Piersanti Mattarella, President of the Regional Government of Sicily, in a bid to frustrate his political reforms. Informer Marino Mannoi later names the killers as Francesco Davì, Salvatore Federico, Santo Inzerillo and Antonio Rotolo.

January 7: U.S. congressmen Richard Howard Ichord Jr. (chairman of the Research and Development Subcommittee of the Armed Services Committee) and Robert Carlton "Bob" Wilson of California (House of Representatives Armed Services Committee) dine with Nugan Hand Bank officer Maurice Bernard "Bernie" Houghton at the Bourbon and Beefsteak Bar and Restaurant in Sydney, Australia. Days later, Houghton flies to Switzerland and on into limbo as an international fugitive.

January 27: Police in Lithgow, New South Wales, Australia, find Frank Nugan — co-founder of the Nugan Hand Bank, recently indicted for stock fraud — shot to death in his car outside town. A note found with the corpse details large loans made to various Nugan Hand customers, including former CIA director William Egan Colby. A June inquest into the slaying reveals that Nugan Hand is insolvent, owing at least $50 million to various creditors. On January 29, Michael Hand meets with Nugan Hand directors, warning that unless they follow orders, they may "finish up with concrete shoes" and are "liable to find their wives being delivered to them in pieces."

February 2: *NBC Nightly News* breaks the story that FBI agents are targeting corrupt members of Congress in a sting operation codenamed "AB-SCAM." The sting targets 31 officials, finally convicting six on charges of bribery and conspiracy.

February 14 : Mafioso-pornographer Michael Zaffarano suffers a fatal heart attack in New York City, while resisting arrest by FBI agents.

February 25: Arizona's Supreme Court overturns the convictions of Max Dunlap and James Robison in the Don Bolles murder, ordering a new trial.

March: Federal agents in West Palm Beach, Fla., arrest Chicago mobster Marshall Caifano for transporting stolen securities valued at $2 million. On May 23, Caifano receives two concurrent 20-year prison terms.

March 7: Roy DeMeo's crew stabs and decapitates suspected police informant Joseph Coppolino, leaving his headless corpse on a street in New York City.

March 21: Jurors in Chester, Pa., convict Mayor John Nacrelli of accepting bribes from gambling racketeer Frank Miller, resulting in a six-year prison term. On the same day, an unidentified shotgunner kills Mafia boss Angelo Bruno in Philadelphia, Pa. Police suspect dissident *consigliere* Antonio "Tony Bananas" Caponigro of ordering the murder. A gang war ensues.

March 24: Las Vegas Mayor Bill Briare honors Moe Dalitz with a "Trendsetter" award.

April: At the Australian inquest into Frank Nugan's January murder, Michael Hand reveals that Nugan Hand Bank is insolvent, with debts of at least $50 million.

April 17: Philadelphia police find mafioso Antonio Caponigro and his cousin/chauffeur Alfred Salerno dead in the trunk of an abandoned car, with $300 in cash stuffed into Caponigro's mouth and anus.

April 29: Despite his enrollment in the federal witness protection program, persons unknown murder Detroit mobster-turned-informant Jeffrey Rockman, AKA "Anthony Star," at his townhouse in Marina Del Rey, Calif.

May 5: Carabinieri Captain Emanuele Basile dies in a Mafia ambush in Monreale, Sicily. Gunmen shoot Basile repeatedly as he carries his four-year-old daughter, but the child escapes injury. The slaying ends Basile's collaboration with Judge Paolo Borsellino in probing Sicilian heroin traffic.

May 9: Palermo chief prosecutor Gaetano Costa signs 55 arrest warrants naming Mafia heroin traffickers. Judge Giovanni Falcone takes charge of the case.

May 12: Roy DeMeo fatally shoots Patrick Penny, a key prosecution witness in Anthony Gaggi's murder trial, as Penny sits in his parked car in Sheepshead Bay, Brooklyn.

June: Mafioso Tommaso Buscetta escapes from custody while on a day-release pass from prison in Sicily. He hides out with fellow mafioso Stefano Bontade, then flees to Brazil. Banker Michael Hand flees Australia, traveling to Fiji under a false identity. Published reports state that Hand is accompanied by CIA agent Theodore "Ted" Shackley Jr.

June 2: Arizona prosecutors drop murder charges against Max Dunlap after key witness John Adamson refuses to testify at Dunlap's retrial. On June 6 the Arizona Attorney General's Office withdraws Adamson's 1977 plea bargain and reinstates his original charge of first-degree murder in the Don Bolles bombing. Prosecutors drop James Robison's murder charge on June 13, when Adamson again refuses to testify.

June 5: Joseph A. Badway, former chauffeur of mafioso Raymond Patriarca, receives a three-month sentence and a $2,000 fine for tax evasion in Providence, R.I.

July1: Congress repeals the federal tax on American gaming devices.

June 17: Nevada's Gaming Control Board orders a "landlord suitability probe" of Moe Dalitz, who owns the land under the new Sundance hotel-casino in downtown Las Vegas. Sundance owners Al Sachs and Herb Tobman receive unanimous approval on June 19, while GCB chairman Harry Reid hedges on Dalitz. The Sundance opens as scheduled on July 2, with Mayor Bill Briare joining Dalitz, Sachs and Tobman to celebrate.

July 2: Chicago Outfit hitman Gerardo Scarpelli and two associates murder William Dauber — boss of various South Side auto chop shops — and his wife Charlotte.

July 5: Rival gunmen execute cocaine dealer Chris Conley in a Cleveland, Ohio, warehouse.

July 11: Mafioso Gabriel Mannarino dies of natural causes in Pittsburgh, Pa. Authorities name John Bazzano Jr. as his successor, but Thomas Ciancutti soon emerges as boss of the local crime family.

August: Former Nicaraguan National Guard Colonel Enrique Bermúdez accepts a CIA offer to lead Guatemala's Legion of September 15, a violent gang of ex–Guardsmen and mercenaries, forerunners of the Nicaraguan "Contra" terrorist movement.

August 6: Mafia gunmen kill chief prosecutor Gaetano Costa in Palermo, Sicily.

August 25: Sicilian police raid two major heroin labs, in Trabia and Carini, arresting mafioso Gerlando Alberti and three Corsican chemists.

September 15: Firefighters discover a heroin lab in Via Villagrazia, Palermo, Sicily.

September 17: A seven-member team of Sandinista guerrillas assassinates Anastasio Somoza at his exile home in Ascunción, Paraguay. The attack with automatic rifles and rocket-propelled grenades also kills Somoza's chauffeur and two other passengers in his car.

September 19: Unknown gunmen murder Philadelphia mafioso John "Johnny Keys" Simone in New York. Police call the slaying a reprisal for Simone's involvement in killing boss Angelo Bruno.

September 20: Roy DeMeo murders and dismembers New York mobster Frank Amato, son-in-law of mafioso Paul Castellano, on Castellano's orders.

October: Pro-Contra Nicaraguans meet in Miami to form the Nicaraguan Revolutionary Armed Forces, pledged to overthrow Sandinista rule with CIA support.

October 2: Mobster Dominic "Junior" Senzarino dies in a shotgun ambush at his home in Youngstown, Ohio.

October 3: Police arrest Maryland congressman Robert Edmund Bauman for soliciting sex from a 16-year-old male prostitute. Bauman enters a court-supervised rehabilitation program for alcoholism and the charge is dropped, but Democratic rival Roy Dyson defeats Bauman in his re-election bid on November 5.

October 17: Jurors in Tucson, Ariz., convict John Adamson of murdering Don Bolles in 1976. Adamson receives a death sentence on November 14.

October 29: Unidentified gunmen kill mafioso "Barracuda Frank" Sindone in South Philadelphia, Pa., allegedly for his involvement in Angelo Bruno's slaying.

November: Media reports place fugitive banker Michael Hand in South America, evading authorities with aid from "former CIA employees."

November 4: Ronald Reagan wins election as the 40th U.S. president.

December 2: Sicilian police log their first arrest of chemist and future prosecution witness Francesco Marino Mannoia, employed by mafioso Stefano Bontade to refine heroin.

December 4: Rhode Island State Police officers arrest mafioso Ray Patriarca for conspiring to kill victim Raymond Curcio in February 1965, after Curcio burglarized the home of Patriarca's brother Joseph. Hospitalized with a claim of chest pains, Patriarca is arraigned on December 5 at Miriam Hospital in Providence. District Court Judge Robert McOsker orders him held without bail pending a hearing on his health.

December 10: South Carolina congressman John Jenrette Jr. resigns from the House of Representatives following his ABSCAM conviction for accepting a $50,000 bribe.

December 16: A hitman posing as a flower deliveryman kills John McCullough, head of mob-controlled Roofers Local 30, at his home in Philadelphia, Pa.

1981 Arizona lawmakers authorize a state lottery. The DEA reports kilos of cocaine selling for $55,000 each in the U.S.

January: California prosecutors charge Nuestra Familia member Robert Rios Sosa with various racketeering offenses including eight murders. Police also question gang associate Raymond F. Johns in the strangulation death of his wife, Maureen Rettig. Senator Paul Laxalt meets with U.S. Attorney General William Smith to protest the FBI-IRS "infestation" of Nevada.

January 3 Florida congressman Richard Kelly's final term expires. Voters have failed to renominate him following his ABSCAM indictment for taking $25,000 in bribes. Upon conviction, Kelly spends 13 months in federal prison.

January 20: Following racketeering convictions based primarily on testimony from informer

Jimmy Fratianno, Los Angeles mafiosi Dominic Brooklier and Samuel Sciortino receive four-year prison terms; Michael "Big Mike Rizzi" Rizzitello receives five years; while Louis Tom Dragna and Jack LoCicero get two years.

January 23: Federal jurors in New York City convict Genovese Family boss Frank "Funzie" Tieri on multiple racketeering charges.

January 31: Jurors in Philadelphia, Pa., convict mafiosi Giovanni "John the Dour Don" Stanfa of lying to a grand jury investigating Angelo Bruno's murder.

February 4: President Reagan names New Jersey contractor Raymond James Donovan as Secretary of Labor. The Senate confirms him, with Senator Orrin Hatch calling Donovan's appointment "one of the most rigorously scrutinized in our countrys' history."

February 12: A television mini-series, *The Gangster Chronicles*, premieres in the U.S., depicting the rise of organized crime during Prohibition. Stars include Michael Nouri as Lucky Luciano, Joe Penny as Bugsy Siegel, and Brian Benben as "Michael Lasker" (renamed to avoid legal action by Meyer Lansky). The program wins a Primetime Emmy for Outstanding Art Direction for a Series.

March: Three London casinos — the Curzon, International Sporting Club and Palm Beach — close their doors. The Palm Beach and International Sporting Club reopen in June.

March 1: Salvatore "Toto" Catalano, a Sicilian immigrant, resigns as boss of the Bonanno Family. Insiders cite his inability to communicate in English as the primary cause.

March 9: President Reagan signs a "finding" that authorizes destabilization of the Nicaraguan government.

March 15: Mafia boss Philip Charles "Chickenman" Testa dies when a pipe bomb explodes on the porch of his home in Philadelphia, Pa. Police blame underboss Pete Casella.

March 30: Mafioso Ray Patriarca is arraigned in New Bedford, Mass., as an accessory before the fact in the 1968 North Attleboro murder of victim Robert "Bobby" Candos.

March 17: Italian police raid banker Licio Gelli's villa in Arezzo, seizing a list of 962 military officers and public officials belonging to the clandestine Masonic lodge Propaganda Due. The ensuing scandal forces Prime Minister Arnaldo Forlani out of office on June 26. Others on the list include murdered banker Roberto Calvi; Prime Minister Silvio Berlusconi; General Vito Miceli, chief of the Italian arm's intelligence service; Mafia-allied banker Michele Sindona; and Victor Emmanuel, Prince of Naples. The Grand Orient Lodge of Italy expels Gelli on October 31.

March 31: Mafioso Alphonse Frank Tieri dies of natural causes at Mount Sinai Hospital in New York City.

April 21: Federal agents capture fugitive Philadelphia mafioso Giovanni "John the Dour Don" Stanfa, indicted earlier on perjury charges. He receives an eight-year prison term.

April 23: Mafioso Stefano Bontade dies in a machine-gun ambush while driving home from his own 42nd birthday party in Palermo, Sicily. His murder sparks the island's "Second Mafia War," continuing into 1983.

April 28: The U.S. House Ethics Committee votes to expel Pennsylvania representative Raymond Lederer from Congress, following his January ABSCAM conviction on charges of accepting $50,000 in bribes. Lederer resigns on April 29 and subsequently receives a three-year prison term, with a $20,000 fine.

May: The owners of Resorts International casino in Atlantic City, N.J., charge David Zarin with 93 counts of theft by deception for unpaid gambling debts accumulated under his $2 million line of credit.

May 5: Members of the Bonanno Family execute three of their own *caporegimes*— Philip Giaccone, Alphonse "Sonny Red" Indelicato and Dominick "Big Trin" Trinchera — at a Brooklyn social club. Undercover FBI agent Joseph Dominick Pistone, AKA "Donnie Brasco," identifies participants in the slaying as John Cerasini, Joseph DeSimone, Louis Giongetti, Joseph Charles "Big Joey" Massino, Dominick "Sonny Black" Napolitano, Benjamin "Lefty" Ruggiero, and Salvatore "Good Looking Sal" Vitale.

May 6: IBT president Frank Fitzsimmons dies from lung cancer in San Diego, Calif. Roy Lee Williams succeeds him as president on May 15.

May 11: Mafioso Salvatore "Totuccio" Inzerillo dies in an ambush while leaving his mistress's home in Palermo, Sicily. Police report that he was shot with the same weapon used to kill Stefano Bontade in April. Testimony before a U.S. Senate subcommittee links IBT president Roy Williams to mafioso Nicholas Civella. Federal prosecutors indict Williams and four co-defendants on May 22, on charges of conspiring to bribe Nevada Senator Howard Cannon. Defiant Teamsters re-elect Williams as their president on June 6, 1981.

May 26: Mafioso Antonio Rotolo strangles rival Santo Inzerillo in Palermo, Sicily, at a meeting called by Inzerillo to discuss the recent murder of his brother Salvatore.

May 27: An unidentified gunman kills "Greek Mob" leader Chelsais "Steve" Bouras at a restaurant in Philadelphia, Pa. Police suspect the Scarfo Mafia family.

June 29: "Wonderland Gang" members William DeVerell, Ronald Launius, David Lind and Joy Miller rob the Los Angeles home of drug dealer Eddie Nash, escaping with cash, drugs and jewelry. Nash suspects porn star John Holmes, who visited his house on June 28, and finds Holmes wearing a ring stolen in the robbery. Holmes identifies the bandits under torture. On July 1, killers strike at gang's house on Wonderland Avenue, executing DeVerell, Launius, and Lind's girlfriend, Barbara Richardson, while leaving Launius's wife Susan badly injured. Lind is absent and survives, later tipping LAPD to Nash's involvement. A search of Nash's home uncovers cocaine valued at $1 million, resulting in a two-year prison sentence. Prosecutors charge Holmes with the murders, but jurors acquit him on June 16, 1982. He subsequently serves 110 days in jail for contempt of court, after refusing to testify under a grant of immunity. Following his death from AIDS in March 1988, Holmes's ex-wife accuses Nash and live-in bodyguard Gregory Diles of the murders. Jurors at their 1990 fail to reach a verdict, but a second panel acquits both defendants. Charged with racketeering in 2000, Nash strikes a plea bargain in September 2001 and admits bribing a juror at his first murder trial. He receives a 4½-year sentence on that charge, plus counts of money-laundering and racketeering, with a $250,000 fine.

July: North Dakota legalizes charitable and non-profit blackjack games. The "Wonderland murders" remain officially unsolved.

July 4: Police in Las Vegas catch Tony Spilotro's "Hole in the Wall" burglary crew looting a furniture store. Crew leader Frank Cullotta turns state's evidence in early 1982.

July 10: Turkish police arrest mobster Nurullah Tevfik Ağansoy for a murder committed in 1980. On January 29, 1981, he is convicted on reduced charges of planting bombs and carrying a gun without license. Ağansoy files a petition for clemency under Turkey's Repentance Law on April 24, 1988, and is subsequently paroled.

July 18: Colombo Family gunmen kill Robert DiLeonardo, brother of Gambino Family member Michael "Mikey Scars" DiLeonardo, in New York City.

July 23: Yakuza "Godfather of Godfathers" Kazuo Taoka dies from a heart attack in Amagasaki, Japan.

July 25: Giuseppe "Pino" Greco and Giuseppe Lucchese bungle an attempt to kill fellow mafioso Salvatore "Totuccio" Contorno in Corleone, Sicily, prompting him to become a police informer.

July 30: Mafioso Calogero "Carlo" Licata shoots himself to death in Bloomfield Hills, Mich.

August 4: Mafioso Salvatore Pieri dies of natural causes in Buffalo, N.Y.

August 10: Guided by the CIA, "Contra" forces from the Legion of September 15, the Nicaraguan Democratic Union and the Nicaraguan Revolutionary Armed Forces merge to create a new Nicaraguan Democratic Force based in Honduras.

August 17: Members of the Bonanno Family execute fellow mafioso Dominick "Sonny Black" Napolitano at a meeting in Brooklyn, N.Y. Police find his corpse, with the hands removed, in Arlington, Staten Island, on August 12, 1982.

August 22: The August 31st issue of *Time* magazine identifies IBT officials Frank Fitzsimmons, Jackie Presser and Bill Presser as FBI informers since 1972. Despite that revelation, Jackie Presser wins re-election to the IBT's international policy committee in February 1983 and is elected as the union's president on April 21, replacing convicted successor Roy Williams in May.

September: A federal grand jury in Florida indicts Rhode Island defendants Raymond Patriarca, Arthur E. Coia, Arthur A. Coia, former state legislator Albert Lepore, and Joseph J. Vaccaro Jr. (of Winchester, Mass.) on racketeering charges. The Coias are officials of the Laborers' International Union of North America, while Lepore is one of their law partners and Vaccaro is a former trustee of a union training school.

September 19: Unknown gunmen execute mafioso Frank Piccolo in Bridgeport, Conn., thus removing him as a witness from a libel suit filed against the NBC network by Las Vegas entertainer and casino owner Wayne Newton. Authorities suspect Paul Castellano of ordering the hit.

October 15: In Providence, R.I., U.S. Magistrate Jacob Hagopian rules that Ray Patriarca is too ill to stand trial for racketeering in Florida.

October 23: Physicians Michael J. Faella and Barbara H. Roberts testify in Providence that Ray Patriarca will probably die within a year, whether or not he is tried for the Curcio slaying. Superior Court Judge Francis Kiely exempts Patriarca from trial on October 27, saying that stress would "endanger his life, if not cause sudden death."

November: Playboy Limited announces the sale of its British gambling operations to Trident Television Limited for $34 million.

November 23: President Reagan signs a National Security Decision Directive authorizing $19.95 million for Nicaraguan Contras.

November 30: Trial opens in Los Angeles for the *Penthouse* libel case, before plaintiff-friendly Judge Kenneth Gale. Moe Dalitz testifies on December 28, admitting personal acquaintance with Sam Giancana and Meyer Lansky.

December: Contras establish fund-raising committees across the U.S., including chapters in

Los Angeles, San Francisco, New Orleans, Houston, and Miami, and Washington, D.C. At the same time, cocaine traffickers Oscar Danilo Blandón and Norwin Meneses meet Contra commander Enrique Bermúdez Varela to discuss funding the movement via drug sales.

1982 Pablo Emilio Escobar Gaviria, leader of Colombia's Medellín Cartel, negotiates a deal with Panamanian general Manuel Antonio Noriega Moreno to ship cocaine through Panama to the U.S. Noriega receives $100,000 per shipment. An FBI report states that Aryan Brotherhood members are recruiting in prisons across the U.S. Expenditures on legal gambling in the U.S. reach $125 billion, with bingo wagering pegged at $3 billion. Nevada casinos report a gross income of $2.7 billion.

January: Federal jurors in California convict Nuestra Familia member Death Row Joe Gonzales on racketeering charges, including 12 counts of murder in Monterey and San Joaquin Counties. The conviction adds 20 years to Gonzales's hopeless sentence.

January 7: With his trial in progress on federal racketeering charges, unknown gunmen execute mafioso Frank "Chickie" Narducci in South Philadelphia, Pa.

January 16: Unknown gunmen murder Corsican mobster and heroin trafficker Marcel Francisci in the parking lot of his apartment house in Paris, France.

January 19: New racketeering indictments in California name defendants Art Beltran, Kenneth Cassie, Raymond Castaneda, Jose Cobos, Raymond Contreras, James Cozad, Anselmo Eddie Dominquez, Afredo Elizalde, Robert Flores, Reynaldo Garcia Jr., Ruben Garnica, Joe Gonzales, Alfredo Guerro, Cesar Gutierrez, Sammy Henegas, David Hernandez, Phillip Lopez, Manuel Montelongo, Guadalupe Ramirez, Ruben Seja, Daniel Serrano, Arturo Serrato, Robert Rios Sosa, William R. Soto, and Eddie Vindiola.

January 23: Nicaraguan Contras recruit ex–fighter pilot Carlos Cabezas to sell cocaine in San Francisco, Calif.

January 28: President Reagan creates the Vice President's Task Force on South Florida, led by Vice President George H.W. Bush. The team combines agents from the Army, ATF, Customs, DEA, FBI, IRS, and Navy to suppress drug trafficking. At the same time, Reagan slashes funding for federal law enforcement agencies, prompting one U.S. Coast Guard officer to call the task force "an intellectual fraud." On the same date, U.S. Attorney General William Smith grants the FBI concurrent jurisdiction with the DEA in cases pertaining to the Controlled Substance Act.

February: The Clermont casino and the Playboy Club close in London, England.

February 17: New Jersey Senator Harrison Williams Jr. receives a three-year prison term following conviction on ABSCAM charges. He resigns from the Senate on March 11 and ultimately serves nine months.

February 26: Chicago loan-shark Frank Renella receives a sentence of seven years in federal prison for violation of the Hobbs Act and for jumping bail.

March: Drug lord Pablo Escobar wins election as an alternate representative to the Colombian Congress from Envigado, campaigning as a populist "Robin Hood" figure, handing out money in Medellín slums, touring the city with Catholic priests, and erecting low-income housing.

March 5: Members of the Gambino Family kill con artists Michael and Nicolina Lizak in retaliation for the murder of family soldier Robert Russo. On the same day, comedian and drug addict John Belushi dies from a "speedball" overdose of cocaine and heroin in a bungalow at Chateau Marmont hotel, in Los Angeles.

March 9: Authorities seize 3,906 pounds of cocaine, valued at over $100 million wholesale, from a hangar at Miami International Airport.

March 15: Police in Philadelphia, Pa., find mafioso Rocco Marinucci dead from multiple gunshot wounds, with three large firecrackers stuffed in his mouth. Investigators subsequently blame Marinucci for the March 1981 bombing that killed Philip "Chickenman" Testa.

March 23: Police in Rome arrest future informer Salvatore "Totuccio" Contorno, interrupting his plan to murder mafioso Giuseppe "Pippo' Calò in retaliation for the slaying of Stefano Bontade. Contorno subsequently prepares a map outlining territories held by various Mafia clans in Palermo.

March 24: Hitman-turned-informer Jimmy Fratianno, now a defense witness in the *Penthouse* libel case, reveals his long personal acquaintance with Judge Kenneth Gale.

April: Colorado lawmakers authorize a state lottery.

April 24: Television host Nick Perry and five accomplices rig a Pennsylvania Lottery drawing to produce the unpopular number "666" for a prize of $3.5 million. Authorities discover the scam before any cash is paid out.

April 30: Mafia gunmen kill Sicilian Communist Party chief and Antimafia Commission member Pio La Torre and his driver, Rosario Di Salvo, in Palermo. Police blame the slayings on La Torre's proposal of new anti–Mafia legislation, drafted on March 30. Nine Mafia bosses receive life sentences for the slayings on January 12, 2007.

May 1: Carabinieri general Carlo Alberto Dalla Chiesa is promoted to serve as prefect of Palermo, to halt the "Second Mafia War."

May 6: Mafioso Salvatore "Sal the Sphinx" Ruggiero Sr. dies in a plane crash offshore from Savannah, Ga. Authorities recover his body on May 14.

May 13: Mafioso Frank Monte dies in an ambush in Philadelphia, Pa., shot five times in the head, back and arms. Published accounts blame Mafia soldiers Joseph Pedulla and Harry "The Hunchback" Riccobene for his slaying. In Los Angeles, jurors in the *Penthouse* libel case exonerate defendant Bob Guccione and his magazine.

June: Mobster-turned-informer "Charles Allen" tells a U.S. Senate subcommittee investigating labor racketeering that Jimmy Hoffa was killed to prevent him from murdering IBT president Frank Fitzsimmons. Allen claims that Hoffa was shot on orders from Tony Provenzano, then "ground up in little pieces, shipped to Florida and thrown into a swamp." Convicted New York mafioso John Franzese returns to prison after violating terms of his November 1978 parole.

June 1: Ten days after IBT president Roy Williams's federal indictment, President Reagan tells the union's national convention, "I hope to be in team with the Teamsters."

June 5: Convicted bank embezzler Roberto Calvi pens a letter to Pope John Paul II, warning that the impending financial collapse of his Banco Ambrosiano may "provoke a catastrophe of unimaginable proportions in which the Church will suffer the gravest damage." The bank fails two weeks later, following discovery of debts totalling $1.5 billion. Funding to the bank's off-shore interest is terminated in July, prompting their chain-reaction collapse.

June 8: Unknown gunmen wound mafioso Harry Riccobene as he emerges from a telephone booth in South Philadelphia, Pa. The Reagan White House launches "Project Democracy" to destabilize the elected government of Nicaragua.

June 10: Convicted banker Roberto Calvi disappears from Rome, traveling through Venice to London, England, on a false passport. On the morning of June 18 a London postman finds Calvi's body hanging under Blackfriars Bridge, his clothing stuffed with bricks and $15,000 in currency. A coroner's inquest on Calvi's death returns an "open" verdict in July 1983, but a private inquiry conducted in December 1998 deems his death a homicide. Mafia informer Francesco Marino Mannoia tells police Calvi was killed for losing syndicate money in the collapse of his Banco Ambrosiano.

June 16: Mafioso Alfio Ferlito and three police escorts die in an ambush during his transfer from one Sicilian prison to another.

June 30: Police in Ontario, Calif., find Mexican Mafia member Tito Marines Jr. murdered on the city's southeast side. They suspect the hit was ordered by drug dealer Mary Lou Davilla Salazar.

July 4: Roy DeMeo's crew murders brothers Anthony and John Romano in New York, as retaliation for their robbery of crew member Peter LaFroscia.

July 9: Judge Kenneth Gale rejects a jury's verdict in the *Penthouse* libel case as "a miscarriage of justice," ordering a new trial. Gale's superiors remove him from the case on August 4.

July 13: Police superintendent Antonio Cassarà releases a report on the Sicilian Mafia, drawn primarily from revelations of informer Salvatore Contorno.

July 20: Federal jurors in Cleveland, Ohio, convict mafioso James "Blackie" Licavoli on RICO charges including illegal gambling, murder for hire, and conspiracy. He receives a 17-year prison term on July 30.

July 31: Dissident mafiosi Victor DeLuca and Joseph Pedulla, associates of Harry Riccobene, wound Philadelphia *caporegime* Salvatore Testa in a street ambush.

August 11: Mafioso Vincenzo Sinagra bungles a contract murder in Palermo, leaving his jammed pistol in the abandoned getaway car. Police arrest him and cousin-accomplice Filippo Marchese before day's end. In England, imprisoned gangsters Reginald and Ronald Kray attend their mother's funeral under heavy police guard.

August 17: A federal judge in Camden, N.J., revokes mafioso Nicodemo Scarfo's bail due to a prior conviction for possession of firearms by a convicted felon.

August 21: Drive-by gunmen strafe mobster Harry Riccobene's car in Philadelphia, Pa., but he escapes injury.

August 23: The District of Columbia begins a lottery. In New York City, Alphonse "Little Al" D'Arco, AKA "The Professor," becomes a "made" member of the Lucchese crime family.

August 25: Disgraced New York congressman Fred Richmond pleads guilty to charges of income-tax evasion, marijuana possession and making an illegal payment of $7,420 to a navy employee who helped arrange contracts for the former Brooklyn Navy Yard. On November 10 Richmond receives a 366-day prison term and a $20,000 fine, ultimately serving nine months.

September: Ex-Sandinista Edén Pastora joins UDN-FARN commander Fernando "El Negro" Chamorro to form the Democratic Revolutionary Alliance as a new Contra army. In Vermont, Attorney General John Easton Jr. rules that video gaming devices fall outside the legal purview of the state Lottery Commission. In Washington, D.C., special prosecutor Leon Silverman declares allegations of Labor Secretary Ray Donovan's underworld involvement — including murder of two state witnesses — "disturbing," but finds insufficient evidence for trial.

September 3: Mafia gunmen on motorcycles murder Prefect Carlo Alberto Dalla Chiesa, his wife and driver in Palermo, Sicily. The triple murder results in passage, on September 11, of anti-Mafia legislation proposed earlier by murder victim Pio La Torre. On July 9, 1983, prosecutors indict 15 mafiosi for the slayings.

September 13: Police in Geneva, Switzerland, arrest Italian fugitive banker Licio Gelli as he attempts to withdraw tens of millions of dollars from a numbered bank account. Although detained in Champ-Dollon Prison pending extradition to Italy, Gelli escapes and flees to South America. Italy creates its second Antimafia Commission. The panel publishes 2,750 files compiled by its predecessor, documenting links between the Mafia and various public officials.

October 14: U.S. Attorney General Smith creates the first Organized Crime Drug Enforcement Task Force.

October 22: CIA headquarters learns of an impending meeting in Costa Rica, held by Contras and Norwin Meneses lieutenant Renato Pena Cabrera, to discuss an exchange of arms for drugs.

November: Minnesota and Oklahoma legalize pari-mutuel betting on horse races.

November 8: The FBI identities Norwin Meneses lieutenants Horacio Pereira, Fernando Sánchez and Troilo Sánchez as sources of cocaine sold by Contra supporters in San Francisco, Calif.

November 15: Washington's state lottery begins operation.

November 30: Rosario Riccobono, Mafia boss of Partanna Mondello, a suburb of Palermo, vanishes forever with eight of his soldiers, while attending a banquet at Michele Greco's estate. Days later, three more of Riccobono's men are gunned down in public and police find his brother, Vito Riccobono, decapitated in his car. Police list all 13 mobsters as casualties of Sicily's "Second Mafia War."

December: Federal prosecutors charge Chicago mobster Joseph Lombardo Sr. with extorting $800,000 from contractor Robert Kendler and attempting to bribe Nevada senator Howard Cannon to kill or delay legislation regulating the trucking industry. Convicted at trial in 1983, Lombardo receives a 15-year sentence for conspiring to bribe Cannon.

December 6: Federal jurors in Denver, Colo., convict mafiosi Eugene "Checkers" Smaldone,

Clarence "Chauncey" Smaldone, and Paul "Fat Paul" Villano for extortionate credit transactions, tax evasion, and conspiracy, resulting in 10-year prison terms.

December 8: Warlocks MC associate Sandra Pennington Basile escapes from the Pennsylvania State Correctional Institution for Women in Muncy, while serving two consecutive life sentences for a double murder committed in Upper Providence Township on March 29, 1974.

December 15: Federal jurors in Chicago convict IBT president Roy Williams, attorney Allen Dorfman, and two co-defendants on charges of attempting to bribe Nevada senator Howard Cannon to defeat a trucking-regulation bill. Williams receives a 55-year prison term on March 31, 1983, and resigns his union office on April 14, replaced as president by Jackie Presser.

December 21: Congress passes the first Boland Amendment, banning U.S. support of efforts to topple Nicaragua's government.

1983 Robert "Black Bob" Vasquez takes command of Nuestra Familia, scrapping the gang's paramilitary structure to establish a governing body known as *La Tabla* ("The Board"). Membership in the new structure consists of three categories: Category 1 includes all new recruits; Category 2 comprises veteran gangsters; while Category 3 is restricted to management-level members. In the U.S., gamblers place legal bets totaling $163 billion; legal casinos report income of $107.5 billion; Atlantic City casinos claim $1.77 billion in gross revenue; pari-mutuel bets total $14.6 billion; bingo games earn $3.1 billion; and state governments claim $2.2 billion from lottery ticket sales totaling $5.6 billion.

January: Colorado launches its state lottery.

January 10: Hitman Roy DeMeo is murdered in New York City. Detectives suspect mafioso Frank DeCiccio, acting on orders from Paul Castellano.

January 15: Meyer Lansky dies in New York City, after a long battle with lung cancer.

January 17: Federal agents raid a Colombian freighter docked in San Francisco Bay, seizing 430 pounds of cocaine and revealing the first public link between Contra guerrillas and illegal drugs.

March: Art Schlichter, quarterback for the Baltimore Colts, admits losing more than $750,000 in illegal bets on professional football games. The National Football League suspends Schlichter.

March 1: Governor Thomas Kean signs a bill prohibiting use of video gaming devices by New Jersey State Lottery Commission.

March 12: Mafioso Nicholas Civella dies from lung cancer in Kansas City, Mo.

March 31: New York State Lottery officials report $645 million in ticket sales over the past 12 months, generating $359 million in state revenue.

April: Moe Dalitz applies for permission to take control of the Sundance hotel-casino from disgraced protégés Al Sachs and Herb Tobman. On June 11, Nevada gaming officials announce that Dalitz will surrender the Sundance to El Cortez casino owner Jackie Gaughan, pending location of a suitable buyer.

April 27: President Reagan addresses Congress, defending support for "Contra" terrorists in Nicaragua.

April 29: Unknown gunmen murder mafioso Pasquale "Pat the Cat" Spirito in South Philadelphia, Pa.

June: Iowa's state legislature authorizes parimutuel betting on horse races.

June 7: IBT president Jackie Presser announces the union's endorsement of President Ronald Reagan for re-election to the White House.

July: President Reagan attends the ILA's national convention, praising union president and longtime mob ally Thomas Gleason as a man of "integrity and loyalty."

July 16: Governor John Spellman signs a bill establishing the Washington State Lottery.

July 23: President Reagan issues Executive Order 12435, creating a President's Commission on Organized Crime. The panel's final report, issued in 1986, is marred by internal dissension. More than half of the commission members write individual opinions, complaining of wasted time and resources, suppression of evidence, and deliberate blindness to sundry "dark places."

July 29: A remote control bomb in Palermo, Sicily, kills anti–Mafia magistrate Rocco Chinnici, bodyguards Salvatore Bartolotta and Mario Trapassi, and Stefano Li Sacchi, the concierge at Chinnici's apartment block. Mafioso Michele Greco receives a life sentence for ordering Chinnici's murder (and many other crimes) on December 16, 1987.

August: DEA agents arrest Sicilian mafioso Benito Zito in Philadelphia, Pa., on charges of selling 2.5 kilos of heroin to undercover agent Stephen Hopson.

September: FBI informers report that Philadelphia's Mafia family has created a hit list of dissident members led by Harry "The Hunchback" Riccobene. Those targeted for death include his brother Robert Riccobene, Richard Gregorio, Thomas Inverato, Joseph Kahan, Frank Martinez, Robert Rego, and Salvatore Tamburrino.

September 6: Hitman David Pardesi, employed by Bada Rajan, kills rival mobster Amirzada Nawab Khan following a court appearance in Mumbai, India.

September 19: President Reagan signs another

secret "finding," authorizing CIA assistance and $19 million for the Contras during fiscal year 1984.

September 21: Rival gangsters murder Bada Rajan in Mumbai, India.

October 9: Federal jurors in Milwaukee, Wis., convict mafioso Frank Balistrieri on five gambling and tax charges, while acquitting him on five other gambling counts. Four co-defendants stand convicted on 19 charges, acquitted on two. Balistrieri receives a four-year prison term and a $15,000 fine on May 29, 1984.

October 11: A federal grand jury in Milwaukee indicts Frank Balistrieri and various associates on charges of using influence to secure loans from the IBT pension fund and using the money to bankroll Las Vegas casinos.

October 14: Gunmen in Philadelphia, Pa., wound mafioso Frank Martinez but he survives the attack.

October 22: Aryan Brotherhood members stab four guards at the federal prison in Marion, Ill., killing Officers Merle Clutts and Robert Hoffman. The slayers receive additional life prison terms.

October 26: Faced with a prison term of life plus 103 years, Cleveland mafioso Angelo Lonardo turns informer for the FBI, hailed as the highest-ranking Mafia defector in U.S. history. In exchange, federal judge John Mandos reduces Lonardo's sentence to time served plus five years' probation on March 10, 1987.

November: An article in the *Sacramento Bee* quotes statements from IRS and Nevada Gaming Control Board agents, claiming that mobsters skimmed 20 percent of the profits from Paul Laxalt's Ormsby House casino during 1971–76.

November 3: Dissident mafioso Salvatore Tamburrino dies after being shot four times in Philadelphia, Pa.

November 18: Mafia soldiers Eddie and Vincent Carini execute victim Verdi Kaja outside his record shop in Brooklyn, N.Y. Prosecutors charge a cousin, Carmine Carini, as a shooter and getaway driver in the murder. Jurors convict him in 1985, resulting in a 25-year prison term.

December: A federal grand jury in Las Vegas, Nev., indicts mob-friendly federal judge Harry Claiborne on charges of bribery, fraud and tax evasion. Jurors fail to reach a verdict at his first trial, in April 1984, resulting in dismissal of the bribery and fraud counts. A second panel convicts Claiborne of tax evasion in July 1984, resulting in a two-year prison term. Congress votes to impeach Claiborne on July 22, 1986, and the Senate convicts him, ordering his removal from office on October 9.

December 3: Nevada's Gaming Control Board issues an "emergency order" suspending gaming licenses of Al Sachs, Herb Tobman, and their Stardust resort in Las Vegas.

December 6: A shotgun blast kills Philadelphia mobster Robert Riccobene in his backyard, as his mother looks on.

December 8: Congress passes the second Boland Amendment, banning CIA, Defense Department, or third-party support for Contra terrorists in Nicaragua.

December 9: The film *Scarface* premieres in America, presenting a fictional view of the "Cuban crime wave" occurring since 1980s Mariel boatlift.

December 10: Four gunmen fire on a car occupied by mafioso Salvatore Testa and several bodyguards in South Philadelphia, Pa., but all escape injury.

December 16: Police in Philadelphia, Pa., arrest Joseph Mastronardo and his sons on charges of running a $50 million-per-year bookmaking ring in Philadelphia, Bucks and Montgomery Counties. State charges are later dismissed.

1984 The DEA reports cocaine selling for $25,000 per kilo across the U.S.

January: FBI informants report that Philadelphia mafioso Nicodemo Scarfo has cancelled the family's "hit list" targeting dissident members.

January 4: Nevada authorities slap Al Sachs and Herb Tobman with a 19-count complaint alleging 222 gaming violations related to a $1.5 million skim at their Stardust casino during 1982–83. The Gaming Control Board proposes a $3.9 million fine, later cut by $900,000 without explanation. All Sachs-Tobman casinos are ordered to close by May 1 if they cannot prove themselves "squeaky-clean." Sachs agrees to the fines on January 8, without admitting guilt. The state revokes his gaming license, and Tobman's, on January 10, while a grand jury indicts nine subordinates on skimming charges.

January 9: DEA Agent Larry Carwell dies in a helicopter crash, while conducting surveillance operations near the Bahamas.

January 11: Detroit mafioso Peter Joseph Licavoli dies from a heart attack in Tucson, Ariz.

January 16: Douglas County District Court Judge Theodore Carlson rules that Nebraska's state lottery law permits use of video lottery devices.

January 17: Tokyo Yakuza boss Yoshio Kodama dies at home, in his sleep, from a stroke.

January 29: An inmate at the federal prison in Oxford, Wis., fatally stabs Correctional Officer Boyd H. Spikerman in hopes that the murder will win him membership in the Aryan Brotherhood. Instead, he receives a life sentence.

February 4: Unknown machine-gunners kill Gambino Family associate Richard DiNome and two guests at his home in New York, allegedly to stop DiNome from becoming a police informer.

February 7: A federal grand jury in Kansas City, Mo., indicts leaders of the local Mafia family on RICO charges including hidden interest in Argent Corporation and skimming from its Las Vegas casinos; skimming from Kansas City's legal bingo games; and the 1978 murder of victim Carl Spero.

February 8: State narcotics agents arrest Ronnie Foster, former national president of the Warlocks MC, at the Wind Gap Truck and Auto Stop in Bushkill Township, Pa.

March: Responding to Judge Carlson's January ruling, state lawmakers ban all video and mechanical lotteries as of January 1, 1985. Canada introduces the Sports Select Baseball sports pool, then abandons it six months later, when losses hit $46 million. At the pool's last drawing, on September 30, 13 players share a $4.8 million jackpot.

March 5: According to a subsequent indictment, Norwin Meneses launches his conspiracy to sell cocaine in San Francisco, Calif., as a means of funding Contra guerrillas in Nicaragua.

March 10: Colombian police and U.S. DEA agents raid Tranquilandia ("Land of Tranquility"), a huge cocaine-processing plant operated by the Medellín Cartel in the jungles of Caquetá, Colombia. Raiders destroy 14 laboratory complexes and 13.8 metric tons of cocaine, 11,800 drums of chemicals, and seven airplanes, with a total value conservatively estimated at $1.2 billion.

March 12: In New Bedford, Mass., Superior Court Judge Elizabeth Dolan denies a prosecution motion to try Ray Patriarca for the 1968 Candos murder, following testimony that Patriarca suffers from coronary artery disease, diabetes, chronic depression and other ailments.

March 13: Joseph Fino, former Mafia boss of Buffalo, N.Y., dies from natural causes.

March 27: Agents of the Reagan White House seek Israeli backing for Contra terrorists in Nicaragua.

March 30: A federal grand jury in New York indicts mafioso Paul Castellano and 23 associates on 78 racketeering charges, including extortion, loan-sharking, and 25 murders.

April: Agents of the Reagan White House seek Saudi backing for Contra terrorists in Nicaragua. In May, Saudi Arabia agrees to finance the Contras with $1 million per month. The first payment arrives on July 6.

April 6: The *Wall Street Journal* reports mining of Nicaraguan harbors by CIA agents.

April 9: Federal jurors in Milwaukee convict mafioso Frank Balistrieri and his two sons, John and Joseph, on extortion charges filed under the Hobbs Act. Frank Balistrieri receives a 13-year sentence on May 29. John and Joseph receive matching eight-year terms on July 30.

April 16: Bonanno Family members Louis "Louie HaHa" Attanasio Jr. and Salvatore "Good Looking Sal" Vitale murder Cesare "The Tall Guy" Bonventre in Garfield, N.J. In Glasgow, Scotland, an underworld "ice cream war" over distribution turf—with ice cream trucks used as cover for illegal drug sales—culminates with an arson fire at the Ruchazie housing estate, killing six members of the Doyle family. Police say 18-year-old Andrew Doyle had refused to sell drugs on his route.

April 26: Ziauddin Ali Akbar, chief of BCCI's Treasury Department, registers the firm Hourcharm Ltd, at his home address in London, England. On May 22, Hourcharm is renamed Capital Commodity Dealers Ltd., then becomes in Capcom Financial Services July. Capcom commences trading in London on September 17, 1984, with a registered net worth of £25 million ($37 million), increasing to £100 million ($160 million) within 12 months.

April 28: Gunmen in Ibague, Colombia, murder army captain Ignasio Luis Arteaga, employed as security chief for a local producer of rice products, Cooperativa Serviarroz Ltd. Authorities subsequently blame Cali Cartel member Henry "The Scorpion" Loaiza-Ceballos for the slaying.

April 30: Medellín Cartel gunmen riding motorcycles assassinate Colombian Minister of Justice Rodrigo Lara Bonilla. A subsequent indictment names Pablo Escobar as the man responsible for Bonilla's murder, listing cartel leaders José Gonzalo Rodríguez Gacha, Fabio Ochoa Vázquez, Jorge Luis Ochoa Vázquez, and Juan David Ochoa Vazquez as material witnesses. Fearing extradition to the U.S., cartel leaders flee to Panama.

May: Contra terrorists in Nicaragua reportedly run out of cash. In London, England, the former Curzon casino reopens as the Aspinall Curzon. Las Vegas entertainer Wayne Newton announces execution of a contract to purchase the Fremont and Stardust casinos for $200 million, the price demanded by owners Al Sachs and Herb Tobman in February. Sachs and Tobman then file suit to block the sale.

May 14: The U.S. Supreme Court rules against mafioso Ray Patriarca and four codefendants in a Florida racketeering case, reinstating indictments dismissed by a lower court and ordering the five to stand trial. On May 22, U.S. Magistrate Jacob Hagopian of Providence, R.I., rules that Patriarca is too ill to face trial in Florida.

May 15: FBI agents observe a meeting of the Mafia Commission held at a private home on Staten Island, N.Y. Attendees include Gambino Family boss Paul Castellano, *caporegime* Frank DeCiccio, and soldier Tommaso "Thomas" Bilotti; Genovese Family boss Anthony "Fat Tony"

Salerno and soldier Carmine Dellacava; Colombo Family boss Gennaro "Gerry Lang" Langella and *caporegime* Ralph "Little Ralphie" Scopo; Lucchese Family underboss Salvatore "Tom Mix" Santoro Sr. and Aniello "Neil" Migliore.

May 27: Mafioso Anthony D'Anna dies in Detroit of natural causes.

June: Gangster Shinobu Tsukasa founds the Kōdō-kai Yakuza clan in Nakamura-ku, Nagoya, Japan. Italy and the United States convene the first meeting of a new Italian-U.S. Working Group on Drug Interdiction. Alabama lawmakers authorize pari-mutuel betting on horse races. Federal prison administrators in the U.S. grant mafioso John Franzese another parole from his 50-year sentence for bank robbery, with supervision extended to March 20, 2020.

June 4: Drug trafficker Norwin Meneses pays for a banquet in San Francisco, Calif., honoring Contra leader and CIA agent Adolfo Calero.

June 13: Yamaguchi-gumi lieutenant Hiroshi Yamamoto founds the Ichiwa-kai Yakuza family in Osaka, Japan.

June 22: Jurors in New York City convict Laborers Local 95 officials Stephen McNair and Joseph Sherman of labor racketeering in connection with an extortion of funds from the Schiavone-Chase Corporation. Prosecutors alleged that the extortion was directed by Genovese Family boss Vincent Gigante. A military court in Ankara arrests Turkish mob boss Behçet Cantürk for membership in Kurdistan Workers' Party.

June 25: Congress denies aid to the Nicaraguan Contras for the third time. Days later, White House operatives Oliver North and Richard Secord arrange private arms sales to the terrorists.

July 2: In a 4-to-3 decision, the U.S. Supreme Court grants New Jersey state officials the authority to require that officers of labor unions representing Atlantic City casino employees must possess "good moral character."

July 11: New England mafioso Raymond Patriarca Sr. dies from complications of diabetes in North Providence, R.I. Son Raymond Jr. succeeds his father as boss of the regional crime family, while caporegime Ilario "Larry Baione" Zannino is promoted to supervise Boston's rackets.

July 17: The *Washington Times* publishes a story detailing leaked by U.S. National Security Council member Oliver North, detailing DEA informant Barry Seal's infiltration into the Medellín Cartel's operation in Panama.

July 18: Mafioso Dominic Brooklier dies from a heart attack at the Tucson Federal Correctional Complex in Arizona.

July 27: A federal grand jury in Miami, Fla., indicts Medellín Cartel leaders Carlos Lehder, Pablo Escobar, Jorge Ochoa and Jose Gonzalo Rodriguez Gacha for drug trafficking, based on evidence collected by Barry Seal in Panama.

July 18: California mafioso Dominic Brooklier dies from a heart attack at the federal government's Metropolitan Correctional Center in Tucson, Ariz. Peter John Milano succeeds Brooklier as boss of the Los Angeles crime family.

July 30: DEA spokesmen inform CIA headquarters that evidence links agency operatives in Costa Rica to known drug traffickers. CIA officials return $36,000 to one convicted dealer while hurrying to bury evidence of their collusion in cocaine smuggling.

September: Paul Laxalt sues the *Sacramento Bee* and its publisher for $250 million, over allegations of casino skimming published in November 1983. The paper responds with a $6 million counterclaim, accusing Laxalt of attempted censorship. Both lawsuits ultimately fail, but Laxalt's attorneys receive $647,454 from the *Bee*'s insurance carrier in April 1988.

September 2: Members of the rival Bandidos and Comancheros motorcycle clubs wage a firefight outside a bar in Milperra, a suburb of Sydney, Australia. The gunfire kills two Bandidos, four Comancheros, and 14-year-old bystander Leanne Walters, while wounding 28 other persons. On June 12, 1987, Sydney jurors deliver convictions on 63 murder counts, 147 manslaughter charges, and 31 counts of affray. Comancheros founder William "Jock" Ross receives a life sentence as the defendant "primarily responsible for the decision that members of his club go to Milperra in force and armed." Other convicted defendants include seven Comancheros and 16 Bandidos.

September 4: After pleading guilty to RICO charge filed in January, Kansas City mobster Anthony Civella receives a five-year prison term; Carl Civella receives a term of 10 to 30 years.

September 13: U.S. State Department spokesmen announce that a decade of Third World crop substitution programs have failed to eradicate cultivation of coca, marijuana and opium poppies in Burma, Mexico, Pakistan and Peru.

September 14: Pennsylvania hitman Salvatore "Salvie" Testa, AKA "The Crowned Prince of the Philadelphia Mob," dies in a candy shop ambush ordered by mafioso Nicodemo Scarfo. The killers dump his corpse in Gloucester Township, N.J.

September 18: A federal grand jury in New York indicts Lucchese Family boss Anthony Corallo and 20 co-defendants for conspiring to dominate the private garbage collection business on Long Island.

September 29: Sicilian authorities reveal that mafioso Tommaso Buscetta has turned informer.

Autumn: Witnesses in Medellín, Colombia, report sightings of fugitive drug cartel leaders Pablo Escobar, Jose Rodríguez, and the Ochoa brothers.

October 10: Congress passes the Boland Amendment, banning any future U.S. funding of Contra terrorists in Nicaragua. The Reagan White House seeks alternate illegal means to support the guerrillas.

October 10–11: The U.S. House and Senate pass the Comprehensive Crime Control Act of 1984, with provisions including a National Narcotics Act, a Controlled Substance Registrant Protection Act (punishing theft of controlled drugs from registered dealers), a Controlled Substances Penalties Amendments Act (increasing prison terms and fines imposed by earlier statutes), an Aviation Drug-Trafficking Control Act (revoking pilot's licenses and aircraft registrations of convicted drug traffickers), Comprehensive Forfeiture Act (permitting seizure of assets held by defendants in RICO cases), and a Dangerous Drug Diversion Control Act (penalizing diversion of legally produced drugs into illicit channels).

October 12: Journalists expose a "Contra Manual" prepared by the CIA for Nicaraguan right-wing terrorists. Congress passes a third Boland Amendment, reiterating its ban on support for the Contras.

October 14: Mexican Mafia member Alfred Arthur Sandoval fatally shoots rival Maravilla gangsters Anthony Aceves and Gilbert Martinez in Los Angeles, wounding victim Manuel Torres in the same attack.

October 31: Police find victims Ray and Marlene Wells shot execution style at their home in Belvedere Park, Calif. Prosecutors later charge Mexican Mafia member Alfred Arthur Sandoval with the slayings.

November: A grand jury in Las Vegas files a 13-count indictment against various officers of Trans-Sterling Corporation, parent company of the scandal-ridden Stardust casino. Trans-Sterling and Karat, Inc., post $50,000 bond on December 15, to cover potential court costs. Trial is scheduled for May 1985 but never convenes.

November 6: Mexican police and U.S. DEA agents stage the "Bust of the Century" in Chihuahua, raiding a large marijuana cultivation and processing complex owned by drug kingpin Rafael Caro Quintero. Raiders destroy an estimated 5,000 to 10,000 tons of high-grade marijuana valued at $2.5 billion. On the same day, voters in California, Missouri, Oregon and West Virginia approve creation of state lotteries; Missouri lawmakers also authorize pari-mutuel betting on horse races, while Oregon amends its constitution to ban casino gambling.

November 12: Sicilian police arrest businessmen Antonio and Ignazio Salvo on charges of Mafia association. Both are later convicted.

November 13: Hitmen kill West End Gang leader Frank "Dunie" Ryan at his Nittolo's Garden Motel in Montreal, Québec.

November 15: Police in Madrid, Spain, arrest Medellín Cartel leader Jorge Ochoa on charges of illegally smuggling fighting bulls from Spain to Colombia. Facing indictments at home and in the U.S., Ochoa mounts legal maneuvers that delay his extradition until July 1986. Meanwhile, the Medellín Cartel threatens to kill five Americans for every Colombian extradited to the United States.

November 26: Authorities in San Francisco, Calif., arrest a Contra officer and a nephew of Norwin Meneses on drug-trafficking charges.

December 2: Unidentified gunmen murder paroled mafioso-turned-informer Leonardo Vitale outside a church in Palermo, Sicily.

December 3: Detective Marcellus Ward suffers fatal gunshot wounds during a joint undercover operation with the DEA in Baltimore, Maryland. Pittsburgh mafioso John Sebastian Larocca dies of natural causes in McCandless, Pennsylania.

December 5: New York mafioso Rosario Gambino receives a 45-year sentence and a $105,000 fine for selling heroin to undercover police officers. Convicted in the same case, relatives Antonio and Erasmo Gambino each receive 30-year terms, with fines of $50,000 and $95,000 respectively; co-defendant Anthony Spatola also receives a 30-year sentence and a $50,000 fine. DEA officials inform CIA headquarters that the Menses family remains active in drug smuggling with Contra leader Sebastian "Guachan" González.

December 14: *The Cotton Club* premieres in U.S. theaters, with Bob Hoskins as Owney Madden, James Remar as Dutch Schultz, Nicolas Cage as "Vincent Dwyer" (i.e., Vincent Coll), and Laurence Fishburne as "Bumpy Rhodes" (i.e., Bumpy Johnson).

December 23: In a bid to divert the Carabinieri's attention from Mafia prosecutions to terrorism, mafiosi dynamite railroad tracks near Bologna, Italy, derailing a train en route from Naples to Milan, killing 16 persons and injuring 200. A court in Florence, Italy, convicts seven defendants of the bombing—including mafioso Giuseppe Calò—on February 25, 1989.

1985 Canadian lottery ticket sales total $2.7 billion.

January 5: Colombia extradites four drug traffickers to Miami. Days later, U.S. authorities are warned of a Medellín Cartel "hit list" including embassy officials, their families, U.S. businessmen and journalists.

January 26: Japan's "Yama-Ichi War" between the Yamaguchi-gumi and Ichiwa-kai Yakuza gangs begins in Suita, Osaka, when Hiroshi Yamamoto sends hitmen to the home of rival Masahisa Takenaka's girlfriend, where they kill Takenaka, underboss Katsumasa Nakayma, and another gangster. The war continues for several years, leaving 36 mobsters dead and many more seriously wounded in an estimated 220 gun battles.

February 7: Drug cartel members kidnap DEA Agent Enrique "Kiki" Camarena Salazar from a streetcorner in Guadalajara, Mexico, and torture him to death. Authorities recover his mutilated corpse on March 5. Lack of cooperation by Mexican authorities in the subsequent investigation prompts U.S. Commissioner of Customs William Von Raab to order a six-day crackdown on traffic crossing the Mexican border.

February 25: A federal grand jury in New York indicts top leaders of the Mafia's Five Families on RICO charges for operating a criminal enterprise known as the "LCN Commission." Specific charges include murder, labor racketeering, and extortion under the Hobbs Act. Defendants include Genovese Family boss Anthony Salerno; Gambino Family boss Paul Castellano and underboss Aniello Dellacroce; Colombo Family acting boss Gennaro Langella; Lucchese Family boss Anthony Corallo and underboss Salvatore Santoro; and Bonanno Family boss Philip Rastelli. Trial begins for eight surviving defendants in September 1986. Jurors convict all eight on 151 separate counts, November 19, 1986.

March: The U.S. State Department grants political asylum to Contra supporters Chepita and Oscar Danilo Blandón, despite DEA warnings that both are "members of a cocaine trafficking organization" smuggling more than 100 kilos per week.

March 15: Raymond Donovan resigns as U.S. Secretary of Labor, after being indicted with six others on charges of fraud and grand theft in New York City. Jurors acquit all seven defendants at trial, on May 25, 1987.

March 30: Police in Rieti, Italy, arrest mafiosi Giuseppe "Pippo" Calò and Antonio "Nino" Rotolo. (Some reports date the arrests from May 31.) Calò faces charges of money-laundering and ordering the 1984 railroad bombing that killed 16 persons. Rotolo is charged with trafficking in heroin.

April: British Columbia launches an independent provincial lottery.

April 4: Jairo Meneses implicates his uncle Norwin in drug trafficking, but the Reagan DOJ declines to file charges. Soon afterward, Norwin Meneses moves to Costa Rica as a DEA informer, targeting his competition.

April 9: Mafia gambling boss Salvatore Lucido dies of natural causes in Detroit.

April 11: Oliver North tells National Security Advisor Robert McFarlane that the Contras are running out of money. Congress rejects Contra funding once again, on April 23.

May 2: A three-year FBI campaign dubbed "Operation Roughrider" culminates with raids in 11 states, jailing 125 Hells Angels, while netting illegal drugs valued at $2 million and an illegal arsenal ranging from Uzi submachine guns to antitank weapons.

May 16: Top DOJ officials order federal prosecutors to cease legal action against indicted IBT president Jackie Presser. Outraged members of Congress demanded an investigation. That probe produces new fraud indictments against Presser in May 1986.

May 31: Italian police arrest mafiosi Giuseppe Calò and Antonio Rotolo at Calò's villa outside Rome. Rotolo is subsequently released on bond.

June: Mobbed-up entertainer Frank Sinatra receives a Presidential Medal of Freedom from Ronald Reagan.

June 25: A federal grand jury in New York indicts Colombo Family boss Carmine "Junior" Persico on murder and extortion charges in the "LCN Commission" case.

July: Montana legalizes video poker machines in licensed liquor establishments. In Philadelphia, Pa., Nicodemo Scarfo orders the murder of Mafia associate Frank "Frankie Flowers" D'Alfonso, for refusal to pay a "street tax." Family soldiers Eugene "Whip" Milano and Salvatore "Salvie" Testa carry out the contract.

July 1: The DEA uses "emergency" regulations to list MDMA as a Schedule I controlled substance.

July 5: Mafioso Joseph Scafidi dies of natural causes in Philadelphia, Pa.

July 23: Medellín Cartel gunmen murder Bogotá Superior Court Judge Tulio Manuel Castro Gil, who earlier indicted Pablo Escobar for the April 1984 murder of Rodrigo Lara Bonilla. On the same day, in South Philadelphia, Pa., unknown gunmen kill mafioso Frank "Frankie Flowers" D'Alfonso on a public street.

July 28: Palermo mafioso Giovanni Motisi murders police officer Beppe Montana, in charge of the search for Sicilian fugitives. Despite a life sentence imposed *in absentia*, Motisi evades arrest and remains at large.

August 6: Fifteen mafiosi ambush policemen Ninni Cassarà and Giovanni Lercara outside Cas-

sarà's home in Sicily, riddling them with 200 bullets while Cassarà's wife looks on.

August 20: Convicted IBT president Roy Williams enters the U.S. Medical Center for Federal Prisoners in Springfield, Mo., to begin serving his bribery sentence. He is paroled in August 1988, due to failing health and prior cooperation with prosecutors.

August 23: A court in Louisville, Ky., awards former Green Bay Packers quarterback Paul Hornung a $1,160,000 judgment against the National Collegiate Athletic Association, which barred him from betting on games while employed as a college football analyst.

September: DEA spokesmen identify Oscar Danilo Blandón as the head of a cocaine distribution organization in Los Angeles. Federal authorities decline to prosecute. In Panama, Contra physician Hugo Spadafora meets three times with DEA agent Robert Nieves in Costa Rica, accusing Contra leader "Guachan" Gonzalez and Panamanian dictator Manuel Noriega of drug trafficking. Noriega remains on the CIA payroll, while Spadafora is beheaded by assassins one week after his last meeting with Nieves. During the same month, mafiosi Giuseppe Lucchese and Vincenzo Puccio murder Giuseppe "Pino" Greco at his home in Ciaculli, Sicily.

October 10: Opening statements begin in the New York City trial of mafioso Paul Castellano and nine co-defendants, charged with operating an international auto-theft ring that shipped stolen cars to Puerto Rico, Kuwait, and other foreign destinations.

October 28: Acting on orders from mafioso Vincent "The Animal" Ferrara, three gunmen execute mobster Vincent James Limoli in Boston, Mass.

November 6: Members of the M-19 terrorist group invade Colombia's Palace of Justice in Bogotá, seizing some 300 hostages. Colombian troops storm the building, resulting in a battle that claims the lives of all 35 guerrillas, plus 11 Supreme Court justices and 48 soldiers. Before they are killed, the invaders burn many court documents, including all outstanding extradition petitions. Most analysts agree that leaders of the Medellín Cartel sponsored the raid.

November 12: As the "LCN Commission" case continues to expand, a federal grand jury in New York indicts Bonanno Family member Anthony "Bruno" Indelicato for the murders of Leonard Coppolla, Carmine Galante, and Guiseppe Turano.

November 27: Cleveland mafioso James Licavoli dies from a heart attack at Oxford Federal Correctional Institution, Oxford, Wis.

December 2: Indicted mafioso Aniello Dellacroce dies in New York from cancer. His death triggers John Gotti's rebellion against Gambino Family boss Paul Castellano.

December 4: Congress modifies its stance on Nicaragua, permitting "intelligence aid" to Contra terrorists.

December 5: Parties to the 10-year *Penthouse* libel suit surrounding Moe Dalitz's La Costa resort settle their case out of court, with letters of mutual admiration and agreement to pay their own legal fees.

December 16: Gunmen dispatched by mafioso John Gotti execute Gambino Family boss Paul Castellano and underboss Tommy Bilotti outside Sparks Steak House in Manhattan.

December 19: A federal grand jury in New York indicts mafioso Michael Franzese and eight associates on RICO charges involving a plot to sell gasoline to local retailers while evading local, state, and federal taxes.

December 20: Journalists Brian Barger and Robert Parry publish the first of five Associated Press stories linking the CIA and Contras to cocaine trafficking. Most national media outlets ignore the reports, while Parry his hounded from his job by Reagan White House officials.

1986 DOJ spokesmen estimate that the American Mafia has 2,500 "made" members nationwide, working in conjunction with thousands of "civilian" associates. President Reagan declares Nicaraguan Contras "the moral equivalent of our [American] Founding Fathers." The Pequot Indian tribe opens a bingo hall in Connecticut, ranked as the world's most profitable by 2004.

January 1: Milwaukee Mafia boss Frank Balistrieri pleads guilty to federal conspiracy and racketeering charges, receiving a 10-year prison term. On January 7 jurors acquit Balistrieri's sons in the same case.

January 12: The *New York Times* runs an article allegedly written by President Reagan, titled "Declaring War on Organized Crime." The piece closes with Reagan's saying: "I believe that if the American people will now give their full support to the war now going on against the mob, we can, in our children's lifetime, perhaps even in our own — obliterate this evil and its awful cost to our nation."

January 19: The made-for-TV movie *Mafia Princess* premieres in the U.S., starring Susan Lucci as Antoinette Giancana and Tony Curtis as her father, Sam Giancana. Sicilian businessman-mafioso Antonio Salvo dies from cancer at a clinic in Bellinzona, Switzerland.

January 21: Federal jurors in Kansas City, Mo., convict Chicago mobsters Joseph Aiuppa, John Cerone, Angelo LaPierta, and Joseph Lombardo

on conspiracy charges related to looting of the IBT Central States Pension Fund and skimming of $2 million from Nevada casinos. Oliver North requests establishment of a Swiss bank account, for use in funneling proceeds of illegal Iranian arms sales to Contra terrorists in Nicaragua. National Security Advisor John Poindexter approves the plan in February.

February 10: In New York City, NYPD Detectives Stephen Caracappa and Louis Eppolito murder diamond merchant Israel Greenwald on orders from Lucchese Family captain Anthony "Gaspipe" Casso. FBI agents recover Greenwald's body in April 2005. In Palermo, the "Maxi Trial" of 474 mafiosi — including 119 tried *in* absentia — begins in a custom-made bunker next door to Ucciardone prison. The trial culminates on December 16, 1987, with 360 defendants convicted and 114 acquitted. By that time, several of those convicted *in absentia* — including Giuseppe "Pino" Greco, Filippo Marchese, Mario Prestifilippo, and Rosario Riccobono — are already dead. Nineteen convicted defendants receive life prison terms, while sentences for the rest total 2,665 years.

February 19: An unidentified machine-gunner kills DEA informant Barry Seal outside a Salvation Army outlet in Baton Rouge, La.

February 20: Sicilian police arrest mafioso Michele Greco, charging him with the 1983 murder of magistrate Rocco Chinnici. Greco receives a life sentence for the crime on December 16, 1987.

March 18: Mafioso Michele "The Shark" Sindona, serving a life sentence for murder in Voghera, Italy, drinks a cup of coffee spiked with cyanide. He dies from the poison on March 22.

March 20: A federal grand jury in New York indicts Genovese Family boss Anthony Salerno and 14 subordinates on 29 felony counts including conspiracy, extortion, and racketeering.

March 21: Colombo Family member Michael J. Franzese pleads guilty to federal racketeering and tax conspiracy charges in New York City. His plea bargain includes a 10-year prison term, five years' probation, and nearly $15 million in fines, forfeiture and restitution.

April 11: Pennsylvania State Police officers arrest Warlocks MC member Daniel Angelo Peruso for stealing a pickup truck in Limerick two months earlier.

April 13: A remote-control car bomb kills Gambino Family *caporegime* Frank DeCiccio outside the Veterans & Friends Social Club on 86th Street in Dyker Heights, Brooklyn.

Mid-April: Guatemalan narcotics officer Celerino Castillo III receives a telegram from DEA agent Robert Nieves in Costa Rica, reporting

Contra involvement in drug-smuggling from Ilopango, El Salvador.

April 28: Police in Minneola, Long Island, N.Y., arrest paroled mafioso John "Sonny" Franzese on two counts of violating his release terms through associating with known criminals. A federal parole board recommends his return to prison on August 20.

May 7: State police officers raid the home of Warlocks MC member Joseph Centurione in Dublin, Pa., arresting Centurione and wife Linda on charges of possession, possession with intent to deliver methamphetamine, receiving stolen property and criminal conspiracy.

May 9: The 9th U.S. Circuit Court of Appeals in San Francisco overturns John Adamson's death sentence in the Don Bolles murder, finding that he improperly was condemned to die after a trial judge had ruled that a prison term was appropriate.

June 5: Gambino Family underboss Salvatore Gravano lures *caporegime* and pornographer Robert "D.B." DiBernardo to a basement office on Stillwell Avenue in Bensonhurst, Brooklyn, and murders him there, afterward disposing of the body secretly. Authorities declare DiBernardo legally dead in December 1992.

June 8: The *Miami Herald* names Oliver North in a front-page story headlined "Despite Ban, U.S. Helping Contras."

June 12: Russian mobster Vladimir Reznikov accosts rival Marat Balagula at the Rasputin nightclub in Brighton Beach, N.Y., brandishing a pistol and demanding $600,000 plus a percentage of Balagula's rackets to spare Balagula's life. Soon after Reznikov leaves, Balagula suffers a heart attack but survives.

June 13: Members of Roy DeMeo's hit team murder Russian mobster Vladimir Reznikov in New York City. Federal jurors in New York convict leaders of the Colombo Family on RICO charges including bribery, conspiracy, and extortion. Following that verdict, the U.S. Attorney's Office files America's first civil RICO complaint against the convicted defendants. Those convicted include boss Carmine "Junior" Persico; underboss Gennaro Langella; former acting boss Anthony Scarpati; *caporegimes* Dominic Cataldo, John DeRoss, Alphonse Persico Jr., and Andrew Russo; soldier Frank "The Beast" Falanga; and family associate Hugh "Apples" MacIntosh.

June 14: Soldiers from the Chicago Outfit bludgeon brothers Anthony and Michael Spilotro to death in a cornfield outside Morocco, Ind., planting them in shallow graves. A local resident discovers the corpses on June 23.

June 16: Mobster Gaetano Milano murders mafioso William Grasso in New Haven, Conn.

Milano receives a 33-year prison term in 1991, reduced to 26 years in October 2008.

June 19: Basketball player Len Bias dies from a cocaine overdose in Riverdale, Md., two days after he was drafted by the Boston Celtics. On July 25 a grand jury indicts teammates David Gregg and Terry Long for possession of cocaine and obstruction of justice. The same panel indicts Brian Tribble, a friend of Bias, for possession of cocaine with intent to distribute.

June 23: U.S. District Court Judge Harold Ackerman of Newark, N.J., names a trustee to operate IBT Local 560, formerly controlled by the Provenzano faction of the Genovese Family.

June 25: The U.S. House of Representatives approves a $100 million Contra Aid package, by a vote of 221–209. The Senate approve funding in August.

June 27: Don Rodgers, a member of the Cleveland Browns football team and 1983 Rose Bowl Most Valuable Player, dies from a cocaine overdose at his home in California. American journalists "discover" the crack cocaine epidemic.

June 30: IRS agents arrest the sons of bookmaker Joseph Mastronardo Sr. in Philadelphia, Pa., on charges of interstate bookmaking and money-laundering. Joseph Jr. later receives a two-year prison sentence, with a $250,000 fine and five years' probation. Brother John is sentenced to three months in prison, a $250,000 fine, and five years' probation.

July 14: A Spanish court agrees to extradite Colombian drug lord Jorge Luis Ochoa Vásquez to the U.S. Despite that ruling, Ochoa disappears on August 17, after receiving a suspended sentence on charges of falsifying documents for transport of fighting bulls from Spain to Colombia.

July 24: A federal grand jury in the Eastern District of New York indicts Genovese Family member Joseph "Joe Glitz" Galizia and three Russian mobsters — Sheldon Levine, Igor Porotsky, and Igor Roizman — on charges of evading $5 million in gasoline excise taxes. In Arkansas, two DEA agents and an officer of the Jefferson County Sheriff's Office die in a helicopter crash at Mount Ida, during a marijuana eradication mission.

July 26: Two accounts held by Manuel Noriega with BCCI in Luxembourg, valued at $11.1 million total, transfer to the account of the Banco Nacionale de Panama at the Union Bank of Switzerland in Zurich, in the name of a firm titled "Finlay International."

July 31: Drug cartel gunmen assassinate Supreme Court Justice Hernando Baquero Borda in Bogotá, Colombia.

August 25–27: DEA agents in southern California debrief an inside Oscar Blandón's drug network, receiving confirmation that cocaine supports the Contras in Nicaragua. The L.A. County Sheriff's Office launches its own investigation, soon discovers that FBI Headquarters has the same information.

September 25: John Gotti faces trial in New York City on charges spanning an 18-year series of crimes, including armored-car robbery, gambling, loan-sharking, and murder.

October 5: Nicaragua's air force shoots down one of Oliver North's illegal Contra resupply planes. White House spokesmen deny U.S. involvement on October 8.

October 10: In New York City, Lucchese Family members Paul Vario, Frank Manzo and Pasquale Raucci plead guilty to RICO conspiracy charges.

October 13: CIA Director William Casey warns Oliver North that "this whole thing [illegal aid to Contra terrorists] is coming unraveled and that things ought to be 'cleaned up.'" North begins shredding of classified documents while he and Casey debate selection of a "fall guy."

October 23: A federal grand jury in Allentown, Pa., indicts 13 members of United Slate, Tile and Composition Roofers, Damp and Waterproof Workers Association and Residential Reroofers Local 30B on charges including RICO conspiracy, mail fraud, solicitation of kickbacks to influence the operation of an employee benefit plan, embezzlement from an employee welfare plan, Hobbs Act extortion, collection of credit and claims by extortionate means, interstate travel in aid of racketeering and embezzlement of union funds. Defendants include Daniel J. Cannon, Robert Crosley, Michael Daly, Edward Hurst, Michael Mangini, Robert Medina, James Nussi, Mark "Buddy" Osborn, Richard Shoenberger, Joseph Traitz, Stephen Traitz Jr., Stephen Traitz III, and Ernest Williams. Jurors convict all of the accused at trial, in November 1987. A federal appellate court affirms the convictions on March 22, 1989.

October 24: A federal grand jury in New York files a 51-count RICO indictment against members of the Colombo Family. Defendants include the current boss, two former bosses, four capos, several soldiers, and two non-"made" associates.

October 27: A combined strike force including FBI and IRS agents, L.A. County Sheriff's officers and local police raid Oscar Blandón's used-car dealership, and a dozen other locations in southern California. On the same day, President Reagan signs a bill authorizing the CIA to spend $100 million in support of the Contras and the controversial Federal Controlled Substance Analogue Enforcement Act, which states that "a controlled substance analogue shall, to the extent intended for human consumption, be treated, for the purposes of any Federal law as a controlled substance

in schedule I" of the Controlled Substance Act of 1970. Reagan also signs the Anti-Drug Abuse Act of 1986, appropriating $1.7 billion to fight the drug crisis. Of that sum, $97 million is allocated to build new prisons, $200 million for drug education and $241 million for treatment. The law also sets mandatory minimum sentences for drug offenses, including 10 years imprisonment for possessing one kilogram of heroin or five kilograms of cocaine, and five years for selling five grams of crack.

October 31: A New Jersey state grand jury indicts Philadelphia mafioso Nicodemo Scarfo for extortion, gambling, loan-sharking, and racketeering.

November: Unidentified gunmen kill Colonel Jaime Ramírez, head of Colombia's anti-narcotics police unit, on a highway near Medellín, wounding his wife and two sons. A DEA informer reports deliveries of Colombian cocaine to a Costa Rican ranch owned by John Hull, with drugs transported from there to Miami concealed in shipments of frozen shrimp.

November 3: The Lebanese magazine *Ash-Shiraa* reveals illegal U.S. arms sales to Iran. On November 13 President Reagan and Attorney General Edwin Meese admit diversion of funds from those sales to Contras in Nicaragua, sparking the Iran-Contra scandal.

November 5: Jurors in New York convict Harry Davidoff, vice president of IBT Local 851, on two counts of extortion and two counts of conspiracy, filed under the Hobbs Act, related to union activities at JFK International Airport.

November 18: Following conviction on racketeering charges in New York, Colombo Family members Carmine "Junior" Persico and Gennaro "Jerry Lang" Langella receive prison terms of 39 years and 65 years, respectively. On the same day, a federal grand jury in Miami indicts Colombian Pablo Escobar, José Rodríguez Gacha, Carlos Lehder, and the Ochoa brothers for RICO violations, naming their Medellín Cartel as the world's largest cocaine-smuggling organization.

November 24: A federal grand jury indicts Genovese Family boss Anthony Salerno and three other mobsters for "exerting influence and control over" Jackie Presser's 1983 election as president of the IBT.

November 25: U.S. Attorney General Edwin Meese acknowledges diversion of funds from illegal Iranian arms sales to Contra terrorists in Nicaragua.

December 2: Police find the corpse of New Jersey–based "Pizza Connection" defendant Gaetano Mazzara on a Brooklyn street corner, stuffed inside a garbage bag.

December 10: Prosecutors drop all charges filed

against Oscar Blandón following October's raids in southern California. Blandón applies for permanent residence in U.S.

December 13: LAPD officers find former Contra mercenary Steven Carr dead from a drug overdose, shortly before his scheduled testimony concerning Contra drug and arms dealing in Costa Rica.

December 17: Medellín Cartel gunmen assassinate Guillermo Cano Isaza, editor-in-chief of the newspaper *El Espectador*, in Bogotá. In October 1995, four defendants — Carlos Martínez Hernández, María Ofelia Saldarriaga, Luis Carlos Molina Yepes, and Pablo Enrique Zamora — are convicted of the slaying, sentenced to prison terms of 16 years, 8 months. An appellate court subsequently overturns the convictions of all except Molina.

December 19: Lawrence Walsh is chosen as independent counsel to investigate the Iran-Contra conspiracy.

December 23: A federal grand jury in the Eastern District of Pennsylvania files a 61-count RICO indictment against 19 defendants associated with Roofers Union Local 30 in Philadelphia. Charges include bribery, embezzlement, and extortion. Separate indictments charge Judges Mario Driggs of Municipal Court and Esther Sylvester from the Court of Common Pleas with single counts of extortion.

December 26: President Reagan grants NASCAR driver Robert Glenn Johnson Jr. a pardon from his 1956 North Carolina moonshining conviction.

December 27: Shortly after the DOJ refuses to prosecute Oscar Blandón, the assistant U.S. attorney assigned to Blandón's case dies in Los Angeles. Investigators call the death a suicide.

December 31: A drug-trafficking suspect kills DEA Agent William Ramos while resisting arrest at Las Milpas, Tex.

1987 January 1: Syndicate gunmen execute James Lee "Jimmy Casino" Stockwell, owner of the mob-connected Mustang Topless Theater, at his condominium in Buena Park, Calif. Stockwell's slaying is the first of several in a struggle to control the club's thriving drug and prostitution trade.

January 5: The U.S. Senate Intelligence Committee votes against release of its report on the Iran-Contra scandal. Senator Patrick Leahy leaks the document on January 8.

January 6: The U.S. Senate creates a select committee to investigate the Iran-Contra conspiracy. Burglars raid Contra headquarters, stealing financial records.

January 7: The House of Representatives creates a select committee to investigate the Iran-Contra conspiracy.

January 12: LAPD and the LASO create a "Freeway Rick Task Force" to investigate activities of drug kingpin Ricky Donnell Ross, AKA "Freeway Ricky," who obtains his cocaine supplies from Contra supporter Oscar Blandón.

January 13: U.S. District Court Judge Richard Queen sentences eight convicted defendants in the "LCN Commission" case. Anthony Salerno, Carmine Persico, Gennaro Langella, and Anthony Corallo receive 100-year terms without parole and $240,000 fines; Salvatore Santoro receives 100 years without parole and a $250,000 fine; Anthony Indelicato received 40 years without parole and a $50,000 fine.

January 15: U.S. Magistrate Edwin Naythons rules that Philadelphia mafioso Nicodemo Scarfo is a public menace, ordering confinement without bail pending trial on extortion charges.

January 16: Bonanno Family boss Philip Rastelli receives a 12-year term in federal prison for directing a labor racketeering conspiracy through IBT Local 814, carried out between 1964 and 1985.

January 20: The U.S. Parole Commission rules that imprisoned ex–IBT president Roy Williams must serve his full 10-year bribery sentence despite failing health. Undercover DEA Agent Raymond Stastny suffers gunshot wounds in Atlanta, Ga., dying on January 26.

January 21: Contra supporter Dennis Ainsworth contacts FBI agents in San Francisco, Calif., informing them that the Contras have "become more involved in selling arms and cocaine for personal gain than in a military effort to overthrow the current Sandinistas."

February: Unknown gunmen in New York City murder gambler and con artist Pasquale "Paddy Bulldog" Varriale. Police say Varriale received $10,000 from the Bonanno Family to bribe a juror in the "Pizza Connection" trial, then failed to deliver.

February 3: Colombian National Police capture Carlos Lehder at a rural hideout outside Medellín. Extradited to the U.S. on February 4, Lehder is convicted of drug smuggling on May 19, 1988, and receives a sentence of life without parole plus 135 years.

February 9: Former National Security Advisor Robert McFarlane attempts suicide.

February 20: Border Patrol Agent John Robert McCravey suffers fatal injuries in a car crash, while chasing human traffickers near Calexico, Calif. He dies on February 23.

February 24: President Reagan denies any memory of authorizing Iran-Contra arms deals.

February 25: The U.S. Supreme Court rules in *California v. Cabazon Band of Indians*, declaring that Indian reservations are exempt from state and local laws banning bingo, draw poker and other card games. The decision ultimately legalizes Indian casinos nationwide.

March 2: Jurors in New York City convict 18 defendants in the "Pizza Connection" trial, which also produced 175 Mafia indictments in Italy.

March 4: President Reagan contradicts his previous denial, admitting responsibility for Iran-Contra arms transactions. On March 11 he claims "laryngitis" as an excuse for dodging further questions.

March 10: U.S. District Court Judge John Mandos reduces Cleveland mafioso Angelo Lonardo's prison term to time served and releases him on five years' probation, in exchange for Lonardo's services as a government informant.

March 12: Massachusetts mafioso Ilario "Larry Baione" Zannino receives cumulative federal sentences of 20 years for illegal gambling and extortion involving victim Donald Smoot, a gambler who owed him $14,000.

March 13: Federal jurors in New York City acquit mafioso John Gotti and five associates on RICO and conspiracy charges, beginning Gotti's reputation as "the Teflon Don."

March 17: Florida mafioso Santo Trafficante Jr. dies at the Texas Heart Institute in Houston.

Spring: Oscar Blandón relocates from Los Angeles to Miami. Ricky Ross subsequently leaves L.A., resulting in disbandment of the Freeway Rick Task Force.

April: The Overseas Private Investment Corporation (OPIC) requests a DOJ investigation of drug trafficker John Hull, related to a $375,000 loan Hull received in March 1984, to build a wood products factory in Quesada City, Costa Rica. Hull subsequently defaulted on the loan. In July the DOJ assigns Senior Litigation Counsel Ellen Meltzer to investigate possible charges of criminal fraud.

April 21: Senate investigators grant John Poindexter immunity from prosecution to compel testimony on the Iran-Contra conspiracy. Lawrence Walsh opposes further immunity grants on April 28.

April 22: U.S. District Court Judge Vincent Broderick in New York City issues an injunction barring mafiosi Anthony Corallo, Christopher Furnari, Gennaro Langella, Carmine Persico, Dominic Montemarano, Anthony Salerno, Salvatore Santoro, Ralph Scopo, and any other member of the Mafia from participating in the affairs of Local 6A of the Cement and Concrete Workers Union or any other labor organization or employee benefit plan as defined in Title 29 of the U.S. Code, and from participation in any aspect of the concrete construction business nationwide.

April 29: William Ciccone, a mentally unbal-

anced resident of Ozone Park, Queens, fires a pistol at mafioso John Gotti outside the Bergin Hunt and Fish Club. Gambino Family members capture Ciccone and transport him to a Staten Island candy store, where he is tortured and shot to death by family associate Joe Watts.

April 30: Adolfo Constanzo kidnaps drug lord Guillermo Calzada and six members of his household from Mexico City. Police discover the first of their mutilated corpses in the Zumpango River on May 8.

May 5: Joint hearings of Congressional select committees begin on the Iran-Contra conspiracy.

May 6: Federal jurors convict Philadelphia mafioso Nicodemo Scarfo of conspiring to extort funds from waterfront developer Willard Rouse III. Ex-CIA director William Casey dies from a brain tumor in Roslyn Harbor, N.Y.

May 8: Joseph Avila, prominent restaurateur and drug dealer, shot to death in Newport Beach, Calif.

May 19: A federal grand jury in New York indicts Mildred Carmella Russo, a clerk in U.S. District Court, for obstruction of justice. The indictment charges that Russo leaked sealed information to Gambino Family members and associates over a 10-year period.

May 21: A federal jury in Los Angeles indicts mafioso Peter and Carmen Milano, with 13 other defendants, of conspiring to violate the RICO Act through drug trafficking, extortion, and obstruction of justice.

May 28: Inundated by drug cartel threats, the Colombian Supreme Court orders annulment of Colombia's extradition treaty with the U.S., by a vote of 13–12. Annulment becomes official on June 25.

June 2: A new cinematic version of *The Untouchables*, starring Kevin Costner as Eliot Ness and Robert De Niro as Al Capone, premieres in New York City.

June 13: Federal jurors in New York convicts Colombo Family members Carmine Persico, Gennaro Langella, John DeRoss, Andrew Russo, Dominic Cataldo and Alphonse Persico on RICO Act charges of operating a criminal enterprise.

June 16: A federal grand jury in New York City returns indictments in "the largest criminal union fraud scheme" ever prosecuted by the DOJ. Defendants Mario Renda, president of First United Fund, vice president Joseph DeCarlo, and financial consultant Martin Schwimmer stand accused of stealing $16 million from two union pension and welfare funds. DeCarlo pleads guilty in June 1987; on February 28, 1989, he receives five years' probation, 500 hours of community service, and a $10,000 fine. Renda pleads guilty in May 1988; on February 28, 1989, he receives a four-year prison term, five years' probation, and fines totaling $125,000. Jurors convict Schwimmer on October 28, 1988; on February 14, 1989, he receives 10 years in prison, five years' probation, a $1.6 million fine, and an order to pay $10 million in back taxes.

June 22: Police find Mary Lou Davilla Salazar, Francisco Delgado Ortiz and Lourdes Flores murdered in a house on Sunkist Street in Ontario, Calif. Detectives charge Mexican Mafia member Reuben "Tupi" Hernandez with the slayings on June 25.

July 7–14: Oliver North testifies before Congress concerning his involvement in the Iran-Contra conspiracy.

August 4: In Philadelphia, Pa., mafioso Nicodemo Scarfo and six codefendants plead not guilty to charges of conspiracy and murder in the July 1985 killing of Frank D'Alfonso.

August 26: Federal prosecutors in New York file a civil RICO complaint against leaders of the Bonanno Family and various labor leaders, seeking court appointment of a trustee to manage Bonanno-dominated IBT Local 814, forfeiture of three properties used for illegal gambling, and divestiture of three hotels and a taxi company.

September 3: Unidentified gunmen kill Carmine Varriale and Frank Santora in Brooklyn, N.Y. Police identify Santora as a Colombo Family member. Varriale is a member of the Lucchese Family and brother of February murder victim Pasquale Varriale.

September 20: Fugitive Italian banker Licio Gelli surrenders to authorities in Switzerland. He receives a two-month prison term on December 22.

October: Police in Invercargill, New Zealand, charge three members of the Road Knights MC with fatally beating a rival — Robert Holvey, of a gang called The Damned — outside a local prison. The charges are later dismissed.

October 11: A teenage gunman assassinates former presidential candidate Jaime Pardo Leal in La Mesa, Colombia. Police blame Medellín Cartel leader José Gonzalo Rodríguez Gacha for the slaying.

October 13: The Manhattan District Attorney's office charges five officials from the New York City District Council of Carpenters — Attilio Bitondo, Martin Forde, Eugene Hanley, John O'Connor and Irving Zeidman — on charges of collaborating with the Gambino Family to extort money from building contractors. All are convicted and sentenced to prison at trial, in 1990.

October 21: Jurors convict Sicilian immigrant Pietro Alfano, owner of an Oregon pizzeria, in the "Pizza Connection" case, resulting in a 15-year prison term.

October 24: The AFL-CIO executive council unanimously votes for readmission of the IBT, with 1.6 million dues-paying members.

November: In Las Vegas, Moe Dalitz sells the Sundance hotel-casino to the Reno-based Fitzgeralds casino chain.

November 8: Vice President George H. W. Bush wins election as America's 41st president.

November 21: Colombian police arrest Jorge Ochoa on a bull-smuggling charge which earlier prompted his extradition from Spain.

November 22: A band of cartel gunmen invade the home of Juan Gomez Martinez, editor of Medellín's daily newspaper El Colombiano. They present a communiqué signed "The Extraditables," threatening assassination of Colombian officials if Jorge Ochoa is extradited to the U.S. A local court releases Ochoa "under dubious legal circumstances" on December 30.

December 7: The UN General Assembly passes Resolution 41/111, declaring an International Day against Drug Abuse and Illicit Trafficking on June 26 of each year, beginning in 1988.

December 15: A court in Florence, Italy, sentences fugitive financier Licio Gelli in absentia to an eight-year prison term for financing right-wing terrorist activity in Tuscany during the 1970s. Gelli already faces a 14-month sentence issues in San Remo, for illegally exporting funds from Italy.

December 22: MDMA is deleted as a Schedule I controlled substance, due to improper "emergency" scheduling by the DEA in 1985.

December 27: Federal jurors in New York convict Gambino Family underboss Joseph "Piney" Armone on charges of racketeering conspiracy involving extortion, bribery and illegal interstate travel to commit bribery. He receives a 15-year sentence and an $820,000 fine on February 22, 1988.

1988 January: Rivals of the Road Knights MC bomb a bank in Waikiwi, New Zealand, to distract police from the subsequent bombing of a local Road Knights clubhouse. A still-unidentified sniper fires on police at the scene of the second bombing.

January 4: Unknown gunmen kill mafioso Vincent "Jimmy" Rotondo outside his home in Brooklyn, N.Y., shortly before his scheduled promotion to serve as underboss of the DeCavalcante Family.

January 12: Mafia gunmen assassinate Giuseppe Insalaco, ex-mayor of Palermo, Sicily, who tried to clean up municipal corruption during 1984.

January 18: Members of the Medellín drug cartel kidnap Andrés Pastrana Arango, son of former Colombian president Misael Pastrana, who has pressured authorities to extradite prominent cocaine traffickers. Police rescue him a week later, and Pastrana wins election as Bogotá's mayor in March.

January 25: Two gunmen presumed to be members of the Medellín drug cartel assassinate Colombian Attorney General Carlos Mauro Hoyos Jiminez in Bogotá.

February: A U.S. Senate subcommittee chaired by Senator John Kerry opens a two-year investigation of BCCI corruption worldwide.

February 2: Sedgwick County Sheriff's Detective Terry McNett dies from gunshot wounds suffered during a drug raid in Wichita, Kan.

February 5: A federal grand jury in Miami indicts Panamanian dictator Manuel Noriega for drug trafficking in collaboration with the Medellín cartel. In Pasadena, Calif., Taiwanese drug traffickers kill DEA Agents George Montoya and Paul Seema during an $80,000 rip-off.

February 17: Swiss authorities extradite Licio Gelli to Italy under tight security, including armored cars, decoy vehicles, and deployment of 100 police sharpshooters.

February 23: New York mafioso Joseph "Piney" Armone receives a 15-year prison term and an $820,000 fine on racketeering charges including bribery and extortion.

March: Italy creates its third Antimafia Commission. Authorities in Sicily arrest 160 persons based on testimony from mafioso-turned-informer Antonino Calderone.

March 11: Robert McFarlane pleads guilty to four counts of withholding information from Congress in the Iran-Contra scandal. On March 16 federal prosecutors indict Oliver North, John Poindexter, Richard Secord, and Iranian businessman Albert Hakim on 23 counts (some later dismissed when the Reagan administration withholds relevant documents).

March 19: In Sicily, magistrate Giovanni Falcone issues 160 arrest warrants based on testimony from Mafia informer Antonino Calderone.

March 23: Contras and Sandinistas sign a truce at Sapoa, Nicaragua. MDMA returns to the Schedule I list of controlled substances in America, following proper procedures.

April: Jurors in New York convict sports agent Norby Walters of fraud and racketeering for signing college players to professional teams before their eligibility expired. Walters, an alleged associate of mafioso Michael Franzese, receives an 18-month sentence on September 17.

April 6: NYPD spokesmen report that fugitive mafioso Armond "Buddy" Dellacroce, son of late Gambino Family underboss Aniello Dellacroce, has died from a drug overdose. In Tampa, Fla., Customs agents inform the U.S. attorney that "probative evidence exists to establish corporate criminality against BCCI as an institution," and

that "current plans for prosecution are to indict BCCI as an institution under the provisions of the RICO statutes." A second memo repeats those statements on May 10.

April 17: Mafioso Anthony Frank "Nino Glasses" Gaggi dies of natural causes while confined at New York's Metropolitan Correctional Center. Federal jurors convict three Genovese Family members on racketeering charges, while acquitting John Joseph DiGilio Sr. *Frank Nitti: The Enforcer* premieres on American television with Anthony LaPaglia in the title role and Vincent Guastaferro cast as Al Capone.

April 29: Florida's state lottery begins operation.

May 4: Plagued by cancer and federal indictments, Jackie Presser begins a four-month leave of absence as IBT president. He undergoes surgery for a brain tumor on May 14.

May 5: New York jurors convict mafiosi Anthony Salerno, Vincent DiNapoli, Matthew Ianniello and Aniello Migliore of racketeering and bid rigging in the construction industry.

May 12: Police find Gambino Family associate George Yudzevich shot to death in California. Yudzevich earlier testified as a prosecution witness at the racketeering trial of mobster Joseph Armone. Detroit mafioso Frank Meli dies of natural causes in Sterling Heights, Mich.

May 16: Los Angeles mafioso Peter Milano receives a six-year term in federal prison for racketeering. His brother Carmen is sentenced to two years for extorting money from California bookmakers and drug dealers.

May 27: Police find recently-acquitted mafioso John Joseph DiGilio Sr. in the Hackensack River, near Carlstadt, N.J. shot five times in the head. Fellow Genovese Family member Louis Auricchio confessed to the slaying in 1998.

May 28: Adolfo Constanzo's gang sacrifices drug dealer Hector de la Fuente and local farmer Moises Castillo at Rancho Santa Elena, 20 miles outside Matamoros, Mexico.

June 28: In Washington, the DOJ files suit to oust senior leaders of IBT President Jackie Presser and other ranking union officers, claiming that they forged a "devil's pact" with organized crime.

June 29: A grand jury in New York indicts Genovese Family *consigliere* Louis Anthony "Bobby" Manna for conspiring to kill Gambino Family boss John Gotti and his brother Gene.

July 2: Unknown gunmen in Mexico murder two presidential election monitors employed by candidate Cuauhtémoc Cárdenas Solórzano. On July 6, following a nationwide breakdown of the government's IBM AS/400 vote-counting machinery, rival candidate Carlos Salinas de Gortari is declared the winner. Many observers brand the result fraudulent.

July 7: A Texas grand jury indicts drug trafficker Ricky Ross on conspiracy charges.

July 9: IBT president Jackie Presser dies from cancer in Cleveland, Ohio. Union leaders name William J. McCarthy as his successor on July 12.

July 10: A court in Bologna, Italy, absolves Licio Gelli of subversive association in a local terrorist bombing which killed 85 people and wounded more than 200 on August 2, 1980, but he receives a five-year sentence for slandering the investigation. An appellate court voids that sentence on July 18, 1990.

July 19: Mexican Mafia member Reuben Tommy "Tupi" Hernandez receives three consecutive life sentences plus 16 years in California, following conviction in a triple murder.

July 31: Federal agents arrest mobster Gerardo Scarpelli for a robbery in Michigan City, Ind. Confronted with wiretap recordings of his conversations with other mafiosi, Scarpelli agrees to inform on other members of the Chicago Outfit.

August 4: Federal jurors in New York City convict seven defendants on racketeering and extortion charges involving the Wedtech Corporation in the Bronx. Those convicted include Congressman Mario Biaggi; Biaggi's son and attorney, Richard; Bronx Borough president Stanley Simon; Wedtech president and chairman of the board John Mariotta; and Small Business Administration chief of staff and regional director Peter Neglia. On November 18 Mario Biaggi and Mariotta receive eight-year prison terms, with fines of $242,750 and $291,550, respectively; Simon gets five years and a $70,350 fine; Neglia gets three years and a $40,200 fine; Richard Biaggi receives two years and is fined $71,250. An eighth defendant, Wedtech counsel Bernard Ehrlich, receives a six-year sentence and a $222,000 fine on January 10, 1989.

August 12: Adolfo Constanzo's cult performs another human sacrifice at Rancho Santa Elena, crediting the ritual for the August 13 release of gang member Ovidio Hernandez and his infant son, recently kidnapped by rival drug traffickers.

August 22: New Canadian legislation imposes a maximum six-month jail term and a $100,000 fine on any person who To advocate legalization of cannabis, promotes consumption of cannabis for medical reasons, advocates use of cannabis hemp for fiber, demonstrates how cannabis is grown, or puts out any newsletters, magazines or videos presenting cannabis in a positively light. Conviction of a second offense brings one year in prison and a $300,000 fine.

August 26: Jurors in New York acquit Lucchese Family members Anthony "Tumac" Accetturo,

Michael Salvatore "Mad Dog" Taccetta, and 18 codefendants on multiple racketeering charges.

August 29: Unknown gunmen execute mobster Wilfred "Willie Boy" Johnson in Brooklyn, N.Y. Johnson has been an active FBI informer inside the Gambino Family since 1969.

September: A U.S. federal investigation dubbed "Dentex" culminates with indictments of 11 defendants in five cities on charges of bribery and kickbacks in awarding health care benefit contracts.

September 2: *The Deceivers* premieres in the U.S., starring Pierce Brosnan as a British officer opposing thugs in India during 1825.

September 6: After exhaustive hearings, DEA administrative law judge Francis Young says that marijuana has clearly established medical uses and should be reclassified as a prescriptive drug. The agency ignores his recommendation.

September 9: Posing as a drug-money-launderer, undercover U.S. Customs agent Robert Mazur meets with Amjad Awan, BCCI's personal banker to Panamanian General Manuel Noriega, at the Grand Bay Hotel in Miami, Fla., secretly recording their conversation.

September 17: Adolfo Constanzo gang member Florentino Ventura kills himself in Mexico City, after murdering his wife and a family friend.

September 18: General Saw Maung assumes command of Myanmar (formerly Burma) as president of a military junta called the State Law and Order Restoration Council (known after November 15, 1997, as the State Peace and Development Council). Ironically, heroin production and exportation increases under military rule.

September 24: Federal jurors in Broward County, Fla., convict imprisoned mafioso Joseph "Piney" Armone on charges of extortion, loan-sharking, and racketeering.

September 25: Mafia assassins murder Judge Antonio Saetta and his son in an ambush outside Palermo, Sicily. Saetta is a member of the Palermo Court of Appeal, and has refused bribes related to that court's impending review of "Maxi Trial" verdicts.

September 26: Unknown gunmen kill Mauro Rostagno, a journalist and anti-drug crusader who has denounced Mafia drug traffickers on local television, in Valderice, Sicily.

September 28: Assassins kill mafioso Giovanni Bontade and his wife at their home in Palermo, Sicily.

October 10: A federal grand jury in Tampa, Fla., indicts Capcom Financial Services Ltd., the British parent company of the Chicago-based Capcom Futures, Inc. (associated with the BCCI), on charges of conspiracy to launder money for the Medellín Cartel and to violate federal narcotics laws.

October 11: Police in Victoria, Australia, kill mobster Graeme Jensen in a lawnmower repair shop, when he resists arrest on suspicion of murder.

October 17: President Reagan signs the Indian Gaming Regulatory Act, creating three classes of gaming permitted on reservations. Class I gaming covers traditional Indian gaming and social gaming for minimal prizes; Class II includes various forms of bingo and non-banked card games; Class III grants limited authority for standard casino gaming.

October 18: Federal jurors in New York City convict IBT Local 875 officers Frank Casalino and Richard Stolfi on racketeering charges. On February 23, 1989, Casalino receives a four-year prison term, while Stolfi gets five years.

October 19: Timothy Smith, imprisoned for embezzlement in 1981 and barred from running any employee benefit plan for the next five years, receives a five-year sentence in Philadelphia, Pa., for income tax evasion and another year for holding a prohibited position, related to his management of another union benefit plan. His sentence also includes five years' probation.

November 5: Drug trafficker Ricky Ross returns to Los Angeles from Cincinnati, Ohio.

November 10: A federal grand IBT Local 473 members Frank Costanzo Jr. and Carmen Parise on charges of extortion and depriving a union member's rights by violence, stemming from threats against union member Jerry Lee Jones.

November 19: Federal jurors in Philadelphia convict mafioso Nicodemo Scarfo on RICO charges including drug trafficking, loan-sharking, extortion and nine counts of murder. Scarfo subsequently receives a 45-year prison term. On the same day, Congress passes the Anti-Drug Abuse Act, creating the Office of National Drug Control Policy, replacing the term "recreational use" with "abuse," and imposing the death penalty for murders related to drug trafficking.

December 1: Carlos Salinas de Gortari takes office as president of Mexico. Despite promises to collaborate with the U.S. in suppressing narcotics traffic, the *New York Times* later deems his administration "synonymous with fraud, corruption and economic devastation."

December 2: David Friedland receives a 15-year prison term in Camden, N.J., pursuant to his September guilty plea on RICO conspiracy charges involving IBT Local 701's pension fund in North Brunswick. His sentence is concurrent with a seven-year term received in 1982 for defrauding the same pension plan.

December 5: A grand jury in Cleveland, Ohio, indicts five officials of IBT Local 432 for racketeering and embezzling $259,000 from the union's welfare fund. Defendants include Salvatore T. "Sam" Busacca, son Salvatore I. Busacca, Pat Lanese, Michael Paventi, and Gary Tiboni. On December 6 the grand jury charges attorney Joseph Kalk with aiding in the crimes. Busacca Sr. is already serving a 10-year sentence for racketeering, imposed in a separate case during August 1987.

December 12: Mafioso Anthony Provenzano dies from a heart attack at a federal penitentiary in Lompoc, Calif.

December 15: A federal grand jury in New York indicts Lucchese Family members James Abbatiello, Michael LaBarbera Jr., and Peter Vario on charges of controlling the concrete industry on Long Island through their positions and influence in Local 66 of the Laborers' International Union of North America.

December 20: In Vienna, Austria, the UN passes a Convention Against Illicit Traffic in Narcotic Drugs and Psychotropic Substances, legally effective as of November 11, 1990.

December 21: William Hainsworth, former administrator for the welfare fund of Plasterers & Cement Masons Local 803 pleads guilty to perjury and embezzling $62,484 from the union fund. Jurors in New York City convict IBT Local 804 secretary-treasurer John F. Long and Local 808 secretary-treasurer John Mahoney Jr. on charges of racketeering, RICO conspiracy, extortion and perjury.

December 22: An appellate court overturns John Adamson's latest death sentence in the bombing murder of Arizona journalist Don Bolles.

December 24: John Gotti Jr. and Michael "Mikey Scars" DiLeonardo become "made" members of the Gambino Family.

1989 Illinois and Iowa legalize riverboat casino gambling. South Dakota legislators approve limited-stakes casino gambling in Deadwood.

January: Authorities in Athens, Greece, approve extradition of fugitive mobster Albert "Caesar" Tocco for trial in Chicago on extortion and racketeering charges. Costa Rican authorities indict John Hull on charges of murder, narcotics trafficking, and "hostile acts" related to a 1985 bombing that killed several journalists.

January 13: Federal jurors in Cleveland, Ohio, convict IBT Local 507 president Garold Friedman and recording secretary Anthony Hughes of racketeering and embezzling more than $700,000 from the union.

February: Outgoing Major League Baseball commissioner Peter Ueberroth and successor Bart Giamatti question Cincinnati Reds player-manager Pete Rose about gambling allegations. *Sports Illustrated* reports the ongoing investigation in its

March 21 issue. On August 24 Rose voluntarily accepts a permanent ban from professional baseball.

February 8: A federal grand jury in San Francisco, Calif., indicts Norwin Meneses for drug-trafficking offenses committed during 1984–85. The indictment and resulting arrest warrant are immediately sealed.

February 14: Adolfo Constanzo's gang sacrifices rival drug dealers Ernesto Diaz and Ruben Garcia at Rancho Santa Elena.

February 21: Oliver North's trial begins in the Iran-Contra conspiracy. On May 4, jurors convict him on three counts and acquit on nine others. North receives a sentence of 1,200 hours community service and $150,000 fine on July 5.

February 24: Businessman Albert Muth pleads guilty in Modesto, Calif., on a charge of mail fraud relating to his acquisition of $750,000 from the pension fund of IBT Local 701 in New Jersey.

February 25: Adolfo Constanzo's cult sacrifices Jose Garcia, a cousin of gang member Ovidio Hernandez, at Rancho Santa Elena.

February 26: *The Revenge of Al Capone* premieres on American television, with Ray Sharkey in the title role. Neil Giuntoli portrays Dutch Schultz, with Scott Paulin cast as Eliot Ness and Jordan Charney as J. Edgar Hoover.

February 27: Twenty-five soldiers of the Medellín Cartel invade the home of emerald magnate Gilberto Molina, 43 miles west of Bogotá, Colombia, during a housewarming party. The gunmen murder 18 persons including Molina, another emerald dealer, a retired police colonel in charge of Mr. Molina's security, plus various bodyguards, guests, and musicians. In Frankfurt am Main, West Germany, police arrest Russian mobster Marat Balagula, a fugitive from justice since his 1986 conviction for credit card fraud in the U.S. They extradite Balagula in December and he receives an eight-year prison term.

February 28: Mafioso Constabile "Gus" Farace fatally shoots undercover DEA agent Everett Hatcher on Staten Island, N.Y., during a meeting to discuss cocaine sales. A nationwide manhunt begins.

March: Yakuza boss Hiroshi Yamamoto retires in Osaka, Japan, whereupon his Ichiwa-kai clan dissolves.

March 3: Robert McFarlane receives two years' probation, a $20,000 fine and 200 hours community service for Iran-Contra offenses.

March 7: Alan S. Cohn, vice president of marketing for United HealthCare, Inc., pleads guilty in Baltimore, Md., on one count of conspiracy to commit mail fraud. United HealthCare subsequently pays a $150,000 civil fine. In Springfield,

Mass., two officials of Iron Workers Local 357 are sentenced for conspiring to embezzle more than $400,000 from the union: Robert Edmund McNulty receives a two-year term, while James Kennedy receives two years' probation.

March 9: Contract killer John "Chokemaster" Sheridan executes club owner Horace "Big Mac" McKenna at his home in Brea, Calif. Employers David "English Dave" Amos and ex-policeman Michael "Mike" Woods assumes control of McKenna's clubs. Sheridan turns informer in January 2000, resulting in the arrest of Amos and Woods on October 26–27. Jurors subsequently convict all three in McKenna's slaying.

March 10: Gerald Thomas Callahan, former secretary-treasurer of Iron Workers Local 357, receives a six-month prison term and two years' probation related to embezzlement of union funds in Springfield, Massachusetts.

March 13: Adolfo Constanzo's cult sacrifices another victim at Rancho Santa Elena. Dissatisfied with the result, Constanzo demands another victim. Gang members drive to South Padre Island, Tex., and kidnap college student Mark Kilroy and return him to the ranch for sacrifice that night.

March 14: Joseph Kinkade, former president of Roofers Local 30/38, pleads guilty to extortion in Allentown, Pa. On March 15 Kinkade and co-defendant Gary McBride plead guilty to multiple racketeering charges. Kinkade and McBride receive prison terms of 18 to 36 months, plus $3,000 fines. In New York City, Federal District judge David Edelstein approves an agreement between the IBT and DOJ, resulting from a RICO complaint filed in June 1988, creating an independent review board to certify union elections in 1991.

March 15: A federal grand jury in Florida indicts attorney Allan F. Meyer for criminal violations in obtaining a $1,075,000 loan from IBT Local 701 in New Jersey. Meyer is the ninth defendant indicted in connection with the local's pension plan.

April: Israeli arms traffickers led by Yair Klein, Pinchas Shahar and Maurice Sarfati deliver 500 Israeli-manufactured machine guns to the Medellín Cartel, including one used to assassinate Colombian presidential candidate Luis Carlos Galán on August 18, 1989. NBC News reveals the transaction on August 21.

April 1: Adolfo Constanzo's gang sacrifices ex-policeman Victor Sauceda at Rancho Santa Elena.

April 8: Mexican federal officers arrest drug lord Miguel Angel Felix Gallardo in a suburb of Guadalajara, holding him on charges related to the kidnap-murder of DEA agent Enrique Camarena.

April 9: Returning to Matamoros from a meeting with Adolfo Constanzo in Brownsville, Tex., gang member Serafin Hernandez drives past a police roadblock. Believing himself magically invisible, he ignores pursuing squad cars and leads them to Rancho Santa Elena. Two more gang members arrive on the scene, regaling officers with tales of black magic and human sacrifice. Excavation begins on April 10, revealing 15 mutilated corpses by April 16. The dead include Mark Kilroy and two renegade narcotics agents, Miguel Garcia and Joaquin Manzo. Three victims remain unidentified today.

April 14: Senator John Kerry releases a report by the U.S. Senate Committee on Foreign Relations Subcommittee on Narcotics, Law Enforcement and Foreign Policy, detailing links between the Nicaraguan Contras and drug traffickers.

April 17: Police raid Adolfo Constanzo's luxury apartment in Atizapan, outside Mexico City.

April 28: Ex-IBT president Roy Williams dies from cardiac disease and emphysema at his farm in Leeton, Mo.

May: DOJ investigator Ellen Meltzer and two FBI agents interview drug trafficker John Hull in Costa Rica. Hull declines to furnish copies of his financial records.

May 2: Gerardo Scarpelli, hitman-turned-FBI informant, hangs himself in a shower stall at the Chicago Metropolitan Correctional Center. On the same day, unknown gunmen kill Russian mobster Michael Markowitz in Brooklyn, New York, presumably because he testified against members of the Genovese and Lucchese Families in federal court.

May 5: Cleveland mobster Morris Kleinman dies in Florida.

May 6: Police surround Adolfo Constanzo's hideout in Mexico City, sparking a 45-minute gun battle that leaves one officer wounded. Inside the flat, Constanzo orders triggerman Alvaro de Leon Valdez to kill him and male lover Martin Quintana. Valdez complies, then surrenders with cult "Godmother" Sarah Aldrete. De Leon receives a 30-year sentence for the double slaying in August 1990. Aldrete receives a 62-year sentence in 1994, while four other cult members are sentenced to 67 years each.

May 11: Vincenzo Puccio is beaten to death at Ucciardone Prison in Palermo, Sicily, by fellow mafioso-inmates Antonino and Giuseppe Marchese (nephews of Mafia boss Filippo Marchese), who plead self-defense. Both are later convicted of murder and sentenced to life imprisonment. On the day of Vincenzo's slaying, gunmen also kill his brother Pietro outside Ucciardone Prison.

May 20: DEA Agent Rickie Finley dies in a plane crash outside Lima, Peru, during "Operation Snowcap."

May 26: Italian police arrest several mafiosi in Palermo, Sicily. Those seized with a cache of weapons include Salvatore "Totuccio" Contorno and his cousin, Gaetano Grado.

June: A shootout in Saugus, Mass., leaves Boston mobster Francis Salemme seriously wounded, allegedly by rival Frank Imbruglia. In Cincinnati, Ohio, a grand jury indicts drug-trafficker Ricky Ross. Antimafia magistrate Giovanni Falcone and his wife when police find a bomb planted next to their beach house in Sicily.

June 6: Anonymous letters signed "Il Corvo" ("The Crow," understood to mean "provocateur") circulate in Sicily, accusing magistrate Giovanni Falcone and police inspector Gianni De Gennaro of bringing mafioso Salvatore Contorno to Sicily to launch a state-sponsored purge of the Corleonesi Mafia faction.

June 17: Police retrieve the corpse of murdered Patriarca Family underboss William P. Grasso from the Connecticut River.

June 20: Authorities find and defuse a powerful bomb at the home of magistrate Giovanni Falcone in Addaura, Sicily, during a conference on Mafia money-laundering with Swiss jurists Carla Del Ponte and Claudio Lehman.

July: Police in Mountain View, Calif., charge Nuestra Familia member Raymond F. Johns with the murder of Nancy Johnson, found beaten and strangled in her home. Indicted drug trafficker John Hull flees Costa Rica, traveling through Haiti and on to the U.S.

July 5: A car bomb kills Antonio Roldan Betancur — governor of Antioquia, the Colombian state surrounding Medellín, while on his way to deliver a speech condemning terrorism. The blast also kills three bodyguards and two bystanders. In Palermo, Sicily, gunmen execute Antonino Puccio, brother of murdered mafiosi Pietro and Vincenzo Puccio.

July 6: A grand jury in New York indicts Pete Rose's bookmaker, Richard Troy, on charges of involvement in a gambling ring run by the Gambino Family.

July 7: Gambino Family members Gene Gotti and John Carneglia receive 50-year prison terms for drug trafficking. Peter Gotti, another brother of boss John Gotti, replaces Gene as the family's *caporegime* in Queens, N.Y.

August 1: The U.S. Chemical Diversion and Trafficking Act of 1988 takes legal effect, regulating 12 precursor chemicals, eight essential chemicals, tableting machines, and encapsulating machines related to production of cocaine in South America.

August 8: Longtime mob–IBT attorney and onetime Las Vegas casino owner Morris Shenker dies in St. Louis, Mo.

August 9: Unidentified gunmen kill Richard Costello Sr., president of ILA Local 1964, and son Richard Jr. at their union office in Ridgefield, N.J. Both are known associates of the Gambino Family.

August 14: President Bush grants executive clemency to two persons convicted of organized crime offenses. He pardons Raymond Joseph Shovelski (convicted in 1974 of conspiracy to accept kickbacks on government contracts) and commutes the sentence of Douglas Bruce Fenimore (1981, receiving and concealing stolen property, interstate transportation of stolen property, and bank robbery).

August 15: The Chicago Mercantile Exchange Clearing House Finance Subcommittee reviews Senate findings on Capcom U.S., a BCCI subsidiary, finding reasonable grounds to charge the firm with violations of CME rules including "Acts of bad faith" (commingling customer funds with house funds); Permitting the Misuse of facilities; Detrimental Act; Uncommercial conduct; Accepting new trades when account undermargined; Transfers of positions with no change in ownership; notification of reduction in capital in excess of 20 percent; and non-compliance with financial requirements. In October, Capcom pays a $500,000 fine and withdraws from CME membership.

August 17: Medellín Cartel gunmen kill Superior Judge Carlos Ernesto Valencia, shortly after he indicts Pablo Escobar for the murder of Guillermo Cano.

August 18: Drug cartel gunmen assassinate former presidential candidate Luis Carlos Galán Sarmiento at a political rally near Bogotá, Colombia. As a result of his murder, President Virgilio Barco Vargas issues an emergency decree reestablishing Colombia's extradition treaty with the U.S. On the same day, in Medellín, assassins kill Valdemar Franklin Quintero, commander of police for Antioquia. A group of cartel leaders calling themselves "The Extraditables" subsequently declares war on the federal government, launching a campaign of narcoterrorism continuing through January 1991. Police arrest congressman and former minister of justice Alberto Santofimio Botero for complicity in Galán's murder on May 13, 2005. Convicted on October 11, 2007, Santofimio receives a 24-year prison term.

August 24: The Chicago Board of Trade expels Capcom UK, a BCCI subsidiary.

August 31: Moe Dalitz dies in Las Vegas, Nev., from cancer and kidney failure.

September 1: An FBI drug sting in Los Angeles nabs several corrupt lawmen assigned to task forces investigating Oscar Blandón and Ricky Ross. In Marseille, France, rival mobsters kill Jose Vanverberghe, brother of "Francis the Belgian."

September 6: A human-trafficking suspect fatally shoots Border Patrol Agent Keith Connelly during an undercover investigation in Fresno, Calif.

September 11: Mafiosi James Gallo and Vincent "Vinny Ocean" Palermo murder independent sanitation contractor Fred Weiss outside his apartment on Staten Island, N.Y.

September 14: Lucchese Family soldiers Anthony Senter and Joseph Testa receive life sentences for participating in a dozen murders committed by Roy DeMeo's hit team.

September 17: Mobster Maya Dolas leads an attack on the rival Joshi gang in Mumbai, India, killing five persons.

October 11: Mafia defector Francesco Marino Mannoia begins collaborating with magistrate Giovanni Falcone in Palermo.

October 16: A federal grand jury indicts De-Cavalcante Family boss Giovanni "John the Eagle" Riggi, his sons, family underboss Girolamo "Jimmy Dumps" Palermo, and soldier Salvatore Timpani on RICO charges involving their control of Laborers Union Local 394 in Elizabeth, N.J. Jurors convict Giovanni Riggi and Timpani on July 20, 1990, while acquitting the other defendants. Riggi receives a 15-year prison term.

October 19: A civil complaint filed in federal court in Newark, N.J., accuses Genovese Family boss Vincent Gigante of conspiring to control IBT Local 560 in Union City by means of racketeering.

October 31: Mafioso Nicodemo Salvatore Scarfo Jr. suffers nine bullet wounds from a masked machine-gunner during a Halloween party at Dante and Luigi's restaurant in Philadelphia, Pa.

November 8: Medellín Cartel gunmen execute Jorge Enrique Pulido, director of JEP Television in Bogotá, Colombia. Richard Secord strikes a bargain with Iran-Contra prosecutors, pleading guilty on one count to receive a sentence of two years' probation.

November 11: A federal grand jury indicts Patriarca Family members Robert "Bobby Russo" Carrozza, Vincent "The Animal" Ferrara, Dennis Lepore, Angelo "Sonny" Mercurio, and Joseph Russo on RICO charges including extortion, loan-sharking and cocaine trafficking.

November 17: A Nassau County grand jury declines to indict John Gotti Jr. on charges of assaulting two men and a woman outside a Long Island nightclub. On the same day, a shootout in Bensonhurst, Brooklyn, kills fugitive mobster Costabile "Gus" Farace Jr., wounding Joseph "Big Joe" Sclafani Sr. and son Joseph Jr.

November 21: Iran-Contra defendant Albert Hakim pleads guilty on one count, receiving a sentence of two years' probation and a $5,000 fine.

November 22: The Mirage hotel-casino opens in Las Vegas, Nev. Gambler Elmer Sherwin wins $4.6 million on opening night, on a Megabucks spin.

November 27: The Arizona Attorney General's office files new murder charges against James Robison in the 1976 bombing death of Don Bolles. A bomb explodes aboard Avianca Airlines Flight 203, en route from Bogotá to Cali, Colombia, killing all 107 persons aboard plus three on the ground. Authorities speculate that Medellín Cartel leaders hoped to kill presidential candidate César Gaviria Trujillo, who missed his scheduled flight. U.S. authorities later convict cartel assassin Dandeny Muñoz Mosquera of the bombing and sentence him to 10 life terms plus 45 years.

November 28: LAPD arrests Ricky Ross on charges stemming from his Cincinnati drug-trafficking indictment.

December: Canada's first permanent legal casino opens at the Fort Garry Hotel in Winnipeg, Manitoba.

December 4: Jurors in Marseille, France, acquit Francis Vanverberghe on heroin-trafficking charges.

December 6: A truck bomb planted by Medellín Cartel terrorists explodes in Bogotá, Colombia, outside headquarters of the Administrative Department of Security. The blast kills 52 persons and wounds at least 1,000.

December 15: Indicted Panamanian dictator Manuel Noriega declares war on the U.S. On the same day, Colombian National Police and soldiers raid a ranch at Tolu, Colombia, killing fugitive Medellín cartel leader José Gonzalo Rodríguez Gacha, his son, and four other associates. An estimated 15,000 people flock to Rodríguez Gacha's funeral on December 17.

December 20: U.S. military forces invade Panama in "Operation Just Cause," seeking to capture and extradite Manuel Noriega. Noriega surrenders on January 3, 1990, and is returned to America for trial. Operation Just Cause claims the lives of 228 soldiers (23 American and 205 Panamanian); estimates of Panamanian civilian deaths range from 200 to 4,000.

1990 Lottery ticket sales in the U.S. total $20 billion, with a net profit to state agencies of $10 billion. West Virginia pioneers the concept of "racinos," allowing the MTR Gaming Group to install slot machines and video lottery terminals at Mountaineer Race Track in Chester.

January: A plea bargain struck by BCCI and federal prosecutors in Tampa, Fla., keeps the corrupt bank alive, with DOJ spokesmen in Washington, D.C., lobbying state regulators to permit continued BCCI operations in their several jurisdictions.

January 19: Detroit mafioso Paul Vitale dies of natural causes in Clinton, Mich.

January 25: President Bush proposes an additional $1.2 billion for America's "war on drugs," including a 50 percent increase in military spending.

February 6: Jurors in Los Angeles convict mafioso Michael Anthony Rizzitello of attempted murder in the shooting of local strip club owner William Carroll.

February 7: A federal grand jury in Chicago indicts mobster Ernest Rocco Infelise on 21 racketeering counts. Jurors convict him on 20 counts, on March 10, 1992, but fail to reach a verdict on a charge that he conspired to murder bookie Hal Smith. Infelise receives a 63-year prison term on August 19, 1993.

February 8: New York jurors acquit "Teflon Don" John Gotti Sr. and codefendant Anthony Guerreri on RICO charges related to the shooting of Carpenters Union Local 608 official John O'Connor.

February 22: Federal prosecutors indict CIA agent and Iran-Contra conspirator Thomas G. Clines on four felony counts of underreporting his income for 1985–86 by at least $260,000 and failing to disclose that he had foreign overseas bank accounts. Jurors convict Clines on September 18. On December 13, 1990, he receives a 16-month prison term and a $40,000 fine.

February 25: Serbian gangsters Aleksandar "Kristijan" Golubović and Dragan "Gagi" Nikolić shoot up a disco bar at Belgrade's Mažestik Hotel while searching for a rival mobster.

March: DEA agents in San Diego, Calif., open an investigation of drug smuggler and Contra supporter Oscar Blandón.

March 5: Cocaine dealers murder New York State Police Criminal Investigator Joseph Aversa during undercover negotiations on Manhattan's Lower East Side.

March 15: A federal grand jury in New York indicts Burmese drug lord Khun Sa on 10 counts alleging that his agents smuggled 3,500 pounds of heroin into New York City during one 18-month period. Additional charges name him as the source of a heroin cache seized in Bangkok, Thailand. U.S. Attorney General Richard Thornburgh acknowledges "no immediate hope" of an arrest.

March 21: Federal agents arrest Illinois mobster Donald "The Wizard of Odds" Angelini on racketeering and gambling charges. At trial Angelini receives a 37-month prison term. Authorities parole him on October 14, 1994.

March 22: A federal grand jury in Boston indicts eight members and associates of the Patriarca Family on RICO charges including murder, extortion, gambling, and other crimes. Defendants include Raymond Patriarca, Vincent "The Animal" Ferrara, J.R. Russo, Robert Carozza, Dennis Lepore, Carmen Tortora, Pasquale Barone and fugitive Angelo Mercurio. Ferrara pleads guilty in 1992 and receives a 22-year sentence. U.S. District Judge Mark Wolf reduces Ferrara's sentence and orders his release on April 12, 2005, after finding that prosecutors illegally withheld evidence that a key witness tried to recant his testimony.

April 1: Sicilian police arrest mafioso Giuseppe Lucchese on multiple murder charges. He later receives a life sentence.

April 7: Federal jurors convict Iran-Contra conspirator John Poindexter on five counts of conspiracy, obstruction of justice, lying to Congress, defrauding the government, and the alteration and destruction of evidence. An appellate court overturns the verdict on November 15, 1991.

April 19: Nuestra Familia member Louie "Dumptruck" Chavez leaves California's Tehachapi State Prison with orders from "generals" Vincent "Chente" Arroyo and Joseph "Pinky" Hernandez to re-establish the gang's regiment in San Jose.

April 27: *The Krays* premieres in London, England, starring real-life twins Gary and Martin Kemp as 1960s mobsters Ronald and Reginald Kray.

May 27: Nuestra Familia member Ronald Shelton is paroled in California and assumes command of the gang's chapter in San Jose.

May 30: A federal grand jury in New York indicts top-level mafiosi in the "windows" case, related to labor racketeering in the construction industry. Defendants include Genovese Family boss Vincent Gigante, underboss Venero Mangano, and soldier Joseph Zito; Colombo Family underboss Benedetto Aloi; Lucchese Family boss Vittorio Amuso, underboss Anthony Casso, and *caporegime* Peter Chiodo; and Gambino Family *caporegime* Peter Gotti. Gigante avoids prosecution by feigning mental illness, wandering the streets in pajamas and muttering incoherently.

June 25: Arizona rancher, liquor distributor and organized crime figure Kemper Marley dies of cancer in La Jolla, Calif.

June 28: The U.S. Supreme Court leaves intact a 1988 appellate court's judgment overturning John Adamson's death sentence in the bombing murder of Arizona reporter Don Bolles.

July: The DOJ's Criminal Division declines to prosecute drug trafficker John Hull on fraud charges, as recommended by Senior Litigation Counsel Ellen Meltzer. The agency's Fraud Section Chief sends a memorandum to the director of the Commercial Litigation Section, recommending a civil lawsuit.

July 4: Fireworks detonated outside the Hells Angels clubhouse on East 3rd Street in Manhattan accidentally kill a 14-year-old neighbor and injure three other persons. In San Jose, Calif., police accuse Nuestra Familia members Victor "Sleepy" Esquibel and Lorenzo "Lencho" Guzman of stabbing gang rival Carlos "Weasel" Mejias outside a liquor store.

July 21: Oscar Blandón tells undercover DEA agents that he is "due to receive $1 million dollars back from the U.S. government."

August: Police find Lucchese Family *caporegime* Bruno Facciola stabbed and shot in the eyes, with a dead canary stuffed in his mouth, after corrupt NYPD detectives finger Facciola as an FBI informer.

August 13: Nuestra Familia member William "Indio" Agundez beats a fellow inmate at the San Jose County jail, allegedly on orders from incarcerated gang leaders.

August 17: Mexican Mafia member Joe "Colorado Red" Ariaz executes victims Daniel Arriaga and Salvador Barrasa in Fontana, Calif., for their failure to pay $30,000 in gang "taxes."

September: The U.S. House Ethics Committee reprimands Massachusetts congressman Barney Frank for his relationship with male prostitute Stephen Gobie. Frank admits paying Gobie for sex "years earlier" and hiring him as an assistant, but claims he fired Gobie upon learning that Gobie ran a prostitution service from Frank's apartment. In Stockton, Calif., members of Nuestra Familia gather for a strategy meeting at the home of Lisa Quevas. Andrew "Mad Dog" Cervantes demotes Louie "Dumptruck" Chavez to second-in-command of the San Jose chapter, serving under new chief Ronald "Lucky" Shelton. Japanese gangsters on Okinawa organize the Okinawa Kyokuryu-kai Yakuza clan, following a rift in the parent organization. Authorities formally designate the group as a criminal organization in June 1992.

September 6: Ricky Ross pleads guilty to drug-trafficking charges in Cincinnati. In Bogotá, Colombian President Cesar Gaviria Trujillo offers drug traffickers who surrender voluntarily reduced prison sentences to be served in Colombia, as an alternative to U.S. extradition.

September 10: *The Lost Capone* premieres on American television, starring Eric Roberts as Al Capone and Adrian Pasdar as lawman-brother Jimmy Capone AKA "Richard Hart."

September 14: *State of Grace* premieres in the U.S., incorporating some actual events in a fictionalized account of the Westies gang in New York City.

September 17: Newly paroled Nuestra Familia member Bobby "Silent" Lopez joins the gangs chapter in San Jose, Calif.

September 18: The film *Goodfellas* premieres in New York City, starring Ray Liotta as Mafia associate-turned-informer Henry Hill. Joe Pesci wins an Academy Award for Best Actor in a Supporting Role.

October 16: A Los Angeles attorney representing corrupt policemen jailed in an FBI drug sting informs the media of Oscar Blandón's involvement with the CIA and Contras. A federal judge quickly issues a gag order.

October 22: Nuestra Familia member William "Indio" Agundez gives a formal statement on the gang's activities to Police Inspector Sandra Williams in San Jose, Calif. Later that day, a gang member attacks Agundez's brother at San Quentin prison, slashing his throat.

October 30: Drug dealers kill undercover Syracuse Police Investigator Wallie Howard Jr. while attempting to rob him of $42,000 in the Bronx, N.Y.

November 6: Colorado voters approve limited-stakes casino gambling in the former mining towns of Black Hawk, Central City and Cripple Creek. On the same day, in New York City, NYPD detectives-turned-hitmen Stephen Caracappa and Louis Eppolito execute Gambino Family member Edward Lino on orders from Lucchese Family member Anthony "Gaspipe" Casso.

November 17: At a Nuestra Familia gang meeting in San Jose, Calif., drug dealer John Blanco names competitor Tony "Little Weasel" Herrera as a police informer. Gang lieutenant Sheldon "Skip" Villanueva issues a "green light" for Herrera's execution. On November 20 gunmen ambush Herrera on Wooser Avenue, shooting him eight times in the head.

November 24: Ex-FBI agent William Roehmer publishes *War of the Godfathers*, a "nonfiction novel" including a chapter on the mythical murder of Moe Dalitz and the federal conviction of his nonexistent killers.

December: Nuestra Familia member Bobby "Silent" Lopez wins promotion to serve as "security director" of the gang's chapter in San Jose, Calif. Ronald "Lucky" Shelton orders member Robert "Fat Cow" Jasso's execution for verbal insubordination.

December 19: Arizona prosecutors refile murder charges against Max Dunlap in the 1976 bombing death of Don Bolles. Dunlap and James Robison are also charged with conspiring to obstruct the Bolles investigation. Confessed murder participant John Adamson renews his promise to testify against the pair, in return for reinstatement of his 1977 plea bargain and 20-year prison term.

December 20: *The Godfather: Part III* premieres in Beverly Hills, Calif., continuing the fictional exploits of the Corleone Mafia family, including a thinly-disguised treatment of Pope John Paul I's alleged murder. The film receives seven Oscar nominations but fails to win in any category.

1991 Louisiana becomes the fourth state to authorize riverboat gambling. In Japan, the Goto-gumi Yakuza clan moves its headquarters from Fujinomiya, Shizuoka Prefecture, to Tokyo.

January: Drug lord brothers Fabio Ochoa Vázquez, Jorge Luis Ochoa Vázquez and Juan David Ochoa Vázquez surrender to Colombian authorities in exchange for reduced prison terms. Jorge and Juan serve five years before their release in July 1996.

January 9: Lucchese Family boss Vittorio "Little Vic" Amuso and underboss Anthony "Gaspipe" Casso name Alphonse "Little Al" D'Arco to serve as acting boss while Amuso and Casso fight federal RICO indictments.

January 10: Clothing manufacturer Libero Grassi publishes an open letter to the Mafia in the Palermo newspaper *Giornale di Sicilia*, condemning Mafia extortion. On the same day, Grassi gives police the names of five alleged extortionists, prompting their arrest in March.

January 25: Colombian journalist Diana Turbay Quintero is killed in Medellín, as police attempt to rescue her from drug cartel kidnappers.

February: Sicilian judge Giovanni Falcone becomes Director of Penal Affairs in the Italian Ministry of Justice.

February 1: Claudio Martelli takes office as Italy's minister of justice, assigning magistrate Giovanni Falcone to prepare new anti–Mafia legislation.

February 5: The Constituent Assembly of Colombia is created to draft a new constitution.

February 8: Ricky Ross receives a 10-year federal prison term for drug trafficking.

February 26: Italy's Supreme Court orders the release of 42 mafiosi convicted in the Maxi Trial of 1986–87. Minister of Justice Claudio Martelli issues a special decree returning them to jail.

March: The Bank of England asks the Price Waterhouse accounting firm to carry out an inquiry on BCCI. On June 24, under the codename "Sandstorm," Price Waterhouse reports that BCCI has "widespread fraud and manipulation" which makes it difficult, if not impossible, to reconstruct the bank's financial history. On July 5, 1991, a court in Luxembourg orders BCCI liquidated because it is hopelessly insolvent, with an estimated $9.5 billion lost or stolen. On the same day, regulators in five countries seize and close BCCI offices. On July 17, British officials reveal that BCCI has used stock in First American Bank as collateral for loans used to conceal fraud at BCCI. The same report declares that BCCI has never turned a profit during its existence.

March 5: President Bush pardons Charles Walker Harrison, convicted in 1966 of unlawful possession of narcotics without having paid transfer tax.

March 15: California jurors convict Nuestra Familia members Lorenzo "Lencho" Guzman and Victor "Sleeper" Esquibel in the July 1990 stabbing death of Carlos "Weasel" Mejias.

March 23: Nuestra Familia member Leonel Jose Cano slashes the throat of Fresno Bulldog gang leader Gabriel Coronado in the Santa Clara County (Calif.) jail. Coronado survives the wound.

April 1: Iowa launches the first gambling boat in recent American history, with individual players limited to $200 in losses per cruise.

April 11: Palermo businessman Libero Grassi appears on national television in Italy, condemning Mafia extortion.

April 12: An order from the DOJ in Washington, D.C., bars Hotel Employees and Restaurant Employees Union president Edward T. Hanley from direct involvement in Atlantic City, N.J., Local 54, after mafioso Philip Leonetti testifies fo Hanley's ties to the Chicago Outfit and Philadelphia mafioso Nicodemo Scarfo.

April 13: Unknown gunmen kill Gambino Family member Bartholomew "Bobby" Boriello outside his home in Bensonhurst, Brooklyn. Investigators say the hit was ordered Lucchese Family underboss Anthony "Gaspipe" Casso.

April 15: Nuestra Familia members Bobby "Silent" Lopez and Ronald "Lucky" Shelton kill PCP dealer Larry Valles in San Jose, Calif., after Valles refuses their demand for 25 percent of his income.

May: California authorities jail Nuestra Familia member Bobby Lopez for parole violations. Jerry "Cripple" Salazar succeeds Lopez as chief of the gang's San Jose chapter.

May 1: Drug cartel soldiers murder Colombian Minister of Justice Enrique Low Murtra in downtown Bogotá.

May 13: Costa Rican authorities request John Hull's extradition to face trial on murder and drug-trafficking charges. The U.S. State Department informs DEA headquarters but takes no further action.

May 17: Costa Rican journalist Jorge Valverde tells DEA Country Attaché Ronald E. Lard that a DEA agent helped drug trafficker John Hull flee Costa Rica in July 1990. The accused agent denies any impropriety on May 30.

May 29: Convicted Ohio mafioso John "Peanuts" Tronolone dies in Florida prior to commencement of a nine-year prison term.

June 12: California jurors convict Mexican Mafia member Joe "Colorado Red" Ariaz of first-degree murder in the death of victim Daniel Arriaga, but fail to reach a verdict in the slaying of Salvador Barrasa. On August 8 Ariaz receives a sentence of 29 years to life in state prison.

June 13: DEA agents secure audio and video tapes of Oscar Blandón negotiating a 50-kilogram cocaine shipment with an agency informer.

June 19: By a secret vote of 51–13, the Constituent Assembly of Colombia incorporates a ban on extradition in the nation's new constitution, effective as of July 5.

June 20: A five-man hit team led by Colombo Family *consigliere* Carmine Sessa storms the home of *caporegime* Vittorio "Little Vic" Orena, but premature gunfire allows Orena to escape.

June 26: Nuestra Familia member Raul "Roy" Reveles stabs fellow gang member Elias Rosas to death in California, for "snitching" on member Pablo "Panther" Pena.

July 5: With extradition to the U.S. legally banned, Medellín cartel boss Pablo Escobar surrenders to Colombian police. President Bush pardons Thomas Leoutsakos (convicted in 1968 for selling methamphetamine) and Laurie Virginia Rossetti (1976, conducting an illegal gambling business).

July 9: CIA officer Alan Fiers Jr. pleads guilty to two misdemeanor counts in the Iran-Contra case. He receives one year probation and 100 hours of community service on January 31, 1992.

July 16: Mexican Mafia members Rene "Boxer" Enriquez and Benjamin "Topo" Peters stab fellow gangster Salvador "Mon" Buenrostro 26 times in an interview room at the Los Angeles County jail. The attack comes in retaliation for Buenrostro insulting gang leader Joe Morgan.

July 22: A court bailiff in Salinas, Calif., kills Nuestra Familia member Daniel Ray Mendoza when Mendoza attempts to seize his pistol, during Mendoza's arraignment on charges of armed robbery, burglary and possession of stolen property.

July 23: DEA contract pilot Harold Wires admits flying fugitive John Hull from Costa Rica to Haiti in 1990. claiming that a DEA agent paid him $700 for the trip. Other informants corroborate the story on August 9 and 12.

July 24: Nuestra Familia member fatally shoots Esteban Guzman in San Jose, Calif., for selling drugs at a price below that set by Nuestra Familia leaders.

July 25: Louie "Dumptruck" Chavez delivers a Nuestra Familia "hit list" to California parole officer E.J. Allen.

July 26: *Mobsters* premieres in the U.S., fictionalizing the rise of Lucky Luciano, Meyer Lansky, Bugsy Siegel and Frank Costello during Prohibition.

July 28: Nuestra Familia members kill victim Martin Bacos in an ambush at Santee Elementary School in San Jose, Calif.

July 29: New York City D.A. Robert Morgenthau indicts BCCI on 12 counts of fraud, money-laundering and larceny. According to the charges, BCCI's "scheme was premised on the fact that banks rely on credit. The essence of the scheme was to convince depositors and other banking and financial institutions, by means of false pretenses, representations, and promises that the BCC Group was a safe financial repository and institution for funds, and thereby defendants acted to persuade depositors and banking and other financial institutions to provide the BCC Group banks with deposits and credit."

July 31: Betty Amato, wife of Pittsburgh mafioso Frank "Sonny" Amato Jr., wins a $12.6 million Pennsylvania Lottery Super 7 jackpot. While FBI agents say "it just seemed too good to be true," investigation results in no charges.

August: Convicted drug trafficker Ricky Ross begins testimony against Los Angeles police officers indicted on corruption charges in connection with his case.

August 8: Federal jurors in Hartford, Conn., convict mafioso Nicholas "Nicky" Bianco on two counts of racketeering. He receives a 138-month prison term on November 25.

August 9: Mafia assassins kill Antonio Scopelliti, a prosecutor scheduled to argue the government's final appeal of the Maxi Trial before Italy's Supreme Court, during his vacation in Calabria, Italy.

August 13: DEA Agent Alan Winn dies in a helicopter crash during drug surveillance operations over the island of Hawaii.

August 18: Unknown gunmen kill gangster Arthur "Fat Boy" Thompson Jr. in Glasgow, Scotland. Police charge Paul John Ferris with the murder, plus attempted murder of Thompson's father, drug-trafficking, and other charges, but jurors acquit him on all counts.

August 21: Alphonse "Little Al" D'Arco steps down as acting boss of the Lucchese Family and flees into hiding.

August 26: Nuestra Familia members gather in San Jose, Calif., at the home of Anthony Guzman, to plot the murders of suspected police informers Sheila Apodaca and Ray "Chocolate" Perez. Police arrest Guzman and gang member and Ronald Shelton, but Shelton sends a message to Bobby Lopez, instructing him to proceed with the murders. Gunmen execute Sheila Apodaca on August 28, then kill Perez on August 29.

August 29: Unidentified gunmen kill anti–Mafia crusader Libero Grassi in Palermo, Sicily. Jurors convict mafiosi Francesco "Ciccio" Ma-

donia and his son Salvatore "Salvino" Madonia of Grassi's murder in October 2006.

September 3: Yakuza boss Susumu Ishii dies in Tokyo, Japan.

September 6: Federal prosecutors indict CIA deputy director for operations Clair E. George on ten counts related to the Iran-Contra conspiracy. His first trial ends with a hung jury on July 13, 1992. On December 9, 1992, a second jury convicts him on two felony counts of lying to Congress.

September 20: A grand jury in New York City indicts Gambino Family *caporegime* Ralph "Ralphie Bones" Mosca, his son Peter, and Joseph Passanante on charges of operating a citywide gambling network.

September 21: Lucchese Family defector Alphonse D'Arco becomes a federal witness against the Mafia.

September 26: Indicted drug trafficker John Hull telephones Inspector Sandalio Gonzalez of the DEA's Office of Professional Responsibility, denying charges that a DEA agent helped him flee Costa Rica in 1990. Hull repeats that denial in a letter penned on October 7. The DEA accepts Hull's word and issues a "letter of clearance" to the accused agent on January 15, 1992.

October 3: Police blame an ongoing Boston gang war for the death of Barry Lazzarini, a restaurateur found bound and bludgeoned at his home in Manomet, Mass.

October 7: Former Assistant Secretary of State for Western Hemisphere Affairs Elliott Abrams pleads guilty to misdemeanor charges in the Iran-Contra conspiracy, receiving two years' probation, 200 hours community service and a $50 fine.

October 21: Nuestra Familia defector Louie "Dumptruck" Chavez agrees to testify against the gang in California.

October 28: Police in New Jersey jail Barry Lesher, a Pennsylvania member of the Warlocks MC after finding him in possession of a machine gun and three unregistered, stolen pistols.

November: Gambino Family underboss Salvatore "Sammy the Bull" Gravano agrees to become a federal witness, admitting participation in 19 murders.

November 1: *Billy Bathgate* premieres in the U.S., starring Dustin Hoffman as Dutch Schultz.

November 3: Nicaraguan National Police arrest Norwin Meneses, Enrique Miranda, and three others in Managua, with 1,593 pounds of cocaine.

November 7: Mexican soldiers kill seven officers of the Federal Judicial Police in Veracruz, allegedly after mistaking them for drug smugglers. On November 27 Mexico's attorney general admits that the soldiers "may have been" guarding 814 pounds of Colombian cocaine. President Carlos Salinas de Gortari orders an investigation, culminating in the brief detention of a general who is subsequently released without trial.

November 10: *The Return of Eliot Ness* premieres on American television, starring Robert Stack for the last time as Eliot Ness in a wholly fictional story.

November 15: BCCI faces a new federal indictment, charging that it illegally bought control of another American bank, Independence Bank of Los Angeles, using Saudi businessman Ghaith Pharaon as a front man. In December, BCCI's liquidators plead guilty to all pending American criminal charges, thus clearing the way for BCCI's formal liquidation. BCCI pays $10 million in fines and forfeits all $550 million of its American assets — a record, at the time, for the largest single criminal forfeiture ever obtained by federal prosecutors.

November 16: Police raid the Lokhandwala Complex in Mumbai, India, sparking a four-hour shootout that leaves seven gangsters dead, including Maya Dolas.

November 18: Mafia gunmen aligned with Vittorio Orena ambush rival mobster Gregory "The Grim Reaper" Scarpa Sr. in New York City, while Scarpa is driving with his daughter and granddaughter. All three escape injury.

November 24: Mafia gunmen kill soldier Hank Smurra in his car in the Sheepshead Bay section of Brooklyn.

November 26: Federal prosecutors indict senior CIA operations officer Duane Ramsdell "Dewey" Clarridge on seven counts related to the Iran-Contra conspiracy.

November 29: Guards at California's Santa Clara County jail find drugs and weapons on the fourth-floor cellblock housing Nuestra Familia gang members. In New York City, Larry Sessa — nephew of Colombo Family *consigliere* Carmine Sessa — escapes injury from an ambush by masked gunmen.

December: Ronald Robert Carey becomes the first IBT president elected by a direct vote of the union's membership.

December 9: LAPD arrests Oscar Blandón on conspiracy and drug-trafficking charges, then drops the case at the request of DOJ officials under Attorney General William Barr.

December 20: *Bugsy* premieres in U.S. theaters, starring Warren Beatty as Bugsy Siegel, Ben Kingsley as Meyer Lansky, and Annette Benning as Virginia Hill. The film wins two Academy Awards, for Best Art Direction–Set Decoration and Best Costume Design.

December 26: Epifano "Fano" Trafficante, brother of mafioso Santo Trafficante Jr. and a convicted felon, dies from natural causes in Tampa, Fla.

December 27: New York mafioso Michael Franzese receives more prison time for violating terms of his 1989 release from 10-year racketeering sentence imposed in 1986.

1992 Sicilian Mafia leaders meet with Russian mobsters in Prague, Czechoslovakia, and with U.S. mafiosi in Switzerland, to coordinate traffick in drugs and weapons. Louisiana approves operation of a gambling casino in New Orleans. President Carlos Salinas de Gortari issues regulations for DEA agents operating in Mexico, including a limit on the number of agents allowed in the country, denial of diplomatic immunity, a ban on carrying firearms, and designation of cities where they may live. Japanese authorities name the Kyoto-based Aizukotetsukai Yakuza clan as a criminal organization under new legislation, prompting a legal challenge from leader Tokutaro Takayama. The Kyoto District Court dismisses Tokutaro's lawsuit in September 1995.

January: Relatives of New Jersey mafioso John "Johnny Boy" D'Amato report him missing. Police locate his bloodstained car but no other trace of D'Amato. Eleven years later, in July 2003, jurors convict defendant Philip Abramo of D'Amato's slaying and four other gangland murders.

January 10: Jurors in New York City convict Gambino Family member George "Big Georgie" Remini on charges of civil contempt and obstructing justice for refusing to testify at the trial of former *caporegime* Thomas Gambino. Remini receives an 18-month prison term.

January 26: Police find Russian mobsters Andrei Kuznetsov and Vladimir Litvinenko shot and partially dismembered in Los Angeles.

January 30: Italy's Supreme Court affirms the sentences imposed on various Maxi Trial defendants in Sicily. Mafia leaders still at large retaliate by drawing up a death list of public officials involved in the trial.

February 23: Gambino Family underboss Joseph "Piney" Armone dies in New York while serving a 15-year prison term.

March 10: Unknown gunmen kill a sister of mafioso-turned-informer Peter "Fat Pete" Chiodo outside her home in Brooklyn, N.Y.

March 12: An assassin on a motorcycle ambushed ex-mayor Salvatore Lima outside of Palermo, Sicily, killing him with multiple gunshots. Police say the Mafia blamed Lima for failing to block confirmation of the earlier Maxi Trial verdicts.

March 13: *American Me*, dramatizing the creation and rise of the Mexican Mafia, premieres in the U.S., starring Edward James Olmos (who also directed). Eme members publicly denounce the film's portrayal of their gang.

March 25: An unknown gunman executes Mexican Mafia veteran Charles "Charlie Brown" Manriquez at the Ramona Gardens housing project in Los Angeles. Manriquez served as a technical advisor to director Edward James Olmos on *American Me*.

March 26: Hells Angels in Montreal, Québec, create the Rockers MC as a "puppet club" for service in the "Québec Biker War."

March 27: Pennsylvania authorities culminate a seven-year investigation with the arrest of Warlocks MC member Eric Martinson and his common-law wife on money-laundering charges related to methamphetamine sales in New York.

April: Turkish mobster Behçet Cantürk imports six tons of morphine base and five tons of marijuana from Pakistan.

April 2: A new RICO trial begins for Gambino Family boss John Gotti in New York City's federal court, on charges including murder, conspiracy to commit murder, loan-sharking, illegal gambling and tax evasion. Jurors convict Gotti on June 23, resulting in a sentence of life imprisonment without parole.

April 16: A court in Milan convicts 33 defendants on fraud charges related to the collapse of Banco Ambrosiano in 1982. Licio Gelli receives a sentence of 18 years and six months, reduced to 12 years on appeal. Former Banco Ambrosiano deputy chairman Carlo De Benedetti receives a sentence of six years and four months, overturned on April 21, 1998.

May: Gambling begins at Rhode Island's first "racino," Twin River Casino and Racing.

May 6: Federal agents in New York City arrest six NYPD officers and one retired officer after a five-month undercover drug operation.

May 13: Paroled Mexican Mafia member Jose "Joker" Gilbert Gonzales murders Ana Lizarraga, a gang counselor at Ramona Gardens housing project in Los Angeles and a consultant on the film *American Me*.

May 15: Federal agents arrest Oscar Blandón and his wife Chepita at an INS office in San Diego, Calif., when they go to pick up Chepita's green card.

May 22: "Retired" Chicago Outfit boss Tony Accardo dies from congestive heart failure at his home in Barrington Hills, Ill.

May 23: Mafia assassins detonate a remote-control bomb on the highway between Palermo International Airport and Palermo proper, killing magistrate Giovanni Falcone, his wife, and three police officers: Rocco Di Cillo, Antonio Montinaro, and Vito Schifani.

June: Members of Laborers Local 110 in St. Louis, Mo., vote local Mafia boss Matthew "Mike" Trupiano Jr. out of the union.

June 1: A grand jury in Santa Clara, Calif., indicts 21 Nuestra Familia members on multiple felony charges. Defendants include Vincent "Chente" Arroyo, Santos "Bad Boy" Burnias, Leonel "Leo" Cano, Andrew "Mad Dog" Cervantes, Anthony "Chico" Guzman, Joseph "Pinky" Hernandez, Timothy "Timo" Hernandez, Bobby "Silent" Lopez, Alice Perez Lomelin, Carlos "Gusano" Mendoza, Irene Nieto, Raul "Ro" Reveles, Jerry "Cripple" Salazar, Herminio "Spankio" Serna, Martin Serna, Ronald "Lucky" Shelton, Carmen Trinidad, James "Huevo" Trujeque, Eddie "Flaco" Vargas, Sheldon "Skip" Villanueva and Celeste Williams.

June 8: Italy's fourth Antimafia Commission begins operations spanning 17 months. Before its dissolution in February 1994, it publishes 13 reports.

June 15: Federal jurors in Manhattan convict Lucchese Family boss Vittorio "Little Vic" Amuso on 54 RICO charges including murder, narcotics trafficking, loan-sharking, labor racketeering, and illegal gambling.

June 16: Federal prosecutors indict ex–Secretary of Defense Caspar Weinberger indicted on two counts of perjury and one count of obstructing justice, related to the Iran-Contra conspiracy.

June 25: Jurors in New York convict Bonanno Family soldier Thomas "Tommy Karate" Pitera on six counts of first-degree murder plus charges of narcotics trafficking. He subsequently receives a life sentence.

July 10: Federal jurors in Miami convict Manuel Noriega on eight counts of drug trafficking, money-laundering and racketeering, resulting in a 40-year prison sentence.

July 16: Sicilian mafioso Gaspare Mutolo begins cooperating with magistrate Paolo Borsellino to solve the murder of Giovanni Falcone.

July 19: A car bomb in Palermo, Sicily, kills magistrate Paolo Borsellino and five police bodyguards: Agostino Catalano, Walter Corsina, Emanuela Loi, Vincenzo Li Muli, and Claudio Traina.

July 27: A stroke kills mafioso Anthony "Fat Tony" Salerno at the Medical Center for Federal Prisoners in Springfield, Mo.

July 30: Called to testify before a U.S. Senate subcommittee investigating the BCCI and its Capcom subsidiaries, Kerry Fox — Vice-President and General Manager of communications and electronics at Martin Marietta and President of two of Rockwell International's major divisions — pleads the Fifth Amendment on grounds of possible self-incrimination.

August: A Nicaraguan court convicts Norwin Meneses of cocaine trafficking. He receives a 30-year sentence in Tipitapa Prison.

September 5: Mafioso Carmine "The Doctor" Lombardozzi, AKA "The Italian Meyer Lansky," dies of natural causes in New York.

September 6: Italian police capture fugitive mafioso Giuseppe "Piddu" Madonia in Sicily.

September 12: Police arrest fugitive mafiosi Gaspare, Paolo and Pasquale Cuntrera at Rome's Leonardo da Vinci–Fiumicino Airport following their expulsion from Venezuela. On the same day, *Teamster Boss: The Jackie Presser Story* premieres on American television, with Brian Dennehy in the title role.

September 17: Mafia assassins execute wealthy Sicilian businessman-mafioso Ignazio Salvo in Santa Flavia, apparently for failing to influence the Maxi Trial appellate verdict.

September 18: Medellín Cartel gunmen kill Myriam Rocio Velez, Superior Judge of Bogotá's Circuit Court, prior to her scheduled sentencing of Pablo Escobar on murder charges.

September 25: A federal grand jury indicts mafioso Santo Trafficante III on charges of bank fraud and money-laundering at the Key Bank of Florida.

October 1: Jurors in Chicago convict Outfit "fixer" Gus Alex on extortion charges.

October 2: Police in Dedham, Mass., blame Boston mobsters for the murder of restaurateur Rocco Scali, shot in the parking lot of a local pancake house.

October 13: Oscar Blandón strikes a deal with federal prosecutors in California, reducing a possible life prison term to four years.

November: Federal jurors convict imprisoned Russian mobster Marat Balagula on charges of bootlegging gasoline. The conviction adds 10 years to his previous eight-year sentence.

November 16: Tommaso Buscetta testifies before Italy's Antimafia Commission, saying that murdered politician Salvatore Lima "was, in fact, the politician to whom Cosa Nostra turned most often to resolve problems for the organisation whose solution lay in Rome."

December 2: An unknown gunman kills Lucchese Family soldier Patrick "Patty" Testa in the garage of a Brooklyn used-car dealership.

December 24: Unidentified gunmen in Queens, N.Y., execute Thomas and Rosemarie Uva, a married couple who support themselves by robbing Mafia social clubs in Little Italy. Police find a submachine gun and a quantity of stolen jewelry in the victims' car. Former ILA president Thomas Gleason dies in New York City. President Bush pardons five defendants in the Iran-Contra scandal, including ex–Secretary of Defense Caspar Weinberger, ex–Assistant Secretary of State for Western Hemisphere Affairs Elliott Abrams, ex–National Security Advisor Robert McFarlane, and three ex–CIA officers: Duane Clarridge, Alan Fiers, and Clair George. Bush also pardons Guillermo Medrano Moreno (convicted in 1967 of importing and selling heroin), Edwin Roberts (1947, illegal whiskey distilling), and Carl Frank Westminster Jr. (1977, possession, sale, and transfer of a controlled substance).

December 25: *Hoffa* premieres in the U.S., starring Jack Nicholson as the vanished IBT president.

1993 Moroccan authorities initiate a cannabis eradication campaign. In Thailand, military forces collaborating with the DEA begin destruction of opium poppy fields in the "Golden Triangle." Black inmates organize the United Blood Nation at the George Mochen Detention Center on Riker's Island, New York City. Ninety-two million gamblers visit casinos in the United States.

January 8: Italian police capture Balduccio di Maggio, former chauffeur for fugitive mafioso Salvatore "Totò" Riina. Di Maggio cooperates with authorities in tracking Riina.

January 11: Arizona defendants Max Dunlap and James Robison are granted separate trials in the 1976 Don Bolles bombing murder.

January 15: Carbinieri officers arrest fugitive Mafioso Totò Riina in Palermo, Sicily.

January 18: Outgoing President Bush pardons Robert Edward Leigh Barnhill (convicted in 1980 of bid rigging in violation of Sherman Antitrust Act), Frederick Irwin Lorber (1962, obtaining marijuana without paying transfer tax), Clyde Henry Umphenour Jr. (1956 and 1961, two counts interstate transportation of forged securities). Bush also commutes the sentence of Aslam Adam (1985, conspiracy to possess with intent to distribute heroin, importation of heroin, and use of mail in committing felony).

February: Inmates Joaquin Alvarado and Jorge Lopez stab fellow prisoner Jose Uribe 37 times in his cell in his cell at the Los Angeles County jail. Authorities say the murder was committed to impress leaders of the Mexican Mafia.

February 1: Taiwan signs a $2.8 billion contract with China Ship Building Corporation (CSBC) for six modified Lafayette Class frigates. The sale requires reversal of French policy against supplying arms to Taiwan. In March, Taiwan's Navy General Headquarters orders CSBC to halt assembly, thereafter assigning the work to a French firm. Yin Ching-feng, head of the Taiwanese navy's Arms Acquisition Office, visits French authorities, pointing out flaws with the frigates and demanding remedial action.

February 7: Milwaukee mafioso Frank Balistrieri dies from a heart attack at his home.

February 19: Members of the Bath Beach and

New Springville Boys gangs kill Staten Island housewife Judith Shemtov during a bungled home invasion. Participants in the raid include future Mafia associates James Calandra, Chris Paciello, and Thomas Reynolds.

March 3: Mafia boss Carlos Marcello dies in his sleep at his home in Metairie, La.

March: Costa Rican authorities repeat their request for John Hull's extradition. The U.S. State Department continues stonewalling.

March 12: Police in Ontario, Calif., capture Mexican Mafia member Regino "The Bull" Deharo after a carjacking and 50-mile televised pursuit. Officer Roger Matthews is wounded by gunfire during the chase. In Mumbai, India, 13 car bombs kill 257 persons and wound another 713. Police blame the "D-Company" syndicate led by fugitive mobster Dawood Ibrahim, acting in retaliation for Hindu-Muslim riots in December 1992 and January 1993.

March 22: John Savoy, defense attorney for Max Dunlap in the Bolles murder case, receives two years' probation on a perjury conviction after telling a grand jury he possessed no relevant records dating from 1977.

March 27: Prosecutors in Palermo, Sicily, accuse former Italian prime minister Giulio Andreotti of acting in criminal collusion with the Mafia.

April 6: Mafia informer Tommaso Buscetta identifies Italy's ex–prime minister Giulio Andreotti as the "national politician" used by former Palermo mayor Salvatore Lima to handle Mafia affairs. Italy's Antimafia Commission releases a report on links between the Mafia's "third level" and various politicians.

April 8: Police arrest fugitive Colombo Family *consigliere* Carmine Sessa and other mafiosi during a meeting outside Manhattan's St. Patrick's Cathedral. Charged with racketeering and murder, Sessa subsequently turns state's evidence against his cohorts.

April 20: Jurors in Phoenix, Ariz., convict Max Dunlap of first-degree murder and conspiracy to obstruct the Bolles bombing investigation. He subsequently receives a life prison term with no parole for 25 years.

May 14: Italian telejournalist Maurizio Costano, known as an anti–Mafia crusader, narrowly escapes death in a car bombing.

May 18: Italian police capture fugitive mafioso Benedetto "The Hunter" Santapaola at a farmhouse outside Catania, Sicily, after 11 years in hiding.

May 24: Roman Catholic Cardinal Juan Jesús Posadas Ocampo and six other persons die in an ambush by Tijuana Cartel soldiers at Mexico's Guadalajara International Airport. A government inquiry concludes that Posadas was mistaken for a drug lord. Investigators blame cartel leaders Juan Francisco Murillo Díaz and Édgar Nicolás Villegas for the attack, but no charges are filed.

May 25: Chicago Outfit boss John "No Nose" DiFronzo and associate Donald "The Wizard of Odds" Angelini receive three-year prison terms for conspiracy and fraud, related to attempted infiltration of an Indian reservation casino.

May 28: Retaliating for the arrest of Totò Riina, Mafia terrorists bomb the Uffizi Gallery in Florence, Italy, killing five persons.

June 25: Mafioso Samuel Rusotti of Rochester, N.Y., dies in prison while serving a 1984 sentence on charges including two murders, three attempted murders, and extortion. In Easton, Pa., Warlocks MC member Eric "Dirt" Martinson receives a sentence of 126 months in federal prison on drug, weapon and money-laundering charges. Martinson's common-law wife, Christine Dickson, is released on time served for persuading Martinson to plead guilty.

June 28: A car bombing in New York City kills police informer Lee Carter. Authorities suspect members of the Hells Angels motorcycle gang, but no charges are filed.

July 2: Mafioso-turned-informer Jimmy Fratianno dies in Oklahoma, from complications of Alzheimer's disease.

July 22: Salvatore Cancemi, acting boss of the Porta Nuova Mafia clan, surrenders to Carabinieri in Palermo, Sicily.

July 27: A federal grand jury in New York indicts mafiosi Steven "Wonderboy" Crea, John Gammarano, Salvatore Lombardi, Dominic Truscello, and Gaetano Vastola on charges of extortion related to housing projects in the Bronx and Brooklyn.

July 27–28: Mafia terrorists detonate car bombs overnight at the Villa Reale Museum and the Pavilion of Contemporary Art in Milan, and the Church of San Giorgio and the Lateran Vicariate in Rome, killing five people and wounding dozens.

July 30: LAPD suspects mobsters Joseph Ippolito and Frankie Ziserto in the stabbing death of Bret Cantor, owner of Hollywood's Dragon Fly club.

August: Ricky Ross leaves federal prison after serving four years. Author Bill Kelly repeats the false tale of Moe Dalitz's "murder" in *Detective Cases* magazine, twisting William Roehmer's original fable to describe an ambush on the Las Vegas Strip in June 1961.

August 4: A Florida judge sentences Harlan Blackburn, an associate of Santo Trafficante Jr., to 24 and a half years in prison for cocaine trafficking.

August 5: Unknown gunmen kill mafioso Michael "Mikey Chang" Ciancaglini in South Philadelphia, Pa., wounding companion Joseph Merlino.

August 24: Chicago mafioso Salvatore DeLaurentis receives an 18½-year prison term for racketeering and income tax evasion.

September 1: A new *Untouchables* series premieres on American television, starring Tom Amandes as Eliot Ness and William Forsythe as Al Capone. The series runs through May 22, 1994, airing 42 episodes.

September 15: Unidentified gunmen murder Catholic priest and anti–Mafia crusader Giuseppe "Pino" Puglisi outside his home in Palermo, Sicily.

September 27: Nuestra Familia member Paul Farfan is shot and killed during a robbery in San Jose, Calif. Police accuse fellow gang members Adam Caris and Louis Oliverez Jr. of killing Farfan and dumping his body in Watson Park.

September 28: Harry Rosenzweig dies in Phoenix, Ariz.

October 15: The Luxor hotel-casino opens in Las Vegas, Nev.

October 20: Gunman John Pappa kills Colombo Family *caporegime* Joseph Scopo outside Scopo's home in New York City. Police arrest Pappa on September 26, 1997, and he later receives a 45-year prison term.

October 26: Prison physicians at Pelican Bay, Calif., diagnose Mexican Mafia leader Joseph "Pegleg" Morgan with inoperable liver cancer, ordering his transfer to a prison hospital at Corcoran. Morgan dies there on November 9. Bosnian authorities try to arrest gangster and war criminal Mušan "Caco" Topalović, but Topalović's 10th Mountain Brigade murders nine officers and eight civilian hostages. Topalović vanishes, but police later claim to have killed him "while trying to escape." Searchers locate his grave in 1996 and 12,000 people attend his funeral on December 2 of that year.

October 31: A large Mafia bomb, planted outside Rome's Olympic Stadium and timed to detonate at the end of the Lazio versus Udinese football match, fails to explode.

November 19: DEA Agent Stephen Strehl dies in a plane crash while conducting surveillance of a suspected indoor marijuana grow site.

November 10: Jurors in Smith County, Tex., convict Ricky Ross on an outstanding drug conspiracy charged, whereupon he returns to prison.

November 25: French prosecutors in Marseille indict Francis Vanverberghe for his role in a year-long gang war. The charges are dismissed for lack of evidence on December 14, 1994.

December: Newspapers report that one-third of all Italian parliament members are under investigation for corruption.

December 2: Drug lord Pablo Escobar and bodyguard Alvaro de Jesús Agudelo die in a shootout with Colombian National Police in Medellín.

December 3: LAPD officers find Mexican Mafia member Ricardo "Rascal" Gonzalez stabbed to death at the Ramona Gardens housing project in East Los Angeles. Serbian gangster Jusuf "Juka" Prazina leaves a hotel in Zagreb, Republic of Croatia, with bodyguards and disappears. Police find his bullet-scarred car abandoned at a railway station in Aachen, Germany, on December 4. Hitchhikers spot his corpse in a canal near the German border on December 31, and detectives trace bullets from Prazina's head to a gun owned by one of his bodyguards. Three suspects are later convicted at trial.

December 4: Officers of Mexico's Federal Judicial Police arrest Tijuana Cartel member Francisco Rafael Arellano Félix in Tijuana. Arellano is extradited to the U.S. on September 16, 2006, and pleads guilty to multiple charges on June 18, 2007. Despite that plea, he is released in El Paso, Tex., on March 5, 2008, and returns to Mexico.

December 9: Taiwanese Naval Captain Yin Ching-feng vanishes, his body subsequently found floating offshore. Military coroners brand his death a suicide, until autopsy results prove that Yin was tortured and bludgeoned to death. Subsequent investigation demonstrates that naval authorities withheld evidence from police. Observers link Yin's murder to Taiwan's unfolding frigate scandal.

December 15: Nuestra Familia members Ronald "Lucky" Shelton and Jerry "Cripple" Salazar confess to ordering six murders in San Jose, Calif. Federal authorities place both gangsters in the witness protection program.

December 17: Arizona jurors acquit James Robison in the Bolles murder case, despite his admission on cross-examination that he asked a fellow jail inmate to arrange the murder of key prosecution witness John Adamson.

December 18: President Bill Clinton signs federal legislation banning manufacture of a home-made drug known as "cat," formally known as methcathinone.

December 26: Former IBT president Dave Beck at Northwest Hospital in Seattle, Wash., at age 99.

December 31: Unknown gunmen murder gangster and saloon bouncer Viv Graham at the Anchor pub in Tyneside, North East England.

1994 Iowa voters eliminate wager and loss limits formerly imposed on riverboat casinos.

January: President Clinton orders a shift in policy from the anti-drug campaigns of previous administrations toward foreign "institution building" in the hope that "strengthening democratic governments abroad will foster law-abiding behavior and promote legitimate economic opportunity." Mexican Mafia member Humberto "Capone" Madrigal suffers gunshot wounds the Ramona Gardens housing project in East Los Angeles. He identifies David "Smilon" Gallardo as the triggerman, then recants the identification.

January 3: Jury selection begins in a federal lawsuit designed to confiscate the New York City clubhouse occupied by Hells Angels, where illegal drugs were seized in 1985.

January 5: New York mafiosi John Gambino, Joseph Gambino, and Lorenzo Mannino plead guilty to federal racketeering charges. All receive 15-year sentences on June 14.

January 6: An "emergency" ruling adds 2C-B to the list of Schedule I controlled substances in the U.S.

January 14: Unknown abductors kidnap mobster Behçet Cantürk in Sapanca, Turkey. Police find him shot dead the following day.

January 24: A federal grand jury in New York indicts Bonanno Family *consigliere* Anthony Spero on racketeering charges including loan-sharking, illegal gambling, murder and extortion.

February: Mexican Mafia members Juan "China Boy" Arias and David "Smilon" Gallardo engage in a Los Angeles shootout with brothers Eduardo and Ricardo Soriano. All participants except Gallardo are wounded.

February 25: Retired mafioso Russell Bufalino dies from natural causes at age 90, in Wilkes Barre, Pa.

March: A U.S. Customs agent finds 3.4 metric tons of ephedrine concealed on a plane traveling from Switzerland to Mexico. The drug, manufactured in India, is earmarked for Mexico's Colima Cartel. DEA agents subsequently learn that the cartel has smuggled 170 tons of ephedrine — enough for 2 billion methamphetamine tablets — into the U.S. over an 18-month period. In Los Angeles, Mexican Mafia hitman Ernest "Chuco" Castro turns state's evidence against the gang, resulting in arrest of 21 Eme members.

March 17: A federal grand jury in Philadelphia, Pa., indicts mafioso Giovanni "John the Dour Don" Stanfa on charges of labor racketeering, extortion, loan-sharking, murder and conspiracy to commit murder. He is convicted on November 21, 1995, subsequently receiving five consecutive life sentences.

March 18: Gambino Family associate Robert Sasso, president of IBT Local 282 in New York City, pleads guilty to extorting money from local contractors.

April 5: A sniper kills mobster Otari Kvantrishvili at a bath house in Moscow, Russia. Prosecutors convict four members of a rival gang on September 29, 2008.

April 17: Italian swindler Licio Gelli receives a 17-year prison term for divulging state secrets and slandering investigators of the Propaganda Due lodge. An appellate court reduces that sentence to house arrest on September 9, 1998.

April 26: Philadelphia mafioso-turned-informer Philip Colletti pleads guilty to the August 1993 murder of Michael Ciancaglini and the attempted murders of victims Steven Mazzone and Joseph "Skinny Joey" Merlino.

May 10: *Getting Gotti* premieres on American television, with Anthony John Denison cast as John Gotti and Ron Gabriel as Salvatore Gravano.

May 14: Nuestra Familia gunmen execute gang member Joseph Anthony Meza for failing to pay a drug debt.

May 31: Authorities at California's San Quentin Prison inadvertently release Nuestra Familia member Adam Caris hours before he is indicted for the 1993 murder of victim Paul Farfan.

June 2: A grand jury in San Jose, Calif., indicts Nuestra Familia members Vincent "Chente" Arroyo, Carlos Mendoza, Deborah Mendoza, Louis Oliverez Jr., Guadalupe Mary Segura and Jeanette Alarcon on multiple felony charges.

June 30: DEA Agent Richard Fass suffers fatal gunshot wounds during an undercover methamphetamine investigation in Glendale, Ariz.

August 2: U.S. State Department spokesmen declare that ongoing requests for John Hull's extradition to Costa Rica on murder and drug-trafficking charges are "not sufficient for presentation in a United States court."

August 12: DEA agents plan a drug sting against imprisoned dealer Ricky Ross.

August 18: An unidentified gunman kills Irish mobster Martin Cahill on a street near his Dublin home. Various published theories blame rival gangsters or the IRA.

August 27: Five DEA agents die when their airplane crashes during a reconnaissance mission near Santa Lucia, Peru, conducted as part of "Operation Snowcap."

September: The DEA concludes Operation Foxhunt, a two-year investigation of a Colombian drug-trafficking ring based in Los Angeles, distributing multi-ton quantities of cocaine to San Francisco, Chicago and New York City. The sweep produces 191 arrests, while seizing 6.5 tons of cocaine and over $13.5 million in cash.

September 13: A car bomb kills Sergei Timofeyev, boss of the Orekhovskaya gang in Moscow, Russia.

September 19: INS agents escort Oscar Blandón out of prison. In October, as a DEA informer, Blandón proposes a drug-smuggling project to sting target Ricky Ross.

September 20: Police in Fresno, Calif., suspect members of the "Armenian Mafia" in the murder of Armenian jeweler Norair Kebabjian, found beaten and shot in his store.

October: Police in the Netherlands seize a 6.4-metric ton shipment of ephedrine bound for Mexico.

October 2: Kansas City mobster Carl "Corky" Civella dies in federal prison, from pneumonia. On the same day, paroled Cleveland gangster Milton "Maishe" Rockman dies from natural causes in Ohio.

October 19: Trafficante Family underboss Frank Diecidue is found hanging at his home in Tampa, Fla. Authorities rule the death a suicide.

October 28: Detroit mafioso Salvatore "Sam" Finazzo dies of natural causes in Sterling Heights, Mich.

November 10: A court in Vilnius, Lithuania, condemns Boris Dekanidze — head of the city's "Vilnius Brigade" crime syndicate — for the murder of journalist Vitas Lingys in 1993. Dekanidze is executed on July 12, 1995.

November 14: Mafioso Nicholas "Nicky" Bianco dies from Lou Gehrig's disease at the U.S. Medical Center for Federal Prisoners in Springfield, Mo.

November 23: President Clinton pardons David Phillip Aronsohn (convicted in 1961 of failure to pay a special occupational tax on wagering), David Christopher Billmaier (1980, possession with intent to distribute amphetamines), Carl Bruce Jones (1983, distribution of marijuana and use of telephone to facilitate marijuana distribution), Candace Deon Leverenz (1972, unlawful distribution of LSD), Theodore Roosevelt Noel (1972, selling whiskey in unstamped containers and making false statement in the acquisition of firearms from licensed dealer), Susan Lauranne Prather (1975, causing marijuana to be transported through the mail), Robert Ronal Raymond (1972, conspiracy to manufacture, receive, possess, and sell firearms silencers), and Charles Coleman Wicker (1975, conspiracy to conduct illegal gambling business).

November 25: Narcotics officers seize 60 pounds of khat in Newark, N.J., arresting Jordanian national Atef al-Yafia.

November 27: Thai authorities and DEA agents conclude "Operation Tiger Trap," targeting heroin traffic by the Shan United Army.

December 20: The *Federal Register* carries a notice of proposed permanent ban the drug 2C-B, supported by the DEA.

1994–97 The "Great Nordic Biker War" between Hells Angels and rival Bandidos MC members claims 11 lives in Scandinavia, with 96 bikers wounded and 74 attempted murders attempted murders recorded. Danish legislators ban motorcycle clubs from owning or renting property for club activities, but the law is later repealed on constitutional grounds.

1994–2002 Canada's "Québec Biker War" between Hells Angels and various rival clubs produces at least 150 murders, plus numerous bombings and other violent incidents, while landing more than 100 bikers in prison.

1995 Southeast Asia's "Golden Triangle" leads the world in opium production, with an annual yield of 2,500 tons. Legal gambling revenue in the U.S. tops $40 billion. Worldwide lottery revenue hits $95 billion: the U.S. leads with $28.7 billion in ticket sales, followed by Germany with $9.2 billion.

January 26: Kansas City mafioso William "Willie Rat" Cammisano Sr. dies from multiple organ failure related to lung disease.

February 7: Mobster Alphonse Gangitano fatally shoots rival Greg Workman in Melbourne, Australia.

February 10: Nuestra Familia gunmen kill Joseph Littlewolf Lincoln during a robbery in Santa Rosa, Calif. Police charge gang members Rafael Ampier Jr. and Javier Zubiate with the murder. They plead not guilty on February 23. Zubiate receives a sentence of 19 years to life on November 2, 1995.

March: Gunmen execute Colombo Family member Joseph Scarpa in New York City. A federal grand jury indicts four Gambino and Lucchese Family members for the slaying on June 5, 1998. DEA agents in California complete their sting on Ricky Ross, arresting him for trying to sell more than 100 kilograms of cocaine to an undercover officer. Convicted at trial in 1996, Ross receives a life sentence, later reduced to 20 years on appeal. He is released to a California halfway house on September 20, 2009.

March 1: An apparent contract killing claims the life of telejournalist Vladislav Nikolayevich Listyev at his apartment house in Moscow, Russia.

March 16: The New York State Senate convenes hearings to investigate the presence of organized crime at Manhattan's Jacob K. Javits Convention Center.

March 17: Imprisoned gangster Ronald Kray dies from a heart attack at England's Wexham Park Hospital.

March 18: A federal grand jury indicts New York mafiosi Joseph and Louis DiNapoli on charges of using phony minority-owned firms to gain control of the city's asbestos-carting industry and win $5 million in city contracts.

March 24: Aryan Brotherhood member Robert Scully is paroled from California's "supermax" Pelican Bay State Prison. He murders a police officer on March 30.

April 13: A grand jury charges Norman DuPont, owner of Manhattan's Ravenite Social Club and a Gambino Family associate, with the murder of car service dispatcher Harmon Fuchs, intended as a warning to a mob rival who owned DuPont money. DuPont subsequently receives a life sentence at trial.

April 17: President Clinton pardons Jack Pakis (convicted in 1972 of operating an illegal gambling business) and Gordon Roberts Jr. (1977, interstate transportation of forged and falsely made securities).

April 22: Mexican Mafia members Jimmy Palma and Richard Anthony Valdez kill gang defector Anthony Moreno and four members of his family in Los Angeles, on orders from gang leaders Luis "Big Homie" Maciel and Raymond "Huero Shy" Shyrock. Palma and Valdez receive death sentences for the murder on June 11, 1997.

April 23: Yakuza gangster Hiroyuki Jo murders Aum Shinrikyo cult member Hideo Murai on live television in Tokyo, Japan, in the presence of 100 reporters and 10 policemen.

April 25: Unknown gunmen kill gangster Vasil Iliev outside a restaurant in Sofia, Bulgaria.

May: The U.S. Sentencing Commission publishes a report noting racial disparities in sentencing for cases involving powder cocaine vs. crack. The commission proposes reducing the discrepancy, but Congress rejects that recommendation for the first time in history.

May 1: A federal grand jury in Los Angeles indicts 22 members and associates of the Mexican Mafia on RICO charges. Defendants include Alex "Pee Wee" Aguirre, Juan "China Boy" Arias, Daniel "Black Dan" Barela, George Bustamante, Reuben "Night Owl" Castro, David "Smilon" Gallardo, Richard "Ricky" Guitierez, Joe "Shakey" Hernandez, Reuben "Tupi" Hernandez, Ronald Ray "Champ" Mendez, Jesse "Pelon" Moreno, Victor "Victorio" Murillo, Benjamin "Topo" Peters, Antonio "Tonito" Rodriquez, Michael "Musclehead" Salinas, Raymond "Huero Shy" Shyrock, Randy "Cowboy" Therrien, and Sammy "Negro" Villalba.

May 6: Warlocks MC member Robert "Mudman" Simon fatally shoots Police Sergeant Ippolito Gonzalez during a routine traffic stop in Franklin Township, Gloucester County, N.J. Sentenced to death for murder, Simon is beaten to death by fellow inmate Ambrose Harris in 1999.

May 7: Police in Franklin Township, Pa., charge Warlocks MC member Robert Ronald "Mudman" Simon with the May 6 fatal shooting of police sergeant Ippolito Gonzalez. Simon is on parole from previous murder conviction for the 1982 slaying of a 19-year-old woman in Carbon County.

May 9: Police find the bodies of murder victims Armando Castillo and Gilbert Hernandez in Upland, Calif. Prosecutors charge Mexican Mafia members David Villa, Ignacio "Toby" Villa, and Cathy Estrada with the slayings on December 27, 1995.

June: Sicilian police capture fugitive mafioso Leoluca Bagarella. Bernardo Provenzano replaces him as the Mafia's "boss-of-bosses."

June 8: FBI agents in New York charge Russian gangster Vyacheslav Ivankov with extorting several million dollars from an investment advisory firm run by two Russian businessmen. Jurors convict him, with two codefendants, in June 1996.

June 9: Colombian National Police arrest Cali Cartel leader Gilberto José Rodríguez Orejuela at his home. He is extradited to the U.S. for trial on December 3, 2004.

June 19: Cali Cartel officer Henry "The Scorpion" Loaiza-Ceballos surrenders to Colombian police. He subsequently receives an 18-year prison sentence for supporting paramilitary terrorist groups.

June 22: A federal grand jury indicts New York mafiosi Joseph Francolino and Alphonse "Allie Shades" Malangone for monopolizing trash collection through control of the Association of Trade Waste Removers of Greater New York, the Kings County Trade Waste Association, and the Greater New York Waste Paper Association. Both are subsequently convicted and imprisoned.

June 24: Cali Cartel officer Victor Julio Patiño-Fomeque surrenders to Colombian police, subsequently receiving a 12-year prison term.

June 29: John R. Bartolomeo, a member of the Hells Angels MC, receives a 35-year prison sentence for killing William "Cats" Michaels, a Devils Disciples MC member suspected of selling drugs on Hells Angels turf in Weymouth, Mass.

July: California journalist Gary Webb, writing for the *San Jose Mercury News*, begins investigation of Oscar Blandón's ties to the Nicaraguan Contras and Ricky Ross.

July 2: The U.S. ban on 2C-B becomes permanent.

July 4: Colombian National Police arrest Cali Cartel officer José Santacruz-Londoño. He escapes from Bogotá's La Picota Prison on January 11, 1996, and flees to Medellín, where he is killed by police while trying to flee, on March 5, 1996.

July 8, 1995: Cali Cartel member Victor Julio Patiño-Fomeque surrenders to Colombian authorities, later receiving a 28-year prison term and a $100,000 fine. He subsequently escapes from jail but is recaptured in Villagorgona on April 15, 1997.

July 17: A sniper kills Bandidos MC member Michael Ljunggren on the E4 motorway, south of Markaryd, Sweden.

July 26: Arizona prison inmate James Robison receives an additional five-year prison term after admitting that he tried to hire a killer to murder Don Bolles bomber John Adamson.

August 3: Cleveland jurors convict Mafia associate Chester "Zip" Liberatore of labor racketeering as business manager of Laborers Local 310.

August 6: Colombian National Police Cali Cartel member Miguel Angel Rodríguez Orejuela at his home. He is extradited to the U.S. on March 11, 2005.

August 10: A car bomb kills 11-year-old Daniel Desrochers near a school in Montreal, Québec. Police speculate that the bomb was set by Hells Angels to kill a member of a rival gang.

August 16: Florida police arrest Patriarca Family boss Francis "Cadillac Frank" Salemme on charges of racketeering, extortion, loan-sharking, money-laundering and gambling. He later turns informer, helping to convict much of the family's leadership.

September 1: Hitmen disguised as police kill Carmela Minniti, wife of mafioso Benedetto "The Hunter" Santapaola, at her home in Catania, Sicily. Journalist Liliana Madeo explains: "She ran his affairs. If she was just a little woman, she wouldn't have been killed." On the same day, New York mafioso Joseph N. Gallo dies from natural causes at age 83.

September 4: James Phillip Hoffa, son of murdered IBT leader Jimmy Hoffa, announces his candidacy for the union presidency, held by incumbent Ron Carey. The campaign grows so contentious that Carey sues Hoffa for libel in September 1996.

September 8: A New York grand jury indicts Colombo Family *caporegime* Thomas Petrizzo and two associates — Kenneth Paskewics and IBT Local 707 president James McNeil — on charges of conspiring to defraud the Long Island union of more than $1.5 million.

September 9: Gambino Family *consigliere* Joseph "Jo Jo" Corozzo Sr. pleads guilty to operating illegal poker machines in Louisiana.

September 11–13: Three psychiatrists tell a New York court that Genovese Family boss Vincent Gigante is unfit to stand trial on a 1990 indictment for contract rigging and a 1993

charge that he conspired to kill 10 rival mobsters.

September 13: Pirates capture the freighter *Anna Sierra* off the coast of Thailand, setting the crew adrift in lifeboats, then repaint the ship in transit to China. Arriving at Beihai on September 15, they use forged papers to sell the *Anna Sierra*'s sugar cargo. Chinese authorities detain the pirates, but later release them without filing charges.

September 17: Three-year-old Stephanie Kuhen dies from gunshot wounds in Los Angeles, after her parents inadvertently drive into a crossfire between Mexican Mafia soldiers and members of the rival Avenues Gang. Bullets also wound her stepfather and infant brother. On September 21 LAPD arrests suspects Vincent Castro Caldera, Hugo David Gomez, Augustin Lizama and Marcos Antonio Luna for the shooting. Two more suspects, Anthony Gabriel Rodriquez Jr. and Manuel Rosales, are arrested on September 27. Jurors convict Gomez, Rodriguez and Rosales on June 3, 1997; all three receive sentences of 54 years to life on August 1, 1997. Luna pleads guilty to assault with a deadly weapon on July 3, 1997. Lizama pleads guilty to a reduced charge of assault on August 29, 1997, and receives a life sentence.

Autumn: Prompted by the August bombing death of Daniel Desrochers, Québec authorities create a special police squad called Carcajou ("Wolverine") to pursue outlaw bikers.

October: DEA agents meet with reporter Gary Webb, seeking to dissuade him from pursuing research on Oscar Blandón and the Contras. Two weeks later, Robert Nieves — the DEA's chief agent in Costa Rica — resigns from the agency.

October 5: Unknown gunmen murder William "Billy" Veasey in Philadelphia, Pa. Police call the shooting an effort to intimidate brother John Veasey, scheduled to testify as a prosecution witness against mafioso John Stanfa.

October 20: Gunman Ernie "Leche" Carillo kills Mexican Mafia members Phillip "Chano" Chavez and his cousin Patricio Rocha in San Bernardino, Calif.

November: DEA headquarters alerts the CIA to Gary Webb's investigation of Contra drug-dealing and warns of his attempts to locate Norwin Meneses.

November 11: The first legal land-based casino in New Orleans, La., files for bankruptcy.

November 14: The film *Casino* premieres in New York City, with Robert De Niro and Joe Pesci starring in a fictionalized portrayal of Tony Spilotro and Frank "Lefty" Rosenthal in Las Vegas.

November 22: NYPD officers find Colombo

Family associate Frank O'Heir shot to death on his mother's grave at St. John's Cemetery in Queens. The shooting, ruled suicide, follows O'Heir's recent guilty plea on charges of selling guns for the Mafia.

November 24: Bonanno Family soldier Benjamin "Lefty Two Guns" Ruggiero dies from lung cancer in New York. Mexican Mafia gunmen in San Bernardino, Calif., kill Ernie "Leche" Carillo in retaliation for his October slaying of Phillip Alvarez and Patricio Rocha.

November 25: *Sugartime* premieres on HBO, starring John Turturro as Sam Giancana and Maury Chaykin as Tony Accardo.

1996 The London-based International Maritime Bureau reports 224 acts of piracy worldwide. The Parliament of Canada passes the Controlled Drugs and Substances Act, repealing the Narcotic Control Act and Parts III and IV of the 1920 Food and Drugs Act, thereby implementing the 1961 Single Convention on Narcotic Drugs, the 1971 Convention on Psychotropic Substances, and the 1988 United Nations Convention Against Illicit Traffic in Narcotic Drugs and Psychotropic Substances. Purdue Pharma markets OxyContin, a time-release formula of oxycodone.

January 1: California begins a three-year moratorium on creation of new card clubs statewide.

January 5: Burmese authorities announce the peaceful surrender of "opium king" Khun Sa. Reported terms include official sanction for continued opium trading in exchange for cessation of Khun Sa's guerrilla war against the government of Myanmar.

January 19: Border Patrol Agent Jefferson L. Barr dies in a shootout with marijuana smugglers near the Rio Grande River, in Texas.

February 17: Indian gangster Koose Muniswamy Veerappan kidnaps nine members of a special police task force assigned to capture him at Marapala, Chamarajanagar. He holds them hostage until the last week of August.

February 27: Mafioso Ilario "Larry Baione" Zannino dies of natural causes at the Medical Center for Federal Prisoners in Springfield, Mo., while serving time for gambling and loan-sharking.

February 29: President Clinton names retired U.S. Army general Barry Richard McCaffrey to serve as director of the White House Office of National Drug Control Policy.

March: Trial convenes for Ricky Ross in San Diego, Calif. Oscar Blandón appears as a prosecution witness and confesses Contra drug-dealing. In October Ross receives a life sentence without parole.

March 8: Chicago mobster Samuel "Black Sam" Carlisi receives a 12½-year sentence for extortion and loan-sharking. He dies in prison from a heart attack on January 2, 1997.

March 12: Former gangster Jack Comer dies in London while recovering from a cerebral hemorrhage.

March 13: A federal grand jury indicts Detroit mafioso Giacomo William Tocco and 16 associates for multiple RICO violations. All are arrested by FBI agents on March 15. Alleged crimes include collection of $234,700 in "street tax" extortion, collection of $38,400 in illegal gambling debts, and receiving $4.2 million from sale of the Edgewater and Frontier hotels in Las Vegas, Nev.

March 28: Trial begins for Nuestra Familia members in Los Angeles, on an indictment returned in 1992. The proceedings are interrupted in June, when Vincent "Chente" Arroyo pleads guilty to robbery and turns state's evidence against his codefendants, in exchange for a 25-year sentence with parole eligibility after 17 years.

March 30: A grand jury in Stockton, Calif., files multiple indictments against Nuestra Familia members. Dioncycio Gerolaga pleads guilty to conducting a criminal enterprise, while George Albert Quinones pleads guilty to conspiracy to distribute narcotics.

April 14: Detroit mafioso Dominick Licavoli dies from cancer in Macomb, Mich.

May 2: The U.S. Organized Crime Drug Enforcement Task Force concludes "Operation Zorro II," crushing a Colombian smuggling network with cells in six states. One of those arrests, Jorge Valazquez, is an NYPD officer and a sergeant in the National Guard.

May 20: Police photograph Colombo Family acting boss Andrew Russo meeting *consigliere* Joel Carace Sr. at Manhattan's Doral Inn. The meeting sends Russo back to prison for violating probation. On the same day, Italian police arrest fugitive mafioso Giovanni Brusca near Agrigento, Sicily. Already convicted and sentenced *in absentia* for the murders of Paolo Borsellino and Giovanni Falcone, Brusca turns informer in February 1999.

May 24: French manufacturers deliver the first assembled Lafayette/Kang Ding Class frigate under Taiwan's multibillion-dollar contract, with defective anti-aircraft defenses and incomplete electronic-combat systems.

June 1: Unknown gunmen kill Chechen mobster and warlord Ruslan Labazanov at his home in Tolstoy-Yurt.

June 16: An unknown gunman kills Danish Bandidos MC member Jan "Face" Krogh Jensen at a highway rest stop in Mjøndalen, Norway.

June 24: In the case of *Western Telcon v. Cali-*

fornia State Lottery, California's Supreme Court rules that the lottery's electronic keno game is an illegal "banked" game.

November: DEA spokesmen report that drug traffickers from China, Colombia, Mexico and Nigeria are "aggressively marketing heroin in the United States and Europe."

July: Colombian authorities release Medellín Cartel members Jorge Luis Ochoa Vázquez and Juan David Ochoa Vásquez from prison.

August 12: Confessed killer John Adamson leaves prison in Arizona and enters the WITSEC program.

August 13: IBT president Ron Carey places Philadelphia Local 107 under federal trusteeship for corruption and ties to organized crime.

August 17: HBO airs *Gotti*, starring Armand Assante as the imprisoned "Teflon Don."

August 18–20: California's *San Jose Mercury News* runs Gary Webb's three-part "Dark Alliance" series, detailing U.S. government involvement in drug trafficking on behalf of the Nicaraguan Contras. The CIA and DOJ launch internal investigations of Webb's claims in early September.

August 27: A hitman employed by mobster Alaattin Çakıcı kills rival Nurullah Tevfik Ağansoy and policeman Celal Babür in Istanbul, Turkey.

September 1: Cali Cartel lieutenant Helmer "Pacho" Herrera-Buitrago surrenders to Colombian authorities.

September 6: The district attorney in Queens, N.Y., charges members of the New Westies gang with murder and operating a drug network that earns more than $17 million yearly. Indicted defendants include gang leader Edward O'Boyle, his brother Daniel, and John McDonnell.

October 3: President Clinton signs the Comprehensive Methamphetamine Control Act of 1996, regulating pseudoephedrine sales and requiring wholesale distributors of over-the-counter cold medicines to register for a DEA license.

October 4: The *Washington Post* attacks Gary Webb's "Dark Alliance" series, seeking to debunk his claims. The *Los Angeles Times* follows suit on October 21.

October 15: IBT Local 707 president James McNeil pleads guilty to helping Colombo Family boss Vittorio "Little Vic" Orena hide payments he received from the $3.65 million purchase of the union's headquarters on Long Island, N.Y.

October 24: Dutch police raid British gangster Curtis "Cocky" Warren's villa in the Netherlands, seizing 400 kilograms of cocaine, 1,500 kilograms of cannabis resin, 60 kilograms of heroin, 50 kilograms of ecstasy, three guns, several hand grenades, several cases of CS gas canisters, $600,000 in U.S. currency, and 400,000 Dutch guilders. At

trial, Warren receives the maximum 12-year sentence.

November: CIA director John Deutsch visits South Central Los Angeles to answer charges that his agency was responsible for proliferation of crack cocaine in U.S. ghettos.

November 3: Detroit mafioso Dominic Bommarito dies of natural causes in Homestead, Fla.

November 5: In a referendum on gambling, Louisiana voters approve video poker games in 33 parishes and ban them in 31, while permitting 15 riverboat casinos and one land-based casino to continue operations.

November 20: Trial begins in Los Angeles for 13 of 22 Mexican Mafia members indicted in May 1995.

December: Imprisoned Lucchese Family member Anthony "Superman" Gioia turns informer after learning that mafioso Frank "Frankie Bones" Papagnio plans to kill Gioia's father. His testimony helps convict more than 60 family members.

December 3: Authorities in Tucson, Ariz., raided a warehouse containing 5.3 tons of cocaine.

December 7: Police find mafioso Joseph Sadano shot dead in his car, parked at a senior citizen's home in Newark, N.J. Informers later say that Sadano was killed for withholding tribute payments from Philadelphia boss Nicodemo Scarfo and refusing to attend family meetings. Jurors acquit suspect Joseph "Skinny Joey" Merlino of Sadano's slaying in March 2004.

December 9: Brooklyn District Attorney Charles Hynes announces the indictment of more than 29 men involved in a gambling operation spanning the country from New York to Las Vegas, Nev. The ring, earning $400 million yearly, is led by James Rossi and Frank Tramontano.

December 13: Arizona state troopers seize a tractor trailer entering the state from Mexico, loaded with 2,700 pounds of marijuana.

December 15: Ron Carey claims victory in his campaign for re-election as IBT president. Rival James P. Hoffa challenges 31,000 ballots, but federal election monitors confirm Carey's victory on December 16.

December 22: Mexican Mafia hitman Johnny Torres testifies in Los Angeles concerning the rules of conduct imposed on Eme members.

1997 Thousands of bogus companies swamp DEA headquarters with new license applications mandated by the Comprehensive Methamphetamine Control Act of 1996. Dutch lawmakers ban 2C-B.

January: Chicago mobster Victor Spilotro dies of natural causes in a Wheeling, W.Va., health-care facility.

January 6: Gunmen kill Tony Spilotro associate Herbert "Fat Herbie" Blitzstein at his home in Las Vegas, Nev. Business partner Joseph DeLuca approaches police in June, confessing his role in the murder. DeLuca pleads guilty in August and provides information resulting in multiple indictments.

January 12: Trial resumes in Los Angeles for seven of 21 Nuestra Familia members indicted in May 1995. Jurors convict all seven on July 14. Eddie "Pajaro" Vargas receives a 60-year prison term on August 15. Herminio "Spankio" Serna and James "Huero" Trujeque are sentenced to death on September 13. Edward "Roach" Aroche, William "Dreamer" Fernandez and Albert "Beto" Guillen are sentenced to life without parole on October 8. Bobby "Silent" Lopez receives a death sentence on November 14.

January 17: A federal grand jury in New York indicts Gambino Family *caporegime* Daniel Marino and two associates, Gary Furio and John Ryan, for wiretapping underboss Salvatore Gravano's home in 1991.

January 23: Detroit mafioso Peter "Bozzi" Vitale dies in Clinton Township, Mich.

February 2: Greek police find Russian syndicate hitman Alexander Viktorovich "Superkiller" Solonik strangled to death, 15 miles outside Athens.

February 28: The film *Donnie Brasco* premieres in the U.S. and Canada, starring Johnny Depp as FBI agent Joseph Pistone, infiltrator of the Bonanno and Colombo Families in New York.

March 19: James P. Hoffa accuses IBT president Ron Carey of illegal re-election campaign activities, including a $95,000 kickback from the owner of a Massachusetts-based direct mail firm. A federal grand jury convenes in Manhattan to investigate the charges on March 26 and indicts two conspirators — Michael Ansara and Martin Davis — on June 6. Ansara later pleads guilty to participating in a kickback scheme. Carey denies all knowledge of the plot, but federal overseers disqualify him from union office on November 17, 1997. Carey takes a leave of absence on On November 25, and the IBT's Independent Review Board expels him from the union on July 27, 1998. James P. Hoffa wins election as IBT president on December 5, 1998.

April: Canadian legislators pass Bill C-95, amending the Criminal Code of Canada to acknowledge crimes committed "for the benefit of, at the direction of, or in association with" a criminal organization. Convictions carry a mandatory minimum sentence of five years in prison and a maximum sentence of 14 years. The law bans membership in designated "outlaw motorcycle gangs" or any other "known criminal organization."

April 20: Police in Leonardtown, Md., arrest three members of the Iron Horsemen MC on charges of beating one man to death and assaulting another in separate incidents on the same day.

April 23: Federal jurors in Manhattan convict Genovese Family *consigliere* James Ida of RICO charges including two murders, labor racketeering, and illegally controlling the Feast of San Gennaro in Little Italy. Ida receives a term of life without parole.

May: *San Jose Mercury News* editor Jerry Ceppos retracts some statements contained in Gary Webb's "Dark Alliance" exposé series. Webb objects and is reassigned to a bureau office 150 miles from his home, resigning from the paper on November 19.

May 29: Jurors in Los Angeles convict Mexican Mafia members Alex Aguirre, Juan Arias, Daniel Barela, Reuben Castro, David Gallardo, Reuben Hernandez, "Shakey Joe" Hernandez, Raymond Mendez, Jesse Moreno, Raymond Shyrock, Benjamin Peters, and Randy Therrien on various charges, while acquitting Victor Murillo. Gallardo and Therrien are sentenced to life without parole on September 2, with Gallardo receiving an additional 300 months. On September 3 Castro, Peters and Shyrock receive sentences of life without parole; Reuben Hernandez receives a life term with possible parole; Arias, Barela, Joe Hernandez, and Moreno are sentenced to 32 years. On September 5 Aguirre and Mendez receive life sentences.

June 1: Drive-by gunmen, presumed to be Crips, kill Death Row Records employee Aaron "Heron" Palmer in Compton, Calif. Palmer videotaped the beating of Crips member Orlando Anderson on the night Tupac Shakur was killed in Las Vegas, Nev.

June 5: Manhattan District Attorney Robert Morgenthau charges 48 members of the East Village "Champion Crew" on charges of drug trafficking and murder.

June 6: Italian police arrest fugitive mafioso Pietro "The Little Gentleman" Aglieri and two lieutenants, Natale Gambino and Giuseppe La Mattina, at an abandoned lemon warehouse in Bagheria, Sicily.

June 7: New Jersey mafioso Simone Rizzo "Sam the Plumber" DeCavalcante dies from a heart attack in Florida.

June 10: Federal prosecutors charge 17 members of the Outlaws MC with racketeering, murder, narcotics trafficking and bombing in Florida, Illinois, Indiana, and Wisconsin.

June 12: Agents of a New Jersey state and federal task force arrest Genovese Family *caporegime* Anthony "Tony Pro" Provenzano on charges of trying to extort half an insurance company from its owner for a $40,000 gambling debt.

June 17: Bulgarian gangster Iliya Pavlov Naydenov survives a car-bombing on the highway between Sofia and Bistritsa.

June 25: Officials from the U.S. and Barbados sign an Agreement Concerning Co-operation in Suppressing Illicit Maritime and Air Trafficking in Narcotic Drugs and Psychotropic Substances in the Caribbean Area.

June 26: A member of the Hells Angels fatally shoots correctional officer Diane Lavigne as she drives home from work in Québec, Canada.

July 1: Police in Long Beach, Calif., arrest Mexican Mafia member Reuben Gomez following a botched home-invasion robbery. On September 27 a grand jury indicts Gomez for that crime and six counts of murder committed since his February release from Pelican Bay State Prison. Prosecutors identify the victims as drug dealers who fell behind in payments to the gang.

July 11: Mexican Mafia member Robert "Gypsy" Cervantes murders victim Paul Fix during a robbery in Placentia, Calif.

July 25: Federal jurors in New York convict Genovese Family boss Vincent Gigante of RICO violations including extortion and conspiracy to commit murder. He receives a 12-year sentence on December 19.

August 12: Hitman Abdul Rauf kills "Bollywood" film producer Gulshan Kumar outside a temple in Mumbai, India. Rauf confesses on January 9, 2001, and receives a life sentence on April 29, 2002, but refuses to name his employers. Eighteen other suspects are acquitted on April 24, 2002.

August 24: Bouncer and Hells Angel Steve Tausan fatally beats drunken customer Kevin Sullivan at the Pink Poodle strip club in San Jose, Calif. Subsequent investigation prompts sweeping police raids against the MC in January 1998, with civil lawsuits resulting.

August 27: The film *Hoodlum* premieres in America, romanticizing the Prohibition-era exploits of Harlem gangster "Bumpy" Johnson (played by Laurence Fishburne). Tim Roth portrays Dutch Schultz, with Andy Garcia cast as Lucky Luciano.

August 28: Members of the dissident Nakanokai Yakuza gang kill Yamaguchi-gumi leader Masaru Takumi and an innocent bystander in the coffee shop of the Oriental Hotel in Kobe, Japan.

September 8: Hells Angels ambush Québec correctional officers Pierre Rondeau and Robert Corriveau en route to pick up prisoners, killing Rondeau. On December 18, 1997, biker-turned-informer Stephane Gagné later tells police that Québec club leader Maurice "Mom" Boucher ordered the shooting and the June murder of Officer

Diane Lavigne to terrorize police. Jurors acquit Boucher at his first trial, in November 1998, but a second panel convicts him in May 2002, resulting in a sentence of life with a minimum of 25 years.

September 12: Police in National City, Calif., break up a drug ring run from prison by Mexican Mafia member Frank "Chino" Macias Madriaga.

September 17: Lucchese Family soldiers James "Jimmy Frogs" Gallione and Mario Gallo confess to killing Constabile Farace in 1989.

September 22: Genovese Family acting boss Liborio "Barney" Bellomo receives a 10-year sentence for ordering the murder of suspected informer Ralph DeSimone, extorting money from waste haulers, and illegally controlling Local 46 of the Mason Tenders Union.

September 24: A federal grand jury in San Diego, Calif., indicts Tijuana Cartel leader Ramon Arellano Félix on drug-trafficking charges. FBI headquarters adds his name to the Bureau's "Ten Most Wanted" list.

September 28: Sicilian police detain mafioso Salvatore "Vito" Vitale, but he escapes before they formally arrest him.

October: Mexican Mafia member Jimmy "Character" Palma, condemned for murdering two children, is stabbed to death by other Death Row inmates at California's San Quentin State Prison.

October 15: Police and federal agents in Frackville, Pa., arrest 10 persons in a raid on a methamphetamine lab. Two of those charges are members of the Warlocks MC.

October 22: Mafia boss Matthew Trupiano Jr. suffers a fatal heart attack at his home in St. Louis, Mo.

November 3: Genovese Family *caporegime* Nicholas "Little Nick" Corozzo pleads guilty to loan-sharking, extortion and selling stolen property in New York.

November 6: Imprisoned Colombo Family associate Hugh "Apples" MacIntosh dies from natural causes at the U.S. Medical Center for Federal Prisoners in Springfield, Mo.

November 10: Police arrest drug lord Adán Amezcua Contreras on weapons charges in Colima, Mexico. The charges are later dismissed.

November 25: A federal grand jury indicts New York mafiosi Rosario "Ross" Gangi and Frank "Curly" Lino, plus 15 associates, for stock fraud.

December: U.S. Attorney General Janet Reno refuses to release a declassified report from the DOJ's Inspector General on federal handling of the Oscar Blandón and Norwin Meneses cases. The U.S. Organized Crime Drug Enforcement

Task Force concludes "Operation Meta," targeting a Mexican narcotics network. Raids in 17 cities, spanning nine states, produce 121 arrests while seizing 133 pounds of methamphetamine, 1,765 pounds of marijuana, and 1,100 kilograms of cocaine.

December 6: Mafioso Michael Santo "Big Mike" Polizzi dies of natural causes in Detroit.

December 18: FBI spokesmen in Indiana announce an investigation of the Indianapolis Police Department, involving charges that officers have robbed drug dealers. Patrolman Myron A. Powell stands accused of fatally shooting drug dealer Michael Highbaugh during a recent botched holdup on December 11. Jurors later convict Powell of murder, resulting in a 65-year prison term.

December 23: President Clinton pardons five participants in organized crime activity: Clio Louise Carson (convicted in 1979 for transmission of wagering information), Glen Edison Chapman (1955 and 1957, two counts of removing, possessing, and concealing non-tax-paid whiskey), George Edward Maynes Jr. (1975, distribution of cocaine), Charley Morgan (1964, unlawful possession of a still and manufacture of mash), and Edward Kenneth Williams Jr. (1979, receiving and selling stolen motor vehicles and aiding and abetting the same).

1998 The IMB reports 198 acts of piracy worldwide, claiming 67 lives. Pirate raids in Malaysian waters increase to 67, from 51 in 1997. The International Narcotics Control Board estimates that 11.5 tones of oxycodone are manufactured worldwide.

January: The CIA declassifies one volume of a two-volume report on its internal investigation of Contra drug-trafficking. The second volume remains classified.

January 7: Mexican Mafia member Luis "Pelon" Maciel receives a death sentence for ordering the murders of Anthony "Dido" Moreno and four relatives.

January 8: To avoid trial in federal court, six associates of the Warlocks MC plead guilty to distributing methamphetamine in Allentown and Easton, Pa. Defendants include Steven Everett, Jeffrey Farnack, Donald Neith, Daniel Peruso, Richard Smith Sr., and David Yeakel.

January 15: Loan-shark Bernard Marchesani dies from cancer in Allen Park, Mich.

January 16: Pirates kill fisherman Israel Job Pineda off the coast of La Herradura, El Salvador. Police subsequently arrest nine other local fishermen for the attack. Gunmen kill mafioso Alphonse Gangitano at his home in the Melbourne suburb of Templestowe, Australia. A corner's report points suspicion at rivals Graham "The Mun-

ster" Kinniburgh and Jason Moran, but no prosecution results.

January 21: Authorities in Santa Clara County, Calif., raid a Hells Angels clubhouse and nine homes occupied by club members, fatally shooting three dogs in the process. Lawsuits filed by Angels later cost police more than $1.8 million.

January 22: A federal grand jury in New York indicts mafioso John Gotti Jr. and 39 associates on racketeering charges that include conspiracy to commit murder and extorting money from the Manhattan strip club Scores. Others charged in the indictment include radio personality John "Goombah Johnny" Sialiano and former Major League Baseball pitcher Dennis "Denny" McLain.

February 10: FBI agents raid the Chicago District Council of Laborers, removing mobsters Frank Caruso Sr. and son Frank Jr. from control of the union, placing it under the trusteeship of attorney Robert Bloch.

March: Fred Hitz, former Inspector General for the CIA, tells Congress that the agency had a secret bargain with the DOJ from 1982 to 1995, permitting the CIA to avoid reporting incidents of drug-trafficking by its agents and assets. Prosecutors in Moscow, Russia, charge presidential cohort Roman Tsepov with extortion. Tsepov flees to the Czech Republic.

March 19: Mafioso Anthony Turra dies in an ambush outside his Philadelphia, Pa., home as he leaves to face trial in federal court on charges including the attempted murder of underboss Joseph Merlino.

March 27: Turkish police arrest mobster Hüseyin Baybaşin and his nephew Gıyasettin Baybaşin on charges of conspiracy to murder, kidnapping and drug smuggling. Both are convicted on February 10, 2001, with Hüseyin Baybaşin receiving a 20-year sentence (increased to life in July 2002), while Gıyasettin Baybaşin gets 11 years.

April: Pirates seize the Malaysian vessel *Petro-Ranger* and divert it to China, where it is impounded by the authorities. Captain Ken Blyth serves 30 days in jail for telling his crew to surrender, while the pirates face no charges and are repatriated to their native Indonesia. Italy's Court of Cassation confirms Licio Gelli's 12-year sentence for fraud in the Banco Ambrosiano case, but Gelli flees to France in May, on the eve of his scheduled surrender.

April 4: Mexican Mafia member Charles "Chacho" Woody murders Victor "Victorio" Murillo in Visalia, Calif.

April 14: Sicilian police capture fugitive mafioso Salvatore "Vito" Vitale. During his transfer from the police station to prison, his wife and three children attack officers in an abortive effort to liberate Vitale.

April 15: Prosecutors in Stockton, Calif., indict Nuestra Familia members Andrew "Mad Dog" Cervantes and David Marquez on charges of conspiracy to commit murder, drug trafficking, racketeering, and robbery.

April 28: A federal grand jury in New York indicts Lucchese Family acting boss Joseph "Little Joe" DeFede and 11 others on extortion and racketeering charges involving the Mafia's control of Manhattan's Garment District. DeFede pleads guilty in December and receives a five-year sentence, leaving prison on February 5, 2002.

May: The U.S. Treasury Department reveals its three-year "Operation Casablanca" probe of international money-laundering, with indictments against four Venezuelan banks, three Mexican banks, and 167 individual defendants. On July 1, 1999, a federal judge in Los Angeles dismisses the case against one bank — Banorte, based in Monterrey, Mexico — and orders the return of $1.4 million seized by authorities.

May 1: Mexican Mafia gunmen strafe the home of suspected informer Armando Ibarra's girlfriend in San Bernardino, Calif., fatally wounding seven-year-old Mindy Flores by mistake. She dies on May 5. On September 1, 1999, police charge Isaac Aguirre, Jesse "Worm" Chavez, and Vincente Meza with murder and attempted murder.

May 14: Frank Sinatra dies in Los Angeles.

May 19: Italian authorities announce that Sicilian drug kingpin Pasquale Cuntrera has been accidentally released from prison, where he was sentenced to 21 years. Spanish police arrest Cuntrera on the Costa del Sol, on May 24, for extradition to Italy.

May 29: *The General* premieres in Irish theaters and across Great Britain, starring Brendan Gleeson as Dublin mobster Martin Cahill.

June: Japan bans 2C-B.

June 1: Mexican narcotics agents arrest Colima Cartel leaders José de Jesús Amezcua Contreras and Luis Ignacio Amezcua Contreras in Guadalajara, on charges of money-laundering and racketeering. On June 10 the *New York Times* reports that most of their charges have been dismissed.

June 2: Mafioso Joseph Russo dies from natural causes in a federal prison.

June 3: While resisting arrest, a drug smuggler shoots and kills Border Patrol Agent Alexander Kirpnick two miles north of the Mexican border in Arizona.

June 12: Police in Philadelphia, Pa., arrest mafioso Ralph Natale for a parole violation, returning him to prison for completion of an 11-year sentence.

July: U.S. Attorney General Janet Reno and Mexico Attorney General Jorge Madrazo Cuellar draft the "Brownsville Agreement," wherein both nations pledge to inform each other about sensitive cross-border law enforcement operations. DEA spokesmen say that the agreement ties their hands in terms of international investigations.

July 24: Chicago Outfit fixer Gus Alex dies from a heart attack in federal prison.

August 3: A car bomb kills mechanic John Furlan at his home in the Melbourne suburb of Coburg, Victoria, Australia. Police suspect mobster Domenic "Mick" Gatto but file no charges.

August 9: LAPD Officer Filbert Henry Cuesta Jr. suffers fatal gunshot wounds at a rowdy wedding attended by Mexican Mafia members. Eme member Catarino "Termite" Gonzalez Jr. faces trial for the slaying on April 30, 2001. Jurors convict Gonzalez on June 21, 2001, resulting in a life prison term.

August 17: French police arrest Turkish gangster Alaattin Çakıcı and two associates at a hotel in Nice, with false passports and $17,000 in U.S. currency. France extradites Çakıcı to Turkey for trial on fraud charges, on December 14, 1999. He spends three years in prison, released on December 1, 2002.

August 19: Gunmen Rico "Smiley" Garcia and Cesar "Lobo" Ramirez execute Nuestra Familia lieutenant Michael "Mikeo" Castillo in Salinas, Calif.

August 29: Bonanno Family soldiers Vincent "Kojak" Giattino and Thomas Pitera murder FBI informer Wilfred "Willie Boy" Johnson in Brooklyn, as a favor to mafioso John Gotti.

September: Legislators in the United Kingdom abolish capital punishment for piracy. The Japanese cargo ship Tenyu vanishes with a cargo of aluminum en route from Indonesia to Korea. Chinese authorities while find it docked at Zhangjiagang in December, its 15 crew members replaced by 16 Indonesians.

September 1: A federal grand jury indicts Lucchese Family member Nicholas "Fat Nicky" DiCostanza and nine members of his "Port Richmond Crew" on charges including arson, drug dealing, extortion, loan-sharking, murder, and witness tampering. The crimes, committed between January 1, 1990, and February 28, 1995, spanned the states of New York and Pennsylvania.

September 9: French police arrest Italian fugitive Licio Gelli in Cannes, seizing gold ingots valued at $2 million from his villa. Authorities deport him to Italy on October 15. In California, a federal grand jury indicts Aryan Brotherhood officer Michael McElhiney on charges of smuggling heroin into the federal prison at Leavenworth, Kan.

September 24: Connecticut authorities charge eight members of the Diablos MC with various crimes, including the 1992 murder of rival James Gang MC member Mike D'Amato in Wallingford. Raymond "Stoney" Stone confesses that slaying and receives a 20-year sentence.

October 23: Federal jurors in Manhattan convict Colombo Family member Gregory Scarpa Jr. on six counts of extortion, loan-sharking, racketeering, tax fraud, and conspiracy to commit murder, while acquitting him on five counts of murder.

October 27: Retaliating for the August slaying of Michael Castillo, Nuestra Familia gunmen kill Cesar Ramirez in Salinas, Calif.

October 30: Police in Salinas foil Rico Garcia's attempt to kill Nuestra Familia "general" Hector "Copas" Gallegos.

November: Pirates board the bulk carrier MV *Cheung Son* in the South China Sea, murder all 23 crewmen, and dump their weighted bodies overboard. Six corpses later surface in fishing nets off the Chinese port of Shantou. The ship is never seen again, but Chinese authorities convict and execute 13 of the alleged hijackers in 2000.

November 10: Rico Garcia crew members Humberto Estrada, Jimmy Guevara, Gabriel Gutierrez, and Paul Salcido shoot Geronimo Garza and Maria Lopez in Salinas, Calif.

November 13: Judge John Corbett O'Meara hands Detroit mobster Giacomo "Jack" Tocco a one-year maximum sentence in a halfway house, with stipulations allowing Tocco to leave and deal with family business during daylight hours. Prosecutors object, and Tocco is resentenced on December 23 to a Federal Medical Facility in Rochester, Minn., released in 1999 after serving less than 11 months. On January 5, 2000, the U.S. 6th Circuit Court of Appeals rules that Judge O'Meara ignored federal sentencing guidelines. The court then sentences Tocco to 34 months with credit for time served. He is released once more on November 21, 2001.

November 19: Mexican Mafia gunmen execute Enrique Delgadillo, Jose Gutierrez, and Richard Serrano in a Montebello, Calif., auto shop.

November 23: Unknown gunmen kill mobster Charles "Mad Charlie" Hegyaljie at his home in Caulfield, Victoria, Australia. Police suspect hitman Dino Dibra but file no charges.

December 20: Gangster Ivo Karamanski and his bodyguard suffer fatal gunshot wounds in Dupnica, Bulgaria. Police blame the shooting on a drunken quarrel. An unknown gunman kills gangster Bindy Johal at a dance club in Vancouver, British Columbia.

December 24: President Clinton pardons 12 convicted participants in organized crime activity: Thomas Earl Burton (1982, attempted possession with intent to distribute cocaine), James William Gardner (1983, conspiracy to distribute cocaine), Sebraien Michael Haygood (1982, importation of cocaine), Warren Curtis Hultgren Jr. (1982, conspiracy to possess with intent to distribute cocaine), Michael Ray Krukar (1988, unlawful distribution of marijuana), Leslie Jan McCall (1988, use of telephone to facilitate cocaine distribution), William Edward Payne (1965, willful attempt to evade excise tax on wagers), Benito Maldonado Sanchez Jr. (1960, possession of marijuana without payment of transfer tax), Vicki Lynn Seals (1979, distribution of PCP), Irving A. Smith (1957, conspiracy to engage in price-fixing), Darrin Paul Sobin (1987, conspiracy to manufacture marijuana), and John Timothy Thompson (1986, use of the telephone to facilitate cocaine distribution).

1999 Afghanistan produced 4,600 tons of opium, prompting an estimate from the U.N. Drug Control Program that the nation produces 75 percent of the world's heroin. Swedish legislators classify prostitution as a form of violence against women, offering a general amnesty to prostitutes and initiating programs to train them for other occupations. Curiously, while the new law permits sale of sexual favors, hiring prostitutes and pimping remain illegal. Aryan Brotherhood leader Barry Mills writes letters to paroled gang members, urging them to expand the gang's activities outside the prison.

January 7: Mexican Mafia gunmen kill Michael Hutto at his home in Colton, Calif. Police named gang members Anthony and Edward Hernandez as prime suspects, stating that Hutto shortchanged Eme members in a drug deal.

January 9: Gunmen murder mobster Vince Mannella outside his home in Fitzroy North, Victoria, Australia.

January 10: Police find Mexican Mafia members Joseph Caldera and Arthur Daniel Flores shot to death in San Bernardino, Calif., naming Anthony and Edward Hernandez as the probable shooters. The Hernandez brothers subsequently receive three consecutive life sentences. *The Sopranos* premieres on HBO, with James Gandolfini cast as "Tony Soprano," a fictional New Jersey mafioso plagued by endless trouble on all sides. The series airs 86 episodes before its cancellation on June 10, 2007, while collecting 88 awards and another 211 nominations.

January 28: Phoenix attorney Neal Roberts, a key figure in the Don Bolles bombing case, dies from coronary artery disease, cirrhosis and emphysema. His former secretary says Roberts admitted involvement in Bolles's slaying, but police suspect his claims were influenced by alcoholism and a craving for attention.

February 2: Police in southern California arrest 16 Mexican Mafia members in predawn raids. Those captures include Marcel "Psycho" Arevalo, Daniel "Sporty" Bravo, Jesse "Shady" Detevis, Frank "Sapo" Fernandez, Juan "Topo" Garcia, David Contreras Gonzales. Fugitives James "Drak" Maxon and Jesus "Dreamer" Ramirez elude authorities.

February 24: Drive-by gunmen wound boxer-mobster Danny Catania outside his home in Hoppers Crossing, Victoria, Australia, resulting in amputation of one leg. Police suspect Andrew Veniamin but file no charges.

February 27: The made-for-television movie *Lansky* premieres in the U.S., starring Richard Dreyfuss as Meyer Lansky and Eric Roberts as Bugsy Siegel.

March: Mexican police arrest Colima Cartel leader Adán Amezcua Contreras on money-laundering charges, then drop the case and release him in May.

March 18: NYPD officers find Bonanno Family *caporegime* Patrick Gerlando Sciascia shot dead in the Bronx. On June 23, 2005, family boss Joseph Charles "Big Joey" Massino confesses to ordering Sciascia's death and receives a life sentence.

March 26: The European Union passes "Agenda 2000," an economic aid program including 7,586 billion euros earmarked for Sicily over a six-year period. Wiretaps on a mafioso's phone subsequently records his instruction, "'They're advising everyone not to make a noise and attract attention because we've got to get our hands on all of this Agenda 2000."

March 31: The International Criminal Tribunal for the former Yugoslavia unseals an indictment issued on September 30, 1997, charging gangster and warlord Željko Ražnatović with 24 charges of crimes against humanity from the Yugoslav wars of 1990–95.

April: Pirates armed with Molotovs cocktails storm the Cypriot-registered oil tanker *Valiant Carrier* in the Malacca Strait, stabbing three of ship's officers and a seven-month-old girl before leaving the ship adrift. Crew members regain control of the vessel and narrowly avert collision with a nearby island.

April 20: Nuestra Familia soldiers Albert "Beto" Avila, Santos "Bad Boy" Burnias, David "Dreamer" Escamila, and Antonio "Chuco" Guillen kill gang "general" Robert "Brown Bob" Viramontes at his home in Campbell, Calif., acting under orders from superiors Tex Hernandez and Gerald Rubalcaba.

April 28: Pirates board an unnamed ship in Indonesia's Bangka Strait, stealing $9,926 and some articles of gold jewelry.

May 14: Nuestra Familia soldiers kill Alberto Avila for failing to destroy the car used in the April slaying of Robert Viramontes. Police charge Santos Burnias, David Escamila, Antonio Guillen and Rudy Moreno with Avila's murder on October 28.

May 26: Mafiosi Alphonse "Allie Boy" Persico and John "Jackie" DeRoss murder rival mobster William "Billy Fingers" Cutolo in New York City. Prosecutors convict both killers in December 2007, although Cutolo's remains — buried with those of his bulldog Alexo — are not discovered until October 2008, during FBI excavation of a field in East Farmingdale, N.Y.

May 29: Two gunmen ambush grocer Joseph Quadara outside a supermarket in Toorak, Victoria, Australia. Police suspect the shooters mistook Quadara for unrelated local mafioso Giuseppe "Joe" Quadara.

June 8: Pirates board a ship bound for Songkhla, Thailand, off the east coast of Malaysia, holding one crewman hostage while 16 more are set adrift in a lifeboat. The raiders steal 2,060 tons of fuel before Chinese authorities intercept and detain the vessel.

June 23: Iowa Senator Charles Grassley introduces the Most Favored Rogue States Act, to amend the Foreign Assistance Act of 1961 by revising the definition of a "major drug-transit country," specifically by deleting the "significantly affecting the United States" requirement.

July 1: U.S. Attorney Alejandro Mayorkas announces a new federal indictment targeting the Mexican Mafia. Defendants include Carlos "Cheeks" Aguilar, Crispin "Conejo" Alvidrez, Fernando "Cuate" Alvidrez, Joe "Inch" Annet, Mario "Whisper" Castillo, Javier Duarte, Margaret Farrell, Dominick "Solo" Gonzalez, Gerardo "Blanco" Jacobo, Guadalupe Juarez, Adrian Nieto, Rolando "Rolo" Ontiveros, Sally Peters, Veronica Rodriquez, Reuben "Toker" Rojas and Suzanne Schoenberg.

July 14: Gambino Family *caporegime* and ILA racketeer Joseph Colozza dies in New York City.

July 25: The made-for-television movie *Bonanno: A Godfather's Story* premieres in the U.S., starring Martin Landau as Joseph Bonanno.

August 5: Gambino Family *caporegime* James "Jimmy Brown" Failla dies from natural causes at a federal prison in Texas.

August 10: Turkish gangster Dündar Kılıç dies at the American Hospital in Istanbul, from cancer of the eye.

August 25: Patriarca Family member Louis R. Failla dies of natural causes in federal prison.

August 29: DEA agents in Miami, Fla., conclude "Operation Ramp Rats I" by arresting 39 drug smugglers, most of them employed at Miami International Airport. "Operation Ramp Rats II" bags another 15 airport workers on September 9.

September: DEA agents conclude "Operation Impunity," arresting 93 persons linked to the Amado Carrillo Fuentes drug-trafficking organization headquartered in Juarez, Mexico. Raiders seize 12,434 kilos of cocaine and over 4,800 pounds of marijuana were seized, along with $19 million in U.S. currency and another $7 million in assets.

September 9: An unknown gunman kills businessman Dimitrios Belias at an underground car park in Brighton, Victoria, Australia. Police blame unpaid underworld debts.

September 15: Imprisoned British gangster Curtis Warren fatally beats inmate Cemal Guclu at Holland's Nieuw Vosseveld prison. Convicted of manslaughter in 2001, Warren receives an additional four years, making him eligible for parole in 2014.

September 24: An Italian court acquits seven-time Prime Minister Giulio Andreotti of conspiring with mafiosi to kill journalist Carmine Pecorelli in 1979. Prosecutors later win reversal of the verdict on appeal.

October: DEA agents cap "Operation Millennium" by arresting 31 members of the original Medellín cartel. A second campaign, "Operation Columbus," targets different traffickers in Colombia, Venezuela, Panama, and the Caribbean, producing 1,290 arrest while raiders seize 900 kilos of cocaine, nine kilos of heroin, 1,097 metric tons of marijuana, 38 weapons, 26 vehicles, 27 boats, three laboratories and one aircraft.

October 1: Ukrainian mobster Leonid Ludwig "Tarzan" Fainberg completes his racketeering prison sentence in the U.S. and is deported to Israel.

October 9: ATF agents in Colorado arrest 37 members of the Sons of Silence MC on weapons and drug-trafficking charges. Raiders seize 35 guns, four hand grenades, two silencers, 20 pounds of methamphetamine, plus several motorcycles and a an unspecified amount of cash. The raids cap a two-year undercover operation.

October 13: Colombian National Police arrest Medellín Cartel officer Fabio Ochoa Vásquez on the same day that 30 cartel associates are jailed in Colombia, Ecuador, and Mexico in "Operation Millennium." U.S. authorities request Ochoa's extradition in December 1999 and finally achieve it in September 2000. At trial in 2003 he receives a 30-year sentence. In Gladstone Park, Victoria, Australia, drug dealer and convicted murderer Carl Anthony Williams suffers a gunshot wound

to the stomach. Police suspect mobsters Jason and Mark Moran, but file no charges.

October 15: Federal jurors deadlock at the heroin conspiracy trial of Aryan Brotherhood officer Michael McElhiney.

October 16: The made-for-television movie Excellent Cadavers premieres in the U.S., starring Chazz Palminteri as murdered Italian magistrate Giovanni Falcone.

October 20: Gerardo Mannella, brother of mobster Vince Mannella, dies in an ambush outside his home in Melbourne, Australia.

October 22: Ten pirates board the Japanese cargo ship Alondra Rainbow, loaded with aluminum ingots, setting 17 crew members adrift on a life raft without food or water. They are rescued a week later, while the hijacked ship—renamed and sailing under a Belizean flag—is later captured by the Indian navy. One of the pirates confesses that his gang planned to exchange the Alondra Rainbow's cargo for weapons to arm separatist guerrillas fighting in Sri Lanka.

November 10: Mafia gambling specialist Dominic Allevato dies in Warren, Mich.

November 19: Mexican Mafia associate Ricardo Cruz receives a sentence of 28 years to life for the murder of Rudy Saenz in Coachella, Calif.

November 25: Prosecutors in San Leandro, Calif., charge gang security director Pietro Garcia with killing ex-member Joseph Meza, slain for stealing drugs from the gang. Police in Broadmeadows, Victoria, Australia, raid a covert methamphetamine lab, seizing 25,000 amphetamine tablets, a pill press, a loaded pistol and 6.95 kg of powders containing methamphetamine, ketamine, and pseudoephedrine with a street value up to AU$20 million. They charge Carl Williams with various felonies, resulting in a seven-year sentence imposed on October 29, 2004.

November 28: Retired mafioso Sam "The Farmer" Frangiamore dies from natural causes.

December 23: President Clinton pardons 12 convicted participants in organized crime activity: Meredith Marcus Appleton II (1990, conspiracy to possess with intent to distribute cocaine and to distribute cocaine), Albert McMullen Cox (1987, bribery of a public official), Elizabeth Marie Frederick (1987, distribution and possession with intent to distribute cocaine), Daniel Clifton Gilmour Jr. (1985, importation of marijuana), Michael Lee Gilmour (1985, importation of marijuana), Jodie David Moreland (1987, conspiracy to possess with intent to distribute marijuana), Mark Edwin Pixley (1991, aiding in the manufacture, by cultivation, of marijuana), Warren David Samet (1968, transporting, concealing, and facilitating the transportation of marijuana that was acquired without paying the tax imposed), Steven

Elliott Skorman (1972, distributing LSD), Richard Beauchamp Steele (1989, conspiracy to eliminate competition by fixing prices in interstate commerce), Daniel Larry Thomas Jr. (1987, illegal use of a communication facility to distribute cocaine), and Martin Harry Wesenberg (1964, willfully failing to pay the special occupational tax on wagering, and aiding and abetting the same).

2000 The IMB reports 469 acts of piracy worldwide, including 72 homicides. More than one-third of the attacks occur in Indonesian waters. In Afghanistan, Taliban leader Mullah Mohammed Omar bans cultivation of opium poppies. The UN Drug Control Program confirms widespread opium eradication. The Hells Angels "patch over" Los Bravos, a local MC in Manitoba, Canada, making the club a Hells Angels chapter.

January 15: Policeman Dobrosav Gavrić assassinates gangster and indicted war criminal Željko Ražnatović in the lobby of Belgrade's Continental Hotel. At trial in 2006, Gavrić receives a 19-year sentence.

January 21: Gunmen employed by gangster Ali Baba Budesh attempt to kill "Bollywood" film producer Rakesh Roshan in Mumbai, India, after Roshan ignores extortion demands.

January 24: Four gunmen execute criminal-politician Gopal Rajwani outside the First Class Magistrate's court in Ulhasnagar, a suburb of Mumbai, India.

January 28: Police in Howell Township, New Jersey, arrest 10 members of The Breed MC on rape and extortion charges related to the gang's control of strip clubs, tattoo parlors and other businesses in Long Branch. The four rape complainants are dancers employed by the gang.

February 1: Nuestra Familia member Hector "Copas" Gallegos waives indictment by a federal grand jury in Los Angeles, pleading guilty on charges of conspiring to murder victims Fred Perez, Roman Herrera, David Mendoza and an individual known only as "Jose." Gallegos also pleads guilty to selling 500 grams of heroin and methamphetamine.

February 21: Mexican Mafia members organize a riot against rival black gangsters at California's Pelican Bay State Prison. The melee occurs on February 23, leaving 28 prisoners injured. Guards shoot three rioters, killing inmate Miguel "Sharky" Sanchez.

February 23: Pirates attack the Japanese tanker MT *Global Mars*, carrying 6,000 metric tons of palm oil, off the coast of Malaysia, holding 17 crew members hostage for 13 days, then setting them adrift in a lifeboat. The crewmen are rescued on March 10, in Thai coastal waters. The ship remains missing.

February 28: The cargo ship MV *Hualien* sails from Hualien harbor, Taiwan, bound for Taipei with 5,381 metric tons of river sand. Authorities blame pirates for the ship's disappearance, with 21 crewmen.

March: French deputies Arnaud Montebourg and Vincent Peillon release their *Parliamentary Report on the Obstacles on the Control and Repression of Financial Criminal Activity and of Money-laundering in Europe*. The report's third section focuses exclusively on "Luxembourg's political dependency toward the financial sector: the Clearstream affair." In the U.S., DEA agents conclude "Operation Tar Pit," targeting smugglers of Mexican black tar heroin, arresting some 200 smugglers and dealers in 12 cities nationwide.

March 10–26: Various drug enforcement agencies carry out "Operation Conquistador," aimed at interdicting cocaine traffic an Panama, Colombia, Venezuela, Bolivia, Ecuador, Suriname, Trinidad & Tobago, Montserrat, Dominica, St. Kitts, Nevis, Antigua, Anguilla, St. Martin, British Virgin Islands, Barbuda, Grenada, Barbados, St. Vincent, St. Lucia, Aruba, Curacao, Jamaica, Haiti, Dominican Republic, and Puerto Rico. Raids result in 2,331 arrests, while seizing 94 cocaine labs, 4,966 kilos of cocaine, 5,402 kilos of coca leaf, 55.6 kilos of heroin, 14 kilos of morphine base, 362.5 metric tons of marijuana, 73.4 kilos of hash oil, 3,370 doses of dangerous drugs, 129 metric tons of solid precursor chemicals, 39,095 gallons of liquid chemical precursors, 13 boats, 172 vehicles, 83 guns, 17,340 rounds of ammunition, $132,772 in cash, and $2,160,845 in other assets.

March 15: President Clinton pardons four convicted organized crime defendants: Everett Gale Dague (convicted in 1982 of conspiracy to obstruct commerce by extortion, extortion, demanding or receiving illegal payments on behalf of a labor union, and demanding or accepting illegal unloading fees from a motor vehicle driver), Terry Stephen Duller (1990, engaging in illegal gambling business), Peter John Thomas (1978, conspiracy to possess cocaine with intent to distribute), and Heather Elizabeth Wilson (1993, use of telephone to facilitate commission of drug-trafficking felony).

April 2: Sicilian mafioso-turned-informer Tommaso Buscetta dies of cancer in New York City.

April 4: LAPD blames Compton drug dealer Vance "Big V" Buchanan for the slaying of Death Row Records associate William "Chin" Walker. In England, paroled gangster Charles Kray — brother of twins Reginald and Ronald Kray — dies from natural causes.

April 7: Police in Delhi, India, disclose a

recorded conversation between Wessel Johannes "Hansie" Cronje, champion of South Africa's national cricket team, and Sanjay Chawla, a representative of an Indian betting syndicate, involving match-fixing negotiations. The United Cricket Board of South Africa fires Cronje on April 11, after he admits accepting between $10,000 and $15,000 from a British bookmaker to "forecast" game results. On June 7 cricketeer Herschelle Herman Gibbs testifies that Cronje offered him $15,000 to score less than 20 points in a match at Nagpur. Cronje details his dealings with bookmakers on June 15, admitting acceptance of $30,000 to fix matches. Players Gibbs and Henry Williams receive six-month suspensions on August 28, while Cronje is banned from cricket for life on October 11.

April 13: Jurors in San Diego, Calif., convicted Mexican Mafia member Frank "Chino" Madriaga on drug and extortion charges. He receives a sentence of 29 years and four months on July 17. DEA agents conclude "Operation Green Air," crushing a marijuana smuggling network based in Los Angeles, which shipped drugs via Federal Express. Agents arrest more than 100 individuals, including 25 FedEx employees, while seizing 34,000 pounds of marijuana plus $4.2 million in cash and assets.

April 25: Gunmen kill Genaro Martinez, brother of high-ranking Mexican Mafia member Eulalio "Lalo" Martinez, in Los Angeles. Jurors convict defendants Anthony Angulo and Ricky Camacho of the murder on March 29, 2001.

April 27: Unknown gunmen kill drug dealer Vance Buchanan in Los Angeles, apparently in retaliation for William Walker's slaying on April 4.

May: California authorities parole Nuestra Familia lieutenant Daniel "Lizard" Hernandez to Santa Barbara. He lasts less than a month before a June arrest on parole violation charges returns him to Corcoran State Prison.

May 2: Prosecutors in Queens, N.Y., charge alleged mafioso Ralph Romano Jr. with second-degree murder in the June 7, 1989, gunshot slaying of former business partner John Spensieri. Jurors convict Romano on November 4, 2001, but an appellate court later overturns that verdict. Convicted a second time on June 3, 2005, Roman receives a sentence of 18 years to life on November 8, 2005.

May 8: Gunmen kill grocer Francesco Benvenuto in Melbourne, Australia. Police suspect mobsters Mark Moran and Andrew Veniamin but file no charges.

May 11: A federal grand jury unseals indictments of Mexican drug lords Benjamin and Ramon Arellano Félix, charging both with 10 counts of drug trafficking, conspiracy, money-laundering and aiding and abetting violent crimes. The U.S. State Department offers a $2 million reward for information leading to their arrest and conviction.

May 16: A single gunshot kills mobster Richard Mladenich at the Esquire Hotel in St. Kilda, Victoria, Australia.

June 15: Drug dealer Carl Williams murders gangster Mark Moran outside his home in Aberfeldie, Victoria, Australia. Police describe the slaying as retribution for Francesco Benvenuto's slaying in May.

June 22: California-based Computer Associates International, one of the world's largest software manufacturers, settles a 1998 shareholders' class-action suit contending that the firm misstated its revenue for 1998–99 by some $500 million to artificially inflate stock prices. CAI agrees to pay the plaintiffs $234 million, while eight company executives subsequently plead guilty on stock fraud charges. Former CEO Sanjay Kumar receives a 12-year prison sentence and an $8 million fine on November 2, 2006.

June 26: *When the Sky Falls*, a film based on the murder of Irish journalist Veronica Guerin, premieres in the United Kingdom. Joan Allen stars as reporter "Sinead Hamilton."

July: The new Scottish Criminal Cases Review Commission seeks access to all Crown documents related to the Glasgow "ice cream war."

July 6: Philadelphia mafioso Anthony "Mad Dog" DiPasquale dies after crashing his car into a tree on Interstate 95 in Bucks County, Pa.

July 7: President Clinton pardons four convicted organized crime defendants: Dane Robert Hessling (1987, distribution and possession with intent to distribute cocaine), Cynthia Lou LeBlanc (1978, conspiracy to distribute and possess methaqualone), Richard Edwin Sacchi (1989, conspiracy to possess cocaine with intent to distribute), James H. Wetzel Jr. (1981, conspiracy to distribute cocaine), and Diane Mae Zeman (1981, use of a telephone to facilitate importation of hashish oil).

July 9: Mexican Mafia gunmen kill four members of the rival Seventh Street Gang in San Bernardino, Calif., in retaliation for encroachment on La Eme's drug territory.

July 22: U.S. Customs agents seize 2.1 million tablets of ecstasy at Los Angeles International Airport. Smuggling ringleader Tamer Adel Ibrahim flees into Mexico, pursued by DEA and FBI agents.

July 30: Indian gangster Koose Muniswamy Veerappan kidnaps "Bollywood" film star Rajkumar, releasing him on November 15 after payment of a 300,000,000 rupee ($6.5 million) ransom.

August: The DEA's "Operation Mountain Express," targeting illegal methamphetamine dealers and producers, culminates with 140 arrests in eight U.S. cities. Raiders seize 10 metric tons of pseudoephedrine tablets (capable of producing approximately 18,000 pounds of methamphetamine), 83 pounds of finished methamphetamine, two pseudoephedrine extraction laboratories, one methamphetamine laboratory, 136 pounds of chemical solvents and reagents, and $8 million in cash.

August 8: Financial scandal envelops Lernout & Hauspie Speech Products, a speech recognition technology company based in Ypres, Belgium, with revelation of fictitious transactions in Korea and accounting irregularities elsewhere. Belgian police arrest founders Jo Lernout and Pol Hauspie, with former CEO Gaston Bastiaens, in April 2001. The firm goes bankrupt on October 25, 2001.

August 22: President Clinton announces delivery of $1.3 billion in foreign aid to Colombia, earmarked for cocaine eradication via purchase of 60 combat helicopters and employment of 800 drug enforcement officers.

August 23: Imprisoned mafioso Anthony Corallo dies of natural causes at a federal prison hospital in Springfield, Mo.

August 26: The DEA, U.S. Customs Service, and the Joint Interagency Task Force-East conclude "Operation Journey," targeting a Colombian drug transportation organization that uses commercial ships in transporting cocaine to 12 countries. From its launch in January 1999, Operation Journey seized 22,489 kilos of cocaine. British authorities release imprisoned mobster Reginald Kray following his diagnosis of inoperable bladder cancer. Kray dies in his sleep on October 1.

September 6: Manhattan District Attorney Robert Morgenthau charges 38 defendants with racketeering and extortion related to Local 608 of the United Brotherhood of Carpenters and Joiners. Defendants include Lucchesse Family acting boss Steven "Wonderboy" Crea; *caporegimes* Joseph "Joey Flowers" Tangorra and Dominick "Crazy Dom" Truscello; soldiers Joseph Datello, Philip DeSimone, Anthony "Razor" Pezzullo, Joseph Truncale, and Arthur Zambardi; Local 608 president Michael Forde; and Local 608 business agent Martin Deveraux. Crea and Tangorra strike plea bargains with the prosecution, while their cohorts are convicted at trial. Forde's 2004 conviction is overturned on appeal, while a second jury acquits him in 2008.

September 8: Police in San Bernardino County, Calif., arrest 11 members of the Mexican Mafia on charges of operating a drug ring linked to Mexican cartels. Those jailed include Alfonzo Aguila, Judy Alvarado, Paul Flores, Danny Hanks, Antonio Hernandez, Santos Hernandez, Adolph Moraga, Raul Ramirez, Sadie Ramirez, Monica Rodriquez, and Alfredo Valdez.

September 13: Canadian journalist Michel Auger suffers six gunshot wounds outside the office of his newspaper, *Le Journal de Montréal*. Police suspect Hells Angels but the case remains officially unsolved.

September 26: As the Taiwan frigate scandal expands, authorities charge fugitive arms dealer Andrew Wang with naval captain Yin Ching-feng's murder. Wang was employed as Thomson CSF agent in Taiwan during negotiations for the Sino-French frigate purchase.

September 27: Assassins mounted on a motorcycle kill drug lord Francis Vanverberghe in Paris, France.

October: Members of the Gypsy Jokers MC enter a bar owned by ex-policeman Don Hancock in Perth, Western Australia. Hancock expels them for harassing his daughter, who works as a barmaid. Later that night, an unknown gunman kills biker William Grierson at a Gypsy Joker camp outside town. The club blames Hancock, but police file no charges.

October 2: A hitman employed by gang boss Nam Cam, né Trương Văn Cam, kills rival racketeer Dung Ha in Haiphong, Vietnam.

October 6: Alfred Arthur Sandoval, the highest-ranking Mexican Mafia member on California's death row at San Quentin, wins a reversal of his capital sentence from the 9th Circuit Court of Appeals in the case of victim Marlene Wells.

October 10: Police in Québec arrest Hells Angels leader Maurice "Mom" Boucher for ordering the random murders of prison officers Diane Lavigne and Pierre Rondeau.

October 14: Indicted mobster Dino Dibra dies in an ambush outside his home in Sunshine, Victoria, Australia.

October 20: President Clinton pardons three convicted organized crime defendants: Cheryl Ada Elizabeth Little (1978, conspiracy with intent to distribute a controlled substance), Joe Clint McMillan (1992, conspiracy to violate the Sherman Antitrust Act), and Jane Marie Schoffstall (1989, possession with intent to distribute methamphetamine).

October 24: Jurors in Los Angeles convict Mexican Mafia members Robert Cervantes, Frank "Sapo" Fernandez, Juan "Topo" Garcia, Roy "Spider" Gavaldon, Dominick "Solo" Gonzalez, Sally Peters, Jimmy "Drak" Sanchez, and Susanne Schoenberg, on racketeering charges. The same panel acquits defendant Adrian Nieto on three counts of conspiracy to commit murder and one count of racketeering.

October 25: Taiwan's government watchdog agency, the Control Yuan, issues impeachment documents for naval commander-in-chief Yeh Chang-tung, Lei Hsueh-ming (in charge of vessels management), and Yao Nung-chung (in charge of weapons procurement) for accepting kickbacks in the ongoing frigate scandal.

October 26: A federal grand jury in Miami, Fla., indicts Trafficante Family *caporegime* Steven Bruno "Uncle Steve" Raffa and 13 other defendants on charges of illegal gambling, money-laundering and racketeering. Other defendants include Julius Chiusano, Joseph Silvestri, Fred Scarola, and Margate police officer Charles Clay. On November 16 police find Raffa hanged at his home, ruling the death a suicide.

October 27: The DEA launches "Operation Liberator," targeting drug traffickers in Puerto Rico, Dominican Republic, Mexico, Haiti, Ecuador, El Salvador, Venezuela, Bolivia, Panama, Belize, Honduras, Suriname, St. Lucia, Guyana, Colombia, Honduras, Antigua, French Guyana, Trinidad & Tobago, and the Cayman Islands. The campaign ends with a series of raids on November 19.

November: Police in New South Wales, Queensland and Western Australia raid clubhouses of the Rebels MC, seizing drugs, firearms, and a pet crocodile.

November 1: Ex-KGB/FSB officer Alexander Valterovich Litvinenko requests political asylum in London, England. Authorities grant his request on May 14, 2001, and Litvinenko becomes a naturalized British subject in October 2006. In Bogotá, the Colombian National Police and DEA conclude "Operation New Generation," launched two years earlier against a drug cartel led by Carlos Mario Castro-Arias. Raiders execute 52 arrest warrants (44 in Colombia, six in New Jersey, two in New York). Overall, the two-year campaign produces 102 arrests, with seizures including 2,110 kilograms of cocaine, 1,400 grams of heroin, six tons of miscellaneous chemicals, and $2.3 million in cash.

November 9: Nuestra Familia member Carlos "Charlie Brown" Alcala pleads guilty in Salinas, Calif., on charges of conspiracy to distribute 500 grams of heroin and methamphetamine.

November 16: Police find mafioso Steve Raffa hanged with an electrical cord at his home in Broward County, Fla. Authorities rule the death a suicide, inspired by his upcoming trial on gambling, loan-sharking and racketeering charges.

November 21: President Clinton pardons five convicted organized crime defendants: Glen David Curry (1982, conspiracy to distribute and possess with intent to distribute cocaine, distributing and possessing with intent to distribute co-

caine, and using a telephone to facilitate distribution of cocaine); John Laurence Silvi and John Laurence Silvi II (1992, conspiracy to bribe a union official); John Donald Vodde and Melinda Kay Stewart Vodde (1989, possession and distribution of cocaine, and aiding and abetting).

November 22: Agents of the DEA, FBI, IRS, and the U.S. Customs Service conclude "Operation Red Tide," targeting international smugglers of cocaine and ecstasy. Raiders arrest 22 suspects in Los Angeles; Boston, Mass.; Las Vegas, Nev.; Phoenix, Ariz.; Anchorage, Alaska; Salt Lake City, Utah; London, England; Frankfurt, Germany; Milan, Italy; and Amsterdam, Holland.

November 26: Mexican Mafia member Mariano Martinez faces trial on federal racketeering charges in Los Angeles. Jurors convict him on February 15, 2001.

December 9: By a vote of five to four, in the case of *Bush v. Gore*, the U.S. Supreme Court reverses a Florida Supreme Court ruling ordering a third count of votes cast in the presidential election. George W. Bush thus "wins" the election, although he received 543,895 fewer individual votes than Gore nationwide, and is inaugurated on January 20, 2001.

December 14: Agents of the DEA, FBI, and the U.S. Customs Service conclude "Operation Impunity II," launched in October 1999 against Mexican-based smugglers of cocaine and marijuana. The campaign produces 155 arrests, plus seizure of 5,490 kilograms of cocaine, 9,526 pounds of marijuana, and $11 million in cash. The U.S. Attorney's Office in Brownsville, Texas, indicts drug kingpin Osiel Cardénas Guillén and seven other members of his organization on various charges.

December 19: Kevin "Spike" O'Neill, president of the Outlaws MC's Wisconsin/Stateline chapter in Racine, receives a life sentence on racketeering charges.

December 22: President Clinton pardons 20 defendants convicted of organized crime offenses: Harlan Richard Billings (1985, conspiracy to possess with intent to distribute in excess of 1,000 pounds of marijuana), William Robert Carpenter (1991, possession of marijuana with intent to distribute), Peter Welling Dionis (1976, conspiracy, importation, and possession with intent to distribute hashish), Peter Bailey Gimbel (1991, conspiracy to distribute cocaine), Martin Joseph Hughes (1987, aiding and abetting the falsification of union records, aiding and assisting in the submission of false tax records, making false statements to a government agency), Daniel Wayne Keys (1977, possession with intent to distribute marijuana), Larry Ray Killough (1985, unlawful distribution of prescription drugs), Pierluigi

Mancini (1985, possession of cocaine with intent to distribute), Edward Francis McKenna (1993, possession with intent to distribute anabolic steroids), Andrew Kirkpatrick Mearns III (1978, conspiracy to distribute and possess with intent to distribute cocaine), Philip James Morin (1984, distribution of cocaine), James William Rogers (1983, conspiracy to commit racketeering), George Wisham Roper II (1974, conspiracy to bribe public officials and to defraud the United States government), Anthony Andrew Schmidt (1985, conspiracy to possess and distribute cocaine), Stanley Sirote (1974, bribery of a public official), Dent Elwood Snider Jr. (1981, use of a telephone to facilitate the distribution of cocaine), Stephanie Marie Vetter (1979, possession with intent to distribute methamphetamine), Thomas Andrew Warren (1975, conspiracy to import marijuana), Michael Lynn Weatherford (1986, aiding and abetting interstate travel in aid of racketeering), and Charles Z. Yonce Jr. (1988, conspiracy to possess with intent to distribute cocaine and aiding and abetting therein).

2001 U.S. gamblers spend $125.6 billion on lottery tickets. The IMB reports 50 acts of piracy during the year's first quarter, with 18 occurring in the South China Sea, 14 in the Malacca Strait, 13 in the Indian Ocean, four off the coast of West Africa, and one in the Philippines. No arrests are recorded in any case. OxyContin draws media attention as a popular recreational drug, with yearly sales in the U.S. topping $2.5 billion.

January 1: Pirates loot five fishing vessels off the coast of Patharghata, Bangladesh, selling their cargo for $5,000. On the same day, three more ships are robbed of $9,000 off Manderbaria, Bangladesh.

January 5: Nuestra Familia officer Daniel "Lizard" Hernandez sends a note to gang member Joseph "Pinky" Hernandez, requesting support for his bid to control the gang's chapter in San Jose, Calif.

January 6: Mexican Mafia members Robert "Gypsy" Cervantes and David Gonzales Contreras receive life sentences without parole for their convictions on federal racketeering and murder charges. California state authorities transfer Cervantes to federal custody on January 7, in a bid to sever his ties with La Eme.

January 12: Spokesmen for the Gypsy Jokers MC claim that police in Adelaide, South Australia, beat a club member for refusing to remove his motorcycle helmet and sunglasses.

January 15: Nuestra Familia officer Daniel "Lizard" Hernandez demands 25 percent of all profits from a counterfeiting operation run by gang associate Jeff Allen. On January 16 Hernan-dez and Robert "Chico" Rose schedule a meeting to discuss gang business in San Jose, plus establishment of chapters in Stockton and Visalia.

January 18: Agents of the DEA, FBI, IRS and the U.S. Customs Service conclude "Operation White Horse," launched in April 2000 against a Colombian cartel smuggling heroin to Philadelphia, Pa. Raiders arrest 111 suspects, while seizing 22 kilograms of heroin, 10 kilograms of cocaine, 15 weapons and approximately $1.3 million in cash.

January 19: Drug lord Joaquín Guzmán Loera escapes from Puente Grande maximum-security prison in Jalisco, Mexico, with aid from bribed guards. Subsequent investigation implicates 78 persons in his escape.

January 20: Daniel Hernandez sends a "red line" message to imprisoned Nuestra Familia leaders seeking impeachment of "general" Gerald "Cuete" Rubalcaba and lieutenant Sheldon Villanueva, with retirement for lieutenant David Cervantes. In Washington, D.C., President Clinton pardons 27 defendants convicted of organized crime offenses: Bernice Ruth Altschul (1992, conspiracy to commit money-laundering), Nicholas M. Altiere (1983, importation of cocaine), Chris Harmon Bagley (1989, conspiracy to possess with intent to distribute cocaine), Scott Lynn Bane (1984, unlawful distribution of marijuana), David Roscoe Blampied (1979, conspiracy to distribute cocaine), Leonard Browder (1990, illegal dispensing of controlled substance and Medicaid fraud), Donna Denise Chambers (1986, conspiracy to possess with intent to distribute and to distribute cocaine, possession with intent to distribute cocaine, use of a telephone to facilitate cocaine conspiracy), Roger Clinton (1985, conspiracy to distribute cocaine and distribution of cocaine), Rickey Lee Cunningham (1973, possession with intent to distribute marijuana), Marcos Arcenio Fernandez (1980, conspiracy to possess with intent to distribute marijuana), Alvarez Ferrouillet (1997, interstate transportation of stolen property, money-laundering, engaging in a monetary transaction with criminally derived property, false statements to government agents, conspiracy to make false statements to a financial institution), Pincus Green (1984, wire fraud, mail fraud, racketeering, racketeering conspiracy, criminal forfeiture, income tax evasion, and trading with Iran in violation of trade embargo), Robert Ivey Hamner (1986, conspiracy to distribute marijuana, possession of marijuana with intent to distribute), Jay Houston Harmon (1982, conspiracy to import marijuana, conspiracy to possess marijuana with intent to distribute, importation of marijuana, possession of marijuana with intent to distribute, conspiracy to import cocaine), Debi Rae Huckleberry (1986, distribution of methamphetamine), Hildebrando Lopez (1981, distribution of cocaine), James Timothy Maness (1985, conspiracy to distribute Valium), John Francis McCormick (1988, racketeering, racketeering conspiracy, aiding and abetting extortion), Charles Wilfred Morgan III (1984, conspiracy to distribute cocaine), Miguelina Ogalde (1981, conspiracy to import cocaine), Richard H. Pezzopane (1988, conspiracy to commit racketeering, mail fraud), Richard Wilson Riley Jr. (1993, conspiring to possess with intent to distribute and to distribute marijuana and cocaine), Michael James Rogers (1977, conspiracy to possess with intent to distribute marijuana), Anna Louise Ross (1988, distribution of cocaine), Bettye June Rutherford (1992, possession of marijuana with intent to distribute), Gregory Lee Sands (1990, conspiracy to distribute cocaine), Marlena Francisca Stewart-Rollins (1989, conspiracy to distribute cocaine), Kevin Arthur Williams (1990, conspiracy to distribute and possess with intent to distribute crack cocaine), Mitchell Couey Wood (1986, conspiracy to possess and to distribute cocaine). Clinton also pardons fugitive racketeer and tax-evader Marc Rich, whose wife has made controversial donations made by Rich's wife to the Clinton Library and the Democratic Party.

January 24: A federal grand jury in New York City indicts mafioso Alphonse Persico for loan-sharking, one day before his scheduled release from a Florida prison. On January 31 another indictment charges him with racketeering and laundering money through a catering hall in Gravesend, Brooklyn. Persico pleads guilty to the new charges on December 20, subsequently receiving a 13-year sentence and a $1 million fine.

January 27: Allegedly acting "on request of the FBI," Daniel Hernandez advises imprisoned Nuestra Familia officers Daniel "Stork" Perez, James "Tibbs" Morado and Cornelio "Corny" Tristan that he is in charge of the gang's street operations, facing opposition from "general" Gerald "Cuete" Rubalcaba and Sheldon Villanueva.

February: Imprisoned Mexican Mafia godfather Benjamin "Topo" Peters dies from cancer in California. Rick Causey, CAO of Enron Corporation, an American energy company based in Houston, Tex., tells company budget managers, "From an accounting standpoint, this will be our easiest year ever. We've got 2001 in the bag."

February 7: Pirates storm the fishing vessel Dilruba off Patharghata, Bangladesh, wounding one crewman with gunfire and stealing supplies valued at $139,373. In California, Nuestra Familia officer Jimmy Sieraoski orders Daniel Hernandez to cease communications with gang member Robert Rose. Hernandez ignores the command.

February 8: Police in Palmdale, Calif., charge Petra Celia Gonzales — wife of Mexican Mafia leader Fred "Sapo" Gonzales and mother of imprisoned gang member Dominique "Nick" Gonzales — with running a mail fraud ring from her home.

February 14: Southside Stockstone gang members Jose Azua and Eric Espinoza receive seven-year prison terms for selling drugs in Los Angeles; codefendant Samuel Zapata is sentenced to five years. From prison, Nuestra Familia officer Daniel Hernandez orders member Ramiro "Goose" Garcia to sever ties with Antonio "Chuco" Guillen in San Jose.

February 19: Daniel Hernandez accuses Jimmy "Travieso" Morales of betraying other Nuestra Familia gang members, marking him for death as a traitor.

February 20: Trial convenes in Allentown, Pa., for four ex-members of Roofers Union Local 30–30b on drug and racketeering charges. On April 6 jurors convict defendants Mark Goodwin, Pietro Joseph Grippi, Joseph Michael Traitz, and Stephen Joseph Traitz III of operating a methamphetamine ring, but acquit all four of murdering drug dealer Robert Hammond on April 14, 1987.

February 21: Bonanno Family *caporegime*-turned-federal witness Albert "Al Walker" Embarrato dies of natural causes in New York City.

February 23: Mobster Anthony Joseph Giacalone dies in Detroit, Mich., from heart and kidney failure.

February 26: Luxembourg's Tribunal d'Arrondissement launches an investigation of Clearstream Banking S.A., the custody and settlement division of Deutsche Börse AG, based on accusations of money-laundering and other offenses contained in the book *Revelation$*, by authors Denis Robert and Ernest Backes. Clearstream suspends CEO André Lussi on May 15 and announces his permanent departure by "mutual agreement" on December 31. Investigation documents Clearstream's prior links to the BCCI, but corporate leaders win a libel suit against Backes and the French magazine *Le Figaro* on March 29, 2004. Despite that judgment in the company's favor, judges reject Clearstream's plea for damages, finding that the accusations are "serious and cross-checked, absent of any animosity, and expressed with caution." By June 1, 2006, Clearstream has obtained 28 judgments against Denis Robert but received only three euros, despite petitions seeking 100,000 to 300,000 per claim.

March: Police in Québec stage "Operation Springtime," arresting 120 Hells Angels and club associates on various charges. At Chittagong, Bangladesh, the crew of the cargo ship *Actuaria* repels a group of pirates attempting to hijack the vessel.

In San Francisco, Calif., unknown assailants fatally beat Mexican Mafia member Michael "Hacha" Ison outside a skid row pool hall. FBI agents and federal prosecutors meet after DNA tests identify a hair from missing IBT president Jimmy Hoffa, found in the backseat of a car owned by Charles "Chuckie" O'Brien. No charges are filed.

March 5: *Fortune* magazine publishes an article titled "Is Enron Overpriced," questioning the corporation's high stock value, trading at a rate of 55 times its earnings. Enron CFO Andrew Fastow tells *Fortune*, "We don't want to tell anyone where we're making money."

March 7: Pirates board the Panamanian tanker *Lingfield* near Bintan, Indonesia, binding and blindfolding the ship's senior officers before escaping with $11,000 from a safe. In California, Nuestra Familia member Hector "Copas" Gallegos, author of the gang's "14 bonds" (rules of conduct), receives a 20-year federal prison term for racketeering in Los Angeles. Codefendant Carlos Alcala is sentenced to 130 months.

March 9: Thai police blame an unspecified "organized crime organization" for boarding the Panamanian cargo ship Jasper offshore from Kosichang, stealing $11,000. In California, Nuestra Familia officer Daniel Hernandez orders Ramiro Garcia to eliminate dissident gang member Mark "Caja" Rodriquez.

March 11: Nuestra Familia "regimental commanders" convene a meeting in California. Daniel Hernandez falsely accuses officers James "Blackie" Enriquez, James "Tibbs" Morado and Sheldon Villanueva of suspicious behavior.

March 15: Six pirates commandeer the Indonesian cargo ship *Inabukwa* off the coast of Malaysia, marooning its crew on a small island, then fleeing with a cargo of pepper and tin ingots valued at $2,170,000. Filipino police seize the ship and arrest the pirates two weeks later.

March 20: Venezuelan pirates board a Swedish yacht off the coast of Trinidad, wounding the captain with gunfire before stealing liquor and cash.

March 22: Defying orders from Nuestra Familia officer Jimmy Sieraoski, Daniel Hernandez names Robert Rose to lead the gang's chapter in San Jose, Calif. In Melbourne, Australia, unknown gunmen execute mobster George Germanos.

March 25: An unknown gunman kills David "Brim Dave" Dudley, a Death Row Records associate, outside the Los Angeles home of Death Row insider Alton "Buntry" McDonald.

March 28: Nuestra Familia officer Joseph "Pinky" Hernandes warns Daniel Hernandez to obey directions issued from Corcoran state prison by Jimmy "Wino" Sieraoski.

March 29: Prosecutors file first-degree murder charges against Mexican Mafia member Jose Luis "Clever" Sanchez for his role in fomenting a riot between black and Hispanic inmates at Pelican Bay State Prison.

March 30: Nuestra Familia member Rico Garcia orders Albert Larez to compile a list of prosecution witnesses against the gang. Daniel Hernandez countermands that order.

April: The Third Yamano-kai Yakuza clan, based in Kumamoto, Kyūshū, Japan, formally dissolves. Police remove it from their list of active criminal groups in November.

April 2: Filipino pirates strafe a fishing boat off the coast of Zamboanga, killing two crewmen and wounding another, then flee without boarding the vessel. In Providence, R.I., a federal grand jury indicts Mayor Vincent "Buddy" Cianci Jr., director of administration Frank Corrente, chief of staff Artin Coloian, and auto garage businessman Richard E. Autiello on racketeering and corruption charges.

April 4: ATF agents arrest six members of the Sons of Silence MC in Iowa, on charges of firearms violations plus trafficking in cannabis, cocaine, and methamphetamine.

April 5: Federal agents in California arrest Nuestra Familia members Paul "Powder" Killinger, Albert Larez, and Jaime "Smokey" Rodriquez. Jurors in New York City convict Bonanno Family *consiglieri* Anthony Spero of racketeering and ordering the murders of victims Vincent Bickelman, Paul Gulino and Louis Tuzzio. Spero receives a life prison term and a $250,000 fine on April 15, 2002.

April 12: California authorities arrest Nuestra Familia member Robert "Wolfie" Haas on charges of parole violation. Police in San Jose also arrest gang member Israel "Silent" Mendoza. Daniel Hernandez names Sylvester "Silvio" Gomez to replace Mendoza, while appointing Anthony "Chino" Morales to lead the gang's Visalia chapter. In Italy, *L'Espresso* magazine publishes a cover story naming Matteo Messina "Diabolik" Denaro as "the new boss of the Mafia."

April 17: Nuestra Familia member Robert "Bubba" Hanrahan leaves prison on parole, bearing a letter from James "Conejo" Perez naming Hanrahan commander of the gang's Salinas, Calif., chapter. That order deposes Armando Heredia, named to the Salinas post by Daniel Hernandez.

April 20: A federal grand jury in Los Angeles indicts 13 Nuestra Familia members on 25 counts of racketeering. Defendants include Henry Cervantes, Jacob Enriquez, Vidal Fabela, Rico "Smiley" Garcia, Tex Hernandez, James Morado, Daniel Perez, Cesar "Lobo" Ramirez, David "Sir

Dyno" Rocha, Gerald Rubalcaba, Cornelio Tristan, Diana Vasquez, and Sheldon Villanueva.

April 22: Nuestra Familia officer Daniel Hernandez removes Eric "Cobra" Martinez from his post as the gang's security chief in Visalia, Calif., while continuing to sow dissension in the ranks.

May: Four pirates board the Panamanian cargo ship Marine Universal while it is anchored in Lagos Harbor, Nigeria, throwing one crewman overboard, then fleeing the vessel. Ex-IBT official and self-proclaimed hitman Frank "The Irishman" Sheeran tells Fox News reporter Eric Shawn that he personally killed Jimmy Hoffa. Sheeran identifies a house where the slaying allegedly occurred.

May 4: A federal grand jury in Cleveland, Ohio, indicts Youngstown congressman James Anthony Trafficant Jr. on 10 counts of bribery, racketeering, obstruction of justice and income tax evasion. Jurors convict him on April 11, 2002, and Trafficant receives an eight-year sentence with a $150,000 fine and forfeiture of $96,000 in illegitimate earnings on July 30, 2002. Congress expels him by a vote of 420-to-1 on July 24, 2002, and Trafficant subsequently loses his bid to be reelected from prison. Paroled on September 2, 2009, he attends a September 6 banquet and announces plans to run again for Congress, telling assembles supporters, "I guess, the same jackass I was."

May 18: Police in Melbourne, Australia, rearrest Carl Williams on drug-trafficking charges, holding him in custody until July 17, 2002.

May 31: Agents of the IRS, U.S. Postal Service, and Pennsylvania State Police raid the homes of Bufalino Family members in eastern Pennsylvania, seizing financial records. Federal agents in Milwaukee, Wis., indicts Edward Anastas, ex-president of the local Outlaws MC chapter, following publication of an indictment charging him with racketeering conspiracy, cocaine conspiracy, and participating in a bombing. Anastas subsequently turns state's evidence against other club members, resulting in a 10-year sentence for defendant Thomas Sienkowski. The 7th Circuit U.S. Court of Appeals vacated that sentence on February 20, 2004.

June: California prison authorities parole Nuestra Familia member Ben "Huero" Chavez. He leaves prison with a letter from gang leaders James "Conejo" Perez and Sheldon "Skip" Villanueva confirming Robert Hanrahan's appointment as commander of the Visalia chapter — a direct challenge to opposing orders from Daniel Hernandez.

June 11: Silvio Berlusconi begins his second term as Italy's prime minister. Allegations of involvement with the Mafia persist, dating from 1973.

June 15: A federal grand jury in Chicago indicts 10 defendants on racketeering charges related to a $10 million insurance fraud scheme in suburban Cicero. Those charged include Cicero Town President Betty Loren-Maltese; former public safety director Emil Schullo; former supervisor, trustee and treasurer Joseph DeChicio; Cicero mob boss Michael Spano Sr. and his son Michael Jr.; trucking executive John LaGiglio and wife Bonnie; former IRS Criminal Investigation Division supervisor Gregory Ross; attorney Charles Schneider; and Frank Taylor, general manager of Specialty Risk Consultants, Inc., a sham company created to handle insurance for Cicero.

June 18: A federal grand jury in Sonoma County, Calif., indicts Nuestra Familia members Luis Aroche, Armando Heredia, Ramiro Garcia, Joseph Hernandez, Alberto Larez, Israel Mendoza, Anthony Morales and Robert Rose on racketeering charges. Jurors in Santa Clara County convict gang members Christopher Carasco, Gustavo Castenada, Jerry Patlin, Steven Pena and Andres Perez of beating another inmate in the county jail.

June 20: Federal, state and local officers conclude "Operation Marquis," an 18-month nationwide investigation targeting a Mexican drug cartel based in Nuevo Laredo, led by members of the former Amado Carrillo Fuentes syndicate. The campaign produces 185 arrest, plus seizures of 8,645 kilograms of cocaine, 23,096 pounds of marijuana, 50 pounds of methamphetamine, and $13 million in cash.

June 25–27: Convening in Las Vegas, Nev., the IBT adopts the concept of "one member, one vote" as a permanent component of the union's constitution. Delegates re-elect James Phillip Hoffa as the IBT's general president.

July: Portugal decriminalizes all recreational drugs for personal consumption. An Italian court sentences fugitive mafioso Luigi Putrone *in absentia* to a life prison term for crimes committed in the 1980s and 1990s.

July 3: Nuestra Familia member Daniel Hernandez signs a secret federal plea bargain in California, admitting one count of conspiracy to conduct a continuing criminal enterprise while sparing himself from a potential life sentence and remaining in place as a government informer.

July 24: Daniel Hernandez convenes a meeting of Nuestra Familia members, informing him that he controls the gang's street operations despite conflicting orders from imprisoned leader Jimmy "Wino" Sieraoski.

July 26: In Paris, France, two motorcycle-riding gunmen murder Djilali Zitouni, a prime suspect in the earlier slaying of gangster Francis Vanverberghe. FBI agents monitoring bribery-related wiretaps in Westbury, Conn., arrest Mayor Philip Giordano on charges of hiring a prostitute to furnish two girls, age nine and 10, for sex. State prosecutors file rape charges on September 11, while a federal grand jury unseals a 14-count indictment on September 21. The unnamed prostitute pleads guilty to state charges on September 19. Federal jurors convict Giordano on March 25, 2003, and he receives a 37-year sentence on June 13. The still-unnamed procurer receives a 10-year sentence on October 17, 2003.

Early August: Armed pirates in three speedboats stop the British yacht *Swan* off the coast of Somalia and hold the crew captive for 10 days, then release them unharmed.

August: Pietro Lunardi, Italy's Minister for Infrastructure and Transportation, raises a storm of protest with a statement that Italians should "learn to live with the Mafia," adding that "everyone should deal with the crime problem in their own way."

August 3: Albanian mobster Alex Rudaj leads a troupe of gunmen into Soccer Fever, a Greek social club in Queens, N.Y., pistol-whipping the owner and routing his patrons. Prosecutors later describe the attack as part of a campaign to invade gambling turf claimed by the Lucchese Family. In California, jurors convict Nuestra Familia member John Sloan of murdering victim Francisco Gonzalez and wounding Francisco Duran in a gang-related shooting.

August 14: Enron Corporation CEO Jeffrey Skilling resigns after six months in office, citing "personal reasons." On August 15 he admits leaving due to Enron's faltering stock prices. Also on August 15, Sherron Watkins, Enron's vice president for corporate development, sends an anonymous letter to company founder Kenneth Lay, warning him of Enron's accounting practices. She writes: "I am incredibly nervous that we will implode in a wave of accounting scandals." Watkins meets with Lay on August 22, delivering a six-page explanation of the company's fraudulent dealings. Lay consults other executives and recommends firing Watkins, then decides against it to avoid litigation.

August 30: DEA agents and local police conclude "Operation Green Clover," targeting ecstasy traffickers in California and Colorado. Raiders arrest 55 suspects, while seizing 85,000 ecstasy tablets, 2.5 kilograms of cocaine, 320 pounds and 4100 plants of marijuana, five pounds of methamphetamine, 40,000 dosage units of LSD, 13 vehicles, 36 weapons, and $1,360,000 in cash.

September 1: A car bomb kills ex-policeman Don Hancock and bookmaker Lou Lewis at Hancock's home in Perth, Western Australia. Authorities suspect members of the Gypsy Jokers MC,

retaliating for the October 2000 murder of biker William Grierson. Jurors acquit the prime suspect on October 29, 2003.

September 5: The DEA and the Dominican Republic's National Drug Control Directorate conclude "Operation Sanctuary," a 12-month investigation of cocaine trafficking and money-laundering. Raiders arrest 43 persons, seizing 2,899 kilograms of cocaine and $2,511,285 in cash.

September 26: DEA agents and local authorities conclude "Operation Black Ice," a seven-month campaign targeting the Jose Serrano heroin trafficking organization. Raiders in Arizona, California and Missouri arrest 11 suspects.

October 7: Retaliating for Al-Qaeda's terrorist attacks of September 11, U.S. troops invade Afghanistan. The war — still in progress as this book went to press — restores Afghanistan as a leading source of heroin worldwide.

October 15: Spokesmen for the law firm of Vinson & Elkins, representing Enron Corporation, announce that Enron has done nothing wrong in its accounting practices. On October 16 company leaders announce that amended financial statements for the years 1997–2000 are required to correct accounting violations. Those "restatements" reduce earnings by $613 million, increase liabilities by $628 million, and reduce equity by $1.2 billion. Kenneth Lay removes Andrew Fastow as CFO on October 25. Enron begins buying back its commercial paper on October 27 and seeks $2 billion in bank financing on October 29. The *New York Times* calls for an "aggressive" SEC investigation on November 1. Enron secures $1 billion in financing from rival Dynegy Corporation on November 2, followed by Dynegy's announcement on November 7 of plans to purchase Enron at an $8 billion "fire-sale price." Enron "corrects" its earning statements once again on November 9, for a further reduction of $591 million during 1997–2000. On November 19 company spokesmen announce impending debts of $9 billion due for repayment in 2002. Dynegy cancels plans to buy Enron on November 28. Enron's European operations file for bankruptcy on November 30, followed by Chapter 11 filings in the U.S. on December 2.

October 18–19: DEA agents in southern California conclude "Operation Triple X," dismantling a major ecstasy ring based in Escondido. Raiders seize 48,000 ecstasy tablets, one pound of methamphetamine, 48 kilos of 3,4-Propene (which could produce 500,000 ecstasy tablets), 700 pounds of camphor oil (which could produce one million ecstasy tablets), 45 gallons of GBL (used to produce GHB), 15 weapons, and $429,000 in cash.

October 22: Mafioso Raffaele Quasarano dies from natural causes in Detroit, Mich.

October 23: British Home Secretary David Blunkett proposes relaxing the classification of cannabis from a class B drug to class C. Authorities ignore his recommendation.

October 28: Bonanno Family soldier John "Porky" Zancocchio and wife Lana plead guilty to charges of loan-sharking and tax evasion in New York City. Porky receives a 71-month sentence and a $300,000 fine on January 21, 2002, while Lana's defense attorney negotiates a term of house arrest. Authorities release John Zancocchio from custody on August 29, 2008.

October 31: Biopharmaceutical ImClone Systems, Inc., asks the FDA to review Erbitux, its new cancer drug. ImClone founder Sam Waksal receives a tip on December 26 that approval will be denied. He tells his daughter to sell her shares and tries to sell his own. Celebrity stockholder Martha Stewart sells her 3,928 shares of ImClone on December 27. The FDA announces its rejection of Erbitux on December 28, and ImClone stock drops 18 percent on December 31.

November: For the third time, Scotland's Criminal Cases Review Commission refers the murder convictions of Thomas Campbell and Joe Steele to the court of appeals.

November 6: Taiwan's government requests legal assistance from Switzerland in the ongoing frigate scandal, citing concerns over fraud, money-laundering and corruption.

November 21: Trial begins in Miami, Fla., for three defendants charged with federal violations including racketeering conspiracy, murder in aid of racketeering, conspiracy to commit murder in aid of racketeering, bank fraud, loan-sharking, passing counterfeit checks and possession of stolen goods. On December 14 jurors convict all three — including Gambino Family members Anthony "Tony Pep" Trentacosta and Frederick Massaro, and Mafia associate Ariel Hernandez. Massaro stands convicted on 21 felony counts; Trentacosta is convicted of RICO conspiracy; and Hernandez is convicted of killing stripper Jeanette Smith, whom he believed to be an FBI informer. Trentacosta dies in prison, in December 2005.

November 23: Sicilian mafioso Giovanni Riina receives a life sentence for four murders committed in 1995.

November 26: Mexican Mafia "street general" John "Stranger" Turscak receives a 30-year sentence for crimes committed while acting as an informer for the FBI's Los Angeles field office.

November 28: Mexican Mafia members assault three LASO deputies at the Inmate Reception Center downtown in Los Angeles.

November 29: Authorities raid the home of mafioso Richard G. Gotti in Valley Stream, N.Y., seizing $12,000 in cash.

December: Scotland's Lord Justice Clerk, Lord Gill, frees Thomas Campbell and Joe Steele from prison pending resolution of their appeal on murder convictions from Glasgow's ice cream war.

December 6: New Zealand yachtsman Sir Peter Blake, winner of the America's Cup in 1995 and 2000, dies in a battle with pirates who attempt to board his schooner *Seamaster* at the mouth of the Amazon River. The U.S. Attorney's Office for the Eastern District of New York indicts members of Staten Island's Mafia-allied New Springville Boys gang on charges of stealing loan-sharking, money-laundering, hijacking a marijuana shipment valued in excess of $1 million, and stealing $240,000 from bank night-deposit boxes nationwide. Defendants include leader Lee D'Avanzo, Ned Bilali, Robert Catanese, Francis Costanzo, William "Big Bill" Fauci, Joseph "Fat Joe" Gambino, and Edward Shamah.

December 10: Mexican Mafia member Antonio Haro slashes the throat of Deputy Chris Varela at the Los Angeles Inmate Reception Center.

December 11: Federal agents strike at the "Warez" network of software pirates, staging raids to seize computers in 27 U.S. cities spanning 21 states. In Scotland, authorities grant bail to Thomas "TC" Campbell and Joseph Steele, sentenced to life imprisonment in 1984 on six counts of murder related to Glasgow's "ice cream wars." A prosecution witness from their trial admits lying under oath.

December 13: Prosecutors in Bergen County, N.J., schedule a pretrial conference for Daniel Provenzano on his recent 44-count racketeering indictment, including charges of state tax evasion, beating debtors, and using a hammer to smash the thumbs of an employee suspected of pilferage. Provenzano pleads guilty on November 6, 2002, and receives a 10-year prison sentence plus a $111,000 fine on September 15, 2003. State authorities deny his first parole bid on December 24, 2005.

December 14: Dominick "Little Dom" Curra, one-time "personal bookie" to mafioso John Gotti, pleads guilty in New York City on charges of trying to sell forged artworks.

December 17: Jurors in Trenton, N.J., convict Joseph V. Lo Re and four codefendants on charges of conspiring to embezzle money from a waterfront union in Bayonne.

2002 Italian authorities report a rift in the Mafia, between factions based in Corleone (led by Leoluca Bagarella and Salvatore Riina) and Palermo (led by Bernardo Provenzano, Matteo Messina Denaro, Antonino Giuffrè, and Salvatore Lo Piccolo).

Indonesia, Bangladesh and India lead the world in pirate attacks with 102, 32 and 18 incidents respectively. In Ontario, Canada, Crown Prosecutor Graeme Williams seeks to have the Hells Angels formally branded a "criminal organization" under prevailing anti-gang legislation.

January 7: Ex-policeman Jack Redlinger faces trial in Atlanta, Ga., on charges of accepting bribes to fix traffic tickets for employees of the Gold Club, a local strip joint whose owner was charged with racketeering in 1999. Redlinger is the last of 17 defendants indicted in the case. In New York, Peter Bacanovic, Martha Stewart's stockbroker, tells SEC attorneys that he and Stewart agreed on December 20, 2001, to sell ImClone shares if the price fell below $60. Stewart confirms that story to the SEC, FBI and federal prosecutors on February 4.

January 8: Four police detectives in Buffalo, N.Y., go to trial on charges of stealing money from an undercover FBI agent posing as a drug dealer. All four have been suspended with pay since their arrest in March 2000.

January 10: Agents of the DEA, IRS, U.S. Customs and the RCMP conclude "Operation Mountain Express III," targeting methamphetamine traffickers in the United States and Canada. The campaign produces more than 300 arrests, plus seizures of nine clandestine methamphetamine labs, 30 tons of pseudoephedrine, 181 pounds of methamphetamine, 96 cars and some $16 million in cash.

January 17: Spokesmen for Enron Corporation announce the dismissal of Arthur Andersen LLP as the company's auditor, citing its accounting advice and the destruction of documents. Andersen leaders reply that they severed their ties to Enron when Enron entered bankruptcy.

January 23: Chris Maskell visits the Barrie, Ontario, home of a businessman who sold him $75,000 worth of "black boxes" built to defraud satellite television companies by programming "smart cards" to avoid payment of monthly fees. Accompanied by Hells Angels Raymond Bonner and Steven Lindsay, Maskell demands a refund. Police subsequently indict the Angels for extortion, leading to designation of the club as a criminal organization.

January 28: Trial begins in Boston for retired Massachusetts state trooper Richard Schneiderman, accused of obstructing the FBI's search for fugitive James "Whitey" Bulger by telling Bulger's relatives that G-men had requested pen registers on their telephones.

January 30: Vowing that he would rather die than return to prison, Pagans MC member Thomas Campbell murders police officer Dennis McNamara in Upper Darby Township, Pa.

February: Self-proclaimed hitman Frank Sheeran visits Detroit, Mich., with author Charles Brandt, pointing out a house where Sheeran claims he killed Jimmy Hoffa.

February 10: Tijuana Cartel leader Ramon Arellano Félix dies in a shootout with police in Mazatlán, Mexico.

February 16: A federal jury in Montgomery, Ala., convicts defendants Anton Pusztai and Anita Yates on charges related to their operation of an Internet website that illegally sold prescription drugs by mail-order. Specific charges include conspiracy to commit violations of the Federal Food, Drug, and Cosmetic Act, conspiracy to commit money-laundering, mail fraud, dispensing misbranded drugs, and operating a drug repackaging facility not registered with FDA. On June 18 Pusztai receives a 15-year prison term, while Yates is sentenced to 6 years.

February 17: Disgraced Moe Dalitz protégé Al Sachs dies from a heart attack.

February 19: Mobster Karim Lala, né Abdul Karim Sher Khan, dies from natural causes in Mumbai, India.

February 23: Police on Long Island, N.Y., arrest 73 members of the Pagans MC after they attack Hells Angels at an indoor motorcycle and tattoo expo called the Hellraiser Ball, leaving one Pagan shot to death and dozens of bikers injured in brawling. On March 12 a federal grand jury indicts all 73 Pagans on racketeering charges.

March: FBI agents announce that they will refer the Hoffa murder case to prosecutors in Oakland County, Mich. In August those authorities report that existing physical evidence is insufficient to support criminal charges. Investigators from Taiwan's Control Yuan report that prices of the nation's frigate deal with France were wrongfully inflated by $2 billion from the original quote, while various Taiwanese politicians and military officers received $26.75 million in kickbacks.

March 6: Unknown arsonists firebomb a tattoo parlor owned by members of the Pagans MC in South Philadelphia, Pa. Police suspect retaliation by Hells Angels for a brawl in New York on February 23.

March 7: FBI agents arrest seven members of the Genovese Family and officers of ILA Local 1588 on charges related to a "money for work" shake-down of dock workers at various New Jersey waterfront shipping terminals. The defendants include Aniello "Sonny" Bello, Carlo Bilancione, Anthony D'Errico, Ralph Esposito, Nicholas Furina, Nicholas Romano, and John Timpanaro.

March 8: The film *I banchieri di Dio* premieres in Italy, starring Omero Antonutti as murdered swindler and bagman Roberto Calvi. In California, federal prosecutors their intention to seek the death penalty against Nuestra Familia member Rico "Smiley" Garcia. In Puebla, Mexico, police arrest fugitive Tijuana Cartel leader Benjamin Arellano Félix.

March 18: FBI headquarters announces the culmination of "Operation Candyman," a 14-month investigation of Internet child pornography. Results include 231 searches and 86 arrests in 27 states. Of those arrested, 27 admit prior molestation of 36 children.

March 21: Mexican Mafia member Frank "Pancho Villa" Martinez faces trial on federal racketeering charges in Los Angeles. Prosecutors say that Martinez led a gang faction called the "Columbia Li'l Cycos," collecting $4.4 million per year in protection payments from drug dealers around MacArthur Park.

March 22: Rene "Boxer" Enriquez retires as a leader of the Mexican Mafia in South Central Los Angeles, emerging as a federal government witness in 2003.

March 24: Québec Hells Angels boss Maurice Boucher faces trial in Montreal on charges of ordering to prison officers killed in 1997. Jurors convict him on May 6, resulting in an automatic life prison term with no parole for at least 25 years.

March 28: Sicilian mafioso Pietro "The Little Gentleman" Aglieri writes to National Anti-Mafia Prosecutor Pierluigi Vigna and Chief Prosecutor of Palermo Pietro Grasso, proposing lenient sentences for gangsters who "dissociate" from the Cosa Nostra without becoming informers.

April 3: LAPD officers find Bloods gang member Alton "Buntry" McDonald shot to death in the Compton ghetto. Unknown members of the rival Fruit Town Piru Crips are suspected.

April 13: In Montreal, Québec, a "mega" trial convenes for 17 Hells Angels charged with drug trafficking and other crimes during a biker war that claimed at least 160 lives. The proceedings begin in a specially-constructed high-security courthouse built at a cost of $20 million.

April 16: Italian police arrest fugitive mafioso Antonino "Nino" Giuffrè. He turns informer for the government in June 2002.

April 22: Mayor Vincent Cianci Jr. of Providence, R.I., faces trial on federal corruption and racketeering charges with codefendants Frank Corrente and Richard Autiello. Jurors convict all three defendants on June 11. Cianci receives a sentence of five years and four months on September 6 and resigns from office. He enters prison at Fort Dix, N.J., on December 6, 2002, and is released to a Boston halfway house on May 30, 2007.

April 27: A brawl between rival Hells Angels and Mongols at the Harrah's Casino & Hotel in Laughlin, Nev., leaves Angels Jeramie Bell and Robert Tumelty dead from gunshot wounds, while Mongol Anthony Barrera is fatally stabbed. Hells Angels Rodney Cox and James Hannigan receive two-year prison terms on February 23, 2007, for their role in provoking the so-called "River Run Riot." Authorities dismiss charges filed against 36 other Hells Angels.

April 29: A federal grand jury in New York indicts Genovese Family member Lawrence "Larry Glitz" Galizia and four associates—Christopher Demenna, Anthony Hooks, Frank Isoldi, and Robert Schwall—on charges of collecting debts for an illegal gambling service run through Costa Rica and making illegal loans in the range of $15,000 to $100,000.

May: A court in Moscow, Russia, convicts ex-KGB/FSB agent Alexander Valterovich Litvinenko on abuse-of-office charges. He receives a 3½-year prison sentence in absentia. A federal court blocks extradition of Colima Cartel leader José de Jesús Amezcua from Mexico to the U.S., on grounds that extradited suspects may not face capital punishment of life imprisonment.

May 1: Police in Port Melbourne, Victoria, Australia, find gangster Victor George Peirce shot dead in his car outside a Bay Street supermarket.

May 2: Former Chicago Police Department chief of detectives William Hanhardt pleads guilty to federal charges of racketeering conspiracy and conspiracy to ship stolen jewels across state lines as part of a police theft ring. He receives a sentence of 15 years and 10 months, reduced on May 25, 2004, to 11 years and nine months. His release is scheduled for January 13, 2012.

May 3: Jurors in Boston, Mass., convict retired policeman Michael Flemmi on charges of concealing weapons for his brother, mafioso-hitman Stephen "The Rifleman" Flemmi.

May 12: Retired mafioso Joseph Bonanno dies from heart failure in Tucson, Ariz. In Winnipeg, Manitoba, Canada, Daniel Tokarchuk fatally shoots Trevor Savioe, a member of the Hells Angels MC. Despite a plea of self-defense, jurors convict Tokarchuk of murder on November 23, 2004.

May 25: Former Gambino Family underboss-turned-prosecution witness Salvatore Gravano and son Gerard plead guilty in Brooklyn, N.Y., to charges of running a multimillion-dollar ecstasy ring on Arizona. Charges against Gravano's wife and daughter are dismissed. On September 6 Salvatore receives a 20-year sentence, while Gerard is sentenced to nine years in prison.

May 26: A shootout between two carloads of Camorra members left five women dead on the outskirts of Naples, Italy. Police described the victims as mobsters themselves, reporting that women have "moved up to the front line" in gangland warfare. Three suspects in the case are also female.

June: During a court appearance in Italy, mafioso Leoluca Bagarella warns government officials that the Mafia is "tired of being exploited, humiliated, oppressed and used like goods exchanged among the various political forces." Nationwide, 300 imprisoned mafiosi launch a hunger strike protesting imposition of strict regulations to cut off their contact with cohorts at large. In the U.S., a federal grand jury indicts British businessmen David Bermingham, Giles Darby and Gary Mulgrew — officers of the firm Greenwich NatWest — on seven counts of wire fraud related to the Enron scandal.

June 3: Lew Wasserman dies in Beverly Hills, Calif.

June 4: A federal grand jury in New York City files racketeering charges against members of the Gambino Family, alleging Mafia control of the Brooklyn and Staten Island waterfronts, looting of ILA benefit plans, and extortion of actor Steven Seagal over several years, demanding $150,000 for each film he made. Defendants include family boss Peter "One-Eyed Pete" Gotti; *caporegimes* Anthony "Sonny" Ciccone and Richard V. Gotti; soldiers Jerome Brancato, Primo Cassarino, Richard G. Gotti, and Peter Piacenti; and associates Richard Bondi, Salvatore Cannata, Thomas Lisi, Carmine Malara, Julius Nasso, Vincent Nasso, Jerome Orsino Jr., and Anthony Pansini. On the same day, James Rigas resigns as president, CEO and vice chairman of scandal-ridden Adelphia Business Solutions, Inc., along with sons John (Adelphia's chairman), Michael (vice chairman and secretary), and Timothy (vice chairman, CFO, and treasurer).

June 9: Defendant Mariano "Chuy" Martinez receives a sentence of life without parole plus 130 years in federal prison for his role in directing Mexican Mafia activity in Los Angeles, under orders from Benjamin "Topo" Peters.

June 10: Imprisoned mafioso John Joseph Gotti dies from throat cancer at the United States Medical Center for Federal Prisoners in Springfield, Mo.

June 12: FBI agents arrest ImClone founder Samuel Waksal for insider trading. Martha Stewart repeats her claim that she had a $60 stop-loss order in place before the FDA rejected ImClone's drug Erbitux. On June 18 Stewart insists she is "fully" cooperating with authorities.

June 15: Federal jurors in Chicago convict Arthur Andersen LLP of obstructing justice by shredding documents related to its audit of Enron Corporation. Andersen surrenders its CPA license and rights to practice before the SEC on August 31. The U.S. Supreme Court reverses Andersen's conviction based on flaws in the jury's instructions.

June 20: A federal grand jury in New York City indicts Gambino Family members Michael DiLeonardo, Frank Fappiano, Edward Garafola and Louis Vallario for exerting illegal influence over firms in Manhattan's Garment District, various construction companies, and wholesale produce distributors.

June 25: Following exposure of mismanagement by internal auditors, WorldCom — America's second-largest long-distance telephone company — admits $3.85 billion in "accounting misstatements." The firm's board of directors fires CFO Scott Sullivan, while controller David Meyers resigns. WorldCom files for Chapter 11 bankruptcy protection on July 21, the largest such filing in U.S. history. An SEC investigation reveals that Sullivan, Meyers, CEO Bernard Ebbers, and WorldCom director of general accounting Buford "Buddy" Yates used fraudulent accounting to inflate the company's assets by $11 billion. Sullivan pleads guilty and receives a five-year sentence in exchange for testimony against Ebbers. Oklahoma's attorney general indicts Ebbers on August 27, 2003, with a superceding indictment issued on November 20, 2003, while federal prosecutors indict him on March 2, 2004. Federal jurors convict Ebbers on March 15, 2005 and he receives a 25-year prison term on July 13. His projected parole date is July 4, 2028. WorldCom emerges from Chapter 11 bankruptcy in 2004 with $5.7 billion in debt. Most of its creditors still await compensation.

July: Italy's National Regulatory Authority for Public Works releases evidence that safeguards against corruption are systematically subverted in Sicily. Palermo's chief prosecutor estimates that 96 percent of all government contracts issued in Sicily are rigged in advance.

July 9: Embarrassed by his close ties to Enron conspirators, President Bush addresses the nation on "corporate responsibility" from New York's Wall Street. He calls for "strict enforcement and higher ethical standards" to "usher in a new era of integrity in corporate America."

July 10: Michael Goldman shoots Alexander Kudryavstev in Melbourne, Australia, later claiming that he acted under orders from mobster Nikolai "The Russian" Radev. Goldman receives a 14-year sentence on May 27, 2004.

July 12: The film *Road to Perdition* premieres in the U.S. and Canada, starring Paul Newman as "John Rooney," a fictionalized version of real-life Prohibition gangster John Patrick Looney of Rock Island, Ill. Stanley Tucci portrays Frank "The Enforcer" Nitti. In London, England, police find potential Enron trial witness Neil Coulbeck dead in a public park.

July 14: Italian police claim to have arrested the entire 15-man Mafia Commission for Agrigento Province during a raid at Santa Margherita Belice. Those jailed include a nobleman, a physician, and a member of the provincial council.

July 22: Justice Jean-Guy Boilard recuses himself from the Montreal Hells Angels "mega" trial, after a defense attorney files a complaint against him in an unrelated case.

July 24: Federal agents arrest five former executives of Adelphia Communications Corporation on charges that they looted the firm of more than $1 billion, using it as their "personal piggy bank." They include ex-chairman, president, and CEO John Rigas; former executive vice president, CFO, chief accounting officer, and treasurer Timothy Rigas; former executive vice president for operations Michael Rigas; ex–vice president of finance James R. Brown; and ex-director of internal reporting Michael C. Mulcahey.

August 7: Québec Superior Court Judge Pierre Beliveau orders a new trial for 17 Hells Angels accused of drug trafficking, gangsterism and conspiracy to commit murder. That trial convenes in September with 16 defendants.

August 23: Jurors in Chicago convict seven defendants of conspiracy to steal $12 million from suburban Cicero via insurance fraud. Those convicted include former Cicero town president Betty Loren-Maltese, mobster Michael Spano Sr. and his son Michael Jr., Joseph DeChicio, John LaGiglio, Bonnie LaGiglio, Charles Schneider, and Emil Schullo.

August 25: Indian gangster Koose Muniswamy Veerappan kidnaps former state minister H. Nagappa. Police find Nagappa murdered in November.

August 28: In Los Angeles, Assistant U.S. Attorney Gregory Jessner charges leaders of the Aryan Brotherhood with multiple murders, conspiracy to commit murder, extortion, robbery and narcotics trafficking.

August 29: Pirates board the yacht *Miss P.* at Careano, Venezuela, beating the captain, ransacking the boat, then stealing a dinghy and outboard motor.

September 5: José Luis Santiago Vasconcelos, chief of the Mexican attorney general's organized crime unit, reports that sisters of imprisoned drug lords Adán, Jesús and Luis Amezcua Contreras now run the Colima Cartel.

September 6: Convicted insurance swindler Artak Jragatsbanyan dies in a shooting at his Los Angeles home. Police suggest that Jragatsbanyan may have been killed by one or more ex-convicts from whom he extorted money.

September 14: "Ginza Tiger" Hisayuki Machii, founder of the Tosei-kai Yakuza clan, dies in Japan at age 79.

September 15: Unknown gunmen wound gangster Radoljub "Rade" Kanjevac and companion Igor Petrović on the St. Sava square in Niš, Serbia.

September 20: INTERPOL officers arrest Indian gangster and terrorist Abu Salem in Lisbon, Portugal, on charges of participating in the 1993 Mumbai bombings, the August 1997 murder of film producer Gulshan Kumar, and the slaying of actress Manisha Koirala's secretary. He remains in custody today.

September 29: Jim and Katie Coolbaugh repulse pirates attempting to board their sailboat *Asylum*, near Punta Hermosa, Colombia. On the same day, gunmen board and ransack the *Morning Dew*, in the same vicinity.

October: The UN Drug Control and Crime Prevention Agency announces Afghanistan is now the world's largest opium producer. General Nicolò Pollari, chief of Italy's Military Intelligence and Security Service, warns of "a concrete risk" that Mafia disappointment with ongoing prosecutions may spark a new series of assassinations. An independent forensic report declares that Italian banker Roberto Calvi was murdered in June 1982.

October 1: A federal grand jury in Arizona returns a 198-count indictment against Kwikmed, Inc., Cymedic Health Group, Inc., four owners of the corporations, and two associated physicians, charging them with operation of websites that sold prescription drugs — including Viagra, Celebrex, Xenical, and Propecia — without legitimate prescriptions, earning more than $28 million in the process. On October 2, 2003, Dr. William J. Clemans pleads guilty to conspiracy, introduction of misbranded drugs into interstate commerce, failure to register a drug manufacturer, mail fraud, and conspiracy to commit money-laundering. On December 16, 2003, Dr. Adalberto Robles Guzman pleads guilty on two counts of tax evasion. In March 2004 Kwikmed owner Janice Gamblin pleads guilty to conspiracy, introduction of misbranded drugs into interstate commerce, mail fraud, money-laundering and failure to register an establishment in which drugs are manufactured, prepared, propagated, compounded, and processed.

October 2: Former Merrill Lynch & Co. assistant Douglas Faneuil pleads guilty to taking a payoff to keep quiet about Martha Stewart's ImClone stock trade.

October 4: Somalian pirates rob the British yacht *Sara of Hamble* in the Indian Ocean, 40 miles south-southeast of Obbia, stealing cash and equipment worth £4000 ($6000).

October 5: Three members of The Breed

MC — Frederick DeCapua, Sanford Gorzelsky and Scott Lear — attack Arne "Ole" Olsen at a café in West Long Branch, N.J., in retaliation for his trial testimony against other club members.

October 12: Five armed and masked pirates board the yacht *Panacea* at Isle Coche, south of Margarita, Venezuela, binding its owners and shooting the captain in one knee.

October 15: Unknown gunmen kill two nephews of murdered drug lord Francis Vanverberghe in Bouches-du-Rhone, France.

October 16: Unknown gunmen kill Henry "Hen Dog" Smith — a former Death Row Records employee and Compton MOB Piru Gang member — while he sits in his car, in Los Angeles. Police find drug dealer Paul Kallipolitis murdered at his home in Sunshine, Victoria, Australia. Officers charge Angelo Mario Venditti with the slaying on July 29, 2008.

October 18: Compton Southside Crip member Jerry "Monk" Bonds, previously questioned in the slaying of rapper Tupac Shakur, dies in a Los Angeles ambush. ImClone founder Sam Waksal admits tipping daughter Aliza to the FDA's impending rejection of Erbitux and trying to sell his own shares in advance.

October 24: A bomb explodes outside gangster Radoljub Kanjevac's apartment in Niš, Serbia. Jurors later convict rival Milan Šević of planting the device.

October 28: Los Angeles defense attorneys for Nuestra Familia member Armando Santa Cruz Heredia file a motion accusing chief prosecution witness Daniel "Lizard" Hernandez of committing crimes under the FBI's protection. The motion seeks dismissal of all charges based on government misconduct.

November 14: James R. Brown, ex–vice president for finance of Adelphia Communications, pleads guilty to conspiracy and fraud in New York City.

November 17: An Italian appellate court reverses the 1999 acquittal of senator for life Giulio Andreotti on charges that he instigated the 1979 murder of journalist Mino Pecorelli. The court sentences Andreotti to 24 years in prison. Another appellate court overturns the latest verdict on October 30, 2003,

November 18: Six of 16 Hells Angels on trial in Montreal, Québec, plead guilty to charges including drug trafficking, gangsterism, and conspiracy to commit murder. The court imposes sentences ranging from four to 14 years.

November 21: Police in Salinas, Calif., arrest Nuestra Familia member Jose Tizcareno for participation in a string of eight bank robberies executed to finance gang activities. Eight other suspects remain at large.

December: British government spokesmen announce that the National Health Service will henceforth supply free heroin "to all those with a clinical need for it." Article 41-bis of the Italian Prison Administration Act, originally passed as Prison Administration Act, Law No. 354 of July 26, 1975, becomes a permanent fixture of the nation's penal code, permitting isolation of selected prisoners to terminate contact with free-world criminal cohorts.

December 9: A federal grand jury in New York indicts Gambino Family *caporegime* Ronald "Ronnie One Arm" Trucchio and soldier-son Alphonse Trucchio on charges of operating a sports betting ring based in Ozone Park, Queens. Prosecutors claim that the network earned $600,000 per week.

December 13: A federal judge in Los Angeles sentences Mexican Mafia enforcer Anthony "Coco" Zaragoza to life imprisonment on racketeering charges.

December 20: President Bush pardons Kenneth Franklin Copley, convicted in 1962 of selling untaxed whiskey in Tennessee.

December 23: Bonanno Family *consigliere* Anthony "T.G." Graziano pleads guilty in New York on charges of loan-sharking, tax evasion, and conspiracy to commit murder. He receives a 25-year sentence, tentatively scheduled for parole on January 6, 2012.

2003 The IMB reports 334 acts of piracy worldwide between January 1 and September 30, up from 271 in 2002.

January 2: Mexican Mafia member Jesus "Gizmo" Rochin turns state's evidence against the gang in California, receiving a 12-year sentence instead of life imprisonment for assault, attempted murder, narcotics conspiracy and racketeering, assault.

January 6: In Chicago, convicted insurance swindlers Bonnie LaGiglio and Michael Spano Jr. are sentenced for their involvement with Specialty Risk Consultants in Cicero, Ill. LaGiglio receives a 41-month prison term for tax fraud, while Spano is sentenced to 6½ years.

January 10: Pirates armed with submachine guns stop a Spanish yacht three miles offshore from Cabo Tres Puntas, Venezuela, stealing cash and credit cards.

January 16: "Operation Tsunami" concludes in Afghanistan, as Canadian soldiers and native police arrest 16 suspected heroin traffickers.

January 19: Associates of Rajendra Sadashiv Nikalje, AKA Chotta Rajan, kill Sharad Shetty, Dawood Ibrahim's financial manager, at the India Club in Dubai.

January 26: Despite law enforcement proclamations of the American Mafia's demise, the *New*

York Times declares that "[r]eports of its death have been greatly exaggerated.... Its membership is diminished; its top bosses are under arrest and the mistakes of some of its leaders show that it is fraying. Despite all that, as other bands of ethnic criminals come and go, the old Mafia persists."

January 29: Five gunmen kill crime boss Kieran Keane and wound companion Owen Treacy in Limerick, Ireland.

February: CFO Fausto Tonna announces a surprise €500 million bond issue by the multinational Italian dairy and food corporation Parmalat SpA. Founder and CEO Calisto Tanzi fires Tonna and replaces him with Alberto Ferraris, who later tells *Time* magazine that he was denied access to company books handled by chief accounting officer Luciano Del Soldato. Ferraris investigates, revealing illegal transactions with the Caymans-based mutual fund Epicurum. Ferraris resigns in November, followed by Del Soldato in December. On December 21 Tanzi admits misappropriating some $800 million. Parmalat collapses with debts of $20 billion. Tanzi receives a 10-year prison term for fraud on December 17, 2008.

February 4: Mexican Mafia member Francisco "Puppet" Martinez receives a life sentence for racketeering in Los Angeles.

February 12: Pagans MC member Thomas Campbell pleads guilty to first-degree murder in the January 2002 execution-style slaying of police officer Dennis McNamara in Upper Darby Township, Pa. Campbell receives a life prison term.

February 14: Acting DEA Administrator John B. Brown III announces the results of "Operation Deja Vu," a seven-month campaign targeting drug traffickers in the Northeastern United States, Puerto Rico, and Colombia. The operation has produced 67 arrests in seven cities, plus seizures including 21 kilograms of heroin, eight pounds of marijuana, 17.4 kilograms of cocaine, 1.9 kilograms of crack cocaine and $438,420 in cash.

February 19: Mexican Mafia member Max "Mono" Torvisco strikes a plea bargain with prosecutors in Los Angeles, receiving a 10-year sentence on racketeering charges with provision that he must serve 85 percent of that term before seeking parole.

February 24: U.S. Attorney General John Ashcroft announces the conclusion of "Operation Pipe Dreams" and "Operation Headhunter," targeting sales of illegal drugs and drug paraphernalia via the Internet. Fifty defendants stand indicted on various charges.

February 26: New Jersey's Division of Gaming Enforcement bans mafioso William "Big Billy" D'Elia from entering any Atlantic City casino under threat of license forfeiture.

March 1: Roland Dumas, former French foreign minister, tells *Le Figaro* that France paid $500 million in bribes to secure its frigate contract with Taiwan. Dumas says the payments were approved by former president Francois Mitterand, with $400 million delivered to Taiwan's ruling KMT party and $100 million to the Chinese Communist Party's Central Committee in Beijing.

March 7: Unknown gunmen fatally wound gangster Iliya Pavlov Naydenov outside his office in Sofia, Bulgaria. He dies en route to a hospital.

March 9: Pirates pursue the yacht *Narena* in the Gulf of Aden, interrupted by the warship *Royal Pascaderas*.

March 14: Thomas Sienkowski, local president of the Outlaws MC in Milwaukee, Wis., receives a 10-year prison term for racketeering. In Matamoros, Mexico, troops capture Gulf Cartel leader leader Osiel Cárdenas Guillén following a shootout with his gunmen.

March 17: Federal jurors in New York City convict mafiosi Primo Cassarino, Anthony "Sonny" Ciccone, Peter Botti, Richard G. Gotti, and Richard V. Gotti on 65 racketeering charges. Cassarino turns informer against other mafiosi in a bid for leniency. Richard V. Gotti is paroled on August 12, 2005; Richard G. Gotti on March 2, 2007. Ciccone has a projected release date of April 24, 2013.

March 18: DEA telecommunications specialist, Elton Lee Armstead falls to his death while installing surveillance gear on a grain silo in Morris, Ill.

March 19: The SEC accuses HealthSouth Corporation—a large health care services provider based in Birmingham, Ala.—and CEO Richard Scrushy of fraudulently inflating the firm's earnings by $1.4 billion. In 2004 the SEC indicts Scrushy on 36 counts of fraud. A Birmingham jury acquits him on June 28, 2005. On October 28, 2005, a federal grand jury in Montgomery indicts Scrushy and ex-governor Don Eugene Siegelman on 30 counts of bribery, extortion, money-laundering, obstruction of justice, and racketeering. On June 29, 2006, Montgomery jurors convict both defendants: Scrushy stands convicted of bribery, conspiracy, and mail fraud, while Siegelman is convicted of bribery, conspiracy, mail fraud, and obstruction of justice. On June 28, 2007, Scrushy is sentenced to six years and 10 months in a prison, plus a $150,000 fine and $267,000 in restitution to United Way of Alabama, and three years' probation. Siegelman is sentenced to seven years and four months in prison, a $50,000 fine, $181,325 restitution of to the state, three years' probation, and 500 hours of community service upon his release. At a subsequent civil trial in Birmingham, on June 18, 2009, Scrushy is ordered to pay HealthSouth investors $2.87 billion in damages.

March 27: Colombian pirates board a yacht off the coast of Puerto Velero, assaulting crew members.

April 3: Mafioso Louis "Big Louie" DeSorbo dies from natural causes in New York City.

April 15: Spokesmen for the DEA and RCMP announce the culmination of "Operation Northern Star," targeting methamphetamine traffickers in the U.S. and Canada. Raids in Chicago; Detroit; Cincinnati; Gulfport, Miss.; Los Angeles; New York; Riverside, Calif.; Montreal; Québec; Vancouver, British Colombia; and Ottawa, Ontario have jailed 66 suspects. An unknown gunman kills Bulgarian mobster Nikolai "The Russian" Radev in Coburg, Victoria, Australia. Police suspect Andrew "Benji" Veniamin and Carl Anthony Williams.

April 16: Royal Australian Navy forces capture the North Korean freighter *Pong Su* with 50 kilograms of heroin aboard, 100 miles southwest of Melbourne. Authorities charge that North Korea's government sponsors narcotics trafficking.

May 12: Police in Winnipeg, Canada, find Kevin Tokarchuk shot to death at his home, one year to the day after his brother killed a member of the Hells Angels MC.

May 14: Robert Stack, the first actor to portray Prohibition agent Eliot Ness, dies in Beverly Hills, Calif.

June: With Prime Minister Silvio Berlusconi on trial for corruption charges, Italy's parliament passes a law granting immunity from prosecution to five top state officials: the prime minister, the state president, the presidents of both parliamentary chambers and the president of the constitutional court. Passage of the law ends Berlusconi's trial. The Constitutional Court revokes the new law on January 23, 2004.

June 4: A federal grand jury indicts Martha Stewart and stockbroker Peter Bacanovic on nine counts related to the ImClone insider-trading scandal. Stewart resigns as CEO of Martha Stewart Living Omnimedia but remains as a board member and chief creative officer. On June 5 she launches a website proclaiming her innocence.

June 6: Male prostitute Shane Chartres-Abbott dies from gunshot wounds in Melbourne, Australia. Hitman Evangelos Goussis later confesses to the slaying and implicates two corrupt policemen.

June 10: ImClone founder Sam Waksal receives a sentence of seven years and three months in federal prison.

June 15: Former Yakuza boss Tokutaro Takayama dies from natural causes in Kyoto, Japan.

June 21: A gunman murders gangsters Jason Moran and Pasquale Barbaro in a van outside a football clinic in Essendon, Victoria, Australia. Police charge rival mobsters Victor Brincat, Alfonso Traglia and Carl Williams with the crime on September 17, 2004. Williams receives a life sentence in May 2007.

June 26: Police in Eugene, Ore., raid a clubhouse of the Free Souls MC, seizing several stolen bikes and charging one member with manufacturing and selling methamphetamine. Italian prosecutors reveal that they are investigating Salvatore "Totò" Cuffaro, former president of Sicily, on charges of collaborating with the Mafia.

July: Police in New Jersey arrest three members of The Breed MC for beating a former member. In Vancouver, British Columbia, RCMP officers launch Project E-Pandora, agreeing to pay informer Michael Plante $500,000 for infiltrating the Hells Angels and another $500,000 after his testimony sends various members to prison.

July 8: The film *Veronica Guerin* premieres in Ireland, starring Cate Blanchett as the murdered Irish journalist and Gerard McSorley as mobster John Gilligan. In Arizona, police stage statewide raids against members of the Hells Angels MC, wounding Michael Wayne Coffelt with gunfire at the Angels clubhouse in Phoenix. On December 6, 2004, Judge Michael Wilkinson of Maricopa County Superior Court declares the Phoenix raid an "attack" violating Arizona search-and-seizure laws.

July 16: Police in Oakland County, Mich., excavate the backyard of a rural home in a futile search for evidence in the 1975 disappearance of Jimmy Hoffa.

July 21: A gunman kills drug dealer Willie Thompson outside a karate club in Chadstone, Victoria, Australia. Police suspect associates of murdered mobster Nikolai "The Russian" Radev but file no charges.

July 24: An unknown gunman murders Wardell "Poochie" Fouse, an associate of Death Row Records CEO Marion "Suge" Knight Jr., in Los Angeles.

August 10: Pirates storm a tanker in the Strait of Malacca, near Port Klang, Kuala Lumpur, looting the ship and steering in into Indonesian waters, where they ask $100,000 ransom for the crew.

July 31: U.S. Attorney General Ashcroft unseals a January indictment of Mexican drug lord Ismael Zambada Garcia and two of his top lieutenants, Vicente Zambada Niebla and Javier Torres Felix, on charges of conspiracy to import and distribute 2,796 kilos of cocaine between August 2001 and

June 2002. The indictments arise from "Operation Trifecta," a 19-month investigation resulting in 240 arrests.

August 18: Police pull the charred corpse of Mark Mallia, an associate of Nikolai "The Russian" Radev, from a storm drain in Sunshine, Victoria, Australia.

September: Police in London, England, reopen their investigation of Roberto Calvi's death.

September 1: Former Yakuza boss Kazuo Nakanishi dies from natural causes in Osaka, Japan.

September 6: Mafioso Marshall Caifano dies in Chicago, at age 92.

September 11: The DOJ and FDA file for an injunction to stop Rx Depot, Inc., from importing Canadian drugs in violation of U.S. federal law. U.S. District Judge Claire Eagen grants a preliminary injunction on November 6. In Montreal, Québec, nine Hells Angels plead guilty to charges of drug trafficking, gangsterism and conspiracy to commit murder, subsequently receiving prison terms of 10 to 15 years. They include Jean-Guy Bourgouin, Rene Charlebois, Denis Houle, Daniel Lanthier, Sylvain Laplante, Gilles Mathieu, Pierre Provencher, Normand Robitaille, and Guillaume Serra. In Tarneit, Victoria, Australia, gunmen execute Housam Zayat, another associate of Nikolai "The Russian" Radev.

October 20: Police find Istvan "Steve" Gulyas and his defacto wife murdered at their home in Sunbury, Victoria, Australia. They were associates of Nikolai Radev, operators of a dating service described by police as a front for prostitution.

October 25: Gunmen shoot alleged mobster Michael Marshall outside his home in South Yarra, Victoria, Australia.

October 28: Cassandra Harvey and son Joshua Harvey plead guilty in St. Louis, Mo., on federal charges of conspiracy to distribute 1,4-butanediol, an analogue of GHB. On January 30, 2004, Cassandra receives a 168-month prison term, while Joshua is sentenced to 100 months.

November: The High Court of Osaka, Japan, orders Yakuza boss Yoshinori Watanabe and three other defendants to pay $80 million in damages for the gang-related slaying of an off-duty policeman in 1995.

November 2: Eleven of 21 indicted Nuestra Familia members plead guilty to racketeering charges in Los Angeles. They include Luis "Roach" Aroche, Vidal "Spider" Fabelaz, Ramiro "Goose" Garcia, Armando "Suave" Heredia, and Diana Vasquez (sentenced to 20 years in prison); Robert "Chico" Rose (15 years); Jacob "Blackie" Enriquez, Cesar "Lobo" Ramirez, and Sheldon "Skip" Villanueva (14 years each); Israel "Silent" Mendoza (12½ years); and Anthony "Chino" Morales (nine years). The U.S. Attorney's office announces that

trial will commence for defendants Henry "Happy" Cervantes, Albert "Bird" Larez, and David "Sir Dyno" Rocha on January 5, 2004.

November 4: Mafioso Frank D. "Sonny" Amato Jr. dies from congestive heart failure in Pittsburgh, Pa.

November 5: President Bush pardons Wisconsin inmate Michael Robert Moelter, convicted in 1988 of conducting an illegal gambling business.

November 17: Police in Melbourne, Australia, jail drug dealer and murderer Carl Williams on charges of threatening a detective and his girlfriend.

November 18: U.S. District Judge Miriam Cedarbaum rejects Martha Stewart's plea to dismiss two of five federal charges filed against her in the ImClone scandal.

November 22: An Italian court convicts attorney Cesare Previti of paying Judge Renato Squillante $434,000 to subvert investigation of a firm owned by Previti's client, Prime Minister Silvio Berlusconi. Previti receives a five-year sentence but remains free on appeal. An appellate court overturns his conviction, but Previti is convicted and sentenced again on December 2, 2005. The Supreme Court of Cassation invalidates that verdict on November 30, 2006, ruling that Milan's trial court lacked jurisdiction in the case.

November 23: Unknown gunmen kill mafioso Adolfo "Big Al" Bruno outside the Our Lady of Mount Carmel Society in Springfield, Mass. On November 26 a federal grand jury indicts successor Anthony Arillotta and seven codefendants on gambling and loan-sharking charges.

November 26: Ex-bankers Ernest Backes and André Strebel file a criminal complaint with the Swiss attorney general against Bank Menatep owner Mikhail Khodorkovsky and two colleagues, Alexei Golubovich and Platon Lebedev, charging them with money-laundering and supporting a criminal organization. Bank Menatep, which failed in 1998 during the "Kremlingate" scandal involving diversion of $4.8 billion in IMF funds, is linked to Clearstream. In April 2006 Clearstream spokesmen declare that while "Menatep may have strange accounts, it wasn't closed because of money-laundering." In an unrelated Russian case, on May 30, 2005, Khodorkovsky receives a nine-year prison sentence. Later that year, Russian prosecutors convict Lebedev of tax evasion, resulting in a nine-year sentence.

December: Russian authorities confiscate 4,000 copies of a newly-published book by former KGB/FSB agent Alexander Litvinenko, *Gang from Lbyanka*, which claims that President Vladimir Putin protected Afghan drug trafficking during his tenure as head of the FSB (July 25, 1998, to August 8, 1999).

December 3: A federal grand jury in Florida indicts three companies and 10 individuals on 108 charges related to illegal sale of controlled substances and other prescription drugs over the Internet. Charges include conspiring to unlawfully distribute Schedule III and IV controlled substances (including weight-loss drugs Bontril, Ionamin, Phentermine, Adipex, and Meridia) without a legitimate medical purpose and outside the usual course of professional practice, money-laundering, and violating the Federal Food, Drug, and Cosmetic Act by introducing into interstate commerce misbranded prescription drugs, including Bontril, Meridia, Xenical, and Viagra. Retired physician Marvin Brown and pharmacist Luke Coukos plead guilty on December 19. Brown surrenders his DEA controlled substance registration, as well as his licenses to practice medicine in Massachusetts and Ohio. Coukos receives a 60-month prison sentence and a $140,318 fine on March 12, 2004.

December 4: Nuestra Familia member Armando "Suave" Heredia receives a sentence of 25 years to life in Salinas, Calif., after pleading guilty to weapons violations and drug conspiracy charges.

December 7: Unknown gunmen kill Bulgarian mobster Konstantin "Samokovetsa" Dimitrov on Dam Square in Amsterdam, Holland.

December 12: As part of "Project Halo," police in Nanaimo, British Columbia, raid and search the local Hells Angels clubhouse.

December 13: Unknown gunmen kill crime boss Graham "The Munster" Allen Kinniburgh outside his home in Kew, Victoria, Australia.

December 14: Confessed hitman Frank Sheeran dies in a nursing home outside Philadelphia, Pa.

December 20: Jurors in Dublin, Ireland, convict five defendants on charges of murdering Limerick crime boss Kieran Keane in January and attempting to murder associate Owen Treacy. Those sentenced to life imprisonment include Christopher "Smokie" Costelloe, Desmond Dundon, Anthony "Noddy" McCarthy, James McCarthy, and David "Frogs Eyes" Stanners.

2004 Mexican pharmaceutical companies legally import 224 tons of pseudoephedrine, twice the amount required to produce legitimate cold medicine. The remainder is converted into methamphetamine for sale in the U.S. The IMB records 325 pirate attacks worldwide, with 30 fatalities. Indonesia and Nigeria lead the list, with 93 and 39 incidents respectively. U.S. citizens lose $78 billion through legal gambling.

January 7: Consumer groups file a lawsuit against OxyContin manufacturer Purdue Pharma Ltd. in Hartford, Conn., claiming that the firm reaped billions in unlawful profit through fraudulent patents and sham lawsuits that blocked generic alternatives to the widely prescribed pain reliever. A federal judge later dismisses that suit — like 120 others before it — but Perdue settles a suit filed by West Virginia's attorney general for $10 million on November 5, in a case that charges Perdue with dishonestly marketing the painkiller.

January 9: Disgraced federal judge Harry Claiborne commits suicide in Las Vegas.

January 15: DEA Administrator Karen Tandy announces the conclusion of "Operation Streamline," targeting the Orlando Ospina drug cartel based in Cali, Colombia. The campaign has produced 11 arrests.

January 20: Police in Montreal, Québec, arrest mafioso Vito Rizzuto on a New York warrant charging him with racketeering conspiracy charges, including loan-sharking and murder, in connection with the 1981 gangland killings of three rival Bonanno crime family *caporegimes*, Philip Giaccone, Alphonse Indelicato, and Dominick Trinchera. Legal maneuvers stall his extradition until August 17, 2006.

January 22: The FDA sends warning letters to three firms in Temple, Tex.— Expedite-Rx (a technological interface), SPC Global Technologies Ltd. (a pharmacy benefits manager), and Employer Health Options, Inc. (a pharmacy benefits manager)— informing them that it considers their drug import program to be illegal and a risk to public health. Expedite-Rx has already received a warning from the Texas State Board of Pharmacy in July 2003 to "immediately discontinue receiving/processing prescription drug orders."

January 27: Trial begins in New York City for Peter Bacanovic and Martha Stewart in the ImClone scandal. On March 5 jurors convict both defendants on four counts each, while acquitting Bacanovic of making false statements. Both receive five-month prison terms on July 15, 2004, with Stewart fined $30,000 and Bacanovic fined $4,000.

January 28: Mexican Mafia members Julio Contreras, Jaime Lopez Jr., Christina Montano, Denise Ortega, Leonard Parmer, Sergio Pulido Perez, Pamela Thompson, and Arthur Genaro Torres plead not guilty on racketeering charges in San Diego, Calif.

February: Police in Montreal, Québec, stage a massive sweep against Hells Angels, issuing arrest warrants for 63 club members charged with drug offenses and gangsterism. In California, journalist Gary Webb loses his job with the state legislature, blaming political harassment for his prior exposure of CIA drug trafficking.

February 18: Italian police arrest 'Ndrangheta boss Giuseppe Morabito at a hideout in Calabria's Aspromonte Mountains.

February 23: Pirates pursue the U.S.-registered sailboat *Klondike* in the Gulf of Aden, between Somalia and Yemen.

February 28: Armed pirated board the yacht *Myriad* at Punta Pargo, Venezuela, firing several random shotgun blasts.

March: The Court of Criminal Appeal in Edinburgh, Scotland, quashes the 1984 murder convictions of Thomas Campbell and Joe Steele in the Glasgow "ice cream war."

March 1: Jurors in Montreal, Québec, convict nine members of the Hells Angels and Rockers MCs on charges of conspiring to commit murder and traffic in drugs between January 1995 and March 2001. Quebec Superior Court Justice Pierre Béliveau sentences the defendants on March 4. The include Richard "Dick" Mayrand (22 years, reduced to 16 years, nine months after time in custody); Luc "Bordel" Bordeleau and Sylvain Moreau (20 years, reduced to 14 years, nine months); André Couture, Érik "Le Pif" Fournier, and Bruno Lefebvre (18 years, reduced to 12 years, nine months); Sébastien "Bass" Beauchamp (13 years, reduced to seven years, nine months); Ronald "Popo" Paulin (12 years, reduced to six years, six months); and Alain Dubois (10 years, reduced to nine years, nine months). Bikers André Chouinard and Michel Rose also plead guilty on March 4, to charges of murder conspiracy, drug trafficking, and participating in gang activity. Chouinard receives a 20-year sentence, while Rose gets 16 years.

March 5: Pirates board and loot the yacht *Saltaire* in the Gulf of Aden, off the coast of Yemen.

March 11: Provincial legislators in Manitoba, Canada, pass the Criminal Property Forfeiture Act, permitting seizure of property owned by any member of a designated "criminal organization," without proof of specific criminal activity.

March 18: Singapore authorities announce their intent to execute Chew Seow Leng, an addict caught with eight ounces of heroin in January. Most of the 400 prison inmates hanged in Singapore since 1994 have been executed for drug offenses.

March 23: Domenic "Mick" Gatto murders mobster Andrew Veniamin at a pizzeria in Carlton, Victoria, Australia. Jurors acquit Gatto on a plea of self-defense in June 2005.

March 27: Camorra gunmen in Naples, Italy, accidentally kill a 14-year-old girl while trying to shoot rival mobster Salvatore Giuliano.

March 31: "Operation Candy Box" culminates with the arrest of 130 suspects in the U.S. and Canada, charged with manufacturing and trafficking in ecstasy and marijuana. Two masked gunmen kill Lewis Moran, father of Jason Moran and stepfather of Mark Moran, at a bar in Bruns-

wick, Victoria, Australia. Companion Bert Wrout is wounded but survives. Jurors convict hitman Evangelos Goussis on May 29, 2008. He receives a life sentence. He receives a life sentence on February 9, 2009.

April: A federal grand jury in Los Angeles five reputed members of the Jerusalem Network, an Israeli crime syndicate, on multiple charges including money-laundering and extortion. Defendants include Gabriel Ben Harosh, Hai Waknine, Yoram El-Al, Thanh Nguyen, and Sasson Barashy.

April 5: Pirates in a fishing boat ram the sailing yacht *Yume Maru* en route from the west coast of Panama to the Galápagos Islands. Five men armed with knives and pistols board the yacht, stealing jewelry, charts, maps, and navigation equipment. In Stavanger, Norway, bandits rob an office of Norsk Kontantservice AS — a firm offering management, control and distribution of cash to Norwegian banks — and kill policeman Arne Sigve Klungland while escaping with 57.4 million kroner ($9.3 million). Authorities initially blame Albanian mafia members, but later blame Oslo resident David Aleksander Toska and 12 accomplices for the crime. Jurors convict all 13 at trial, with sentences totaling 181 years imposed on March 10, 2006. On January 19, 2007, an appellate court upholds 12 of the verdicts, while acquitting defendant Thomas Thendrup. Ten days later the Norwegian Supreme Court adds another 27 years to the sentences of those still deemed guilty.

April 7: A federal grand jury in Rochester, N.Y., indicts mobsters Dominic "Sonny" Celestino and Francesco "Frank" Frassetto for conspiring to loot a local bank and wire the money to Miami, Fla.

April 8: In San Francisco, Calif., a federal grand jury in returns a six-count indictment against Texas-based Reliant Energy Services, Inc., and four of its officers — Jackie Thomas, a former vice president of Reliant's Power Trading Division; Reggie Howard, a former director of Reliant's West Power Trading Division; Lisa Flowers, a term trader for Reliant's West Power Trading Division; and Kevin Frankeny, Reliant's manager of western operations — for their role in precipitating California's recent electricity crisis. On August 15, 2005, Reliant announces a $445 million settlement resolving civil litigation claims against the company in California, Oregon and Washington. In March 2007 Reliant pays a $22.2 million penalty in addition to a $13.8 million credit provided in a settlement with the Federal Energy Regulatory Commission

April 11: On Easter Sunday pirates board a yacht anchored at Chateau Belair, Saint Lucia, in the eastern Caribbean, threatening the owners with knives.

April 16: Officers of the New Hampshire State Police Special Investigations Unit arrest Outlaws MC member John Nowoselski for possession of 12 illegal weapons. Jurors convict him on October 29.

April 26: Second-generation mafioso and long-time fugitive Nofio Pecoraro Jr. pleads guilty in Louisiana on charges of conspiring to commit mail fraud and structuring of monetary instruments at Certified Lloyd's Insurance Company of Covington. He receives a 21-month prison term and a $75,000 fine on August 18.

April 29: Mafioso Gaetano Badalamenti dies from heart failure at the Devens Federal Medical Center in Ayers, Mass.

May 3: French magistrate Renaud Van Ruymbeke receives an anonymous letter accusing Clearstream Banking AG of illegal secret transactions. One June 14 magistrate Dominique Talancé receives a similar letter with a CD-ROM listing numbered bank accounts. Between those events, on June 2, the European Commission declares that "Clearstream Banking AG and its parent company Clearstream International SA infringed competition rules by refusing to supply cross-border securities clearing and settlement services, and by applying discriminatory prices." In January 2006 both magistrates declared the case closed, on the grounds that the anonymous list of accounts has been proved fraudulent. On August 15, 2005, Reliant spokesmen announce a $445 million settlement resolving lawsuits filed by officials in California, Oregon and Washington. In March 2007 Reliant agrees to pay a $22.2 million penalty on top of a $13.8 million credit fixed in an earlier settlement with the Federal Energy Regulatory Commission.

May 8: Police find hitman Lewis Caine shot dead on a street in Brunswick, Victoria, Australia. Police arrest suspects Keith Faure and Evangelos Goussis for the murder on May 19. Jurors convict both defendants on November 5, 2005.

May 16: Authorities find police informer Terrence Hodson and his wife Christine murdered at their home in Kew, Victoria, Australia.

May 17: Jurors in Camden, N.J., convict Pagans MC member Richard Hill or raping a woman during a supposed club initiation ceremony on August 17, 2001. Hill receives a 35-year prison term on September 16, with a mandatory 29-year minimum.

May 20: President Bush grants executive clemency to four persons convicted of organized criminal activity. He pardons Paul Jude Donnici (Missouri, 1993, illegal transmission of wagering information) and Kenneth Lynn Norris (Oklahoma, 1993, illegally dumping toxic waste). Bush also commutes the sentences of Bobby Mac Berry

(North Carolina, 1997, conspiracy to manufacture and possess with intent to manufacture marijuana) and Geraldine Gordon (Nevada, 1989, distribution of and conspiracy to distribute phencyclidine).

May 28: Forensics experts hired by Fox News claim they have found blood traces at a home in Oakland County, Mich., named by late mobster Frank Sheeran as the scene of Jimmy Hoffa's murder. Prosecutors search the house, removing floorboards. In Oklahoma, Governor Brad Henry signs America's first state legislation limiting sale of pseudoephedrine to pharmacies and requiring retailers to sell pseudoephedrine products from behind the counter, with purchasers showing identification and signing a register. DEA agent Terrance Loftus dies in a plane crash near Chicago's Midway International Airport while returning from an evidence delivery to Kansas City.

June 3: "Operation United Eagles" culminates in the arrest of drug traffickers Jorge Arrellano Félix and Efrain Perez by Mexican federal agents.

June 4: A court in Ho Chi Minh City, Vietnam, convicts mobster Nam Cam of ordering rival Dung Ha's murder in October 2000. A firing squad executes Nam and four associates on May 7, 2004.

June 6: Federal authorities parole drug lord Griselda Blanco and deport her from the U.S. to her native Colombia.

June 8: In La Mesa, Calif., Mexican Mafia member Ricardo "Rock" Marquez pleads guilty to possession of an unregistered automatic rifle and conspiracy to distribute 33,000 ecstasy tablets. Federal jurors in New York convict Adelphia Communications Corporation founder John Rigas on multiple charges of fraud. He receives a 15-year prison sentence on June 27, 2005.

June 9: Police in Melbourne, Australia, charge Carl Williams with conspiracy to murder mafioso Mario Condello. On June 17 officers charge Condello and lawyer George Defteros with conspiring to kill Carl Williams and his brother George.

June 12: Lucchese Family bookmaker Louis Barone pleads guilty to manslaughter in the December 22, 2003, shooting of Albert Circelli Jr. at a nightclub in East Harlem, N.Y. The homicide occurred after Circelli insulted the singing talent of Barone's girlfriend.

June 17: Venezuelan authorities find the captain of the French yacht *Les Chouans* shot to death aboard his boat near Ensenada Medina, presumably slain by pirates.

June 29: In Rochester, N.Y., mobster Francesco Frassetto and his two sons stand accused of conspiring to distribute cocaine between August 1997 and February 2000. Additional charges cite a February 2000 heroin transaction.

June 30: Lucchese Family acting boss Louis "Louie Bagels" Daidone receives a life sentence on conviction of loan-sharking and conspiracy to murder victims Bruno Facciola and Thomas Gilmore, slain as suspected government informers.

July 2: Cuban police arrest Colombian drug lord Luis Hernando Gómez Bustamante at Havana's José Martí International Airport, after he presents a false passport to immigration officials.

July 7: A federal grand jury in Houston, Tex., indicts Enron founder Kenneth Lay on 11 counts of securities fraud and related charges.

July 8: Federal jurors in Manhattan convict former Adelphia Communications founder John Rigas on conspiracy and fraud charges.

July 13: U.S. officials deport Russian gangster Vyacheslav Ivankov to face trial for murdering two Turkish nationals in 1992. Russian jurors acquit him on July 18, 2005.

July 14: Police in Graz, Austria, arrest Turkish parole violator and fugitive Alaattin Çakıcı, deporting him on October 19 to face trial on multiple charges, including the contract murder of his ex-wife. Ultimate conviction brings Çakıcı a total of 36 years and eight months in prison.

July 25: The Rite Aid pharmacy chain agrees to pay $7 million in settlement of charges that the company submitted false prescription claims to U.S. government health insurance programs.

July 28: Police raid a clubhouse of the Gypsy Jokers MC in Portland, Ore., smashing through walls in an effort to locate club members suspected of stealing motorcycles, detaining one member in handcuffs so long that he soils himself. The Jokers file a $50,000 federal lawsuit, settled out of court by city attorneys in summer 2007.

August: Gary Webb lands a job with the weekly *Sacramento News & Review* at half his former salary. When his ex-wife garnishes his wages, Webb is forced to sell his house and move into his mother's home at a retirement village. In Washington, D.C., the DEA issues guidelines for physicians regarding prescription of pain medication, then withdraws them without notice in early October.

August 16: A motorist finds International Boxing Federation super flyweight champion Robert Quiroga stabbed to death along Interstate Highway 10 in San Antonio, Tex. Two years later, police charge Bandidos MC member Richard "Scarface" Merla with the slaying. Merla pleads guilty in September 2007, telling the court, "I don't regret it. I don't have no remorse. I don't feel sorry for him and his family. I don't and I mean that."

August 20: A federal grand jury in Los Angeles indicts Mexican Mafia members Merced Cambrero, Fernando Cazares, Alejandro Martinez and Gilbert Saldana for weapons and civil rights violations in the 1999 racist murder of black victim Kenneth Kurry Wilson. In Florida, FBI agents arrest fugitive Massachusetts mafioso Frankie Roche, sought for parole violations. During the arrest, Roche is "accidentally" shot in the back but survives his wound.

August 27: Narcotics officers in Salinas, Calif., arrest Nuestra Familia leader Robert Patrick "Bubba" Hanrahan at his home, seizing a kilogram of methamphetamine, six ounces of cocaine, a pistol, $4,600 in cash, plus drug and gang-related paraphernalia.

August 30: Police in Oslo, Norway, arrest Lars Harnes — a member of the Bandidos MC and fugitive from prison on charges of robbery, sexual assault and torture — for a new bank robbery. In Amsterdam, Holland, 13 Hells Angels appear in court on charges related to the February murders of three fellow club members, resulting from a botched cocaine deal.

August 31: Drive-by gunmen strafe a welding shop owned by Hells Angels in Edmonton, Alberta, Canada. Police suspect members of the Bandidos MC.

September: Turning informer in exchanged for reduced prison time, Bonanno Family boss Joseph Charles "Big Joey" Massino begins recording his conversations with underboss Vincent Basciano. Two Hells Angels in Barrie, Ontario, face trial for extorting money from a local businessman and committing the crime "for the benefit or at the direction of a criminal organization."

September 2: Eighteen associates of the Vagos MC are arraigned in Sacramento, Calif., on charges of drug trafficking, weapons offenses, and receiving stolen property.

September 4: Police in Thomastown, Victoria, Australia, arrest the local Hells Angels sergeant-at-arms on charges of a prohibited person in possession of a weapon, possessing ammunition without a license, trafficking amphetamines and handling and disposing of stolen goods.

September 9: Police in Wangaratta, Victoria, Australia arrested Sherwin Williams, sergeant-at-arms of the Outcasts MC, on firearms charges and one count of unlawful imprisonment.

September 11: Roman Tsepov, cohort of President Vladimir Putin, falls ill in St. Petersburg, Russia, and dies on September 24. An autopsy reveals that he was poisoned with unspecified radioactive material, similar to that later used in the 2006 murder of Alexander Litvinenko.

September 12: Québec Superior Court Justice Jerry Zigman sentences Hells Angels Walter Stadnick and Donald Stockford to 20 years in prison on charges including conspiracy to commit murder, drug trafficking and gangsterism.

September 13: A fight between rival chapters of the Nomads MC leaves three members injured, two by gunfire, in Islington, New South Wales, Australia. Police pursue other members for 60 miles before catching them in the Hawkesbury River hamlet of Mooney Mooney.

September 15: A federal grand jury in Manhattan indicts six defendants on charges of labor racketeering, extortion, and fraud in a scheme that swindled New York's Metropolitan Transportation Authority out of $10 million. Defendants include Gambino Family members Richard Calabro, Edward Garafola, son Mario Garafola, and John "Johnny Rhino" Vitiello; Laborers Union Local 79 business agent Junior Campbell; and developer Frederick Contini.

September 16: Across Canada, police stage 34 coordinated raids on clandestine methamphetamine labs, arresting 17 suspects and seizing more than 20,000 pounds of ephedrine valued at $14.5 million, plus $3.5 million in cash. Several of those detained are Hells Angels.

September 18: Mami Kitamura, wife of Kitamura-gumi Yakuza leader Jitsuo Kitamura, orders the death of three victims in Omuta, Fukuoka, Japan, to avoid repayment of a debt. Jitsuo and their two eldest sons, Takashi and Takahiro Kitamura, execute victims Sayoko Takami, her son, and a teenage family friend. On September 20 they also murder Sayoko's younger son. Police arrest Mami Kitamura on September 21, and she confesses the slayings on September 22. Mami and Takahiro are condemned to die at trial, on October 17, 2006. Jitsuo and Takashi receive death sentences on February 28, 2007.

September 22: Police in Amsterdam arrest "Big Willem" van Boxtel, ex-president of the local Hells Angels chapter, on charges of accepting €250,000 in advance for a €1 million contract to kill mobster Willem Holleeder. On September 29 van Boxtel admits that real estate tycoon Willem Endstra asked to "do something" to Holleeder, but he denies taking the contract which prompted the Angels to expel him.

September 25: A Tasmanian drug company publishes details of its genetically-engineered opium poppies — thebaine oripavine poppy 1, or top1—mutants which do not produce morphine or codeine. In Henry Clay Township, Pa., two members of the Pagans MC use clubs to beat four patrons of the Traveler's Restaurant. Suspect Warren Lee McDaniel of West Virginia waives extradition on November 21. Second suspect Blair Jones Jr. is the son of a former Unionville police chief.

September 27: Eight members of Nuestra Familia plead guilty in Los Angeles on federal racketeering and drug trafficking charges. They in-

clude Henry Cervantes, Joseph Hernandez, Tex Hernandez, Alberto Larez, James Morado, Daniel Perez, Gerald Rubalcaba, and Cornelio Tristan. In Québec Superior Court, Justice Jerry Zigman sentences Hells Angels Walter Stadnick and Donald Stockford to 18 months in prison, with $100,000 fines, for running a drug network.

September 29: Jurors in Montreal, Québec, convict five members of the Bandidos MC on 22 charges from gangsterism and drug trafficking to weapons possession and arson. In Taunton, Mass., Outlaws MC member Joseph Noe faces arraignment on charges of kidnapping and beating Patrick Rooslet, a member of the rival Disciples MC.

October: Acting on information from mafioso Joseph Massino, FBI agents in New York excavate a mob graveyard in Queens known as "The Hole." Bureau spokesmen identify Massino as their source on February 4, 2005. He receives a life prison term on June 23, 2005, but the U.S. Bureau of Prisons website includes no record of his incarceration.

October 4: Mafioso and JFK assassination suspect Fred "The Wolf" Randaccio dies from natural causes in Sicily, at age 97. In Whyalla, South Australia, hotel patrons brawl with members of an outlaw MC. Spokesmen for Holland's National Prosecution Department announce that the body is investigating every Hells Angels chapter in the Netherlands on suspicion the club is a cover for a criminal organization.

October 7: Jurors in Texarkana, Ark., convict Timothy Pilgreen on charges of first-degree murder and attempted murder, for ramming six members of the Outlaws MC with a stolen pickup truck on October 29, 2003, killing two and injuring four. On October 8 the panel recommends life imprisonment.

October 12: Australia's Northern Territory News reports that murder victim Marshall Haritos, found beaten to death at his girlfriend's apartment in Parap, a Darwin suburb, is a member of the Coffin Cheaters MC suspected of running a $2 million amphetamine laboratory. His family denies the charge.

October 14: Federal prosecutors in Boston, Mass., charge 13 men with conspiracy to distribute more than $2 million worth of oxycodone in Gloucester between October 2003 and June 2004. The charges name Carlos Espinola, a member of the Red Devils MC, as the gang's primary supplier.

October 18: Indian gangster Koose Muniswamy Veerappan dies in a shootout with officers of the Tamil Nadu State Special Task Force near Moolakadu, Tamil Nadu, India. In death, police blame Veerappan's gang for 184 murders, poaching 200 elephants, smuggling of ivory worth $2.6 million and 10,000 tons of sandalwood worth $22 million.

October 19: Authorities in Placer County, Calif., charge Vagos MC members James Cross, Ryan Patrick Hill, and Nicholas Matteson with planning to kill a fellow member whom they feared might betray their plans of defection to the Hells Angels. The U.S. Organized Crime Drug Enforcement Task Force concludes "Operation Money Clip," an international investigation of money-laundering and drug trafficking. The campaign produces 83 arrests, while officers seize 2,526 kilograms of cocaine, 74 pounds of crystallized methamphetamine, 2.8 pounds of methamphetamine, 40,265 pounds of marijuana, and one kilogram of heroin, 45 cars, two guns, and $4.7 million in cash.

October 26: FBI spokesmen and Manhattan U.S. Attorney David Kelley announce the arrest of Alex Rudaj and 21 other "Albanian Mafia" members on federal racketeering charges.

October 28: Serbian gangster Radoljub Kanjevac survives a car-bombing in Nis.

October 29: DEA agent John Balchunas suffers fatal gunshot wounds in a struggle with two assailants in Milwaukee, Wis., dying on November 5.

October 30: Gunfire wounds two bikers during a clash between the Viet Nam Vets MC and Warrior Brotherhood MC in Palm Springs, Calif. Police jail suspects David Edmond Caudillo, William Garrett Morrow, George Allen Sanchez, and Gary Lane Stroup on charges including suspicion of assault with a deadly weapon, possession of a ballistic vest during the commission of a felony, and possession of an illegal knife.

November: Officers of the Manitoba Integrated Organized Crime Task Force launch "Project Defense," targeting Hells Angels and other high-level drug traffickers in Manitoba, Canada. In Numazu, Shizuoka, Japan, the Kyokuto-Sakurai-Soke-Rengokai Yakuza clan officially disbands. Police lift its designation as a criminal organization in May 2005.

November 2: Thirty members of the Coffin Cheaters and Rebels MCs agree to pay for damage caused aboard the *Spirit of Tasmania II* ferry on October 31.

November 3: The Australian Crime Commission reports activity by 97 organized crime groups nationwide, including amphetamine producers, outlaw motorcycle clubs, networks of firearms dealers, car "rebirthing" groups and sexual exploitation rings, plus identity theft and card-skimming groups that specialize in stealing the codes from magnetic strips on credit cards. New technology enables such groups to earn $4 billion yearly from fraud alone.

November 4: Pagans MC associate Gregory Spangler suffers stab wounds outside the Blue Star Hotel in Lancaster, Pa. On November 8 police charge Hells Angel Terence "Cracker" McCracken with aggravated assault, terroristic threats and simple assault.

November 5: College students brawl with members of the Jus Brothers MC in Stockton, Calif., leaving student Mark Steven Donahue stabbed to death. Police charge club members Robert Kenneth Memory, Frankie Joe Prater, and his wife Teresa with Donahue's slaying, holding them in lieu of $1 million bond.

November 6–7: Canadian police raid more than 50 businesses and homes in Vancouver, Surrey, Langley, North Vancouver, Coquitlam and Maple Ridge, British Columbia, targeting Hells Angels, Italian, and Vietnamese organized crime groups.

November 12: Québec Superior Court Justice Fraser Martin sentences former Hells Angel Stephane Faucher to two years in prison for contempt of court after Faucher refuses to testify as a police informant. The sentence extends Faucher's previous 12-year sentence for gangsterism, drug trafficking and conspiracy.

November 17: President Bush pardons Gerald Douglas Ficke (Nebraska, 1992, structuring currency transactions to evade reporting requirements) and Fred Dale Pitzer (Ohio, 1976, interstate transportation of falsely made securities).

November 28: An unknown gunman kills Black Pistons MC member Dean "Ellwood" Glaum at a gas station in Montgomery, Ala.

November 29: The Outlaws MC opens a prospect chapter in Moscow, Russia, days after the announcement of a newly-formed Hells Angels chapter.

November 30: A judge in Lynn, Mass., orders Hells Angels James Costin and Thomas Duda Jr. held without bail on charges of police lieutenant Vernon Coleman at a local café.

December 3: Two police officers in Cairns, Queensland, Australia, suffer injuries in a tavern brawl with members of the Bandidos MC.

December 4: Pennsylvania State Police officers arrest Nigerian immigrant Shafi Haji-Hussein Brmaji with 52 pound of khat in Luzerne County's Sugarloaf Township. Jurors deadlock at Brmaji's trial on May 5, 2006. A second panel subsequently convicts him of drug trafficking. Brmaji's appeal is denied on April 9, 2010.

December 8: Following a routine traffic stop in Manchester, N.H., state police seize 600 grams of cocaine, plus marijuana, Vicodin, Viagra and $12,000 in cash from Outlaws MC associate Michael Hunt. Prosecutors charge Hunt with drug trafficking on December 9.

December 10: Gary Webb shoots himself to death in Sacramento, Calif., less than 24 hours after the theft of his motorcycle. Obituaries brand him a "discredited" journalist, while Internet websites spin conspiracy theories surrounding his death.

December 14: Sicilian mafioso Giuseppe Riina receives a 14-year sentence for extortion, Mafia association and money-laundering.

December 15: Convicted on 50 counts of writing "excessive" prescriptions for opioid painkillers to chronic pain patients, Dr. William Hurwitz of McLean, Va., receives four 25-year federal sentences and forty-six 15-year sentences, all to run concurrently. The Fourth Circuit Court of Appeals overturns his conviction on August 22, 2006, due to errors by the trial judge. A second trial begins on March 26, 2007. On April 27 jurors convict Hurwitz on 16 counts of drug trafficking. He receives a sentence of four years and nine months on July 13, 2007, and is released on January 9, 2009.

December 20: California investigators launch a probe of Mexican Mafia finances after gang leader Frank Macias "Chino" Madriaga amasses $40,000 in his inmate account at Pelican Bay State Prison. In Toledo, Ohio, former Outlaws MC international president James "Frank" Wheeler receives a life prison term for racketeering and conspiracy to distribute drugs, in addition to his pre-existing 16½ years on similar charges in Florida.

December 21: The U.S. Marshals Service adds Randy Mark Yager, Chicago president of the Outlaws MC, to its 15 Most Wanted list as a fugitive from racketeering charges.

December 27: Police find former Renegades MC member Ronald Becht and wife Susan murdered at their small engine repair shop in Buffalo, N.Y. Investigators suspect gang involvement. In Adelaide, South Australia, police suspect outlaw bikers of stealing one truck and burning two others at a Dry Creek garage. Police in Orange County, Calif., charge Hells Angel Rodrigo Jose Requejo with fatally stabbing one victim and wounding the dead man's twin brother.

December 29: Hells Angel Robert Garceau dies from cancer at California's Novato Community Hospital, while awaiting an appellate court's disposition of his 1993 double-murder conviction.

December 31: Russian legislators strip the Federal Sport Agency of its power to grant casino licenses.

2005 Somalian pirates hijack 35 ships, disrupting UN supply lines of food into the war-torn and tsunami-ravaged nation.

January 1: Five members of the Pagans MC beat Hells Angel Vincent Heinrich in Woodland Township, N.J. In Edmonton, Alberta, Canada, a gunman kills Redd Alert gang member Russell Adams and a companion at Lou's Bar and Grill. Police charge suspect Lyle Chaywee Buffalo with first-degree murder, attempted murder and possession of a weapon dangerous to public peace.

January 3: Hells Angels East Coast leader John "John the Baptist" LaFranco responds to the Heinrich beating and other recent incidents by declaring war on the rival Pagans.

January 6: Shotgunners kill Lynn and Fred Gilbank in Ontario, Canada. Police charge Satan's Choice MC member Ion Croitoru and Andre Gravelle with the slayings, but prosecutors drop the charges on June 12, 2006. Later that month, Croitoru pleads guilty to extortion and forfeits $10,000 bail.

January 7: Police in Hamilton, Ontario, Canada, charge professional wrestler Ion "The Terrible Turk" Croitoru with murdering attorney Lyn Gilbank and her husband Frank at their home on November 16, 1998. At the time, Croitoru was a member of the Satan's Choice MC. Prosecutors say Lyn Gilbank was targeted for defending a client who testified against members of a local crime family. After spending seven months in prison, Croitoru was released on $100,000 in August, then is arrested on December 2, 2005, for violating his bail terms. Police also file a new extortion charge against him. Ontario Attorney General Michael Bryant drops the murder charges on June 12, 2006, whereupon Croitoru pleads guilty to extortion and violating the terms of his bail. As punishment, he forfeits $10,000 of his bond.

January 14: A member of the Club Deroes MC assaults a woman at a hotel in Bunbury, Western Australia, then fires a pistol at bystanders outside. Officers of the Gang Response Unit arrest a suspect in Dwellingup on January 19. In South Philadelphia, Pa., drive-by gunmen kill Hells Angels vice president Tom Wood. Police seek local Pagans leader Steven "Gorilla" Mondevergine for questioning.

January 20: Trial begins for Hells Angel Terence "Cracker" McCracken, charged with stabbing a member of the Pagans MC in November 2004.

January 21: Pennsylvania mafioso Ralph Natale receives a 13-year prison term in Camden, N.J., with credit for five years spent in custody as an informer and prosecution witness at various federal trials.

January 25: Police seeking fugitive mafioso Bernardo Provenzano raid homes in Sicily, arresting 46 suspected Mafia collaborators.

January 28: Police in Berlin, Germany, arrest five persons on suspicion of fixing professional soccer matches. Those charged include bookmaker

Milan Šapina, his brother Philip, referee Robert Hoyzer, and three Hertha Berliner Sport-Club players: Alexander Madlung, Nando Rafael and Josip Šimunić, accused of throwing a German Cup match on September 22, 2004. On February 2 prosecutors announce raids on the premises of 19 more suspects, seizing evidence that implicates 25 persons — including 14 players and three more referees — in fixing 10 matches during 2004. Hoyzer confesses to fixing and betting on matches, then turns state's evidence against his codefendants. The German Football Association suspends him on February 10, then bans him for life on April 29. Police file new charges against Hoyzer on February 12, citing evidence that he fixed more matches than originally acknowledged. On November 17, 2005, Hoyzer receives a prison term of two years and five months, while referee Dominik Marks gets 18 months and Milan Šapina receives a sentence of two years and 11 months. Their appeals are denied in December 2006.

February: Dutch prosecutors charge imprisoned British gangster Curtis Warren with running an international drug-smuggling cartel from his cell. Although convicted, Warren successfully appeals and wins parole on June 30, 2007, seven years ahead of his projected release date on other charges.

February 4: Federal prosecutors inform the press of Bonanno Family boss Joe Massino's role as an informer. On June 23 Massino receives a life sentence for racketeering, seven counts of murder, arson, extortion, loan-sharking, illegal gambling, conspiracy and money-laundering.

February 11: Pirates pursue the Australian yacht *Cardonnay* en route from Panama to the Galápagos Islands, but fail to overtake their target.

February 28: Philip Giordano, former city budget manager for Waterbury, Conn., pleads guilty in federal court to bribery, federal income tax fraud and violating campaign laws for accepting donations on behalf of ex-mayor Philip Giordano, in exchange for continuing a donor's $100,000 street-sweeping contract.

March: Japanese mobster Kiyoshi Takayama is promoted to the rank of *wakagashira* ("eldest son") in the Kodo-kai Yakuza clan, based in Nakamura-ku, Nagoya. Kenichi Shinoda, AKA Shinobu Tsukasa, forms the Hirota-gumi clan.

March 2: FBI agents arrest Armando Botta Jr. and Frank Depergola, ex-employees of the Massachusetts Career Development Institute in Springfield, on loan-sharking charges.

March 3: President Bush pardons Charles Russell Cooper, convicted of bootlegging in South Carolina, in 1959.

March 8: Captains of the yachts *Gandalf* and *Mahdi* repel pirates off the coast of Yemen, sinking one speedboat and wounding two attackers.

March 9: Louisiana State Police officers arrest "Godfather of dog fighting" Floyd Boudreaux and his son Guy at their home in Broussard, charging both with 57 felony counts of dog fighting and two counts of animal cruelty. Jurors acquit both defendants on October 17, 2008.

March 15: In the midst of financial scandal and an SEC investigation, the governing board of American International Group, Inc.— a New York–based insurance company and 18th-largest public company on Earth — forces CEA Maurice Greenberg to resign. New York Attorney General Eliot Spitzer files a criminal complaint against AIG, Greenberg, and ex–CFO Howard Smith on May 26. Those charges are dismissed in 2006, but Greenberg pays a $15 million civil settlement that same year in a case alleging fraudulent financial practices.

March 18: Drug dealer Derek "Yardie Derek" McDuffus stabs gangster Desmond "Dessie" Noonan in Manchester, England. Noonan dies en route to a local hospital. Police charge McDuffus with murder on June 15 and he is later convicted.

April: Kiyoshi Takayama becomes a formal member of Japan's Fifth Yamaguchi-gumi syndicate, assuming the rank of *wakagashira-hosa* (deputy underboss) in June.

April 4: Police arrest 14 alleged mafiosi on gambling charges in Queens, N.Y.

April 7: The Serious Organised Crime and Police Act receives royal assent in Great Britain.

April 12: Massachusetts mafioso Vincent "The Animal" Ferrara leaves federal prison after when U.S. District Judge Mark L. Wolf reduces his sentence, citing evidence of prosecutorial misconduct at trial in 1992.

April 19–20: DEA agents and other authorities cap "Operation Cyber Chase" a year-long investigation targeting international Internet pharmaceutical traffickers operating in the United States, India, Asia, Europe and the Caribbean. The campaign produces 20 arrests in the U.S., Costa Rica and India.

April 25: A federal grand jury in Chicago indicts Joseph Lombardo and 13 other Outfit members in "Operation Family Secrets," with specific charges including 18 murders committed since the 1970s. In New York City, federal prosecutors announce that the Rigas family, disgraced founders and leaders of Adelphia Communications Corporation, will forfeit nearly its entire fortune to create a $715 million fund for compensation of investors who lost money when the firm collapsed in 2002. On June 20 ex–CEO John Rigas receives a 15-year prison term, while son and former CFO Timothy gets 20 years. On November 22 government spokesmen tell reporters that former executive vice president Michael Rigas will soon plead guilty on felony charges. In Chicago, federal prosecutors cap "Operation Family Secrets" by charging Frank Calabrese Sr. and other high-profile Outfit members murder, racketeering, extortion, and illegal gambling.

April 28: The world's most expensive legal casino, Wynn Las Vegas Hotel Resort and Casino, opens in Las Vegas, Nev.

May: Researchers at the Ernest Gallo Clinic and Research Center in Emeryville, Calif., announce successful laboratory inhibition of the AGS3 gene, curbing desire for heroin in rodents.

May 5: Armed pirates board the sailing sloop Ten Large off Ayerabu Island, Indonesia, stealing all the cash on board.

May 13: Three pirates raid the catamaran Madam, anchored off Carenero, Venezuela, threatening owners Bruno and Catherine Millet with knives before stealing binoculars, shoes and some portable electronics.

May 17: A federal grand jury in Pittsburgh, Pa., indicts Carl Valenti and 12 other defendants on charges of heroin trafficking.

May 27: In Rochester, N.Y., William A. Hunter pleads guilty on federal charges of conspiring to distribute marijuana with mobster Francesco "Frank" Frassetto and his two sons, Frank Jr. and Philip.

Late May: Pirates attack the yacht Caramba off Negril, Jamaica, stealing money, electronics, a tool kit and several head sails.

May 29: Yakuza boss Toi Inagawa dies from illness in Japan.

June: Mobster Brandon Croteau sells drugs to an undercover state police trooper in Springfield, Mass., and is charged with drug trafficking. He subsequently pleads guilty and receives a 10-year prison term.

June 6: The U.S. Navy guided-missile destroyer USS Gonzalez fires .50-caliber machine guns to prevent pirates from boarding the motor vessel Tigris in the Indian Ocean, off the coast of Somalia.

June 8: Prosecutors in Seattle, Wash., charge 28 members of the Bandidos MC with racketeering, kidnapping, assault, and drug and firearms violations. Defendants include international president George Wegers, national treasurer Christopher Horlock, and national sergeants-at-arms Jimmie Garman and Hugh Henschel. All 28 defendants subsequently plead guilty on reduced charges. In Washington, D.C., President Bush pardons Texas defendant James Edward Reed, convicted in 1975 of conspiracy to possess with intent to distribute marijuana.

June 14: DEA Administrator Karen Tandy announces the conclusion of "Operation Mallorca," a 27-month investigation targeting four Colombian-based money brokers who funneled drug proceeds through the Colombian Black Market Peso Exchange. The campaign produces 36 arrests, plus seizures including 947 kilograms of cocaine, seven kilograms of heroin, 21,650 pounds of marijuana, and $7.2 million in cash.

June 15: A federal grand jury in Orange County, Calif., files racketeering and drug trafficking charges against Mexican Mafia members Orlando Alvarado, Francisco Amaya, Eddie Armenta, Jose Arvizu, Abel Azevedo, Jose Becerra, Rogelio Cardenas, Joseph Castro, Robert Cervantes, Marco Diaz, Arthur Duran, Ismael Esquivel, Sandra Flores, Juan Holguin, Mario Jiminez, Anthony Lebron, Freddie Luevano, Abraham Magallon, Jose Martinez, David Melgoza Jr., Ramon Meza Jr., Lawrence Morales, Frank Nerida, Long Nguyen, Robert Ocampo, Freddie Ojeda, Peter "Sana" Ojeda, Francisco Rodriquez, Mia Rodriquez, Oscar Ruiz, Mario Saucedo, Rafael Torres, David Trujillo, and Octavio Valenzuela.

June 26: A Washington Post survey finds 58 casinos, 2,000 gaming halls and some 70,000 slot machines in Moscow, Russia.

June 27: Pirates seize the MV Semlow, bearing food for tsunami victims from Mombasa, Kenya, to Bosasso, Somalia, and hold the ship for 100 days.

June 29: "Operation Site Down," a two-year, 11-nation investigation of film and software piracy, culminates with 70 raids in the U.S. and 20 more in 10 other countries. Raiders shut down eight major distribution servers while identifying more than 120 cyber-pirates. By May 6, 2008, 40 defendants have struck plea bargains including forfeiture of 118 computers, 13 laptops, 28 keyboards and monitors, 4,567 bootleg CDs and DVDs, 28 PlayStations and Xboxes, seven computer towers, five digital cameras, and other hardware.

June 30: Four pirates board a sailing yacht anchored at Saline Joniche, Calabria, Italy, holding the owner at gunpoint while they steal cash and computer equipment.

July: Deputy "drug czar" Scott Burns tells Congress that the Clinton administration's "strategy to reduce drug use in America is not focused on one illicit drug at the expense of another, but seeks to reduce all illicit drug use." In Canada, "Project E-Pandora" culminates with the arrest of 18 Hells Angels on various charges. Overall, the year-long investigation has indicted 45 defendants, while raiders have seized more than 20 kilograms of cocaine; more than 20 kilograms of methamphetamine; more than 70 kilograms of marijuana; 250 kilograms of Methylamine; two methamphetamine labs; prohibited weapons including pistols, fully automatic firearms, silencers,

11 sticks of dynamite, and four hand grenades; and more than $200,000 in cash.

July 14: Modern buccaneers pursue the sailboat *Sandpiper* past Isle De Malpelo, en route from Panama to the Galápagos Islands.

July 19: Authorities in Rome indict mafioso Giuseppe Calò, bank swindler Licio Gelli, businessmen Ernesto Diotallevi and Flavio Carboni, and Carboni's girlfriend Manuela Kleinszig for the 1982 murder of Roberto Calvi. Trial convenes on October 5 and continues until June 6, 2007, when Judge Mario Lucio d'Andria dismisses the charges for lack of evidence. The DEA's "Operation Money Trail Initiative" culminates with the indictment of Mexican money broker Saul Saucedo-Chaidez, AKA "The Engineer," on charges of moving $42 million between the U.S. and Mexico.

July 24: Assembled members of the IBT and Service Employees International Union vote to withdraw from the AFL-CIO. IBT president James P. Hoffa predicts that seven more unnamed international unions would soon bolt and join the Teamsters.

July 29: Yoshinori Watanabe retires as fifth *kumicho* (godfather) of Japan's Yamaguchi-gumi crime syndicate, succeeded by Kenichi Shinoda. Shinoda names Kiyoshi Takayama as his underboss on August 8.

August: The Tokyo-based Kokusui-kai Yakuza clan forges an alliance with the larger Yamaguchi-gumi syndicate.

August 1: At California's San Quentin prison, three Nuestra Familia members assault an inmate wearing Mexican Mafia tattoos.

August 4: Pirates board the American catamaran *Tortilla Flat* at Laguna Grande, Golfo De Cariaco, Venezuela, wounding the owner with a machete and stealing the boat's dinghy.

August 8: Nuestra Familia leaders order attacks on white inmates at San Quentin, sparking a fight with 70 prisoners involved.

August 12: Police in Ústí nad Labem, Czech Republic, arrest fugitive Sicilian mafioso Luigi Putrone. A Czech court orders his extradition on June 21, 2006.

August 17: A federal grand jury in Newark, N.J., indicts 16 defendants on charges of loan-sharking, sports bookmaking, numbers running, and football-ticket gambling. Those charged include Michael "Tona" Borelli, Joseph Bruno, Ludwig "Ninny" Bruschi, Alex Conigliaro, Michael Crincoli, John Dennis, Lawrence "Larry Fab" Dentico, Russell Fallacara, John Grecco, Peter Grecco, Nicholas "Nicky the Snake" Ladagona, Joseph "Billy Nap" Napolitano, Steve Pastore, Gregory Richardson, Joseph "Big Joe" Scarbrough, and John Yeswita. Dentico, an associate

of the Genovese Family, pleads guilty on August 16, 2006, and receives a 51-month sentence, leaving prison on May 12, 2009.

August 18–19: DEA agents join other foreign, federal, state and local authorities to close "Operation Three Hour Tour," a 10-month investigation of three Mexican and Colombian drug transportation syndicates and their 27 U.S. distribution groups. The campaign produces 164 arrest, plus seizure of 3,163 pounds of cocaine, 55 pounds of methamphetamine, 15 pounds of heroin, 9.5 ounces of crack cocaine, 10,000 doses of ecstasy, 58 vehicles, 216 pounds of marijuana, 52 guns, and $5.5 million in cash.

August 25: A sniper kills gangster-sportsman Georgi Andreev Iliev at a restaurant in Sunny Beach, Bulgaria.

August 26: Taiwanese Premier Frank Hsieh asks Swiss authorities to maintain a freeze on bank accounts held by fugitive murder suspect Andrew Wang and members of his family. The Swiss demand a promise that Wang will not face the death penalty if arrested. Premier Hsieh agrees.

August 29: The DOJ announces indictments against eight former executives of the major accounting firm KPMG, in what reporters call the largest tax evasion scheme in U.S. history. A ninth defendant is an outside attorney paid to write letters for KPMG assuring clients that their tax shelters "more likely than not" would withstand IRS audits. The announcement includes word that KPMG will pay a $456 million fine to settle charges of illegal marketing of tax shelters. The first installment of $256 million is due on September 1, 2005, with two remaining payments of $100 million due on June 30, 2006, and December 31, 2006. KPMG also agrees to cooperate in prosecution of its former officers.

August 30: FBI agents in New York City arrest Judge David Gross and 10 other men on a variety of charges related to the Genovese Family's illegal operations. Gross is charged with conspiring to launder Mafia funds through a restaurant in Freeport, N.Y. Attorney General Alberto Gonzales announces the culmination of "Operation Wildfire," targeting methamphetamine traffickers in 200 cities nationwide. The campaign produces 427 arrests, plus seizures including 56 clandestine labs, 209 pounds of methamphetamine, 201,035 tablets of pseudoephedrine, 158 kilograms of pseudoephedrine powder, 224,860 tablets of ephedrine, 123 weapons and 28 vehicles.

September 1: Governor Arnold Schwarzenegger commutes the state life sentences of Nuestra Familia leaders Joseph Hernandez, Tex Hernandez, James Morado, Gerald Rubalcaba, and Cornelio Tristan, permitting their transfer to federal custody.

September 16: Police arrest Camorra leader Paolo Di Lauro at an apartment in the Secondigliano neighborhood of Naples, Italy.

September 21: Chicago mobster Albert Tocco dies from a stroke at the federal prison in Terre Haute, Ind.

September 22: FBI agents and NYPD officers arrest five mafiosi in connection with the 1992 murders of husband-wife bandits Thomas and Rose Marie Uva, who specialized in robbing Mafia social clubs.

September 23: In São Paulo, Brazil, *Veja* magazine exposes the "Whistle's Mafia" scandal, involving bribery of soccer referees Paulo José Danelon and Edílson Pereira de Carvalho to fix International Federation of Association Football matches. Pereira de Carvalho admits accepting payoffs to fix several Brazilian National Championship matches. Police arrest suspected gambling ringleader Nagib Fayad in Piracicaba on September 25. The São Paulo Football Sporting Justice Court bans both referees for life on October 31.

September 28: President Bush pardons five defendants convicted of organized crime offenses: Adam Wade Graham (1990, conspiracy to deliver 10 or more grams of LSD), Rufus Edward Harris (1963, possession and selling of untaxed whiskey), Larry Paul Lenius (1989, conspiracy to distribute cocaine), Larry Lee Lopez (1985, conspiracy to import marijuana), and Mark Lewis Weber (1981, selling Quaalude tablets and marijuana).

October: Dutch police raid Hells Angels clubhouses in Amsterdam, Haarlem, Harlingen, IJmuiden, Kampen and Rotterdam, seizing €70,000 ($103,285) in cash plus an arsenal of weapons including 20 pistols, a submachine gun, a flame thrower, a grenade launcher, and hand grenades. In Japan, the nation's largest Yakuza clan — the Yamaguchi-gumi — forges an alliance with the Fifth Aizukotetsu-kai.

October 6: The Swiss Federal Commission approves release of bank records relevant to the Taiwan frigate scandal.

October 8: Pirates capture the cargo ship MV *Torgelow* near El-Maan, Somalia, holding it for 53 days.

October 12: Pirates seize the MV *Miltzow* at Merka, Somalia, releasing the ship and its cargo of UN food on October 14.

October 26: Mafioso Michael Rizzitello dies from heart disease in California, while serving a 33-year prison sentence for attempted murder. In Sofia, Bulgaria, unknown gunmen kill shady banker Emil Kyulev.

October 28: Taiwanese State Public Prosecutor-General Wu Ying-chao unseals Swiss bank files related to the nation's $2.8 billion frigate kickback scandal. DEA agents arrest 30 members of the Black Mafia Family in eight states, seizing 2.5 kilos of cocaine, numerous weapons, plus $3 million in cash and assets.

October 29: Brazilian police kill gang leader Erismar Rodrigues Moreira in the Rocinha slum of Rio de Janeiro.

October 30: Four pirates armed with guns and machetes board a yacht anchored Bahia del Sol, El Salvador, then flee when confronted by the captain, firing shots as they retreat.

November: Pirates storm the Canadian ketch *Alioth* off Isla Borracha, Venezuela, binding captain and crew before sexually assaulting a female passenger. Mexican officials admit that drug cartels have artificially inflated national demand for pseudoephedrine, vowing to reduce imports to a legitimate level for production of cold medicine and to reduce the number of retail outlets nationwide from 51,000 to 17,000.

November 5: Pirates armed with automatic weapons and grenade launchers attack a luxury liner, *The Seabourn Spirit*, off the coast of Somalia, wounding one crewman before the ship escapes.

November 13: Gunmen wound indicted drug dealer Antonio Sergi in his car, in Melbourne, Australia.

November 17: "Operation Sweet Tooth," an Organized Crime Drug Enforcement Task Force investigation of ecstasy and marijuana traffickers, culminates with 291 arrests in the U.S. and Canada. Raiders 931,300 MDMA tablets, 1,777 pounds of marijuana, and $7.75 million in cash.

Late November: An armed yachtsman repels would-be pirates from his vessel at Isla Piritu, Venezuela.

November 30: "Operation Northern Impact," an Organized Crime Drug Enforcement Task Force investigation of international cocaine and marijuana traffickers based in Mexico, culminates with the arrest of 53 suspects on charges including drug conspiracy and money-laundering. Raiders seize 341 kilograms of cocaine, 2,258 pounds of marijuana, and $1.4 million in cash. On the same day, DEA agents cap "Operation High Step" with arrests of 78 heroin traffickers in Boston, Chicago, New York City and Orlando, Fla. Raiders seize 78 kilograms of heroin, 39 kilograms of cocaine, 20 weapons, and $1.4 million in cash.

December 1: Mobster Anthony Arillotta receives a three-year prison term in Springfield, Mass., for loan-sharking and illegal gambling.

December 4: Four pirates board and loot the Canadian sailing vessel *Nomotos*, anchored at Porlamar, Venezuela. In Japan, Yakuza boss Kenichi Shinoda begins serving a six-year prison sentence for illegal firearms possession, originally imposed in 1997.

December 7: Connecticut police arrest Diablos

MC member Jerry Louis Fantauzzi on charges of selling drugs in Meriden and Waterbury. Fantauzzi receives a 10-year sentence on November 20, 2006.

December 8: "Operation Cali Exchange," an international investigation of cocaine traffickers, produces 24 indictments and 18 arrests plus seizures including 2,107 kilograms of cocaine, 518 pounds of marijuana, and $7 million in cash.

December 9: Patrick Balsamo smashes windows of a Staten Island grocery store owned by Salvatore Sciandra, following complaints of sexual harassment from Balsamo's daughter, an employee at the store. Sciandra's brother — Genovese Family *caporegime* Carmine Sciandra— approaches Balsamo with a baseball bat and suffers a gunshot wound to the stomach.

December 12: Prosecutors in Springfield, Mass., indict mobster Frankie Roche for the murder of Adolfo "Big Al" Bruno. Serbian mobster Kristijan Golubović receives a six-year sentence in Belgrade on illegal arms and racketeering charges, later reduced to 4 years. He is released on January 9, 2009.

December 13: Crips founder Stanley "Tookie" Williams III dies by lethal injection at San Quentin prison for four murders committed in 1979.

December 15: DEA agents arrest Albert Saltiel-Cohen, owner of three of the world's largest anabolic steroid manufacturers, to climax "Operation Gear Grinder." In addition to the Saltiel-Cohen arrest, agents jail four other suspects in California and Texas, while identifying more than 2,000 buyers of illegal steroids.

December 16: Five nocturnal pirates rob the sailboat *Monkey's Business* and another vessel at Cow Bay, Saint Thomas, Jamaica.

December 19: Genovese Family boss Vincent Gigante dies from complications of heart disease at the U.S. Medical Center for Federal Prisoners in Springfield, Mo. In New York City the National Association of Securities Dealers (now the Financial Industry Regulatory Authority) announces a levy of $19.4 million in fines against the investment firms Merrill Lynch; Pierce, Fenner & Smith; Wells Fargo Investments; and Linsco/ Private Ledger Corporation for suitability and supervisory violations related to sales of Class B and Class C mutual fund shares. Merrill Lynch pays $14 million of the fine.

December 20: President Bush pardons six defendants convicted of organized crime offenses: Carl Eugene Cantrell (1980, possession with intent to distribute marijuana), Harper James Finucan (1980, possession with intent to distribute marijuana), Bobby Frank Kay Sr. (1959, operation of an illegal distillery), Charles Elis McKinley (1950,

violation of Internal Revenue Service liquor laws), John Gregory Schillace (1988, conspiracy to possess cocaine with intent to distribute), and Wendy Rose St. Charles (1984, conspiracy to conduct a narcotics enterprise, and distribution of cocaine).

2006 A UN World Drug Report calls methamphetamine the most abused hard drug on Earth, with 26 million known addicts, including 1.4 million in the United States. Globally, the highest concentration is in East and Southeast Asia. The IMO reports 61 incidents of piracy in the year's first quarter, including 20 unsuccessful attacks in January. U.S. gambling revenue in legal casinos hits $32 billion.

January: Police in Vancouver, British Columbia, arrest 10 Hells Angels on charges of gun-running and drug trafficking.

January 2: Rival Israeli mobsters Yaakov Alperon and Amir Mulner meet to resolve their differences at a hotel north of Tel Aviv. The meeting turns violent, with Mulner stabbed in the neck. In March 2006, police charge Alperon and his brother Reuven with "making threats, attempted assault, and intentionally damaging a car."

January 13: FBI agents arrest fugitive Chicago Outfit member Joseph "Joey the Clown" Lombardo Sr. in Elmwood Park, Ill., home of longtime friend Dominic Calarco.

January 14: Pirates hijack the German yacht *Wado Ryu*, anchored off Racha Yas Island, Phuket, Thailand. Authorities find the boat adrift on January 19.

January 17: Mexican Mafia member Roberto Ramiro Marin receives a 15-year sentence in San Diego, Calif., after pleading guilty to charges of conspiracy to distribute methamphetamine.

January 18: "Operation Husky" culminates with police raids on Hells Angels hangouts in the Canadian provinces of Alberta, Ontario, and Québec. Police arrest 27 suspects, while seizing illegal drugs valued at $2.3 million plus unspecified numbers of weapons, vehicles, and large amounts of cash.

January 24: The USS *Winston S. Churchill* captures a suspected pirate ship, the MV *Safina al-Birsarat*, off Somalia's coast. Indian crewmen say that 10 Somalis found on board hijacked the dhow near Mogadishu on January 15 and thereafter used it to attack merchant ships. The *Churchill's* crew delivers the pirates to Kenya for trial. The pirates receive seven-year prison terms in November 2006. In Hampton County, Mass., a grand jury indicts Keith Gallagher Sr., national vice president of the Diablos MC, on three counts each of trafficking in cocaine and drug violations in a school zone, and one count of possession of marijuana.

January 27: DEA agents and NYPD narcotics

officers cap "Operation Bronx Tale" with 21 arrests targeting members of a Panama-based heroin trafficking syndicate run by Silverio Guzman.

January 30: Ireland's High Court approves seizure of a 77-acre ranch owned by convicted gangster John Gilligan. Gilligan loses his appeal of the order on December 19, 2008.

January 31: Kenneth Lay and Jeffrey Skilling face trial in federal court for the Enron scandal. Jurors convict both defendants on May 25, 2006, finding Lay guilty on 10 counts and Skilling guilty on 19. Lay dies while on vacation in Snowmass, Colo., on July 5, 2006, prior to sentencing, and the trial judge vacates Lay's conviction on October 17, 2006. Skilling receives a prison term of 24 years and four months on October 26, 2006.

February 1: DEA agents cap "Operation Liquid Heroin" with the arrest of 22 Colombian nationals, charged with smuggling over 20 kilograms of heroin into the U.S. Methods include use of human "swallowers," surgical implantation of drug packets in puppies, plus concealment of drugs in body creams, aerosol cans, pressed into bead shapes, and sewn into the lining of purses and double-sided luggage.

February 6: New Jersey State Police spokesmen announce the culmination of "Operation Slapshot," an undercover investigation of illegal gambling inside the National Hockey League. Those indicted on various charges include Rick Tocchet, an assistant coach for the Phoenix Coyotes; Janet Jones, wife of NHL legend Wayne Gretzky; and suspended state trooper James Harney. On February 8 investigators name San Jose Sharks center Jeremy Roenick and Toronto Maple Leafs center Travis Green as persons implicated in the conspiracy, with ties to Philadelphia's Mafia family. On August 3, 2006, Harney pleads guilty to conspiracy, promoting gambling and official misconduct, confessing his partnership with Tocchet in the betting ring. He receives a six-year prison term on August 3, 2007. Defendant James Ulmer of Swedesboro, N.J., pleads guilty to conspiracy and promoting gambling on December 1, 2006. Tocchet pleads guilty to identical charges on May 25, 2007. Unknown gunmen kill lawyer-mobster Mario Condello at his home in Melbourne, Australia.

February 14: A federal grand jury in Spokane, Wash., indicts five members and associates of the Hells Angels MC on charges including racketeering, conspiracy to racketeer, murder, attempted murder, intimidation, extortion, robbery and trafficking in stolen motor vehicles and motor vehicle parts. Those charged include Spokane chapter president Richard Allen Fabel, Joshua Binder, Paul Foster, Ricky Jenks, and Rodney Lee Rollness.

February 15: Police in Manitoba, Canada, arrest 13 persons on charges including drug trafficking, extortion, proceeds of crime, and organized crime related offenses. Three of those jailed are Hells Angels.

February 16: Kansas City mafioso Anthony Thomas "Tony Ripe" Civella suffers a fatal heart attack while golfing in Phoenix, Ariz.

February 19: Four pirates board a French yacht anchored in Endeavour Harbour, on Tawila Island, in the Red Sea, stealing an outboard motor.

February 21: Pirates board and loot two yachts, the *Kumara* and *Ten Large*, anchored off Malaysia's Tioman Islands.

February 27: William V. Musto, ex-mayor of Union City, N.J., convicted of racketeering in 1982, dies from complications of Alzheimer's disease.

March 1: Malaysian pirates rob the yacht *Cin Cin*, anchored among the Tioman Islands.

March 2: Two boatloads of pirates pursue the yacht *Serenity* in Indonesia waters, but fail to overtake it.

March 3: Prosecutors in Detroit, Mich., indict reputed mafioso Jack V. Giacalone and 14 codefendants on illegal gambling charges. Jurors later convict Giacalone at trial.

March 5: Syndicate hitman Richard "The Iceman" Kuklinski dies of natural causes while imprisoned at Trenton, N.J.

March 6: Israeli authorities extradite drug trafficker Zeev Rosenstein for trial in the U.S. on charges of smuggling ecstasy. He subsequently receives a 12-year prison term, with stipulation that he serve the time in Israel.

March 9: Congress passes the Combat Methamphetamine Epidemic Act to regulate retail sales of ephedrine, pseudoephedrine, and phenylpropanolamine used to manufacture illegal drugs. The law takes effect on September 30, imposing daily and monthly purchase limits, mandating placement of products beyond direct customer access, use of sales logbooks, and customer ID verification. In southern California, ATF agents cap "Operation 22 Green" by arresting 25 members of the Vagos MC on firearms and narcotics charges. Agents also seize 95 illegal weapons, plus drugs, two stolen motorcycles, and $6,000 in cash.

March 14: Disgraced Moe Dalitz protégé Herb Tobman dies from a heart attack in Las Vegas. The first in a series of Aryan Brotherhood racketeering trials begins in Orange County, Calif. Defendants Tyler "The Hulk" Bingham, Christopher Overton Gibson, Edgar "The Snail" Hevle, and Barry "The Barron" Mills face federal charges of ordering or participating in 15 murders or attempted murders since 1981. Defense attorneys make their closing arguments on July 13. Jurors convict all four defendants on July 28. The panel deadlocks while considering penalties on September 15, resulting in life sentences.

March 15: The UN Security Council urges any naval forces operating off Somalia to take action against suspected pirates.

March 18: An unidentified sniper kills Hells Angels MC member Anthony William Benesh III outside a restaurant in Austin, Tex. Police suspect members of the rival Bandidos. Off the coast of Somalia, the USS *Cape St. George* and USS *Gonzalez* exchange gunfire with pirates, killing one buccaneer and wounding five.

March 20: Businessman Antonios Sajih "Tony" Mokbel misses a court date in Melbourne, Australia, concerning charges filed against him for importing cocaine from Mexico in 2000. Initially believed dead, Mokbel is arrested in Athens, Greece, on June 5, 2007, and extradited to Australia for trial on May 17, 2008.

March 21: Police in Reggio Calabria, Italy, arrest five alleged in connection with the October 16, 2005, ambush murder of Dr. Francesco Fortugno, vice president of Calabria's regional council.

March 23: Police in Italy, Spain, and Morocco arrest dozens of persons in Italy, Spain, and Morocco while seizing 20 tons of cocaine, 17,000 tons of hashish, and €15,000 cash. All of those jailed are said to be members or associates of the Calabrian 'Ndrangheta. In New York City, a federal grand jury indicts Colombo Family members Carmine, John, and Joseph Baudanza on charges of operating a "pump and dump" stock scam. The brothers plead guilty on April 17, 2007, and all are sentenced to prison. Carmine is paroled on October 30, 2009; Joseph has a projected release date of February 18, 2011; John is scheduled for release on August 2, 2015.

March 26: Brooklyn District Attorney Charles Hynes announces the culmination of "Operation Kings Flush," resulting in arrests of 10 men charged with earning $45 million per year from illegal bookmaking in New York City.

March 27: Police in Catanzaro, Calabria, Italy, find four persons shot to death in gangland execution style. On the same day, Italian authorities seize a "narco submarine" used by the 'Ndrangheta to transport cocaine from Colombia to Italy. In Rochester, N.Y., mafioso Philip Frassetto and his brother plead guilty to federal charges of heroin trafficking, implicating their father, veteran mobster Francesco "Frank" Frassetto.

March 28: Police arrest 17 alleged drug traffickers in Reggio di Calabria, Italy.

March 30: Gambino Family underboss Anthony "The Genius" Megale pleads guilty to ex-

tortion in Connecticut. He receives an 86-month prison term on April 3, scheduled for release on July 18, 2014. DEA spokesmen announce the climax of "Operation Omni Presence," a multi-jurisdictional international investigation targeting a drug syndicate that smuggled cocaine from Mexico to New York City. Raiders arrest 11 suspects, while seizing 194 kilograms of cocaine and $474,000 in cash.

March 31: Cleveland mafioso-turned-informer Angelo Lonardo dies in his sleep at age 95.

April 1: Great Britain activates a new Serious Organised Crime Agency, merging the National Crime Squad, the National Criminal Intelligence Service, the National Hi-Tech Crime Unit, the investigative and intelligence sections of HM Revenue & Customs on serious drug trafficking, and the Immigration Service's responsibilities for organized immigration crime.

April 4: Somali pirates seize the South Korean fishing boat *Dong Won 628*. The guided missile destroyer USS *Roosevelt* and Dutch frigate HNLMS *De Zeven Provinciën* give chase and fire warning shots, then retreat when the pirates threaten to execute 25 crew members. The hijackers hold their prize for 117 days before collecting $800,000 ransom. In Sicily, fugitive mafioso Bernardo Provenzano mentions Matteo Messina Denaro as his possible successor.

April 6: Federal jurors in New York City convict ex–NYPD detectives Stephen Caracappa and Louis Eppolito on racketeering charges, including eight murders committed as Mafia hitmen. On June 5 both receive life sentences without parole. A judge voids their convictions on June 30, noting that the statute of limitations has expired on a key charge of racketeering conspiracy. A federal appellate court reinstates the convictions on September 17, 2008. On March 6, 2009, Caracappa received life plus 80 years, while Eppolito is sentenced to life in prison plus 100 years. Both defendants are also fined more than $4 million each.

April 8: Police unearth eight corpses from a farmer's field near Shedden, Ontario, Canada. On April 9 the victims are identified as Bandidos MC members George Jesso, George Kriarakis, John Muscedere, Luis Manny Raposo, Francesco Salerajno, and Paul Sinopoli; plus prospective member Jamie Flanz and club associate Michael Trotta. On April 10 authorities charge five defendants with first-degree murder. They include Bandidos Brent Gardiner, Wayne Kellestine, and Frank Mather, plus common-law couple Eric Niessen and Kerry Morris. On May 5 prosecutors reduce charges for Niessen and Morris, naming them as accessories after the fact. On June 16 police in Winnipeg charge Bandidos Marcelo Aravena,

Dwight Mushey, and Michael Sandham with first-degree murder.

April 11: Police capture fugitive mafioso Bernardo Provenzano outside Corleone, Sicily, after 43 years in hiding.

April 13: Officers of the National Police Corps arrest an unnamed Moroccan citizen in Tarifa, Spain, on charges of affiliation with the Mafia. Authorities in Calabria, Italy, crack down on local mobsters, arresting Camorra boss Salvatore Terracciano and 11 associates, plus 'Ndrangheta leader Giuseppe Arena and chief lieutenant Francesco Gentile.

April 14: Police in Messina, Sicily, arrest five suspects in a sweep targeting Mafia and Camorra members.

April 18: President Bush pardons three defendants convicted of organized crime offenses: Karen Marie Edmonson (1978, distribution of methamphetamine), Mark Reuben Hale (1991, defrauding two Texas savings and loan institutions of $5 million), Karl Bruce Weber (1985, possession of cocaine with intent to distribute).

April 19: DEA agents in Los Angeles arrest 31 members of the Eastside Wilmas Gang and the Highland Park Gang on drug trafficking charges. Raiders seize eight pounds methamphetamine, one pound of cocaine, 23 vehicles, 14 firearms and $90,000 in cash.

April 20: Spanish police on the Balearic Islands of Majorca arrest fugitive Italian financier Marco Rodolfo del Vento, AKA "The Doctor," said to be an agent of Sicilian mafioso Biagio Crisafulli.

April 22: Ten pirates board the British yacht *Idle Vice* of Kip near Kannyakumari, Cape Comorin, India, stealing a life raft and other property.

April 24: Authorities in Philadelphia, Pa., stop intercept Joseph Mastronardo on his way home from Florida, seizing $500,000 from his car and another $2 million from his home.

April 30: Somalian pirates hijack a cargo ship, killing one of the crew, then release the vessel on May 7.

May: Italian police expose a sports corruption scandal involving six of the nation's top soccer teams: Juventus Football Club, Football Club Internazionale Milano, Associazione Calcio Milan, ACF Fiorentina, Società Sportiva Lazio, and Reggina Calcio. On July 4 Italian Football Federation prosecutor Stefano Palazzi calls for Juventus, AC Milan, ACF Fiorentina, and SS Lazio to be demoted from Serie A status, with penalty points imposed against each. On August 13 Palazzi seeks demotion of Reggina Calcio to Serie B, with penalty points and a fine equivalent to £68,000. On August 17 Reggina club president Pasquale "Lillo" Foti is fined £20,000 and banned from the game for 30 months. On the coast of Somalia, pirates hold three vessels hostage while demanding $500,000 ransom for each.

May 1: Glenn Merritt, president of the Bandidos MC's chapter in Bellingham, Wash., pleads guilty on federal charges of distributing methamphetamine and trafficking in motorcycle parts. He receives a four-year prison term in November.

May 2: Mexico's congress passes a bill legalizing the private personal use of all drugs, including opium and all opiate-based narcotics. President Vicente Fox Quesada promises to sign the bill, then changes his mind on May 3, under pressure from the U.S., and sends back to congress for changes.

May 3: Bernardo Provenzano faces trial for Mafia murders committed during the 1980s, participating via video-link from a maximum-security jail in Terni, Italy. Bandidos MC member Britt Anderson pleads guilty to threatening a federal informer in Seattle, Wash.

May 5: Merchants in Palermo, Sicily, celebrate a "Pizzo Free Day" of symbolic liberation from Mafia protection rackets. In Seattle, Wash., George Wegers — national president of the Bandidos MC — pleads guilty to federal racketeering charges, while prosecutors drop 14 other felony counts. He receives a two-year sentence in October.

May 6: Cuban-born mobster Jose Miguel Battle Sr., né Ramon Iglesias, pleads guilty to racketeering charges in New Jersey. He receives a 20-year prison term on January 15, 2007, and dies in custody on August 6, 2007.

May 10: Yakuza boss Seijiro Matsuo announces his retirement as leader of the Dōjin-kai clan in Kurume City, Fukuoka. War ensues between clan headquarters and the dissident Kyushu-Seidō-kai splinter group based in Ohmuta.

May 11: Mobsters Armando Botta and Frank Depergola plead guilty to loan-sharking in Springfield, Mass.

May 12: Officers of the *Guardia di Finanza* in Palermo, Sicily, freeze €30 million in assets owned by Mafia associate Ottavio Lo Cricchio, including a horse racing track.

May 13: Palermo's *Guardia di Finanza* strikes again, freezing villas and other assets of Mafia associate Vincenzo Piazza valued at €17.5 million.

May 14: While investigating corruption in Italy's athletic clubs, magistrate Giuseppe Narducci calls for all soccer "elites" to aid his inquiries.

May 15: Gambino Family member Gregory De Palma faces trial in Manhattan on racketeering charges. Jurors convict him on June 6, resulting in a 12-year sentence. De Palma dies at Butner

Federal Medical Prison in Butner, N.C., on November 20, 2009.

May 17: Camorra boss Paolo Di Lauro receives a 30-year sentence in Naples, Italy, on charges of Mafia association, extortion and drug smuggling. DEA spokesmen announce the culmination of "Operation Twin Oceans," targeting the Pablo Rayo-Montano cocaine syndicate based in Colombia. The three-year campaign has produced more than 100 arrests, plus seizures including 52 tons of cocaine and nearly $70 million in assets. FBI agents search a farm in Milford Township, Mich., for Jimmy Hoffa's remains, but leave empty-handed.

May 21: Authorities in Pittsburgh, Pa., dismiss Carl Valenti's RICO charges. FBI agents allege witness tampering. In Kurume, Fukuoka Prefecture, dissident factions of the Dōjin-kai Yakuza clan engage in gun battles for turf, following the retirement of boss Seijiro Matsuo.

May 22: Jurors in Melbourne, Australia, convict boxer-turned-gangster Danny Catania of setting a man on fire. Catania receives a six-year-minimum sentence.

May 26: Sicilian mafioso-turned-informer Francesco Marino Mannoia receives €1 million from the government to start a legitimate business. On the same day, anti–Mafia candidate Rita Borsellino loses Sicily's regional presidential election to incumbent and alleged Mafia associate Salvatore "Totò" Cuffaro.

May 31: A grand jury in Norristown, Pa., charge Joseph Vito Mastronardo Jr. and brother John with bookmaking and criminal conspiracy. Police arrest the brothers on June 5, seizing $2.7 million found in their possession. On the same day, a federal grand jury in New Jersey indicts mafioso William "Big Billy" D'Elia on charges of laundering $600,000 in illegal drug proceeds.

June 7: Prosecutors in Chicago release transcripts of recordings made by informer Frank Calabrese Jr., of conversations with his father, Outfit loan-shark Frank Calabrese Sr. In Buffalo, N.Y., authorities jail Mafia associate Leonard Mordino and 10 other alleged participants in a cocaine-trafficking ring.

June 9: Unknown gunmen kill alleged mafioso Domenico Farina in Catania, Sicily. In Connecticut, a grand jury indicts Genovese Family member Matthew "Matty the Horse" Ianniello for racketeering and collecting $500,000 from corrupt trash haulers.

June 10: Italy's *Guardia di Finanza* seizes property worth €1.2 million from Francesco Cannizzo, alleged boss of the Tortoriciani Mafia clan in Messina, Sicily.

June 12: Carabinieri officers arrest mafioso Salvatore Lupo in Catania, Sicily. In New Jersey, De-

Cavalcante Family *consigliere* Stefano "Steve the Truck Driver" Vitabile receives a life sentence for ordering the January 1992 murder of acting boss John D'Amato, motivated by D'Amato's rumored bisexuality.

June 16: Albanian mobster Alex Rudaj receives a 27-year sentence in New York City for racketeering and extortion. French gangster Jacques "Mad Jacky" Imbert receives a four-year prison term in Marseille, for extorting money from a Paris businessmen in the 1990s (reduced to two years on appeal, on January 2, 2008). The Detroit *Free Press* publishes a 56-page FBI memo from January 1976, contending that Jimmy Hoffa was murdered by mobsters who feared his re-election as IBT president.

June 19: Mafioso Francesco Frassetto pleads guilty to federal drug trafficking charges in Rochester, N.Y. In Palermo, Sicily, prosecutors charge legislator Gaspare Giudice with Mafia association, fraudulent bankruptcy, money-laundering and extortion. A court subsequently acquits him.

June 20: The city of San Jose, Calif., settles a Hells Angels lawsuit by agreeing to pay the club nearly $800,000 for shooting three dogs during raids against the local clubhouse and nine bikers' homes conducted on January 21, 1998. Previous settlements in the same case include $990,000 from the Santa Clara County Sheriff's Department, plus some $50,000 each from the cities of Santa Clara and Gilroy. The settlements follow an April 2005 ruling by the 9th U.S. Circuit Court of Appeals which found the raids to be unnecessarily intrusive. In Palermo, Sicily, police cap a four-year Mafia investigation — "Operation Gotha" — with dawn raids netting 45 prisoners.

June 21: Czech officials announce fugitive mafioso Luigi Putrone's extradition to Italy. In Manhattan, DEA spokesmen announce the climax of "Operation Double Identity," resulting in arrests of 56 Colombian heroin traffickers.

June 25: John Denoncourt, an associate of the Hells Angels MC, suffers fatal gunshot wounds outside a pizzeria in Manchester, N.H. On June 27 police charge Christopher Legere, a member of the rival Outlaws, with his murder.

July 2: Pirates in the Strait of Malacca board two UN-chartered ships bearing construction supplies to tsunami-ravaged Aceh, on Sumatra, Indonesia. They damage equipment on one ship, while stealing cash and personal belongings from crewmen on the other.

July 9: The dramatic series *Brotherhood* premieres on HBO. Although set in New Hampshire, the series is a thinly-veiled pastiche of Boston mobster James "Whitey" Bulger and his brother William, former president of the Massachusetts State Senate. After three seasons, the series is canceled in April 2009.

July 19: Jurors in Melbourne, Australia, convict hitman Carl Anthony Williams of killing victim Michael Marshall. Williams receives a 27-year sentence.

July 21: France's Consultative Commission on National Defence Secrets declines to release documents requested by investigating magistrates Renaud Van Ruymbeke and Xaviere Simeoni in the Taiwan frigates scandal. In Philadelphia, Pa., police arrest 15 members of The Breed MC on charges of trafficking in methamphetamine worth more than $11.25 million between May 2005 and June 2006. Raiders seize 22 pounds of crystal meth, nearly $500,000 in cash and bank deposits, 44 firearms, 10 homemade bombs, 24 motorcycles, and various other vehicles.

July 26: DEA agents in Seattle, Wash., arrest 14 Somali immigrants on charges of shipping imported khat aboard commercial airliners around the state of Washington, and to Illinois, Maine, Massachusetts, Minnesota, Ohio, Utah, and Washington, D.C. In New York, DEA agents and state police officers cap "Operation Somalia Express" by arresting 31 persons on charges of smuggling more than 25 tons of khat, valued in excess of $10 million, from the Horn of Africa to the U.S. During the 18-month campaign, raiders have seized five tons of khat and $2 million in cash.

July 28: Federal jurors in Santa Ana, Calif., convict four Aryan Brotherhood leaders on charges of conspiracy to commit murder to extend their control over drug trafficking, gambling and other prisoners.

August 2: A superior court judge in San Diego, Calif., sentences three Mexican Mafia members following their conviction on kidnapping charges. Julio Contreras and Arthur Torres receive life terms, while Francisco Gongora is sentenced to 28 years.

August 4: A Colombian appellate court in Ibaque seeks to reduce the prison term imposed on Cali Cartel member Henry Loaiza-Ceballos from 18 to 11 years, thus making him eligible for immediate release. Prosecutors counter on December 19 by accusing Loaiza-Ceballos of complicity in the terrorist murders of 100 victims around Trujillo between 1988 and 1990.

August 8: Four members of the Outlaws MC and a female companion suffer gunshot wounds in South Dakota's Custer State Park. Police arrest two Canadian Hells Angels as suspects in the shooting.

August 10: Police discover a "Mafia graveyard" on property near the former hideout of mafioso Bernardo Provenzano, outside Corleone, Sicily. Excavation reveals two skulls with shotgun wounds, a sternum with bullets wounds, two jawbones, and several human vertebrae. In Massachusetts, a federal appellate court affirms the 2005 reduction of sentence for Boston mafioso Vincent "The Animal" Ferrara.

August 11: Sicilian politician Onofrio Fratello receives an 18-month suspended prison term after admitting his affiliation with the Mafia.

August 14: Mexican Mafia member Jose Becerra pleads guilty to federal racketeering charges in Los Angeles. He receives a 37-month prison term on December 18. In Ibaque, Colombia, an appellate court seeks to free Cali Cartel officer Henry Loaiza-Ceballos with seven years remaining on his 18-year prison term. Authorities block that effort on December 19, by charging Loaiza-Ceballos with the murders of 100 victims slain by paramilitary groups his cartel supported between 1988 and 1994.

August 15: President Bush pardons six defendants convicted of organized crime offenses: Randall Leece Deal (1972, liquor law violations & conspiracy to viol liquor laws), William Henry Eagle (1972, possessing an unregistered still, carrying on the business of a distiller without giving the required bond, and manufacturing mash on other than lawfully qualified premises), Kenneth Clifford Foner (1991, conspiracy to impede functions of the FDIC, commit embezzlement as a bank officer, make false entries in the records of an FDIC-insured bank, and commit bank fraud), Victoria Diane Frost (1994, conspiracy to possess and distribute L-ephedrine hydrochloride), John Louis Ribando (1976 and 1978, possession with intent to distribute marijuana), and Jerry Dean Walker (1989, possession with intent to distribute cocaine). DEA Administrator Karen Tandy announces the culmination of "Operation Black Gold Rush," targeting traffickers in black tar heroin. The campaign produces 138 arrests in 15 U.S. cities and 10 indictments in eight federal judicial districts, along with state charges. Raiders seize more than 17 kilos of heroin and some $500,000 in cash.

August 16: FBI agents and Washington State Police raid a Hells Angels clubhouse in Spokane, Wash., seeking suspects and evidence related to a club brawl with rival Mongols at the Harrah's Casino in Laughlin, Nev., on April 27, 2002. On the same day, U.S. Coast Guard officers capture fugitive Mexican drug lord Eduardo Arellano Félix aboard the yacht *Dock Holiday*, 15 miles off the coast of Baja California Sur. Arellano Félix receives a life prison term on November 5, 2007, after pleading guilty to money-laundering and running a criminal enterprise. In Hasbrouck Heights, N.J., FBI agents arrest mafioso-turned-informer Peter "Petey Cap" Caporino and his wife on illegal gambling charges. Caporino pleads guilty in July 2007 and receives a seven-year prison term on September 7, 2007.

August 17: Authorities in Montreal, Québec, extradite mafioso Vito Rizzuto to face trial on federal racketeering charged in Brooklyn, N.Y. On May 4, 2007, Rizzuto pleads guilty to being present at the 1981 murder of Bonanno Family *caporegimes* Philip Giaccone, Alphonse Indelicato, and Dominick Trinchera. He receives a 10-year sentence, to be followed by a three-year supervised release.

August 27: Police in San Antonio, Tex., find Richard Cobia Jr. and Lewis Lopez shot to death on the city's south side. Prosecutors later charge and convict Mexican Mafia members in the double murder.

August 28: Unknown killers, presumed to be vengeful members of the 'Ndrangheta, slaughter businessman Angelo Cottarelli, his wife and son, at their home near Brescia, Italy. Police report that all three victims were tortured, perhaps for information related to missing money obtained through a series of frauds.

August 31: Mobster Anthony "Little Tony" Zizzo vanishes after leaving his Chicago home. Police find his car abandoned at a restaurant in Melrose Park, Ill., but report "no signs of foul play." Zizzo remains missing.

September: The UN Office on Drugs and Crime reports that Afghanistan's opium harvest will be a world record of 6,100 metric tons — approximately 92 percent of the world's total supply. Unknown gunmen kill 18-year-old Salvatore Montani, a relative of mobster Andrea Montani, in Naples, Italy. In Ontario, Canada, police cap an 18-month investigation of the Hells Angels MC with raids netting 27 prisoners, illegal drugs valued in excess of $3 million, and other property including automobiles worth $300,000, motorcycles valued at $140,000, and $470,000 in cash.

September 5: Police in London, England, arrest Raffaele Caldarelli, a fugitive Sicilian mafioso facing a 20-year sentence imposed in 1999 on drug and weapons charges.

September 11: Israeli gangster Hai Waknine receives a 10-year federal prison term for racketeering in Los Angeles.

September 12: A court in Mumbai, India, convicts four members of Mushtaq "Tiger" Memon's family for their role in deadly terrorist bombings of March 1993. Michael Plante, testifying at the drug trial of Hells Angels member Ronaldo Lising and codefendant Nima Ghavami, admits that he has received $500,000 from the RCMP as an informer, with a promise of $500,000 more at the conclusion of his testimony. Plante also received a car, a motorcycle, and airline tickets to Mexico,

plus other fringe benefits. In Los Angeles, Mexican Mafia leader Peter Ojeda pleads guilty to federal narcotics and racketeering charges. He receives a 14-year sentence on December 18.

September 13: A federal grand jury in Los Angeles indicts 185 Mexican Mafia members on RICO conspiracy and narcotics trafficking charges. Defendants include Jose Juan Alvarez, Elvin Ambrocio, Araceli Bravo, Luis Castro, Reuben "Night Owl" Castro, Noe Chavez, Ronaldo "Casper" Cruz, Melida "La Dona" Flores, Juana Fuentes, Jorge Sanchez Monroy, Juan Morales Montes, Marlon David Penate, Jose Morales Perez, Michael "Mousie" Pineda, Jesusita Ramirez, Mervyn Nelson Sanchez, Edwin Schaad, and Efrain Ruiz Torres.

September 15: Police in Trapani, Italy, detain two businessmen and a wine maker for questioning in the August 28 murders of Angelo Cottarelli and his family.

September 20: Bonanno Family *caporegimes* Louis "Louie HaHa" Attanasio Jr. and Peter Calabrese plead guilty in New York City to the April 1984 murder of Cesare "The Tall Guy" Bonventre. Both receive 15-year federal prison terms.

September 25: Police in Cambridgeshire, England, cap "Operation Keymer" with a series of raids on marijuana growers continuing through October 6. Nine raids result in 12 arrests and seizure of some 28,000 plants valued at £2.5 million.

September 26: Andrew Fastow strikes a plea bargain with federal prosecutors in the Enron case, accepting a 10-year prison term and two years' probation, plus forfeiture of $23.8 million. He is scheduled for release on December 17, 2011. Cali Cartel leaders Gilberto and Miguel Rodríguez Orejuela receive 30-year federal prison terms in Miami, Fla., after pleading guilty to charges of conspiring to import cocaine. On November 16 both brothers plead guilty to an additional count of conspiring to engage in money-laundering, receiving concurrent sentences of 87 months.

September 28: "Operation Triple Play," a joint DEA-RCMP investigation of ecstasy traffickers, jails 19 suspects. Raiders seize more than 50,000 ecstasy pills valued in excess of $1 million, several guns, and over $100,000 in cash.

October: U.S. Postal Inspection Service agents raid the home of "D.C. Madam" Deborah Jeane Palfrey, seizing documents related to prostitution and money-laundering, while a court order freezes Palfrey's bank accounts containing more than $500,000.

October 3: Mexican Mafia member Marco Diaz pleads guilty to federal racketeering conspiracy charges in Los Angeles.

October 5: Russian President Vladimir Putin

announces passage of new legislation mandating relocation of all Russian casinos to "uninhabited areas" beginning on July 1, 2009. The designated locations for approved gambling include Kaliningrad; Azov City, Krasnodar; Sibirskaya Moneta, Altai Krai; and Russky Island, Primorski.

October 7: A gunman murders journalist Anna Stepanovna Politkovskaya in the elevator of her apartment building in Moscow, Russia. Prosecutors bring three suspects — including one FSB agent — before the Moscow District Military Court in October 2008. On November 25 their attorney says an unnamed politician may have ordered the slaying. Jurors acquit the defendants on February 19, 2009. Russia's Supreme Court overturns the acquittals on June 25, 2009, and orders a new trial.

October 13: Pirates board the Austrian yacht *Yab Yum*, anchored off Navimca Cumana, Venezuela, stealing two outboard engines.

October 14: Unknown gunmen wound gangster-turned-prosecution witness Michael "Eyes" Pastras in Brunswick, Victoria, Australia.

October 16: Aging mafioso Clarence "Chauncey" Smaldone dies of natural causes at a hospice in Denver, Colo.

October 30: Unidentified gunmen murder Giovanni Montani, another seemingly innocent relative of imprisoned mobster Andrea Montani, in Naples, Italy. In Palermo, Sicily, agents of the *Guardia di Finanza* seize goods and real estate worth €104 million from businessman Angelo Prisinzano, accused of Mafia association.

October 31: Mafioso Michael James Genovese dies of natural causes in Pittsburgh, Pa., at age 87. Unknown gunmen kill three persons in Naples, Italy, during a turf war between rival Camorra families. Eleven prosecutors assigned to anti–Mafia campaigns in Catania, Sicily, resign after budget cuts require them to personally finance their investigations.

November: Federal prosecutors in New Jersey charge mafioso William "Big Billy" D'Elia with soliciting the murder of a codefendant in his money-laundering case. D'Elia pleads guilty to reduced charges of money-laundering conspiracy and witness tampering on March 12, 2008. He receives a nine-year prison term on November 24, 2008. His projected release date is August 13, 2014.

November 1: The Stardust Resort and Casino closes after 48 years of operation in Las Vegas, Nev. On the same day, former KGB/FSB officer Alexander Litvinenko suddenly falls ill in London, England, dying on November 23. Postmortem examination reveals that he was poisoned with radioactive polonium-210. Litvinenko's widow accuses Russian agents of his murder.

November 2: Police suspect Camorra members in the near-fatal stabbing of a victim in Naples, Italy.

November 3: Italy's government vows to post 1,000 extra police officers in Naples following a rash of violence that has claimed 12 lives in 10 days.

November 6: Pirates seize the coal ship MV *Veesham I*, registered in the United Arab Emirates, demanding $150,000 ransom for release of 14 crewmen. Agents of Somalia's Islamic Courts Union liberate the ship and capture the pirates on November 8. In Wilmington, Del., police fatally shoot Pagans MC member Derek J. Hale while trying to arrest him. On November 9, Delaware State Police Sergeant Melissa Zebley names Hale as one of 12 Pagans sought for drug trafficking.

November 7: In Somalia, troops from the Union of Islamic Courts storm the hostage oil tanker *Veesham I*, killing two of six pirates aboard and capturing the rest.

November 9: Nuestra Familia member Leticia Salcido receives an eight-year prison term in Salinas, Calif., for drug trafficking.

November 12: Police arrest fugitive Nuestra Familia member Robert Patrick "Bubba" Hanrahan at San Ysidro, Calif., as he re-enters the U.S. from Mexico.

November 13: In San Diego, Calif., Patricia Palacios — wife of imprisoned Mexican drug lord Gilberto Camacho — receives a two-year federal prison term for laundering cartel money. She also forfeits her house, cars and jewelry to the government. In Detroit, a federal judge sentences two members of the Devil's Disciples MC and five associates to prison terms ranging from 30 to 97 months, following their convictions on charges of manufacturing methamphetamine.

November 14: DEA agents cap "Operation Burnout" with arrests of 10 persons in Pittsburgh, Pa. The suspects — and two still at large — stand accused of selling fentanyl-laced heroin which has killed at least 10 addicts since June.

November 17: Somalia's Supreme Islamic Courts Council bans use and distribution of khat, sparking street protests in Kismayo.

November 22: Howard Roberts, deputy chief of police for Nottinghamshire, England, advocates legalization of heroin and provision of the drug to addicts without charge under Britain's National Health Service. He estimates that a yearly supply of heroin would cost £12,000 per user, while addicts steal at least £45,000 worth of property a year. In Montreal, Québec, police cap "Operation Coliseum" by jailing 91 alleged Mafia members and associates. One of those arrested is alleged godfather Nicolo Rizzuto, charged with gangsterism, conspiracy and importing drugs.

December 1: In Montreal, Québec, police arrest a provincial customs officer and two other persons on charges of conspiring with the Rizzuto crime family. Authorities still seek 87 other defendants. In Mexico, Felipe de Jesús Calderón Hinojosa assumes office as president, declaring war on drug traffickers.

December 4: Judges in Palermo grill Villabate mobster Antonino Mandala on charges of Mafia association. On the same day, Spanish prosecutors meet in Alicante to discuss organized crime at a conference organized by the State General Prosecutor. In Boston, Mass., mafioso Carmen "The Big Cheese" DiNunzio pleads not guilty to charges of extortion and illegal gambling.

December 5: In Messina, Sicily, Judge Bruno Finocchiaro sentences mafioso Luigi Galli and 17 members of his Giostra crime family to prison terms totaling 218 years. Journalists in northern Italy report that bands of thieves are hijacking truckloads of Parmesan cheese for black-market sale.

December 11: A federal judge in Los Angeles orders convicted Israeli racketeer Hai Waknine to pay his victims $646,000 in restitution. In Mexico, federal authorities launch "Operation Michoacan" against the La Familia Michoacana drug cartel. By early 2010 the campaign claims the lifes of 50 Mexican soldiers, 100 police officers, and 500 cartel gunmen. New England mafioso-turned-federal informer Angelo "Sonny" Mercurio dies from a pulmonary embolism in Little Rock, Ark.

December 12: Police in San Bernardino, Calif., arrest 43 Mexican Mafia members and associates on conspiracy charges. Several of those detained are members of the San Manuel Indian Tribe.

December 18: Mexican Mafia kingpin Peter Ojeda receives a 14-year federal prison term after pleading guilty racketeering and narcotics violations in Santa Ana, Calif.

December 19: Judge Antonella Pappalardo acquits David Costa, regional councilor of the Union of Christian and Centre Democrats, on charges of Mafia association in Palermo, Sicily. Leaders of the European Union voice concern over escalating gangland-style murders in Bulgaria, slated to join the EU in January 2007.

December 20: Minister for Justice Michael McDowell announces that the government will consider passage of U.S.-style racketeering statutes as part of a proposed legislative crackdown on organized crime. Authorities in Naples, Italy, log the city's 75th gangland murder for 2006.

December 21: Carabinieri officers in Bari, Italy, arrest eight women accused of Mafia association, while announcing their search for 100 more local suspect. President Bush grants executive clemency

to seven defendants convicted of organized crime offenses. He pardons William Sidney Baldwin Sr. (1981, conspiracy to possess marijuana), Marie Georgette Ginette Briere (1982, possession of cocaine with intent to distribute), George Thomas Harley (1984, aiding and abetting the distribution of cocaine), Patricia Ann Hultman (1985, conspiracy to possess with intent to distribute and to distribute cocaine), Eric William Olson (1984, conspiracy to possess with intent to distribute, possession with intent to distribute, possession of, and use of hashish), and Thomas R. Reece (1969, violating the Internal Revenue Code pertaining to alcohol). Bush also commutes the 262-month prison term of Phillip Anthony Emmert (1992, conspiracy to distribute methamphetamine) to five years' supervised release.

December 22: Fugitive Camorra boss Raffaele Caldarelli is jailed in London, England, while British authorities prepare his extradition to Italy.

December 24: Rino Foschi, sporting director of Sicily's Serie A soccer league, received a severed goat's head at his home in Palermo. Police interpret the "gift" as a Mafia warning.

December 26: Imprisoned Mexican Mafia member Reuben Castro, already serving life for murder, pleads not guilty to new federal racketeering charges in Los Angeles.

December 27: "Drug mafia" gunmen kill 16 victims during a wild night of violence in Rio de Janeiro, Brazil.

December 28: Canadian authorities grant bail to 14 defendants, including a former customs agent, an Air Canada baggage handler and a taxi driver, arrested before Christmas on charges of conspiring to import cocaine through Pierre Elliott Trudeau International Airport in Dorval, Québec. *Guardia di Finanza* officers in Palermo, Sicily, report 430 seizures of goods valued at €490 million, including 49 companies, from local mafiosi. In Caserta, Italy, police seize goods valued at €10 million from waste-handling entrepreneur Cipriano Chianese.

December 29: Federal prosecutors in Florida announce the indictment of 96-year-old mafioso Albert "Chinky" Facchiano on charges of racketeering and witness intimidation. Italian police detain model Mercedes Brito from the Dominican Republic — unrelated to a Venezuelan model of the same name — as she deplanes with 98 packets of cocaine in her stomach, weighing 2.6 pounds and valued at nearly £1million. Serbian Prime Minister Vojislav Kostunica announces that his government has been purged of underworld corruption. Alleged Genovese Family associate Charles Steinberg pleads guilty to federal racketeering charges in Fort Lauderdale, Fla. In Somalia, guerrilla warriors of Transitional Federal Parliament, supported by Ethiopian troops, capture Mogadishu. Local sales of khat quickly resume.

2007 Eleven U.S. states permit casino gambling, while Indian tribes operate 354 gaming facilities on reservations in 28 states. South African legislators pass Criminal Law Amendment Act 32, targeting human traffickers and sex offenders. Legal slot machines in the U.S. reap profits of $25 billion. The International Narcotics Control Board reports 75.2 tons of oxycodone manufactured worldwide. The U.S. has the highest per capita consumption rate, followed by Canada, Denmark, Australia, and Norway.

January 1: Francesco Forgione, head of Italy's parliamentary anti–Mafia commission, blames underworld manipulation of health-care contracts for a spate of recent deaths in Palermo hospitals.

January 2: Prosecutors in Palermo, Sicily, oppose Judge Marina Pino's plan to dismiss murder charges in the August 1989 Mafia slaying of policeman Nino Agostino and his wife. Police in Catania arrest fugitive mafioso Carmelo Puglisi. In Brezno, Central Slovakia, prosecution witness Matej Zachar dies in a fall from the window of his sixth-floor apartment, jeopardizing the murder case filed against mob boss Mikuláš Černák. Mexican authorities launch "Operation Baja California" against drug smugglers, fielding a force of 2,620 soldiers, 21 airplanes, nine helicopters, 28 ships, 247 tactical vehicles and 10 drug-sniffing dogs.

January 3: Italian detectives seek Vatican assistance in deciphering a "Mafia Bible," recently published in Latin by Sicilian mafioso Matteo Messina Denaro. London's *Daily Mail* exposes Eastern European "baby factories" operating in Athens, Greece, run by Albanian and Russian mobsters, where Bulgarian and Romanian women selected for physical beauty produce "made-to-order" newborns for international sale.

January 5: Unknown gunmen murder Sumiyoshi-kai Yakuza boss Ryoichi Sugiura in Tokyo, Japan. Hours later, Sumiyoshi-kai retaliate by firing on local Yamaguchi-gumi offices.

January 7: Police in Manchester, England, announce their search for Ann Hathaway, wife of an imprisoned mobster, sought for her involvement in a crime network spanning Western Europe. Police in Hong Kong arrest 101 alleged Triad gangsters on various charges.

January 8: Police in Florence, Italy, report the capture of fugitive Sicilian mafioso Antonino Finocchiaro and a female companion.

January 9: Federal jurors in Los Angeles convict Aryan Brotherhood leaders Robert "Blinky" Griffin and John "Youngster" Stinson on five counts of murder. In Israel, Public Security Minister Avi Dichter announces a campaign to dis-

rupt underworld control of bottle recycling programs.

January 10: A court in Skopje, Macedonian, sentences fugitive Stanislava Poletan *in absentia* for conspiring to import 486 kilos of cocaine. Octavio Líster, chief of the Dominican Republic's Corruption Prevention Department, announces indictments against multiple defendants charged with embezzling millions from the Finance Ministry's Pensions and Retirements Department.

January 11: Federal agents arrest Italian mobster Giuseppe Giambrone in Fort Myers, Fla., on charges of making a false statement on an immigration form in 2003.

January 12: Federal prosecutors in Chicago charge John Thomas Ambrose, a former supervisory inspector of the U.S. Marshals Service's Great Lakes Regional Fugitive Task Force, with leaking information on protected witnesses to mobsters facing prosecution. Jurors convict Ambrose on April 27, 2009. His presumed release date from federal prison is September 10, 2013.

January 15: Colombian police arrest Eugenio Montoya Sanchez, a fugitive leader of the Norte Del Valle Cartel, after a shootout with his bodyguards.

January 16: Italian prosecutors announce discovery of new evidence linking art dealer Gianfranco Becchina and the Mafia to sale of stolen artifacts in Japan, during 1991.

January 18: Scotland Yard detectives arrest fugitive "godmother" Ann Hathaway, wife of imprisoned killer and drug trafficker Antonio Rinzivillo, on a warrant issued in Italy.

January 19: Ex–federal prosecutor George Phillips, now head of the Mississippi Department of Public Safety, asks Louisiana officials to reduce the prison term of "Dixie Mafia" member Bobby Joe Fabian, based on his aid in solving a murder case.

January 20: Mexican authorities extradite Gulf Cartel leader Osiel Cárdenas Guillén to Houston, Tex., for trial on drug trafficking charges. British police announce that they have identified the slayer of Alexander Litvinenko as former Russian spy Andrei Lugovoi. The Crown Prosecution Service calls for Lugovoi's extradition on May 22, followed by a formal request from the British Foreign Office on May 28. Russian authorities refuse extradition on July 5, 2007.

January 22: The IMB reports that incidents of piracy decreased worldwide in 2006, while increasing in Nigerian waters. In Budapest, Hungary, defendant Laszlo Wapper receives a 15-year sentence for killing mobster Bulcsu Slavy, AKA "The King of Balaton," in 1997 and hiding the corpse in a friend's garage for seven years.

January 23: Trial begins in New York City for

mafioso brothers Anthony and Chris Colombo, charged with racketeering. Jurors deadlock in the case, whereupon Anthony pleads guilty to reduced charges on June 26, 2007.

January 26: Police in Buzias, Romania, arrest two brothers and their wives on charges of human trafficking, money-laundering and electronics theft in European Union countries. In Skopje, Macedonia, Justice Minister Mihajlo Manevski launches a two-year program of cooperation with Italy's Ministry of Justice and the Sicilian-based International Institute of Higher Studies in Criminal Sciences, to suppress organized crime. In Biloxi, Miss., convicted racketeer and drug trafficker Howard Leroy Hobbs announces plans to seek re-election as Harrison County's sheriff, a post he held for 12 years prior to being imprisoned in 1984. Hobbs loses the election and dies on March 3, 2008.

January 27: President Felipe Calderón vows to wage "permanent war" against organized crime in Mexico.

January 28: NYPD officers find beating victim Roberta Shalaby outside a Hells Angels clubhouse in Manhattan's East Village. A search of the clubhouse reveals no evidence linking Angels to the assault, and club members subsequently sue the city for damages.

January 29: NYPD SWAT officers raid a Hells Angels clubhouse, briefly detaining several members who are subsequently released without charges.

January 30: DOJ spokesmen in New York announce the arrest of 11 Gambino Family members and two Sicilian mafiosi — Francesco Nania and Vito Rappa — on charges including racketeering, loan-sharking, extortion, bribery of a federal official, money-laundering, attempted bank fraud, check forgery, interstate travel in aid of racketeering, and smuggling conspiracy. Police in Scotland arrest Brian Howes and Kerry Ann Shanks on charges filed by a federal grand jury in Arizona, on September 27, 2006, accusing them of operating clandestine methamphetamine labs across the U.S.

January 31: Alexander Yelin, deputy chief of the Russian Interior Ministry's department on organized crime, announces that "more than 2,000 industrial entities have fallen under criminal control" since the demise of Soviet communism. Deputy Interior Minister Oleg Safonov reports that 446 crime syndicates "with a complex internal structure" presently operate in Russia. In New York City, federal agents arrest 13 Gambino Family members and associates on charges of extortion, racketeering, loan-sharking and money-laundering. Massachusetts Attorney General Martha Coakley warns that expansion of legal

gambling threatens the state with increased organized crime and higher expenses for law enforcement.

February: Sicilian authorities seize assets valued at €30 million, held by front men for mafioso Antonio Rotolo.

February 1: Genovese Family *caporegime* Renaldi "Ray" Ruggiero pleads guilty to federal racketeering charges in Fort Lauderdale, Fla.

February 2: DOJ spokesmen report that unspecified disciplinary action has been taken against Assistant U.S. Attorney Jeffrey Auerhahn in Boston, because he "engaged in professional misconduct and exercised poor judgment" during prosecution of New England racketeers in the early 1990s.

February 5: Unknown gunmen kill Yakuza boss Ryoichi Sugiura as he drives through Tokyo, Japan.

February 10: A federal grand jury in Brooklyn, N.Y., charges 19 members of the Bonanno Family with multiple racketeering offenses. Defendants include acting underboss Nicholas Santora and acting *consigliere* Anthony Rabito.

February 11: A gun battle between drug dealers, vigilante "militia" forces, and police claims nine lives in Rio de Janeiro, Brazil. Israeli Minister Daniel Friedman announces plans to appoint new judges and prosecutors whose sole job will be to preside over cases involving organized crime.

February 12: Social-Democratic Party general board member Slavko Linic accuses Croatian Prime Minister Ivo Sanader of "protecting the Mafia." Pirates pursue the yacht *Gypsy Moth IV* in the Gulf of Aden but fail to board the vessel.

February 13: Police in Naples, Italy, impound the entire suburban neighborhood of Casalnuovo, built with laundered underworld funds. Raiders seal 50 new buildings containing more than 300 flats, plus 22 small villas, all valued in excess of $84 million.

February 15: Police in Tokyo, Japan, find Kazuyoshi Kudo, head of the Kokusui-kai Yakuza clan, shot dead at his home. Evidence suggests a suicide.

February 16: Drug cartel gunmen kill six victims in Baja California, Chihuahua, Michoacán, Nuevo Leon, and Sinaloa, Mexico. Officers of Mexico's Federal Preventive Police arrest 10 suspects, with five officers wounded in the process.

February 19: Israeli police commander Moshe Karadi resigns in the midst of scandal linking senior officers to leaders of organized crime. Near Guatemala City, Guatemala, police find three visiting Salvadorean politicians and their driver dead in a burned and bullet-riddled car. The victims include Central American Parliament members Eduardo D'Aubuisson, Jose Ramon Gonzalez, and William Pichinte.

February 21: Authorities in Guatemala charge four policemen with the February 19 murders of three Salvadorean politicians.

February 25: Pirates hijack the MV *Rozen*, a UN-chartered cargo ship delivering food to northeastern Somalia. Somali authorities arrest four suspects on February 27, while four others retain command of the ship and 12 hostage crewmen. The remaining hijackers release the *Rozen* and two other captured vessels on April 6.

February 26: Guatemalan President Oscar Berger blames organized criminal gangs for the fatal shooting of four policemen held at Boqueron prison in Cuilapa, on suspicion of murdering three visiting Salvadorean politicians. The shooting sparks a 12-hour riot, resulting in the arrest of the prison's director and 21 employees.

February 28: Sandro De Bernardin, Italy's ambassador to Israel, protests recent comments by an Israeli commission of inquiry into suspected police corruption warning that Israel was "going the way of Sicily." Attorney General Alberto Gonzales announces the culmination of "Operation Imperial Emperor," targeting Mexican drug lord Victor Emilio Cazares-Gastellum. Raiders arrest 66 cartel members nationwide, bringing the total of arrests over 20 months to 400. Seizures during the campaign include 27,229 pounds of marijuana, 9,512 pounds of cocaine, 705 pounds of methamphetamine, 227 pounds of pure methamphetamine, 11 pounds of heroin, 100 guns, 94 vehicles, and $45.2 million in cash. In Melbourne, Australia, drug dealer Carl Williams pleads guilty to killing mobsters Mark Mallia, Jason Moran and Lewis Moran, plus conspiracy to murder rival Mario Condello. Williams receives multiple life prison terms. A fellow inmate beats him to death at HM Prison Barwon on April 19, 2010.

March 4: Ex-Israeli mobster Ron Gonen announces publication of a memoir detailing his life in organized crime and reports that he was recently expelled from WITSEC after 18 years in hiding, for co-authoring the book with writer Dave Copeland.

March 6: Prosecutors in Montreal, Québec, release documents accusing Mafia underboss Francesco del Balso and accomplice Lorenzo Giordano of operating an illegal bookmaking syndicate that earned some $500 million between December 2004 and November 2005.

March 7: Spokesmen for the United Nations World Food Program announce that piracy has prevented the agency from delivering 2,400 metric tons of food to Somalia. In Sicily, police arrest 21 alleged mafiosi, including boss Cesare Lombardozzi in Agrigento.

March 8: British mobster Terry Adams receives a seven-year sentence for money-laundering, and

is ordered to pay £750,000 compensation for the £1m he laundered. In southern Romania, police capture fugitive Italian mobster Antonio Constantin, sentenced to 25 years *in absentia* for his role as a senior member of the Sacra Corona Unita crime syndicate.

March 10: Police in San Bernardino County, Calif., find an abandoned truck containing marijuana valued at $20 million.

March 13: Mafioso Francesco Madonia dies at a prison hospital in Naples, Italy, while serving a life sentence for murder.

March 15: Police in Frankfurt, German, arrest Serbian businessman Andrija Drašković on an Italian warrant charging him with international organized crime activity. In Mexico City, police raid the palatial home of Zhenli Ye Gon, alleged supplier of precursor chemicals to illegal methamphetamine produces. The raiders seize $207 million, 18 million pesos, €200,000, 113,000 Hong Kong dollars, 11 gold Mexican coins, a large cache of jewelry, seven vehicles, and a drug lab under construction. Officers miss Zhenli but arrest nine other persons.

March 16: Dutch officials in The Hague debate plans to extradite fugitive 'Ndrangheta member "Francesco S." to Italy. The alleged drug trafficker has been jailed in Amsterdam since June.

March 18: Police in Galati, Romania, arrest loan-shark and "Yakuza pawn" Takahiro Kawaguchi, sought by INTERPOL officers since 2004. In Belgrade, Serbia, ex–police chief Marko Nicovic claims that Kosovo police and Albanian military units are controlled by "the notorious Muslim Albanian mafia." U.S. Coast Guard officers find 42,845 pounds of cocaine aboard the Panamanian flagged motor vessel *Gatun*, near Isla de Coiba, Panama.

March 19: Police stage pre-dawn raids in Naples, Italy, jailing some 200 suspected Camorra members. Police dogs in Johor Baru, Malaysia, uncover a cache of pirated CDs and DVDs valued at $3 million. Officers arrest three suspects, while local mobsters place a bounty on the dogs, called Flo and Lucky. Offshore from Parque Nacional Colba, Panama, a strike force of Panamanian police and DEA agents seize a boat carrying 19.4 metric tons of cocaine, arresting 12 crewmen.

March 20: Mexican authorities seize $207 million in cash from a drug cartel warehouse in Mexico City.

March 21: Two pirate craft pursue a yacht in the Red Sea, off the coast of Yemen, but the raiders fail to board their target.

March 22: Washington's State Gambling Commission announces plans to revoke the license of Frank S. Nakayama, a security supervisor at

Ringo's Little Vegas Casino in Spokane Valley, based on his association with the Hells Angels MC.

March 27: Police in Belgium, France, Italy and Luxembourg stage 40 coordinated raids in a crackdown on organized crime in the European Union, sparked by reports linking two Italian members of the European Parliament to the Mafia. In Kiev, Ukraine, unknown gunmen murder Russian businessman Maxim "Mad Max" Kurochkin outside a courthouse where his trial in progress on blackmail charges.

March 28: "Operation Eliminacion," conducted by the New York Organized Crime Drug Enforcement Strike Force, produces 11 arrests in New York and Colombia, targeting members of a Colombian heroin trafficking ring.

March 29: Federal prosecutors in Detroit, Mich., release an indictment issued under seal on December 15, 2006, charging 17 members of the Black Mafia Family with drug trafficking and money-laundering. Defendants include gang founders Demetrius and Terry Flenory. In November 2007 the brothers plead guilty to running a continuing criminal enterprise. Terry Flenory is scheduled for release on January 7, 2032. His brother's presumed release date is February 25, 2032.

March 30: Genovese Family associates Joseph Dennis Colasacco, Charles Steinberg and Mitchell Weissman receive federal prison terms in Fort Lauderdale, Fla., after pleading guilty to RICO conspiracy charges. Steinberg is released on June 16, 2009. Weissman is paroled on December 23, 2009. Colasacco's tentative release date is October 18, 2011.

March 31: Police on Gran Canaria Island arrest an unnamed Spanish national, described as a co-founder of "The Corporation," a Cuban-American crime syndicate based in Florida. During the arrest, officers seize assets valued in excess of $27 million.

April 1: Pirates capture the UAE-registered dhow MV *Nimatullah*, anchored off Mogadishu, Somalia, with 800 tons of cargo and 14 crewmen aboard.

April 2: Judge Peter Moss of Ireland's Woolwich Crown Court sentences drug lord Brian Brendan Wright to 30 years in prison for running an international cocaine network. In Peru, President Alan Garcia authorizes use of military aircraft to destroy clandestine drug labs and smugglers' airstrips in the Amazon jungle. In Tijuana, Mexico, police arrest Victor Magno Escobar, an ex-policeman and officer of the Tijuana Cartel. In San Antonio, Tex., U.S. District Judge Fred Biery sentences Mexican Mafia informer William "Willow" Covarrubias to two years in prison for

failing a drug test and pistol-whipping a man in August 2006, over a $150 debt.

April 3: Police in Baja California, Mexico, arrest ex-policeman Víctor Magno Escobar Luna—AKA "The Cop Killer"—on charges of leading a ransom kidnapping gang.

April 4: Italy's parliamentary anti–Mafia committee urges all political parties to refrain from fielding candidates indicted for underworld associations in May's primary elections. In Palermo, police arrest Bartolo Pellegrino, former deputy chief of Sicily's regional government, on charges of Mafia association. Police in Toronto, Canada, raid a Hells Angels clubhouse, detaining 15 bikers on drug and weapons charges after seizing 500 liters of GHB valued at $996,000, nine kilograms of cocaine, two kilograms of hashish, plus quantities of oxycodone and Viagra, 72 guns, three pairs of brass knuckles, and $21,000 in cash.

April 5: Spokesmen for the UAE order all ships bearing their nation's flag to vacate Somalian waters following seizure of the MV *Nimatullah* and MV *Nishan* for ransom. Yakuza gangster Kaneyoshi Kuwata dies from natural causes at home, in Osaka, Japan.

April 6: Authorities in Corleone, Sicily, lift a 40-year ban on wearing of hoods by Easter penitents. Masking was outlawed in the 1960s to discourage Mafia assassins.

April 8: Somali pirates release the MV *Nimatullah* and the UN-chartered MV *Rosen*. Authorities refuse to discuss any ransom payments.

April 10: Trial begins in New York City for Gambino Family members Alfred DiCongilio and Dominick "Skinny Dom" Pizzonia, on federal charges related to the 1992 murders of husband-wife bandits Thomas and Rose Marie Uva. Jurors convict Pizzonia of racketeering conspiracy on May 11, but acquit him of extortion and murder. The panel acquits DiCongilio on all charges. Pizzonia receives a 15-year sentence on September 5. His presumptive release date is February 28, 2020.

April 12: Police in the Brazilian state of Pernambuco arrest 20 suspected members of a "killing firm" responsible for 1,000 contract murders in the past five years. In Monterey County, Calif., Nuestra Familia member Robert Patrick "Bubba" Hanrahan receives a 13-year sentence for drug trafficking.

April 17: Tetsuya Shiroo, a senior member of the Yamaguchi-gumi Yakuza clan, shoots Mayor Iccho Itoh outside his re-election campaign headquarters in Nagasaki, Japan. The Nagasaki District Court condemns Tetsuya on May 26, 2008, but an appellate court commutes his death sentence to life imprisonment on September 29, 2009. Also in Japan, historians Hirofumi Hayashi and Yoshiaki Yoshimi announce discovery of documents in archives from the Tokyo war crimes trials of 1945–46, documenting induction of Chinese "comfort women" into sexual slavery.

April 18: Drug cartel gunmen in Tijuana, Mexico, invade a hospital to liberate their captive boss, touching off a battle with police and soldiers that leaves three people dead.

April 19: Massachusetts prosecutors charge ex-convict Fotios "Freddy" Geas with the murder of mafioso Adolfo "Big Al" Bruno. On April 20 they charge mobster Brandon Croteau as a participant in the slaying.

April 23: The U.S. Coast Guard seizes 20 tons of cocaine valued at $600 million from a Panamanian-flagged off California's coast.

April 27: A grand jury in Springfield, Mass., indicts murder suspect Fotious Geas, his brother Ty, and mafioso Anthony Arillotta on charges of conspiring to extort funds from poker machine owners Carlo and Gennaro Sarno. In California's Coachella Valley, "Operation Clean House" culminates with the arrest of 13 Mexican Mafia members, in raids that seize more than 50 guns, one pipe bomb, several vehicles, and $15,000 in cash. Suspects charged with conspiracy to distribute narcotics and other crimes include Jovita Aguirre, James Angle, Rodolfo Baldemar Zuñiga, Chad Wayne Baringer, Oscar Bustos, Chris Huerta, Joe Huerta, Jose Chavez Huerta, Maria Carmen Huerta, Franchesca Martina Ochoa, Alicia Rodriguez, Tony Rodriguez, Juan Carlos Rosas, and Ernest Julian Sanchez.

April 29: Federal jurors in Detroit acquit Jack V. Giacalone, son of imprisoned mafioso Vito Giacalone, on gambling and racketeering charges.

May 2: ATF agents and local police arrest three members of the Free Souls MC in Eugene, Ore. Raiders seize 10 stolen motorcycles, various firearms, plus quantities of marijuana, hashish oil, and methamphetamine.

May 4: Canadian mafioso Vito Rizzuto pleads guilty in New York City to participating in the 1981 murder of three Bonanno Family members. On May 25 he receives a 10-year prison term, followed by three years' supervised parole.

May 5: FBI agents arrest 40 members and associates of the Highwaymen MC in Detroit, Mich., on charges including racketeering, murder for hire, assault, police corruption, cocaine trafficking, vehicle theft, and mortgage and insurance fraud. The raiders seize 29 illegal firearms.

May 7: Fugitive Mafia wife Ann Hathaway returns to Manchester, England, following deportation from Italy. In Melbourne, Australia, jurors convict hitman Carl Anthony Williams of three murders and one attempted murder, resulting in a life prison term. A fellow prisoner beats Williams to death on April 19, 2010.

May 8: Troops from Mexico's 51st Infantry Battalion, assigned to "Operation Michoacán," kill four members of the La Familia drug cartel in a pitched battle at Apatzingan, Michoacán. Three soldiers are also wounded.

May 9: Three current and former executives of Purdue Pharma plead guilty in Abingdon, Va., to criminal charges that they misled regulators, doctors and patients about the drug's risk of addiction and its potential to be abused. The firm agrees to pay $600 million in fines, while the individual defendants are fined a total of $34.5 million. In Albania, the newspaper *Koha Jone* that 15 "Mafia" clans control organized crime nationwide. Authorities in Washington County, Md., arrest Pagans MC leader Jay Carl Wagner for possession of a regulated firearm after conviction of a violent crime. Wagner pleads guilty on March 5, 2008, and receives a 30-month prison term on August 8, 2008.

May 10: Police in San Francisco, Calif., report that an unnamed victim has survived critical wounds in a drive-by shooting described as a "Mafia-style execution." Military leaders from Indonesia and Malaysia agree to cooperate on patrols against pirates in the Malacca Strait.

May 12: Japanese journalist Taichiro Kajimura reports discovery of 30 Dutch government documents submitted to the post-war Tokyo tribunal as evidence of forced prostitution during 1944, in Magelang, Java. NYPD officers arrest Colombo Family member John "Sonny" Franzese for parole violation, after watching him share doughnuts with other mafiosi. Police in Gosnells, Western Australia, jail Gypsy Jokers Dean Alan Adams and Peter Floyd Robinson for beating a man with metal pipes, outside a bar.

May 13: Last confirmed sighting of Colombian drug lord Griselda Blanco, at Bogotá's El Dorado International Airport. Brooklyn Supreme Court Justice Guy Mangano Jr. vacates the 1985 murder conviction and 25-year sentence of Mafia associate Carmine Carini, ordering a new trial on reduced charges of second-degree murder. Carini confesses the slaying on June 12 and is released on the basis of time served.

May 14: Drug cartel soldiers kill federal prosecutor Jose Nemesio Lugo in Mexico City and high-ranking narcotics officer Jorge Altriste in Tijuana, Baja California. The *New York Post* announces FBI collaboration with Italian authorities on "The Pantheon Project," a joint effort to limit emigration of Sicilian mafiosi to the U.S. Police in Sussex, England, prepare to extradite Italian fugitive Enrico Mariotti, convicted in 1995 for the 1977 kidnap-murder of millionaire Duke Massimiliano Grazioli by the Magliana gang and sentenced to 25 years *in absentia*. Trial begins in the Supreme Court of British Columbia for three Hells Angels indicted during "Project E-Pandora." Proceedings related to defendants David Francis Giles, Richard Andrew Rempel, and David Roger Revell continue until February 20, 2008, with a ban on publication of details. Jurors acquit all three defendants on March 26, 2008.

May 15: Somali pirates seize the Tanzanian-flagged boats *Mavuno 1* and *2*, holding them and their 24 crewmen hostage until November 4. In Mexico, separate attacks by cartel gunmen claim the lives of federal prosecutor Jose Nemesio Lugo in Mexico City, and top police official Jorge Altriste in Tijuana. Anto Djapic, president of the Croatian Party of Rights, claims that 10 percent of all Croatians are linked to drug trafficking, either as dealers or addicts.

May 16: Forty cartel gunmen invade the town of Cananea, Mexico, killing four policemen, kidnapping a fifth officer and two civilians. A police counterattack kills eight of the raiders. Emanuil Yordanov, Bulgaria's former Interior Minister, tells the FOCUS News Agency that most "Mafia-style" murders committed nationwide since 2001 "were linked in some way or another to the major sponsors of the former governments." Pirates intercept the Canadian yacht *Arioso II* in the Atlantic Ocean, 250 miles northwest of Cape Verde, but the crew repels boarders.

May 17: Aging Genovese Family member Renaldi "Ray" Ruggiero receives a 14-year sentence in Miami, Fla., after pleading guilty to RICO charges in February. His sentence also includes two years' supervised parole, a $35,000 fine, and forfeiture of $10,000 previously seized by federal agents. Somali pirates capture two South Korean fishing boats with 24 crewmen aboard, prompting an IMB alert advising all ships to remain at least 200 nautical miles offshore. Police in Preston, Lancashire, England, arrest fugitive mafioso Gennaro Panzuto on suspicion of killing four victims in Naples, Italy.

May 18: A court in London, England, orders convicted money-launderer Terry Adams to pay £4.8 million in legal fees to three law firms that defended him under Britain's free legal aid scheme. The judge also orders Adams to pay £800,000 in prosecution costs. On May 21 Adams receives an order to file reports detailing his income for the next 10 years. In Nagakute, Japan, "retired" Yamaguchi-gumi mobster Hisato Obayashi surrenders to police after a two-day standoff during which he killed a policeman, shot his two children, and held his wife hostage.

May 20: A UN-chartered cargo ship eludes pirates off the coast of Somalia.

May 22: Bahrain's Maritime Liaison Office is-sues a piracy warning to all vessels passing the coast of Somalia. Chinese authorities follow with a similar advisory on May 23.

May 23: More than 15,000 Italian college students demonstrate against Mafia violence in Palermo, Sicily, outside a prison where various mafiosi are incarcerated. In Ibbenbüren, German, two members of the Bandidos MC shoot a rival Hells Angel at his Harley-Davidson shop. Both are convicted of murder and sentenced to life imprisonment on June 11, 2008. In San Diego, Calif., DEA spokesmen announce the climax of "Operation Jacket Racket," targeting Colombian drug traffickers who hide contraband in the lining of clothing and baby blankets. Indictments charge 44 defendants with drug trafficking, money-laundering and counterfeiting.

May 28: Trial begins in Sicily for mafiosi Bernardo Provenzano and Toto Riina, charged with four gangland murders committed in 1969.

May 29: Somali pirates release the St. Kitts–flagged *Mariam Queen* following payment of $100,000 ransom. Indonesia's Supreme Court condemns five defendants—a Dutchman, a Frenchman, and three Chinese nationals—convicted of running an ecstasy factory capable of producing a million tablets per week.

May 30: Sheriff's deputies in Snohomish County, Wash., raid the homes of four Hells Angels suspected of various crimes. In New York City, a federal grand jury indicts Genovese Family boss Danny "The Lion" Leo on charges of extortion and loan-sharking. Leo pleads guilty in 2008 and receives a five-year prison term, with a projected release date of October 7, 2011.

June 1: A judge in London, England, sentences 10 members of an auto-theft ring that earned £4.5 million from sale of 190 stolen vehicles. Defendants include Omar Abbas (five years), Anthony Holt (four years), Robert Taylor (2 years), Mark Danlardy (18 months), Michael Kingsley (15 months), Jason Okoh (12 months), Terrance Harding (nine months), David Adams (200 hours of community service), Emma Rayfield (75 hours of community service), and Matthew Wilson (12 months suspended).

June 2: Somali pirates hijack the Danish ship MV *Danica White*. U.S. Navy ships sink several small pirate craft, but buccaneers aboard the *Danica White* escape into Somali territorial waters.

June 4: Somali pirates execute a crewman from the Taiwanese fishing vessel the *Ching Fong Hwa 168* when a ransom deadline passes with no money paid.

June 6: Gambino Family associate Robert DeCicco survives three gunshot wounds in Bath Beach, Brooklyn.

June 7: NYPD officers find Genovese Family soldier Rudolph Izzi shot to death in bed at his Brooklyn home. A federal grand jury in California charges members of Nuestra Familia from Bakersfield, Fontana, and Fresno with conspiracy to distribute methamphetamine, cocaine, marijuana and ecstasy. Defendants include Crystal Castro, Fidel Ramon Castro, William Eugene Connelly, Maria Victoria Marquez Pulido, Julia Quiroz, Vincent Rivera, and Juan Villalobos Arias. Spanish police arrest international arms dealer Monzer al Kassar on charges of arming Colombian drug traffickers, while Romanian authorities jail accomplices Tareq Mousa al Ghazi and Luis Felipe Moreno-Godoy.

June 9: Prosecutors at the trial of mafiosi Giuseppe Maniaci and Salvatore Micali, in Messina, Sicily, claim that the Mafia planned to kidnap actress Maria Grazia Cucinotta and hold her for ransom.

June 10: Brazilian police search the home of President Luiz Inácio Lula da Silva's brother in São Bernardo do Campo, as part of a nationwide crackdown on illegal gambling, money-laundering and police corruption that has jailed 87 suspects in Mato Grosso do Sul state.

June 11: Federal jurors in Spokane, Wash., convict three former Hells Angels on multiple felony charges. Defendant Richard Allen "Smilin' Rick" Fabel stands convicted of several racketeering counts, including mail fraud and extortion. Joshua Binder is convicted of conspiracy to commit racketeering and attempted interference with commerce by threats or violence, while jurors deadlock on his participation in the 2001 murder of victim Michael Walsh. Rodney Lee Rollness faces a mandatory life sentence for murder, racketeering, conspiracy to commit racketeering and several other crimes, including trafficking in stolen motorcycles. The panel fails to reach a verdict against defendant Ricky Jenks. Fabel receives a seven-year sentence on September 17.

June 12: *O Globo*, a newspaper in Rio de Janeiro, Brazil, charges that underworld gamblers used bribes and death threats to fix the results of February's carnival parade, ensuring victory for the Beija-Flor samba school run by mobster Anisio Abraao David. In Chicago, mobster Michael Marcello admits paying witness Nicholas Calabrese $4,000 per month to withhold information from federal agents. The plead bargain carries a sentence of seven to 10 years in prison.

June 13: The Swiss Bundeskanzlei (Federal Chancellery) delivers $34 million to Taiwan from bank accounts held by various alleged participants in the ongoing frigate scandal. Dutch authorities

release British drug trafficker Curtis "Cocky" Warren from prison after serving 10 years of a 12-year sentence. IMB spokesmen call for naval forces of all nations to collaborate in suppressing Somali piracy. In Palermo, Sicily, unknown motorcycle gunmen kill mafioso Nicolo Ingarao. Yakuza gunmen execute mobster Zenji Tsurumaru in Kurume, Fukuoka, Japan.

June 16: Ex-NYPD detective and convicted Mafia hitman Louis Eppolito writes to the Associated Press, blaming media bias for his conviction.

June 18: Hells Angels member Christopher Wayne Hudson assaults an exotic dancer, then shoots three male victims in Melbourne, Australia, killing attorney Brendan Keilar. Hudson pleads guilty to murder and attempted murder on May 12, 2008. In Houston, Tex., Kenneth Rice — former chief of Enron Corporation's high-speed Internet unit — receives a 27-month prison term for his role in the company scandal.

June 19: Yakuza gunmen kill Hidenori Irie in Kurume, Fukuoka, Japan. The "Family Secrets" trial of Chicago Outfit members begins in federal court. On September 10 jurors convict Frank Calabrese Sr. and other defendants of a racketeering conspiracy that included murder, extortion, and loan-sharking. A hearing to determine guilt in 18 gangland murders convenes on September 11. On September 27 jurors find that Frank Calabrese Sr. participated in seven of the slayings. Judge James Zagel denies a motion for a new trial on April 10, 2008, based on allegations that Calabrese threatened one of his jurors. Calabrese receives a life sentence on January 28, 2009. Codefendant Joey Lombardo receives a life sentence from Judge Zagel on February 2, 2009.

June 20: Mexican Mafia member Robert Romero pleads guilty to federal RICO charges in San Diego, Calif.

June 22: Colombian police arrest fugitive Guatemalan drug lord Otto Roberto Herrera Garcia, at large since his escape from a Mexican prison in 2005. Somali pirates release the Indian cargo ship Al Haqeeq after payment of an undisclosed ransom.

June 24: Police in Sicily arrest reputed leaders of nine Mafia families. In Forest Park, Ga., Outlaws MC member Frank Rego Vital dies in a shootout with rival members of the Renegades MC. Two Renegades survive multiple bullet wounds.

June 25: Mexican Mafia associates Edna Davis, Angela Esparza, Jessie Munoz and Mary Lou Vega plead guilty to federal RICO charges in San Diego, Calif.

June 26: Newly declassified CIA documents

confirm the agency's recruitment of mafiosi to kill Fidel Castro in the early 1960s.

June 27: More than 1,000 Brazilian police invade the Alemao slum district of Rio de Janeiro to uproot a drug syndicate. The resultant pitched battle claims 19 lives. Unknown gunmen kill Serbian mobster Ramiz Delali outside his apartment building in Sarajevo.

June 28: Senegalese authorities find an abandoned boat drifting near the resort of Mbour, with 1.2 metric tons of cocaine aboard.

July 1: A new ordinance in Moscow, Russia, closes slot machine parlors smaller than 100 square meters and those with fewer than 50 machines.

July 2: Chief U.S. District Judge Mark Wolf asks the Massachusetts Board of Bar Overseers to initiate disciplinary proceedings against federal prosecutor Jeffrey Auerhahn for his collaboration in FBI misconduct surrounding investigation of the New England Mafia.

July 4: Italy's Anti-Vivisection League complains of "savage" illegal horse races employing injured animals dopes with performance-enhancing drugs, staged in Catania, Palermo, and Siracuse, Sicily. Police admit preventing seven of an estimated 300 illegal races over the past year.

July 9: Cuban authorities deport fugitive drug lord Luis Hernando Gómez Bustamante to Colombia. DEA agents collect him for extradition to the U.S. on July 19. In Washington, "D.C. Madam" Deborah Jeane Palfrey releases her telephone records for public viewing on the Internet, while her attorney sends 54 CD-ROM copies to researchers, activists, and journalists.

July 10: The U.S. Attorney's office announces indictments of various Nuestra Familia members in California, on charges of racketeering and conspiracy to distribute methamphetamine, cocaine, marijuana and ecstasy. Defendants include: Ernesto Bravo Tejeda of Madera; Oscar Campos Padilla of Castroville; Andrea Cadena, Mario Diaz Jr., Alvaro Cobian Gomez, Valdemar Salazar Cambunga and Jason Michael Stewart Hanson of Los Banos; Sophia Corella Sanchez of Marina; Edward Fuentes of Merced; Marcos Anthony Gomez Jr. and Benjamin Santos Castro of San Francisco; Gabriel Caracheo, Faustino Gonzales, Manuel Somora Cadena and Pedro Anthony Rios III of Salinas; Ernest Paul Killinger of Orangevale; Manuel Gauna and Gerardo Lopez Mora of Salinas; Thurman Lee Maxwell of Warren, Ohio; Richard Mendoza of Castroville; Bismark Martin Ocampo of Petaluma; David Perez Ramirez of Manteca; Larry Sixto Amaro of Hanford; Leo Torres of Dos Palos; Fernando Villapando of Moreno Valley; and Jose Angel Villasenor of Fremont. A joint communiqué from the IMO and

the UN World Food Programme warns that "the actions of pirates operating in the waters off Somalia threaten the sea lanes in the region and could endanger the fragile supply line for food assistance to Somalis." In southern Italy, police arrest 60 suspected 'Ndrangheta members on charges ranging from drug trafficking, human trafficking, and insurance fraud.

July 11: Secretary-General Ban Ki-moon announces plans to raise the issue of Somali piracy before the UN Security Council.

July 13: Mafioso Giuseppe Lo Baido dies in a shotgun ambush outside his home in Palermo, Sicily. Federal jurors in Chicago convict Canadian newspaper mogul Conrad Moffat Black on three counts of mail and wire fraud and one count of obstruction of justice, while acquitting him of racketeering. Black receives a 78-month prison term, plus a $125,000 fine and an order to compensate his victims in the amount of $6.1 million. An appellate court affirms his conviction on June 25, 2008.

July 15: Police in Sicily arrest mafioso-turned-informer Calogero Pulci on new charges of Mafia association. In New York City, ex-judge David Gross pleads guilty to laundering more than $400,000 for the Genovese Family. Gross receives a three-year prison term on November 16, 2007.

July 16: Louisiana senator David Bruce Vitter calls a press conference to apologize for using the prostitution services of "D.C. Madam" Deborah Jeane Palfrey at least five times between October 1999 and February 2001. In Reggio Calabria, Italy, police capture fugitive 'Ndrangheta leader Giuseppe Bellocco after 10 years in hiding. Police in Barcelona, Spain, arrest former MP Eduardo Planells on charges of bribery, prevarication and fraud, claiming that he provided work and residence permits to members of the Russian Mafia. Armed pirates board and loot the yacht *Star Isi* at Madang, Papua New Guinea, leaving its owners badly injured.

July 19: Newly released FBI documents claim that mafioso Frank Cotroni of Montreal, Québec, discusses possible assassination of U.S. Supreme Court Chief Justice Warren Burger with New York mobsters Joseph Gambino and Phillip Rastelli in 1979. In London, England, Albanian mobster Kujtim Spahiu receives a 33-year sentence for killing victim Prel Marku outside a social club in October 2006. The court acquits codefendants Lulzi Bici, 21, and Muhammed Mehmeti. In Sofia, Bulgaria, Vanyo Tanov resigns as chief of the nation's police agency assigned to investigate organized crime, blaming a "political smokescreen" that conceals corruption in the "higher echelons of power."

July 20: The *New York Post* breaks news of an

FBI investigation into point-rigging by National Basketball Association referee Tim Donaghy. On July 27 the Associated Press identifies Donaghy's accomplice as James Battista, former owner of a sports bar in Havertown, Pa. Donaghy appears in a Brooklyn federal court on August 15 and pleads guilty to conspiracy to engage in wire fraud and transmitting wagering information through interstate commerce, naming Thomas Martino as the middleman who passed information to Battista. The judge fines Donaghy $500,000 and orders payment of $30,000 in restitution. On June 10, 2008, Donaghy's lawyer files court documents charging that two other NBA referees fixed Game 6 of the 2002 Western Conference Finals between the Los Angeles Lakers and Sacramento Kings. On June 19, 2008, the NBA filed a demand that Donaghy reimburse the league $1.4 million, including $577,000 of his pay and benefits over four seasons, plus legal fees and other expenses related to the investigation. Donaghy receives a 15-month prison sentence on July 29, 2008. Battista and Martino receive sentences of 15 months and 366 days, respectively. Authorities release Donaghy after 11 months, but he is arrested for parole violation in August 2009. He is released on November 4, 2009, after completing his original sentence.

July 25: FBI agents and officers of China's Public Security Bureau cap "Operation Summer Solstice" with arrests of 25 software pirates, accused of distributing bootleg computer programs valued in excess of $2 billion. The raiders also seize more than 290,000 CDs, worth $500 million. In Atlanta, Ga., U.S. Attorney David Nahmias unseals an indictment charging 16 members of the Black Mafia Family with drug trafficking. Defendants include Dionne Beverly, Fleming Daniels, Ramon Dobson, Lamar Fields, Victor Hammonds, Jamal Mitchell, Franklin Nash, Derek Pitts, and Darryl Taylor.

July 26: BBC News exposes a Bulgarian child-trafficking ring that offers toddlers for sale at a price of €60,000 (£40,000) per child. In Boston, Mass., U.S. District Judge Nancy Gertner orders the federal government to pay $101.75 million Peter Limone, Joseph Salvati, and relatives of two deceased codefendants framed for murder by the FBI and Mafia in 1967.

July 27: Somali pirates demand $1.5 million for the release of five crewman aboard the hijacked Danish vessel MV *Danica White*.

July 30: The U.S. House of Representatives passes a resolution condemning Japan's forcible induction of sex slaves during World War II. In Glasgow, Scotland, gangster Thomas "Tam" McGraw dies from a heart attack at his home.

August: U.S. State Department spokesmen report that Afghanistan's opium poppy production has increased 15 percent over 2006. Afghanistan now accounts for 95 percent of the world's opium.

July 31: FBI agents raid clubhouses of the Outlaws MC in Brockton and Taunton, Mass., arresting club members on various charges.

August 2: Officers of Spain's Guardia Civil stage raids on the Costa del Sol, arresting 14 persons in five towns on 51 charges including drug trafficking, money-laundering, and forging official documents. Those jailed include five Italians (all alleged Camorra members), six Moroccans, and three Spaniards. Raiders seize seven properties, four firms and 60 vehicles, all valued at a total of €5 million, plus 2.5 tons of hashish and several guns. In Québec, Canada, Czech tennis player Tomáš Berdych loses the Montreal Masters tournament, then complains of match-fixing by Russian mobsters at a recent tournament in Poland. Unknown assassins in the southern Mexican state of Guerrero kill two federal agents who participated in the August 2 raid on Zhenli Ye Gon mansion, in Mexico City.

August 3: Guatemala's congress votes to collaborate with the UN in creation of a new International Commission Against Impunity in Guatemala, designed to dismantle violent criminal organizations believed to be responsible for widespread crime and the paralysis in the country's justice system. In Palermo, Sicily, police arrest fugitive mafioso Franco Franzese.

August 6: Australian Federal Police spokesmen complain that Italian authorities have stalled extradition of Calabrian drug traffickers indicted in 2004, on charges of smuggling cocaine Melbourne. London's *Daily Mail* exposes Mafia involvement in commercial tuna "ranching" in the Mediterranean Sea, around Malta.

August 7: Brazilian police arrest Colombian drug lord Juan Carlos Ramirez Abadia, AKA "Lollypop," in Aldeia da Serra.

August 8: Italian authorities blame Camorra members for setting recent disastrous wildfires and firing rifle shots at an emergency helicopters over Quindici, near Naples.

August 9: Police in China's Fujian Province arrest a "snakehead" human trafficker and detain 12 illegal emigrants posing as a Shaolin Temple martial arts team.

August 10: Italian authorities release wiretap evidence linking Gambino Family soldier Francesco "Franky Boy" Calì to Sicilian mafiosi involved in drug trafficking and money-laundering. On the same day, police in Sicily arrest Mayor Rosario Bordonaro of Baucina, two former employees of Torretta's town hall, and 14 residents of Boccadifalco on charges of Mafia association.

August 12: Police in London, England, announce that millions of pounds stolen from Italy's Banco Ambrosiano by deceased swindler Roberto Calvi have been traced to a bank in the Bahamas. Italian anti–Mafia investigators report that 105,000 assault rifles sidetracked from the U.S. Army have been sold by mafiosi to Iraq's interior ministry. Drive-by gunmen kill Hells Angel Gerry Tobin on the M40 motorway in Warwickshire, England.

August 13: Pirates board a Malaysian barge in the Malacca Strait, kidnapping two Indonesian crewmen.

August 15: While German prosecutors place Russian mobster "Alexander A." on trial for racketeering, unknown gunmen execute six Italian immigrants, all suspected members of the 'Ndrangheta, outside a pizzeria in Duisburg, Germany. Police in San Luca, Italy, arrest 31 suspects on August 29. In Bellevue, Western Australia, police arrest two members of the Gypsy Jokers MC on charges of unlawfully possessing weapons, ammunition, and a large sum of cash.

August 16: Federal agents and local police raid Outlaws MC clubhouses in Daytona Beach, Jacksonville, and Ormond Beach, Fla. The Jacksonville raid nets 60 weapons. On the same day, U.S. Attorney General Alberto Gonzales announces a federal indictment of 16 Outlaws in Detroit, Mich., on charges including assault and drug distribution. DEA spokesmen in Dallas, Tex., announce the culmination of "Operation Puma," a 30-month investigation of cocaine and marijuana trafficking across the U.S.-Mexican border. Raiders arrest 30 suspects, while seizing several million dollars worth of drug-related assets.

August 17: Actor Steven Seagal tells the *Los Angeles Times* that an FBI investigation of his alleged ties to organized crime ruined his film career.

August 18: Unknown gunmen kill Yoshihisa Onaka, leader of the Dōjin-kai Yakuza clan, in Kurume, Fukuoka, Japan.

August 19: Pietro Grasso, Italy's anti–Mafia commissioner, identifies the 'Ndrangheta as Europe's most powerful crime syndicate.

August 20: Owners of 17 Italian restaurants hold an anti–Mafia press conference in Berlin, Germany, declaring that recent gangland murders have left Germany's Italian community "shaken to the core."

August 22: Danish officials announce the release of a cargo ship following payment of ransom to Somali pirates.

August 23: Somali pirates release the Danish vessel *Danica White* following payment of an unspecified ransom. An Organized Crime Drug Enforcement Task Force caps the second phase of "Operation Imperial Emperor," targeting drug traffickers and money-launderers in southern Cal-

ifornia. Raiders arrest 59 suspects, while seizing 664 pounds of cocaine, 142 pounds of methamphetamine, 434 pounds of marijuana, three firearms, 14 vehicles and $5,170,896 in cash.

August 24: Russian police arrest mobster-businessman Vladimir Kumarin on charges of banditry, organizing a gang, and attempting to murder business rival Sergei Vasiliev in 2006. Jurors convict Kumarin of fraud and money-laundering on November 12, 2009, resulting in a 14-year sentence.

August 27: Russian police arrest 10 suspects in the October 2006 assassination of journalist Anna Politkovskaya. Those jailed include a Chechen gang leader and FSB Lieutenant Colonel Pavel Ryaguzov. Police in Tijuana, Mexico, blame drug cartel assassins for the deaths of three decapitated victims found at a local garbage dump.

August 28: Police in Bishop's Stortford, Hertfordshire, England, blame a £600 drug deal for a shooting that leaves three men dead, with two women and a three-year-old girl wounded by two Asian gunmen.

August 29: A federal judge in Boston, Mass., grants mafioso Francis "Cadillac Frank" Salemme a hearing on claims that prosecutors unfairly interrogated him without his lawyer present in November 1999, then used his words to indict him.

August 30: "Operation Gangland" culminates in San Diego, Calif., as a grand jury indicts 23 members of the Mexican Mafia on 46 felony charges including extortion, firearms violations, narcotics sales, assault, and solicitations for murder. Defendants include Richard Buchanan, Refugio Castellanos Servin, Juan Carlos Cordero, Raul Antonio Cruz, Jorge Cuevas Mendoza, Jose Luis Espinoza. Juan Antonio Hornback, Judy Ann Huerta, Ruby Jacqueline Mendez, David Pael Martinez, Luis Hector Munoz Jr., Jaime Perez, Patrick Ralph Ponce, Max Ponce Jr., Eden Portugal Macias, Antonio Padilla, Gerardo Robles, Victor Ruby, Manuel Solarez, Anthony Gabriel Valles, Raul Vega Mejia, Mark Villasenor, and Jose Zepeda.

August 31: Police in Thessaloniki, Greece, arrest an unnamed 23-year-old suspect in the local machine-gun slaying of a Russian mobster who killed the suspect's uncle in Russia, during 2005. Two more suspects remain at large.

September: South Korea's government names Bae Jeong-ja, foster daughter of Japanese Prime Minister Hirobumi Ito, as a collaborator who recruited Korean "comfort women" as sex slaves for Japanese occupation troops during World War II.

September 3: Italian president Giorgio Napolitano calls for an "effective mobilization of the state and civil society" against organized crime.

September 7: Officials in Guyana announce the

creation of an emergency radio network for boaters to report pirate attacks along the nation's coastline and interior rivers.

September 10: Police in Colombia's Valle del Cauca Province capture fugitive drug lord Diego Montoya.

September 11: Citing fears of torture, Judge D.D. Sitgraves in Los Angeles rejects an Italian extradition request for alleged mafioso Rosario Gambino.

September 14: The Irish Examiner newspaper reports that six members of Limerick's McCarthy-Dundon gang were recently robbed by mobsters in Varna, Bulgaria, after traveling there for target shooting at a local gun range. Authorities in Montreal, Québec, Mafia revoke the parole of hitman Moreno Gallo, released in 1983 from a life sentence imposed for the 1973 murder of drug dealer Angelo Facchino.

September 19: Police in Palermo, Sicily, announce the arrest of Giuseppe Lipari, charged with helping mafioso Bernardo Provenzano dodge arrest for 40 years.

September 24: French President Nicolas Sarkozy offers to protect UN World Food Program shipments to Somalia with warships. DEA agents join officers of the FDA's Office of Criminal Investigations and the U.S. Postal Inspection Service to close "Operation Raw Deal," targeting international traffickers in anabolic steroids, human growth hormone and insulin growth factor. Raiders seize 56 steroid labs across the U.S. and arrest 124 suspects, while confiscating 11.4 million steroid dosage units were seized, 242 kilograms of raw steroid powder from China, 27 pill presses, 71 weapons, 25 cars, three boats, and $6.5 million in cash.

September 25: Australian tennis star Patrick Hart "Pat" Cash claims that Russian mobsters are trying to fix matches on the Association of Tennis Professionals World Tour. Chinese authorities announce that they have crushed more than 4,000 criminal gangs nationwide since February 2006, referring 340 cases for prosecution.

September 26: Police in Florence, Italy, serve forty arrest warrants on charges of Mafia association, illegal money lending, extortion, theft, robbery, blackmail, fraud, whitewashing and drug trafficking.

September 28: FBI agents in Sullivan County, N.Y., arrest Deputy Sheriff Philip Etkin on extortion charges, claiming that he collected $3,500 from a Middletown resident in return for lifting a nonexistent Mafia murder contract.

September 29: Police in Tokyo, Japan, accuse Yakuza gangsters of hiding fugitive Tatsuya Ichihashi, sought since September 18 for the strangulation murder of English teacher Lindsay Hawker.

Investigators in Naples, Italy, report that Mafia bosses have held secret meetings at local police stations.

October 1: Police in Palermo, Sicily, arrest fugitive mafioso Enrico Scalavino, accused of Mafia association, drug trafficking and extortion.

October 4: Kentucky Attorney General Greg Stumbo and officials in Pike County sue Purdue Pharma L.P. for millions of dollars in damages resulting in abuse of the firm's drug OxyContin. In Hong Kong, Taiwanese mobster "King Duck" Chen Chi-Li — boss of the United Bamboo Gang — dies in hospital from pancreatic cancer.

October 8: Italy's Anti-Mafia Investigation Department issues 32 arrest warrants for suspects in Palermo, Naples, and Genoa.

October 10: A federal grand jury in New York City indicts three Genovese Family associates and four other defendants on charges related to a string of violent home invasions in New Jersey and New York.

October 15: Bruno Piccolo, an 'Ndrangheta member turned government witness, hangs himself at a police safe house in Locri, Italy.

October 17: While maintaining claims of innocence, immigrant restaurateur Ciro Schiattarella agrees to extradition from Aberdeen, Scotland, to his native Naples, Italy, where he faces trial for association with the 'Ndrangheta.

October 18: The film *American Gangster* premieres in New York City, starring Denzel Washington as convicted drug lord Frank Lucas.

October 19: Pirates storm the Canadian yacht *Ciel & Mar* off the coast of Madagascar, injuring both owners. Police in Surrey, British Columbia, find six persons murdered in a high-rise apartment, reporting that five were slain in a drug-related shooting while the sixth, fireplace repairman Ed Schellenberg, was an innocent bystander. Prosecutors charge defendants. Prosecutors subsequently charge defendants Jamie Bacon, Cody Haevischer, Matthew Johnson, Dennis Karbovanec and Sophon Sek with the "Surrey Six" slayings.

October 21: The Comoran-flagged cargo ship MV *Jaikur II* eludes pirates off Barawa, Somalia, after delivering supplies from the UN World Food Program.

October 22: A report issued by the Confesercenti Italia, an association of small businesses, claims that organized crime represents the single largest segment of Italy's economy, with annual receipts exceeding $127 billion.

October 24: Police in Sicily arrest Gaetana Conti on charges of delivering her 20-year-old son, police informer Sebastiano Mazzeo, to Mafia killers in 1991. Elsewhere in Italy, officers arrest a dozen suspects linked to international money-laundering by the Rizzuto Mafia family in Montreal, Québec.

October 26: Police in Mexicali, Baja California, arrest Tony Gonzales-Rodriguez Jr., alleged second-in-command of the Mexican Mafia, and deliver him to U.S. authorities for trial on drug-trafficking charges.

October 28: The American guided missile destroyer USS *Porter* sinks two pirate boats moored to the hostage Japanese-flagged chemical tanker *Golden Nori*, seized by hijackers off the coast of Somalia.

October 30: Somali pirates seize a North Korean cargo ship near Mogadishu, but crewmen soon regain control of the vessel. Italian authorities announce the birth of mafioso Raffaele Cutolo's daughter, sired by artificial insemination from prison under court order, following a extended litigation.

November 1: Federal prosecutors in New York drop Mafia-related murder charges filed against ex–FBI agent Lindley DeVecchio, citing "conflicting evidence" in the case. At Manzanillo, Mexico, police seize a Colombian cargo ship bearing 23.5 tons of cocaine valued in excess of $400 million.

November 4: Italian police capture fugitive mafioso Salvatore Lo Piccolo outside Palermo, after 20 years in hiding. Somali pirates release the South Korean fishing boats *Mavuno 1* and *Mavuno 2*, and their 24 crewmen, seized for random six months earlier.

November 5: Somali pirates release a Taiwanese fishing vessel 5½ months after seizing it. In Rome, national anti–Mafia prosecutor Pietro Grasso announces that the Mafia's "Cupola," or ruling commission, "has been demolished." Police in Giardinello, Sicily, arrest fugitive mafioso Salvatore Lo Piccolo, his son Sandro, and two other gangsters: Andrea Adamo and Gaspare Pulizzi.

November 7: Police in Sweden call on the nation's Minister of Justice to establish a "Swedish FBI," tasked to suppress criminal activity by motorcycle gangs and Russian mobsters. In Palermo, Sicily, police announce discovery of a list comprising the Mafia's "Ten Commandments," during a raid on a fugitive mafioso's home.

November 8: Yakuza assassins accidentally kill innocent civilian Hiroshi Miyamoto at a hospital in Kurume, Fukuoka, Japan.

November 9: RCMP officers execute a seizure order against a Hells Angels clubhouse in Nanaimo, British Columbia.

November 11: Paramilitary police arrest fugitive 'Ndrangheta member Cosimo Romanello, in hiding since June 2004, at his home in Siderno, Italy. Graeme Pearson retires from his post as director of the Scottish Crime and Drug Enforcement

Agency, calling for broader police authority to confiscate property owned by drug traffickers.

November 12: Yakuza member Shigeki Koga suffers fatal gunshot wounds in Kurume, Fukuoka, Japan.

November 13: Days after a leading prosecutor's announcement that the Mafia's ruling commission no longer exists, police in Sicily announce their raid on "a summit of Mafia dons," jailing fugitives Andrea Gioe, Vincenzo Mangione, Domenico Serio, and brother Nunzio Serio. Elsewhere authorities serve 70 warrants in Catania and Syracuse, jailing more suspects on charges of Mafia association, drug trafficking, extortion and usury. In Pomona, Calif., two gunmen fatally wound Mexican Mafia member Frank "Frankie B" Buelna at Characters Sports Bar.

November 16: Three mafiosi receive prison terms for extortion in Palermo, Sicily. The defendants include Francolino Spadaro (16 years), Giovanni Di Salvo (14 years), and Lorenzo D'Aleo (10½ years). On the same day, the ministers of internal affairs for Serbia and Slovakia, Dragan Jočić and Robert Kalinak, sign an agreement to collaborate in fighting organized crime.

November 20: The lower house of the Dutch parliament unanimously passes a motion urging Japan to financially compensate the women forced into sexual slavery during World War II.

November 21: A court in Rome, Italy, announces the acquittal of three defendants charged with killing banker Roberto Calvi in 1982. The court blames unnamed mafiosi for Calvi's slaying.

November 22: China's state news media announces that five Hollywood studios have sued a Chinese Internet service provider and an Internet café accused of selling downloads of various recent hit films.

November 26: Douglas McCarron, president of the United Brotherhood of Carpenters, institutes temporary emergency supervision over Manhattan East Side Local 157, following charges of bribery, no-show business agents, and link to Manhattan's Mafia families. The local's top three officers resign. In Rome, Italian Justice Minister Clemente Mastella calls for cancellation of a fictional TV series, "The Boss of All the Bosses," based on the life of mafioso Salvatore Riina, which portrays him as a hero. Network producers cancel the show on November 29.

November 27: An ambush in Kurume, Fukuoka, Japan, kills Yakuza leader Yoshikazu Matsuo and his chauffeur.

November 28: British businessmen David Bermingham, Giles Darby and Gary Mulgrew plead guilty to one count of wire fraud related to the Enron scandal. On February 22, 2008, all three defendants receive 37-month prison terms, plus an order for payment of $7.3 million in restitution to the Royal Bank of Scotland. They enter separate American prisons between April 30 and May 9, 2008, with prospective release dates in January 2011. Canada's House of Commons unanimously approves a draft motion urging Japan to make a "formal and sincere apology" to "comfort women" enslaved as prostitutes during World War II. Terra Securities ASA, a Norwegian security firm that sold various financial instruments, filed for bankruptcy, one day after the Financial Supervisory Authority of Norway withdraws its permission to operate, based on charges that Terra misinformed eight municipalities in Norway as to the risk of their investments.

November 29: Police in Montreal, Québec, cap "Operation Nanti" by arresting 10 persons suspected of drug trafficking in conjunction with the local Mafia.

December: The city council of Amsterdam, Holland, revokes the business license of the Yab Yum brothel owned by members of the Hells Angels MC. Spanish police cap their "Project Valkiria" with arrests of eight Hells Angels on various charges.

December 2: Somali pirates release the MV *Al Marjan* and its 22 crewmen, captured in October. Unknown kidnappers abduct popular singer Paulo Sergio Gómez Sánchez after a concert in Morelia, Michoacán, Mexico. Police find his tortured, strangled corpse on December 3, blaming drug cartel members who had warned Gómez to stay out of Morelia.

December 3: Fugitive mafioso Daniele Emmanuello dies in a shootout with police at Villarosa, Sicily. Unidentified gunmen Francesco and Luigi Comberiati, sons of imprisoned 'Ndrangheta boss Vincent Comberiati, outside a bar in Petilia Policastro, Italy.

December 4: Police in Sicily arrest 46 suspected mafiosi, while filing new charges against 23 already in custody. Pirates attack an ExxonMobil oil tanker in the Niger Delta of southern Nigeria, killing one crewman and wounding another.

December 5: LASO officers arrest five Mexican Mafia members on charges related to the March 2006 murder of victim Robert Whitehead. Defendants include George Bravo, Maria Dolores Llantada, Angelita Martinez, Yvonne Montes, and David Shahagun.

December 7: Retired tennis star John McEnroe voices concern that the Russian Mafia and other factions of organized crime use extortion to fix tennis matches.

December 8: Suspected drug cartel members kill Mexican crime reporter Gerardo Israel García Pimentel during a high-speed chase near his home, in Uruapan, Michoacán.

December 10: Yakuza boss Osamu Yano receives a death sentence in Tokyo, Japan, for his role in five murders committed during 2002 and 2003. Somali pirates demand $1 million ransom for release of the chemical tanker MV *Golden Nori* and its 22 crewmen, seized on October 28. President Bush grants executive clemency to 13 defendants convicted of organized crime offenses. He pardons John Edward Casto (1990, distribution of cocaine), Jackie Ray Clayborn (1993, manufacturing marijuana), Debbie Sue Conklin (1990, conspiracy to distribute methamphetamine), John Fornaby (1991, conspiracy to distribute cocaine), Daniel Ray Freeman (1963, violation of Internal Revenue liquor laws), Paul Dwight Hawkins (1990, conspiracy to import marijuana), Roger Paul Ingram (1987, conspiracy to possess with intent to distribute ecstasy), William Charles Jordan (2000, managing and conducting an illegal gambling business), Billy Joe LaForce (1991, conspiracy to possess marijuana with intent to distribute), John F. McDermott (1995, receiving kickbacks in defense procurement contracts), William James Norman (1970, possession of an unregistered distillery, carrying on the business of a distiller without giving the required bond, possession and custody of a still without the required sign outside the premises, working at a distillery without the required sign outside the premises, unlawfully producing distilled spirits from mash and similar material), Charles Eddie Trobaugh (1965, liquor law violations), and Steven Wayne Whitlock (1990, conspiracy to import marijuana). Bush also commutes the 235-month sentence of Michael Dwayne Short (1992, aiding and abetting the distribution of cocaine base), reducing it to five years' supervised parole.

December 12: Somali pirates free the Japanese chemical tanker MV *Golden Noori*, six weeks after its capture. Agazio Loiero, governor of Calabria, Italy, declares a "state of emergency" due to Mafia looting of the region's health system. Sicilian immigrant Emanuele "Lino" Saputo — founder of a major cheese-producing firm in Montreal, Québec — denies allegations of Mafia association aired by Italian police. Francesco Forgione, president of Italy's Antimafia Commission, tells reporters that the Mafia earns $220 billion yearly from investments in foreign multinational companies such as Gazprom — Russia's largest corporation and the world's largest extractor of natural gas. Police in Winnipeg, Canada, cap "Project Drill" by raiding a Hells Angels clubhouse, arresting 14 persons after seizing marijuana, guns, and $70,000 in cash.

December 13: Jurors in New York City acquit Genovese Family member Carmine Polito on charges of murdering loan-shark Sabotino Lombardi and wounding his cousin Michael D'Urso in 1994.

December 13: Under pressure from Amnesty International, the European Parliament in Strasbourg, Austria, passes a resolution calling for the Japanese government to formally acknowledge its responsibility for sexual slavery conducted in occupied territories during World War II.

December 14: Italian police capture fugitive Camorra boss Edoardo Contini in a Naples suburb, after seven years in hiding. In Montreal, Québec, mafioso Francesco Del Balso waives his right to a preliminary inquiry on charges of attempting to extort cash from industrialist John Xanthoudakis.

December 17: Spokesmen for the East African Seafarers' Assistance Programme announce that Somali pirates have attacked an Italian-flagged container ship, the MV *Jolly Turchese*, en route to Mombassa, Kenya. Owners of the ship deny the report on December 18. Rival members of the Hells Angels and Bandidos brawl in Ibbenbüren, Germany, on the first day of a civil lawsuit involving both MCs. Police in Grants Pass, Ore., arrest six members of the Vagos MC for the August beating of a member who planned to quit the club. Charges include first-degree burglary, second-degree robbery, coercion and second-degree kidnapping. In Kurume, Fukuoka, Japan, leaders of the rival Dōjin-kai and Kitamura-gumi Yakuza clans announce a cease-fire in their latest gang war. Hostilities officially cease on February 5, 2008. New Jersey Attorney General Anne Milgram announces the indictment of 32 Lucchese Family members and associates on racketeering charges that include a scheme to provide imprisoned members of the Bloods with drugs. Defendants include *caporegimes* Joseph "Joey Dee" DiNapoli, Matthew Madonna, and Ralph Perna. Police in Germany and Italy arrest four suspects in the slaying of six Italian mobsters at Duisberg, Germany.

December 19: Gambino Family *caporegime* Gregory "Big Georgie" DeCicco pleads guilty to running a loan-sharking operation from 1999 to 2007.

December 20: The Supreme Court of Canada refuses to hear an extradition appeal filed by Sicilian mafioso Alfonso Caruana. In Italy, police arrest supermarket magnate Giuseppe Grigoli on charges of Mafia association. The U.S. Marshals Service adds fugitive Mexican Mafia member David Gonzalez Sauceda to its 15 Most Wanted list.

December 21: Thousands gather for an anti–Mafia concert in Corleone, Sicily.

December 22: Yakuza boss Kakuji Inagawa dies of natural causes in Japan.

December 23: Armed pirates board a charter yacht off the coast of Saint Vincent in the Caribbean, looting the craft and wounding both passengers aboard.

December 24: Italy's largest cement company, Italcementi S.p.A., announces suspension of its Sicilian operations as a protest against Mafia extortion demands.

December 27: A judge in Rosemead, Calif., orders Mexican Mafia "shot-caller" Eulalio "Lalo" Martinez to stand trial for the murder of victim Donald "Pato" Schubert. Authorities in Vigone, northern Italy, blame mobsters for a stable fire that killed 20 racehorses and caused £1.5 million in property damage.

December 28: Jurors in New York City convict mafioso Alphonse Persico of murdering William Cutolo in May 1999. In Rosarito, Mexico, soldiers seize 200 guns from the town's police department for ballistics comparison with bullets retrieved from the bodies of drug-murder victims. Unknown gunmen murder camorrista Francesco Verde in Naples, Italy. In Palermo, Sicily, an appellate court reduces the 14-year prison sentence of mafioso Giuseppe Salvatore Riina, received in 2004, to eight years and 10 months.

December 29: Federal agents disarm the entire police force of Playas de Rosarito, in Baja California, on suspicion that the officers collaborate with drug cartels.

2008 January: New York mafioso John Edward Alite pleads guilty to two murders, four murder conspiracies, at least eight shootings and two attempted shootings as well as armed home invasions and armed robberies in New York, New Jersey, Pennsylvania and Florida.

January 1: Retired mafioso Salvatore "Bill" Bonanno dies from a heart attack at his home in Tucson, Ariz.

January 3: After five years of fruitless searching, British disc jockey Peter Lloyd Price announces that he will seek Mafia aid in locating his biological father, believed to be a Sicilian.

January 5: A Sicilian court orders Salvatore Riina and six other mafiosi to pay the family of murdered judge Paolo Borsellino €3.3 million. The Czech newspaper *Mladá fronta DNES* quotes official sources claiming that organized crime has influenced national defense contracts.

January 7: Detroit mafioso Vincent "Little Vince" Meli dies of bone cancer at St. John Macomb-Oakland Hospital in Warren, Mich.

January 9: The IMB reports a 300-percent increase in pirate attacks off Somalia's coast, compared to a 10-percent increase worldwide.

January 15: Italian police cap "Operation Viola" by arresting 51 members of a Nigerian syndicate specializing in drug smuggling and human trafficking. Elsewhere in Europe, officers jail an additional 15 suspects.

January 16: Five reputed mafiosi in Montreal, Québec— Francesco Arcadi, Lorenzo Giordano, Paolo Renda, Nicolo Rizzuto, and Rocco Sollecito — waive preliminary hearings on charges of extortion, illegal betting, and importing drugs and weapons, electing to proceed with trial. In Palermo, Sicily, police arrest 39 members of Salvatore Lo Piccolo's Mafia faction. In Leeds, England, police charge Blue Angels MC member Paul Miller with attempted murder, following the shooting of motorcycle shop owner Andrew Malham.

January 18: A court in Palermo convicts Sicilian president Salvatore "Totò" Cuffaro on charges of Mafia association. Cuffaro receives a sentence of five years in solitary confinement. In Serbia, gangster Sretko "The Beast" Kalini receives a 40-year prison term for multiple murders, kidnappings, terrorist acts, and the March 2003 assassination of Serbian Prime Minister Zoran Djindjic.

January 20: A judge in Palermo sentences 38 mafiosi to prison terms totaling more than 400 years. The stiffest sentences, 20 years each, go to Franco Bonura and Antonino Rotolo, leaders of the Uditore and Pagliarelli Mafia factions. Thirty Hells Angels and Outlaws MC members brawl at England's Birmingham International Airport. Police charge 12 combatants, seizing weapons including brass knuckles, hammers, and a meat cleaver.

January 21: Italian newspapers announce that jailed mafioso Gaspare Pulizzi has turned informer against Salvatore Lo Piccolo and other underworld leaders. Mafioso Antonio Rotolo receives a 13-year prison term in Palermo, Sicily. Mexican security forces arrest Sinaloa Cartel leader Alfredo Beltrán Leyva in Culiacán, seizing $900,000 in cash and luxury watches.

January 23: Mafiosi Anthony Arillotta, Fotios "Fredd" Geas, and brother Ty Gease face trial on extortion conspiracy charges in Springfield, Mass. Jurors acquit all three defendants on January 28. Russian police arrest mobster Semion "The Brainy Don" Mogilevich in Moscow.

January 24: Police in Moscow arrest Russian mobster Semion Yudkovich Mogilevich on tax-evasion charges. They release him on July 24, 2009, claiming that the charges "are not of a particularly grave nature," and he disappears prior to trial. The FBI lists Mogilevich as one of its ten most wanted fugitives on October 22, 2009.

January 26: Sicilian President Salvatore "Totò" Cuffaro resigns amid reports that Italy's national government plans to oust him on charges of Mafia association. Somali pirates seize an Oman-flagged fishing vessel off the coast of Puntland.

January 30: Police in Caltanissetta, Sicily, arrest Mario Colombini — CEO of Italcementi SpA, Italy's biggest cement manufacturer — on charges of Mafia association. Venezuelan police find Colombian drug lord Wilber Alirio Varela Fajardo murdered at a resort hotel in the state of Mérida.

January 31: Officers in Palermo, Sicily, arrest mafioso Andrea Bonaccorso for the June 2007 slaying of victim Nicola Ingarao. Unknown gunmen kidnap Chechen mobster Movladi "Lord Lenin" Atlangeriyev outside a restaurant in Moscow, Russia. Atlangeriyev remains missing and presumed dead. In Fargo, N.D., police seize 600 pounds of khat at Hector International Airport.

February 1: Somali pirates seize a Danish-flagged tug boat, the *Svitzer Korsakov*, holding the vessel and six crewmen for ransom. They release the hostages and vessel on March 17, following payment of $700,000 ransom.

February 2: Italian immigrant and alleged mafioso Giuseppe Massimo Chindamo receives a 25-year sentence for fatally stabbing an ex-girlfriend in London, England, in 1995. The court also orders payment of nearly £100,000 in compensation to his victim's family.

February 4: Suspected Russian gunmen murder Irish mobster Paddy Doyle in Estepona, Spain.

February 5: Televised political debates in Poland reveal Russian mobster Semion Mogilevich's control of the Hungarian firm Eural-Trans-Gaz, which signed a contract to provide Poland with natural gas in 2003.

February 6: Federal agents in Brooklyn, N.Y., arrest 50 Gambino Family members and associates — including imprisoned Sicilian mafioso Antonio Rotolo — on various charges including labor racketeering and five counts of murder. In Perth, Australia, the Gypsy Jokers MC loses its legal appeal against the 2003 West Australia Corruption and Crime Commission Act, requiring dismantling of its fortified headquarters.

February 10: Police retrieve the corpse of Mafia boss Giovanni Bonanno — a fugitive since January 2006 — from an unmarked grave outside Palermo, Sicily.

February 11: A U.S. naval ship shells the waterfront at Eyl, Somalia, to prevent resupply of pirate ships.

February 12: Police blame Mafia gunmen for the murders of brothers Gianpaolo and Giuseppe Riina, in Partinico, Sicily. Their father was killed near the same spot, 10 years earlier. Authorities in Sicily guard a Catholic bishop who refused to officiate at the funeral of mafioso Crocefisso Emanuello.

February 13: Imprisoned mafiosi Michele Greco dies of natural causes at a hospital in Rome, Italy. Police raids in London, England, jail 22 persons linked to a £100 million cocaine-smuggling ring. Somali troops exchange gunfire with pirates attempting to resupply the captured tugboat *Svitzer Korsakov*.

February 18: Police in Reggio Calabria, Italy, arrest 'Ndrangheta boss Pasquale "The Supreme One" Condello, with his son and nephew.

February 19: Sheriff's deputies in Pima County, Ariz., seize 150 dogs and arrest six participants in a network that breeds dogs for illegal fighting.

February 20: Italian authorities release a 230-page report detailing criminal activities and international connections of the 'Ndrangheta crime syndicate.

February 23: Nuestra Familia reorganizes its leadership structure under David "DC" Cervantes, with new written directives for gang leaders transferred from state to federal custody in 2005.

February 28: A spokesman for Serbian Prime Minister Branislav Ristivojevic tells reporters that the country will file lawsuits at the International Court of Justice against the U.S. and any other nations that officially recognize "the fictitious Mafia state" in Kosovo and Metohija province.

March: A report from the Pew Centre, a Washington think tank, reveals that one in 100 American adults — some 2.3 million — are now in prison. Nearly half of all federal inmates are confined for nonviolent drug offenses.

March 2: Police in Palermo, Sicily, jail three persons on charges of harboring fugitive mafiosi Salvatore and Sandro Lo Piccolo prior to their capture in November 2007.

March 4: Authorities in Calabria, Italy, seize property valued in excess of $220 million from members of the 'Ndrangheta.

March 5: Prosecutors in Italy charge highly-decorated anti–Mafia policeman Riccardo Ravera with extortion and trafficking in stolen artworks. Detectives say he helped steal art valued over £6 million from the summer home of Italy's royal family in 2004, later returning 42 pieces when only 34 were reported missing. Members of the Hells Angels and Outlaws MC's brawl at a motorcycle rally in Germany. Thai police arrest international arms dealer Viktor Bout and codefendant Andrew Smulian on charges filed in the U.S., including conspiracy to arm terrorists in Colombia.

March 7: Sicilian grocer Fabio Messina opens a new supermarket in Palermo, announcing that it will carry only products sold by firms which refuse to meet Mafia extortion demands. Police in Sydney, Australia, arrest members of a Korean-based sex trafficking syndicate.

March 8: Czech police blame an ongoing "Mafia" war for a shooting that leaves two Russian victims wounded near Prague's Old Town Square.

March 9: As its stock prices plummet, Canadian cheese producer Saputo, Inc., files defamation suits against three Canadian media groups that have publicly linked former CEO Lino Saputo to Mafia money-laundering.

March 10: The *New York Times* reports that New York Governor Eliot Laurence Spitzer has spent an estimated $80,000 on a prostitution service called Emperors Club VIP. Spitzer announces his resignation on March 12, effective on March 17. On July 16 the *Times* reports that Spitzer used campaign funds to hire prostitutes. In November 2008, prosecutors announce that Spitzer will not face criminal charges.

March 11: A judge in Palermo, Sicily, commutes mafioso Salvatore Ferranti's prison term to house arrest, on grounds that the 460-pound prisoner is too fat to survive in jail. In Naples, Italy, officers seize assets worth €150 million from Gaetano Iorio, a businessman linked to the Camorra's Casalesi clan. In Calabria, prosecutors announce that members of the 'Ndrangheta have used computers to siphon £10million from an Italian government bank account, transferring the money to Egypt via Bologna. Police in Tijuana, Mexico, capture fugitive drug cartel leader Gustavo Rivera Martinez.

March 12: A federal grand jury in Detroit indicts four police officers and a member of the Highwaymen MC on bribery and drug trafficking charges.

March 17: Otto Friedli, a founder of the original Hells Angels chapter, dies in California.

March 18: Unidentified gunmen murder Russian mobster Marat Balagula in Brooklyn, N.Y.

March 20: Police in the Republic of Moldova seize 200 kilos of Afghan heroin valued at €10 million.

March 23: Unknown gunmen execute 'Ndrangheta member Luca Megna and wound his five-year-old daughter, leaving her comatose in Calabria, Italy.

March 24: President Bush grants executive clemency to four defendants convicted of organized crime offenses. He pardons William L. Baker (1980, distribution of a controlled substance and falsifying records); Anthony C. Foglio (1996, distribution of marijuana); and William Marcus McDonald (1984, distribution of cocaine, possession of cocaine with intent to distribute). Bush also commutes the sentence of Robert Michael Milroy (1975, importation of heroin). Somali pirates steal two UN World Food Program training boats from the docks at Merca.

March 25: Paramilitary police in Catania, Sicily, arrested local Mafia boss Francesco Montagno Bozzone and 14 associates on charges of extortion, drug trafficking and possessing illegal weapons. Apparently retaliating for Luca Megna's slaying on March 23, assassins in Calabria, Italy, kill rival 'Ndrangheta member Giuseppe Cavallo and wound his wife. Authorities in Bergen County, N.J., announce the arrest of 45 participants in a gambling ring that earned $1 million per month. Raiders in that case seize 45 arrested in illegal Bergen County gambling ring seize more than $5 million in cash, five cars, and five pounds of marijuana.

March 26: In Washington, D.C., bankruptcy court examiner Michael Missal unseals a report detailing "significant improper and imprudent practices" by New Century Financial Corporation, America's second-largest sub-prime mortgage lender. Federal regulators sue three former NCFC officers on December 7, 2009, accusing them of misleading company investors about the firm's prospects.

March 27: Walter Veltroni, head of Italy's Democratic Party, brands Silvio Berlusconi and his Forza Italia Party as tools of the Mafia. On the same day, 'Ndrangheta gunmen execute Francesco Capicchiano in Calabria, Italy. British Columbia's Supreme Court rules against prosecutors attempting to Hells Angels member David Francis Giles on a charge of possessing cocaine for the benefit of a criminal organization.

March 29: Mob boss Anthony "The British Bulldog" Burnes suffers fatal gunshot wounds outside a pub in Liverpool, England.

March 31: U.S. District Judge Nicholas Garaufis sentences Bonanno Family member Vincent "Vinny Gorgeous" Basciano to life imprisonment for the 2001 murder of a rival New York gangster.

April 4: Somali pirates seize the French luxury liner Le Ponant with 30 crew members aboard. Following payment of $2 million ransom on April 11, French troops in helicopters capture six of the buccaneers and recover the money.

April 7: An unknown gunman kills mobster-turned-author Georgi Stoev in Sofia, Bulgaria. On the same day, while France deploys elite GIGN commandos to Djibouti, pending raids against Somali pirates, local militiamen fire on pirates commanding the captured yacht Le Ponant.

April 10: Police in Kennewick, Wash., raid a Gypsy Joker MC clubhouse, seizing stolen property and weapons, arresting four members for possession of methamphetamine.

April 16: French commandos fly six captures Somali pirates to Paris, where they are charged with hostage-taking, hijacking and theft on April 18.

April 17: Massachusetts mafioso Frankie Roche pleads guilty on federal charges of murder in aid of racketeering. He admits accepting $10,000 to kill Adolfo "Big Al" Bruno in November 2003.

April 20: Somali pirates armed with grenade launchers capture the Spanish tuna fishing boat Playa de Bakio, with 26 crewmen aboard. Spanish authorities announce the boat's release on April 26, following payment of a $1.2 million ransom.

April 21: Pirates fire on a Japanese oil tanker in the Gulf of Aden, off the coast of Yemen, spilling several hundred gallons of fuel at sea. They also seize a freighter from Dubai, the Al-Khaleej.

April 22: Somali security forces liberate the Al-Khaleej, arresting seven pirates. The hijackers and four accomplices receive life prison terms on April 28.

April 24: Police in Eugene, Ore., arrest Mongols MC members Nathan A. Cassidy, Justin J. "Mooch" DeLoretto, and Matthew A. Weiss with attempted assault on detectives, after they allegedly tried to run a police car off the road.

April 25: Spanish police recapture fugitive Moroccan drug lord Mohamed Ouazzani, who escaped from prison in 2007.

April 26: A shootout between rival drug cartels in Tijuana, Mexico, leaves 15 dead and seven wounded. Police recover 21 cars, 54 guns, and 1,500 shell casings.

April 28: The U.S., Great Britain, France and Panama introduce a draft resolution to the UN Security Council aimed at combating maritime piracy for ransom in Somali waters and the Gulf of Aden, authorizing use of "all necessary means" to fight buccaneers.

May 1: Incarcerated Gulf Cartel leader Osiel Cárdenas Guillén hosts a "Day of the Child" party for 2,000 guests in Ciudad Acuña, Coahuila, Mexico, including food, music, clowns, and ponies. On the same day, relatives find "D.C. Madam" Deborah Jeane Palfrey hanging in a storage shed outside her mother's home in Tarpon Springs, Fla. Authorities rule her death a suicide.

May 6: DEA spokesmen in California announce the climax of "Operation Sudden Fall," an undercover operation on the San Diego State University campus. The campaign has jailed 96 suspects, including 75 students accused of selling or buying cocaine, marijuana, or ecstasy.

May 8: Drug cartel gunmen murder Edgar Millan Gomez, director of national police operations against drug traffickers, at his home in Mexico City.

May 9: Assassin's kill Esteban Robles, chief of Mexico City's anti-kidnap squad.

May 10: Presumed cartel soldiers murder Juan

Antonio Roman Garcia, deputy chief of police in Ciudad Juarez, Mexico.

May 17: Somali pirates seize the *Victoria*, a Jordanian-flagged ship carrying sugar, then release it on May 23.

May 23: Police in San Luca, Italy, arrest 'Ndrangheta boss Giuseppe Nirta.

May 25: Pirates seize the Dutch freighter *Amiya Scan* off Somalia's coast, holding its nine crewmen hostage until June 25.

May 26: Police raids in Caserta, Italy, jail 50 alleged Camorra members.

May 27: Police in Holdenville, Okla., arrest six suspects in a dogfighting and drug-trafficking ring. One of those detained is a former NFL football player.

May 28: Drug raids in Culiacán, Mexico, leave seven policemen dead and four wounded. Somali pirates seize two cargo ships, the MV *Arean* and MV *Lehmann*, in the Gulf of Aden.

May 29: Indicted Gambino Family boss Nicholas "Little Nick" Corozzo surrenders in New York after four months in hiding. He pleads guilty to racketeering charges in July 2008 and receives a prison term of 13.5 years on April 17, 2009. A sentence of 4.5 to 13.5 years is imposed for state gambling offenses on April 28, 2009. His presumed release date is March 2, 2020.

May 30: Somali pirates seize a German cargo ship, the *Lehmann Timber*, releasing it and its crew on July 8, after payment of a $750,000 ransom.

May 31: Federal officials in Washington, D.C., announce application of drug-trafficking laws to impose financial sanctions on Mexican cartels, the 'Ndrangheta, and the Kurdistan Workers' Party, as well as certain individuals in Afghanistan, Turkey, and Venezuela.

June 2: The UN Security Council passes a resolution authorizing foreign navies to patrol Somalian waters and intercept pirates.

June 4: Federal agents in New York City arrest Thomas Gioeli, acting boss of the Colombo Family, and seven associates on charges of racketeering conspiracy, extortion, robbery, and murder. On the same day, New York mafioso Francesco "Franky Boy" Cali pleads guilty to conspiring to extort funds from trucker Joseph Vollaro in Staten Island. Incarcerated at Brooklyn's Metropolitan Detention Center, Cali is released on April 6, 2009.

June 5: Federal prosecutors in Massachusetts charge mafioso Fotios Geas with the murder of Adolfo "Big Al" Bruno. A federal grand jury in San Diego, Calif., indicts nine imprisoned Mexican Mafia members for conspiracy to distribute methamphetamine. Defendants include Marco Corrado, Jorge Lopez-Herrera, Maria "Kika"

Madriaga, Jose Alberto "Bat" Marquez, Rolando "Rolo" Montemayor, Julia Morones, Ruben Santos, Brian Mark "Dusty" Smith, and Juan Manuel "Manny" Velarde.

June 6: The mayor of Eyl, Somalia, complains that regional soldiers in Puntland have joined forces with pirates. The accusation prompts his dismissal on June 9.

June 9: DEA agents and local authorities seize 262 tons of hashish in Afghanistan, capping "Operation Albatross" with the world's largest single-drug seizure on record. Twelve suspects face various charges.

June 13: Spanish police arrest 20 members of the Russian Tambov Gang in Madrid, the Balearic islands and the coastal resorts of Malaga and Marbella.

June 14: An unidentified assassin fatally stabs anti-corruption activist Giuseppe Basile outside his home in Puglia, Italy.

June 15: Somalia's interim government hires the French private security firm Secopex to combat piracy, at a price of $75–$150 million annually for three years.

June 19: Members of the Mongrel Mob gang set fire to the rival Road Knights MC clubhouse in Invercargill, New Zealand, stealing two motorcycles. Police charge two suspects with arson on September 6.

June 21: Police and Humane Society investigators raid a dog-fighting facility in Atmore, Ala.

June 23: Somali pirates storm a yacht in the Gulf of Aden, taking its captain and three European tourists hostage.

June 26: Cartel gunmen kill federal police commander Igor Labastida and a bodyguard at a restaurant in Mexico City, also wounding three other guards and several civilians. In Kentucky, five members of the Iron Horsemen MC receive federal prison terms totaling 16 years for drug trafficking.

July 8: Somali pirates release the cargo vessel MV *Lehmann Timber* following receipt of $750,000 ransom.

July 20: Somali pirates hijack a Japanese-owned bulk carrier, the MV *Stella Maris*, with 20 crewmen aboard.

July 22: The Italian Senate passes a bill granting immunity from criminal prosecution to the nation's the President, Prime Minister, and Speakers of the Senate and Lower House, as long as they remain in office. All four face active charges of Mafia association.

July 25: Estonia urges the European Union to take stronger action against Somali piracy.

July 29: Police in Berywn Heights, Md., raid the home of Mayor Cheye Calvo, following delivery of a box containing 32 pounds of marijuana, addressed to his wife. The case collapses when officers fail to provide a search warrant.

July 30: ATF and FBI agents raid several Chicago properties linked to the Outlaws MC.

August 4: A federal grand jury in Tampa, Fla., indicts mafioso John Gotti Jr. on conspiracy charges including cocaine smuggling and three counts of murder.

August 6: French prosecutors in the Taiwan frigate scandal dismiss the case for "lack of evidence," after seven years of investigation. Police in San Luca, Italy, arrest Paolo Nirta, head of the Nirta-Strangio 'Ndrangheta clan.

August 7: Police in Toronto, Canada, arrest fugitive 'Ndrangheta boss Giuseppe Coluccio. He is extradited to Rome on August 19. The IMB warns of pirate "mother vessels" lurking in the Gulf of Aden.

August 8: Pirates attack, but fail to capture, a bulk carrier in the Gulf of Aden.

August 9: Somali pirates release two German hostages upon receipt of $1 million ransom. Four pirates armed with machetes board the sailboat *Sunday's Child*, anchored at Guatemala's Monkey Bay Marina, killing owner Dan Dryden and wounding his wife before looting the vessel. Authorities subsequently charge brothers Carlos Ernesto Lemus Hernandez and Elfido Concepcion Lemus Hernandez with murder.

August 12: Somali pirates capture the Thai cargo ship *Thor Star*, with 28 persons aboard, and the Nigerian tugboat MT *Yengeoa Ocean*. Jurors in San Bernardino, Calif., recommend execution Mexican Mafia associates Lorenzo Arias and Luis "Maldito" Mendoza, convicted of murder. Both are formally sentenced to death on September 9. Jurors in Modesto, Calif., convict Nuestra Familia enforcer Felix "Gato" Lopez of second-degree murder and other charges related to a fatal shooting at a local tattoo parlor.

August 13: Police in Sioux Falls, S.D., seize 106 pounds of khat.

August 14: Members of AK81, a street gang affiliated with the Hells Angels MC, fatally shoot Turkish gang member Osman Nuri Dogan in Tingbjerg, Denmark.

August 15: Mexican Mafia member Juvenal Vega-Soto receives a life sentence in San Diego, Calif., for conspiracy to distribute methamphetamine.

August 19: Somali pirates seize the Malaysian palm oil tanker MT *Bunga Melati Dua*, with 39 crewmen aboard. They release the ship and hostages on September 29, following payment of ransom.

August 21: Somali pirates capture three vessels — the German cargo ship MV *BBC Trinidad* with nine crewmen, the Iranian bulk carrier MV *Iran Deyanat* with 29 crew, and a Japanese cargo ship MT *Irene* — in coastal waters. They release the MV *BBC Trinidad* and MT *Irene* on September 11, following payment of ransom.

August 22: Genovese Family *consigliere* Dominick Cirillo leaves prison on parole. A multinational naval coalition, dubbed Combined Task Force 150, establishes a Maritime Security Patrol Area in the Gulf of Aden.

August 23: Somali pirates fire on another Japanese cargo ship in the Gulf of Aden but fail to board it.

August 26: California Attorney General Jerry Brown announces that Citigroup has agreed to pay nearly $18 million in refunds and fines to settle charges that it wrongly took funds from the accounts of credit card customers. The payments include $14 million in restitution to 53,000 customers nationwide.

August 27: Police in Tijuana, Mexico, blame drug cartels for the slayings of three headless victims found in a local rubbish dump.

August 28: Mexican Mafia leader Salvador Orozco Hernandez and brother Alfred Hernandez receive 10-year sentences in San Bernardino, Calif., after pleading guilty to attempted murder.

August 29: Pirates seize the Malaysian tanker MT *Bunga Melati 5* in the Gulf of Aden, off Yemen's coast, with 41 crewmen aboard, demanding $8.2 million in ransom.

September 2: Somali pirates seize the French yacht *Carre d'as* with two persons aboard, demanding $1 million ransom. French troops storm the boat on September 15, killing one hijacker and arresting six others, while freeing the hostages.

September 3: Somali pirates in the Gulf of Aden seize an Egyptian cargo ship with 25 crew aboard.

September 5: Malaysian authorities dispatch three naval ships to guard merchant vessels in the Gulf of Aden. Spanish police arrest fugitive Colombian drug lord Edgar Guillermo Vallejo-Guarin, AKA "Beto the Gypsy," at a hotel in Madrid.

September 7: Crewmen aboard three separate ships repel pirate attacks in the Gulf of Aden. A minister from Somalia's autonomous Puntland region announces the capture of 14 pirates.

September 8–12: ATF agents instruct 40 Mexican police and military officers in techniques for suppressing small-arms trafficking.

September 10: Somali pirates miss a Greek cargo ship but seize a South Korean bulk carrier with 22 crewmen aboard, releasing it on October 16.

September 11: Mexican Mafia members Arthur Garcia and Ricardo Polanco receive prison terms of 55 and 50 years, respectively, for the 2005 murder of victim Frankie "Frankie B" Buelna in Pomona, Calif. A Basque tuna trawler eludes Somali pirates.

September 15: Somali pirates hijack the chemical tanker MT *Stolt Valor*, from Hong Kong, with 33 crewmen aboard. In Morelia, Michoacán, Mexico, drug cartel gunmen lob grenades into a crowd, killing eight persons and wounding more than 100.

September 16: French commandos liberate the hijacked yacht *Carre d'as* in Somalia. "Operation Solare" culminates with the arrests of more than 200 persons in the U.S., Italy, Mexico and Guatemala, targeting drug traffickers from Mexico's Gulf Cartel and the 'Ndrangheta.

September 16–17: Across the U.S., federal agents and local police cap "Project Reckoning" with the arrest of 175 persons linked to Mexico's Gulf Cartel. Overall, the 15-month campaign has jailed 507 defendants while seizing 711 kilograms of cocaine, 1,039 pounds of methamphetamine, 19 pounds of heroin, 51,258 pounds of marijuana, 176 vehicles, 167 weapons and $60.1 million in cash.

September 17: Janette V. Amaya, a "tax collector" for the Mexican Mafia, receives a six-year sentence in San Diego, Calif., after pleading no contest to a charge of transporting heroin for sale. Police in Pavia, Italy, arrest fugitive 'Ndrangheta boss Francesco Pelle on murder charges. In Montreal, Québec, mafiosis Nicolo Rizzuto, Rocco Sollecito, Paolo Renda, Francesco Arcadi, Francesco Del Balso and Lorenzo Giordano plead guilty on charges of conspiracy to traffic drugs, extort, run illegal bookmaking and possess illegal goods. In Naples, Italy, suspected Camorra gunmen murder six African immigrants suspected of smuggling drugs. The slayings prompt an immigrant riot on September 18.

September 18: Somali pirates capture a Greek chemical tanker, the MV *Centauri*, with 25 crew members, marking the 55th recognized seizure in coastal waters. A police raid in Culiacán, Mexico, nets $26 million in case, four pounds of marijuana, and two guns from the home of a Sinaloa Cartel member.

September 20: Frank Valenti, former top mafioso in Rochester, N.Y., dies of natural causes at a nursing home in Sugar Land, Tex., at age 97.

September 21: Pirates in speedboats seize a Greek bulk carrier, the MV *Captain Stephanos*, with 19 crewmen. They release the ship and hostages on December 8.

September 22: Viktor Bout's extradition hearing begins in Bangkok, Thailand. Police in Campania, Italy, arrest Camorra member Alfonso Cesarano in connection with the murders of six African immigrants, while 500 troops patrol the district.

September 23: The U.S. Navy ship *John Lenthall* fires on two suspected pirate vessels off the coast of Somalia.

September 24: Leonard Epps, target of a Mexican Mafia murder plot in San Bernardino, Calif., files a $50 million lawsuit against six gang members and associates for conspiracy to commit murder, negligence and intentional infliction of mental distress.

September 25: Somali pirates hijack the Ukrainian cargo vessel MV *Faina*, with 21 persons aboard. Its cargo includes 33 army tanks and large amounts of ammunition. A Russian warship arrives on September 26, but pirates hold their prize until a $3.2 million ransom is paid on February 5, 2009.

September 26: Somali pirates seize the Liberian-flagged oil tanker MV *Genius* and 19 crewmen, holding it until ransom is paid on November 21.

September 27: Somali hijackers release three captive ships — the MV *Al Monsourah*, MT *Bunga Melati 5*, and MV *Stella Maris*— after receiving a total of $5.2 million in ransom.

September 28: A sniper fires five shots into the exercise yard of a jail in Varces, France, killing one inmate with ties to organized crime and wounding another. Officers capture the shooter nearby, "with the gun still hot."

September 29: Raids in Casal di Principe, Italy, result in seizure of apartments, businesses and other property owned by Camorra boss Giuseppe Setola.

October 2: Mexican Mafia member Albert Angel "Spanky" Amaya receives a sentence of 25 years to life in San Bernardino, Calif., for extortion and carjacking.

October 3: Jurors in Palm Beach, Fla., convict Gambino Family *caporegime* Vincent Artuso on charges of RICO conspiracy, mail fraud, wire fraud, and money-laundering.

October 5: Unknown gunmen execute Notorious MC member Todd O'Connor in the Sydney suburb of Tempe, Australia.

October 8: Members of the racist street gang AK81 engage in a shootout with immigrant rivals in Copenhagen, Denmark. Immigrant gangsters retaliate by attacking AK81 members in Odense, on October 9.

October 9: NATO ships join an international naval force patrolling Somali waters against piracy. Pirates release 20 Filipino seamen and 29 Iranians captured on various ships in recent months, while seizing the Panamanian-flagged vessel MV *Wail* with 11 crew.

October 10: Somali pirates seize a Panamanian-flagged Greek chemical tanker with 20 crewmen aboard. Payment of ransom secures the release of two other ships, the MV *Iran Deyat* and MT *Irene*.

October 12: Troops from semiautonomous Puntland (in northeastern Somalia) storm a hijacked ship, killing two pirates but failing to liberate the vessel.

October 13: Former bookie and casino boss Frank "Lefty" Rosenthal dies from a heart attack at his home in Miami Beach, Fla.

October 14: Puntland troops storm the Panamanian-flagged vessel hijacked on October 9, capturing 10 pirates and liberating 11 crewmen. The raiders lose one man killed, with three wounded. In Naples, Italy, police announce reports that Camorra members have issued a murder contract on author Roberto Saviano, whose book *Gomorra* describes the syndicate's inner workings. In Tokyo, Japan, members of the Gotogumi Yakuza clan vote to expel leader Tadamasa Goto. He begins study for the Buddhist priesthood in April 2009.

October 15: Somali pirates hijack a Japanese-operated bulk carrier, the MV *African Sanderling*, with 21 crewmen in the Gulf of Aden. They release the ship and hostages on January 12, 2009.

October 16: Somali pirates seize eight fishing vessels with 96 crewmen, demanding ransom for their safe return. They release the crew of MV *Bright Ruby* upon receiving cash. In Montreal, Québec, mafiosi Francesco Arcadi and Francesco Del Balso receive 15-year prison terms; codefendant Nicolo Rizzuto is released on three years' probation. On the same day, Pennsylvania State Attorney General Tom Corbett announces the culmination of "Operation Underground," a drug investigation targeting the Warlocks MC. Raiders seize 68 firearms, $53,000 cash, cutting agents, chemicals and a hand-written manual to making the drug, *Your No-Nonsense Guide for Making Meth*. Four suspects — Michael Spadafora, Randy Cronrath, Holly Cronrath, and Michael Sexton — are charged with various offenses.

October 18: Colombian drug trafficker Luis Hernando Gómez Bustamante pleads guilty to federal racketeering charges in Washington, D.C. He admits smuggling 500,000 kilograms of cocaine into the United States between 1990 and 2004.

October 21: FBI agents climax a three-year undercover narcotics investigation by serving 160 search warrants in seven states, arresting more than 60 members of the Mongols MC. Somali officials announce the liberation of a hijacked Indian dhow and its 13 crew members, following a battle between "freelance coast guards" and pirates. In Eugene, Ore., police arrest members of three allied motorcycle clubs — Brother Speed, the Gypsy Jokers, and the Outsiders — on weapons charges.

October 22: Drive-by gunmen kill Bandidos MC member Ross Brand outside the gang's clubhouse in Geelong, Victoria, Australia. A companion suffers nonfatal wounds. Police capture Sinaloa Cartel boss Jesus "The King" Zambada García following a shootout in Mexico City. On the same day, police arrest federal narcotics investigator Édgar Enrique Bayardo del Villar on charges of collaborating with Zambada.

October 23: A French warship captures nine pirates armed with anti-tank missiles in the Gulf of Aden. Somali buccaneers threaten to kill various hostages in retaliation. Russia asks Somali authorities for carte blanche to hunt pirates in coastal waters.

October 24: Drug cartel gunmen kill narcotics prosecutor Andres Dimitriadis and two bodyguards near his home in Cuernavaca, Mexico.

October 25: Pirates board and loot a French vessel off the southern coast of Nigeria. Federal officers capture drug lord Eduardo Arellano Félix after a shootout in Tijuana, Mexico.

October 28: Crewmen aboard five separate commercial ships foil pirate attacks in the Gulf of Aden.

October 29: Somali pirates seize the Turkish freighter MV *Yasa Neslihan* with a crew of 20, releasing it after payment of ransom on December 6.

October 31: Pirates storm an oil industry support vessel off the coast of Cameroon, kidnapping 10 of its 15 crewmen. Víctor Gerardo Garay Cadena, acting commander of Mexico's Federal Preventive Police, resigns amid accusations of corruption. On December 2 prosecutors charge Garay with protecting the Beltrán Leyva Cartel.

November 3: A federal grand jury in New York City indicts Genovese Family *caporegime* Michael Coppolla on racketeering charges, including extortion and conspiracy to extort members of ILA Local 1235, wire fraud, conspiracy to commit identification document fraud, and murder.

November 7: Somali pirates seize the Danish cargo ship *CEC Future* and 13 crewmen, releasing ship and hostages after payment of ransom on January 16, 2009. Mexican federal police agents in Reynosa, Tamaulipas, arrest Jaime González Durán, founder of the drug cartel army known as *Los Zetas*.

November 10: Somali pirates hijack the Filipino chemical tanker MT *Stolt Strength* with 23 crew, marking the 83rd seizure for 2008. They release the ship and crewmen on April 21, 2009.

November 12: Pirates commandeer the Turkish

chemical tanker *Karagol* with 14 crewmen aboard, in the Gulf of Aden while the British frigate *Cumberland* and Russian frigate *Neustrashimy* chase others away from a Danish target. Raiders release the Karagol on January 12, 2009. Former Taiwan president Chen Shui-bian launches a hunger strike in Taipei, protesting his arrest on charges of corruption and money-laundering.

November 13: Gunmen presumed to be drug cartel soldiers assassinate crime reporter Armando Rodriguez in Ciudad Juarez, Mexico. Pirates seize a Chinese fishing vessel with 24 crewmen off the northern coast of Kenya.

November 15: Somali pirates hijack the Japanese-owned *Chemstar Venus* and the Saudi supertanker *Sirius Star*, seizing 48 hostages. They release the *Sirius Star* on January 9, 2009.

November 16: A Russian frigate pursues Somali pirates, following a foiled assault on another Saudi ship. Australian police raid a Rebels MC clubhouse, arresting two members for the October slaying of Bandidos member Ross Brand.

November 17: A car bomb kills Israeli crime boss Yaakov Alperon at the Tel Aviv Central Bus Station, wounding three bystanders. Police in Mexico City arrest Rodolfo de la Guardia García, ex-director of Mexico's INTERPOL office, on charges of protecting the Beltran Leyva Cartel.

November 18: A court in Mombassa arraigns eight defendants on piracy charges. The Indian naval frigate *Tabar* sinks a suspected pirate "mother ship" in the Gulf of Aden, then pursues two smaller attack boats without overtaking them. Nearby, pirates seize a Thai ship and an Iranian cargo vessel, capturing 41 hostages. They release the Iranian ship on January 9, 2009.

November 19: FBI agent Samuel Hicks suffers fatal gunshot wounds during a joint DEA-FBI drug raid in Pittsburgh, Pa. Ricardo Gutiérrez Vargas, current chief of Mexico's INTERPOL office, is jailed on suspicion of collaborating with drug cartels.

November 20: The UN Security Council votes unanimously to impose sanctions on pirates, arms smugglers, and "perpetrators of instability" in Somalia. Egyptian authorities meet with representatives of nations bordering the Red Sea to craft policies for curbing Somali piracy. Police in Bogotá, Colombia, tear-gas protesters enraged by a crackdown on DMG, a pyramid scheme suspected of laundering drug money. DMG founder David Murcia and six associates face money-laundering charges, while 59 others have fled the country.

November 21: Federal agents arrest Noé Ramírez Mandujano, former chief of Mexico's anti-organized crime agency, on charges of protecting drug cartels.

November 24: Shipping magnates from around the world seek a military blockade of the Somali coast against pirates.

November 25: President Bush grants executive clemency to five defendants convicted of organized crime offenses. He pardons Andrew Foster Harley (wrongful use and distribution of marijuana and cocaine at the U.S. Air Force Academy); Robert Earl Mohon Jr. (conspiracy to distribute marijuana); and Ronald Alan Mohrhoff (unlawful use of a telephone in a narcotics felony). Bush commutes the prison terms of John Edward Forte and James Russell Harris, both convicted of cocaine offenses. On the same day, pirates capture the chemical tanker *Biscaglia* in the Gulf of Aden.

November 26: Guinean pirates attack a Chinese fishing vessel off the coast of Sierra Leone, engaging in a shootout with naval gunboats that leaves four raiders dead and several more in custody.

November 27: Jurors in Nottingham, England, convict seven members of the Outlaws MC on charges of murdering Hells Angel Gerry Tobin in August 2007. Defendants Malcolm Bull, Ian Cameron, Sean Creighton, Dane Garside, Karl Garside, Simon Turner, and Dean Taylor receive life prison terms.

November 30: Somali pirates fire on the U.S. cruise liner M/S *Nautica*, with more than 1,000 people on board, but fail to board the ship. Rival drug smugglers from Mexico and Guatemala fight a pitched battle on the border between their respective nations, leaving 18 persons dead.

December 1: FBI agents arrest Mayor Larry Langford of Birmingham, Ala., on federal charges including conspiracy, bribery, fraud, money-laundering and filing false income tax returns. Also named in the indictment are local lobbyist Albert LaPierre and investment banker William Blount from Montgomery, Ala.

December 2: A federal grand jury in Chicago indicts seventeen defendants on charges of conspiracy to possess and distribute cocaine or heroin or both. Defendants include 10 Cook County sheriff's correctional officers, one Chicago policeman, and four police officers from Hervey, Ill. LAPD arrests two participants in a dog fighting ring, while rescuing 17 animals.

December 3: The newspaper *El Universal* reports that 5,031 Mexicans have died since January 1 in acts of violence stemming from organized crime, including 35 murdered in the past 24 hours.

December 4: Pirates attack an oil-services vessel in Nigerian waters, kidnapping two foreign workers. Danish warships sink a suspected pirate craft off the coast of Somalia, capturing seven suspects and delivering them to police in Yemen.

December 5: Authorities in Nashville, Tenn., arrest 11 persons on charges of running America's largest cock-fighting syndicate.

December 6: Pirates attack but fail to capture a Dutch container ship, 480 miles offshore from Dar es Salaam, Tanzania.

December 8: The EU launches its anti-piracy task mission off the Somali coast, preparing to relieve NATO warships.

December 9: FBI agents arrest Illinois Governor Milorad "Rod" Blagojevich on federal charges including conspiracy to commit mail and wire fraud and solicitation of bribery. A DOJ complaint accuses Blagojevich of running several "pay to play" schemes, including attempting "to obtain personal gain ... through the corrupt use" of his authority to fill Barack Obama's vacated United States Senate seat. On April 3, 2009, a federal grand jury indicts Blagojevich, his brother Robert, and four other defendants on multiple felony charges.

December 10: Felix Batista, an anti-kidnapping expert for the private security firm ASI Global, is abducted from a restaurant in Saltillo, Coahuila, Mexico.

December 11: Ex-IBT president Ron Carey dies from lung cancer in Queens, N.Y.

December 13: Indian naval forces capture 23 pirates in the Gulf of Aden.

December 16: Three Hells Angels receive prison terms in Hanover, Germany, for assaulting members of the rival Bandidos MC in March 2006. Eleven other Angels receive suspended jail terms for the same incident. Somali pirates attack a tugboat off the coast of Yemen. The UN Security Council approves land and air attacks on pirate bases in Somalia.

December 17: Helicopters launched by an international anti-piracy force foil the attempted hijacking of a Chinese cargo ship in Somali waters. Bosnian gangster Ismet "Ćelo" Bajramović shoots himself to death at home, in Sarajevo.

December 21: Drug cartel terrorists kidnap, torture, and decapitate a police commander and seven off-duty soldiers, leaving their heads at a shopping center in Chilpancingo, Mexico, with a note threatening further retaliation for army drug raids.

December 25: A German military helicopter pursues Somali pirates following a failed attack on an Egyptian ship. One helicopter suffers gunshot wounds.

December 30: DEA spokesmen in Nashville, Tenn., announce the culmination of "Project Reckoning, Phase II," targeting elements of Mexico's Gulf Cartel. The two-week campaign has jailed 41 suspects in Nashville, plus 30 more in Texas, Mississippi, Nevada, Kentucky, North Carolina, and Oklahoma.

December 31: Mexican authorities report 5,630 drug-related murders nationwide for 2008.

2009 January 1: Somali pirates capture their first ship of the new year, the Egyptian cargo vessel *Blue Star*, with 28 crewmen aboard.

January 2: A French warship captures eight Somali pirates, while EU forces foil a separate attack on the Greek oil tanker *Kriti Episkopi*. Mexican police arrest Alberto Espinoza Barrón, a leader of the La Familia Michoacána drug cartel.

January 4: The French warship Jean de Vienne foils two attempted hijackings in the Gulf of Aden, apprehending 19 pirates.

January 6: Drug cartel soldiers disrupt a newscast from the Televisa TV station in Monterrey, Mexico, with gunfire and hand grenades. They leave a note reading: "Stop reporting just on us. Report on the narco's political leaders."

January 7: Somali pirates release the Turkish cargo ship MV *Yasa Neslihan* upon receipt of an unspecified ransom payment.

January 8: The U.S. Navy announces formation of a new international force under American command, to battle pirates off the Somali coast.

January 11: One day after releasing the Saudi supertanker *Sirius Star*, five Somali pirates drown after their boat capsizes. One corpse is recovered with $150,000 on cash.

January 13: Pirates fail in their attempt to capture a Norwegian cable ship off the coast of Nigeria. A Russian warship foils a pirate attack on a Dutch container ship in the Gulf of Aden.

January 14: Mehdi Seyyed, president of the Bandidos MC in Sweden, receives a nine-year prison sentence on two counts of attempted murder, related to car-bombings in Gothenburg, during September 2006.

January 15: Three hundred Australian members of the Rebels MC attend funeral services for member Edin "Boz" Smajović, recently murdered at the Macarthur Auto Centre in Campbelltown, New South Wales.

January 17: Disgraced ex–FBI agent John Connolly receives a 40-year prison term for his role in the 1982 Mafia slaying of a gambler in Miami, Fla.

January 20: Unknown gunmen fire at drug-trafficker Jamie Bacon as he drives through Abbotsford, British Columbia.

January 22: A resident of Abbotsford, British Columbia, suffers gunshot wounds during an apparent robbery of a marijuana grow-operation. Police in Tijuana, Mexico, arrest Santiago Meza Lopez, a "disposal expert" accused of dissolving

300 corpses in acid for cartel leader Teodoro García Simental.

January 23: Colombian drug cartel financial manager Eugenio Montoya Sanchez pleads guilty in Miami, Fla., to charges of conspiring to import cocaine and obstruction of justice by murder. On April 28 he receives a 30-year prison term. In Abbotsford, British Columbia, drive-by gunmen wound two alleged gang members.

January 24: Mexican authorities stage "Operation Clean House," arresting a dozen high-ranking government officials in Mexico City on charges of collaboration with the Sinaloa Cartel. Drug traffickers in Surrey, British Columbia, wound one victim in a shooting at his home.

January 26: Mobster Paul Schiro receives a 20-year federal prison term in Chicago, following conviction of participating in a racketeering conspiracy that included murder, gambling, loan-sharking and squeezing businesses for "street tax."

January 27: Unknown gunmen kill Hells Angels MC associate Andrew Cilliers outside his home in Surrey, British Columbia.

January 28: Japan's defense minister sends naval ships to join in anti-piracy patrols off Somalia's coast.

January 29: Somali pirates hijack a German gas tanker, the MV *Longchamp*, in the Gulf of Aden, capturing 13 crewmen.

January 29: Police in Vancouver, British Columbia, blame drug-traffickers for the murder of elderly resident William Peter Canning.

February 1: Tyson Edwards suffers fatal stab wounds in a gang-related altercation outside a nightclub in downtown Vancouver, British Columbia.

February 2: Suspected drug traffickers murder James Ward Erickson in a Surrey, British Columbia, apartment.

February 3: Ukraine's Foreign Ministry announces that Somali pirates have released the Antigua-flagged, Turkish-owned cargo ship MV *Bosphorus Prodigy*. Gang-related shootings claim two lives in British Columbia: Raphael Baldini in Surrey, and Brianna Helen Kinnear in Coquitlam. Outside Cancún, Mexico, police find torture-slaying victims, identified as retired General Mauro Enrique Tello Quiñónez, recently chosen as a special drugs consultant to the mayor Benito Juárez municipality, his aide and chauffeur.

February 4: Police in Philadelphia, Pa., arrest Warlocks MC member Daniel "Dirty Dick" McElheney during a raid on his home that uncovers six rifles, 10 pistols and various illegal drugs. Federal prosecutors in New York City unseal a 38-count indictment charging 13 members of the Genovese Family racketeering and other offenses,

including violent extortions of individuals and businesses, loan-sharking, narcotics trafficking and operation of illegal gambling businesses.

February 5: Police in Ontario, Canada, announce the results of a crackdown on child pornography, resulting in arrests of 31 sex offenders and the rescue of two young victims. Officials estimate that 65,000 child pornographers remain active in Canada, with another 600,000 in the U.S. In Mexico City, police capture drug trafficker Gerónimo Gámez García.

February 6: Gang related violence claims two more victims in British Columbia — William Wayne Cloud, stabbed in Vancouver, and Kevin LeClair, shot in Langley.

February 8: Suspected drug traffickers wound a victim with gunfire in a Vancouver, British Columbia, parking lot.

February 10: Soldiers pursuing leads to the slaying of Mauro Enrique Tello Quiñónez seize control of a police station in Cancún, Mexico.

February 11: The USS *Vella Gulf* detains seven suspected pirates off the Somali coast. Dutch authorities extradite five Somali pirates to the Netherlands for trial. Police in Vancouver, British Columbia, describe Nicholas Gordon Smith as the victim of "a targeted hit" by drug dealers.

February 12: A helicopter from the USS *Vella Gulf* fires warning shots at pirates attempting to board the Indian-flagged vessel *Premdivya*, off the Somali coast. Nine pirates surrender, with weapons including rocket-propelled grenades. A Russian nuclear-powered heavy missile cruiser, *Peter The Great*, captures 10 more pirates, similarly armed, during their attack on an Iranian-flagged fishing trawler. Cartel gunmen assassinate Detective Ramón Jasso Rodríguez, chief of the state police homicide division for Nuevo León, Mexico.

February 14: Michigan authorities raid an Eaton Rapids methamphetamine lab operated by the Highwaymen MC, seizing processed drugs, 40 pounds of anhydrous ammonia, and various other chemicals. The raiders arrest one suspect.

February 15: The Mexican Navy and U.S. Coast Guard join forces to seize seven tons of cocaine from a fishing vessel in international waters, off Mexico's Pacific coast.

February 16: A gang-related shooting leaves one man wounded outside a strip club in Surrey, British Columbia. On the same day in Surrey, unknown gunmen kill Nicole Alemy as she drives her husband's Cadillac. Her spouse, Koshan Alemy, has a record of arrests for possession of a restricted weapon, possession of a weapon with an altered serial number, and other firearms offenses.

February 17: The SEC charges Texas financier Robert Allen Stanford with multiple violations of

U.S. securities laws for alleged "massive ongoing fraud" that involves $8 billion in certificates of deposits. FBI agents raid three of Stanford's offices, while the SEC amends its complain on February 27, describing the fraud as "a massive Ponzi scheme." On February 22 agents announce ongoing investigation of Stanford's rumored links to Mexican drug cartels. G-men arrest him on June 18, 2009. In Surrey, British Columbia, Shane Alan Messent — a "person known to police" — suffers fatal gunshots during a gang-related home invasion.

February 19: Armed pirates attack a tug and barge in the Malacca Strait, en route to Singapore, kidnapping two crewmen.

February 20: Public Safety Secretary Roberto Orduna resigns his post in Ciudad Juárez, Mexico, following drug cartel threats to slaughter policemen if he remains on the job.

February 22: Unidentified gunmen wound a "man known to police" in east Vancouver, British Columbia. Five gunmen presumed to be cartel assassins attack the convoy of Governor José Reyes Baeza Terrazas in Chihuahua, Mexico, killing one bodyguard.

February 23: FBI agents and local police raid prostitution operations in 29 U.S. cities, arresting 55 pimps, 55 customers, and 464 adult prostitutes, while rescuing 48 juveniles. Raiders seize assets including illegal drugs, cars, computers, and $438,000 in cash.

February 24: Mexican authorities extradite drug lord Miguel Ángel Caro Quintero to the U.S. On the same day, cartel assassins murder the mayor of Vista Hermoza, in Michoacán. DEA agents stage "Operation Xcellerator," raiding operations of the Sinaloa Cartel in California, Maryland, and Minnesota. The raiders arrest 755 persons and seize a "super lab" capable of producing 12,000 ecstasy pills per hour.

February 25: Chinese and Danish and warships foil two separate attacks by pirates off Somalia's coast. The ATF releases a report stating that 90 percent of all firearms confiscated from Mexican drug traffickers originate in the U.S. DEA Acting Administrator Michele Leonhart announces the climax of Operation Xcellerator," a 21-month investigation targeting Mexico's Sinaloa Cartel. Raiders arrest 52 suspects in California, Minnesota and Maryland. Overall, the campaign has produced 755 arrests, with seizures including more than 12,000 kilograms of cocaine, more than 16,000 pounds of marijuana, more than 1,200 pounds of methamphetamine, more than 8 kilograms of heroin, approximately 1.3 million pills of ecstasy, 149 vehicles, three aircraft, three maritime vessels, 169 weapons, $59.1 million in cash, and $6.5 million in other assets.

February 26: Suspected gangsters kill Cory Stephen Konkin in his car, in Maple Ridge, British Columbia.

February 27: U.S. Attorney General Eric Holder announces results of a crackdown no Mexico's Sinaloa Cartel, resulting in 755 arrests, with 52 suspects jailed in the past week alone. Police in Surrey, British Columbia, blame gangsters for a "target" shooting that leaves one man wounded.

February 28: The yacht *Serenity*, with two persons aboard, vanishes while en route from the Seychelles to Madagascar. One crewman phones his family on March 24, saying he has been kidnapped by Somali pirates. Some 1,800 Mexican troops arrive in Ciudad Juárez, as part of a new offensive against drug cartels.

March: A Swedish court sentences Bosnian "Gambling King" Rade Kotur to 14 years in prison on charges of instigating a murder, illegal gambling, and evading taxes on income of 463 million kroner ($74 million) between January 1, 2005, and November 13, 2007.

March 2: Suspected drug cartel gunman injure four policemen in two simultaneous shootings, in the town of Uruapan, Michoacán. Police blame gangsters for the fatal shooting of Sukhwinder Singh Dhaliwal in Vancouver, British Columbia.

March 3: Drug traffickers stage three shootings in British Columbia, killing victim Sunil Mall in East Vancouver; slaying a young woman and wounding her male companion in a Burnaby apartment, and strafing a suspected drug house in Surrey. A German warship captures nine Somali pirates, delivering them to Kenyan authorities for trial on March 10. In Guatemala, Catholic Bishop Rodolfo Valenzuela Núñez of Verapaz denounces organized crime that has "led to a climate of insecurity and mistrust among the people," claiming at least 33 lives since 2008.

March 4: Police in San Angelo, Tex., serve organized crime warrants on five persons suspected in the March 2 slaying of victim Kevin Harris. The defendants and alleged gang members include Breeana Andrews, Kelley Edgar Fryar Jr., Woody Joe Jackson, Caree Nelson, and Randy Eugene Stripland.

March 5: Drive-by gangsters wound a man at his home in Vancouver, British Columbia. Police in Gosnells, Western Australia, charge Gypsy Jokers MC members Dean Alan Adams and Peter Floyd Robinson with beating victim Petera Heta Haimona outside a local bar on May 12, 2007. In Belgrade, Serbia, Interior Minister Ivica Dačić tells the 6th Annual Ministerial Conference on Border Security Cooperation in South East Europe that "fighting organized crime is priority." Colorado journalists link former Denver Broncos players Rod Bernstine and Reggie Rivers to the

Gin Rummy Club, an illegal gambling establishment that left some athletes deeply in debt and prompted two losers to kill themselves. Sheriff Thomas Dart of Cook County, Ill., files a federal lawsuit against Craigslist, an Internet advertising network, charging that the company promotes prostitution. The lawsuit seeks an injunction barring ads for erotic services from Craigslist, plus reimbursement exceeding $100,000 for prostitution cases filed during the past year.

March 6: Mark Steinagel, spokesman for the Utah Division of Real Estate, announces ongoing investigations of mortgage fraud and other crimes in Provo, where nine defendants have already been convicted and imprisoned. Suspected drug traffickers fatally shoot Lionel Yisheng Tan in a "targeted attack" at a gas station in Vancouver, British Columbia.

March 9: Mexican soldiers arrest 26 members of the Tijuana Cartel, including enforcer Ángel Jácome Gamboa, one state police officer, and one city policeman.

March 10: Suspected drug traffickers execute two male victims at an apartment in Vancouver, British Columbia. Mexico's Ministry of Defense orders six French military helicopters for use in the war on drugs.

March 12: Police in Adelaide, Australia, arrest a member of the Gypsy Jokers MC for shooting a former Hells Angel and a member of the Newboys gang outside the group's clubhouse. The U.S. Department of Homeland Security reveals "last resort" plans to use National Guardsmen to prevent Mexican drug violence from crossing the border.

March 15: Police in Langley, British Columbia, say the shooting of Laura Lynn Lamoureux "is linked to the street-level drug trade and has the signature of being a targeted murder."

March 17: A federal grand jury in Philadelphia, Pa., indicts 22 defendants on charges related to a $3.6 million cocaine distribution ring. Those charged include a state correctional officer and Thomas "The Boss" Zaroff Jr., president of the Outlaws MC in Philadelphia. Police in Adelaide, South Australia, charge a member of the Gypsy Jokers MC with attempted murder for shooting a member of the rival Newboys gang.

March 19: Somali pirates seize the St. Vincent-flagged Titan, with 24 crewmen aboard. A Turkish warship foils a pirate attack on a Turkish commercial ship in the Gulf of Aden. Police blame "a targeted shooting" for the murder of Marc Bontkes at Hi-Knoll Park, in Surrey, British Columbia. Mexican soldiers capture Sinaloa Cartel leader Vicente Zambada Niebla, son of drug lord Ismael Zambada García.

March 21: A crowd of some 150,000 people gathers in Naples, Italy, to protest organized crime and corruption.

March 22: Somali pirates fire automatic weapons and rocket-propelled grenades at three cargo ships, but fail to capture any of their targets. Australian police arrest four bikers following a clash between Hells Angels and Comancheros at Sydney's Kingsford Smith Airport, which leaves one man beaten to death. Drug cartel gunmen kill Édgar Garcia, officer in charge of kidnap-extortion investigations for the state police in Michoacán.

March 24: Mexican authorities offer rewards of $2 million per head for the capture of 24 notorious drug cartel leaders, with rewards of $1 million each for 13 of their primary lieutenants. Police in Sydney, Australia, arrest Bandidos MC Sergeant-at-Arms Mahmoud Dib on weapons charges, following a series of drive-by shootings.

March 25: Pirates hijack the MT *Nipayia*, a Greek-owned and Panama registered ship with a crew of 19, 450 miles east of Somalia's southern coast. Mexican soldiers capture fugitive drug trafficker Héctor Huerta Ríos in Monterrey.

March 26: Somali pirates seize the MT *Bow Asir*, a Norwegian tanker with a crew of 27. Police in Ciudad Juárez, Mexico, discover the corpse of Deputy U.S. Marshal Vincent Bustamante, a fugitive from justice since his failure to attend a March 18 court hearing on charges of stealing and selling government property. Secretary of State Hillary Clinton announce the planned delivery of eight Black Hawk helicopters to Mexican security forces, for use against drug cartels.

March 29: Ships of the international anti-piracy task force capture seven pirates in the Gulf of Aden, after an attack on a German naval supply ship. Drive-by gunmen in Sydney, Australia, wound Hells Angels MC member Peter Zervas, whose brother died in a brawl with rival Comancheros one week earlier. Police in Vancouver, British Columbia, acknowledge a recent explosion of gang violence, including 45 shootings — 17 of them fatal — since January.

March 30: Police in Abbotsford, British Columbia, publicly blame mobster-brothers Jamie, Jarrod, and Jonathan Bacon for the slaying of Sean "Smurph" Murphy, a street-level drug dealer for the Red Scorpions Gang.

March 31: Officers in Abbotsford, British Columbia, repeat their charges against the Bacon brothers after another Red Scorpions member — Ryan Richards — is fatally shot. In Montreal, Québec, hitman-turned-informer Gerald Gallant pleads guilty to 27 counts of murder and 12 counts of attempted murder, spanning the years 1978–2003, during a war between the Hells Angels and rival Rock Machine MC. In Kansas City,

Mo., FBI agents serve several search warrants "as part of an investigation possibly linked to organized crime."

April 1: Federal prosecutors in Detroit charge Devil's Disciples MC president Jeff G. Smith with illegal possession of body armor by a convicted felon. Smith and 16 other club members also face charges of using a telephone for drug trafficking. Somali pirates capture a tourist yacht with sever persons aboard, near the Seychelles.

April 2: FBI agents and police in Puerto Rico arrest 35 suspected members of a drug trafficking ring blamed for seven murders. In Detroit, FBI agents arrest Devil's Disciples MC president Jeff "Fat Dog" Garvin Smith and 17 other members on charges including drug trafficking and weapons violations. Although the raiders seize 42 firearms, 3,000 rounds of ammunition, three bullet-proof vests, $12,000 in cash, 15 slot machines, 1,000 Vicodin and OxyContin pills, 1.5 pounds of methamphetamine and 55 pounds of marijuana, charges against all the prisoners except Smith are subsequently dismissed. Police in Mexico City arrest Vicente Carrillo Leyva, son of drug lord Amado Carrillo Fuentes.

April 3: Police in Sydney, Australia, arrest Hells Angels MC member Christian Manu Birch after a traffic stop and search reveals a concealed pistol, a bulletproof vest, and "a large amount of liquid, allegedly drug-making chemicals." RCMP officers in British Columbia arrest mobster Jamie Bacon on murder charges related to the October 2007 "Surrey 6" slayings.

April 4: Somali pirates seize a German container vessel, the *Hansa Stavanger*, in the Indian Ocean. Police in Vancouver, British Columbia, blame drug traffickers for the shooting of an unidentified man found dead in his car.

April 5: Somali pirates hijack a small Yemeni boat.

April 6: Somali pirates seize the Taiwanese ship *Win Far 161* with 29 crewmen, near the Seychelles. Other raiders hijack a British-owned bulk carrier, the *Malaspina Castle*, in the Gulf of Aden.

April 8: Somali pirates board the *Maersk Alabama*, a U.S.-flagged cargo ship, then flee as crewmen overpower them. In Santa Barbara, Calif., Hells Angels chapter president Archie Schaffer pleads not-guilty on charges of brandishing a firearm, making criminal threats, street terrorism, reckless driving and committing a crime for the benefit of the club, in an incident dating from January 17. Police in California's Antelope Valley stage a series of raids against the drug-dealing Lancas 13 gang, arresting 26 suspects. Alleged leader Tory Larson faces 14 felony counts of conspiring to sell narcotics, and other offenses.

April 10: French forces free a sailboat captured by Somali pirates the previous week. Owner Florent Lemacon and two pirates die in the exchange of gunfire. Italian journalists blame Mafia corruption for the government's failure to replace homes leveled by a catastrophic earthquake in November 1980. A "shoot and scoot" team from the D-Company syndicate led by fugitive mobster and terrorist Dawood Ibrahim kills attorney Naushad Kasim in Mumbai, India.

April 11: Somali pirates hijack the Italian-flagged tugboat *Buccaneer*, with 16 crew aboard, in the Gulf of Aden.

April 12: Somali pirates capture two Egyptian fishing boats in the Gulf of Aden.

April 14: Somali pirates seize the Lebanese-owned cargo ship MV *Sea Horse* and the Greek-managed MV *Irene E.M.* A U.S.-flagged cargo ship, the *Liberty Sun*, repels attackers on the same day. The *Sea Horse* is released on April 20, after payment of a $100,000 "reward."

April 15: Canadian police "dismantle" the Hells Angels MC in Québec, with a series of raids that jail 123 club members and associates on charges of first-degree murder, attempted murder, gangsterism or drug trafficking. Underworld gunmen kill Betty "Big Sister" Yan, a Chinese immigrant with known criminal connections, in Vancouver, British Columbia. French naval forces in the Indian Ocean foil a pirate attack on a Liberian-registered vessel and raid the buccaneers' "mother ship," arresting 11 suspects.

April 16: Antonio Maria Costa, executive director of the UN's Office on Drugs and Crime, warns that organized crime "has gone global," posing a security threat to cities, countries and entire regions of Earth.

April 17: Pennsylvania Attorney General Tom Corbett petitions the state's Supreme Court to start a grand jury probe of public corruption and organized crime.

April 18: Somali pirates attack two ships off the Horn of Africa, seizing the Belgian-flagged *Pompei*, while NATO forces thwart the second raid and capture several pirates. Dutch commandos liberate 20 fishermen on a Yemeni dhow hijacked earlier. In New York City, Gambino Family *caporegime* Nicholas "Little Nick" Corozzo receives a 13½-year prison term for ordering a Brooklyn murder that claimed the life of an innocent bystander. Police in Columbiana, Ala., blame drug-trafficking for the deaths of five men found tortured and shot to death in an apartment.

April 19: John Phillip Hernandez — suspected of procuring 339 military-style weapons and delivering them to Mexican drug cartels — receives an eight-year federal prison term in Houston, Tex., after pleading guilty to one count of making a false statement to a gun dealer. Gunmen attack a Mexican prison convoy transporting leaders of the Beltrán Leyva Cartel, killing eight federal officers. In Michoacán, police capture boss Rafael Cedeño Hernández and 43 other members of La Familia Michoacána at a christening party for a gangster's newborn infant.

April 20: The Maltese-flagged MV *Atlantica* evades pirate pursuers in the Gulf of Aden. Nigerian pirates seize the *Aleyna Mercan* near Port Harcourt, releasing its captain and chief engineer on April 22.

April 21: Spanish police arrest 22 Hells Angels in five provinces, on charges of illicit association, extortion, drug and weapons trafficking. In New York City, Somali pirate Abduwali Abdukhadir Muse faces piracy charges related to seizure of the *Maersk Alabama*.

April 22: Police in Durango, Mexico, find the corpses of two undercover federal agents with a note reading "Neither priests nor rulers will ever get El Chapo"—an allusion to remarks made by Archbishop of Durango Héctor González Martínez about Sinaloa Cartel leader Joaquín Guzmán Loera, AKA *El Chapo* ("Shorty").

April 23: Australian police stage coordinated nationwide raids against the Rebels MC, seizing methamphetamine, heroin, cocaine, firearms, cash, stolen goods and stolen vehicles.

April 25: Pirates seize the Maltese-flagged MV *Patriot* in the Gulf of Aden. Israeli private security officers foil an attack on an Italian cruise ship off Somalia's east coast.

April 26: Pirates attack four Yemeni tankers escorted by a coast guard vessel, en route to Aden. Three ships escape, while the oil tanker *Qana* is captured. Coast Guardsmen wound two pirates and capture five more, later liberating the *Qana* and arresting 11 more suspects. The Turkish cruiser *Ariva 3* repels attackers near the Yemeni island of Jabal Zuqar.

April 28: Spanish naval forces capture nine pirates and deliver them to the Seychelles Coast Guard. A Russian tanker repels attackers off the Somali coast. A Russian warship summoned to assist captures a vessel with 29 suspected pirates aboard. In Chicago, federal jurors convict Deputy U.S. Marshal John T. Ambrose of leaking information about a key government witness to mobsters.

May 1: Portuguese special forces foil a Somali pirate attack on an oil tanker, seizing explosives from 19 captured suspects, but later release them. Hours later, another band of pirates hijacks the Maltese-flagged cargo ship *Ariana*, southwest of the Seychelles. Police in Vancouver, British Columbia, say that teenage kidnap-murder victims Dilsher Singh Gill and Joseph Randay were involved in drug trafficking.

May 3: French naval forces capture three pirate vessels off the Somali coast, including a "mother ship" loaded with Kalashnikov rifles and rocket launchers.

May 4: South Korean snipers in a helicopter chase Somali pirates away from a North Korean freighter. Elsewhere in the area, the Russian destroyer *Admiral Panteleyev* frees eight Iranian hostages held by Somali pirates for more than three months.

May 5: Somali pirates hijack the German cargo ship MV *Victoria* in the Gulf of Aden.

May 7: Somali pirates capture the Netherlands Antilles–flagged MV *Marathon* in the Gulf of Aden.

May 13: The U.S. guided missile cruiser *Gettysburg* and South Korean destroyer ROKS *Munmu the Great* join forces to foil a pirate attack on the Egyptian vessel MV *Amira*, in the Gulf of Aden. Seventeen pirates are arrested.

May 15: Police in Vancouver, British Columbia, arrest eight members of the United Nations Gang, AKA the Global United Nations Syndicate (GUNS), on charges of conspiring to murder members of the rival Red Skorpions gang. Also charges is former Satan's Choice MC member Ion Croitoru.

May 16: A gang related shooting in Cloverdale, British Columbia, kills bystander Christopher Roy Whitmee while wounding a man "well-known to police."

May 17: Gulf Cartel soldiers disguised as policemen liberate 50 inmates from a prison in Zacatecas, Mexico.

May 18: Somalia's fractured government appeals for international aid to create a coast guard, promising to wipe out off-shore piracy. In Queensland, Australia, Rebels MC member Michael Paul Falzon receives a 10-year prison term for trafficking in methamphetamine.

May 19: Gypsy Jokers MC President Leonard Mark Kirby and another member suffer gunshot wounds in a drug-related clash with rival bikers in Perth, Western Australia. In Naples, Italy, police arrest 68 Camorra members on charges of murder, drug trafficking and money-laundering. Jurors in Portland, Maine, convicted 15 members of the Iron Horsemen MC of smuggling cocaine and marijuana from Mexico between 2004 and 2007.

May 21: Police in Moscow, Russia, arrest mob boss Otari Totochiya with 3.2 grams of hashish, filing charges of possessing a controlled substance.

May 22: Italian naval forces thwart a Somali pirate attack on a U.S.-flagged container vessel, arresting nine suspects.

May 23: Former South Korean President Roh Moo-hyun, embroiled in allegations of widespread corruption, leaps to his death from a cliff near the village of Bongha. He leaves a suicide note calling his life "difficult" and apologizing for making "too many people suffer."

May 26: A Swedish warship foils a pirate attack in the Gulf of Aden, detaining seven prisoners. In Paris, France, leaders of the Church of Scientology face trial on charges of organized fraud and illegal pharmaceutical activity, which could force dissolution of the group nationwide.

May 27: Mexican federal officers arrest 10 mayors and 20 other local officials in Michoacán, on charges of collaborating with the drug cartel known as La Familia Michoacána. Police in Maple Ridge, British Columbia, call fatal shooting victim Sarjbit Nagra the latest victim in an ongoing drug war. Officers arrest suspected gunman Hershan "Shawn" Singh Bains on June 26.

May 31: Iranian police arrest ex–trade minister Abdul Falah Sudani at Baghdad International Airport, as he attempts to flee the country. Sudani is a central figure in an unfolding corruption scandal, involving widespread fraud and misappropriation of sums estimated in "hundreds of millions of dollars."

June 8: A shootout between drug cartel gunmen and Mexican troops in Acapulco leaves two soldiers and 16 gangsters dead in the resort city's hotel zone.

June 11: Jeffrey Qi Feng Bian suffers fatal stab wounds during a robbery at his illegal massage parlor in Yaletown, British Columbia. Police charge suspects Justin Lam and Derick Chin Wai Wong with his slaying on June 21.

June 13: Mauricio Fernandez, a mayoral candidate in Mexico City, tells supporters that drug traffickers have contacted all leading political contenders nationwide, soliciting their loyalty before July's elections.

June 15: Police capture Gulf Cartel lieutenant Juan Manuel Jurado Zarzoza at a resort in Cancun, Mexico. Gunmen kill mobster Desmond "Tuppence" Moran, brother of gang patriarch Lewis Moran, in Ascot Vale, Victoria, Australia.

June 16: Police in Melbourne, Australia, arrest three suspects in the murder of Desmond Moran. They include sister-in-law Judy Moran (widow of Lewis Moran), Suzanne Kane (sister-in-law of Jason Moran), and Kane's partner, Geoffrey Amour.

June 20: Drive-by shooters kill Lebanese gangster Mohammed Haddara in Altona, Victoria, Australia. Ahmed Hablas, nephew of rival mobster Macchour Chaouk, surrenders to police and admits the slaying on June 21, claiming self-defense in the wake of his kidnapping by Haddara gang members.

June 22: Police in San Jose, Calif., charge three members of the Vagos MC with gang-raping a woman kidnapped for that purpose on May 4.

June 26: Gunmen presumed to be cartel assassins fail in an effort to kill Ernesto Cornejo Valenzuela, anti-drug candidate for mayor of Benito Juárez, Sonora, Mexico.

June 29: In New York City, stock swindler Bernard Madoff receives a federal prison term of 150 years, following his March guilty plea to 11 felony charges. Prosecutors announce their pursuit of other principals in the conspiracy that bilked Madoff's investors out of an estimated $65 billion.

June 30: Police in Abbotsford, British Columbia, say murder victim Jaswant Rai was "well known" to police as a member of the Red Scorpions Gang.

July 1: Russian Prime Minister Vladimir Putin orders the closure of all Moscow casinos, in a "reform" move that banishes gambling to four special zones located thousands of miles from the nation's capital.

July 2: Federal agents and local police stage coordinated raids on dog-fighting rings in Illinois, Iowa, Missouri, Oklahoma and Texas, arresting 30 persons on various charges and seizing more than 400 dogs.

July 7: Cartel gunmen storm a house in Galeana, Chihuahua, Mexico, killing anti-crime activist Benjamin LeBaron and his brother-in-law Luis Widmar.

July 11: Mexican authorities arrest three leaders of La Familia Michoacána. Cartel soldiers retaliate by attacking police in eight cities throughout western Mexico. In Morelia, Michoacán, gunmen kill three policemen and two soldiers in a raid on Federal Preventive Police headquarters.

July 12: Drug cartel assassins murder five Mexican federal agents in separate attacks throughout Michoacán state.

July 14: Cartel killers kidnap, torture, and murder 12 more federal officers in Michoacán, Mexico. On the same day, published reports identify Julio César Godoy Toscano — elected to Mexico's Congress on July 5 as a leading member of the La Familia Michoacána drug cartel. He flees into hiding as a fugitive.

July 16: Police in Burnaby, British Columbia, call the murder of John William Hanna — found dead in a burned-out car — a "target hit" by gangsters.

July 17: Mexico's federal government fields military and naval forces to "surround" the crime-infested state of Michoacán. By July 21, 3,500 troops are deployed statewide. In New South Wales, Australia, members of the state police anti-gang squad "accidentally" provides Hells Angels with a list of home addresses for all known members of the rival Comancheros MC.

July 23: Federal agents sweep New Jersey and New York, jailing 44 persons on charges of public corruption and international money-laundering. Those arrested include three New Jersey mayors, five rabbis, and one alleged trafficker in human kidneys.

July 27: Assassins execute drug cartel lieutenant Jose Daniel Gonzalez Galeana, from Ciudad Juárez, Mexico, outside his home in El Paso, Tex. Authorities confirm his role as a police informer.

July 28: A sniper kills mobster Vyacheslav Ivankov at a restaurant on Khoroshevskoye Road in Moscow, Russia.

July 29: British police arrest "Dodgy" Dave Courtney on weapons charges. Jurors acquit him on December 10.

July 30: Mexican federal police arrest Armando "The Bachelor" Quintero Guerra and Nazario Moreno González, financial managers of La Familia Michoacána, in Uruapan. Spokesmen for Mexico's Secretariat of National Defense announce that troops have killed six cartel gunmen in Guayuameo, Michoacán.

August 6: A shootout between Mexican police and cartel gunmen leaves 13 persons dead and 22 wounded in Pachuca. While officers rescue several kidnapped federal agents, cartel guerrillas launch a series of drive-by shootings and grenade attacks on police stations nationwide.

August 7: Police in Tijuana, Mexico, arrest Tijuana Cartel lieutenant Manuel Invanovich Zambrano Flores, seizing 10 rifles, seven pistols, and 4,000 rounds of ammunition.

August 9: Mexican authorities announce that they have foiled a plot by the Sinaloa Cartel to assassinate President Felipe de Jesús Calderón Hinojosa.

August 11: Authorities in New York City publish a report detailing how the Waterfront Commission of New York Harbor "became its own bastion of lawlessness, employing the same corrupt, self-serving methods of the pier-based gangsters it was supposed to pursue."

August 12: Danish police jail three members of the AK81 gang on charges of beating two immigrants in Hellerup, a Copenhagen suburb, during April. On the same day, the United Brotherhood of Carpenters places its New York chapter under emergency trusteeship, while firing three chapter officers indicted on federal racketeering charges. Those dismissed include Michael J. Forde, John Greaney, and Brian Hayes.

August 13: Police and FBI agents detain 60-odd members of the Gypsy Jokers MC in Nampa, Ida., interrogating them and photographing them for future reference.

August 15: Mexican authorities capture Héctor Manuel Oyarzabal Hernández, a leader of La Familia Michoacána, with seven subordinates.

August 18: Sheriff's officers in Oconee and Pickens Counties, N.C., raid illegal gambling dens and arrest 18 persons. A judge releases all 18 on personal recognizance.

August 20: DEA agents announce the breakup of a Mexican drug operation based in Chicago, responsible for importing two tons of cocaine per month.

August 25: Mexican police arrest another leader of La Familia Michoacána, Manuel Alejandro Sotelo Barrera, with five subordinates in Manzanillo, Colima.

September 3: Drug cartel gunmen in Ciudad Juárez, Mexico, execute 18 patients at an addiction treatment clinic, after lining them up against a wall.

September 9: Colombian drug lord Fabio Enrique Ochoa Vasco pleads guilty to federal drug-trafficking charges in Tampa, Fla., receiving a 17½-year prison term and forfeiting assets valued in excess of $15 million.

September 15: DEA agents cap "Operation Heavy Cargo" by arresting 23 persons in Miami, Fla., and Puerto Rico. The suspects — including eight American Airlines employees — face charges of conspiracy to possess with intent to distribute in excess of 9,000 kilograms of cocaine, smuggled aboard commercial aircraft.

September 16: Cartel gunmen raid another drug rehabilitation clinic in Ciudad Juárez, Mexico, killing 10 people.

October 22: Federal agents and local police stage synchronized raids against members of Mexico's La Familia Michoacána drug cartel in cities from Boston and St. Paul, Minn., to Raleigh, N.C., jailing more than 300 defendants and placing 20 children in protective custody. Raiders seize substantial quantities of illegal drugs, weapons, and cash.

October 15: DEA agents crack a drug-smuggling ring allegedly active since 1990, centered on Florida's Orlando International Airport. Those jailed include an American Airlines baggage handler.

October 29: Jurors in Toronto, Ontario, convict six Bandidos MC members on 44 counts of first-degree murder and four counts of manslaughter in the April 2006 slayings of eight fellow club members. Those convicted include Marcelo Aravena, Brett Gardiner, Wayne Kellestine, Frank Mather, Dwight Mushey, and Michael Sandham.

December 1: Federal jurors announce a deadlock in the racketeering trial of John Gotti Jr., resulting in a mistrial.

December 5: Jurors in Manhattan convict Mark Jakubek, a former Port Authority of New

York and New Jersey field operations manager, on state charges of enterprise corruption (equivalent to racketeering). Also convicted is accomplice and ex-colleague Anthony Fontanetta.

December 15: The Mexican Air Force receives five U.S. military helicopters for transport and reconnaissance missions against drug cartels.

December 16: Mexican marines kill drug lord Marcos Arturo Beltrán Leyva and three associates during a raid on his hideout in Cuernavaca. One marine also dies in the two-hour battle, while three more suffer wounds from hand grenades.

December 18: Unidentified gunmen kill Nick Rizzuto Jr., son of mafioso Vito Rizzuto, in Montreal, Québec.

December 22: Drug cartel gunmen in Mexico City murder the mother, aunt and two siblings of Melquisedet Angulo, a marine killed in the raid that claimed Arturo Beltrán Leyva's life six days earlier.

2010 January 1: Suspected cartel gunmen kidnap Jose Luis Romero, a crime reporter for the Linea Directa radio station, in Los Mochis, Sinaloa, Mexico. Hours later, assassins murder Jesus Escalante, chief of investigations for the Sinaloa state police, after he launches an investigation of the kidnapping.

January 2: Authorities in India suspend Assistant Commissioner of Police Prakash Wani and four subordinates, following circulation of a videotape that shows them dancing with gangsters at a Christmas Eve party hosted by crime boss Chotta Rajan in Mumbai. Mexican federal agents arrest drug lord Carlos Beltrán Leyva in Culiacán, Sinaloa.

January 3: Police in Reggio Calabria, Italy, blame 'Ndrangheta members for a bomb explosion at a local courthouse.

January 4: A court in China's Guizhou Province sentences 18 defendants to 20-year prison terms for involvement in organized crime. Twelve defendants are members of the Yushan Gang, convicted of racketeering, illegal mining, operating gambling dens, intentional injuring, rape and other felonies. In Chihuahua, Mexico, 13 drug-related shootings claim 29 lives, including two state policemen and a female activist who led protests against alleged police brutality. Federal agents in Tijuana, Mexico, detain seven local policemen on charges of collaborating with drug cartels.

January 5: Gunmen murder crime reporter Boris "Bobi" Tsankov outside a fast-food restaurant in downtown Sofia, Bulgaria. Later in the day, police arrest crime bosses Stefan Bonev and Krasimir Marinov. Andrew Merola, reputed leader of the Gambino Family in northern New Jersey, pleads guilty in Newark on federal charges

of gambling, loan-sharking, fraud and labor racketeering during a Newark hearing. He faces up to 20 years in prison. Police in Naples, Italy, arrest 14 Camorra members.

January 6: Italian prosecutor Pietro Grasso announces a new "Mafia campaign" in response to the 'Ndrangheta bombing of a courthouse in Reggio Calabria. In Greeley, Colo., building contractor Mark Strodtman receives a 31-year prison term for racketeering, based on his part in a mortgage fraud scheme. Chinese gangster Bing Yi Chen, AKA "Ah Ngai," receives a 35-year sentence for a 2007 double-murder in Toronto, Canada.

January 7: A military firing squad in Shijiazhuang, China, executes seven gangsters recently convicted of murder, arms trafficking, gambling and other crimes that spanned six decades in Hebel Province.

January 8: Li Zhuang, a former attorney for mob boss Gong Gangmo, receives a 30-month prison term in China's Chongqing municipality for falsifying evidence and jeopardizing testimony. Li appeals the verdict, then admits to falsifying evidence on February 2. Authorities in Mumbai, India, arrest police "shootout specialist" Pradeep Sharma and several other officers on charges of murdering gangster Ramnarayan Gupta and staging his death to appear as the result of a gunfight. Cartel gunmen attack Mexican troops on routine patrol in the state of Michoacán. The shootout leaves one soldier and four hitmen dead. Disbarred attorney Kenneth Dunn received a 43-month prison term in Fort Lauderdale, Fla., on charges of laundering money and committing other crimes committed for the Bonanno Family. Soaring crime rates in Tancítaro, Michoacán, Mexico, prompt disbandment of the local police department, while state police and soldiers assume responsibility for public safety.

January 9: Police find the corpses of murdered mob bosses Ivaylo "Yozhi" Evtimov and Yulian "Kunfuto" Lefterov on Plana Mountain, in western Bulgaria. Death threats delay the scheduled extradition Marisa Merico — daughter of Calabrian godfather Emilio di Giovine and wife of henchman Bruno Merico — from England to Italy.

January 11: Suspected mafiosi gun down Nicolo Romeo, owner of an animal feed business in Corleone, Sicily, who ignored Mafia extortion demands.

January 12: Police in Bologna and Rosarno, Italy, arrest 17 suspected 'Ndrangheta members on various charges, including violent attacks on immigrant workers. In Chongqing, China, reputed gang boss Yue Ning and 30 associates face trial on charges of pimping, firearms possession, bribery, and other crimes. Federal police in La

Paz, Baja California Sur, arrest Tijuana Cartel lieutenant Teodoro "El Teo" García Simental.

January 13: Bulgarian authorities declare mobster Nikolai "The Little Margin" Marinov a fugitive after he misses a court appearance in Sofia, where he is charged with conspiring to murder three people.

January 14: Indonesian police arrest Chinese businessman Anggodo Widjoj for bribing two members of the nation's Corruption Eradication Commission. Commission spokesmen announce that embezzlement has cost the agency $2.2 trillion. In New York City, federal prosecutors announce that they will not retry John Gotti Jr. on racketeering charges.

January 15: Alleged mafioso John Gotti Jr. announces that he has completed a still-unpublished children's book, *Children of Shaolin Forest*, and plans to pursue a career as a writer.

January 16: Police in Belgrade arrest Serbian gangster Kristijan Golubović, his mother, and five associates on charges of narcotics trafficking.

January 23: An appellate court in Palermo, Sicily, affirms two previous convictions against former president (now senator) Salvatore "Totò" Cuffaro, with an aggravating charge of favoring the Mafia. Cuffaro receives a seven year prison term and vows to resign all political offices while appealing his verdict before the Supreme Court of Cassation.

January 30: Cartel assassins ambush Mexican federal agents on Michoacán's Highway Occidente, wounding seven officers.

January 31: Suspected cartel gunmen murder 16 teenagers at a party in Ciudad Juárez, Mexico. None of those slain has any known criminal ties.

February 3: Francisco Flores, a member of the Florencia 13 street gang, received a sentence of life imprisonment without parole in Santa Ana, Calif., following conviction on federal charges of conspiring to commit murder and attempted murder and violent crime in aid of racketeering.

February 17: Federal prosecutors in Manhattan charge mafiosi Anthony Arillotta and Arthur Nigro, former acting boss of the Genovese Family, with the November 2003 murder of Massachusetts mobster Adolfo Bruno. Other charges filed include racketeering, extortion and gambling conspiracies.

February 17–18: A two-day series of drug raids in Jersey City, N.J., jails 37 members of the Bloods street gang, while confiscating 32 ounces of PCP, 35 "bricks" of heroin, two pistols, $87,000 in cash, and unspecified quantities of OxyCodone, marijuana, and cocaine.

February 23: NYPD officers arrest members of an identity theft ring that sold more than 200 fake

drivers' to convicted criminals at prices ranging from $7,000 to $10,000 each.

February 24: In Houston, Tex., Gulf Cartel "symbolic leader" Osiel Cárdenas Guillén receives a 25-year federal prison term without possibility of parole.

March 4: Following the outbreak of a turf war between "Los Zetas" gunmen and the Gulf Cartel in Reynosa, Tamaulipas, Mexico, Mexican Navy special forces fire on underworld combatants from helicopters. On March 5 local Red Cross spokesmen announce that its doctors will no longer risk their lives to treat wounded persons in combat zones.

March 5: Hells Angels MC member Arnold Loto strikes a plea bargain with prosecutors in Sydney, Australia, related to a fatal airport brawl in March 2009. He pleads guilty to charges of riot and affray, while a murder charge is dismissed. In Queens, N.Y., police arrest 45 drug dealers at Far Rockaway's Hammel Houses, 41 bags of crack, 230 bags of marijuana, plus unspecified amounts of heroin and OxyContin.

March 14: Drive-by shooters kill three persons affiliated with the U.S. consulate in Mexico City, wounding two children in the process.

March 15: NYPD narcotics officers sweep the Amsterdam Houses next-door to Lincoln Center, arresting 28 members of two rival drug-dealing gangs.

March 17: Mexican drug lord Jose Barrientos-Rodriguez pleads guilty in Atlanta, Ga., on federal charges of conspiracy and possession of cocaine with intent to distribute. He receives a 22-year prison term on August 4.

March 19: Mexican soldiers in Monterrey mistakenly kill two innocent university graduate students during a shootout with drug traffickers.

March 23: Spokesmen for the Obama administration in Washington, D.C., pledge increased support for Mexico in the war against drug cartels.

March 30: Drug cartel gunmen launch seven coordinated assaults on Mexican troops in various locations. Troops kill 18 attackers while capturing 50 assault rifles, 61 grenades, several grenade launchers, eight homemade bombs, and six armored vehicles.

April: Ukrainian security forces arrest Russian mobster Aslan Usoyan on a charge of entering the country illegally using false documents.

April 1: Federal agents in Detroit arrest 80 members of two local motorcycle clubs — the Highwaymen and Outlaws — on various charges including conspiracy to commit murder. Bahamian police launch "Operation Tsunami," targeting smugglers of drugs and firearms around Freeport, Grand Bahama. The raids jail 15 suspects by April 12. Cartel gunmen blockade roads in Reynosa, Mexico, and exchange gunfire with soldiers. One gangster dies, while others strike a state police checkpoint in Tampico, killing one policeman, wounding another and a civilian bystander.

April 3: Chicago police announce the culmination of drug raids resulting in 41 arrests, plus seizure of drugs valued at $500,000, 11 guns, five vehicles and $142,899 in cash.

April 8: Two members of the Outlaws MC, Kenneth Koonrad and Michael Scavone, plead guilty to participation in a $3.6 million cocaine distribution ring active from July 2008. State narcotics agents cracked the ring on March 6, 2009, resulting in prior guilty pleas from nine other Outlaws.

April 9: Authorities in Trois-Rivières, Québec, slap the Hells Angels with a $12,000 tax bill for the club's defunct headquarters, closed by police in 2009.

April 15: Hells Angels associate Lloyd MacDonald receives a 10-year sentence for possession of cocaine and other illegal drugs, plus various firearms, including two submachine guns.

April 16: Great Britain bans the synthetic stimulant mephedrone and its related chemical compounds.

April 17: A brawl allegedly erupts between Hells Angels and members of the Outlaws MC outside a bar in Minneiska, Minn. By April 21, local police have found no evidence confirming the fight.

April 19: Police in Belmont, Colo., arrest local resident Bela Geczy on 10 counts of securities fraud and one count of organized crime related to his management of firms including California Oil, Dharma Holdings, Dharma Leeward, and Dharma Post, which cost investors $17 million. Police in Memphis, Tenn., arrest more than 100 persons in a neighborhood known as an "open air drug market."

April 20: Hells Angels MC prospect Allen Morrison receives an 8½-year prison term in Winnipeg, Canada, on charges of selling cocaine valued at $625,000 to undercover police in 2007. Another Hells Angels associate, Blaine Doner, receives a seven-year sentence in Ottawa, Ontario, for conspiring with the club to control drug trafficking through violence and intimidation. Federal prosecutors in New York City release indictments charging 14 members of the Gambino Family on charges of racketeering, murder, and sex trafficking of a minor for their involvement in a child-prostitution ring operated via Craigslist on the Internet. In an unrelated case, Genovese Family associate Frank Schwamborn receives an 11-year federal prison term for securities fraud. Provincial legislators in Manitoba, Canada, pro-

pose amendments to the Manitoba Evidence Act which would create a process for listing "key criminal organizations" and eliminating the need to legal proceedings.

April 21: Hells Angels associate Wayne Holmes pleads guilty in Winnipeg, Canada, on charges of conspiracy to traffic drugs. He receives an 8½-year sentence. Police capture Beltran Leyva cartel lieutenant Gerardo Alvarez-Vazquez and 17 associates after a shootout at his home in Huixquilucan de Degollado, a suburb of Mexico City. In Monterrey, Mexico, cartel gunmen storm two hotels, abducting three registered guests and two receptionists. In Ontario, Calif., federal agents and state police arrest 27 members of the Black Angels gang on drug-trafficking charges, alleging that narcotics revenue was funneled to the Mexican Mafia.

April 22: Jurors in Adelaide, South Australia, convict Hells Angels MC member Dionisios Papadopoulos of trafficking methamphetamine. He receives a five-year sentence, extending the penalty for a prior conviction on blackmail charges. In Tokyo, Japan, Masami Yamamoto — president of the multinational computer hardware and information technology services company Fujitsu Limited — defends the firing of predecessor Kuniaki Nozoe, who has threatened to sue over claims linking him to organized crime. Media reports claim that Fujitsu offered Kuniaki ¥270 million in hush money to avoid litigation.

April 24: Cartel gunmen in Michoacán attack a convoy carrying Genaro García Luna, Mexico's Secretary of Public Safety, killing two bodyguards and two bystanders. Hours later, another hit team lobs grenades at a police station in Morelia, damaging three vehicles. In Manchester, N.H., police jail the co-owner of Luigi's Pizza Bar & Grille for firing gunshots during a brawl between Hells Angels and a rival club outside his restaurant. Defendant Petros Kostakis claims bikers were "storming the place."

April 25: Convicted drug dealer Aerock Wade Hallberg receives a five-year prison term in Winnipeg, Canada, for his role in an $8,000 transaction that earned him $25. Hallberg tells his judge that he "did it for the chicks."

April 27: Convicted Panamanian drug lord Manuel Noriega arrives in France from the U.S. and is remanded to prison without bail pending trial on money-laundering charges.

May 4: Taiwan's Ministry of Justice proposes an amendment to the country's Criminal Code, permitting seizure of any illegally acquired assets of fugitive defendants who have been in hiding for more than six months.

May 20–25: Gun battles erupt in Kingston, Jamaica, as government forces seek to arrest

Michael Christopher "Dudus" Coke, head of the drug-smuggling Shower Posse. Bullets and explosions claim at least 60 lives around the Tivoli Gardens housing project, before authorities suppress resistance and announce that Coke is nowhere to be found.

May 26: Police in Buenos Aires, Argentina, arrest Angie Sanclemente Valencia, a fashion model once crowned as Colombia's "Coffee Queen," on charges of smuggling cocaine. Originally caught with 121 pounds of coke in her luggage, while boarding a flight from Buenos Aires to Cancun, Mexico, Sanclemente Valencia has been a fugitive in hiding since December 2009.

May 27: A judge in Montreal, Québec, orders reputed mafioso Moreno Gallo's deportation to Italy. Police in Cancun, Mexico, arrest Gregorio Sanchez — the city's mayor and a gubernatorial candidate in the state of Quintana — on charges of collaborating with to two drug cartels. A federal judge formally indicts Sanchez on June 1.

June 8: FBI agents in New York City arrest nine Armenian mobsters on racketeering charges. Defendants include Bruno Krasniqi, Saimir Krasniqi, Elton Sejdaris, Erkliant Sula, Skender Cakoni, Gjovalin Berisha, Nazih Nasser, Plaurent Cela, and Gentian Nikolli. Also in Manhattan, federal jurors convict Anthony Cuti and William Tennant, former CEO and CFO of Duane Reade, Inc., on charges of securities fraud.

June 9: Imprisoned mafioso Luciano Aviello tells reporters that his brother Antonio murdered British subject Meredith Kercher in Perugia, Italy, in 2007. Kercher's former roommate, Amanda Knox, stands convicted of the slaying.

June 10: Former NYPD detective Luis M. Batista receives a 15-year federal prison term following conviction on charges of conspiracy to distribute narcotics, bank fraud and conspiracy to commit bank fraud, and obstruction of justice. DEA Acting Administrator Michele Leonhart announces the climax of "Project Deliverance," capped by 429 arrests in 16 states. Overall, the 22-month campaign against Mexican drug cartels has produced 2,266 arrests, with seizures including 1,262 pounds of methamphetamine, 2.5 tons of cocaine, 1,410 pounds of heroin, 69 tons of marijuana, 501 weapons, 527 vehicles, and $154 million in cash.

June 15: In New York City, U.S. Attorney Loretta Lynch announces four indictments charging 17 defendants with participation in health care fraud and money-laundering schemes in the Eastern District of New York Federal agents search offices of 12 durable medical equipment retail companies in South Brooklyn that were operated by the defendants, also seizing assets from bank accounts maintained by the defendants' retail

companies. Mexican authorities extradite drug-trafficker Pedro Antonio Bermudez to Brooklyn, N.Y., for trial on federal charges.

June 16: A joint task force of Colombian police and U.S. federal agents climax "Operation Pacific Rim" with the arrest of drug lord "Don Claudio" in eastern Colombia. Officers describe him as the brains behind a "super cartel" called El Dorado. A cohort, Luis Agustin Caicedo Velandia — AKA "Don Lucho"— awaits extradition from Argentina to the U.S.

June 17: Manhattan's U.S. attorney charges 38 defendants in a nationwide mortgage-fraud conspiracy. FBI agents arrest 17 defendants on the same day, all accused of perpetrating a scheme involving over $15 million in fraudulent loans using fake pay stubs, W-2 forms, and tax returns.

June 22: Jamaican authorities appeal for calm, following the capture of drug lord Michael Christopher Coke, caught while attempting to flee from Kingston disguised as a woman.

June 24: Defendant Jamali Brockett receives a 287-month federal prison term in Brooklyn, N.Y., following conviction of sex trafficking young girls and women and interstate transportation of women for the purposes of prostitution.

July 7: Federal jurors in Brooklyn, N.Y., convict Colombo Family underboss John "Sonny" Franzese on racketeering conspiracy charges. Also convicted are Mafia associates Joseph DiGorga, Christopher Curanovic, and John Capolino.

July 16: The DOJ's Medicare Fraud Strike Force charges 94 defendants in Florida, Louisiana, New York and Texas with participating in schemes to submit more than $251 million in false Medicare claims. The defendants include physicians and owners of various health care companies. In Philadelphia, Pa., federal prosecutors unseal indictments charging three police officers and four civilian defendants with conspiracy to distribute heroin.

July 21: Agents of the Nuevo Leon Attorney General's Office begin excavation of a drug cartel graveyard outside Monterrey. Corpses of 51 murder victims are exhumed by July 24.

July 22: Colombian drug-trafficker and terrorist Gerardo Aguilar Ramirez receives a 27-year federal prison term in Manhattan.

July 29: "Operation Slow Play," a 10-month DEA investigation, culminates with the arrests of 20 suspects in Hartford, Conn. Raiders seize 26 kilograms of cocaine, two kilograms of crack cocaine, one firearm, several vehicles, and $650,000 in cash.

August 5: A federal grand jury in Los Angeles indicts 15 defendants on charges of conspiring to distribute ecstasy. Raids by DEA agents and officers of the Beverly Hills Police Department have seized over 1.1 million MDMA tablets during the preceding investigation.

August 12: Federal prosecutors in Manhattan indict nine members of a major oxycodone distribution ring.

August 13: Unknown gunmen kill crime boss Macchour Chaouk in the backyard of his Melbourne, Australia, home. Family members blame rival mobster Ahmad Haddara, seeking to avenge the June 2009 slaying of his son. Six hours later, two men die in a barroom shooting on Lyons Street. Police arrest a suspect in Chaouk's slaying a short time later.

August 15: Drug cartel soldiers kidnap Edelmiro Cavazos Leal, the mayor of Santiago in Mexico's Nuevo Laredo State. Police find his bullet-riddled corpse beside a road near Monterrey on August 18.

August 16: Mexican authorities extradite Juarez Cartel member Felipe Dominguez-Vargas to Texas for trial on drug-trafficking charges.

August 17: A federal grand jury in Miami, Fla., indicts 27 defendants for their roles in a drug-smuggling operation based at Miami International Airport. DEA agents arrest 18 subjects, while nine remain at large. Defendants include Nelson Albarracin, Angel Reyes, Renzo Oberto, Josue Rubio, James Pena, Yunier Perez Cruz, Reginald Richard, Alfredo Barreto, Balbino Armando Ramos, Jose Alfonso Medina, Robert Marquez, Michael Boveda, Hasiel Gonzalez Rodriguez, Lazaro Nunez, Elio Sanchez, Carlos Ramones, Hugo Morales, Luis Neda, Jose Neda, Francisco Gonzalez, Rolando Rubio, Carlos Antonio Jorges Mendez, Alexander Suarez, Francisco Jose Sotelo, Milton Humberto Felix, Jorge Luis Rodriguez, and Alexander Valdes. In New York City, Colombian drug-trafficker and terrorist Erminso Cuevas Cabrera receives a 29-year prison term for importing tons of cocaine into the U.S.

August 19: DEA agents in San Juan, Puerto Rico, arrest six defendants in a drug sting involving 150 kilos of cocaine valued at $2.4 million.

August 22: Dutch police arrest Irish gangster and parole violator John Traynor in Amstelveen, North Holland, holding him for extradition to complete a seven-year prison term at home.

August 24: In Fort Lauderdale, Fla., mafioso Roberto Settineri pleads guilty to helping attorney Scott Rothstein operate a $1.2 billion Ponzi scheme. Rothstein's prior guilty plea clears the way for prosecution of 20 co-defendants, charged with extortion, drug trafficking, attempted homi-

cide and other crimes "arising from their alleged affiliation with Santa Maria di Gesù, a Sicilian mafia family." In New York City, agents of the New York Joint Organized Crime Task Force arrest Albanian gangsters Florian Veshi and Almir Rrapo on racketeering enterprise that include murder, kidnapping, narcotics trafficking, extortion, robbery, arson, obstruction of justice, and interstate transportation of stolen goods.

August 25: Mexican troops raid a ranch owned by drug traffickers near the Texas border, 14 miles from the town of San Fernando, in the state of Tamaulipas. Three suspects and one soldier die in the ensuing firefight. Afterward, troops discover the corpses of 72 murder victims — 58 men and 14 women — inside a building on the property. Guillermo Valdez, Mexico's intelligence chief, reports that more than 28,000 drug-related murders have occurred since December 1, 2006. On the same day, in Providence, R.I., Dorothy St. Laurent and son Anthony plead guilty to federal charges of interstate extortion, in violation of the Hobbs Act. Their indictment charges that both extorted cash from bookmakers on behalf of husband/father Anthony St. Laurent Sr., a reputed Mafia associate. In Brooklyn, N.Y., federal prosecutors announce the indictment of 12 Bloods street gang members on charges including racketeering, murder, drug distribution, and firearms offenses.

August 30: Mexican police arrest Texas-born drug lord Edgar Valdez — variously known as "La Barbie," "El Comandante" and "El Guero" — at a home outside Mexico City.

September 12: Beltran Leyvan drug cartel leader Sergio Villareal Barragan, AKA "El Grande," surrenders without resistance to a strike force of Mexican soldiers in Puebla, east of Mexico City.

September 16: The U.S. Substance Abuse and Mental Health Services Administration reports a 9 percent increase in use of illegal drugs during 2009, over figures from 2008. Use of marijuana increased 7 percent, use of ecstasy increased 27 percent, and use of methamphetamine increased 60 percent. Nonmedical use of prescription drugs also increased 20 percent.

September 19: HBO premieres a new series, *Boardwalk Empire*, based on the career of mobster Enoch "Nucky" Johnson in Atlantic City, N.J. Steve Buscemi stars as "Nucky Thompson," with Stephen Graham cast as Al Capone, Michael Stuhlbarg as Arnold Rothstein, and Joseph Riccobene as Frankie Yale.

Bibliography

The books and articles listed below were consulted during compilation of the chronology. Space prohibits listing of the individual newspaper articles that contributed other items, but a suggestion of their scope may be gained from perusing the published yearly indexes for major papers including the *Chicago Tribune, Los Angeles Times, New Orleans Times-Picayune, New York Times, The Times* of London, *USA Today* and the *Washington Post.*

Abadinsky, Howard. *Organized Crime.* New York: Wadsworth, 2002.

Abdalyan, Ani. "Money Laundering Regulation in Canada." *Assurances* 64 (October 1996): 395–421.

Abele, Gruppo. "Synthetic Drugs Trafficking in Three European Cities: Major Trends and the Involvement of Organized Crime." *Trends in Organized Crime* 8 (2004): 38–66.

Adams, James Ring. "Losing the Drug War: Drugs, Banks, and Florida Politics; Narcotics Trading Flourishes in the Sunshine State Not Only Because of Demand, but Also Because It Is a Major Source of Campaign and Other Political Funding." *American Spectator* 21 (September 1988): 2–24.

_____. "Medellin's New Generation." *American Spectator* 24 (December 1991): 22–25.

Adler, Patricia. *Wheeling and Dealing: An Ethnography of an Upper Level Drug Dealing and Smuggling Community.* New York: Columbia University Press, 1985.

Alain, Marc. "The Rise and Fall of Motorcycle Gangs in Quebec." *Federal Probation* 59 (June 1995): 54–57.

Albanese, Jay. *Contemporary Issues in Organized Crime.* Monsey, N.Y.: Criminal Justice Press, 1995.

_____. *Organized Crime in America,* 3d ed. Cincinnati: Anderson, 1998.

_____. *Organized Crime in Our Times.* Cincinnati: Anderson, 2004.

_____. *Prediction and Control of Organized Crime: A Risk Assessment Instrument for Targeting Law Enforcement Efforts.* Washington, D.C.: National Institute of Justice, 2001.

Alberti, Adriana. "Political Corruption and the Role of Public Prosecutors in Italy." *Crime, Law and Social Change* 24 (1995): 273–92.

Albini, Joseph. *The American Mafia: Genesis of a Legend.* New York: Appleton-Century Crofts, 1971.

_____. "The Distribution of Drugs: Models of Criminal Organization and Their Integration." Thomas Meiczkowski (ed.), *Drugs, Crime and Social Policy: Research Issues and Concerns.* Boston: Allyn and Bacon, 1992.

_____. "Mafia as Method: A Comparison Between Great Britain and U.S.A. Regarding the Existence and Structure of Types of Organized Crime." *International Journal of Criminology and Penology* 3 (1975): 295–305.

Albini, Joseph, R. Rogers, and Julie Anderson. "Russian Organized Crime and Weapons of Terror: The Reality of Nuclear Proliferation." Delbert Rounds (ed.), *International Criminal Justice: Issues in a Global Perspective.* Needham Heights, MA: Allyn and Bacon, 2000.

Albrecht, Hans-Jorg. "Money Laundering and the Confiscation of the Proceeds of Crime — A Comparative View on Different Models of the Control of Money Laundering and Confiscation." T.G. Watkin (ed.), *The Europeanisation of Law.* Oxford: Alden Press, 1998.

Albrecht, Hans-Jorg, and Cyrille Fijnaut. *Containment of Transnational Organized Crime: Comments on the UN Convention of December 2000.* Strafrecht, Germany: Max-Planck-Institute Fur Auslandisches und Internationales, 2002.

Alexander, Herbert, and Gerald Caiden (eds.). *The Politics and Economics of Organized Crime.* New York: Macmillan, 1985.

Alexander, Robert. *The Rise and Progress of British Opium Smuggling, and Its Effects Upon India, China, and the Commerce of Great Britain. Four Letters Addressed to the Right Honourable the Earl of Shaftesbury.* London: Seeley, Jackson, and Halliday, 1856.

Alexander, Shana. *The Pizza Connection: Lawyers, Drugs, Money, Mafia.* New York: Weidenfeld & Nicolson, 1988.

Allen, Edward. *Merchants of Menace.* Springfield, IL: Thomas, 1962.

Allsop, Kenneth. *The Bootleggers.* New Rochelle, N.Y.: Arlington House, 1961.

Amir, Menachem. "Aging and Aged in Organized Crime." *Journal of Offender Counseling, Services and Rehabilitation* 13 (1989): 61–85.

_____. "Organized Crime and Organized Criminality Among Georgian Jews in Israel." R.J. Kelly (ed.), *Orga-*

nized Crime: A Global Perspective. Totowa, N.J.: Rowman and Littlefield, 1986.

Anastasia, George. *Blood and Honor: Inside the Scarfo Mob—The Mafia's Most Violent Family.* Philadelphia: Camino Books, 2004.

_____. *The Goodfella Tapes.* New York: Avon, 1998.

_____. *The Last Gangster.* New York: HarperCollins, 2004.

Anbinder, Tyler. *Five Points: The Nineteenth-Century New York City Neighborhood That Invented Tap Dance, Stole Elections and Became the Worlds Most Notorious Slum.* New York: The Free Press, 2001.

Anderson, Annelise. *The Business of Organized Crime: A Cosa Nostra Family.* Stanford, CA: Hoover Institution Press, 1979.

Anderson, Robert. "From Mafia to Cosa Nostra." *American Journal of Sociology* 61 (November 1965): 302–10.

Aniskiewicz, Rick. "Corruption and Organized Crime: Historical Tends and Contemporary Issues." *Law Enforcement Intelligence Analysis Digest* 5 (Winter 1990): 25–31.

_____. "Metatheoretical Issues in the Study of Organized Crime." *Journal of Contemporary Criminal Justice* 10 (December 1994): 314–24.

Anslinger, Harry. *The Protectors: The Heroic Story of the Narcotics Agents, Citizens, and Officials in Their Unending, Unsung Battles Against Organized Crime in America and Abroad.* New York: Farrar, Straus, 1964.

Anslinger, Harry, and William Charles Oursler. *The Murderers: The Story of the Narcotic Gangs.* New York: Farrar, Straus and Cudahy, 1961.

Anson, Robert. *"They've Killed the President!"* New York: Bantam, 1975.

Anthony, Jason, Amani Harrison, Patrick Linehan, and Jeffery Palker. "Securities Fraud." *American Criminal Law Review* 36 (Summer 1999): 1095–155.

Appleton, Peter, and Doug Clark. *Billion $$$ High: The Drug Invasion of Canada.* Montreal: McGraw-Hill Ryerson, 1990.

Arlacchi, Pino. *Mafia Business: The Mafia Ethic and the Spirit of Capitalism.* London: Verso, 1987.

_____. "The Mafioso: From Man of Honour to Entrepreneur." *New Left Review* (November/December 1979): 53–72.

_____. *Men of Dishonor: Inside the Sicilian Mafia.* New York: William Morrow, 1992.

_____. "Nations Build Alliances to Stop Organized Crime." *Global Issues* 6 (2001): 27–30.

Arnold, Guy. *The International Drugs Trade.* New York: Routledge, 2004.

Aromaa, Kauko (ed.). *Eastern Crime: A Selection of Reports on Crime in the St. Petersburg Region and the Baltic Countries, 1993–1999.* Helsinki: National Research Institute of Legal Policy, 1999.

Aronowitz, Alexis. "Smuggling and Trafficking in Human Beings: The Phenomenon, the Markets That Drive It and the Organisations That Promote It." *European Journal on Criminal Policy and Research* 9 (Summer 2001): 163–95.

Asbury, Herbert. *All Around the Town: Murder, Scandal, Riot and Mayhem in Old New York.* New York: Alfred A. Knopf, 1934.

_____. *The Barbary Coast: An Informal History of the San Francisco Underworld.* New York: Alfred A. Knopf, 1933.

_____. *The French Quarter: An Informal History of the New Orleans Underworld.* Garden City, N.Y.: Garden City Publishing, 1938.

_____. *The Gangs of Chicago: An Informal History of the Chicago Underworld.* New York: Thunder's Mouth Press, 1986.

_____. *The Gangs of New York: An Informal History of the Underworld.* New York: Alfred A. Knopf, 1928.

_____. *Gem of the Prairie: An Informal History of the Chicago Underworld.* New York: Alfred A. Knopf, 1940.

_____. *The Great Illusion: An Informal History of Prohibition.* Garden City, N.Y.: Doubleday, 1950.

_____. *Sucker's Progress: An Informal History of Gambling in America.* New York: Dodd, Mead, 1938.

Ashley, Richard. *Cocaine: Its History, Uses and Effects.* New York: Warner Books, 1976.

Ashman, Charles. *The CIA-Mafia Link.* New York: Manor Books, 1975.

Ashman, Charles, and Rebecca Sobel. *The Strange Disappearance of Jimmy Hoffa.* New York: Manor Books, 1976.

Astorga, Luís. *Drug Trafficking in Mexico: A First General Assessment.* Mexico City: MOST, 2000.

Atkins, Ace. *White Shadow.* New York: Putnam, 2006.

Atwood, Barrett, and Molly McConville. "Money Laundering." *American Criminal Law Review* 36 (Summer 1999): 901–27.

Australian Institute of Criminology. *Art Crime: Protecting Art, Protecting Artists, and Protecting Consumers.* Canberra: The Australian Institute of Criminology, 2000.

Baba, Yoko. "Vietnamese Gangs, Cliques, and Delinquents." *Journal of Gang Research* 8 (Winter 2001): 1+.

Bäckman, Johan. *The Inflation of Crime in Russia: The Social Danger of the Emerging Markets.* Helsinki: National Research Institute of Legal Policy, 1998.

Bacon, John. "The French Connection Revisited." *International Journal of Intelligence and Counterintelligence* 4 (Winter 1990): 507–23.

Bailey, John, and Roy Godson. *Organized Crime and Democratic Governability: Mexico and the U.S.-Mexican Borderlands.* Pittsburgh: University of Pittsburgh Press, 2000.

Balboni, Alan. *Beyond the Mafia.* Reno: University of Nevada Press, 1996.

Ballezza, R A. "YACS (Yugoslavian/Albanian/Croatian/Serbian) Crime Groups: An FBI Major Crime Initiative." *FBI Law Enforcement Bulletin* 7 (November): 7–12.

Balsamo, William, and Carpozi, George. *Under the Clock: The Inside Story of the Mafia's First Hundred Years.* Far Hills, N.J.: New Horizon Press, 1988.

Bannister, Paul, and John Stafford. *Deadly Deception: Twenty One Years Undercover Without a Badge.* San Diego: Images Press, 1991.

Barger, Ralph, and Keith Zimmerman. *Hell's Angel: The Life and Times of Sonny Barger and the Hell's Angels MC.* New York: William Morrow, 2000.

Barlett, Donald, and James Steele. *Empire.* New York: W.W. Norton, 1979.

Barrett, Richard. "Confronting Tax Havens, the Offshore Phenomenon, and Money Laundering." *International Tax Journal* 23 (Spring 1997): 12–42.

Barry, Kathleen. *Female Sexual Slavery.* New York: Avon, 1981.

Barton, David. "The Kansas City Experience: Crack Organized Crime Cooperative Task Force." *Police Chief* 55 (January 1988): 28–30.

Barzini, Luigi. *From Caesar to the Mafia: Persons, Places and Problems in Italian Life.* New York: The Library Press, 1971.

_____. *The Italians.* New York: Atheneum, 1964.

Bauer, Hans-Peter, and Peter Martin. "Global Standards for Money Laundering Prevention." *Journal of Financial Crime* 10 (July 2002): 69–72.

Bauer, Robert. "Methamphetamine in Illinois: An Examination of an Emerging Drug." *Illinois Criminal Justice Information Authority Research Bulletin* 1 (2003): 1–12.

Baum, Dan. *Smoke and Mirrors: The War on Drugs and the Politics of Failure.* Boston: Little, Brown, 1996.

Beal, Clifford. *Quelch's Gold: Piracy, Greed, and Betrayal in Colonial New England.* Westport, CT: Greenwood, 2007.

Beare, Margaret. "Corruption and Organized Crime: Lessons from History." *Crime, Law and Social Change* 28 (1997): 155–72.

_____. *Criminal Conspiracies: Organized Crime in Canada.* Scarborough, Ontario: Nelson Canada, 1996.

_____ (ed.). *Critical Reflections on Transnational Organized Crime, Money Laundering, and Corruption.* Toronto: University of Toronto Press, 2004.

_____. "Organized Corporate Criminality: Tobacco Smuggling Between Canada and the U.S." *Crime, Law and Social Change* 37 (April 2002): 225–43.

Beare, Margaret, and Frederick Martens. "Policing Organized Crime: The Comparative Structures, Traditions and Policies within the United States and Canada." *Journal of Contemporary Criminal Justice* 14 (November 1998): 398–427.

Beare, Margaret, and Stephen Schneider. *Tracing of Illicit Funds: Money Laundering in Canada.* Ottawa: Solicitor General Canada, 1990.

Beaufait, Howard. "The Case of William Potter." Oliver Bayer (ed.), *Cleveland Murders.* New York: Duell, Sloan and Pearce, 1947.

Behan, Tom. *The Camorra.* London: Routledge, 1996.

_____. *See Naples and Die: The Camorra and Organised Crime.* London: I.B. Tauris, 2002.

Behr, Edward. *Prohibition: Thirteen Years That Changed America.* New York: Arcade, 1996.

Belenko, Steven. *Crack and the Evolution of Anti-Drug Policy.* Westport, CT: Greenwood, 1993.

Bell, Daniel. "Crime as an American Way of Life." F. A. J. Ianni (ed.), *The Crime Society: Organized Crime and Corruption in America.* New York: New American Library, 1976.

_____. "The Myth of the Cosa Nostra." *New Leader* 46 (1963): 12–15.

Bequai, August. *Organized Crime: The Fifth Estate.* Lexington, MA: Lexington Books, 1979.

Berdal, Mats, and Monica Serrano. *Transnational Organized Crime & International Security: Business as Usual?* Boulder, CO: Lynne Rienner, 2002.

Bergreen, Laurence. *Capone: The Man and the Era.* New York: Simon & Schuster, 1994.

Berman, Susan. *Easy Street.* New York: Dial Press, 1981.

_____. *Lady Las Vegas.* New York: TV Books, 1996.

Bernstein, Jonas. "A Fistful of Rubles." *American Spectator* 29 (January 1996): pp. 28–30+.

Bernstein, Lee. *The Greatest Menace: Organized Crime in Cold War America.* Boston: University of Massachusetts Press, 2002.

Best, Joel, and David Luckenbill. *Organizing Deviance,* 2d ed. Englewood Cliffs, N.J.: Prentice-Hall, 1994.

Bewley-Taylor, David. *The United States and International Drug Control, 1909–1997.* New York: Cassell, 1999.

Biden, Joseph. *The Sicilian Connection: Southwest Asian Heroin En Route to the United States*: Report. Washington, D.C.: U.S. Government Printing Office, 1980.

Bilek, Arthur. *The First Vice Lord: Big Jim Colosimo and the Ladies of the Levee.* Nashville: Cumberland House, 2008.

Birks, Peter. *Laundering and Tracing.* New York: Oxford University Press, 1995.

Black, David. *Triad Takeover: A Terrifying Account of the Spread of Triad Crime in the West.* London: Sidgwick & Jackson, 1991.

Black, J. Anderson. *Organized Crime.* Broomall, PA: Mason Crest, 2003.

Black, Larry. "Organized Crime and the Teamsters." *MacLean's* (June 29, 1987): 44.

Blakey, G. Robert, and Richard Billings. *The Plot to Kill the President.* New York: Times Books, 1981.

Blecker, Robert. "Beyond 1984: Undercover in America; Serpico to Abscam." *New York Law School Law Review* 28 (1984): 823–1024.

Bloch, Herbert. "The Gambling Business: An American Paradox." *Crime and Delinquency* 8 (October 1962): 355–64.

Block, Alan. *The Business of Crime: Documentary Study of Organized Crime in American Economy.* Boulder, CO: Westview Press, 1991.

_____. *East Side–West Side: Organizing Crime in New York 1930–1950.* Swansea, Wales: University College Cardiff Press, 1980.

_____. *Masters of Paradise.* New Brunswick, N.J.: Transaction, 1991.

_____. "The Snowman Cometh: Coke in Progressive New York." *Criminology* 17 (May 1979): 75–99.

Block, Alan, and William Chambliss. *Organizing Crime.* New York: Elsevier, 1981.

Block, Alan, and Sean Griffin. "Transnational Financial Crime: Crooked Lawyers, Tax Evasion, and Securities Fraud." *Journal of Contemporary Criminal Justice* 18 (November 2002): 381–93.

Block, Alan, and Frank Scarpitti. "Casinos and Banking: Organized Crime in the Bahamas." *Deviant Behavior* 7 (1986): 301–12.

_____, and _____. *Poisoning for Profit: The Mafia and Toxic Waste in America.* New York: W.W. Morrow, 1985.

Block, Alan, and Constance Weaver. *All Is Clouded by Desire: Global Banking, Money Laundering, and International Organized Crime.* Westport, CT: Praeger, 2004.

Block, Ann. "Aw! Your Mother's in the Mafia: Women Criminals in Progressive New York." *Contemporary Crises* 1 (January 1977): 5–22.

Blue, Laura. "The Dirt on the Don." *Time* (October 18, 2004): 36–38.

Blum, Howard. *Gangland: How the FBI Broke the Mob.* New York: Simon & Schuster, 1993.

Blumenthal, Ralph. *Last Days of the Sicilians at War with the Mafia: The FBI Assault on the Pizza Connection.* New York: Times Books, 1988.

Blumenthal, Sid (ed.), *Government by Gunplay.* New York: Signet, 1976.

Boehm, Randolph. "Organized Crime and Organized Labor." *Journal of Social and Political Studies* 2 (Summer 1977): 91–105.

Bologna, Jack. *Handbook on Corporate Fraud: Prevention, Detection, and Investigation.* Boston: Butterworth-Heinemann, 1993.

Bolz, Jennifer. "Chinese Organized Crime and Illegal Alien Trafficking: Humans as a Commodity." *Asian Affairs* 22 (Fall 1995): 147–58.

Bonanno, Bill. *Bound by Honor.* New York: St. Martin's, 1999.

Bonanno, Joseph, and Sergio Lalli. *A Man of Honor: The Autobiography of Joseph Bonanno.* New York: Simon & Schuster, 1983.

Bonanno, Rosalie, and Beverly Donofrio. *Mafia Marriage: My Story.* New York: William Morrow, 1990.

Bonavolonta, Jules, and Brian Duffy. *The Good Guys: How*

We Turned the FBI 'Round—and Finally Broke the Mob. New York: Simon & Schuster, 1996.

Bonnie, Richard, and Charles Whitebread. *Marijuana Conviction: A History of Marihuana Prohibition in the United States.* Charlottesville: University Press of Virginia, 1974.

Booth, Martin. *The Dragon Syndicates: The Global Phenomenon of the Triads.* New York: Carroll & Graf, 1999.

_____. *The Triads: The Growing Global Threat from the Chinese Criminal Societies.* New York: St. Martin's, 1991.

Bossard, André. "Mafias, Triads, Yakuza and Cartels: A Comparative Study of Organized Crime." *Crime and Justice International* 14 (December 1998): 5–32.

_____. *Transnational Crime and Criminal Law.* Chicago: Office of International Criminal Justice, University of Illinois at Chicago, 1990.

Bottom, Bob. *Without Fear or Favour.* South Melbourne, Australia: Sun Books, 1984.

Bourgois, Philippe. *In Search of Respect: Selling Crack in El Barrio.* Cambridge: Cambridge University Pres, 1995.

Bowden, Mark. *Killing Pablo: The Hunt for the World's Greatest Outlaw.* New York: Atlantic Monthly Press, 2001.

Bradford, Alfred. *Flying the Black Flag: A Brief History of Piracy.* Westport, CT: Greenwood Press, 2007.

Bradley, Craig. "Racketeers, Congress, and the Courts: An Analysis of RICO." *Iowa Law Review* 65 (June 1980): 837–97.

Brandt, Charles. *"I Heard You Paint Houses": Frank "The Irishman" Sheeran and the Inside Story of the Mafia, the Teamsters, and the Last Ride of Jimmy Hoffa.* Hanover, N.H.: Steerforth Press, 2004.

Brashler, William. *The Don: The Life and Death of Sam Giancana.* New York: Harper and Row, 1977.

Bremner, Brian. "How the Mob Burned the Banks: The Yakuza Is at the Center of the $350 Billion Bad Loan Scandal." *Business Week* (January 29, 1996): 42–43.

Brennan, Bill. *The Frank Costello Story: The True Story of the Underworld's Prime Minister.* Derby, CT: Monarch Books, 1962.

Brennan, Steve. *The Gigantic Book of Pirate Stories.* New York: Skyhorse, 2007.

Bresler, Fenton. *The Trail of the Triads: An Investigation into International Crime.* London: Weidenfeld & Nicolson, 1980.

Brewton, Pete. *The Mafia, CIA & George Bush.* New York: S.P.I. Books, 1992.

Brill, Stephen. *The Teamsters.* New York: Simon & Schuster, 1978.

British Columbia Coordinated Law Enforcement Unit. *An Examination of Safeguards Against the Influence and Infiltration of Organized Crime Within Law Enforcement in British Columbia.* Vancouver, B.C.: Drug Strategies Section, Policy Analysis Division, Coordinated Law Enforcement Unit, Ministry of Attorney General, 1991.

Brock, David. "The World of Narco-Terrorism." *American Spectator* 22 (June 1989): 24–48.

Broomhall, Bruce, and Allen Castle. *Action against Transnational Organised Crime: Tackling Money Laundering in the Context of Institution-Building in the Asia Pacific.* Vancouver, B.C.: International Centre for Criminal Law Reform and Criminal Justice Policy, University of British Columbia, 1998.

Brown, Rick, Ronald Clarke, Bernard Rix, and James Sheptycki. *Tackling Organised Vehicle Crime: The Role of the National Criminal Intelligence Service.* London: Home Office, 2004.

Brown, Waln. "Black Female Gangs in Philadelphia." *International Journal of Offender Therapy and Comparative Criminology* 21 (1977): 221–28.

Browning, Frank, and John Gerassi. *The American Way of Crime.* New York: G.P. Putnam's Sons, 1980.

Bruinsma, Gerben, and Wim Bernasco. "Criminal Groups and Transnational Illegal Markets." *Crime, Law and Social Change* 41 (2004): 79–94.

Bruning, Fred. "Taking Money from Gangsters: Political Leaders Have Permitted the Mafia to Flourish and Infiltrate Extensively What Is Laughingly Called Legitimate Business." *Maclean's* (October 7, 1991): 15.

Buckwalter, Jane. *International Perspectives on Organized Crime.* Chicago: Office of International Criminal Justice, University of Illinois at Chicago, 1990.

Burbank, Jeff. *Las Vegas Babylon.* New York: M. Evans, 2005.

_____. *License to Steal.* Reno: University of Nevada Press, 2000.

Bureau of Narcotics, U.S. Treasury Department. *"Mafia": The Government's Secret File on Organized Crime.* New York: HarperCollins, 2007.

Burke, Tod, and Charles O'Rear. "Home Invaders: Asian Gangs in America." *Police Studies* 13 (Winter 1990): 154.

Burns, Eric. *The Spirits of America: A Social History of Alcohol.* Philadelphia: Temple University Press, 2003.

Burnstein, Scott. *Motor City Mafia: A Century of Organized Crime in Detroit.* Chicago: Arcadia, 2006.

Burris-Kitchen, Deborah. *Female Gang Participation: The Role of African American Women in the Informal Drug Economy and Gang Activities.* Lewiston, N.Y.: Edwin Mellen Press, 1997.

Butler, Brendan. *Police and Drugs: A Follow-Up Report.* Brisbane, Australia: Queensland Criminal Justice Commission, 1999.

Bynum, Timothy. *Organized Crime in America: Concepts and Controversies.* Monsey, N.Y.: Criminal Justice Press, 1987.

Byrne, John. "Bank Secrecy Act Compliance in the 1990s: Banking Industry Efforts Are Rewarded." *Bankers Magazine* 179 (January/February 1996): 15–22.

Byrne, John, and Mary Johannes. "What You Should Know About Money Laundering Law." *ABA Banking Journal* 77 (July 1985): 69–70+.

Cain, Michael. *The Tangled Web.* New York: Skyhorse, 2007.

Calder, James. "Al Capone and the IRS: State Sanctioned Criminology of Organized Crime." *Crime, Law and Social Justice* 17 (1992): 1–23.

Campagna, Daniel, and Donald Poffenberger. *The Sexual Trafficking in Children: An Investigation of the Child Sex Trade.* Dover, MA: Auburn House, 1988.

Campbell, Anne. "Girls, Gangs, Women and Drugs." *Women and Criminal Justice* 7 (1995): 107.

_____. *The Girls in the Gang.* Cambridge, MA: Blackwell, 1991.

Canadian Security Intelligence Service. *Transnational Criminal Activity: A Global Context.* Ottawa: Canadian Security Intelligence Service, 1998.

Canfield, Michael, and Alan Weberman. *Coup d'état in America.* New York: Third Press, 1975.

Cantalupo, Joseph, and Thomas C. Renner. *Body Mike: An Unsparing Expose by the Mafia Insider Who Turned on the Mob.* New York: Villard Books, 1990.

Capeci, Jerry. *The Complete Idiot's Guide to the Mafia.* Indianapolis: Alpha Books, 2002.

_____, and Gene Mustain. *Gotti: Rise and Fall.* Toronto: Penguin Books Canada, 1996.

Caputo, David. *Organized Crime and American Politics.* Morristown, N.J.: General Learning Process, 1974.

Carey, Arthur, and Howard McLellan. *Memoirs of a Murder Man.* New York: Doubleday, Doran, 1930.

Carlo, Philip. *Gaspipe: Confessions of a Mafia Boss.* New York: William Morrow, 2008.

_____. *The Ice Man: Confessions of a Mafia Contract Killer.* New York: St. Martin's Griffin, 2007.

Carpenter, Teresa. *Mob Girl: A Woman's Life in the Underworld.* New York: Simon & Schuster, 1992.

Carter, Barbara. "Race, Sex, and Gangs: Reform School Families." *Trans Action* 11 (November/December 1973): 36–43.

Carter, David. "International Organized Crime: Emerging Trends in Entrepreneurial Crime." *Journal of Contemporary Criminal Justice* 10 (December 1994): 239.

Cassella, Stefan. *Federal Money Laundering Cases.* Washington, D.C.: U.S. Department of Justice, 2000.

Castillo, Celerino, and Dave Harmon. *Powderburns: Cocaine, Contras and the Drug War.* Oakville, Ontario: Mosaic Press, 1994.

Castillo, Fabio. *La Coca Nostra.* Bogotá, Colombia: Editorial Documentos Periodísticos, 1991.

Catania, Enzo. *Mafia.* New York: St. Martin's, 1978.

Catanzaro, Raimondo. "Enforcers, Entrepreneurs, and Survivors: How the Mafia Has Adapted to Change." *British Journal of Sociology* 36 (March 1985): 34–57.

_____. *Men of Respect.* New York: The Free Press 1988.

_____. "Supply and Demand of Protection in Interpretations of the Mafia: A Reply to Gambetta." *Polis* 8 (December 1994): 465–68.

_____. "Violent Social Regulation: Organized Crime in the Italian South." *Social & Legal Studies* 3 (2 June 1994): 267.

Chalk, Peter. "Southeast Asia and the Golden Triangle's Heroin Trade: Threat and Response." *Studies in Conflict & Terrorism* 23 (April/June 2000): 89–106.

Chandler, David. *Brothers in Blood: The Rise of the Criminal Brotherhoods.* New York: Dutton, 1975.

Chang, Dae. "World Ministerial Conference on Organized Transnational Crime." *International Journal of Comparative and Applied Criminal Justice* 23 (Fall 1999): 141–80.

Chapkis, Wendy. "Trafficking, Migration, and the Law: Protecting Innocents, Punishing Immigrants." *Gender & Society* 17 (2004): 923–37.

Chappell, Duncan, and Marilyn Walsh. "Receiving Stolen Property: The Need for Systematic Inquiry into the Fencing Process." *Criminology* 11 (February 1974): 484–97.

Charbonneau, Jean-Pierre. *The Canadian Connection: An Expose on the Mafia in Canada and Its International Ramifications.* Montreal: Optimum Publishing, 1976.

Chardak, Sharon. "Airport Drug Stops: Defining Reasonable Suspicion Based on the Characteristics of the Drug Courier Profile." *Boston College Law Review* 26 (May 1985): 693–726.

Che, Wai-Kin. "The Triad Societies in Hong Kong in the 1990s." *Police Studies* 13 (Winter 1990): 151–53.

Chen, An. "Secret Societies and Organized Crime in Contemporary China." *Modern Asian Studies* 39 (2005): 77–107.

Chepesiuk, Ron. *Hard Target: The United States War Against International Drug Trafficking, 1982–1997.* Jefferson, N.C.: McFarland, 1999.

_____. *War on Drugs: An International Encyclopedia.* Santa Barbara: ABC-Clio, 1999.

Chimbos, Peter. "Some Trends of Organized Crime in Canada: A Preliminary Review." *Canadian Bar Journal* 12 (1969): 347.

Chin, Ko-lin. *Chinatown Gangs: Extortion, Enterprise, and Ethnicity.* New York: Oxford University Press, 1996.

_____. *Chinese Subculture and Criminality: Non Traditional Crime Groups in America.* New York: Greenwood Press, 1990.

_____. "The Emergence of Asian Organized Crime Problems and Perspectives." *Law Enforcement Intelligence Analysis Digest* 6 (Summer 1991): 45–47.

_____. *Smuggled Chinese: Clandestine Immigration to the United States.* Philadelphia: Temple University Press, 1999.

_____. "The Social Organization of Chinese Human Smuggling." David Kyle and Rey Koslowskie (eds.), *Global Human Smuggling: Comparative Perspectives.* Baltimore: Johns Hopkins University Press, 2001.

Chiocca, Olindo. *Mobsters and Thugs: Quotes from the Underworld.* Toronto: Guernica Editions, 2000.

Chu, Yiu Kong. *The Triads as Business.* London: Routledge, 2000.

Chubb, Judith. "The Mafia, the Market, and the State in Italy and Russia." *Journal of Modern Italian Studies* 1 (Spring 1996): 273–91.

Cilluffo, Frank, and George Salmoiraghi. "And the Winner Is… the Albanian Mafia." *Washington Quarterly* 22 (Autumn 1996): 21–5.

Cirules, Enrique. *The Mafia in Havana.* Melbourne, FL: Ocean Press, 2004.

Clark, Norman. *Deliver Us from Evil: An Interpretation of American Prohibition.* New York: Norton, 1976.

Clarke, Donald. *In the Reign of Rothstein.* New York: Vanguard, 1929.

Clarke, Ronald, Rick Kemper and Laura Wyckoff. "Controlling Cell Phone Fraud in the U.S.: Lessons for the UK 'Foresight' Prevention Initiative." *Security Journal* 14 (2001): 7–22.

Clarke, Thurston, and John Tigue Jr. *Dirty Money: Swiss Banks, the Mafia, Money Laundering, and White Collar Crime.* New York: Simon & Schuster, 1975.

Clawson, Patrick, and Rensselaer Lee. *The Andean Cocaine Industry.* New York: St. Martin's, 1996.

Clutterbuck, Richard. "Peru: Cocaine, Terrorism and Corruption." *International Relations* 12 (August 1995): 77–92.

_____. *Terrorism, Drugs, and Crime in Europe.* London: Routledge, 1990.

Cohen, A. K. "The Concept of Criminal Organization." *British Journal of Criminology* 17 (April 1977): 97–111.

Cohen, Mickey. *Mickey Cohen—in My Own Words.* Englewood Cliffs, N.J.: Prentice-Hall, 1975.

Cohen, Rich. *Tough Jews: Fathers, Sons, and Gangster Dreams.* New York: Vintage, 1999.

Coleman, James. "The Business of Organized Crime: A Cosa Nostra Family." *American Journal of Sociology* 88 (July 1982): 235.

Coles, Nigel. "It's Not What You Know—It's Who You Know That Counts: Analysing Serious Crime Groups as Social Networks." *British Journal of Criminology* 41 (Autumn 2001): 580–94.

Collier, William, and Edwin Westrate. *The Reign of Soapy Smith: Monarch of Misrule.* New York: Doubleday, Doran, 1935.

Conklin, John. *The Crime Establishment: Organized Crime and American Society.* Englewood Cliffs, N.J.: Prentice-Hall, 1973.

Cook, Beryl. "Hard Drugs: The Crisis Now: Island Nations

Face Expanding Drug Trafficking." *Pacific Islands Monthly* 61 (August 1991): 35–38.

Cook, Fred. *Mafia!* Greenwich, CT: Fawcett, 1973.

———. *The Pinkertons.* Garden City, N.Y.: Doubleday, 1974.

———. *The Secret Rulers: Criminal Syndicates and How They Control the U.S. Underworld.* New York: Duell, Sloan and Pearce, 1966.

———. *A Two-Dollar Bet Means Murder.* New York: Dial Press, 1961.

Cooley, Robert. *When Corruption Was King: How I Helped the Mob Rule Chicago, Then Brought the Outfit Down.* New York: Carroll & Graf, 2005.

Cooney, John. *The Annenbergs.* New York: Simon & Schuster, 1982.

Coontz, Phyllis. "Managing the Action: Sports Bookmakers as Entrepreneurs." *Deviant Behavior* 22 (May-June 2001): 239–66.

Corbitt, Michael, and Sam Giancana. *Double Deal: The Inside Story of Murder, Unbridled Corruption, and the Cop Who Was a Mobster.* New York: William Morrow, 2003.

Cordasco, Francesco. *The White Slave Trade and the Immigrants: A Chapter in American Social History.* Detroit: Blaine Ethridge Books, 1981.

Cottino, Amedeo. "Sicilian Cultures of Violence: The Interconnections between Organized Crime and Local Society." *Crime, Law and Social Change* 32 (2000): 103–13.

Courakis, Nestor. "Financial Crime Today: Greece as a European Case Study."

European Journal on Criminal Policy and Research 9 (Summer 2001): 197–219.

Courtwright, David. *Forces of Habit: Drugs and the Making of the Modern World.* Cambridge, MA: Harvard University Press, 2001.

Cowan, Rick, and Douglas Century. *Takedown: The Fall of the Last Mafia Empire.* New York: Berkley, 2002.

Cressey, Donald. *Criminal Organization: Its Elementary Forms.* London: Heinemann Educational Books, 1972.

———. "The Functions and Structure of Criminal Syndicates." *President's Commission on Law Enforcement and Administration of Justice Task Force Report: Organized Crime.* Washington, D.C.: U.S. Government Printing Office, 1967.

———. *Organized Crime and Criminal Organizations.* Cambridge, UK: W. Heffer & Sons, 1971.

———. *Theft of the Nation: The Structure and Operations of Organized Crime in America.* New York: Harper & Row, 1969.

Criminal Intelligence Service Canada. *Annual Reports on Organized Crime in Canada.* Ottawa: CISC, 1997–2004.

———. *Asian Organized Crime Report.* Ottawa: CISC, 1986.

———. "East European-based Organized Crime." *CISC Annual Report, 2001.* Ottawa: CISC, 2001.

———. "Illegal Gaming." *Criminal Intelligence Service Canada Annual Report on Organized Crime, 2000.* Ottawa: Criminal Intelligence Service Canada, 2000.

Crittle, Simon. *The Last Godfather: The Rise and Fall of Joey Massino.* New York: Berkley, 2006.

Cummings, John, and Ernest Volkman. *Goombata: The Improbable Rise and Fall of John Gotti and His Gang.* Boston: Little, Brown, 199.

Curry, G. David. "Crime Crusades and Corruption: Prohibition in the United States, 1900–1987." *American Journal of Sociology* 96 (November 1990): 798.

Curtis, Glenn. *Involvement of Russian Organized Crime Syndicates, Criminal Elements in the Russian Military, and Regional Terrorist Groups in Narcotics Trafficking in Central Asia, Caucasus, and Chechnya.* Washington, D.C.: Library of Congress, 2002.

Curtis, Glenn, Seth Elan, Rexford Hudson and Nina Kollars. "Transnational Activities of Chinese Crime Organizations." *Trends in Organized Crime* 7 (2002): 19–59.

Curtis, Ken. *Pimpin Ain't Easy: An Education on "The Life."* Lakewood, OH: Condos on the Moon, 2006.

Curzon, Sam. *Legs Diamond.* New York: Belmont Tower Books, 1973.

Davis, James. *Street Gangs: Youth, Biker, and Prison Groups.* Dubuque: Kendall/Hunt, 1982.

Davis, John. *Mafia Dynasty: The Rise and Fall of the Gambino Crime Family.* New York: HarperCollins, 1993.

———. *Mafia Kingfish: Carlos Marcello and the Assassination of John F. Kennedy.* New York: McGraw-Hill, 1989.

Davis, Peter. "Corruption as a Fundamental Element of Organized Crime." *Police Studies* 12 (Winter 1989): 154–59.

Davis, Roger. "Outlaw Motorcyclists: A Problem for Police." *FBI Law Enforcement Bulletin* 51 (October 1982): 12–15; 51 (November 1982): 16–22.

Daye, Douglas. *A Law Enforcement Sourcebook of Asian Crime and Cultures: Tactics and Mindsets.* Boca Raton: CRC Press, 1997.

de Borchgrave, Arnaud. "Organized Crime's Global Shadow." *World and I* 12 (1997): 48–53.

de Champlain, Pierre. *Mobsters, Gangsters and Men of Honour. Cracking the Mafia Code.* Toronto: HarperCollins, 2004.

Decker, Scott, G. David Curry, and Kent Joscelyn. "Gangs, Gang Homicides, and Gang Loyalty: Organized Crimes or Disorganized Criminals." *Journal of Criminal Justice* 30 (July/August 2002): 343–52.

De Franco, Edward. *Anatomy of a Scam: A Case Study of a Planned Bankruptcy by Organized Crime.* Washington, D.C.: National Institute of Law Enforcement and Criminal Justice, 1973.

De Grazia, Jessica. *DEA: The War Against Drugs.* London: BBC Books, 1991.

Delap, Breandan. *Mad Dog Coll: An Irish Gangster.* Dublin: Mercier Press, 1999.

del Frate, Anna, and Giovanni Pasqua (eds.). *Responding to the Challenges of Corruption.* Rome: United Nations Interregional Crime and Justice Research Institute, 2000.

Demaris, Ovid. *The Boardwalk Jungle.* New York: Bantam, 1986.

———. *Captive City: Chicago in Chains.* New York: Lyle Stuart, 1969.

———. *The Last Mafioso.* New York: Times Books, 1981.

Demont, John. "First Rum, Now Drugs. Atlantic Coastal Security Is a Constant Challenge." *MacLean's* (May 13, 2002): 46+.

DenBoer, Monica. "Fight Against Organized Crime in Europe: A Comparative Perspective." *European Journal on Criminal Policy and Research* 9 (Autumn 2001): 259–72.

Denisova, Tatyana. "Trafficking in Women and Children for Purposes of Sexual Exploitation: The Criminological Aspect." *Trends in Organized Crime* 6 (Spring/Summer 2001): 30–36.

Denton, Sally, and Roger Morris. *The Money and the Power: The Making of Las Vegas and Its Hold on America, 1947–2000.* New York: Alfred A Knopf, 2001.

Desjardins, Fred. "Hell on Wheels." *Canadian Crime and Justice* (November 1989): 14–15.

———. "The Mob in Canada." *Canadian Police News* 3 (Summer 1989): 7–8.

———. "Organized Crime Begins with Black Handers." *Canadian Police News* 3 (Summer 1989): 8.

DeStefano, Anthony. *King of the Godfathers: Joseph Massino and the Fall of the Bonanno Crime Family*. New York: Citadel, 2007.

Devito, Carlo. *Encyclopedia of International Organized Crime*. New York: Facts on File, 2005.

Diapoulos, Peter, and Steven Linakis. *The Sixth Family*. New York: Dutton, 1976.

Dick, Andrew. "When Does Organized Crime Pay? A Transaction Analysis." *International Review of Law and Economics* 15 (1995): 25.

Dickie, John. *Cosa Nostra: A History of the Sicilian Mafia*. New York: Palgrave Macmillan, 2004.

Dietche, Scott. *Cigar City Mafia: A Complete History of the Tampa Underworld*. New York: Barricade Books, 2004.

_____. *The Silent Don: The Criminal Underworld of Santo Trafficante Jr*. New York: Barricade Books, 2007.

DiFonzo, Luigi. *St. Peter's Banker*. New York: Franklin Watts, 1983.

Dorman, Michael. *Payoff: The Role of Organized Crime in American Politics*. New York: McKay, 1972.

Dombrink, John. "The Criminal Elite: Professional and Organized Crime." *Contemporary Sociology* 13 (September 1984): 586.

Dombrink, John, and James Meeker. "Beyond 'Buy and Bust': Nontraditional Sanctions in Federal Drug Law Enforcement." *Contemporary Drug Problems* 13 (Winter 1986): 711–40.

Donaldson, William. *Brewer's Rogues, Villains, and Eccentrics: An A–Z of Roguish Britons Through the Ages*. London: Orion Books, 2004.

Dorn, Nicholas. *Traffickers: Drug Markets and Law Enforcement*. London: Routledge, 1992.

Douglass, Joseph Jr. "Organized Crime in Russia: Who's Taking Whom to the Cleaners?" *Conservative Review* 6 (May/June 1995): 23–27.

_____. *Red Cocaine: The Drugging of America*. Atlanta: Clarion House, 1990.

Downey, Patrick. *Gangster City: The History of the N.Y. Underworld 1900–1935*. New York: Barricade Books, 2004.

Drosnin, Michael. *Citizen Hughes*. New York: Bantam, 1985.

Du, Phuc Long, and Laura Ricard. *The Dream Shattered: Vietnamese Gangs in America*. Boston: Northeastern University Press, 1996.

Dubro, James. *Dragons of Crime: Inside the Asian Underworld*. Toronto: Octopus, 1992.

_____. *Mob Mistress*. Toronto: Macmillan of Canada, 1988.

_____. *Mob Rule: Inside the Canadian Mafia*. Toronto: Macmillan of Canada, 1985.

Dunn, Guy. "The Russian Mafia." *The World Today* 51 (January 1995): 20.

Dupont, Alan. "Transnational Crime, Drugs, and Security in East Asia." *Asian Survey* 39 (May/June 1999): 433–55.

Easton, Stephen. *Marijuana Growth in British Columbia*. Vancouver: Fraser Institute, 2004.

Ebbe, Obi. "Political-criminal Nexus. The Nigerian Case: Slicing Nigeria's 'National Cake.'" *Trends in Organized Crime* 4 (Spring 1999): 29–59.

Edelhertz, Herbert. *The Containment of Organized Crime*. Lexington, MA: D.C. Heath, 1984.

_____ (ed.). *Major Issues in Organized Crime Control: Symposium Proceedings, Washington, D.C., Sept. 25–26, 1986*. Washington, D.C.: U.S. Government Printing Office, 1987.

Edmonds, Andy. *Bugsy's Baby: The Secret Life of Mob Queen Virginia Hill*. Secaucus, N.J.: Carol, 1993.

Edwards, Adam, and Peter Gill. *Transnational Organised Crime: Perspectives on Global Security*. London: Routledge, 2003.

Edwards, Peter. *Blood Brothers: How Canada's Most Powerful Mafia Family Runs Its Business*. Toronto: Key Porter, 1990.

_____. *The Northern Connection: Inside Canada's Deadliest Mafia Family*. Toronto: Optimum International, 2006.

Edwards, Peter, and Michel Auger. *The Encyclopedia of Canadian Organized Crime: From Captain Kidd to Mom Boucher*. Toronto: McClelland & Stewart, 2004.

Edwards, Peter, and Antonio Nicaso. *Deadly Silence: Canadian Mafia Murders*. Toronto: Macmillan Canada, 1993.

Ehrenfeld, Rachel. *Narco Terrorism*. New York: Basic Books, 1990.

Einstein, Stanley, and Menachem Amir. *Organized Crime: Uncertainties and Dilemmas*. Chicago: University of Illinois at Chicago, 1999.

Eisenberg, Dennis, Uri Dan, and Eli Landau. *Meyer Lansky: Mogul of the Mob*. New York: Paddington Press, 1979.

Eliot, Marc. *Down 42nd Street: Sex, Money, Culture, and Politics at the Crossroads of the World*. New York: Warner Books, 2001.

Elliott, Charles. "A Maybe Baby: Adoption Fraud Aided by the Internet." *White Paper* 15 (March/April 2001): 35–37, 44–46.

Emrich, Robert Louis. *The Basis of Organized Crime in Western Civilization*. Washington, D.C.: President's Commission on Law Enforcement and Administration of Justice, 1966.

Engelman, Larry. *Intemperance*. New York: Free Press, 1979.

English, T. J. *Born to Kill: America's Most Notorious Vietnamese Gang, and the Changing Face of Organized Crime*. New York: William Morrow, 1995.

_____. *Havana Nocturne: How the Mob Owned Cuba and Then Lost It to the Revolution*. New York: William Morrow, 2008.

_____. *Paddy Whacked: The Untold Story of the Irish American Gangster*. New York: Harper Collins, 2005.

_____. *The Westies: Inside the Hell's Kitchen Irish Mob*. New York: Putnam, 1990.

Enright, Laura. *Chicago's Most Wanted: The Top Ten Book of Murderous Mobsters, Midway Monsters, and Windy City Oddities*. Dulles, VA: Potomac Books, 2005.

Erez, Edna. "Women as Victims and Survivors in the Context of Transnational Crime," in Natalia Ollus and Sami Nevala (eds.), *Women in the Criminal Justice System: International Examples and National Responses*. Monsey, N.Y.: Criminal Justice Press, 2001.

European Union. *European Union Organised Crime Situation Report, 2004*. Luxembourg: Office for Official Publications of the European Communities, 2004.

Evans, Richard, and Christopher Aaron. "Organised Crime and Terrorist Financing in Northern Ireland." *Jane's Intelligence Review* 14 (September 2002): 26–29.

Evica, George. *And We Are All Mortal*. West Hartford, CT: University of Hartford, 1978.

Fabre, Guilhem. *Criminal Prosperity: Drug Trafficking, Money Laundering and Financial Crises After the Cold War*. London: Routledge Curzon, 2003.

Facts on File Yearbooks. New York: Facts on File, 1948–2009.

Farrell, Ronald, and Carole Case. *The Black Book and the Mob: The Untold Story of the Control of Nevada's Casinos*. Madison: University of Wisconsin Press, 1995.

Fatić, Aleksandar. "Anti-Corruption and Anti-Organized Crime Policy in Serbia: Regional Implications." *Journal of Southeast European & Black Sea Studies* 4 (2004): 315–24.

Feder, Sid, and Joachim Joesten. *The Luciano Story.* New York: David McKay, 1954.

Federal Bureau of Investigation. *An Analysis of the Threat of Japanese Organized Crime to the United States and Its Territories.* Washington, D.C.: U.S. Government Printing Office, 1992.

_____. *20th Century FBI Files. Declassified Documents from the Federal Bureau of Investigation, Volume 10: Mafia, Organized Crime, and Gangsters.* Washington, D.C.: Federal Bureau of Investigation, 2001.

_____. *Vietnamese Activity in the United States: A National Perspective.* Washington, D.C.: U.S. Government Printing Office, 1993.

Fensterwald, Bernard. *Coincidence or Conspiracy?* New York: Zebra, 1977.

Fentress, James. *Blood and Honor, from the Mafia's Sicilian Roots to Its Domination of American Crime.* New York: Birch Lane Press, 1998.

_____. *Rebels and Mafiosi: Death in a Sicilian Landscape.* Ithaca: Cornell University Press, 2000.

Feve, Sabrina. "Trafficking of People." *Harvard Journal on Legislation* 38 (Winter 2001): 279–90.

Fiandaca, Giovanni (ed.). *Women and the Mafia: Female Roles in Organized Crime Structures.* New York: Springer, 2007.

Fiaschetti, Michael. *You Gotta Be Rough: The Adventures of Detective Fiaschetti of the Italian Squad.* Garden City, N.Y.: Doubleday, Doran, 1930.

Fijnaut, Cyrille, and James Jacobs. *Organized Crime and Its Containment: A Transatlantic Initiative.* Boston: Kluwer Law and Taxation Publishers, 1991.

Filippone, Robert. "The Medellin Cartel: Why We Can't Win the Drug War." *Studies in Conflict and Terrorism* 17 (October/December 1994): 323–44.

Financial Action Task Force. *Report on International Money Laundering.* Paris: Financial Action Task Force, 2001.

Finckenauer, James. *Chinese Transnational Organized Crime: The Fuk Ching.* Washington, D.C.: National Institute of Justice, 2001.

_____. "Russian Transnational Organized Crime and Human Trafficking." David Kyle and Rey Koslowski (eds.), *Global Human Smuggling: Comparative Perspectives.* Baltimore: Johns Hopkins University Press, 2001.

Finckenauer, James, and Elin Waring. *The Russian Mafia in America: Immigration, Culture and Crime.* Boston: Northeastern University Press, 1998.

_____. "Threat of Russian Organized Crime." *Canadian Journal of Criminology* 44 (January 2002): 104–7.

Finkelstein, Monte. *Separatism, the Allies and the Mafia: The Struggle for Sicilian Independence, 1943–1948.* Bethlehem, PA: Lehigh University Press, 1998.

Finlay, Tom, and Catherine Matthews. *Motorcycle Gangs: A Literature Search.* Toronto: University of Toronto Centre of Criminology, 1996.

Fiorentini, Gianluca, and Sam Peltzman (eds.). *The Economics of Organised Crime.* Cambridge: Cambridge University Press, 1995.

Fischer, Steve. *When the Mob Ran Vegas.* Boys Town, NE: Berkline Press, 2005.

Fisher, David. *Killer: Autobiography of a Hit Man for the Mafia.* Chicago: Playboy Press, 1973.

Fitch, Robert. *Solidarity for Sale: How Corruption Destroyed the Labor Movement and Undermined America's Promise.* New York: Public Affairs, 2006.

Flatte, Michael, and Alexi Coweett. "Drugs and Politics: An Unhealthy Mix." *Harvard International Review* 8 (January/February 1986): 29–31.

Flood, Susan. *Illicit Drugs and Organized Crime: Issues for a Unified Europe.* Chicago: Office of International Criminal Justice, 1991.

Florez, Carl, and Bernadette Boyce. "Columbian Organized Crime." *Police Studies* 13 (1990): 81–88.

Flynn, Stephen. "World Wide Drug Scourge: The Expanding Trade in Illicit Drugs." *Brookings Review* 11 (Winter 1993): 6–11.

Flynn, Stephen, and Gregory Grant. *The Transnational Drug Challenge and the New World Order: The Report of the CSIS Project on the Global Drug Trade in the Post Cold War Era.* Washington, D.C.: Center for Strategic & International Studies, 1993.

Fong, Robert. "A Comparative Study of the Organizational Aspects of Two Texas Prison Gangs: Texas Syndicate and Mexican Mafia." *Dissertation Abstracts International, A: The Humanities and Social Sciences* 48 (1987): 1545A.

Foreman, Laura (ed.). *True Crime: Mafia.* New York: Time-Life Books, 1993.

Fortenay, Charles. *Estes Kefauver.* Knoxville: University of Tennessee Press, 1980.

Fowler, Gene. *Beau James: The Life and Times of Jimmy Walker.* New York: Viking Press, 1949.

Fox, Stephen. *Blood and Power: Organized Crime in Twentieth Century America.* New York: William Morrow, 1989.

Fraley, Oscar. *4 Against the Mob.* New York: Popular Library, 1961.

Franzese, Michael, and Dary Matera. *Quitting the Mob: How the "Yuppie Don" Left the Mafia and Lived to Tell His Story.* New York: HarperCollins, 1992.

Fraser, Frank, and James Morton. *Mad Frank: Memoirs of a Life of Crime.* London: Time Warner, 1995.

_____. *Mad Frank's Diary: A Chronicle of the Life of Britain's Most Notorious Villain.* London: Virgin Books, 2000.

Freeman, Bill, and Marsha Hewitt. *Their Town: The Mafia, the Media and the Party Machine.* Toronto: J. Lorimer, 1979.

Fried, Albert. *The Rise and Fall of the Jewish Gangster in America.* New York: Holt, Rinehart and Winston, 1980.

Friedman, Allen, and Ted Schwarz. *Power and Greed: Inside the Teamsters Empire of Corruption.* New York: Franklin Watts, 1989.

Friedman, Robert. *Red Mafiya: How the Russian Mob Has Invaded America.* New York: Little, Brown, 2000.

Friedrichs, D. O. (ed.). *State Crime.* 2 vols. Hants, United Kingdom: Dartmouth, 1998.

Friman, H. Richard. *Narcodiplomacy: Exporting the U.S. War on Drugs.* Ithaca: Cornell University Press, 1996.

Friman, H. Richard, and Peter Andreas. *Illicit Global Economy and State Power.* New York: Rowman & Littlefield, 1999.

_____. "International Pressure and Domestic Bargains: Regulating Money Laundering in Japan." *Crime, Law and Social Change* 21 (April 1994): 253–66.

Furiati, Claudia. *ZR Rifle: The Plot to Kill Kennedy and Castro.* Melbourne, Australia: Ocean Press, 1994.

Furstenberg, Mark. *Violence and Organized Crime.* Washington, D.C.: U.S. Government Printing Office, 1969.

Fuss, Charles. *Sea of Grass: The Maritime Drug War, 1970–1990.* Annapolis: Naval Institute Press, 1996.

Gage, Nicholas (ed.). *Mafia, USA.* Chicago: Playboy Press, 1972.

_____. *The Mafia Is Not an Equal Opportunity Employer.* New York: McGraw-Hill, 1971.

Galante, Pierre, and Louis Sapin. *The Marseilles Mafia: The Truth Behind the World of Drug Trafficking.* London: W. H. Allen, 1979.

Galeotti, Mark. "Albanian Gangs Gain Foothold in European Crime Underworld." *Jane's Intelligence Review* 13 (November 2001): 25–7.

_____ (ed.). *Russian and Post-Soviet Organized Crime.* London: Ashgate/Dartmouth, 2002.

Gallant, Thomas. "Brigandage, Piracy, Capitalism, and State-Formation: Transnational Crime from a Historical World-Systems Perspective." Josiah Heyman (ed.), *From States and Illegal Practices.* New York: Berg, 1999.

Gambetta, Diego. "Fragments of an Economic Theory of the Mafia." *Archives Europeennes De Sociologie* 29 (1988): 127–45.

_____. *The Sicilian Mafia: The Business of Private Protection.* London: Harvard University Press, 1993.

Gambino, Richard. *Vendetta.* Garden City, N.Y.: Doubleday, 1977.

Gardiner, John. *The Politics of Corruption: Organized Crime in an American City.* New York: Russell Sage Foundation, 1970.

Gardner, Paul. *The Drug Smugglers: A True Story.* London: Hal, 1989.

Garrison, Omar. *Howard Hughes in Las Vegas.* New York: Lyle Stuart, 1970.

Gately, William, and Yvette Fernández. *Dead Ringer: An Insider's Account of the Mob's Colombian Connection.* New York: D.I. Fine, 1994.

Gay, Bruce, and James Marquart. "Jamaican Posses: A New Form of Organized Crime." *Journal of Crime and Justice* 16 (1993): 139.

Gaylord, Mark. "The Chinese Laundry: International Drug Trafficking and Hong Kong's Banking Industry." *Contemporary Crises* 14 (March 1990): 23–37.

Geffray, Christian. "Introduction: Drug Trafficking and the State." *International Social Science Journal* 53 (September 2001): 421–26.

Gentry, Curt. *J. Edgar Hoover: The Man and the Secrets.* New York: W.W. Norton, 1991.

Giancana, Antoinette, and Thomas Renner. *Mafia Princess: Growing Up in Sam Giancana's Family.* New York: Morrow, 1984.

Giancana, Sam, and Chuck Giancana. *Double Cross: The Explosive, Inside Story of the Mobster Who Controlled America.* New York: Warner Books, 1992.

Gilinskiy, Yakov. "Organized Crime in Russia: Domestic and International Problems" in Emilio C. Viano (ed.), *Global Organized Crime and International Security.* Brookfield, VT: Ashgate, 1999.

Gilmore, William, and Alastair Brown. *Drug Trafficking and the Chemical Industry: Chemical Precursors and International Criminal Law.* Edinburgh: Edinburgh University Press, 1996.

Gilpin, Raymond. "Macroeconomic Implications of Money Laundering in a Small Open Economy." *BSL Bulletin* 2 (October 1996): 18–22.

Glaser, Lynn. *Counterfeiting in America: The History of an American Way to Wealth.* New York: C.N. Potter, 1968.

Glass, Mary. *Nevada's Turbulent '50s.* Reno: University of Nevada Press, 1981.

Goddard, Donald. *Joey: A Biography.* New York: Harper & Row, 1974.

Godson, Roy. "International Crime Control Strategy." *Trends in Organized Crime* 4 (Fall 1998): 1–3.

_____. "Special Focus: The International Fight Against Money Laundering." *Trends in Organized Crime* 4 (Summer 1999): 1–7.

Godson, Roy, and William Olson. "International Organized Crime." *Society* 32 (1995): 18–29.

Godson, Roy, and Phil Williams. "Strengthening Cooperation Against Transnational Crime." *Survival* 40 (August 1998): 66–88.

Goldberg, Jeffrey. "The Mafia Is Self-Destructing." *New York* 28 (January 1995): 9–22.

Goldfarb, Ronald. *Perfect Villains, Imperfect Heroes: Robert F. Kennedy's War Against Organized Crime.* New York: Random House, 1995.

Goldstock, Ronald, and Dan Coenen. "Controlling the Contemporary Loanshark: The Law of Illicit Lending and the Problem of Witness Fear." *Cornell Law Review* 65 (January 1980): 127–289.

_____, and _____. *Extortionate and Usurious Credit Transactions: Background Materials. Perspectives on the Investigation and Prosecution of Organized Crime.* Ithaca: Cornell Institute on Organized Crime, 1978.

Goldstock, Ronald, Martin Marcus and Il Thacher. *Corruption and Racketeering in the New York City Construction Industry: Final Report of the N.Y. State Organized Crime Task Force.* New York: NYU Press, 1990.

Gomez-Cespedes, Alejandra. "Federal Law Enforcement Agencies: An Obstacle in the Fight Against Organized Crime in Mexico." *Journal of Contemporary Criminal Justice* 15 (November 1999): 352–69.

_____. "Organized Crime in Mexico." Fiona Brookman (ed.), *Qualitative Research in Criminology.* Brookfield, VT: Ashgate, 1999.

Goode, James. *Wiretap: Listening in on America's Mafia.* New York: Simon & Schuster, 1988.

Goodey, Jo. "Sex Trafficking in Women from Central and East European Countries: Promoting a 'Victim-Centred' and 'Woman-Centred' Approach to Criminal Justice Intervention." *Feminist Review* 76 (2004): 26–45.

Gootenberg, Paul (ed.). *Cocaine: Global Histories.* New York: Routledge, 1999.

Gordon, Robert. "Criminal Business Organizations, Street Gangs and 'Wanna-Be' Groups: A Vancouver Perspective." *Canadian Journal of Criminology* 42 (January 2000): 39–60.

Gorman, Joseph. *Kefauver.* New York: Oxford University Press, 1971.

Gosch, Martin, and Richard Hammer. *The Last Testament of Lucky Luciano.* Boston: Little, Brown, 1974.

Grabosky, Peter, Russell Smith, and Gillian Dempsey. *Electronic Theft: Unlawful Acquisition in Cyberspace.* Oakleigh, Australia: Oxford University Press, 2001.

Graham, Fred. *The Alias Program.* Boston: Little, Brown, 1977.

Grascia, Andrew. "The Truth About Outlaw Bikers and What You Can Expect if They Come to Your Town." *Journal of Gang Research* 11 (2004): 1–16.

Gray, James Henry. *Booze: When Whiskey Ruled the West.* Saskatoon: Fifth House, 1995.

Greenberg, Gerald. *Historical Encyclopedia of U.S. Independent Counsel Investigations.* Westport, CT: Greenwood Press, 2000.

Grennan, Sean, Marjie Britz, and Jeffrey Rush, and Thomas Barker. *Gangs: An International Approach.* Upper Saddle River, N.J.: Prentice-Hall, 2000.

Griffin, Joe, and Don DeNevi. *Mob Nemesis: How the FBI Crippled Organized Crime.* Amherst, N.Y.: Prometheus Books, 2002.

Groden, Robert, and Harrison Livingstone. *High Treason.* New York: Berkley, 1990.

Grosse, Robert. *Drugs and Money: Laundering Latin America's Cocaine Dollars.* New York: Praeger, 2001.

Gugliotta, Guy, and Jeff Leen. *Kings of Cocaine: Inside the*

Medellin Cartel an Astonishing True Story of Murder, Money, and International Corruption. New York: Simon & Schuster, 1989.

Gunst, Laurie. *Born Fi' Dead: A Journey Through the Jamaican Posse Underworld.* New York: Henry Holt, 1995.

Haller, Mark. "Bureaucracy and the Mafia: An Alternative View." *Journal of Contemporary Criminal Justice* 8 (1982): 1–10.

———. "Illegal Enterprise: A Theoretical and Historical Interpretation." *Criminology* 28 (1990): 207–35.

———. *Life Under Bruno: The Economics of an Organized Crime Family.* Conshohocken: Pennsylvania Crime Commission, 1991.

Halstead, Boronia. "Use of Models in the Analysis of Organized Crime and Development of Policy." *Transnational Organized Crime* 4 (1998): 1–24.

Hamilton, R. B. "Triad and Crime Gangs of Vietnamese Origin." *Royal Canadian Mounted Police Gazette* 49 (1987): 1–7.

Hammer, Richard. *Playboy's Illustrated History of Organized Crime.* Chicago: Playboy Press, 1975.

Hammersley, Richard, Furzana Khan, and Jason Ditton. *Ecstasy and the Rise of the Chemical Generation.* New York: Routledge, 2001.

Handelman, Stephen. *Comrade Criminal: Russia's New Mafiya.* New Haven: Yale University Press, 1995.

———. "Inside Russia's Gangster Economy." *New York Times Magazine* (January 24, 1993): 12+.

———. "The Russian 'Mafiya.'" *Foreign Affairs* 73 (March 1, 1994): 83.

Hanson, Kitty. *Rebels in the Streets: The Story of New York's Girl Gangs.* Englewood Cliffs, N.J.: Prentice-Hall, 1964.

Haq, Ikramul. *Pakistan, from Hash to Heroin.* Lahore: Annoor, 1991.

Hargreaves, Clare. *Snowfields: The War on Cocaine in the Andes.* New York: Holmes & Meier, 1992.

Harper, Rosalyn, and Rachel Murphy. "Analysis of Drug Trafficking." *British Journal of Criminology* 40 (Autumn 2000): 746–49.

Harris, Graham. *Treasure and Intrigue: The Legacy of Captain Kidd.* Toronto: Dundurn Press, 2002.

Harris, Maz. *Bikers: Birth of a Modern Day Outlaw.* London: Faber and Faber, 1985.

Harvison, C. W. *The Horsemen.* Toronto: McClelland and Stewart, 1967.

Haun, Charles. "'Bloody July,'" in Alvin Hamer (ed.), *Detroit Murders.* New York: Duell, Sloan and Pearce, 1948.

Haycraft, John. *The Italian Labyrinth: Italy in the 1980s.* London: Secker & Warburg, 1985.

Heffernan, Ronald. "Homicides Related to Drug Trafficking [Based on a Study Conducted in the 46th Police Precinct, Bronx, N.Y.]." *Federal Probation* 46 (September 1982): 3–7.

Heimel, Paul. *Eliot Ness.* Nashville: Cumberland House, 2000.

Helfand, Neil. *Asian Organized Crime and Terrorist Activity in Canada, 1999–2002.* Washington, D.C.: Library of Congress, 2003.

Henriques, Julian. "The Gunmen, Saints and the Ghetto." *New Society* 53 (August 1980): 306.

Henstell, Bruce. *Sunshine and Wealth: Los Angeles in the Twenties and Thirties.* San Francisco: Chronicle Books, 1984.

Herbert, David, and Howard Tritt. *Corporations of Corruption: A Systematic Study of Organized Crime.* Springfield, IL: Charles Thomas, 1984.

Hermann, Donald. "Organized Crime and White Collar Crime: Prosecution of Organized Crime Infiltration of Legitimate Business." *Rutgers Law Journal* 16 (1985): 589–632.

Hersh, Seymour. *The Dark Side of Camelot.* New York: Little, Brown, 1997.

Hess, Henner. *Mafia & Mafiosi: Origin, Power and Myth.* New York: New York University Press, 1996.

Higham, Charles. *Howard Hughes.* New York: G.P. Putnam's Sons, 1993.

Hill, Gregg, and Gina Hill. *On the Run: A Mafia Childhood.* New York: Time Warner, 2004.

Hill, Henry, and Gus Russo. *Gangsters and Goodfellas: Wiseguys, Witness Protection, and Life on the Run.* New York: M. Evans, 2004.

Hill, Herbert. "The Mob and Labor-Management Corruption in the Garment Industry." *New Politics* 8 (Summer 2000): 68–82.

Hill, Peter. *Japanese Mafia: Yakuza, Law, and the State.* Oxford: Oxford University Press, 2003.

Hill, Timothy. "Outlaw Motorcycle Gangs: A Look at a New Form of Organized Crime." *Canadian Criminology Forum* 3 (Fall 1980): 26–35.

Himmelstein, Jerome. *The Strange Career of Marihuana: Politics and Ideology of Drug Control in America.* Westport, CT: Greenwood Press, 1983.

Hinckle, Warren, and William Turner. *The Fish Is Red: The Story of the Secret War Against Castro.* New York: Harper & Row, 1981.

———, and ———. *Deadly Secrets.* New York: Thunder's Mouth Press, 1992.

Hishon, Robert. *Tax Fraud and Money Laundering.* Houston: John Marshall, 1993.

Hodgson, Douglas. "Combating the Organized Sexual Exploitation of Asian Children: Recent Developments and Prospects." *International Journal of Law and the Family* 9 (April 1995): 23–53.

Hoffa, James. *The Trials of Jimmy Hoffa.* Chicago: Henry Regnery, 1970.

Hoffa, James, and Oscar Fraley. *Hoffa: The Real Story.* New York: Stein & Day, 1975.

Hoffman, Paul, and Ira Pecznick. *To Drop a Dime.* New York: Putnam, 1976.

Hoffman, William, and Lake Headley. *Contract Killer: The Explosive Story of the Mafia's Most Notorious Hit Man, Donald "Tony the Greek" Frankos.* New York: Thunder's Mouth Press, 1992.

Holdren, John. "Reducing the Threat of Nuclear Theft in the Former Soviet Union." *Arms Control Today* 26 (March 1996): 14–20.

Holt, Simma. *The Devil's Butler.* Toronto: McClelland and Stewart, 1972.

Homer, Frederic, and David Caputo. "Conceptual and Operational Problems of Studying Organised Crime." *Society and Culture* 4 (July 1973): 163–78.

———, and ———. *Guns and Garlic: Myths and Realities of Organized Crime.* West Lafayette, IN: Purdue University Press, 1974.

Hooper, Columbus, and Johnny Moore. "Women in Outlaw Motorcycle Gangs." *Journal of Contemporary Ethnography* 18 (1990): 363–87.

Hopkins, A.D. "Benny Binion," in Jack Sheehan (ed.), *The Players.* Reno: University of Nevada Press, 1997.

Hopsicker, Daniel. *Barry & "The Boys": The CIA, the Mob and America's Secret History.* Noti, OR: Mad Cow Press, 2001.

Horan, James. *The Pinkertons: The Detective Dynasty That Made History.* New York: Bonanza Books, 1967.

_____, and Howard Swiggett. *The Pinkerton Story*. London: William Heinemann, 1952.

Hors, Irene. "Fighting Corruption in Developing Countries and Emerging Economies: The Role of the Private Sector." *African Security Review* 8 (1999): 23–32.

Hoshino, Kanehiro. "A Study on the Attitudes of the Members of Semi National Criminal Gangs Toward Their Association and Subsidiary Association: III. Control and Cohesiveness of the Association." *Reports of National Research Institute of Police Science* 27 (July 1986): 14–27.

Hougan, Jim. *Spooks: The Haunting of America—The Private Use of Secret Agents*. New York: Bantam, 1979.

Huang, Frank, and Michael Vaughn. "A Descriptive Analysis of Japanese Organized Crime: The Boryokudan from 1945 to 1988." *International Criminal Justice Review* 2 (1992): 19–57.

Huang, Hua-Lun. "Let Senior Brothers/Sisters Meet Junior Brothers/Sisters: The Categorical Linkages Between Traditional Chinese Secret Associations and Modern Organized Chinese Underground Groups." *Journal of Gang Research* 11 (2004): 47–68.

Huang, Hua-Lun, John Wang, and George Fox. "From Religious Cult to Criminal Gang: The Evolution of Chinese Triads (Part 1)." *Journal of Gang Research* 9 (Summer 2002): 25–32.

Hubbard, Robert, Daniel Murphy, Fergus O'Donnell, and Peter de Freitas. *Money Laundering and Proceeds of Crime*. Toronto: Irwin Law, 2004.

Humphrey, Caroline. "Russian Protection Rackets and the Appropriation of Law and Order." Josiah Heyman (ed.), *States and Illegal Practices*. New York: Berg, 1999.

Humphreys, Adrian. *The Enforcer: Johnny Pops Papalia, A Life and Death in the Mafia*. New York: HarperCollins, 2002.

Humphreys, Adrian, and Lee Lamothe. *The Sixth Family: The Collapse of the New York Mafia & the Rise of Vito Rizzuto*. Toronto: Wiley, 2006.

Hunt, Thomas, and Martha Macheca-Sheldon. *Deep Water: Joseph P. Macheca and the Birth of the American Mafia*. New York: iUniverse, 2006.

Huston, Peter. *Tongs, Gangs, and Triads: Chinese Crime Groups in North America*. San Jose, CA: Authors Choice Press, 2001.

Hutchinson, John. "The Anatomy of Corruption in Trade Unions." *Industrial Relations* 8 (February 1969): 135–50.

Hutchison, Robert A. *Vesco*. New York: Avon Books, 1976.

Ianni, Francis. *Black Mafia: Ethnic Succession in Organized Crime*. New York: Simon & Schuster, 1974.

Ianni, Francis, and Elisabeth Reuss-Ianni. *A Family Business: Kinship and Social Control in Organized Crime*. New York: New American Library, 1973.

_____, and _____. *The Crime Society: Organized Crime and Corruption in America*. New York: New American Library, 1976.

Iannuzzi, Joseph, and James Morton. *Joe "Dogs" Iannuzzi: The Life and Times of a Real Life Mobster*. New York: Simon & Schuster, 1993.

Ichniowski, Casey and Anne Preston. "The Persistence of Organized Crime in New York City Construction: An Economic Perspective." *Industrial and Labor Relations Review* 42 (July 1989): 549–65.

Imai, Takeyoshi. "The Hiding of Wealth: Organised Crime in Japan." *Journal of Financial Crime* 10 (July 2002): 63–68.

Jacobs, Bruce, and James Short Jr. *Dealing Crack: The Social World of Streetcorner Selling*. Boston: Northeastern University Press, 1999.

Jacobs, James. *Organized Crime and Its Containment: A Transatlantic Initiative*. Leiden, Netherlands: Brill, 1991.

Jacobs, James, Coleen Friel, and Robert Radick. *Gotham Unbound: How New York City Was Liberated from the Clutches of Cosa Nostra*. New York: New York University Press, 1999.

Jacobs, James, Christopher Panarella, and Jay Worthington. *Busting the Mob: The United States vs. Cosa Nostra*. New York: New York University Press, 1994.

Jacobs, James, and Thomas Thacher. "Attacking Corruption in Union Management Relations: A Symposium." *Industrial and Labor Relations Review* 42 (July 1989): 501–7.

Jackall, Robert. *Wild Cowboys: Urban Marauders and the Forces of Order*. Cambridge: Harvard University Press, 1997.

Jacquemet, Marco. *Credibility in Court: Communicative Practices in the Camorra Trials*. Cambridge: Cambridge University Press, 1996.

Jamieson, Alison. *The Antimafia: Italy's Fight Against Organized Crime*. London: MacMillan, 2000.

_____. "Mafia and Political Power 1943–1989." *International Relations* 10 (May 1990): 13–30.

_____. *Terrorism and Drug Trafficking in the 1990s*. Hants, United Kingdom: Dartmouth, 1994.

_____. "Transnational Organized Crime: A European Perspective." *Studies in Conflict and Terrorism* 24 (September/October 2001): 377–87.

Jamieson, Ruth. "Contested Jurisdiction Border Communities' and Cross-border Crime—The Case of Akwesasne." *Crime, Law and Social Change* 30 (1998): 259–72.

Jeffers, H. Paul. *The Napoleon of New York: Mayor Fiorello La Guardia*. New York: John Wiley & Sons, 2002.

Jenkins, Philip. "Narcotics Trafficking and the American Mafia: The Myth of Internal Prohibition." *Crime, Law and Social Change* 18 (November 1992): 303–18.

Jenkins, Philip, and Gary Potter. "The Politics and Mythology of Organized Crime: A Philadelphia Case Study." *Journal of Criminal Justice* 15 (1987): 473–84.

Jennings, Dean. *We Only Kill Each Other*. Englewood Cliffs, N.J.: Prentice-Hall, 1967.

Jensen, Holger. "Hiding the Drug Money: Criminals Are Using Canada to Launder Billions of Dollars in Drug Profits." *Maclean's* 102 (October 23, 1989): 42+.

Jessome, Phonse. *Somebody's Daughter: Inside the Halifax/Toronto Pimping Ring*. Halifax, NS: Nimbus, 1996.

Jester, Jean. "An Analysis of Organized Crime's Infiltration of Legitimate Business." *Criminal Justice* 5 (1974).

Johnson, David. *Illegal Tender: Counterfeiting and the Secret Service in Nineteenth Century America*. Washington, D.C.: Smithsonian Institution Press, 1995.

_____. *The Japanese Way of Justice: Prosecuting Crime in Japan*. New York: Oxford University Press, 2001.

Johnson, Malcolm. *Crime on the Labor Front*. New York: McGraw-Hill, 1950.

Johnston, David. *Temples of Chance*. New York: Doubleday, 1992.

Jones, Siôn, David Lewis, and Philip Maggs. *The Economic Costs of Fraud. A Report for the Home Office and Serious Fraud Office*. London: National Economic Research Associates, 2000.

Jordan, David. *Drug Politics: Dirty Money and Democracies*. Norman: University of Oklahoma Press, 1999.

Joselit, Jenna. *Our Gang: Jewish Crime and the New York Jewish Community, 1900–1940*. Bloomington: Indiana University Press, 1983.

Joseph, Janice. "Jamaican Posses and Transnational Crimes." *Journal of Gang Research* 6 (Summer 1999): 41–47.

Josephson, Matthew. *The Robber Barons: The Great American Capitalists, 1861–1901*. New York: Harcourt, Brace, 1934.

Junninen, Mika, and Kauko Aromaa. *Crime Across the Border: Finnish Professional Criminals and Estonian Crime Opportunities*. Helsinki: National Research Institute of Legal Policy, 1999.

_____. "Professional Crime Across the Finnish-Estonian Border." *Crime, Law and Social Change* 34 (December 2000): 319–47.

Kahn, Gordon, and Al Hirschfeld. *The Speakeasies of 1932*. New York: Glenn Young Books, 1932.

Kaihla, Paul. "The Cocaine King: How a Poor Colombian Became Canada's Biggest Drug Baron and Got Away." *MacLean's* (July 10, 1995): 28–33.

_____. "The People Smugglers: Canada Is a Top Destination in the Global Trade in Humans; How Criminals Victimize the Innocent." *Maclean's* (April 29, 1996): 16–20+.

Kaiser, Robert. *"RFK Must Die!"* New York: Grove Press, 1970.

Kakimi, Takashi. "Organized Crime in Japan: The Boryokudan Groups." *Police Chief* 55 (1988): 161–62.

Kalimtgis, Konstandinos, David Goldman, and Jeffrey Steinberg. *Dope, Inc*. New York: New Benjamin Franklin House, 1978.

Kamstra, Jerry. *Weed: Adventures of a Dope Smuggler*. New York: Harper & Row, 1974.

Kantor, Seth. *Who Was Jack Ruby?* New York: Everest House, 1978.

Kaplan, David, and Alec Dubro. *Yakuza: The Explosive Account of Japan's Criminal Underworld*. Reading, MA: Addison-Wesley, 2003.

Kaplan, John. *The Hardest Drug: Heroin and Public Policy*. Chicago: University of Chicago Press, 1983.

_____. *Marijuana: The New Prohibition*. New York: Meridian Books, 1970.

Karpis, Alvin. *The Alvin Karpis Story*. New York: Coward, McCann & Geohegan, 1971.

Katcher, Leo. *The Big Bankroll: The Life and Times of Arnold Rothstein*. New York: Harper & Brothers, 1959.

Kattoulas, Velisarios. "Bright Lights, Brutal Life: Women Smuggled into Japan Are Forced into Sex Business by Yakuza." *Far Eastern Economic Review* 163 (August 3, 2000): 50–55.

_____. "Young, Fast and Deadly: Japan's Bosozoku, Teenage Biker Gangs." *Far Eastern Economic Review* 164 (February 1, 2001): 64–67.

Katz, Leonard. *Uncle Frank: The Biography of Frank Costello*. New York: Drake, 1973.

Kavanagh, Susan. "Organized Crime in the Marine Ports." *Royal Canadian Mounted Police Gazette* 60 (1998): 9–10.

Kavieff, Paul. *The Life and Times of Lepke Buchalter: America's Most Ruthless Labor Racketeer*. New York: Barricade Books, 2006.

_____. *The Purple Gang*. Fort Lee, N.J.: Barricade Books, 2000.

_____. *The Violent Years*. New York: Barricade Books, 2001.

Keating, William, and Richard Carter: *The Man Who Rocked the Boat*. New York: Harper & Brothers, 1956.

Keefe, Rose. *Guns and Roses: The Untold Story of Dean O'Banion, Chicago's Big Shot before Al Capone*. Nashville: Cumberland House, 2003.

Keene, Linda. "Asian Organized Crime." *FBI Law Enforcement Bulletin* 58 (October 1989): 13–17.

Kefauver, Estes. *Crime in America*. New York: Greenwood Press, 1951.

Kelly, Liz, and Linda Regan. *Stopping Traffic: Exploring the Extent of, and Responses to, Trafficking in Women for Sexual Exploitation in the UK*. London: Home Office, Police Research Series, 2000.

Kelly, Robert. *Encyclopedia of Organized Crime in the United States*. Westport, CT: Greenwood, 2000.

_____. "The Nature of Organized Crime." Herbert Edelhertz (ed.), *Major Issues in Organized Crime Control*. Washington, D.C.: National Institute of Justice, 1987.

_____. "Trapped in the Folds of Discourse: Theorizing About the Underworld." *Journal of Contemporary Criminal Justice* 8 (1992): 11–35.

_____. *The Upperworld and the Underworld: Case Studies of Racketeering and Business Infiltrations in the United States*. New York: Kluwer Academic, 1999.

Kelly, Robert, Ko-Lin Chin, and Jeffrey Fagan. "The Dragon Breathes Fire: Chinese Organized Crime in New York City." *Crime, Law and Social Change* 19 (1993): 245–69.

_____. "Lucky Money for Little Brother: The Prevalence and Seriousness of Chinese Gang Extortion." *International Journal of Comparative and Applied Criminal Justice* 24 (Spring 2000): 62+.

Kelly, Orr. "How the Mafia Invades Business." *U.S. News & World Report* 82 (June 13, 1977): 21–23.

Kelton, Harold. "Characteristics of Organized Criminal Groups." *Canadian Journal of Criminology and Corrections* 13 (January 1971): 68–78.

Kennedy, Robert. *The Enemy Within*. New York: Harper & Row, 1960.

Kennedy, William. *O, Albany*. New York: Viking Penguin, 1983.

Kenney, Dennis, and James Finckenauer. *Organized Crime in America*. Belmont, CA: Wadsworth, 1995.

Kerry, John. *A New Kind of War: National Security and the Globalization of Crime*. New York: Simon & Schuster, 1997.

Kersten, Joachim. "Street Youths, Bosozoku, and Yakuza: Subculture Formation and Societal Reactions in Japan." *Crime and Delinquency* 39 (1993): 277–95.

Kimeldorf, Howard. *Reds or Rackets? The Making of Radical and Conservative Unions on the Waterfront*. Berkeley: University of California Press, 1988.

King, Rufus. *Gambling and Organized Crime*. Washington, D.C.: Public Affairs Press, 1969.

Kirby, Cecil, and Thomas Renner. *Mafia Assassin: The Inside Story of a Canadian Biker*. Toronto: Methuen, 1986.

Kirkpatrick, Sidney, and Peter Abrahams. *Turning the Tide: One Man Against the Medellin Cartel*. New York: Dutton, 1991.

Kleinknecht, William. *The New Ethnic Mobs: The Changing Face of Organized Crime in America*. New York: Free Press, 1996.

Kline, Harvey. *Colombia: Democracy Under Assault*. Boulder, CO: Westview Press, 1995.

Knight, Ronnie, John Knight and Peter Wilton. *Gotcha!* London: Pan, 2003.

Knoedelseder, Bill. *Stiffed: A True Story of MCA, the Music Business, and the Mafia*. New York: HarperCollins, 1993.

Knowles, Gordon. "Deception, Detection, and Evasion: A Trade Craft Analysis of Honolulu, Hawaii's Street Crack-Cocaine Traffickers." *Journal of Criminal Justice* 27 (1999): 443–55.

Kobler, John. *Ardent Spirits: The Rise and Fall of Prohibition*. New York: G.P. Putnam's Sons, 1973.

_____. *Capone: The Life and Times of Al Capone*. New York: Da Capo Press, 2003.

Kohn, George. *Dictionary of Culprits and Criminals*. Metuchen, N.J.: Scarecrow Press, 1986.

Ko-lin Chin. *Chinatown Gangs: Extortion, Enterprise, and Ethnicity*. New York: Oxford University Press, 2000.

Kominek, Jiri. "Albanian Organised Crime Finds a Home in the Czech Republic." *Jane's Intelligence Review* 14 (October 2002): 34–35.

Konigsberg, Eric. *Blood Relation*. New York: HarperCollins, 2005.

Konstam, Angus. *Pirates: Predators of the Seas*. New York: Skyhorse, 2007.

Konstantinova, Elizabeth. "Bulgarian Gangs Provide Key Link in European Trafficking Chain." *Jane's Intelligence Review* 14 (November 2002): 26–29.

Kopp, Pierre. *Political Economy of Illegal Drugs*. New York: Routledge, 2004.

Koskoff, David. *Joseph P. Kennedy*. Englewood Cliffs: Prentice-Hall, 1974.

Kray, Reggie. *Born Fighter*. London: Arrow, 1991.

Kristol, William. "The Business of Organized Crime: A Cosa Nostra Family." *Annals of the American Academy of Political and Social Science* 448 (March 1980): 184.

Krott, Rob. "Vietnamese Gangs in America." *Law and Order* 49 (May 2001): 100+.

Kryshtanovskaia, Olga. "Illegal Structures in Russia." *Sociological Research* 35 (July/August 1996): 60–80.

_____. "Russia's Mafia Landscape: A Sociologist's View." *Current Digest of the Post Soviet Press* 47 (October 1995): 1–5.

Kung, Cleo. "Supporting the Snakeheads: Human Smuggling from China and the 1996 Amendment to the U.S. Statutory Definition of 'Refugee.'" *Journal of Criminal Law and Criminology* 90 (Summer 2000): 1271–316.

Kwitny, Jonathan. *The Crimes of Patriots: A True Tale of Dope, Dirty Money, and the CIA*. New York: W.W. Norton, 1987.

_____. *Vicious Circles: The Mafia's Control of the American Marketplace, Food, Clothing, Transportation, Finance*. New York: W.W. Norton, 1979.

Kyle, David, and John Dale (eds.). *Global Human Smuggling: Comparative Perspectives*. Baltimore: Johns Hopkins University Press, 2001.

Lacey, Robert. *Little Man: Meyer Lansky and the Gangster Life*. Boston: Little, Brown, 1991.

LaLumia, Joseph. "Mafia as a Political Mentality." *Social Theory and Practice* 7 (Summer 1981): 179–92.

Lamb, Kevin. "The Causal Factors of Crime: Understanding the Sub Culture of Violence." *Mankind Quarterly* 36 (Fall 1995): 105–16.

Lamothe, Lee, and Adrian Humphreys. *The Sixth Family: The Collapse of the New York Mafia and the Rise of Vito Rizzuto*. Toronto: John Wiley & Sons, 2006.

Lamothe, Lee, and Antonio Nicaso. *Bloodlines: The Rise and Fall of the Mafia's Royal Family*. Toronto: HarperCollins, 2001.

_____. *Global Mafia: The New World Order of Organized Crime*. Toronto: MacMillan Canada, 1994.

Lampert, Nick. "Law and Order in the USSR: The Case of Economic and Official Crime." *Soviet Studies* 36 (July 1984): 366–85.

Landesco, John. *Organized Crime in Chicago*. Chicago: University of Chicago Press, 1929.

Lane, Kris. *Pillaging the Empire: Piracy in the Americas, 1500–1750*. London: M.E. Sharp, 1998.

Langer, John. "A Preliminary Analysis: Corruption of Political, Economic, Legal and Social Elements in Communities Involved in International Drug Trafficking and Its Effects on Police Integrity." *Police Studies* 9 (Spring 1986): 42–56.

Lanning, Kenneth. *Child Pornography and Sex Rings*. Washington, D.C.: Federal Bureau of Investigation, 1984.

Laplante Laurent. "Counteracting Criminal Biker Gangs: A Losing Battle Without Public Support." *Justice Report* 11 (1996): 9–10.

Lardner, James, and Thomas Reppetto. *NYPD: A City and Its Police*. New York: Henry Holt, 2000.

Lashly, Arthur. *Illinois Crime Survey*. Chicago: Illinois Association for Criminal Justice and the Chicago Crime Commission, 1929.

Lasky, Victor. *It Didn't Start with Watergate*. New York: Dell, 1977.

_____. *J.F.K.—The Man and the Myth*. New York: Dell, 1977.

Latimer, Dean, and Jeff Goldberg. *Flowers in the Blood: The Story of Opium*. New York: Franklin Watts, 1981.

Lavigne, Yves. *Good Guy, Bad Guy: Drugs and the Changing Face of Organized Crime*. Toronto: Random House of Canada, 1991.

_____. *Hell's Angels at War*. Toronto: HarperCollins, 1999.

_____. *Hell's Angels: Into the Abyss*. Toronto: Harper Collins, 1996.

_____. *Hell's Angels: Taking Care of Business*. Toronto: HarperCollins, 1989.

Lee, Bill. *Chinese Playground: A Memoir*. New York: Rhapsody Press, 1999.

Lee, Henry. *How Dry We Were*. Englewood Cliffs, N.J.: Prentice-Hall, 1963.

Lee, Martin, and Bruce Shlain. *Acid Dreams: The Complete Social History of LSD: The CIA, the Sixties, and Beyond*. New York: Grove Weidenfeld, 1992.

Lee, Rensselaer. "Cocaine Mafia." *Society* 27 (January/February 1990): 53–62.

_____. "Dynamics of the Soviet Illicit Drug Market." *Crime, Law and Social Change* 17 (May 1992): 177–233.

_____. "Global Reach: The Threat of International Drug Trafficking." *Current History* 94 (May 1995): 207–11.

Leet, Duane, George Rush, and Anthony Smith. *Gangs, Graffiti and Violence: A Realistic Guide to the Scope and Nature of Gangs in America*. Incline Village, NV: Copperhouse, 2000.

Lehr, Dick, and Gerard O'Neill. *Black Mass: The Irish Mob, the Boston FBI and a Devil's Deal*. New York: Public Affairs, 2000.

Lerner, Michael. *Dry Manhattan: Prohibition in New York City*. Cambridge: Harvard University Press, 2007.

Leuchtag, Alice. "Merchants of Flesh: International Prostitution and the War on Women's Rights." *Humanist* 55 (March/April 1995): 11–16.

Levchuk, Sergei. "Returning to an Earlier Topic: Baby Merchants Are Arrested; Their Bosses Are at Large; Ukrainian Mafia Has Found Its Niche Doing Shady Business in Europe." *Current Digest of the Post Soviet Press* 47 (December 6, 1995): 19.

Levi, Michael. *Fraud: Organization, Motivation and Control*. Brookfield, VT: Ashgate, 1999.

_____. "Money Laundering and Its Regulation." *Annals of the American Academy of Political and Social Science* 582 (2002): 181–94.

_____. "Offender Organization and Victim Responses: Credit Card Fraud in International Perspective." *Journal of Contemporary Criminal Justice* 14 (November 1998): 368–83.

_____. "Organising and Controlling Payment Card Fraud: Fraudsters and Their Operational Environment." *Security Journal* 16 (2003): 21–30.

Levi, Michael, and David Sherwin. *Fraud: The Unmanaged Risk: An International Survey of the Effects of Fraud on Business*. London: Ernst & Young, 2000.

Lewis, George. "Social Groupings in Organized Crime: The Case of the La Nuestra Familia." *Deviant Behavior* 1 (1980): 129–43.

Lewis, Norman. *The Honored Society*. New York: G.P. Putnam's Sons, 1964.

Lewis, Oscar. *Sagebrush Casinos*. Garden City, N.Y.: Doubleday, 1953.

Liddick, Donald. *An Empirical, Theoretical, and Historical Overview of Organized Crime*. Lewiston, N.Y.: Edwin Mellen Press, 1999.

_____. *The Global Underworld: Transnational Crime and the United States*. Westport, CT: Greenwood, 2004.

_____. *Government for Sale: Political Fundraising, Patron/Client Relations and Organized Criminality*. Lima, OH: Wyndham Hall Press, 2001.

_____. *The Mob's Daily Number: Organized Crime and the Numbers Gambling Industry*. Lanham, MD: University Press of America, 1999.

Light, Ivan. "The Ethnic Vice Industry, 1880–1944." *American Sociological Review* 42 (June 1977): 464–79.

Lilley, Peter. *Dirty Dealing: The Untold Truth About Money Laundering*. London: Kogan Page, 2000.

Lintner, Bertil. *Blood Brothers: The Criminal Underworld of Asia*. New York: Palgrave Macmillan, 2003.

_____. *The Politics of the Drug Trade in Burma*. Nedlands, WA: Indian Ocean Centre for Peace Studies, 1993.

Lippens, Ronnie. " Rethinking Organizational Crime and Organizational Criminology." *Crime, Law and Social Change* 35 (June 2001): 319–31.

LiPuma, Edward. "Capitalism and the Crimes of Mythology: An Interpretation of the Mafia Mystique." *Journal of Ethnic Studies* 17 (Summer 1989): 1–21.

Lombardo, Robert. "Black Hand: Terror by Letter in Chicago." *Journal of Contemporary Criminal Justice* 18 (November 2002): 394–409.

_____. "Organized Crime: A Control Theory." *Criminal Organizations* 6 (1991): 8–13.

_____. "The Social Organization of Organized Crime in Chicago." *Journal of Contemporary Criminal Justice* 10 (December 1994): 290–313.

Long Song, John Huey, and John Dombrink. "Asian Emerging Crime Groups: Examining the Definition of Organized Crime." *Criminal Justice Review* 19 (Summer 1994): 228–43.

Longrigg, Clare. *Mafia Women*. London: Chatto & Windus, 1997.

Louderback, Lew. *The Bad Ones*. Greenwich, CT: Fawcett Gold Medal, 1968.

Lowther, Nicola. "Organized Crime and Extortion in Russia: Implications for Foreign Companies." *Transnational Organized Crime* 3 (Spring 1997): 23–38.

Lukas, J. Anthony. *Nightmare*. New York: Viking, 1976.

Lund, Robert. *Virginia State Crime Commission Report of Research Consultants Study on the Impact of Organized Crime and Related Criminal Activities of Pari Mutuel Wagering on Horse Racing*. Richmond: The Commission, 1973.

Lunde, Paul. *Organized Crime: An Inside Guide to the World's Most Successful Industry*. London: Dorling Kindersley, 2004.

Lupsha, Peter. "Drug Trafficking: Mexico and Colombia in Comparative Perspective." *Journal of International Affairs* 35 (Spring/Summer 1981): 95–115.

_____. "Individual Choice, Material Culture, and Organized Crime." *Criminology* 19 (May 1981): 3–24.

_____. "La Cosa Nostra in Drug Trafficking." *Organized Crime in America: Concepts and Controversies* (1987): 31–41.

_____. "Organized Crime in the United States," in R.J. Kelly (ed.), *Organized Crime: A Global Perspective*. Totowa, N.J.: Rowman and Littlefield, 1986.

Lupsha, Peter, and Kip Schlegal. *The Political Economy of Drug Trafficking: The Herrera Organization*. Albuquerque: University of New Mexico, 1980.

Lusane, Clarence. *Pipe Dream Blues: Racism and the War on Drugs*. Boston: South End Press, 1991.

Lyman, Michael, and Gary Potter (eds.). *Drugs and Society: Causes, Concepts and Control*. Cincinnati: Anderson, 1998.

_____, and _____. *Organized Crime*. Upper Saddle River, N.J.: Prentice Hall, 1997.

Lynch, Denis. *Criminals and Politicians*. New York: Macmillan, 1932.

Maas, Peter, *Underboss: Sammy the Bull Gravano's Story of Life in the Mafia*. New York: HarperCollins, 1997.

_____. *The Valachi Papers*. New York: Pocket Books, 1986.

Mabry, Donald. *The Latin American Narcotics Trade and U.S. National Security*. New York: Greenwood Press, 1989.

Maccabee, Paul. *John Dillinger Slept Here*. Saint Paul: Minnesota Historical Society Press, 1995.

MacDonald, Scott. *Dancing on a Volcano: The Latin American Drug Trade*. New York: Praeger, 1988.

Mackay, James, and Gerry Blackwell. *Phone Pirates: Long Distance Theft: What It Is, How It Happens and How to Protect Your Phone Bills from Hackers, Phone Breakers and Organized Crime*. Ajax, Ontario: Telemanagement Press, 1993.

Mackenzie, Simon. *Organised Crime and Common Transit Networks*. Canberra: Australian Institute of Criminology, 2002.

MacLaren, Alasdair. *Impact on Canada of Corrupt Foreign Officials in Other Countries*. Ottawa: Solicitor General Canada, 2000.

Maclean, Don. *Organized Crime*. New York: Ballantine Books, 1972.

_____. *Pictorial History of the Mafia*. New York: Galahad Books, 1974.

MacNamara, Donald, and Philip Stead. *New Dimensions in Transnational Crime*. New York: John Jay Press, 1982.

Madinger, John, and Sydney Zalopany. *Money Laundering: A Guide for Criminal Investigators*. Boca Raton: CRC Press, 1999.

Maguire, Keith. "Fraud, Extortion and Racketeering: The Black Economy in Northern Ireland." *Crime, Law and Social Change* 20 (December 1993): 273–92.

Mahan, Sue (ed.). *Beyond the Mafia: Organized Crime in the Americas*. Thousand Oaks, CA: Sage, 1998.

Maheu, Robert, and Richard Hack. *Next to Hughes*. New York: HarperCollins, 1993.

Mahon, Gigi. *The Company That Bought the Boardwalk*. New York: Random House, 1980.

Main, James. "The Truth About Triads." *Policing* 7 (1991): 144–63.

Makarenko, Tamara. "Colombia's New Crime Structures Take Shape." *Jane's Intelligence Review* 14 (April 2002): 16–19.

Malarek, Victor. *Merchants of Misery*. Toronto: MacMillan, 1989.

_____. *The Natashas: Inside the New Global Sex Trade*. New York: Arcade, 2004.

Malkin, Lawrence. "The Dilemma of Dirty Money." *World Policy Journal* 18 (Spring 2001): 13.

Maltz, Michael. "On Defining Organized Crime. The Development of a Definition and Typology." *Crime and Delinquency* 22 (July 1976): 338–46.

Mannion, James. *101 Things You Didn't Know About the Mafia: The Lowdown on Dons, Wiseguys, Squealers and Backstabbers*. Avon, MA: Adams Media, 2005.

Manzer, Alison. *A Guide to Canadian Money Laundering Legislation*. Markham, Ontario: LexisNexis Canada, 2004.

Marez, Curtis. *Drug Wars: The Political Economy of Narcotics*. Minneapolis: University of Minnesota Press, 2004.

Marrs, Jim. *Crossfire*. New York: Carroll & Graf, 1989.

Marshall, Jonathan. *Drug Wars: Corruption, Counterinsurgency, and Covert Operations in the Third World*. Forestville, CA: Cohen & Cohen, 1991.

Martens, Frederick. "Transnational Enterprise Crime and the Elimination of Frontiers." *International Journal of Comparative and Applied Criminal Justice* 15 (Spring 1991): 99–107.

Martin, John, and Anne Romano. *Multinational Crime: Terrorism, Espionage, Drug & Arms Trafficking*. Newbury Park, N.J.: Sage, 1992.

Martineau, Pierre. *I Was a Killer for the Hells Angels. The Story of Serge Quesnal*. Toronto: McClelland & Stewart, 2003.

Marx, G. T. *Undercover: Police Surveillance in America*. Los Angeles: University of California Press, 1988.

Masciandaro, Donato (ed.). *Global Financial Crime: Terrorism, Money Laundering, and Off Shore Centres*. Burlington, VT: Ashgate, 2004.

Mason, Kevin. "Russian Organized Crime." *Case Western Reserve Journal of International Law* 30 (Winter 1998): 341.

Mathers, Chris. *Crime School: Money Laundering*. Toronto: Key Porter Books, 2004.

Matthew, Richard, and George Shambaugh. "Sex, Drugs, and Heavy Metal: Transnational Threats and National Vulnerabilities." *Security Dialogue* 29 (June 1998): 163–75.

Maximenkov, Leonid, and Conrad Namiesniowski. *Organized Crime in Post-Communist Russian: A Criminal Revolution*. Ottawa: Canadian Security Intelligence Service, 1994.

Maxwell, Gavin. *Bandit*. New York: Harper & Brothers, 1956.

Maylam, Simon. "Prosecution for Money Laundering in the UK." *Journal of Financial Crime* 10 (October 2002): 157–58.

Maysh, Jeff. *Brown Bread Fred*. London: John Blake, 2007.

McCarthy, Kevin. *Twenty Florida Pirates*. Sarasota: Pineapple Press, 1994.

McCauley, Martin. *Bandits, Gangsters and the Mafia: Russia, the Baltic States and the CIS Since 1992*. London: Longman, 2001.

McChesney, Fred. *Money for Nothing: Politicians, Rent Extraction, and Political Extortion*. Cambridge: Harvard University Press, 1997.

McClellan, John. *Crime Without Punishment*. New York: Popular Library, 1963.

McClintick, David. *Swordfish: A True Story of Ambition, Savagery, and Betrayal*. New York: Pantheon, 1993.

McConville, Molly. "Global War on Drugs: Why the United States Should Support the Prosecution of Drug Traffickers in the International Criminal Court." *American Criminal Law Review* 37 (Winter 2000): 75–102.

McCormack, David. *Racketeer Influenced Corrupt Organizations, RICO: Federal and State Civil and Criminal RICO*. Euless, TX: Knowles Law Book Publishers, 1989.

McCormick, Kirk, and Brian Stekloff. "Money Laundering." *American Criminal Law Review* 37 (Spring 2000): 729–56.

McCoy, Alfred. *The Politics of Heroin: CIA Complicity in the Global Drug Trade*. New York: Lawrence Hill Books, 1991.

_____. "Requiem for a Drug Lord: State and Commodity in the Career of Khun Sa," in Josiah Heyman (ed.), *States and Illegal Practices*. New York: Berg, 1999.

McCuen, Gary. *The International Drug Trade*. Hudson, WI: G.E. McCuen Publications, 1989.

McDonogh, Gary. "The Sicilian Mafia: The Business of Private Protection." *Anthropological Quarterly* 69 (April 1996): 97–98.

McGovern, G. P. "Growing Threat of Russian Organized Crime." *Law and Order* 47 (February 1999): 66–68.

McGuire, Phillip. "Jamaican Posses: A Call for Cooperation Among Law Enforcement Agencies." *Police Chief* 55 (January 1988): 20.

_____. "Outlaw Motorcycle Gangs: Organized Crime on Wheels." *National Sheriff* 37 (1986): 68–75.

McIllwain, Jeffrey. "Organized Crime: A Social Network Approach." *Crime, Law and Social Change* 32 (December 1999): 301–24.

_____. *Organizing Crime in Chinatown: Race and Racketeering in New York City, 1890–1910*. Jefferson, N.C.: McFarland, 2004.

McIntosh, Mary. *The Organization of Crime*. London: Macmillan, 1975.

McKeown, Patrick. "Computer Crimes and Criminals." *National Forum* 72 (Summer 1992): 46–47.

McPhaul, Jack. *Johnny Torrio: First of the Gang Lords*. New Rochelle, N.Y.: Arlington House, 1970.

McSweeney, Sean. "The Sicilian Mafia and Its Impact on the United States." *FBI Law Enforcement Bulletin* 56 (February 1987): 1–10.

Melanson, Philip. *The Robert F. Kennedy Assassination*. New York: S.P.I. Books, 1994.

Meltzer, Peter. "Keeping Drug Money from Reaching the Wash Cycle: A Guide to the Bank Secrecy Act." *Banking Law Journal* 108 (May/June 1991): 230–55.

Méndez, Juanh. *The "Drug War" in Colombia: The Neglected Tragedy of Political Violence*. Americas Watch Report. New York: Human Rights Watch, 1990.

Menzel, Sewall. *Cocaine Quagmire: Implementing the U.S. Anti Drug Policy in the North Andes Colombia*. Lanham, MD: University Press of America, 1997.

Mermelstein, Max. *The Man Who Made It Snow*. New York: Simon & Schuster, 1990.

Merrinier, James. *Grafters and Goo Goos: Corruption and Reform in Chicago, 1833–2003*. Carbondale: Southern Illinois University Press, 2004.

Merz, Charles. *The Dry Decade*. Seattle: University of Washington Press, 1930.

Messick, Hank. *The Beauties and the Beasts*. New York: David McKay, 1973.

_____. *John Edgar Hoover*. New York: David McKay, 1972.

_____. *Lanksy*. New York: G.P. Putnam, 1971.

_____. *Of Grass and Snow: The Secret Criminal Elite*. Englewood Cliffs, N.J.: Prentice-Hall, 1979.

_____. *Razzle Dazzle*. Covington, KY: For the Love of Books, 1995.

_____. *Secret File*. New York: G.P. Putnam's Sons, 1969.

_____. *The Silent Syndicate*. New York: Macmillan, 1967.
_____. *Syndicate Abroad*. New York: Macmillan, 1969.
_____. *Syndicate in the Sun*. New York: Macmillan, 1968.
_____. *Syndicate Wife*. New York: Macmillan, 1968.
Messick, Hank, and Joe Barboza. *Barboza*. New York: Dell, 1975.
Messick, Hank, and Burt Goldblatt. *Gangs and Gangsters*. New York: Ballantine, 1974.
_____. *Kidnapping: The Illustrated History*. New York: Delacorte, 1974.
_____. *The Mobs and the Mafia*. New York: Ballantine, 1972.
_____. *The Only Game in Town*. New York: Thomas Y. Crowell, 1976.
Messick, Hank, and Joseph Nellis. *The Private Lives of Public Enemies*. New York: Peter H. Wyden, 1973.
Meyer, Kathryn, and Terry Parssinen. *Webs of Smoke: Smugglers, Warlords, Spies, and the History of the International Drug Trade*. Lanham, MD: Rowman & Littlefield, 1998.
Michaux, Denise. "Drug Courier Profiles and the Infringement of Fourth Amendment Rights." *New York Law School Journal of Human Rights* 9 (Spring 1992): 435–60.
Middlemiss, Jim. "White-Collar Fraud: The New Organized Crime." *Bottom Line* (March 1998): 17.
Milhorn, H. Thomas. *Crime: Computer Viruses to Twin Towers*. Boca Raton: Universal Publishers, 2005.
Milito, Lynda, and Reg Potterton. *Mafia Wife: My Story of Love, Murder, and Madness*. New York: HarperCollins, 2004.
Mills, James. *The Underground Empire: Where Crime and Governments Meet*. New York: Doubleday, 1986.
Minniti, Maria. "Membership Has Its Privileges: Old and New Mafia Organizations." *Comparative Economic Studies* 37 (Winter 1995): 31–47.
Mitchell, Leonard, and Peter Rehak. *Undercover Agent: How One Honest Man Took on the Drug Mob and Then the Mounties*. Toronto: McClelland & Stewart, 1989.
Mitgang, Herbert. *Once Upon a Time in New York*. New York: Free Press, 2000.
Miyazawa, Setsuo. "Scandal and Hard Reform: Implications of a Wiretapping Case to the Control of Organizational Police Crimes in Japan." *Kobe University Law Review* 23 (1989): 13–27.
Modjeska, Lee. "The NLRB and the Mob." *Labor Law Journal* 37 (September 1986): 625–31.
Moldea, Dan. *Dark Victory: Ronald Reagan, MCA, and the Mob*. New York: Viking, 1986.
_____. *The Hoffa Wars*. New York: Paddington Press, 1978.
_____. *Interference*. New York: William Morrow, 1989.
Molidor, Christian. "Female Gang Members: A Profile of Aggression and Victimization." *Social Work* 41 (May 1996): 251–57.
Montgomery, Randel. "The Outlaw Motorcycle Subculture." *Canadian Journal of Criminology and Corrections* 18 (October 1976): 332–42; 19 (October 1977): 356–61.
Moon, Robert. *Biker Women: Outlaw Motorcycle Gangs*. Windsor, Ontario: Windsor Police Force, 1987.
Moore, James. *Very Special Agents: The Inside Story of America's Most Controversial Law Enforcement Agency—The Bureau of the Alcohol, Tobacco, and Firearms*. Champaign: University of Illinois Press, 2001.
Moore, Joan. *Going Down to the Barrio: Homeboys and Homegirls in Change*. Philadelphia: Temple University Press, 1991.
Moore, Mark. *Buy and Bust*. Lexington, MA: D.C. Heath, 1977.

_____. "Organized Crime as a Business Enterprise." Herbert Edelhertz (ed.), *Major Issues in Organized Crime*. Washington, D.C.: National Institute of Justice, 1987.
Moore, Robin, and Barbara Fuca. *Mafia Wife*. New York: Macmillan, 1977.
Moore, Richter, Jr. "Twenty-First Century Law to Meet the Challenge of Twenty First Century Organized Crime." *Futures Research Quarterly* 11 (Spring 1995): 23.
_____. "Wiseguys: Smarter Criminals and Smarter Crime in the 21st Century." *Futurist* 28 (September/October 1994): 33–37.
Moran, Nathan. "Emerging Trends: Transnational Drug Production and Trafficking." *Crime & Justice International* 18 (June 2002): 5–6, 23–24.
Moore, William. *The Kefauver Committee and the Politics of Crime*. Columbia: University of Missouri Press, 1974.
Morello, Celeste. *Before Bruno: The History of the Philadelphia Mafia: Book 1—1880–1931*. Philadelphia: Jeffries & Manz, 2000.
Morgan, John. *Prince of Crime*. New York: Stein and Day, 1985.
Mori, Cesare. *The Last Struggle with the Mafia*. London: Putnam, 1933.
Morrison, David. "The Pentagon's Drug Wars." *National Journal* 18 (Sept. 6, 1986): 2104–109.
Morrow, Robert. *First Hand Knowledge: How I Participated in the CIA-Mafia Murder of President Kennedy*. New York: S.P.I. Books, 1992.
_____. *The Senator Must Die*. Santa Monica: Roundtable, 1988.
Mortimer, W. Golden. *History of Coca: "The Divine Plant" of the Incas*. San Francisco: And/Or Press, 1974.
Morton, James. *Bent Coppers*. London: Time Warner, 1994.
_____. *East End Gangland*. London: Time Warner, 2001.
_____. *Gangland: London's Underworld*. London: Little, Brown, 1992.
_____. *Gangland Australia*. Melbourne: Melbourne University Press, 2007.
_____. *Gangland Bosses: The Lives of Jack Spot and Billy Hill*. London: Little, Brown, 2004.
_____. *Gangland: The Contract Killers*. London: Little, Brown, 2006.
_____. *Gangland: The Early Years*. London: Little, Brown, 2004.
_____. *Gangland International*. London: Little Brown, 1999.
_____. *Gangland: The Lawyers*. New York: St. Martin's Press, 2001.
_____. *Gangland Soho*. London: Piatkus Books, 2008.
_____. *Gangland Today*. London: Little, Brown, 2003.
_____. *Gangland 2: The Underworld in Britain and Ireland*. London: Trafalgar Square, 1995.
_____. *The Krays*. London: The National Archives, 2008.
_____. *Sex, Crimes and Misdemeanours*. London: Time Warner, 2000.
_____. *Supergrasses and Informers*. London: Time Warner, 2002.
Morton, James, and Hilary Bateson. *Conned: Scams, Frauds and Swindles*. London: Portrait, 2007.
Morton, James, and Frank Fraser. *Mad Frank*. London: Little, Brown 1994.
_____. *Mad Frank's Britain*. London: Virgin Books, 2002.
_____. *Mad Frank's London*. London: Virgin Books, 2002.
_____. *Mad Frank's Diary*. London: Virgin Books, 2001.
_____. *Mad Frank's Underworld History of Britain*. London: Virgin Books, 2007.
Morton, James, and Susanna Lobez. *Gangland Australia*. Melbourne: Melbourne University Press, 2007.

Morton, James, and "Ms. X." *Calling Time on the Krays*. London: Time Warner, 1997.

Morton, James, and Leonard Read. *Nipper Read: The Man Who Nicked the Krays*. London: Time Warner, 2002.

Mosquera, Richard. "Asian Organized Crime." *Police Chief* 60 (October 1, 1993): 65.

Motto, Carmine. *Undercover*. Springfield, IL: Thomas, 1971.

Mouzos, Jenny. *International Traffic in Small Arms: An Australian Perspective*. Canberra: Australian Institute of Criminology, 1999.

Mueller, Harald. "Fissile Material Smuggling: German Politics, Hype and Reality." *Arms Control Today* 24 (December 1994): 7–10.

Mullady, Frank, and William Kofoed. *Meet the Mob*. New York: Belmont Books, 1961.

Murdoch, Catherine. *Domesticating Drink: Women, Men, and Alcohol in America, 1870–1940*. Baltimore: Johns Hopkins University Press, 1998.

Murphy, Mark. *The True Story of the Biker, the Mafia & the Mountie*. New York: Avalon House, 1998.

Musto, David. *The American Disease: Origins of Narcotic Control*. Oxford: Oxford University Press, 1999.

Myers, Gustavus. *The History of Tammany Hall*. New York: Boni & Liveright, 1917.

Myers, Willard III. "The Emerging Threat of Transnational Organized Crime from the East." *Crime, Law and Social Change* 24 (August 1995): 181–222.

Nack, William. *My Turf: Horses, Boxers, Blood Money, and the Sporting Life*. New York: Da Capo Press, 2003.

Nadelmann, Ethan. *Cops Across Borders: The Internationalization of U.S. Criminal Law Enforcement*. University Park: Pennsylvania State University Press, 1993.

_____. "International Drug Trafficking and U.S. Foreign Policy." *Washington Quarterly* 8 (Fall 1985): 86–104.

Natarajan, Mangai. "Varieties of Drug Trafficking Organizations: A Typology of Cases Prosecuted in New York City." *Journal of Drug Issues* 28 (Fall 1998): 1005–25.

Natarajan, Mangai, and Mike Hough (eds.). *Illegal Drug Markets: From Research to Prevention Policy*. Monsey, N.Y.: Criminal Justice Press, 2000.

National Council on Crime and Delinquency. *Seminars on Organized Crime's Infiltration of Legitimate Business*. New York: The Council, 1971.

National Criminal Intelligence Service. *UK Threat Assessments*. London: NCIS, 2000–2003.

National White Collar Crime Center. *IFCC 2002 Internet Fraud Report*. Richmond: NWCC, 2003.

Naylor, R. Thomas. *Hot Money*. Toronto: McClelland and Stewart, 1987.

_____. "Mafias, Myths, and Markets: On the Theory and Practice of Enterprise Crime." *Transnational Organized Crime* 3 (1997): 1–45.

_____. *Wages of Crime: Black Markets, Illegal Finance, and the Underworld Economy*. Ithaca: Cornell University Press, 2002.

Neff, James. *Mobbed Up*. New York: Dell, 1989.

Nelli, Humbert. *The Business of Crime: Italians and Syndicate Crime in the United States*. Chicago: University of Chicago Press, 1981.

Neumann, Robert. *Twenty-Three Women: The Story of an International Traffic*. New York: Dial Press, 1940.

Nevala, Sami, and Kauko Aromaa. *Organised Crime, Trafficking, Drugs: Selected Papers Presented at the Annual Conference of the European Society of Criminology, Helsinki 2003*. Helsinki: United Nations European Institute for Crime Prevention and Control, 2004.

New Jersey State Commission of Investigation. *Local Government Corruption*. Trenton: The Commission, 1992.

_____. *Report and Recommendations on Casino Gambling*. Trenton: The Commission, 1977.

_____. *Report and Recommendations on Organized Crime Infiltration of Dental Care Plan Organizations*. Trenton: The Commission, 1981.

New York State Organized Crime Task Force. *An Analysis of Russian Emigre Crime in the Tri State Region*. New York: The Task Force, 1996.

_____. *Corruption and Racketeering in the New York City Construction Industry: Final Report to Governor Mario M. Cuomo*. New York: New York University Press, 1990.

Newman, Peter. *Bronfman Dynasty*. Toronto: McClelland & Stewart, 1978.

Newton, John. *Organised Plastic Counterfeiting*. London: The Stationery Office, 1995.

Newton, Michael. *Encyclopedia of Robberies, Heists, and Capers*. New York: Facts on File, 2002.

Nicaso, Antonio. *Rocco Perri: The Story of Canada's Most Notorious Bootlegger*. Mississauga, Ontario: John Wiley & Sons Canada, 2004.

Nicaso, Antonio, and Lee Lamothe. *Bloodlines: The Rise & Fall of the Mafia's Royal Family*. Toronto: HarperCollins, 2001.

_____, and _____. *Global Mafia: The New World Order of Organized Crime*. Toronto: Macmillan Canada, 1995.

Nickel, Steven. *Torso*. Winston-Salem, N.C.: John F. Blair, 1989.

Nieves, R J. "Cocaine Cartels: Lessons from the Front." *Trends in Organized Crime* 3 (Spring 1998): 13–29.

Noble, Ronald. "Russian Organized Crime A Worldwide Problem." *The Police Chief* 62 (June 1995): 18.

North, Mark. *Act of Treason*. New York: Carroll & Graf, 1991.

Nown, Graham. *The English Godfather: Owney Madden*. London: Ward Lock, 1987.

Nyhuus, Ken. "Chasing Ghosts — Asian Organized Crime Investigation in Canada." *Royal Canadian Mounted Police Gazette* 60 (1998): 46–55, 63.

O'Brien, Joseph, and Andris Kurins. *Boss of Bosses: The Fall of the Godfather — The FBI and Paul Castellano*. New York: Simon & Schuster, 1991.

O'Day, Patrick. "The Mexican Army as Cartel." *Journal of Contemporary Criminal Justice* 17 (August 2001): 278–95.

Oglesby, Carl. *The Yankee and Cowboy War*. Kansas City: Sheed Andrews & McMeel, 1976.

Ognall, Leopold Horace. *Extortion*. London: Collins, 1960.

Ohlemacher, Thomas. "Racketeering and Restaurateurs in Germany: Perceived Deficiencies in Crime Control and Effects on Confidence in Democracy." *British Journal of Criminology* 42 (Winter 2002): 60–76.

_____. "The Sicilian Mafia: The Business of Private Protection." *Kolner Zeitschrift Fur Soziologie Und Sozialpsychologie* 47 (June 1995): 391.

_____. "Viewing the Crime Wave from the Inside: Perceived Rates of Extortion among Restaurateurs in Germany." *European Journal on Criminal Policy and Research* 7 (1999): 43–61.

O'Kane, James. *The Crooked Ladder*. New Brunswick, N.J.: Transaction, 1994.

Oleinik, Anton. *Organized Crime, Prison, and Post-Soviet Societies*. Burlington, VT: Ashgate, 2003.

Olla, Roberto. *The Godfathers: Lives and Crimes of the Mafia Mobsters*. London: Alma Books, 2007.

O'Neal, Scott. "Russian Organized Crime: A Criminal

Hydra." *FBI Law Enforcement Bulletin* 69 (May 2000): 1–5.

O'Neill, Amy. *International Trafficking in Women to the United States: A Contemporary Manifestation of Slavery.* Washington, D.C.: Central Intelligence Agency, 1999.

O'Neill, Gerard, and Dick Lehr. *The Underboss.* New York: St. Martin's Press, 1989.

Ontario Police Commission. *Report to the Attorney General for Ontario on Organized Crime.* Ontario: The Commission, 1964.

Ontario Police Commission on Organized Crime. *Report on the Royal Commission on Gambling.* Toronto: Government of Ontario, 1962.

Ontario Provincial Police. *Canada's Outlaw Motorcycle Gangs (Criminal Ties to the Province of Ontario).* Toronto: OPP Intelligence Branch, 1987.

Oppenheimer, Andres. *Bordering on Chaos: Guerrillas, Stockbrokers, Politicians, and Mexico's Road to Prosperity.* Boston: Little, Brown, 1996.

Ospina-Velasco, Jaime. "Combating Money Laundering and Smuggling in Colombia." *Journal of Financial Crime* 10 (October 2002): 153–56.

Ostrander, Gilman. *Nevada: The Great Rotten Borough.* New York: Alfred A. Knopf, 1966.

Osuna, Rick. *The Night the Defeos Died: Reinvestigating the Amityville Murders.* Las Vegas: Noble Kai Media, 2003.

Pace, Denny. *Concepts of Vice, Narcotics, and Organized Crime.* Englewood Cliffs, N.J.: Prentice Hall, 1991.

Pace, Denny, and Jimmie Styles (eds.). *Organized Crime: Concepts and Controls.* Englewood Cliffs, N.J.: Prentice Hall, 1983.

Padilla, Felix. *The Gang as an American Enterprise.* New Brunswick, N.J.: Rutgers University Press, 1992.

Pantaleone, Michele. *The Mafia and Politics.* London: Chatto & Windus, 1966.

Paoli, Letizia. *Mafia Brotherhoods.* Oxford: Oxford University Press, 2003.

_____. "The Paradoxes of Organized Crime." *Crime, Law and Social Change* 37 (January 2002): 51–97.

Paoli, Letizia, and Bruce Bullington. "Drug Trafficking in Russia: A Forum of Organized Crime?" *Journal of Drug Issues* 31 (Fall 2001): 1007–38.

Paradis, Peter. *Nasty Business: One Biker Gang's Bloody War Against the Hells Angels.* Toronto: HarperCollins, 2002.

Paris, Peter. "Corruption as a Fundamental Element of Organised Crime." *Police Studies* 12 (1989): 154–59.

Parker, Robert. *Rough Justice: The Truth about the Richardson Gang.* London: Fontana Books, 1981.

Parliament of the Commonwealth of Australia. *Asian Organised Crime in Australia. Discussion Paper by the Parliamentary Joint Committee on the National Crime Authority.* Canberra: Parliament of the Commonwealth of Australia, 1995.

Passas, Nikos. *Organized Crime.* Hants, United Kingdom: Dartmouth, 1995.

_____. "Structural Analysis of Corruption: The Role of Criminogenic Asymmetries." *Transnational Organized Crime* 4 (Spring 1998): 42–55.

Passas, Nikos, and David Nelken. "The Thin Line Between Legitimate and Criminal Enterprises: Subsidy Frauds in the European Community." *Crime, Law and Social Change* 19 (1993): 223–43.

Paternostro, Silvana. "Mexico as a Narco Democracy." *World Policy Journal* 12 (Spring 1995): 41–47.

Paust, Jordan. *International Criminal Law: Cases and Materials.* Durham: Carolina Academic Press, 1996.

Pearce, Frank, and Michael Woodiwiss. *Global Crime Connections: Dynamics and Control.* Toronto: University of Toronto Press, 1993.

Pearson, Geoffrey. "Drugs at the End of the Century." *British Journal of Criminology* 39 (1999): 477–87.

Pegram, Thomas. *Battling Demon Rum: The Struggle for a Dry America, 1800–1933.* Chicago: Ivan R. Dee, 1998.

Pennsylvania Crime Commission. *Health Care Fraud: A Rising Threat.* St. David's, PA: The Commission, 1981.

_____. *Racketeering and Organized Crime in the Bingo Industry.* Conshohocken, PA: The Commission, 1992.

_____. *Racketeering in the Commercial Loan Brokerage Industry.* Harrisburg, PA: The Commission, 1980.

Pepper, William. *Orders to Kill.* New York: Warner, 1995.

Perl, Raphael. "The North Korean Drug Trade: Issues for Decision Makers." *Transnational Organized Crime* 4 (Spring 1998): 81–88.

Petacco, Arrigo. *Joe Petrosino.* New York: Macmillan, 1974.

Peterson, Robert. *Crime & the American Response.* New York: Facts on File, 1973.

Peterson, Virgil. *Barbarians in Our Midst.* Boston: Little, Brown, 1952.

_____. "The Career of a Syndicate Boss." *Crime and Delinquency* 8 (1962): 339–54.

_____. *The Mob: 200 Years of Organized Crime.* Ottawa, IL: Green Hill, 1983.

Petrakis, Gregory. *The New Face of Organized Crime.* Dubuque: Kendall/Hunt, 1992.

Petro, Sylvester. *Power Unlimited: The Corruption of Union Leadership: A Report on the McClellan Committee Hearings.* Westport, CT: Greenwood Press, 1959.

Phelan, James. *Howard Hughes: The Hidden Years.* New York: Random House, 1976.

Phillips, Charles, and Alan Axelrod. *Cops, Crooks, and Criminologists: An International Biographical Dictionary of Law Enforcement.* New York: Checkmark Books, 2000.

Pietrusza, David. *Rothstein: The Life, Times, and Murder of the Criminal Genius Who Fixed the 1919 World Series.* New York: Carroll & Graf, 2003.

Pileggi, Nicholas. *Casino: Love and Honor in Las Vegas.* New York: Simon & Schuster, 1995.

_____. *Wiseguy: Life in a Mafia Family.* New York: Simon & Schuster, 1985.

Pilon, Juliana. "The Bulgarian Connection: Drugs, Weapons, and Terrorism." *Terrorism* 9 (1987): 361–71.

Pimentel, Stanley. "Nexus of Organized Crime and Politics in Mexico: Mexico's Legacy of Corruption." *Trends in Organized Crime* 4 (Spring 1999): 9–28.

Piper, Michael. *Final Judgment: The Missing Link in the JFK Assassination Conspiracy.* Washington, D.C.: Wolfe Press, 1993.

Pistone, Joseph, and Richard Woodley. *Donnie Brasco: My Undercover Life in the Mafia.* New York: New American Library, 1988.

Pitkin, Thomas, and Francesco Cordasco. *The Black Hand: A Chapter in Ethnic Crime.* Totowa, N.J.: Littlefield, Adams, 1977.

Pizzo, Stephen, Mary Fricker, and Paul Muolo. *Inside Job: The Looting of America's Savings and Loans.* New York: HarperCollins, 1991.

Plate, Thomas. *The Mafia at War.* New York: New York Magazine Press, 1972.

Polk, Kenneth. *Antiquities Market Viewed as a Criminal Market.* Hong Kong: University of Hong Kong, 2001.

Pontell, Henry, and Alexander Frid. "International Financial Fraud: Emerging Trends and Issues," in Delbert Rounds (ed.), *International Criminal Justice: Issues in a Global Perspective.* Needham Heights, MA: Allyn and Bacon, 2000.

Poppa, Terrence. *Druglord: The Life and Death of a Mexican Kingpin*. New York: Pharos Books, 1990.

Porello, Rick. *The Rise and Fall of the Cleveland Mafia*. New York: Barricade Books, 1995.

_____. *Superthief*. Novelty, OH: Next Hat Press 2006.

_____. *To Kill the Irishman: The War That Crippled the Mafia*. Novelty, OH: Next Hat Press, 2004.

Porter, Bruce. *Blow: How a Small Town Boy Made $100 Million with the Medellín Cocaine Cartel and Lost It All*. New York: HarperCollins, 1993.

Posner, Gerald. *Warlords of Crime: Chinese Secret Societies the New Mafia*. New York: McGraw-Hill, 1988.

Possamai, Mario. *Money on the Run: Canada and How the World's Dirty Profits Are Laundered*. Toronto: Viking, 1992.

Potter, Gary. *Criminal Organizations: Vice, Racketeering, and Politics in an American City*. Prospect Heights, IL: Waveland Press, 1994.

Potter, William. "Before the Deluge? Assessing the Threat of Nuclear Leakage from the Post Soviet States." *Arms Control Today* 25 (October 1995): 9–16.

_____. "Nuclear Exports from the Former Soviet Union: What's New, What's True." *Arms Control Today* 23 (January/February 1993): 3–10.

Powell, Stewart. "Busting the Mob." *U.S. News and World Report* 100 (February 3, 1986): 24–29.

President's Commission on Law Enforcement and Administration of Justice. *The Challenge of Crime in a Free Society*. Washington, D.C.: U.S. Government Printing Office, 1967.

_____. *Task Force Report: Organized Crime*. Washington, D.C.: U.S. Government Printing Office, 1967.

President's Commission on Organized Crime. *America's Habit: Drug Abuse, Drug Trafficking and Organized Crime*. Washington, D.C.: United States Printing Office, 1986.

_____. *The Cash Connection: Organized Crime, Financial Institutions and Money Laundering*. Washington, D.C.: U.S. Government Printing Office, 1984.

_____. *The Edge: Organized Crime, Business and Labor Unions. Interim Report*. Washington, D.C.: U.S. Government Printing Office, 1985.

_____. *The Impact: Organized Crime Today*. Washington, D.C.: U.S. Government Printing Office, 1987.

_____. *Organized Crime and Gambling. Record of Hearing VII*. Washington, D.C.: U.S. Government Printing Office, 1985.

_____. *Organized Crime and Labor Management Racketeering in the United States. Record of VI*. Washington, D.C.: U.S. Government Printing Office, 1985.

_____. *Organized Crime of Asian Origin: Record of Hearing III*. Washington, D.C.: U.S. Government Printing Office, 1984.

Pringle, Patrick. *Jolly Roger: The Story of the Great Age of Piracy*. Mineola, N.Y.: Dover, 2001.

Punch, Maurice. "In the Underworld: An Interview with a Dutch Safe Breaker." *Howard Journal of Criminal Justice* 30 (May 1991): 121–39.

Quebec Police Commission Inquiry on Organized Crime. *The Fight Against Organized Crime in Québec*. Québec: Government of Québec, 1976.

_____. *Organized Crime and the World of Business: Report of the Commission of Inquiry on Organized Crime and Recommendations*. Québec: Editeur officiel du Québec, 1977.

Quimby, Ernest. "Drug Trafficking and the Caribbean Connection: Survival Mechanisms, Entrepreneurship and Social Symptoms." *Urban League Review* 14 (Winter 1990): 61–70.

Quinn, James. "Angels, Bandidos, Outlaws, and Pagans: The Evolution of Organized Crime Among the Big Four 1% MCs." *Deviant Behavior* 22 (July-August 2001): 379–99.

Raab, Selwyn. *Five Families: The Rise, Decline, and Resurgence of America's Most Powerful Mafia Empires*. New York: St. Martin's Press, 2006.

Ragano, Frank, and Selwyn Raab. *Mob Lawyer*. New York: Charles Scribner's Sons, 1994.

Raine, Linnea, and Frank J. Cilluffo (eds.). *Global Organized Crime: The New Empire of Evil*. Washington, D.C.: Center for Strategic and International Studies, 1994.

Rake, Alan. "Drugged to the Eyeballs." *New African* (June 1995): 16–19.

Rakoff, Jed, and Howard Goldstein. *RICO: Civil and Criminal Law and Strategy*. New York: Law Journal Seminars-Press, 1989.

Rappleye, Charles, and Ed Becker. *All American Mafioso: The Johnny Roselli Story*. New York: Barricade Books, 1995.

Raymond, Janice. "The New UN Trafficking Protocol." *Women's Studies International Forum* 25 (September-October 2002): 491–502.

Rebovich, Donald. *Local Prosecution of Organized Crime: The Use of State RICO Statutes*. Washington, D.C.: U.S. Department of Justice, 1993.

Rebovich, Donald, and Jenny Layne. *National Public Survey on White Collar Crime*. Morgantown, WV: U.S. Department of Justice, 2000.

Recio, Gabriela. "Drugs and Alcohol: U.S. Prohibition and the Origins of the Drug Trade in Mexico, 1910-1930." *Journal of Latin American Studies* 34 (February 2002): 21–42.

Rector, Milton. "Sentencing the Racketeer." *Crime and Delinquency* 8 (1962): 385–89.

Reed, Jeffrey. "Identity Theft: CACP Partners with Other Law Enforcement Organizations to Combat Growing Problem." *Canadian Police Chief Magazine* (Winter 2003): 14–15.

Redo, Slawomir. *Organized Crime and Its Control in Central Asia*. Huntsville, TX: Office of International Criminal Justice, Inc., 2004.

Reeve, Arthur. *The Golden Age of Crime*. New York: Mohawk Press, 1937.

Reichel, Philip (ed.). *Handbook of Transnational Crime and Justice*. Thousand Oaks, CA: Sage, 2005.

Reid, Ed. *The Grim Reapers: The Anatomy of Organized Crime in America*. Chicago: Henry Regnery, 1969.

_____. *Mafia*. New York: Random House, 1952.

_____. *The Shame of New York*. New York: Random House, 1953.

Reid, Ed, and Ovid Demaris. *The Green Felt Jungle*. New York: Pocket Books, 1964.

Renard, Ronald. *The Burmese Connection: Illegal Drugs and the Making of the Golden Triangle*. Boulder, CO: L. Rienner, 1996.

Rengert, George. *The Geography of Illegal Drugs*. Boulder, CO: Westview Press, 1996.

Repetto, Thomas. *American Mafia: A History of its Rise to Power*. New York: Henry Holt, 2004.

_____. *Bringing Down the Mob: The War Against the American Mafia*. New York: Macmillan, 2006.

Resendiz, Rosalva, and David Neal. "International Auto Theft: The Illegal Export of American Vehicles to Mexico," in Delbert Rounds (ed.), *International Criminal Justice: Issues in a Global Perspective*. Boston: Allyn and Bacon, 1998.

Reuss-Ianni, Elizabeth. *A Community Self Study of Organized*

Crime. New York: Criminal Justice Coordinating Council, 1973.

Reuter, Peter. "The Decline of the American Mafia." *The Public Interest* 120 (1995): 89–99.

———. *Disorganized Crime: Economics of the Invisible Hand*. Cambridge, MA: MIT Press, 1983.

———. *Racketeering in Legitimate Industries: A Study in the Economics of Intimidation*. Santa Monica: Rand, 1987.

———. "Racketeers as Cartel Organizers." Herbert Alexander and Gerald Caiden (eds.). *The Politics and Economics of Organized Crime*. Lexington, MA: Lexington Books, 1984.

Reuter, Peter, and Jonathan Rubinstein. *Illegal Gambling in New York: A Case Study in the Operation, Structure, and Regulation of an Illegal Market*. Washington, D.C.: U.S. Department of Justice, 1982.

Reuter, Peter, and Edwin Truman. *Chasing Dirty Money: The Fight Against Money Laundering*. Washington, D.C.: Institute for International Economics, 2004.

Reynolds, David, and Grant Newsham. "Managing the Mob: Techniques to Limit the Risks and Costs of Doing Business in Markets Tainted by Organised Crime." *Journal of Financial Crime* 8 (June 2001): 325–31.

Reynolds, Frank, and Michael McClure. *Freewheelin Frank, Secretary of the Angels, as Told to Michael McClure*. New York: Grove Press, 1967.

Reynolds, Marylee. *From Gangs to Gangsters: How American Sociology Organized Crime, 1918–1994*. Guilderland, N.Y.: Harrow and Heston, 1995.

Rhodes, Eric. "The Sicilian Mafia: The Business of Private Protection." *Acta Sociologica* 39 (1996): 251–54.

Rhodes, Robert. *Organized Crime: Crime Control vs. Civil Liberties*. New York: Random House, 1984.

Rice, Berkeley. *Trafficking: The Boom and Bust of the Air America Cocaine Ring*. New York: Scribner, 1989.

Rich, Kim. *Johnny's Girl: A Daughter's Memoir of Growing Up in Alaska's Underworld*. New York: Morrow, 1993.

Richard, Amy. *International Trafficking in Women to the United States: A Contemporary Manifestation of Slavery and Organized Crime*. Washington, D.C.: Central Intelligence Agency, 2000.

Richards, James. *Transnational Criminal Organizations, Cybercrime, and Money Laundering: A Handbook for Law Enforcement Officers, Auditors and Financial Investigators*. Boca Raton: CRC Press, 1999.

Richards, Lenore. "Trafficking in Misery: Human Migrant Smuggling and Organized Crime." *Royal Canadian Mounted Police Gazette* 63 (2001): 19–23.

Richardson, Charlie. *My Manor: The Autobiography of Charlie Richardson*. London: Sidgwick & Jackson, 1991.

Richardson, Eddie. *The Last Word: My Life as a Gangland Boss*. London: Headline, 2005.

Riis, Jacob. *The Battle with the Slum*. New York: Macmillan, 1902.

Roache, Francis. "Organized Crime in Boston's Chinatown." *Police Chief* 55 (January 1988): 48–51.

Roberts, Paul, and Norman Snider. *Smokescreen: One Man Against the Underworld*. Toronto: Stoddart, 2001.

Robinson, Jeffrey. *The Laundrymen: Inside Money Laundering, the World's Third Largest Business*. New York: Arcade, 1996.

———. *The Merger: How Organized Crime Is Taking Over Canada and the World*. Toronto: McClelland and Stewart, 1999.

Rockaway, Robert. *But He Was Good to His Mother*. Jerusalem: Gefen Publishing House, 1993.

Roemer, William. *Accardo: The Genuine Godfather*. New York: Ivy Books, 1995.

———. *The Enforcer*. New York: Ivy Books, 1994.

———. *Roemer: Man Against the Mob*. New York: Ivy Books, 1989.

———. *War of the Godfathers*. New York: Ivy Books, 1990.

Roggiero, Vincenzo. "The Encounter Between Big Business and Organized Crime." *Capital and Class* 26 (1985): 93–104.

Rogozinski, Jan. *Pirates!: Brigands, Buccaneers, and Privateers in Fact, Fiction, and Legend*. New York: Da Capo Press, 1996.

Rome, Florence. *The Tattooed Men: An American Woman Reports on the Japanese Criminal Underworld*. New York: Delacorte Press, 1975.

Ronderos, Juan. "Transnational Drugs Law Enforcement." *Journal of Contemporary Criminal Justice* 14 (November 1998): 384–97.

Rosen, Charley. *The Wizard of Odds: How Jack Molinas Nearly Destroyed the Game of Basketball*. New York: Seven Stories Press, 2001.

Roslin, Alex. "Crooked Blue Line." *This Magazine* 34 (May/June 2001): 16–21.

Rosoff, Stephen, Henry Pontell, and Robert Tillman. *Looting America: Greed, Corruption, Villains, and Victims*. Upper Saddle River, N.J.: Prentice Hall, 2003.

Rothman, Hal. *Neon Metropolis*. New York: Routledge, 2002.

Rothman, Hal, and Mike Davis (eds.). *The Grit Beneath the Glitter*. Berkeley: University of California Press, 2002.

Rothstein, Carolyn, and Donald Clarke. *Now I'll Tell*. New York: Vantage Press, 1934.

Rowan, Roy. "How the Mafia Loots JFK Airport." *Fortune* 115 (June 22, 1987): 54–57.

Royal Canadian Mounted Police. *Aboriginal Organized Crime and Tobacco, Weapons and Gaming*. Ottawa: RCMP, 1992.

———. *Drug Situation in Canada — 2003*. Ottawa: RCMP, 2004.

———. *The Globalization of Organized Crime: How Powerful Crime Groups Are Corrupting Our Communities*. Ottawa: RCMP, 2004.

———. *Marihuana Cultivation in Canada: Evolution and Current Trends*. Ottawa: RCMP, 2002.

———. "Outlaw Motorcycle Gangs in Canada." *Royal Canadian Mounted Police Gazette* 61 (August 1999): 15–37.

Rubio, Mauricio. "Violence, Organized Crime, and the Criminal Justice System in Colombia." *Journal of Economic Issues* 32 (June 1998): 605–10.

Rudolph, Robert. *The Boys from New Jersey: How the Mob Beat the Feds*. New York: William Morrow, 1992.

Ruggiero, Vincenzo. "Crime Inc.: The Story of Organized Crime." *British Journal of Criminology* 32 (Spring 1992): 234–35.

———. "Criminal Franchising: Albanians and Illicit Drugs in Italy," in Mangai Natarajan and Mike Hough (eds.), *Illegal Drug Markets: From Research to Prevention Policy*. Monsey, N.Y.: Criminal Justice Press, 2000.

———. "Drug Economics: A Fordist Model of Criminal Capital?" *Capital and Class* 55 (Spring 1995): 131–50.

———. *Organized and Corporate Crime in Europe: Offers That Can't Be Refused*. Brookfield, VT: Dartmouth, 1996.

———. "Organized Crime in Italy: Testing Alternative Definitions." *Social and Legal Studies* 2 (June 1993): 131–48.

———. "Trafficking in Human Beings: Slaves in Contemporary Europe." *International Journal of the Sociology of Law* 25 (1997): 231–44.

_____. "War Markets: Corporate and Organized Criminals in Europe." *Social and Legal Studies* 5 (March 1996): 5–20.

Rush, Robert, and Frank Scarpitti. "Russian Organized Crime: The Continuation of an American Tradition." *Deviant Behavior* 22 (November-December 2001): 517–40.

Russell, Thaddeus. *Out of the Jungle: Jimmy Hoffa and the Remaking of the American Working Class.* New York: Knopf, 2001.

Russo, Gus. *The Outfit.* New York: Bloomsbury, 2003.

_____. *Supermob.* New York: Bloomsbury, 2006.

Russo, Gus, and Henry Hill. *Gangsters and Goodfellas: Wiseguys … and Life on the Run.* Edinburgh, Scotland: Mainstream, 2005.

Ryan, Patrick. "Organized Crime II." *Journal of Contemporary Criminal Justice* 9 (1993): 175–267.

Ryan, Patrick, and George Rush. *Understanding Organized Crime: A Reader.* Thousand Oaks, CA: Sage, 1997.

Saba, Richard. "The Demand for Cigarette Smuggling." *Economic Inquiry* 33 (April 1995): 189–202.

Sadowsky, Sandy, and H. B Gilmour. *Wedded to Crime: My Life in the Jewish Mafia.* New York: Putnam, 1992.

Saga, Junichi, and John Bester. *Confessions of a Yakuza: A Life in Japan's Underworld.* Tokyo: Kodansha International, 1995.

Saggio, Frankie, and Fred Rosen. *Born to the Mob: The True-Life Story of the Only Man to Work for All Five of New York's Mafia Families.* New York: Thunder's Mouth Press, 2004.

Sakurada, Keiji. "Yakuza Storming the Corporate Ship." *Tokyo Business Today* 62 (April 1994): 46–47.

Salerno, Ralph. "Organized Crime: An Unmet Challenge to Criminal Justice." *Crime and Delinquency* 15 (1969): 333–40.

_____. "Syndicate Personnel Structure." *Canadian Police Chief* 55 (July 1967): 7.

Salerno, Ralph, and John Tompkins. *The Crime Confederation.* New York: Popular Library, 1969.

Salzano, Julie, and Stephen Hartman. "Cargo Crime." *Transnational Organized Crime* 3 (Spring 1997): 39–49.

Sanger, Daniel. *Hell's Witness.* Toronto: Penguin, 2005.

Sann, Paul. *Kill the Dutchman!* New Rochelle, N.Y.: Arlington House, 1971.

Santino, Umberto. "The Financial Mafia: The Illegal Accumulation of Wealth and the Financial Industrial Complex." *Contemporary Crises* 12 (September 1988): 203–43.

Santoro, Marco. "The Mafia and Protection. Three Questions and a Proposal." *Polis* 9 (August 1995): 285–99.

Saposs, David. *Labor Racketeering: Evolution and Solutions.* Urbana: University of Illinois, 1958.

Sato, Ikuya. "Crime as Play and Excitement: A Conceptual Analysis of Japanese Bosozoku (Motorcycle Gangs)." *Tohoku Psychologica Folia* 41 (1982): 64–84.

Satter, David. *Darkness at Dawn: The Rise of the Russian Criminal State.* New Haven: Yale University Press, 2003.

Saviano, Roberto, *Gomorrah: A Personal Journey into the Violent International Empire of Naples' Organized Crime System.* New York: Farrar, Straus and Giroux, 2007.

Savona, Ernesto. *European Money Trails.* London: Harwood Academic, 1999.

_____ (ed.). *The World Report on Money Laundering.* London: Harwood Academic, 2000.

Scarne, John. *The Mafia Conspiracy.* North Bergen, N.J.: Scarne Enterprises, 1976.

Schatzberg, Rufus, and Robert Kelly. *African American Organized Crime: A Social History.* New Brunswick, N.J.: Rutgers University Press, 1997.

Schatzberg, Rufus, Robert Kelly, and Ko-lin Chin (eds.). *Handbook of Organized Crime in the United States.* Westport, CT: Greenwood Press, 1994.

Schegel, Kip. "Violence in Organized Crime: A Content Analysis of the Decavalcante and DeCarlo Transcripts," in Tim Bynum (ed.), *Organized Crime in America: Concepts and Controversies.* Munsey, N.Y.: Criminal Justice Press, 1987.

Scheim, David. *Contract on America.* New York: S.P.I. Books, 1988.

Schenk, John and Kesser. "Born to Raise Hell Inc." *Maclean's* (August 22, 1977): 30–33.

Schiavo, Giovanni. *The Truth About the Mafia and Organized Crime in America.* El Paso: Vigo Press, 1962.

Schlesinger, Arthur. *Robert Kennedy and His Times.* New York: Ballantine, 1978.

Schloenhardt, Andreas. *Organised Crime and the Business of Migrant Trafficking: An Economic Analysis.* Canberra: Australian Institute of Criminology, 1999.

Schmidt-Nothen, Berthe. "Motorcycle Gangs." *International Criminal Police Review* 390 (August/September 1985): 170–79.

Schneider, Jane. "Women and the Mafia; Le Donne, Le Mafia." *Journal of Modern Italian Studies* 1 (Fall 1995): 179–82.

Schneider, Stephen. "Combating Organized Crime in (and by) the Private Sector: A Normative Role for Canada's Forensic Investigative Firms." *Journal of Contemporary Criminal Justice* 14 (November 1998): 351–67.

_____. *Money Laundering in Canada: An Analysis of RCMP Cases.* Toronto: Nathanson Centre for the Study of Organized Crime and Corruption, York University, 2003.

_____. "Transnational Organized Crime and the Business Community." *Canadian International Lawyer* 4 (2000): 95–99.

Schoenberg, Robert. *Mr. Capone.* New York: HarperCollins, 1992.

Schramm, R.R. "Organized Crime: A Canadian Approach." *Police Chief* 55 (January 1989): 32–34.

Schroeder, William R. "Money Laundering: A Global Threat and the International Community's Response." *FBI Law Enforcement Bulletin* 70 (May 2001): 1–9.

Schwarz, Ted. *Joseph P. Kennedy.* New York: John Wiley & Sons, 2003.

Scott, Cathy. *Murder of a Mafia Daughter.* Fort Lee, N.J.: Barricade Books, 2002.

Scott, Kenneth. *Counterfeiting in Colonial America.* New York: Oxford University Press, 1957.

Scott, Peter (ed.). *The Assassinations: Dallas and Beyond.* New York: Vintage, 1976.

_____. *Deep Politics and the Death of JFK.* Berkeley: University of California Press, 1993.

Scott, Peter, and Jonathan Marshall. *Cocaine Politics: Drugs, Armies, and the CIA in Central America.* Berkeley: University of California Press, 1991.

Seidman, Harold. *Labor Czars: A History of Labor Racketeering.* New York: Liveright, 1938.

Selvaggi, Guiseppe, and William Packer. *The Rise of the Mafia in New York: From 1896 Through World War II.* Indianapolis: Bobbs-Merrill, 1978.

Servadio, Gaia. *Mafioso: A History of the Mafia from Its Origins to the Present Day.* London: Secker & Warburg, 1976.

_____. *To a Different World: In the Land of the Mafia.* London: Hamish Hamilton, 1979.

Serio, Joseph. " An Overview of Money Laundering." *Crime & Justice International* 18 (December 2002): 23.

Sevick, James. *Precursor and Essential Chemicals in Illicit Drug Production: Approaches to Enforcement. Issues and Practices in Criminal Justice.* Washington, D.C.: U.S. Dept. of Justice, 1993.

Sexton, Jean. "Controlling Corruption in the Construction Industry: The Quebec Approach." *Industrial and Labor Relations Review* 42 (July 1989): 524–35.

Seymour, Christopher. *Yakuza Diary: Doing Time in the Japanese Underworld.* New York: Atlantic Monthly Press, 1996.

Shannon, Susan. "Global Sex Trade: Humans as the Ultimate Commodity." *Crime & Justice International* 15 (May 1999): 5–25.

Shehu, Abdullah. *Money Laundering: The Challenge of Global Enforcement.* Hong Kong: University of Hong Kong, 2001.

Shelley, Louise. "The Trade in People in and from the Former Soviet Union." *Crime, Law and Social Change* 40 (2003): 231–49.

_____. "Transnational Organized Crime in the United States." *Kobe University Law Review* (1998): 77–91.

_____. "Transnational Organized Crime: The New Authoritarianism." Peter Andreas and H. Richard Friman (eds.), *Illicit Global Economy and State Power.* Lanham, MD: Rowman & Littlefield, 1999.

Sher, Julian. *The Road to Hell: How the Biker Gangs Conquered Canada.* Toronto: Knopf Canada, 2003.

Sheridan, Walter. *The Fall and Rise of Jimmy Hoffa.* New York: Saturday Review Press, 1972.

Sherrid, Samuel. "The Mathematics of Loan Sharking." *Police Chief* 42 (February 1975): 59.

Shibata, Yoko. "Quaking Lenders: How Gangsters Complicate Japan's Banking Crisis." *Global Finance* 10 (January 1996): 40–41.

Short, Martin. *Crime Inc.: The Story of Organised Crime.* London: Arrow Books, 1997.

Shvarts, Alexander. "The Russian Mafia: Do Rational Choice Models Apply?" *Michigan Sociological Review* 15 (Fall 2001): 29–63.

Siegel, Larry. *Criminology.* Belmont, CA: Wadsworth, 2000.

Sikes, Gini. *8 Ball Chicks: A Year in the Violent World of Girl Gangsters.* New York: Anchor Books, 1997.

Simard, Réal, and Vastel Michael. *The Nephew: The Making of a Mafia Hitman.* Scarborough, Ontario: Prentice-Hall Canada, 1988.

Siong Thye Tan. "Money Laundering and E-Commerce." *Journal of Financial Crime* 9 (February 2002): 277–85.

Siragusa, Charles, and Robert Wiedrich. *The Trail of the Poppy: Behind the Mask of the Mafia.* Englewood Cliffs, N.J.: Prentice-Hall, 1966.

Skolnick, Jerome. *House of Cards.* Boston: Little, Brown, 1978.

Sloane, Arthur. *Hoffa.* Cambridge: MIT Press, 1991.

Smith, Dwight. *The Mafia Mystique.* New York: Basic Books, 1975.

_____. "Organized Crime and Entrepreneurship." *International Journal of Criminology and Penology* 6 (1978): 161–77.

_____. "Paragons, Pariahs and Pirates: A Spectrum Based Theory of Enterprise." *Crime and Delinquency* 26 (July 1980): 358–86.

_____. "Wickersham to Sutherland to Katzenbach: Evolving an 'Official' Definition for Organized Crime." *Crime, Law and Social Change* 16 (1991): 135–54.

Smith, Dwight, and Ralph Salerno. "The Use of Strategies in Organized Crime Control." *Journal of Criminal Law, Criminology and Police Science* 91 (March 1970): 101–11.

Smith, Greg. *Made Men: The True Rise-and-Fall Story of a New Jersey Mob Family.* New York: Berkley Books, 2003.

Smith, Harold. *Transnational Crime: Investigative Responses.* Chicago: Office of International Criminal Justice, University of Illinois at Chicago, 1989.

Smith, John. *The Animal in Hollywood.* Fort Lee, N.J.: Barricade Books, 1998.

_____. *Running Scared.* Fort Lee, N.J.: Barricade Books, 1995.

_____. *Sharks in the Desert.* Fort Lee, N.J.: Barricade Books, 2005.

Smith, Laurence. *Counterfeiting: Crime Against the People.* New York: W.W. Norton, 1944.

Smith, Michael. *Why People Grow Drugs: Narcotics and Development in the Third World.* London: Panos, 1992.

Smith, Robert, and George Fox. "Dangerous Motorcycle Gangs: A Facet of Organized Crime in the Mid-Atlantic Region." *Journal of Gang Research* 9 (Summer 2002): 33–44.

Smith, Russell. *Identity-related Economic Crime: Risks and Countermeasures.* Canberra: Australian Institute of Criminology, 1999.

_____. *Organisations as Victims of Fraud, and How They Deal with It.* Canberra: Australian Institute of Criminology, 1999.

Smith, Russell, Michael Holmes, and Philip Kaufman. *Nigerian Advance Fee Fraud.* Canberra: The Australian Institute of Criminology, 1999.

Smitten, Richard. *The Godmother: The True Story of the Hunt for the Most Bloodthirsty Female Criminal in Our Time, Griselda Blanco.* New York: Pocket Books, 1993.

Sondern, Frederic. *Brotherhood of Evil: The Mafia.* New York: Farrar, Straus, and Cudahy, 1959.

South African Law Commission. *Money Laundering and Related Matters.* Pretoria: The Commission, 1996.

Southerland, Mittie. "Applying Organization Theory to Organized Crime." *Journal of Contemporary Criminal Justice* 9 (1993): 251+.

Special Report No. 13, Public Affairs Series: The Mafia Today. Los Angeles: Knight, 1977.

Spencer, Jon. "Crime on the Internet: Its Presentation and Representation." *Howard Journal of Criminal Justice* 38 (1999): 241–51.

Staats, Gregory. "Changing Conceptualizations of Professional Criminals: Implications for Criminology Theory." *Criminology* 15 (May 1977): 49–66.

Stana, Richard. *Investigating Money Laundering and Terrorist Financing: Federal Law Enforcement Agencies Face Continuing Coordination Challenges.* Washington, D.C.: National Institute of Justice, 2004.

Starr, John. *The Purveyor.* New York: Holt, Rinehart & Winston, 1961.

Steinke, Gord. *Mobsters & Rumrunners of Canada.* Edmonton: Folklore, 2003.

Sterling, Claire. *The Octopus: How the Long Reach of the Sicilian Mafia Controls the Global Narcotics Trade.* New York: Simon & Schuster, 1990.

_____. "Redfellas: Inside the Russian Mafia." *New Republic* 210 (April 11–15, 1994): 19.

_____. *Thieves' World: The Threat of the New Global Network of Organized Crime.* New York: Simon & Schuster, 1994.

Stern, Richard. "How the Mafia Manipulates Stocks." *Forbes* 144 (December 15, 1989): 42.

Stevens, Jay. *Storming Heaven: LSD and the American Dream.* New York: Atlantic Monthly Press, 1987.

Stewart, Christopher. *Hunting the Tiger*. New York: St. Martin's Press, 2008.

Stich, Rodney. *Crimes of the DEA-DOJ and the Mafia*. Richmond: Silverpeak, 2008.

_____. *Defrauding America: Encyclopedia of Secret Operations by the CIA, DEA, and Other Covert Agencies*. Richmond, VA: Silverpeak, 1998.

_____. *FBI, CIA, the Mob, and Treachery*. Richmond: Silverpeak, 2007.

Stille, Alexander. *Excellent Cadavers: The Mafia and the Death of the First Italian Republic*. New York: Vintage, 1995.

Stoecker, Sally, and Louise Shelley (eds.). *Human Traffic and Transnational Crime: Eurasian and American Perspectives*. Lanham, MD: Rowman & Littlefield, 2005.

Stoever, Heino. "Crack Cocaine in Germany: Current State of Affairs." *Journal of Drug Issues* 32 (Spring 2002): 413–22.

Stone, Michelle. "La Eme Gang Emerging as Organized Crime Threat." *Crime and Justice International* 15 (March 1999): 13+.

Strong, Simon. *Whitewash: Pablo Escobar and the Cocaine Wars*. London: Macmillan, 1995.

Stuart, Mark. *Gangster #2: Longy Zwillman: The Man Who Invented Organized Crime*. Secaucus, N.J.: Lyle Stuart, 1985.

Simis, Konstantin. *USSR, the Corrupt Society: The Secret World of Soviet Capitalism*. New York: Simon & Schuster, 1982.

Sukharenko, Aexander. "The Use of Corruption by 'Russian' Organized Crime in the United States." *Trends in Organized Crime* 8 (Winter 2004): 118–29.

Summers, Anthony. *The Arrogance of Power*. New York: Viking, 2000.

_____. *Conspiracy*. New York: McGraw-Hill, 1980.

_____. *Official and Confidential*. New York: G.P. Putnam's Sons, 1993.

Sward, Keith. *The Legend of Henry Ford*. New York: Russell & Russell, 1968.

Swartz, Bruce. "Helping the World Combat International Crime." *Global Issues* 6 (2001): 9.

Swisher, Karin. *Drug Trafficking. Current Controversies*. San Diego: Greenhaven Press, 1991.

Szymkowiak, Kenneth. *Sokaiya: Extortion, Protection, and the Japanese Corporation*. Armonk, N.Y.: M.E. Sharpe, 2002.

Taft, Philip. *Corruption and Racketeering in the Labor Movement*. Ithaca: New York State School of Industrial and Labor Relations, Cornell University, 1970.

Takagi, Paul, and Tony Platt. "Behind the Gilded Ghetto: An Analysis of Race, Class and Crime in Chinatown." *Crime and Social Justice* 9 (Spring/Summer 1978): 2–25.

Talbot, David. *Brothers: The Hidden History of the Kennedy Years*. New York: Free Press, 2007.

Talese, Gay. *Honor Thy Father*. Cleveland: World, 1971.

Tallberg, Martin. *Don Bolles*. New York: Popular Library, 1977.

Tamm, Quinn. "Organized Crime and Legitimate Businesses." *Police Chief* 42 (February 1975): 54–56.

Tanzi, Vito. *Money Laundering and the International Financial System*. Washington, D.C.: International Monetary Fund, 1996.

Taylor, Carl. *Girls, Gangs, Women, and Drugs*. East Lansing: Michigan State University Press, 1993.

Taylor, Clyde. "Links Between International Narcotics Trafficking and Terrorism." *Department of State Bulletin* 85 (August 1985): 69–74.

Teresa, Vincent, and Thomas Renner. *My Life in the Mafia*. Garden City, N.Y.: Doubleday, 1973.

Thacher, Thomas. "Combating Corruption and Racketeering: A New Strategy for Reforming Public Contracting in New York City's Construction Industry." *New York Law School Law Review* 40 (1995): 113–42.

Thayer, Nate. "Cambodia: Asia's New Narco State?" *Far Eastern Economic Review* 158 (November 1995): 24–27+.

Thomas, Ralph. "Organized Crime in the Construction Industry." *Crime and Delinquency* 23 (July 1977): 304–11.

Thompson, Craig, and Raymond Allen. *Gang Rule in New York: The Story of a Lawless Era*. New York: Dial Press, 1940.

Thompson, David. "Medellin, Colombia: The Untold Story." *Conflict* 11 (January/March 1991): 69–88.

Thompson, Hunter. *Hell's Angels: A Strange and Terrible Saga*. New York: Random House, 1967.

Thompson, Nathan. *Kings: The True Story of Chicago's Policy Kings and Numbers Racketeers*. Chicago: Bronzeville Press, 2003.

Thompson, Nelson. *The Dark Side of Camelot*. Chicago: Playboy Press, 1976.

Thornton, Mark. *The Economics of Prohibition*. Salt Lake City: University of Utah Press, 1991.

Thouin, Andre. "Outlaw Motorcycle Gangs Around the World." *Royal Canadian Mounted Police Gazette* 61 (August 1999): 51–57.

Thoumi, Francisco. *Political Economy and Illegal Drugs in Colombia*. Boulder, CO: L. Rienner, 1995.

Tomass, Mark. "Mafianomics: How Did Mob Entrepreneurs Infiltrate and Dominate the Russian Economy?" *Journal of Economic Issues* 32 (2 June 1998): 565–74.

Tosches, Nick. *The Devil and Sonny Liston*. Boston: Little, Brown, 2000.

_____. *Dino*. New York: Dell, 1992.

_____. *King of the Jews: The Arnold Rothstein Story*. London: Hamish Hamilton, 2005.

_____. *Power on Earth*. Westminster, MD: Arbor House, 1986.

Touhy, Roger, and Ray Brennan. *The Stolen Years*. Cleveland: Pennington Press, 1959.

Trahair, Richard. "Organized Crime: A Global Perspective." *Australian and New Zealand Journal of Sociology* 23 (November 1987): 473–76.

Trethewy, Steve, and Terry Katz. "Motorcycle Gangs or Motorcycle Mafia?" *Police Chief* 65 (April 1998): 53–60.

Trocki, Carl. *Opium, Empire and the Global Political Economy: A Study of the Asian Opium Trade, 1750–1950*. London: Routledge, 1999.

Truman, Edwin, and Peter Reuter. *Chasing Dirty Money: Progress on Anti-Money Laundering*. Washington, D.C.: Institute for International Economics, 2004.

Tullis, F. LaMond. *Unintended Consequences: Illegal Drugs and Drug Policies in Nine Countries*. Boulder, CO: L. Rienner, 1995.

Tunnell, Kenneth. "The Business of Crime: A Documentary Study of Organized Crime in the American Economy." *Criminal Justice Review* 18 (1993): 297–98.

_____. "Corporations of Corruption: A Systematic Study of Organized Crime." *Contemporary Sociology* 15 (March 1986): 223–24.

Tuohy, John. *When Capone's Mob Murdered Roger Touhy*. Fort Lee, N.J.: Barricade Books, 2001.

Turkus, Burton, and Sid Feder. *Murder, Inc.* New York: Da Capo Press, 1992.

Turner, Wallace. *Gamblers' Money*. Boston: Houghton Mifflin, 1965.

Turner, William, and John Christian. *The Assassination of Robert F. Kennedy.* New York: Random House, 1978.

Tyler, Gus. *Organized Crime in America: A Book of Readings.* Ann Arbor: University of Michigan Press, 1967.

Uchiyama, Ayako, and Hoshino Kanehiro. "The Changes in Way of Life of Boryokudan Members After Enforcement of the Anti Organized Crime Law." *Reports of National Research Institute of Police Science* 34 (December 1993): 99–112.

Ugochukwu Uche, Chibuike. "Nigeria: Bank Fraud." *Journal of Financial Crime* 8 (February 2001): 265.

Ulrich, Christopher, and Timo Kivimäki. *Uncertain Security: Confronting Transnational Crime in the Baltic Sea Region and Russia.* Lanham, MD: Lexington Books, 2002.

Unger, Robert. *The Union Station Massacre.* Kansas City: Andrews McMeel, 1997.

United Nations. *Existing International Legal Instruments, Recommendations and Other Documents Addressing Corruption.* Vienna, Austria: United Nations, 2001.

_____. *Global Programme Against Corruption: Anti-Corruption Tool Kit.* Vienna, Austria: United Nations, 2001.

_____. *Protocol Against the Smuggling of Migrants by Land, Air and Sea, Supplementing the United Nations Convention against Transnational Organized Crime.* New York: United Nations, 2000.

_____. *Revised Draft Protocol Against the Illicit Manufacturing of and Trafficking in Firearms, Their Parts and Components and Ammunition, Supplementing the United Nations Convention Against Transnational Organized Crime.* New York: United Nations, 2000.

_____. *The United Nations Convention against Transnational Organized Crime.* Palermo, Sicily: United Nations, 2000.

_____. *World Drug Report, 2005.* New York: United Nations, 2005.

United States Advisory Commission on Intergovernmental Relations. *Cigarette Bootlegging: A State and Federal Responsibility.* Washington, D.C.: U.S. Government Printing Office, 1977.

United States Department of Justice. *National Drug Threat Assessment, 2005.* Washington, D.C.: Department of Justice, 2005.

United States Department of State. "Arresting Transnational Crime." *Global Issues* 6 (2001).

_____. "The Fight Against Money Laundering." *Economic Perspectives* 6 (2001).

_____. *International Narcotics Control Strategy Report.* Washington, D.C.: Department of State, 2005.

_____. "Responses to Human Trafficking." *Global Issues* 8 (2001).

_____. *Trafficking in Persons Report.* Washington, D.C.: Department of State, 2003.

United States Dept. of Transportation. *Cargo Theft and Organized Crime: A Deskbook for Management and Law Enforcement.* Washington, D.C.: Department of Transportation, 1972.

United States Department of the Treasury and Department of Justice. *The National Money Laundering Strategy for 1999.* Washington, D.C.: Department of the Treasury, Department of Justice, 1999.

United States Federal Bureau of Investigation. *Wanted by the FBI the Mob: FBI Organized Crime Report. 25 Years After Valachi.* Washington, D.C.: U.S. Department of Justice, 1988.

United States General Accountability Office. *Cigarette Smuggling: Information on Interstate and U.S.-Canadian Activity.* Washington, D.C.: U.S. Government Printing Office, 1998.

_____. *Nontraditional Organized Crime: Law Enforcement Officials' Perspectives on Five Criminal Groups.* Washington, D.C.: U.S. Government Printing Office, 1989.

_____. *Suspicious Banking Activities: Possible Money Laundering by U.S. Corporations Formed for Russian Entities.* Washington, D.C.: U.S. Government Printing Office, 2000.

_____. *Terrorism and Drug Trafficking: Testing Status and Views on Operational Viability of Pulsed Fast Neutron Analysis Technology.* Washington, D.C.: U.S. Government Printing Office, 1999.

United States House of Representatives, Commission on Security and Cooperation in Europe. *Crime and Corruption in Russia.* Washington, D.C.: U.S. Government Printing Office, 2000.

_____, Committee on Banking and Financial Services. *The Counterfeiting of U.S. Currency Abroad.* Washington, D.C.: U.S. Government Printing Office, 1996.

_____, _____. *Money Laundering Activity Associated with the Mexican Narco Crime Syndicate.* Washington, D.C.: U.S. Government Printing Office, 1997.

_____, _____. *Organized Crime and Banking.* Washington, D.C.: U.S. Government Printing Office, 1996.

_____, Committee on Energy and Commerce. *Unfair Foreign Trade Practices: Criminal Components of America's Trade Problem.* Washington, D.C.: U.S. Government Printing Office, 1996,

_____, Committee on Foreign Affairs. *Air Piracy in the Caribbean Area.* Washington, D.C.: U.S. Government Printing Office, 1968.

_____, _____. *Connection Between Arms and Narcotics Trafficking.* Washington, D.C.: U.S. Printing Office, 1989.

_____, _____. *The Threat of International Organized Crime.* Washington, D.C.: U.S. Government Printing Office, 1994.

_____, Committee on Government Operations. *The Federal Effort Against Organized Crime.* Washington, D.C.: U.S. Government Printing Office, 1968.

_____, Committee on International Relations. *Drugs in Asia: The Heroin Connection.* Washington, D.C.: U.S. Government Printing Office, 1996.

_____, _____. *Global Organized Crime.* Washington, D.C.: U.S. Government Printing Office, 1996.

_____, Committee on the Judiciary. *Administration's Efforts Against the Influence of Organized Crime in the Laborer's International Union of North America.* Washington, D.C.: U.S. Government Printing Office, 1997.

_____, _____. *Cigarette Bootlegging.* Washington, D.C.: U.S. Government Printing Office, 1978.

_____, _____. *New Jersey–New York Waterfront Commission Compact.* Washington, D.C.: U.S. Government Printing Office, 1953.

_____, _____. *Oversight Hearing on Organized Crime Strike Forces.* Washington, D.C.: U.S. Government Printing Office, 1989.

_____, _____. *Threat Posed by the Convergence of Organized Crime Drug Trafficking, and Terrorism.* Washington, D.C.: U.S. Government Printing Office, 2001.

_____, _____. *Waste, Fraud, and Abuse at Federally Funded Wastewater Treatment Construction Projects: The Potential Effects of Organized Crime Infiltration and Labor Racketeering in the N.Y. Construction Industry.* Washington, D.C.: U.S. Government Printing Office, 1989.

_____, Committee on Merchant Marine and Fisheries. *Panama Gunrunning.* Washington, D.C.: U.S. Government Printing Office, 1980.

_____, _____. *Yacht Hijacking and Drug Smuggling.* Washington, D.C.: U.S. Government Printing Office, 1978.

_____, Select Committee on Assassinations. *Investigation of the Assassination of President John F. Kennedy.* Washington, D.C.: U.S. Government Printing Office, 1979.

_____, Select Committee on Narcotics Abuse and Control. *The Federal Strategy on the Southwest Border.* Washington, D.C.: U.S. Government Printing Office, 1990.

_____, _____. *Narcotics Control in Mexico.* Washington, D.C.: U.S. Government Printing Office, 1988.

United States Senate, Caucus on International Narcotics Control. *Threat to U.S. Trade and Finance from Drug Trafficking and International Organized Crime.* Washington, D.C.: U.S. Government Printing Office, 1997.

_____, Committee on Appropriations. *International Crime, Terrorism, and Narcotics.* Washington, D.C.: U.S. Government Printing Office, 1996.

_____, Committee on Banking, Housing and Urban Affairs. *The Counterfeit Deterrence Act of 1990.* Washington, D.C.: U.S. Government Printing Office, 1990.

_____, Committee on Commerce. *Effects of Organized Criminal Activity on Interstate and Foreign Commerce.* Washington, D.C.: U.S. Government Printing Office, 1972.

_____, Committee on Foreign Relations. *The Drug Trade in Mexico and Implications for U.S. Mexican Relations.* Washington, D.C.: U.S. Government Printing Office, 1995.

_____, _____. *Loose Nukes, Nuclear Smuggling, and the Fissile Material Problem in Russia and the NIS.* Washington, D.C.: U.S. Government Printing Office, 1995.

_____, _____. *Treaty Between the U.S. and the Federal Republic of Nigeria on Mutual Legal Assistance in Criminal Matters.* Washington, D.C.: U.S. Government Printing Office, 1992.

_____, Committee on Governmental Affairs. *Arms Trafficking, Mercenaries and Drug Cartels.* Washington, D.C.: United States Government Printing Office, 1991.

_____, _____. *Asian Organized Crime.* Washington, D.C.: United States Government Printing Office, 1992.

_____, _____. *Gambling and Organized Crime.* Washington, D.C.: U.S. Government Printing Office, 1962.

_____, _____. *Hotel Employees & Restaurant Employees International Union.* Washington, D.C.: U.S. Government Printing Office, 1984.

_____, _____. *Illicit Traffic in Weapons and Drugs Across the United States Mexican Border.* Washington, D.C.: U.S. Government Printing Office, 1977.

_____, _____. *International Narcotics Trafficking.* Washington, D.C.: U.S. Government Printing Office, 1981.

_____, _____. *The New International Criminal and Asian Organized Crime.* Washington, D.C.: U.S. Government Printing Office, 1993.

_____, _____. *Organized Crime.* Washington, D.C.: U.S. Government Printing Office, 1988.

_____, _____. *Organized Crime and Illicit Traffic in Narcotics.* Washington, D.C.: U.S. Printing Office. 1963.

_____, _____. *Organized Crime and Use of Violence.* Washington, D.C.: U.S. Government Printing Office, 1980.

_____, _____. *Organized Crime in Chicago.* Washington, D.C.: U.S. Government Printing Office, 1983.

_____, _____. *Organized Crime: 25 Years After Valachi.* Washington, D.C.: U.S. Government Printing Office, 1988.

_____, _____. *Organized Criminal Activities: South Florida and U.S. Penitentiary, Atlanta, Ga.* Washington, D.C.: U.S. Government Printing Office, 1980.

_____, _____. *Profile on Organized Crime Mid-Atlantic Region.* Washington, D.C.: U.S. Government Printing Office, 1983.

_____, _____. *Russian Organized Crime in the United States.* Washington, D.C.: U.S. Government Printing Office, 1996.

_____, _____. *Structure of International Drug Trafficking Organizations.* Washington, D.C.: U.S. Printing Office, 1989.

_____, _____. *Teamsters Central States Pension Fund.* Washington, D.C.: U.S. Government Printing Office, 1977.

_____, Committee on Interstate and Foreign Commerce. *Waterfront Investigation.* Washington, D.C.: U.S. Government Printing Office, 1953.

_____, Committee on the Judiciary. *Crack Trafficking in Rural America.* Washington, D.C.: U.S. Government Printing Office, 1990.

_____, _____. *Labor Violence and the Hobbs Act.* Washington, D.C.: U.S. Government Printing Office, 1984.

_____, _____. *Organized Crime in America.* Washington, D.C.: U.S. Government Printing Office, 1983.

_____, _____. *The Piracy and Counterfeiting Amendments Act of 1981.* Washington, D.C.: U.S. Government Printing Office, 1981.

_____, _____. *Racketeering in the Sale and Distribution of Cigarettes.* Washington, D.C.: U.S. Government Printing Office, 1977.

_____, _____. *Witness Protection Program.* Washington, D.C.: U.S. Government Printing Office, 1978.

_____, Committee on Labor and Human Resources. *Drugs and Terrorism.* Washington, D.C.: U.S. Government Printing Office, 1994.

_____, _____. *Oversight of Department of Labor's Investigation of Organized Crime Involving Union Workers.* Washington, D.C.: U.S. Government Printing Office, 1982.

_____, Government Operations Committee. *Organized Crime and Illicit Traffic in Narcotics.* Washington, D.C.: U.S. Government Printing Office, 1964.

_____, Impeachment Trial Committee. *Report of the Senate Impeachment Trial Committee on the Articles Against Judge Walter L. Nixon.* Washington, D.C.: U.S. Government Printing Office, 1989.

_____, Select Committee on Improper Activities in the Labor or Management Field. *Investigation of Improper Activities in the Labor Or Management Field.* Washington, D.C.: U.S. Government Printing Office, 1959.

_____, Special Committee to Investigate Organized Crime in Interstate Commerce. *Investigation of Organized Crime in Interstate Commerce.* Washington, D.C.: U.S. Government Printing Office, 1951.

United States Secret Service. *Counterfeiting and Forgery.* Washington, D.C.: Secret Service. 1991.

Unsinger, Peter, and Harry W More. *The International Legal and Illegal Trafficking of Arms.* Springfield, IL: Thomas, 1989.

Vaksberg, Arkadii. *The Soviet Mafia: A Shocking Expose of Organized Crime in the U.S.S.R.* New York: St. Martin's Press, 1992.

Valentine, Douglas. *The Strength of the Wolf: The Secret History of America's War on Drugs.* New York: Verso, 2004.

Valle, James, and Aileen Ikegami and Rod Crisp. *Summary Results from the Methamphetamine Lab Cookers Survey June 2001–December 2002.* Riverside, CA: Inland Narcotic Clearing House, 2003.

Van de Mortel, Elma, and Peter Cornelisse. "The Dynamics of Corruption and Black Markets: An Application of Catastrophe Theory." *Public Finance* 49 (1994): 195–208.

Van den Anker, Christien. *The Political Economy of New*

Slavery. Houndmills, United Kingdom: Palgrave Macmillan, 2004.

Van Duyne, Petrus. "Mobsters Are Human Too: Behavioural Science and Organized Crime Investigation." *Crime Law and Social Change* 34 (December 2000): 369–90.

_____. "Money Laundering: Pavlov's Dog and Beyond." *Howard Journal of Criminal Justice* 37 (November 1998): 359–74.

_____, and Alan Block. "Organized Cross Atlantic Crime." *Crime, Law and Social Change* 22 (1994): 127–47.

Van Duyne, Petrus, Matjaz Jager, Klaus Von Lampe, and James Newell (eds.). *Threats and Phantoms of Organised Crime, Corruption and Terrorism: Critical European Perspectives*. Netherlands: Wolf Legal, 2004.

Varese, Federico. "Is Sicily the Future of Russia? Private Protection and the Rise of the Russian Mafia." *Archives Europeennes De Sociologie* 35 (1994): 224–58.

_____. *The Russian Mafia: Private Protection in a New Market Economy*. New York: Oxford University Press, 2001.

Velie, Lester. *Desperate Bargain*. New York: Reader's Digest Press, 1977.

Vellinga, Menno. *The Political Economy of the Drug Industry: Latin America and the International System*. Gainesville: University Press of Florida, 2004.

Viano, Emilio. *Global Organized Crime & International Security*. Brookfield, VT: Ashgate, 1999.

_____. *Transnational Organized Crime: Myth, Power, and Profit*. Durham: Carolina Academic Press, 2003.

Victor, Michael. "The Crime Society: Organized Crime and Corruption in America." *Social Science Journal* 15 (October 1978): 89–91.

Villano, Anthony, and Gerald Astor. *Brick Agent: Inside the Mafia for the FBI*. New York: Quadrangle, 1977.

Vito, Gennaro (ed.). "Organized Crime." *Journal of Contemporary Criminal Justice* 8 (1992): 1–79.

Volkman, Ernest. *Gangbusters: The Destruction of America's Last Great Mafia Dynasty*. New York: Avon, 1998.

Volkman, Ernest, and John Cummings. *The Heist: How a Gang Stole $8,000,000 at Kennedy Airport and Lived to Regret It*. New York: Franklin Watts, 1986.

Volkov, Vadim. "The Political Economy of Protection Rackets in the Past and the Present." *Social Research* 67 (2000): 709–44.

_____. *Violent Entrepreneurs: The Use of Force in the Making of Russian Capitalism*. Ithaca: Cornell University Press, 2002.

Volz, Joseph, and Peter Bridge. *The Mafia Talks*. Greenwich, CT: Fawcett, 1969.

Voronin, Yuriy. *Measures to Control Transnational Organized Crime*. Washington, D.C.: National Institute of Justice, 2000.

Waisberg Commission. *Report of the Royal Commission into Certain Sectors of the Construction Industry*. Toronto: Government of Ontario, 1974.

Waldorf, Dan. *Careers in Dope*. Englewood Cliffs, N.J.: Prentice-Hall, 1973.

Waldron, Lamar, and Tom Hartmann. *Ultimate Sacrifice: John and Robert Kennedy, the Plan for a Coup in Cuba, and the Murder of JFK*. New York: Carroll & Graf, 2006.

Walker, William. *Drugs in the Western Hemisphere: An Odyssey of Cultures in Conflict*. Wilmington, DE: Scholarly Resources, 1996.

_____. "International Responses to the Threat of Nuclear Smuggling from Russia." *Medicine, Conflict and Survival* 12 (January/March 1996): 53–57.

Wallace, Marnie. *Exploring the Involvement of Organized Crime in Motor Vehicle Theft*. Ottawa: Statistics Canada, 2002.

Walsh, George. *Gentleman Jimmy Walker: Mayor of the Jazz Age*. New York: Praeger, 1974.

Walsh, James. "Triads Go Global." *Time* (February 8, 1993): 37–41.

Walton, Kenneth P. "Organized Crime and Medical Fraud." *FBI Law Enforcement Bulletin* 55 (October 1986): 21–24.

Wang, John. "Illegal Chinese Immigration into the United States: A Preliminary Factor Analysis." *International Journal of Offender Therapy and Comparative Criminology* 45 (June 2001): 345–55.

Wanner, Barbara. "Yakuza in Japan: 'Organized Crime' That Is Out in the Open." *Terrorism, Violence, and Insurgency Report* 11 (1993): 13–22.

Ward, Dick. "Gray Area Phenomena: The Changing Nature of Organized Crime and Terrorism." *Criminal Justice International* 11 (March-April 1995): 1, 4, 18.

Warner, Kenneth. "Cigarette Excise Taxation and Interstate Smuggling: An Assessment of Recent Activity." *National Tax Journal* 35 (December 1982): 483–90.

Waters, Harold. *Smugglers of Spirits: Prohibition and the Coast Guard Patrol*. New York: Hastings House, 1971.

Waugh, Daniel. *Egan's Rats: The Untold Story of the Gang That Ruled Prohibition-Era St. Louis*. Nashville: Cumberland House, 2007.

Webb, Billy. *Running with the Krays: My Life in London's Gangland*. Edinburgh: Mainstream, 1993.

Webster, William, Arnaud De Borchgrave, and Frank Cilluffo (eds.). *Russian Organized Crime and Corruption: Putin's Challenge*. Washington, D.C.: Center for Strategic and International Studies, 2000.

Weisel, Deborah. *Contemporary Gangs: An Organizational Analysis*. Washington, D.C.: National Institute of Justice, 2002.

Weiss, Gary. *Born to Steal: When the Mafia Hit Wall Street*. New York: Warner, 2003.

Welli, Humbert. "A Brief History of American Syndicate Crime," in Timothy Bynum (ed.), *Organized Crime in America: Concepts and Controversies*. Monsey, N.Y.: Criminal Justice Press, 1986.

Wendland, Michael. *The Arizona Project*. Kansas City: Sheed Andrews & McMeel, 1977.

Wethern, George, Vincent Colnett. *A Wayward Angel*. New York: R. Marek, 1978.

Whelan, David. "Organized Crime, Sports Gambling and Role Conflict: Victimization and Point Shaving in College Basketball." *Dissertation Abstracts International: The Humanities and Social Sciences* 54 (July 1993): 327.

Whiting, Robert. *Tokyo Underworld: The Fast Times and Hard Life of an American Gangster in Japan*. New York: Pantheon Books, 1999.

Widgren, Jonas. "Global Arrangements to Combat Trafficking in Migrants." *Migration World Magazine* 23 (1995): 19–25.

Wilde, Sam. *Barbarians on Wheels*. Secaucus, N.J.: Chartwell Books, 1977.

Wilkens, Russell. "Biker Gangs: Getting Away with Murder." *Reader's Digest* 151 (November 1997): 54–60.

Williams, James, and Margaret Beare. "The Business of Bribery: Globalization, Economic Liberalization, and the 'Problem' of Corruption." *Crime, Law and Social Change* 32 (2000): 115–46.

Williams, Phil. "Emerging Issues: Transnational Crime and Its Control." Graeme Newman (ed.), *Global Report on Crime and Justice*. New York: Oxford University Press, 1999.

_____. "The Nature of Drug Trafficking Networks." *Current History* 97 (April 1998): 154–59.

_____. "Transnational Criminal Organizations: Strategic Alliances." *The Washington Quarterly* 18 (Winter 1995): 57.

Williams, Phil (ed.). *Illegal Immigration and Commercial Sex: The New Slave Trade.* Portland, OR: Frank Cass, 1999.

_____ (ed.). *Russian Organized Crime: The New Threat?* London: F. Cass, 1997.

Williams, Phil, and Paul Woessner. "The Real Threat of Nuclear Smuggling." *Scientific American* 274 (January 1996): 40–44.

Williams, Phil, and Dimitri Vlassis (eds.). *Combating Transnational Crime: Concepts, Activities and Responses.* Portland, OR: Frank Cass, 2001.

Willis, Clint (ed.). *Mob: Stories of Death and Betrayal from Organized Crime.* New York: Thunder's Mouth Press, 2001.

_____ (ed.). *Wise Guys: Stories of Mobsters from Jersey to Vegas.* New York: Thunder's Mouth Press, 2003.

Winer, Jonathan. "Alien Smuggling: Elements of the Problem." *Transnational Organized Crime* 3 (Spring 1998): 50–58.

Wing Lo, T. "Political-criminal Nexus. The Hong Kong Experience: Minimizing Crime and Corruption." *Trends in Organized Crime* 4 (Spring 1999): 60–80.

Winter-Berger, Robert. *The Washington Pay-Off: An Insider's View of Corruption in Government.* New York: Dell, 1972.

Wismer, Catherine. *Sweethearts.* Toronto: J. Lorimer, 1980.

Witkin, Gordon. "The New Opium Wars: The Administration Plans to Attack the Lords of Heroin." *U.S. News and World Report* (October 10, 1994): 39–41+.

_____. "One Way, $28,000: Why Smuggling Aliens into America Is a Boom Business." *U.S. News and World Report* 122 (April 14, 1997): 39+.

Wolf, Daniel. *The Rebels: A Brotherhood of Outlaw Bikers.* Toronto: University of Toronto Press, 1991.

Wolf, George, and Joseph DiMona. *Frank Costello: Prime Minister of the Underworld.* New York: William Morrow, 1974.

Wolf, Marvin, and Katherine Mader. *Fallen Angels: Chronicles of L.A. Crime and Mystery.* New York: Ballantine, 1988.

Wolfe, Donald. *The Black Dahlia Files.* New York: Regan, 2005.

Wolff, Kay, and Sybil Taylor. *The Last Run: An American Woman's Years Inside a Colombian Drug Family, and Her Dramatic Escape.* New York: Viking, 1989.

Wolseley, G.J. *Narrative of the War with China in 1860.* London: Longman, Green, Longman & Roberts, 1862.

Woodiwiss, Michael. *Organized Crime and American Power.* Toronto: University of Toronto Press, 2002.

Woodard, Colin. *The Republic of Pirates: Being the True and Surprising Story of the Caribbean Pirates and the Man Who Brought Them Down.* Orlando: Harcourt, 2007.

Wright, Alan. *Organised Crime.* Portland: Willan, 2006.

Wright, Rosalind. "Putting the Crooks Out of Business! The Financial War on Organised Crime and Terror." *Journal of Financial Crime* 10 (April 2003): 366–69.

Xhudo, Gus. "Men of Purpose: The Growth of Albanian Criminal Activity." *Transnational Organized Crime* 2 (Spring 1996): 1–20.

Yallop, David. *In God's Name: An Investigation into the Murder of Pope John Paul I.* London: Jonathan Cape, 1984.

Yangwen Zheng. *The Social Life of Opium in China.* Cambridge: Cambridge University Press, 2005.

Yates, Rowdy. "A Brief History of British Drug Policy, 1950–2001." *Drugs: Education, Prevention & Policy* 9 (2002): 113–24.

Yeager, Matthew. "The Gangster as White Collar Criminal: Organized Crime and Stolen Securities." *Issues in Criminology* 8 (Spring 1973): 49–73.

Youngblood, Jack, and Robin Moore. *The Devil to Pay.* London: Anthony Gibbs & Phillips, 1961.

Zabludoff, Sidney. "Colombian Narcotics Organizations as Business Enterprises." *Transnational Organized Crime* 3. 2 (Summer 1998): 20–49.

Zalisko, Walter. "Russian organized crime." *Law and Order* 47 (October 1999): 219–27.

Zanin, Brenda. "Renewal of Project North Star: Combined Effort Builds Clout Against Organized Crime." *Gazette* (Royal Canadian Mounted Police) 63 (2002): 24–26.

Zeiger, Henry. *The Jersey Mob.* New York: New American Library, 1975.

_____. *Sam the Plumber.* New York: Signet Books, 1970.

Zendzian, Craig. *Who Pays? Casino Gambling, Hidden Interests, and Organized Crime.* New York: Harrow and Heston, 1993.

Zhang, Sheldon, and Ko-lin Chin. *Characteristics of Chinese Human Smugglers.* Rockville, MD: U.S. Dept of Justice, 2004.

Zhang, Sheldon, and Mark Gaylord. "Bound for the Golden Mountain: The Social Organization of Chinese Alien Smuggling." *Crime, Law and Social Change* 25 (1996): 1–16.

_____. "Enter the Dragon: Inside Chinese Human Smuggling Organizations." *Criminology* 40 (November 2002): 737–68.

Zimmermann, Tim, and Alan Cooperman. "The Russian Connection." *U.S. News and World Report* 119 (October 23, 1995): 56–58+.

Zion, Sidney. *Loyalty and Betrayal: The Story of the American Mob.* San Francisco: Collins, 1994.

Zoffi, P. *Organised Crime Around the World.* Monsey, N.Y.: United Nations European Institute for Crime Prevention and Control, 1998.

Zuckerman, Michael. *Vengeance Is Mine.* New York: Macmillan, 1987.

Index